Exam 70-210

MCSE
Windows® 2000 Professional
TRAINING GUIDE

New Riders

Gord Barker, MCSE
Douglas Harrison, MCSE

MCSE Training Guide: (70-210) ICA Windows 2000 Professional

Copyright © 2000 by New Riders Publishing

International Standard Book Number: 0-7357-0965-3

Library of Congress Catalog Card Number: 00-100408

Printed in the United States of America

First Printing: July, 2000

04   03   02   01   7   6

Interpretation of the printing code: The rightmost double-digit number is the year of the book's printing; the rightmost single-digit number is the number of the book's printing. For example, the printing code 00-1 shows that the first printing of the book occurred in 2000.

Trademarks

Warning and Disclaimer

PUBLISHER
David Dwyer

ASSOCIATE PUBLISHER
Al Valvano

EXECUTIVE EDITOR
Stephanie Wall

PRODUCT MARKETING MANAGER
Stephanie Layton

PUBLICITY MANAGER
Susan Nixon

ACQUISITIONS EDITOR
Nancy Maragioglio
Ann Quinn

MANAGING EDITOR
Sarah Kearns

DEVELOPMENT EDITOR
Chris Zahn

PROJECT EDITOR
John Rahm

COPY EDITOR
Daryl Kessler

TECHNICAL REVIEWERS
Larry Chambers
Marc Savage
Ed Tetz

SOFTWARE DEVELOPMENT SPECIALIST
Michael Hunter

INDEXER
Christine Karpeles

PROOFREADER
Debra Neel

COMPOSITOR
Wil Cruz

MANUFACTURING COORDINATOR
Jim Conway

Contents at a Glance

Table of Contents

PART I: Exam Preparation

4 Monitoring and Optimizing System Performance and Reliability   263

6 Implementing, Managing, and Troubleshooting Nework Protocols and Services   407

PART II: Final Review

PART III: Appendixes

About the Authors

Gord Barker currently works as a Consultant for Microsoft Canada Co. in Edmonton, Alberta, Canada. He has been assigned as an Enterprise Strategy Consultant with Telus for the past three years and currently holds an MCSE designation for Windows NT 4.0. Recently, he has been assisting Telus in designing a Windows 2000 Active Directory, implementing it as a Windows 2000 domain and over 5000 Windows 2000 Professional desktops prior to the launch of the product. Gord lives in Edmonton, Alberta with his wife Christina.

Doug Harrison is a Microsoft Certified Systems Engineer (MCSE), Microsoft Certified Database Administrator (MCDBA), and Master Certified Novell Engineer (MCNE). Doug has been working with Windows 2000 since Beta 2. Doug currently works as the Technical Education Manager at PBSC Computer Training in Toronto, Canada. Doug has been teaching Novell and Microsoft certified training for the past four years. Prior to his carrier in the training world, he worked as a network administrator and software developer for a consulting engineering firm. Doug currently lives in Toronto with his family Tracey and Mikayla.

Robert L. Bogue is the Chief Operating Officer of AvailTek, Inc. AvailTek is a software development and systems integration company headquartered in Carmel, IN. Robert has contributed to over 100 book projects and numerous magazine articles and reviews. Robert is MCSE, CNA, A+, Network+, and I-Net+ certified. When he's not busy killing trees or getting certified he enjoys pushing the envelope with new technology. Robert can be reached at Rob.Bogue@AvailTek.com.

Rory McCaw is currently a Microsoft Certified Trainer for a Canadian Certified Technical Education Centre. Rory holds numerous Microsoft certifications and has developed and delivered presentations for Microsoft at Comdex on Windows 2000. Prior to training, Rory worked for an Internet solution provider where he was responsible for the implementation and administration of Microsoft LANs, WANs, and network security.

CD-ROM Content

Alain Guilbault is a senior consultant with Network Technology Professionals in Calgary Canada. He has been in the computer industry for more than 10 years as a technical instructor and consultant. Alain and his wife Sara have recently welcomed a baby boy named Alexander to their family.

Larry Chambers is a Network Consultant for a major systems integration firm. He has worked for the past 12 years in the computer industry with a recent focus on Microsoft Technologies for the last 5 years. He is an MCSE, an MCSD and also maintains a CNE certification. He would like to thank his wife Denise, daughter Courtney and recent son (happy one month birthday Dylan) for letting him take time to do what he enjoys.

About the Technical Reviewers

Marc Savage, MCSE, CNE, MCT, A+, is the Director of Education for PBSC Computer Training Centers, one of the largest training centers in Canada. Marc is an experienced system/network engineer with consulting and teaching experience in large and small client/server networks. He has spent many years in the industry training and developing course material.

Edward Tetz graduated from Saint Lawrence College in Cornwall, Ontario with a diploma in Business Administration in 1990. He spent a short time in computer sales, which turned into a computer support position. He has spent the last eight years providing system and LAN suport for small and large organizations. In 1994 he added training to his repertoire. He is both a Microsoft Certified Trainer and a Microsoft Certified Systems Engineer. He has experience with Apple Macintosh, IBM OS/2, and all Microsoft operating systems. He is currently an Information Technology Coordinator and an instructor for PBSC Computer Training, delivering certified training in most Microsoft products. He would like to thank his wife, Sharon, and their children, Emily and Mackenzie. If not for their love, support, and understanding, he would not be able to find the time or will to write and edit.

Dedication

Dedicated to Tracey and Mikayla. Thank you for the support during this project!—D.H.

Acknowledgments

I would like to thank all the people involved in this project, Chris Zahn and Nancy Maragioglio for their assistance. A special thank you to my wife Christina for patience and understanding during the evenings and weekends spent in the creation of this book.—G.B.

I would like to thank Chris Zahn, Marc Savage, and Larry Chambers, for all the great suggestions and edits. Thanks!—D.H.

Tell Us What You Think!

As the reader of this book, *you* are our most important critic and commentator. We value your opinion and want to know what we're doing right, what we could do better, what areas you'd like to see us publish in, and any other words of wisdom you're willing to pass our way.

As the Executive Editor for the Certification team at New Riders Publishing, I welcome your comments. You can fax, email, or write me directly to let me know what you did or didn't like about this book—as well as what we can do to make our books stronger.

Please note that I cannot help you with technical problems related to the topic of this book, and that due to the high volume of mail I receive, I might not be able to reply to every message.

When you write, please be sure to include this book's title, author, and ISBN number (found on the back cover of the book above the bar code), as well as your name and phone or fax number. I will carefully review your comments and share them with the author and editors who worked on the book.

Fax: 317-581-4663

Email: stephanie.wall@newriders.com

Mail: Stephanie Wall
            Executive Editor
            Certification
            New Riders Publishing
            201 West 103rd Street
            Indianapolis, IN 46290 USA

How to Use This Book

New Riders Publishing has made an effort in the second editions of its Training Guide series to make the information as accessible as possible for the purposes of learning the certification material. Here, you have an opportunity to view the many instructional features that have been incorporated into the books to achieve that goal.

CHAPTER OPENER

Each chapter begins with a set of features designed to allow you to maximize study time for that material.

List of Objectives: Each chapter begins with a list of the objectives as stated by Microsoft.

Objective Explanations: Immediately following each objective is an explanation of it, providing context that defines it more meaningfully in relation to the exam. Because Microsoft can sometimes be vague in its objectives list, the objective explanations are designed to clarify any vagueness by relying on the authors' test-taking experience.

OBJECTIVES

This chapter helps you prepare for the MCSE Windows 2000 Professional exam by covering the following objectives:

Manage and troubleshoot driver signing.

▶ One of the areas in earlier versions of Windows that has caused support problems is the area of device drivers. To that end Microsoft has developed a rigorous driver testing program to ensure that device drivers function correctly. Providing digital signatures of the binary code being installed guarantees that it has passed these tests. Managing the policy that governs these checks can have significant impact on the stability of your system.

Configure, manage, and troubleshoot the Task Scheduler.

▶ The Windows 2000 Task Scheduler can be used to schedule programs and batch files to run at regular intervals or specific times. You can also have Task Scheduler execute programs or scripts when certain operating system events occur. Using Task Scheduler to periodically run maintenance tasks or when some problem occurs can improve your system's stability.

Manage and troubleshoot the use and synchronization of offline files.

▶ The increase in the use of laptop computers indicates the need for access to information when you are traveling and without a network connection. With offline files, you can continue to access network files and programs when you are not connected to the network, and automatically save the changes you make to your files the next time you reconnect to your networ

CHAPTER 4

Monitoring and Optimizing System Performance and Reliability

Chapter Outline: Learning always gets a boost when you can see both the forest and the trees. To give you a visual image of how the topics in a chapter fit together, you will find a chapter outline at the beginning of each chapter. You will also be able to use this for easy reference when looking for a particular topic.

STUDY STRATEGIES

▶ Disk configurations are a part of both the planning and the configuration of NT Server computers. To study for Planning Objective 1, you will need to look at both the following section and the material in Chapter 2, "Installation Part 1." As with many concepts, you should have a good handle on the terminology and know the best applications for different disk configurations. For the objectives of the NT Server exam, you will need to know only general disk configuration concepts—at a high level, not the nitty gritty. Make sure you memorize the concepts relating to partitioning and know the difference between the system and the boot partitions in an NT system (and the fact that the definitions of these are counter-intuitive). You should know that NT supports both FAT and NTFS partitions, as well as some of the advantages and disadvantages of each. You will also need to know about the fault-tolerance methods available in NT—stripe sets with parity and disk mirroring—including their definitions, hardware requirements, and advantages and disadvantages.

Of course, nothing substitutes for working with the concepts explained in this objective. If possible, get an NT system with some free disk space and play around with the Disk Administrator just to see how partitions are created and what they look like.

You might also want to look at some of the supplementary readings and scan TechNet for white papers on disk configuration.

▶ The best way to study for Planning Objective 2 is to read, memorize, and understand the use of each protocol. You should know what the protocols are, what they are used for, and what systems they are compatible with.

As with disk configuration, installing protocols on your NT Server is something that you plan for, not something you do just because it feels good to you at the time. Although it is much easier to add or remove a protocol than it is to reconfigure your hard drives, choosing a protocol is still an essential part of the planning process because specific protocols, like spoken languages, are designed to be used in certain circumstances. There is no point in learning to speak Mandarin Chinese if you are never around anyone who can understand you. Similarly, the NWLink protocol is used to interact with NetWare systems; therefore, if you do not have Novell servers on your network, you might want to rethink your plan to install it on your servers. We will discuss the uses of the major protocols in Chapter 7, "Connectivity." However, it is important that you have a good understanding of their uses here in the planning stage.

Study Strategies: Each topic presents its own learning challenge. To support you through this, New Riders has included strategies for how to best approach studying in order to retain the material in the chapter, particularly as it is addressed on the exam.

INSTRUCTIONAL FEATURES WITHIN THE CHAPTER

These books include a large amount and different kinds of information. The many different elements are designed to help you identify information by its purpose and importance to the exam and also to provide you with varied ways to learn the material. You will be able to determine how much attention to devote to certain elements, depending on what your goals are. By becoming familiar with the different presentations of information, you will know what information will be important to you as a test-taker and which information will be important to you as a practitioner.

EXAM TIP

Remember the Syntax of the Files The syntax of the unattended.txt and UDF files is complex. Create a sample using the Setup Manager and thoroughly review them before the exam. The code generated by the unattended.bat file is especially useful if you want to see the correct syntax associated with using the unattended text and UDF file together.

Exam Tip: Exam Tips appear in the margins to provide specific exam-related advice. Such tips may address what material is covered (or not covered) on the exam, how it is covered, mnemonic devices, or particular quirks of that exam.

Note: Notes appear in the margins and contain various kinds of useful information, such as tips on the technology or administrative practices, historical background on terms and technologies, or side commentary on industry issues.

---

268   Part I   EXAM PREPARATION

INTRODUCTION

This chapter is mainly concerned with the performance and reliability of your computer. The techniques available in Windows 2000 range from digital signing of device drivers and operating system files to running a command-based Recovery Console in the event the system will not even boot.

To make the most of the hardware you have available, you need to take steps to optimize its use and to prevent the operating system from being modified without your consent. Finally, you need to be able to recover the system in the case of a catastrophic failure.

MANAGING AND TROUBLESHOOTING DRIVER SIGNING

Manage and troubleshoot driver signing.

A new feature in Windows 2000 Professional is the ability to digitally sign both drivers and operating system files. This is the assurance that a particular file has met a certain level of testing and that the file has not been overwritten by the installation program of another application. The application of driver signing is governed by a policy set using the System program in the Control Panel.

NOTE

Strange But True Although it sounds backward, it is true: Windows NT boots from the system partition and then loads the system from the boot par

Digitally Signing a File

Digitally signing a file is the process by which you can guarantee that a particular file comes from the source that it claims to. Since any file can be signed, it is necessary to be able to handle all formats of files, including binary files. A technique called catalog file signing is used to provide digital signing information about files without modifying the file itself.

In catalog file signing, a CAT file is created for each driver or operating system file that is being signed. The CAT file includes a hash of the binary file. A hash is the result of a mathematical operation on some data (in this case, the binary file) that is sensitive to any changes made in the source data. In this way, any change to the

WARNING

Don't Overextend Your Partitions and Wraps It is not necessary to create an extended partition on a disk; primary partitions might be all that you need. However, if you do create one, remember that you can never have more than one extended partition on a physical disk.

Objective Coverage Text: In the text before an exam objective is specifically addressed, you will notice the objective is listed to help call your attention to that particular material.

Warning: In using sophisticated information technology, there is always potential for mistakes or even catastrophes that can occur through improper application of the technology. Warnings appear in the margins to alert you to such potential problems.

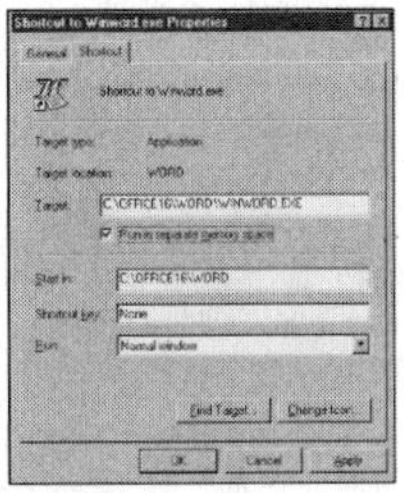

STEP BY STEP

5.1 Configuring an Extension to Trigger an Application to Always Run in a Separate Memory Space

1. Start the Windows NT Explorer.

2. From the View menu, choose Options.

3. Click the File Types tab.

4. In the Registered File Types list box, select the desired file type.

5. Click the Edit button to display the Edit File Type dialog box. Then select Open from the Actions list and click the Edit button below it.

6. In the Editing Action for Type dialog box, adjust the application name by typing **cmd.exe /c start /separate** in front of the existing contents of the field (see Figure 5.15).

FIGURE 5.15
Configuring a shortcut to run a Win16 application in a separate memory space.

Step by Step: Step by Steps are hands-on tutorial instructions that walk you through a particular task or function relevant to the exam objectives.

Figure: To improve readability, the figures have been placed in the margins wherever possible so they do not interrupt the main flow of text.

IN THE FIELD

SHARABLE RESOURCES

Some of the resources used by device drives are reserved for specific devices and some can be shared between devices.

The Interrupt Request (IRQ) uses a Programmable Interrupt Controller (PIC) to request a service for the device. When a request is seen, the current operation is suspended and control given to the device drive associated with the IRQ number (1–15). This resource therefore cannot be shared between devices.

The Input/Output (I/O) port is a memory block used by the device to communicate the service it is requesting. This is tied to the IRQ number and therefore is dedicated to a device.

The Direct Memory Access (DMA) is a direct channel between the device and the computer's memory. The DMA controller supports a number of channels (usually seven) and they are shared between devices (one at a time).

A device memory block is a portion of system memory mapped to the internal memory of the device (usually). This is dedicated to the device and cannot be used by any other process (including Windows 2000 Professional).

In the Field Sidebar: These more extensive discussions cover material that perhaps is not as directly relevant to the exam, but which is useful as reference material or in everyday practice. In the Field may also provide useful background or contextual information necessary for understanding the larger topic under consideration.

REVIEW BREAK

Choosing a File System

But if the system is designed to store data, mirroring might produce disk bottlenecks. You might only know whether these changes are significant by setting up two identical computers, implementing mirroring on one but not on the other, and then running Performance Monitor on both under a simulated load to see the performance differences.

This summary table offers an overview of the differences between the FAT and NTFS file systems.

Review Break: Crucial information is summarized at various points in the book in lists or tables. At the end of a particularly long section, you might come across a Review Break that is there just to wrap up one long objective and reinforce the key points before you shift your focus to the next section.

CASE STUDIES

Case Studies are presented throughout the book to provide you with another, more conceptual opportunity to apply the knowledge you are developing. They also reflect the "real-world" experiences of the authors in ways that prepare you not only for the exam but for actual network administration as well. In each Case Study, you will find similar elements: a description of a Scenario, the Essence of the Case, and an extended Analysis section.

CASE STUDY: REALLY GOOD GUITARS

ESSENCE OF THE CASE

Here are the essential elements in this case:

- need for centralized administration
- the need for WAN connectivity nation-wide
- a requirement for Internet access and e-mail
- the need for Security on network shares and local files
- an implementation of Fault-tolerant systems

SCENARIO

Really Good Guitars is a national company specializing in the design and manufacturer of custom acoustic guitars. Having grown up out of an informal network of artisans across Canada, the company has many locations but very few employees (300 at this time) and a Head Office in Churchill, Manitoba. Although they follow the best traditions of hand-making guitars, they are not without technological savvy and all the 25 locations have computers on-site which are used to do accounting, run MS Office applications, and run their custom made guitar design software. The leadership team has recently begun to realize that a networked solution is essential to maintain consistency and to provide security on what are becoming some very innovative designs and to provide their employees with e-mail and Internet access.

RGG desires a centralized administration of its

continues

Essence of the Case: A bulleted list of the key problems or issues that need to be addressed in the Scenario.

Scenario: A few paragraphs describing a situation that professional practitioners in the field might face. A Scenario will deal with an issue relating to the objectives covered in the chapter, and it includes the kinds of details that make a difference.

Analysis: This is a lengthy description of the best way to handle the problems listed in the Essence of the Case. In this section, you might find a table summarizing the solutions, a worded example, or both.

CASE STUDY: PRINT IT DRAFTING INC.

continued

too, which is unacceptable. You are to find a solution to this problem if one exists.

ANALYSIS

The fixes for both of these problems are relatively straightforward. In the first case, it is likely that all the programs on the draftspeople's workstations are being started at normal priority. This means that they have a priority of 8. But the default says that anything running in the foreground is getting a 2-point boost from the base priority, bringing it to 10. As a result, when sent to the background, AutoCAD is not getting as much attention from the processor as it did when it was the foreground application. Because multiple applications need to be run at once without significant degradation of the performance of AutoCAD, you implement the following solution:

1. On the Performance tab of the System Properties dialog box for each workstation, set the Application Performance slider to None to prevent a boost for foreground applications.

2. Recommend that users keep the additional programs running alongside AutoCAD at a minimum (because all programs will now get equal processor time).

The fix to the second problem is to run each 16-bit application in its own NTVDM. This ensures that the crashing of one application will not adversely affect the others, but it still enables interoperability between the applications because they use OLE (and not shared memory) to transfer data. To make the fix as transparent as possible to the users, you suggested that two things be done:

1. Make sure that for each shortcut a user has created to the office applications, the Run in Separate Memory Space option is selected on the Shortcut tab.

2. Change the properties for the extensions associated with the applications (for example, .XLS and .DOC) so that they start using the /separate switch. Then any file that is double-clicked invokes the associated program to run in its own NTVDM.

CHAPTER SUMMARY

KEY TERMS

Before you take the exam, make sure you are comfortable with the definitions and concepts for each of the following key terms:

- FAT
- NTFS
- workgroup
- domain

This chapter discussed the main planning topics you will encounter on the Windows NT Server exam. Distilled down, these topics revolve around two main goals: understanding the planning of disk configuration and understanding the planning of network protocols.

◆ Windows NT Server supports an unlimited number of inbound sessions; Windows NT Workstation supports no more than 10 active sessions at the same time.

◆ Windows NT Server accommodates an unlimited number of remote access connections (although Microsoft only supports up to 256); Windows NT Workstation supports only a single remote access connection.

Key Terms: A list of key terms appears at the end of each chapter. These are terms that you should be sure you know and are comfortable defining and understanding when you go in to take the exam.

Chapter Summary: Before the Apply Your Knowledge section, you will find a chapter summary that wraps up the chapter and reviews what you should have learned.

EXTENSIVE REVIEW AND SELF-TEST OPTIONS

At the end of each chapter, along with some summary elements, you will find a section called "Apply Your Knowledge" that gives you several different methods with which to test your understanding of the material and review what you have learned.

Chapter 1 PLANNING   **23**

APPLY YOUR KNOWLEDGE

This section allows you to assess how well you understood the material in the chapter. Review and Exam questions test your knowledge of the tasks and concepts specified in the objectives. The Exercises provide you with opportunities to engage in the sorts of tasks that comprise the skill sets the objectives reflect.

Exercises

1.1   Synchronizing the Domain Controllerys

The following steps show you how to manually synchronize a backup domain controller within your domain. (This objective deals with Objective Planning 1.)

Estimated Time: Less than 10 minutes.

1. Click Start, Programs, Administrative Tools, and select the Server Manager icon.

2. Highlight the BDC (Backup Domain Controller) in your computer list.

3. Select the Computer menu, then select Synchronize with Primary Domain Controller.

12.2   Establishing a Trust Relationship between Domains

The following steps show you how to establish a trust relationship between multiple domains. To complete this exercise, you must have two Windows NT Server computers, each installed in their own domain. (This objective deals with objective Planning 1.)

Estimated Time: 10 minutes

1. From the trusted domain select Start, Programs, Administrative Tools, and click User Manager for Domains. The User Manager.

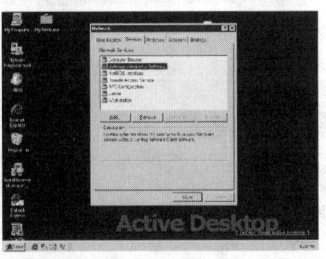

FIGURE 1.2
The login process on a local machine.

2. Select the Policies menu and click Trust Relationships. The Trust Relationships dialog box appears.

4. When the trusting domain information has been entered, click OK and close the Trust Relationships dialog box.

Review Questions

1. List the four domain models that can be used for directory services in Windows NT Server 4.

2. List the goals of a directory services architecture.

3. What is the maximum size of the SAM database in Windows NT Server 4.0?

4. What are the two different types of domains in a trust relationship?

5. In a trust relationship which domain would contain the user accounts?

Exercises: These activities provide an opportunity for you to master specific hands-on tasks. Our goal is to increase your proficiency with the product or technology. You must be able to conduct these tasks in order to pass the exam.

Review Questions: These open-ended, short-answer questions allow you to quickly assess your comprehension of what you just read in the chapter. Instead of asking you to choose from a list of options, these questions require you to state the correct answers in your own words. Although you will not experience these kinds of questions on the exam, these questions will indeed test your level of comprehension of key concepts.

6. Can a local account be used in a trust relation-ship? Explain. .

7. In a complete trust domain model that uses 4 dif-ferent domains, what is the total number of trust relationships required to use a complete trust domain model?

A. Single-domain model

B. Single-master domain model

C. Multiple-master domain model

D. Complete-trust domain model

5. What must be created to allow a user account from one domain to access resources in a differ-ent domain?

A. Complete Trust Domain Model

B. One Way Trust Relationship

C. Two Way Trust Relationship

D. Master-Domain Model

Exam Questions

The following questions are similar to those you will face on the Microsoft exam. Answers to these questions can be found in section Answers and Explanations, later in the chapter. At the end of each of those answers, you will be informed of where (that is, in what section of the chapter) to find more information..

1. ABC Corporation has locations in Toronto, New York, and San Francisco. It wants to install Windows NT Server 4 to encompass all its loca-tions in a single WAN environment. The head office is located in New York. What is the best domain model for ABC's directory services implementation?

A. Single-domain model

B. Single-master domain model

C. Multiple-master domain model

D. Complete-trust domain model

2. JPS Printing has a single location with 1,000 users spread across the LAN. It has special print-ers and applications installed on the servers in its environment. It needs to be able to centrally manage the user accounts and the resources. Which domain model would best fit its needs?

Exam Questions: These questions reflect the kinds of multiple-choice questions that appear on the Microsoft exams. Use them to become famil-iar with the exam question formats and to help you determine what you know and what you need to review or study more.

Answers to Review Questions

1. Single domain, master domain, multiple-master domain, complete-trust domain. See section, Windows NT Server 4 Domain Models, in this chapter for more information. (This question deals with objective Planning 1.)

2. One user, one account, centralized administra-tion, universal resource access, synchronization. See section, Windows NT Server 4 Directory Services, in this chapter for more information. (This question deals with objective Planning 1.)

6. Local accounts cannot be given permissions across trusts. See section, Accounts in Trust Relationships, in this chapter for more informa-tion. (This question deals with Planning 1.)

Answers and Explanations: For each of the Review and Exam questions, you will find thorough explanations located at the end of the section.

Suggested Readings and Resources

The following are some recommended readings on the subject of installing and configuring NT Workstation:

1. Microsoft Official Curriculum course 770: *Installing and Configuring Microsoft Windows NT Workstation 4.0*

   • Module 1: Overview of Windows NT Workstation 4.0

   • Module 2: Installing Windows NT Workstation 4.0

2. Microsoft Official Curriculum course 922: *Supporting Microsoft Windows NT 4.0 Core Technologies*

   • Module 2: Installing Windows NT

   • Module 3: Configuring the Windows NT Environment

3. *Microsoft Windows NT Workstation Resource Kit Version 4.0* (Microsoft Press)

   • Chapter 2: Customizing Setup

   • Chapter 4: Planning for a Mixed Environment

4. Microsoft TechNet CD-ROM

   • *MS Windows NT Workstation Technical Notes*

     • MS Windows NT Workstation Deployment Guide – Automating Windows NT Setup

     • An Unattended Windows NT Workstation Deployment

5. Web Sites

   • www.microsoft.com/train_cert

   • www.prometric.com/testingcandidates/ assessment/chosetest.html (take online

Suggested Readings and Resources: The very last element in every chapter is a list of additional resources you can use if you want to go above and beyond certification-level material or if you need to spend more time on a particular subject that you are having trouble understanding.

Introduction

MCSE Training Guide: Windows 2000 Professional is designed for advanced users, technicians, and system administrators with the goal of certification as a Microsoft Certified Systems Engineer (MCSE). It covers the Installing, Configuring, and Administering Microsoft Windows 2000 Professional exam (70-210). According to Microsoft, this exam measures your ability to implement, administer, and troubleshoot Windows 2000 Professional as a desktop operating system in any network environment.

This book is your one-stop shop. Everything you need to know to pass the exam is in here, and Microsoft has approved it as study material. You do not have to take a class in addition to buying this book to pass the exam. However, depending on your personal study habits or learning style, you may benefit from buying this book *and* taking a class.

Microsoft assumes that the typical candidate for this exam will have a minimum of one year's experience implementing and administering any desktop operating system in a network environment.

How This Book Helps You

This book offers you a self-guided tour of all the areas covered by the Installing, Configuring, and Administering Microsoft Windows 2000 Professional exam and teaches you the specific skills you'll need in order to achieve your MCSE certification. You'll also find helpful hints, tips, real-world examples, and exercises, as well as references to additional study materials. Specifically, this book is set up to help you in the following ways:

◆ **Organization.** The book is organized by individual exam objectives. Every objective you need to know for the Installing, Configuring, and Administering Microsoft Windows 2000 Professional exam is covered in this book. We have attempted to present the objectives in an order that is as close as possible to that listed by Microsoft. However, we have not hesitated to reorganize them where needed to make the material as easy as possible for you to learn. We have also attempted to make the information accessible in the following ways:

  ◆ The full list of exam topics and objectives is included in this introduction.

  ◆ Each chapter begins with a list of the objectives covered in that chapter.

  ◆ Each chapter also features an outline that provides you with an overview of the material and the page numbers where particular topics can be found.

  ◆ The objectives are repeated where the material most directly relevant to it is covered (unless the whole chapter addresses a single objective).

  ◆ The CD-ROM included with this book contains, in PDF format, a complete listing of the test objectives and where they are covered within the book.

◆ **Instructional features**. This book is designed to provide you with multiple ways to learn and reinforce the exam material. The following are some of the helpful methods:

  ◆ *Objective Explanations*. As mentioned previously, each chapter begins with a list of the objectives covered in the chapter. In addition, immediately following each objective is an explanation in a context that defines it more meaningfully.

  ◆ *Study Strategies*. Early in each chapter you will also find strategies for approaching the studying and retaining of the material in the chapter, particularly as it is addressed on the exam.

  ◆ *Exam Tips*. Exam tips appear in the margin to provide specific, exam-related advice. Such tips may address what material is covered (or not covered) on the exam, how it is covered, mnemonic devices, or particular quirks of that exam.

  ◆ *Review Breaks and Summaries*. Crucial information is summarized at various points in the book in lists or tables. Each chapter ends with a summary as well.

  ◆ *Key Terms*. A list of key terms appears near the end of each chapter.

  ◆ *Notes*. These appear in the margins and contain various kinds of useful information such as tips on technology or administrative practices, historical background on terms and technologies, or side commentary on industry issues.

◆ *Warnings*. When using sophisticated information technology, there is always the potential for mistakes or even catastrophes that occur because of improper application of the technology. Warnings appear in the margins to alert you to such potential problems.

◆ *In the Fields*. These more extensive discussions cover material that may not be directly relevant to the exam, but is useful as reference material or in everyday practice. In the Fields may also provide useful background or contextual information necessary for understanding the larger topic under consideration.

◆ *Case Studies*. Each chapter's text concludes with a Case Study. The cases are meant to help you understand the practical applications of the information covered in the chapter.

◆ *Step by Steps*. These are hands-on, tutorial instructions that walk you through a particular task or function relevant to the exam objectives.

◆ *Exercises*. Found at the end of the chapters in the "Apply Your Knowledge" section, exercises are performance-based opportunities for you to learn and assess your knowledge.

◆ **Extensive practice test options.** The book provides numerous opportunities for you to assess your knowledge and practice for the exam. The practice options include the following:

  ◆ *Review Questions*. These open-ended questions appear in the "Apply Your Knowledge" section at the end of each chapter. They allow you to quickly assess your comprehension of what you just read in the chapter. Answers to the questions are provided later in a separate section entitled "Answers to Review Questions."

◆ *Exam Questions*. These questions also appear in the "Apply Your Knowledge" section. Use them to help you determine what you know and what you need to review or study further. Answers and explanations are provided in a separate section entitled "Answers to Exam Questions."

◆ *Practice Exam*. A Practice Exam is included in the "Final Review" section. The Final Review section and the Practice Exam are discussed later in this list.

◆ *ExamGear*. The special Training Guide version of the *ExamGear* software included on the CD-ROM provides further practice questions.

NOTE For a description of the New Riders *ExamGear, Training Guide* software, please see Appendix C, "Using the *ExamGear, Training Guide* Edition Software."

◆ **Final Review.** This part of the book provides you with three valuable tools for preparing for the exam.

   ◆ *Fast Facts*. This condensed version of the information contained in the book will prove extremely useful for last-minute review.

   ◆ *Study and Exam Prep Tips*. Read this section early on to help you develop study strategies. It also provides you with valuable exam-day tips and information on exam/question formats such as adaptive tests and case study-based questions.

◆ *Practice Exam*. A practice test is included. Questions are written in styles similar to those used on the actual exam. Use it to assess your readiness for the real thing.

The book includes several other useful features, such as the sections titled "Suggested Readings and Resources" at the end of each chapter, which directs you toward further information that could aid you in your exam preparation or your actual work. There are valuable appendices as well, including an overview of the Microsoft certification program (Appendix A), and a description of what is on the CD-ROM (Appendix B).

For more information about the exam or the certification process, contact Microsoft:

   Microsoft Education: 800-636-7544

   Internet: `ftp://ftp.microsoft.com/ Services/MSEdCert`

   World Wide Web: `http://www.microsoft.com/ train_cert`

   CompuServe Forum: GO MSEDCERT

WHAT THE INSTALLING, CONFIGURING, AND ADMINISTERING MICROSOFT WINDOWS 2000 PROFESSIONAL EXAM (70-210) COVERS

The Installing, Configuring, and Administering Microsoft Windows 2000 Professional Exam (70-210) covers the Windows 2000 Professional topics represented by the conceptual groupings or units of the test objectives. The objectives reflect job skills in the following areas:

- ◆ Installing Windows 2000 Professional
- ◆ Implementing and Conducting Administration of Resources
- ◆ Implementing, Managing, and Troubleshooting Hardware Devices and Drivers
- ◆ Monitoring and Optimizing System Performance and Reliability
- ◆ Configuring and Troubleshooting the Desktop Environment
- ◆ Implementing, Managing, and Troubleshooting Network Protocols and Services
- ◆ Implementing, Monitoring, and Troubleshooting Security

Before taking the exam, you should be proficient in the job skills represented by the following units, objectives, and subobjectives:

Installing Windows 2000 Professional

Perform an attended installation of Windows 2000 Professional.

Perform an unattended installation of Windows 2000 Professional.

- ◆ Install Windows 2000 Professional by using Windows 2000 Server Remote Installation Services (RIS).
- ◆ Install Windows 2000 Professional by using the System Preparation Tool.

- ◆ Create unattended answer files by using Setup Manager to automate the installation of Windows 2000 Professional.

Upgrade from a previous version of Windows to Windows 2000 Professional.

- ◆ Apply update packs to installed software applications.
- ◆ Prepare a computer to meet upgrade requirements.

Deploy service packs.

Troubleshoot failed installations.

Implementing and Conducting Administration of Resources

Monitor, manage, and troubleshoot access to files and folders.

- ◆ Configure, manage, and troubleshoot file compression.
- ◆ Control access to files and folders by using permissions.
- ◆ Optimize access to files and folders.

Manage and troubleshoot access to shared folders.

- ◆ Create and remove shared folders.
- ◆ Control access to shared folders by using permissions.
- ◆ Manage and troubleshoot Web server resources.

Connect to local and network print devices.

- ◆ Manage printers and print jobs.

- ◆ Control access to printers by using permissions.

- ◆ Connect to an Internet printer.

- ◆ Connect to a local print device.

Configure and manage file systems.

- ◆ Convert from one file system to another file system.

- ◆ Configure file systems by using NTFS, FAT32, or FAT.

Implementing, Managing, and Troubleshooting Hardware Devices and Drivers

Implement, manage, and troubleshoot disk devices.

- ◆ Install, configure, and manage DVD and CD-ROM devices.

- ◆ Monitor and configure disks.

- ◆ Monitor, configure, and troubleshoot volumes.

- ◆ Monitor and configure removable media, such as tape devices.

Implement, manage, and troubleshoot display devices.

- ◆ Configure multiple-display support.

- ◆ Install, configure, and troubleshoot a video adapter.

Implement, manage, and troubleshoot mobile computer hardware.

- ◆ Configure Advanced Power Management (APM).

- ◆ Configure and manage card services.

Implement, manage, and troubleshoot input and output (I/O) devices.

- ◆ Monitor, configure, and troubleshoot I/O devices, such as printers, scanners, multimedia devices, mouse, keyboard, and smart card reader.

- ◆ Monitor, configure, and troubleshoot multimedia hardware, such as cameras.

- ◆ Install, configure, and manage modems.

- ◆ Install, configure, and manage Infrared Data Association (IrDA) devices.

- ◆ Install, configure, and manage wireless devices.

- ◆ Install, configure, and manage USB devices.

Update drivers.

Monitor and configure multiple processing units.

Install, configure, and troubleshoot network adapters.

Monitoring and Optimizing System Performance and Reliability

Manage and troubleshoot driver signing.

Configure, manage, and troubleshoot the Task Scheduler.

Manage and troubleshoot the use and synchronization of offline files.

Optimize and troubleshoot performance of the Windows 2000 Professional desktop.

- ◆ Optimize and troubleshoot memory performance.
- ◆ Optimize and troubleshoot processor utilization.
- ◆ Optimize and troubleshoot disk performance.
- ◆ Optimize and troubleshoot network performance.
- ◆ Optimize and troubleshoot application performance.

Manage hardware profiles.

Recover systems and user data.

- ◆ Recover systems and user data by using Windows Backup.
- ◆ Troubleshoot system restoration by using Safe Mode.
- ◆ Recover systems and user data by using the Recovery Console.

Configuring and Troubleshooting the Desktop Environment

Configure and manage user profiles.

Configure support for multiple languages or multiple locations.

- ◆ Enable multiple-language support.
- ◆ Configure multiple-language support for users.
- ◆ Configure local settings.

- ◆ Configure Windows 2000 Professional for multiple locations.

Install applications by using Windows Installer packages.

Configure and troubleshoot desktop settings.

Configure and troubleshoot fax support.

Configure and troubleshoot accessibility services.

Implementing, Managing, and Troubleshooting Network Protocols and Services

Configure and troubleshoot the TCP/IP protocol.

Connect to computers by using dial-up networking.

- ◆ Connect to computers by using a virtual private network (VPN) connection.
- ◆ Create a dial-up connection to connect to a remote access server.
- ◆ Connect to the Internet by using dial-up networking.
- ◆ Configure and troubleshoot Internet Connection Sharing.

Connect to shared resources on a Microsoft network.

Implementing, Monitoring, and Troubleshooting Security

Encrypt data on a hard disk by using Encrypting File System (EFS).

Implement, configure, manage, and troubleshoot local Group Policy.

Implement, configure, manage, and troubleshoot local user accounts.

- ❖ Implement, configure, manage, and troubleshoot auditing.

- ❖ Implement, configure, manage, and troubleshoot account settings.

- ❖ Implement, configure, manage, and troubleshoot account policy.

- ❖ Create and manage local users and groups.

- ❖ Implement, configure, manage, and troubleshoot user rights.

Implement, configure, manage, and troubleshoot local user authentication.

- ❖ Configure and troubleshoot local user accounts.

- ❖ Configure and troubleshoot domain user accounts.

Implement, configure, manage, and troubleshoot a security configuration.

HARDWARE AND SOFTWARE YOU'LL NEED

As a self-paced study guide, *MCSE Training Guide: Windows 2000 Professional* is meant to help you understand concepts that must be refined through hands-on experience. To make the most of your studying, you need to have as much background on and experience with Windows 2000 Professional as possible. The best way to do this is to combine studying with work on Windows 2000 Professional. This section gives you a description of the minimum computer requirements you need to enjoy a solid practice environment.

You will find that many of the concepts presented in this book explore the use of Windows 2000 Professional within a Windows 2000 networked environment. To fully practice some of the exam objectives, you will need access to two (or more) computers networked together. You will also find that access to both the Windows 2000 Professional and Server products is beneficial. The following presents a detailed list of hardware and software requirements:

- ❖ Windows 2000 Professional (and optionally Windows 2000 Server)

- ❖ Windows 95/98 and/or Windows NT 4.0 Workstation (this software is required to test upgrade paths to Windows 2000 Professional)

- ❖ A server and a workstation computer on the Microsoft Hardware Compatibility List

- ❖ Pentium 133MHz (or better) (Pentium 200 recommended)

- ❖ 2GB hard disk with a minimum of 650MB of free space

- ❖ VGA (or Super VGA) video adapter and monitor

- ❖ Mouse or equivalent pointing device

- ❖ CD-ROM drive

- ❖ Network Interface Card (NIC) or modem connection to the Internet

- ❖ Presence of an existing network, or use of a two-port (or more) miniport hub to create a test network

- ❖ 64MB of RAM (128MB recommended)

It can be easy to obtain access to the necessary computer hardware and software in a corporate business environment. It can be difficult, however, to allocate enough time within the busy workday to complete a self-study program. Most of your study time will occur after normal working hours, away from the everyday interruptions and pressures of your regular job.

ADVICE ON TAKING THE EXAM

More extensive tips are found in the Final Review section titled "Study and Exam Prep Tips," but keep this advice in mind as you study:

◆ **Read all the material.** Microsoft has been known to include material not expressly specified in the objectives. This book has included additional information not reflected in the objectives in an effort to give you the best possible preparation for the examination—and for the real-world experiences to come.

◆ **Do the Step by Steps and complete the Exercises in each chapter.** They will help you gain experience using the specified methodology or approach. All Microsoft exams are task- and experienced-based and require you to have experience actually performing the tasks upon which you will be tested.

◆ **Use the questions to assess your knowledge.** Don't just read the chapter content; use the questions to determine what you know and what you don't. If you are struggling at all, study some more, review, then assess your knowledge again.

◆ **Review the exam objectives.** Develop your own questions and examples for each topic listed. If you can develop and answer several questions for each topic, you should not find it difficult to pass the exam.

NOTE

> **Exam-Taking Advice** Although this book is designed to prepare you to take and pass the Installing, Configuring, and Administering Microsoft Windows 2000 Professional certification exam, there are no guarantees. Read this book, work through the questions and exercises, and when you feel confident, take the Assessment Exam and additional exams using the *ExamGear, Training Guide Edition* test software. This should give you a good indication of whether you are ready for the real thing.
>
> When taking the actual certification exam, make sure you answer all the questions before your time limit expires. Do not spend too much time on any one question. If you are unsure, answer it as best as you can; then mark it for review when you have finished the rest of the questions. (This advice will not apply if you are taking an adaptive exam, however. In that case, take your time on each question. There is no opportunity to go back to a question.)

Remember, the primary object is not to pass the exam—it is to understand the material. After you understand the material, passing the exam should be simple. Knowledge is a pyramid; to build upward, you need a solid foundation. This book and the Microsoft Certified Professional programs are designed to ensure that you have that solid foundation.

Good luck!

NEW RIDERS PUBLISHING

The staff of New Riders Publishing is committed to bringing you the very best in computer reference material. Each New Riders book is the result of months of work by authors and staff who research and refine the information contained within its covers.

As part of this commitment to you, the NRP reader, New Riders invites your input. Please let us know if you enjoy this book, if you have trouble with the information or examples presented, or if you have a suggestion for the next edition.

Please note, however, that New Riders staff cannot serve as a technical resource during your preparation for the Microsoft certification exams or for questions about software- or hardware-related problems. Please refer instead to the documentation that accompanies the Microsoft products or to the applications' Help systems.

If you have a question or comment about any New Riders book, there are several ways to contact New Riders Publishing. We will respond to as many readers as we can. Your name, address, or phone number will never become part of a mailing list or be used for any purpose other than to help us continue to bring you the best books possible. You can write to us at the following address:

New Riders Publishing
Attn: Executive Editor
201 W. 103rd Street
Indianapolis, IN 46290

If you prefer, you can fax New Riders Publishing at 317-581-4663.

You also can send email to New Riders at the following Internet address:

nrfeedback@newriders.com

NRP is an imprint of Pearson Education. To obtain a catalog or information, contact us at nrmedia@newriders.com. To purchase a New Riders book, call 800-428-5331.

Thank you for selecting *MCSE Training Guide: Windows 2000 Professional.*

Exam Preparation

This chapter covers topics associated with installing Windows 2000 Professional. It helps you prepare for the exam by addressing the following exam objectives:

Perform an attended installation of Windows 2000 Professional.

▶ As a system support professional working with Windows 2000 you will need to know how to install Windows 2000. No matter how you install Windows 2000 you will find that knowledge of the manual installation process will help you fully understand the installation process and how to troubleshoot a failed installation.

Perform an unattended installation of Windows 2000 Professional.

- **Install Windows 2000 Professional by using Windows 2000 Server Remote Installation Services (RIS).**

- **Install Windows 2000 Professional by using the System Preparation Tool.**

- **Create unattended answer files by using Setup Manager to automate the installation of Windows 2000 Professional.**

▶ In most large environments you will want to use automated tools to assist in the deployment of Windows 2000. Microsoft has introduced a number of tools to speed up the deployment of Windows 2000. These objectives ensure that support professionals understand all of the options available for the deployment of Windows 2000.

Upgrade from a previous version of Windows to Windows 2000 Professional.

- **Apply update packs to installed software applications.**

- **Prepare a computer to meet upgrade requirements.**

CHAPTER 1

Installing Windows 2000 Professional

▶ It is very rare that you will be installing Windows 2000 in brand new environments. In most situations you will be installing Windows 2000 into existing environments and will be required to upgrade existing systems. This objective ensures you understand the issues associated with upgrading existing Windows 9x and Windows NT environments to Windows 2000.

Deploy service packs.

▶ Microsoft is rapidly developing new features and fixes for their products. This objective ensures that you understand the role the Service Pack plays in your environment. Service Packs are more than just bug fixes—they are the primary vehicles Microsoft has to release new features.

Troubleshoot failed installations.

▶ Anyone installing a product should be able to troubleshoot problems when they pop up. This objective covers a number of common installation problems that you may encounter with Windows 2000.

▶ When studying for this chapter I suggest you sit down and install Windows 2000 no fewer than five times. Although the installation process is not the most exciting process in the world, it is very structured. The more times you see it, the easier it will be to recognize the major phases of the installation process. No matter what type of installation you are performing (with the exception of disk imaging), you will always see the four phases of the installation process.

After fully exploring manual (attended) installations of the Windows 2000 product, you should focus on automating the installation process. Do not try to get too fancy—simply use the Setup Manager to create an unattended text file and uniqueness database file.

I suggest you read about the RIS and RIPrep processes but don't get caught up in the details. To fully understand these services you need a solid background in Active Directory. This technology is covered in great detail on other exams. For the purposes of this exam, you need to understand only the technology required to support the RIS process—not details relating to specific services.

INTRODUCTION

Chapter 1 covers the installation of Windows 2000. The chapter starts with an overview of the Windows 2000 product line. During the discussion of the installation a number of questions are presented so that you will be fully prepared to complete the installation of Windows 2000. Topics include system requirements, disk configurations, file systems, licensing, and workgroup versus domain model. The installation process is also covered in detail so you will be able to identify the steps involved in installing Windows 2000.

Automated installations of Windows 2000 are also covered in this chapter. We explore the use of unattended text files, Remote Installation Services, and the process of imaging a hard drive. At the end of the chapter you will be able to identify the Windows 2000 technologies that assist in the automated installation of Windows 2000.

The chapter ends with a discussion of the upgrade process for legacy Windows 9x and Windows NT operating systems.

WINDOWS 2000 PRODUCTS

Windows 2000 represents the latest version of Microsoft's Windows NT technology. The Windows 2000 product line includes four versions of the product. This section briefly summarizes each of these products and the major differences among them.

Windows 2000 Professional is the workstation operating system of choice in a Windows 2000 environment. Windows 9x and Windows NT 4.0 Workstations must be replaced if companies are to fully utilize the features of Windows 2000 (software deployment, Group Policies, and Active Directory, to name a few).

Windows 2000 Server includes all of the features of Windows 2000 Professional, but it is optimized to offer network services. Windows 2000 Server is ideal for file and print services and Web services.

Windows 2000 Server offers improved network management and supports Microsoft Active Directory (AD). AD represents one of the most significant changes to the Microsoft Windows product line.

NOTE

Windows 2000 and the Alpha Platform Windows NT and Beta releases of Windows 2000 provide support for the Alpha platform. You should note that Microsoft has discontinued support for the Alpha platform.

Windows 2000 Server supports Symmetric Multiple Processing (SMP). Windows 2000 Server supports four processors. This platform supports 4GB of RAM on an Intel-based system.

Windows 2000 Advanced Server is an enhanced version of the Windows 2000 Server product. Advanced Server is designed to support larger enterprise-level services. Advanced Server includes all of the capabilities of the Server product with the addition of clustering (both application fail over and network load balancing). Windows 2000 Advanced Server supports SMP for up to eight processors. Windows 2000 Advanced Server supports 8GB of RAM.

Windows 2000 Data Center Server is the powerhouse of the Microsoft server products. Data Center Server includes all of the features of Advanced Server but is "souped up" to support up to 32 processors and 64GB of RAM. Data Center Server is the product of choice for very large analytical processing environments.

BEFORE YOU BEGIN INSTALLATION

Once you have determined the version of Windows 2000 you need to install, you must consider a number of options regarding its installation. Ensure that you have answers to the following questions before you begin your installation:

◆ Does your system meet the minimum hardware requirements?

◆ Have you determined the optimal disk partition configuration for your system?

◆ Which file system is appropriate for your environment?

◆ Which licensing mode should be used (for server installations)?

◆ Will you be installing your system into a workgroup or domain?

The following sections provide an overview of these configuration options.

NOTE **Symmetric Multi Processors (SMP)** SMP support lets a Windows 2000 Server support more than one processor. This allows applications to run on multiple processors simultaneously (if they are multithreaded applications). SMP can greatly improve the performance of some applications.

NOTE **SMP and Data Center Server** At the time of writing this text, the Data Center Server product had not been released. Microsoft's documentation states that the product will support a total of 32 processors. At this time it is not clear if the retail Data Center Server product will support 32 processors. Most likely you will need to purchase an OEM (Original Equipment Manufacturer) version of the product to obtain support for 32 processors.

EXAM TIP **What Product Is Right for Your Environment?** Expect questions on the exam that require you to identify the right product for a specific environment. To answer these questions you must understand the platform on which each product runs and for what use Microsoft intended it.

Hardware Requirements

Table 1.1 lists the minimum hardware requirements to install and operate Windows 2000 Professional and Windows 2000 Server.

TABLE 1.1		
WINDOWS 2000 PROFESSIONAL/SERVER MINIMUM HARDWARE REQUIREMENTS		
Component	*Windows 2000 Professional Requirements*	*Windows 2000 Server Requirements*
Processor	Pentium 133MHz (or higher)	Pentium 133MHz (or higher)
Memory	64MB for Intel-based processors	128MB for Intel-based processors (256MB recommended)
Hard Disk	One or more hard disks with a minimum of 2GB on the system partition (with a minimum of 650MB of free space)	One or more hard disks with a minimum of 2GB on the system partition (with a minimum of 1GB of free space)
Network	One or more network adapters	One or more network adapters
Display	Video display adapter and monitor with video graphics adapter (VGA) resolution or higher	
Other	CD-ROM drive A high-density 3.5-inch disk drive Keyboard and mouse	

Before installing any of the Windows 2000 products you should ensure that your hardware meets the minimum standards just listed.

Disk and Partition Options

Windows 2000 supports two types of disk storage. The first, called *basic storage,* is one you will most likely be familiar with. The second is new to Windows 2000 and is called *dynamic storage.*

Basic storage is similar to disks found in the Windows 95/98 and Windows NT 4.0 environments. Basic storage consists of disks that contain primary partitions and extended partitions with logical drives. You can have up to four primary partitions, or up to three primary partitions and one extended partition per physical hard disk.

Dynamic storage consists of a disk that contains volumes rather than partitions. To create a dynamic disk you must convert a basic disk into a dynamic disk. Dynamic storage offers the following advantages over basic storage:

◆ Volumes can be extended to include noncontiguous space on the available disks.

◆ There is no limit on the number of volumes you can create on a single disk.

◆ Disk configuration information is stored on the disk instead of the Windows registry. Configuration information is also replicated to all other dynamic disks so that one disk failure will not cause all dynamic storage to become unavailable.

Once converted to dynamic, you cannot convert a disk back to basic without removing all existing volumes from the disk. If you want to convert a basic disk into a dynamic disk you must ensure that a minimum of 1MB of free (unallocated) space is available on your basic disks. This area is needed to track dynamic disk configuration information. Without it the conversion process cannot proceed.

Managing Partitions on Basic Disks

Basic disks allow for a number of different partition configurations. A *partition* is an area of a physical hard disk that functions as though it were a separate unit. There is a limit of four partitions per physical disk.

A *primary partition* is a partition that can contain the files necessary to boot a particular operating system. A primary partition cannot be further subpartitioned. There can be up to four primary partitions per physical disk.

NOTE **Dynamic Disks and the Installation Process** You do not need to be an expert on Windows 2000 dynamic disks to understand the Windows 2000 installation process. It is discussed in this chapter only so you don't limit your options when you install Windows 2000.

If you partition your hard disks so that 1MB of unallocated space is not available on the end of your drive, you must repartition your hard disk to create the space. If you repartition your disks you will need to reinstall Windows 2000. In short, if you ever think you might want to convert your disks to dynamic, make sure you leave the unpartitioned space at the end of your hard drive before you install Windows 2000.

NOTE **Dynamic Disk and Windows 9x/Windows NT** Dynamic disks are not supported on Windows 95/98 or Windows NT. If you are dual-booting your system and you convert your disk from basic to dynamic, you will no longer be able to access the partitions (called volumes if converted to a dynamic disk) from Windows 9x or Windows NT.

NOTE **Basic Disks Versus Dynamic Disks** A hard disk must either be basic or dynamic. You cannot combine the store types on one disk.

NOTE

Reverting from Dynamic to Basic Disks   To change a dynamic disk back into a basic disk, you must delete all volumes from the dynamic disk. (The procedure would be to open the Disk Management Console and right-click the drive letter to convert [under the Volume column]. This menu should include an entry to delete the volume.) Once you have done this, then through Disk Management, right-click the dynamic disk that you want to change back to a basic disk, and then click Revert to Basic Disk.

A primary partition is needed for a Windows 2000 system partition. The system partition is needed to load Windows 2000 (it contains NTLDR and NTDETECT.COM). Only a primary partition can be used for the system partition.

Windows 2000 also uses a Boot partition. The Boot partition contains the actual Windows 2000 operating system files. The system partition can be on the same partition but does not have to be.

You are limited to four primary partitions per physical disk. In some situations, however, you may require more partitions. To assist in breaking the four-partition limit, you have the ability to create an *extended partition.* Extended partitions are similar to primary partitions in that they define areas of space on a physical hard drive.

The main differences between primary partitions and extended partitions are as follows:

◆ There can be only one extended partition per physical hard disk.

◆ Extended partitions need to be divided into logical drives.

◆ The only limit that exists on the number of logical drives is the number of letters in the alphabet.

◆ Logical drives cannot be configured as bootable (they cannot become a Windows 2000 system partition).

During installation, the Windows 2000 Setup program examines the hard disk to determine its existing configuration. The Setup program will allow you to create new partitions. Microsoft suggests that you create only the partition on which you will install Windows 2000. Once Windows 2000 is installed and operational, you can use the Disk Management utility to manage disk configurations.

Microsoft recommends that you install Windows 2000 on a partition with a minimum of 2GB. As previously mentioned, Windows 2000 requires only 650MB of free disk space. However, the recommended 2GB partition allows for flexibility in the future. In many cases, software will require space on the boot partition of the system.

If you are planning to convert your basic disks to dynamic disks, ensure that your disk has a minimum of 1MB of unpartitioned space free.

Windows 2000 File Systems

Before you decide which file system to use, you should understand the benefits and limitations of each file system. Changing a volume's existing file system can be time-consuming, so choose the file system that best suits your long-term needs. If you decide to use a different file system, you must back up your data and then reformat the volume using the new file system. However, you can convert a FAT or FAT32 volume to an NTFS volume without formatting the volume (like most disk operations, however, it is recommended that you back up your data before the conversion).

The following sections provide an overview of the differences between FAT, FAT32, and NTFS file systems.

FAT

File Allocation Table (FAT) is a file system that has been around for a very long time and is currently supported by most operating systems on the market.

The primary benefit of using FAT is that it is supported by Windows NT 3.5x/4.0, Windows 95/98, Windows 3.x, and DOS. For this reason, FAT is an exceptional choice for systems that are required to dual-boot between Windows 2000 and one (or more) of the previously mentioned operating systems.

The version of FAT supported by Windows 2000 has a number of additional features that are not supported by systems running DOS. When used under Windows 2000, the FAT file system supports the following additional features:

- ◆ Long filenames up to 255 characters
- ◆ Multiple spaces
- ◆ Multiple periods
- ◆ Filenames are not case-sensitive but do preserve case

The FAT file system is a logical choice for systems where dual-boot capabilities are required. FAT is also a good choice for small partitions (less then 400MB) because it has very low system overhead.

FAT has other advantages as well: There are many tools and utilities available to address problems and recover data, and you can start the computer with an MS-DOS bootable floppy disk on Intel-based machines that are experiencing startup failures.

For all the benefits of FAT, it should be recognized that it has a number of major limitations that should make you stop and think before it becomes your file system of choice on your Windows 2000 system.

The primary limitations of FAT are as follows:

◆ FAT is inefficient for larger partitions. As files grow in size, they may become fragmented on the disk, causing slower access times. FAT also uses inefficient cluster sizes. A cluster is the smallest unit of storage on a partition. If the cluster size is too large, you can end up with lots of wasted space on the partition.

◆ FAT provides no local security. The FAT file system does not support local security, so there is no way to prevent a user from accessing a file if the user can log in to the local operating system.

◆ FAT does not support compression, encryption, remote storage, mount points, and disk quotas under Windows 2000.

FAT32

The FAT32 file system is very similar to FAT. FAT32 was introduced in the Microsoft product line with Windows 95 OSR 2. The primary difference between FAT and FAT32 is that FAT32 supports a smaller cluster size, so it does not have as much wasted space as that associated with larger partitions.

Like FAT, FAT32 supports long filenames, multiple spaces, multiple periods, and preserves case while not being case-sensitive.

FAT32 also has its limitations, however:

◆ FAT32 has no local security. It does not support local security, so there is no way to prevent a user from accessing a file if he or she can log in to the local operating system.

◆ FAT32 does not support compression, encryption, remote storage, mount points, or disk quotas under Windows 2000.

◆ FAT32 is not supported by all versions of Windows 95 and is not supported by DOS and Windows NT. You need to be careful when deciding to use it. If you plan to dual-boot your system, ensure that all the operating systems you are using support FAT32. If they do not, the FAT32 partitions will not be accessible to those operating systems.

NTFS

NTFS is the file system of choice on most systems running Windows 2000. NTFS offers the following benefits:

◆ **Support for long filenames.** NTFS supports long filenames up to 255 characters.

◆ **Preservation of case.** NTFS is not case-sensitive, but it does have the capability to preserve case for POSIX compliance.

◆ **Recoverability.** NTFS is a recoverable file system. It uses transaction logging to automatically log all files and directory updates so that in case of a system failure the operating system can redo failed operations.

◆ **Security.** NTFS provides folder- and file-level security for protecting files.

◆ **Compression.** NTFS supports compression of files and folders to help save disk space.

◆ **Encryption.** NTFS supports file-level encryption. This gives a user the ability to encrypt sensitive files so that no one else can read the files.

◆ **Disk quotas.** NTFS partitions support user-level disk quotas. This gives an administrator the ability to set an upper limit on the amount of space that a user can use on a partition. Once the user reaches his limit, he is not allowed to store more information on the partition.

◆ **Sparse files.** These are very large files created by applications in such a way that only limited disk space is needed. NTFS allocates disk space only to the portions of a file that are written to.

◆ **Size.** NTFS partitions can support much larger partition sizes than FAT. NTFS can support partitions up to 16 *exabytes* in size (this is equal to 16 billion gigabytes).

Using NTFS gives you enhanced functionality and scalability compared to FAT and FAT32.

The main limitation of NTFS is that other operating systems do not support it and it has high system overhead. If you need to dual-boot your system or have partitions less than 400MB in size, it is recommended that you format your partitions with FAT or FAT32.

Licensing Mode

Every installation of Windows 2000 requires a license. When you purchase a copy of Windows 2000 you receive a license for the single instance of the operating system you are installing. You also are required to have a Client Access License (CAL) for all clients that are attaching to your server over the network.

Windows 2000 Servers support two licensing modes: Per Seat and Per Server.

The Per Seat licensing mode requires that a Client Access License be purchased for each client that will access your server over the network. In environments where clients will be accessing multiple servers, this licensing mode works well.

The Per Server licensing mode requires that a license be purchased for each connection to a server. This is the preferred licensing mode in environments where a limited number of clients attach to the network or there are only a small number of servers.

The right licensing mode for your environment can be determined by completing a few simple calculations. To determine the number of CALs required for a Per Seat installation, simply count the total number of clients that will be accessing resources over the network. To determine the number of Per Server licenses required, count the total number of connections required for each server in your environment (clients requesting resources from your server). Compare the numbers. The mode that requires the fewest number of licenses is preferred for your environment.

When calculating the total number of licenses required, remember that access to the following services does not require a CAL:

◆ Anonymous or authenticated access to a computer running Internet Information Server (IIS)

◆ Telnet and File Transfer Protocol (FTP) connections

If you are in doubt, select Per Server. Microsoft allows you to perform a one-time server license conversion from Per Server to Per Seat. Per Seat to Per Server license conversions are not allowed.

Workgroup Versus Domain Models

During the installation of Windows 2000 you must choose the type of network security group to which you want to belong. Your choices are between a domain model and a workgroup model. This section quickly describes each model and the information required to join the security group.

Workgroup Model

A workgroup is a logical grouping of computers created to assist in the organization of equipment. Under the workgroup model, each computer that is part of a workgroup maintains its own security database. Because security data is managed at each machine separately, the workgroup model is limited to small groupings of machines. To join a workgroup during the installation process, you need only know the name of the workgroup.

Domain Model

The domain model is similar to the workgroup model in that it creates logical groupings of computer equipment. The primary difference between the workgroup and domain models is that the domain model supports a centralized database of security information.

NOTE **Licensing Mode** Licensing issues make for great scenario questions. Ensure that you know what options you have for licensing and how to calculate the total number of CALs required based on different licensing scenarios.

Joining a domain requires the following:

- ◆ The Domain Name Service (DNS) name of the domain (for example, `Microsoft.com`).

- ◆ A computer account must exist for the computer you are installing. Before a computer can join a domain, a computer account must exist in the domain. Your network administrator, prior to the installation process, can create the computer account. You can also create the computer account during the installation process if you have authority to add domain computer accounts. (In Chapter 7, "Implementing, Monitoring, and Troubleshooting Security," see the sections titled "User Rights" and "Built-In Groups" for details on the rights required to create computer accounts.)

- ◆ A domain controller and DNS server must be available on the network.

INSTALLING WINDOWS 2000 PROFESSIONAL—AN OVERVIEW

Once you have planned your Windows 2000 installation, you can start the installation process. This section provides an overview of the installation process and emphasizes the configuration information required during each phase of the installation.

The Windows 2000 installation process is broken into following phases:

1. Running the setup program

2. Completing the Setup Wizard

3. Installing networking components

4. Completing the installation

> **EXAM TIP**
>
> **The Four Phases of the Installation**
> As you study the upcoming sections, make sure you learn the different phases of the installation process. You can expect to be asked where certain configuration options are set during installation.

Phase 1—Running the Setup Program

To begin the Windows 2000 installation you will need to start your computer and access the Windows 2000 installation files. You have four ways to start the installation process:

◆ Boot the system, load the appropriate drivers to access the CD-ROM, and load the setup program from the command prompt by executing the WINNT.EXE command.

◆ Create a Windows 2000 boot disk using the MAKEBOOT command (run the MAKEBOOT A: command, found in the BOOTDISK directory of the Windows 2000 installation CD). Booting from a Windows 2000 boot disk will cause the setup program to run automatically.

◆ If your computer supports booting from the CD-ROM you can boot the system from the CD-ROM with the Windows 2000 CD in the drive. This will cause the setup program to run automatically.

◆ You can also create a network client and attach to the installation files over the network.

The first phase of the installation process is often referred to as the "text-mode" portion of the installation. During this portion of the installation you are asked for the basic installation information. This information is required to prepare the installation partition and copy required installation files to the hard disk.

The text-mode setup process completes the following steps:

1. Setup loads a minimal version of Windows 2000 into memory.

2. The text-mode portion of setup starts.

3. You are prompted to load third-party RAID/SCSI drivers. To load drivers, press F6.

4. The setup program prompts you to select a boot partition for this installation of Windows 2000 (the boot partition is where Windows 2000 is run from).

5. The setup program prompts you for the file system you would like for the partition. If you have created a new partition, you are asked for the file system type. If you have selected an existing partition, you are asked if you would like to convert it to NTFS.

6. Setup copies files to the hard disk and saves configuration information.

7. Setup restarts the computer and then starts the Graphical User Interface (GUI) portion of the installation.

Phase 2—Completing the Setup Wizard

After the text-mode installation has restarted your computer, the GUI-mode installation begins. This is where a large number of configuration options are specified.

Once the setup program has installed Windows 2000 security features and detected hardware devices, the Setup Wizard prompts you for the following information:

1. Regional settings

2. Name and organization

3. Product key

4. Computer name and password for the local Administrator account

5. Time and date

Phase 3—Installing Networking Components

This phase of the installation process guides you through the configuration of the Windows 2000 networking components. During this portion of the installation the following occurs:

1. Setup detects your network adapter(s). If setup cannot detect your adapter, you must provide the appropriate drivers on a disk. After configuring your network adapter, Windows 2000 will attempt to locate a DHCP server on the network.

2. Setup then prompts you to choose to install networking components with typical or custom settings. The typical installation includes the following options:

   ◆ Client for Microsoft Networks

   ◆ File and Print Sharing for Microsoft Networks

   ◆ TCP/IP

3. Setup prompts you to join a workgroup or a domain.

4. Setup installs and configures the Windows 2000 components that you specified.

After installing the networking components, the setup program moves to the final phase of installation.

Phase 4—Completing the Installation

The final phase of installation completes the following:

◆ Copies the remaining files to your system

◆ Applies the configuration you selected

◆ Saves your configuration to the local hard disk

◆ Removes temporary files

◆ Restarts the computer

As soon as the system restarts, the Network Identification Wizard runs. This wizard asks whether you are the only user who will be accessing this system, or can other users access it as well. If you indicate that you are the only user, you are assigned administrative privileges on the local machine.

MANUALLY INSTALLING WINDOWS 2000 PROFESSIONAL

Perform an attended installation of Windows 2000 Professional.

The next two sections focus on how a technician would install Windows 2000 Professional at the computer rather than remotely or through an automated process. Two methods are available: installation from a CD and installation from a network.

Installing from a Local CD

Installing from a local CD-ROM is one of the easiest ways to install Windows 2000. This option makes sense, however, only if you are installing a small number of computers, or a nonstandard configuration, because it is time-consuming.

To install Windows 2000 from the local CD-ROM you must gain access to the CD in one of three ways:

◆ Boot the system and load the appropriate drivers to access the CD-ROM.

◆ Create a Windows 2000 boot disk using the MAKEBOOT command (run the MAKEBOOT A: command, found in the BOOTDISK directory of the Windows 2000 installation CD, to create a boot disk). Booting from a Windows 2000 boot disk will cause the setup program to run automatically.

◆ Boot the system from the CD-ROM with the Windows 2000 CD in the drive (this option is supported only on computers that can boot from the CD-ROM). This will cause the setup program to run automatically.

If you booted from a Windows 2000 Boot disk or from a Windows 2000 installation CD, the setup program will run automatically. Alternatively, you will have to run the setup program manually. Depending on the operating system you use to boot the computer you will run either WINNT.EXE or WINNT32.EXE.

If you are using DOS to access your CD-ROM you will run WINNT.EXE to start the setup process. If you are installing Windows 2000 over Windows 95/98 or Windows NT (performing either an upgrade or a new installation) you will run WINNT32.EXE to start the setup process.

Both WINNT and WINNT32 support a number of command switches that allow for customization of the installation process. Table 1.2 presents the command switches associated with WINNT. Table 1.3 presents the command switches associated with WINNT32. To use a switch, type the command, followed by a space, followed by the switch.

TABLE 1.2	

WINNT.EXE COMMAND SWITCHES

Switch	*Description*
/a	Enables accessibility options.
/e:command	Executes a command before the final phase of setup.
/i:inf_file	Specifies the filename of the setup information file. The default is Dosnet.inf. A setup information file is used to automate the installation.
/r:folder	Specifies an optional folder to be installed.
/rx:folder	Specifies an optional folder to be copied.
/s:source_path	Specifies the location of the Windows 2000 installation files.
/t:temp_drive	Specifies the location where temporary files should be copied during installation.
/u:script_file	Specifies an unattended text file (this will be discussed in greater detail in upcoming sections).
/udf:id, file	Used in conjunction with an unattended text file (to be discussed in greater detail in upcoming sections).

EXAM TIP

Command Switches and the Exam
You will need to remember the command switches associated with both the WINNT and WINNT32 setup programs.

TABLE 1.3

WINNT32.EXE COMMAND SWITCHES

Switch	Description
/copydir:folder	This option creates an additional folder with the systemroot. For example, if the source folder contains a folder called Private_drivers that has modifications just for your site, you can type **/copydir:Private_drivers** to have setup copy that folder to your installed Windows 2000 folder. The new folder location would be C:\Winnt\ Private_drivers. You can use /copydir to create as many additional folders as you want.
/copysource: folder name	Creates an additional folder within the systemroot (just like the copydir option). Setup deletes the files after the installation is complete.
/cmd:command	Executes a command before the final stage of setup.
/cmdcons	Copies additional files to the hard disk that are necessary to load a command-line interface for repair and recovery.
/debug level:file	Creates a debug log at a specified level.
/s:source_path	Specifies the location of the Windows 2000 installation files. You can specify multiple paths to speed up the installation process.
/syspart:drive	Copies setup startup files to a hard disk and marks the drive as active. This allows you to move the hard disk to another computer to complete the installation. You must use the /tempdrive option with this switch.
/tempdrive:drive	Specifies the location where temporary files should be placed.
/checkupgradeonly	Checks your computer for upgrade compatibility with Windows 2000. For Windows 95 or Windows 98 upgrades, setup creates a report named Upgrade.txt in the Windows installation folder. For Windows NT 3.51 or 4.0 upgrades, it saves the report to the Winnt32.log in the installation folder.

Switch	*Description*
/makelocalsource	Instructs setup to copy all installation source files to your local hard disk. Use /makelocalsource when installing from a CD to provide installation files when the CD is not available later in the installation.
/unattend:file	Specifies an unattended text file (to be discussed in greater detail in upcoming sections).
/Udf:id, udf_file	Used in conjunction with an unattended text file (to be discussed in greater detail in upcoming sections).

NOTE

Making Boot Disks Windows NT users will notice that the /b option is no longer supported by WINNT or WINNT32. A floppyless install is now the default installation mode. You can run a program called MAKEBOOT from the Bootdisk folder on the root of the Windows 2000 installation CD, if you want to use a floppy disk to start the install.

Installing Over a Network

In environments where you are installing a large number of systems you will find that installing over the network is preferred to local CD-based installations. Generally, installing over the network is easier to manage and is much faster than CDs.

To install Windows 2000 over a network, run the setup program from a shared network folder. The setup program copies the required file to the local system and then starts the installation process. This process is very similar to the CD-based installation but has the following additional requirements:

◆ A distribution server with a copy of Windows 2000 installation files must be available.

◆ You must have network client software so that client computers can attach to the distribution server.

◆ Client computers must have an existing 685MB partition (1GB is highly recommended). This partition is required so the installation files can be copied from the distribution server to the client before installation starts.

Once you meet these requirements you will be able to start a networked installation of Windows 2000. Step by Step 1.1 shows you how to do just that.

STEP BY STEP

1.1 Networked Installation of Windows 2000

1. Start the local computer and initialize the client network software.

2. Connect to the distribution server.

3. Run WINNT.EXE or WINNT32.EXE (and any command switches you require) to start the setup program. A temporary folder called Win_nt.~ls will be created. This folder contains the temporary installation files required to install Windows 2000.

4. Setup will restart the computer. Upon reboot, Phase 1 of the installation will begin.

AUTOMATING THE INSTALLATION PROCESS

Perform an unattended installation of Windows 2000 Professional.

Microsoft has greatly improved the tools available to deploy Windows 2000 Professional. Windows 2000 can be installed in three ways: manual installation from CD, imaging, or Remote Installation Services (RIS) images.

In most large deployments of Windows 2000 it would be impractical to install each server and workstation using the traditional CD-based installation. Instead, Microsoft has tools that leverage the fact that most systems can be installed using standardized configurations. Using Windows 2000 deployment tools such as RIS, deployments will be automated so that the only user intervention the installations will require is to turn the computer on.

Due to the power that these new deployment tools offer and the importance of this technology to companies planning large installations of Windows 2000 Professional, it is essential that you are able to analyze deployment scenarios to determine the most effective tool to get the job done.

Creating Unattended Installation Files

Although the computers on most networks are not identical, they usually have a number of similarities. It is possible to create a script file that will automate the installation process so that little or no user intervention is required during the installation process.

Using setup scripts offers a number of benefits for most deployments. The following list includes some of these benefits:

◆ Little or no user intervention is required so the chance of human error is reduced.

◆ You can be assured that all machines installed have consistent and correct configurations.

◆ Staff with little or no knowledge of Windows 2000 can complete installations.

Files Used for Unattended Installation

Two different files are used during an unattended installation. The first file is called an unattended text file (sometimes referred to as an answer file). This file contains all of the information necessary to install Windows 2000. The second file is called a Uniqueness Database File (UDF). Most large deployment systems have a standard configuration that will be applied to each system. However, there will always be a number of settings that must be unique to each machine (the computer name, for example). The unattended text file is used to configure all of the standard options for each machine (one file for each type of hardware platform in your environment); the UDF file is used to configure the unique aspects of each individual computer.

The UDF file is optional. You can create a unique unattended text file for each computer in your environment. In most situations, however, this solution is impractical, because the management of the unattended text files becomes difficult. Most organizations will assess the operational requirements of each computer being installed and categorize them into major groupings. An unattended text file would then be created for each category of system. A UDF file would also be needed so that the unique configuration options for each individual computer, within each category, could be included in the installation process.

Both the answer and UDF files can be created using the Windows 2000 Setup Manager or using a simple text editor. The Setup Manager is part of the Windows 2000 Resource Kit and can be installed by running Setup.exe from the \Support\tools folder on the Windows 2000 distribution CDs.

The Setup Manager allows you to do the following:

◆ Create answer and UDF files using an easy-to-use graphical interface

◆ Specify computer-specific or user-specific information

◆ Include application setup scripts in the answer files

◆ Create answer files (winnt.sif) that can be used if booting from the installation CD

◆ Automatically create a networked distribution folder for the installation files

In the next two sections we will explore the contents of an unattended text file and a UDF file, and the Setup Manager.

Creating an Unattended Text File

Using an unattended text file allows the administrator to start the installation of Windows 2000 and walk away. The installation process reads the unattended text file and uses the information contained within it to configure the system.

To install Windows 2000 using an unattended text file, use the /u switch after the WINNT or WINNT32 command. The syntax of this command is as follows:

```
WINNT /u:"answer file" /s:"source path where the Windows
➡2000 installation files can be found"
```

or

```
WINNT32 /unattend:"answer file" /s:"source path where the
➡Windows 2000 installation files can be found"
```

where:

◆ /u or /unattend is the switch specifying that this is an unattended installation.

◆ "answer file" is the name of the answer file that you have created (the default name is Unattended.txt).

◆ /s is the switch to point to the location of the Windows 2000 installation files.

◆ "source path" is the location of the Windows 2000 installation files (the I386 directory for an Intel installation).

The main purpose of the unattended text file is to answer all of the prompts that the person performing the installation would manually enter during the installation. You can use the same unattended text file across a number of computers. If you use the same unattended text file in this way, however, you will need to revisit each computer after the installation is complete to configure unique aspects of each computer (unless a Uniqueness Database File (UDF) is used—more on this later).

Following is a sample unattended text file (you can find a copy of this file on the Windows 2000 CD in the I386 directory). This file can be opened using any text editor. The information found in Unattended.txt is categorized into section headings, parameters, and values associated with those parameters. The sample file contains a fraction of the total number of section headings and parameters supported during unattended installations. (For a complete listing, see the *Microsoft Windows 2000 Unattended Setup Parameters Guide: Answer File Parameters for Unattended Installation of Microsoft Windows 2000*, Microsoft Corporation, Revision 1.5 April 9, 1999, available at `http://www.microsoft.com/TechNet/win2000/win2ksrv/technote/unattend.asp`.)

EXAM TIP

Command Syntax Matters You are sure to get a question regarding the syntax of the unattended text file. If you can memorize the syntax, these are easy marks.

As you review this file, note that information is organized in the following format:

```
[Section Heading]
; Comments
; Comments
Parameter = value
```

The file contents are listed here:

```
; Microsoft Windows NT Workstation Version 5.0 and
; Windows NT Server Version 5.0
; (c) 1994 - 1998 Microsoft Corporation. All rights
; reserved.
;
; Sample Unattended Setup Answer File
;
; This file contains information about how to automate the
; installation
; or upgrade of Windows NT Workstation and Windows NT
; Server so the
; Setup program runs without requiring user input.
;
; For information on how to use this file, read the
; appropriate sections
; of the Windows NT 5.0 Resource Kit.

[Unattended]
Unattendmode = FullUnattended
OemPreinstall = NO
TargetPath = WINNT
Filesystem = LeaveAlone

[UserData]
FullName = "Your User Name"
OrgName = "Your Organization Name"
ComputerName = "COMPUTER_NAME"

[GuiUnattended]
TimeZone = "004"
; Sets the Admin Password to NULL
AdminPassword = *
; Turn AutoLogon on
AutoLogon = Yes
;For Server installs

[LicenseFilePrintData]
AutoMode = "PerServer"
AutoUsers = "0"

[GuiRunOnce]
; List the programs that you want to lauch when the machine
; is logged into for the first time
; "Notepad %WINDIR%\Setuperr.log"
```

```
[Display]
BitsPerPel = 4
XResolution = 800
YResolution = 600
VRefresh = 70

[Networking]
; When set to YES, setup will install default networking
; components. The components to be set are
; TCP/IP, File and Print Sharing, and the Client for
; Microsoft Networks.
InstallDefaultComponents = YES

[Identification]
JoinWorkgroup = Workgroup
```

Information in the Unattended.txt file is divided into main sections. Table 1.4 provides explanations of the section headings and parameters found in a typical Unattended.txt file.

TABLE 1.4

SECTION HEADINGS AND PARAMETERS IN A TYPICAL UNATTENDED TEXT FILE

Section Heading	Option (Values)	Description
Unattended This section header is used to identify whether an unattended installation is being performed. This section is required in an Unattend.txt file; otherwise, the answer file will be ignored.	UnattendMode (Values: GuiAttended / ProvideDefault / DefaultHide / ReadOnly / FullUnattended)	This parameter defines the unattended mode to be used during GUI-mode setup. The default value is DefaultHide when the key is not specified. When this key is specified, text-mode setup is fully automated with or without the necessary answers. GuiAttended specifies that the GUI-mode section of setup is attended. When specified, the end-user will be required to answer all questions in the GUI-mode portion of setup before setup completes. This mode is useful in preinstallation scenarios in which the OEM or administrator wants to automate only text-mode setup. *continues*

TABLE 1.4	*continued*

SECTION HEADINGS AND PARAMETERS IN A TYPICAL UNATTENDED TEXT FILE

Section Heading	Option (Values)	Description
		ProvideDefault specifies that answers in the answer file are defaults. In this case, setup will display these default answers to the user, who may change them if desired. This is useful in preinstallation scenarios where the OEM or administrator wants to give persons setting up the machine the option to change the predefined default answers (especially network options).
		DefaultHide specifies that answers in the answer file are defaults. Unlike the ProvideDefault value, setup will not display the user interface to end users if all the answers relating to a particular wizard page are specified in the answer file. If only subsets of the answers on a page are specified, the page will be displayed with the provided answers. The user will be able to modify any of the answers on the displayed page. This is useful in deployment scenarios where an administrator may only want end users to provide the administrator password on the computer. This is the default behavior if unattended mode is not specified.

Section Heading	*Option (Values)*	*Description*
		ReadOnly specifies that answers in the answer file are read-only if the wizard pages containing these answers are displayed to the end user. Just like the DefaultHide parameter, no user interface is displayed to the user if all answers on a page are supplied in the answer file. Unlike the DefaultHide parameter, however, the user can only specify new answers on a displayed page. This is useful in scenarios where an administrator wants to force specific answers on a page.
		FullUnattended specifies that GUI mode is fully unattended. If a required setup answer is not specified in the answer file, an error will be generated. This is useful in deployment scenarios where a complete hands-off installation is required and an unspecified answer is an error in the answer file.
	Repartition (Values: Yes/No)	Specifies whether all partitions on the first drive on the client computer should be deleted and the drive reformatted with the NTFS file system.
	FileSystem (Values: ConvertNTFS/ LeaveAlone)	This key specifies whether the primary partition should be converted to NTFS or left alone.

continues

TABLE 1.4   *continued*

SECTION HEADINGS AND PARAMETERS IN A TYPICAL UNATTENDED TEXT FILE

Section Heading	Option (Values)	Description
	NtUpgrade (Values: Yes/No)	This key determines whether a previous version of Windows 2000 Professional or Server, Windows 2000 Advanced Server, or Windows 2000 Datacenter Server should be upgraded.
	Win9xUpgrade (Values: Yes/No)	The Win9xUpgrade key determines whether previous installations of Windows 95 or Windows 98 should be upgraded to Windows 2000. Yes indicates that the Windows installation should be upgraded, and No means do not upgrade the installation if found. The default is No. This parameter is necessary only when using an answer file to upgrade an existing Windows 9x computer to Windows 2000. It is valid only if used in conjunction with Winnt32.exe.
	TargetPath (Values: * or <path name>)	This key determines the installation folder in which Windows 2000 should be installed. * indicates that setup should generate a unique folder name for the installation. This is usually WINNT, unless that folder already exists. In that case, setup will install into WINNT.*X* (where X is between 0 and 999) if that folder does not already exist.

Section Heading	*Option (Values)*	*Description*
		\<path name\> is the user-defined install folder and should not include the drive letter. To specify the target drive, the /tempdrive command line option to Winnt32.exe or /t option to Winnt.exe must be specified.
UserData This section is used to specify user-specific data into the installation process—specifically, the user's name, organization, computer name, and product ID.	FullName (Value: \<string\>)	The FullName key is used to specify the user's full name. If the key is empty or missing, the user is prompted to enter a name.
	OrgName (Value: \<string\>)	This key is used to specify an organization's name. If the OrgName key is empty or missing, the user is prompted to enter an organization name.
	ComputerName (Value: \<string\>)	This key is used to specify the computer name. If the ComputerName key is empty or missing, the user is prompted to enter a computer name. If the value is *, setup generates a random computer name based on the organization name specified. The computer name specified should contain no more than 64 characters. If more than 64 characters are used for the ComputerName parameter, the computer name will be truncated to 64 characters.

continues

| TABLE 1.4 | *continued* |

SECTION HEADINGS AND PARAMETERS IN A TYPICAL UNATTENDED TEXT FILE

Section Heading	*Option (Values)*	*Description*
	ProductID (Value: \<string>)	The ProductID key specifies the Microsoft Product Identification (Product ID) number. This parameter sets the Product ID for all computers installed using this unattended text file to the same value. This could cause issues when calling Microsoft product support.
GuiUnattended This section is used to specify settings for the GUI portion of the installation. It can be used to indicate the time zone and to hide the administrator password page.	AdminPassword (Values: \<password>/*)	This key sets up the administrator account password. If the value is *, setup will set the Administrator password to NULL.
	AutoLogon (Values: Yes/No)	This key, if set to Yes, sets up the computer to auto-logon once with the Administrator account. The default behavior is No. The key is not valid on upgrades. If you specify an AdminPassword, that password will be used to perform the auto-logon process. The password will be deleted from the copy of the answer file left on the computer after the installation is complete.

Section Heading	*Option (Values)*	*Description*
	AutoLogonCount (Value: \<integer\>)	This key lists the number of times that the computer should automatically log on using the administrator account and password specified. The value is decremented after each logon and the feature is disabled after the specified number of logon attempts is complete. It is useful only when AutoLogon = Yes. A reboot is required to decrement the counter.
	TimeZone (Value: \<index\>)	The TimeZone key determines the time zone of the computer. If the key is empty, the user is prompted to select a time zone.
	ProfilesDir (Value: \<path to profile directory\> Default: %systemdrive%\ Documents and Settings)	The ProfilesDir key is used to specify the location of Windows 2000 profiles. This parameter is valid only on clean installs of Windows 2000 and is ignored on upgrades. The ProfilesDir parameter is useful in scenarios that require new installations to use the same profile directory as Windows NT 4.0. For example, ProfilesDir = %systemroot%\Profiles. The directory specified must contain an environment variable such as %systemdrive% or %systemroot%.

continues

TABLE 1.4 | *continued*

SECTION HEADINGS AND PARAMETERS IN A TYPICAL UNATTENDED TEXT FILE

Section Heading	Option (Values)	Description
	DetachedProgram (Value: <detached program string>)	The DetachedProgram key is used to indicate the path of the custom program that should run concurrently with the setup program. If the program requires any arguments, the Arguments key must be specified.
	Arguments (Value: <arguments string>)	The Arguments key indicates that arguments or parameters accompany the custom program that should run concurrently with the setup program.
LicenseFilePrintData This section is only applied to Windows 2000 Server installations. It enables you to specify the licensing option you want to use for your server (such as, per server or per seat licensing and the number of licenses).	AutoMode (Values: PERSEAT/ PERSERVER)	The AutoMode key determines whether Windows 2000 Server, Windows 2000 Advanced Server, or Windows 2000 Datacenter Server is to be installed in a per seat or a per server license mode. If AutoMode = PERSERVER, the AutoUsers key must also be specified. PERSEAT indicates that a client access license has been purchased for each computer that accesses the server. PERSERVER indicates that client access licenses have been purchased for the server to allow a certain number of concurrent connections to the server.

Section Heading	Option (Values)	Description
		If AutoMode is empty or missing, the user will be prompted to select the license mode.
	AutoUsers (Value: integer)	This key is valid only if AutoMode = PerServer. The integer value indicates the number of client licenses purchased for the server being installed. The minimum value allowed is 5 (less than 5 will cause the install to fail).
GuiRunOnce This section specifies a command you want run when the installation completes for the first time and the computer is rebooted. This is useful if you want to install additional software on the computer after the operating system is installed.		
Display This section allows you to specify the display settings you want applied.	BitsPerPixel (Value: <valid bits per pixel>)	This key specifies the <valid bits per pixel> for the graphics device being installed. For example, a value of 8 (2^8) implies 256 colors; 16 implies 65,536 colors.
	Xresolution (Value: <valid x resolution>)	This key specifies a <valid x resolution> for the graphics device being installed.
	Yresolution (Value: <valid y resolution>)	This key specifies a <valid y resolution> for the graphics device being installed.
	Vrefresh (Value: <valid refresh rate>)	This key specifies a <valid refresh rate> for the graphics device being installed.

continues

TABLE 1.4	*continued*

**SECTION HEADINGS AND PARAMETERS IN A TYPICAL
UNATTENDED TEXT FILE**

Section Heading	Option (Values)	Description
		Be very careful with these settings. An improperly configured refresh rate can damage your monitor.
Networking	InstallDefault Components	When set to Yes, setup will install default networking components.
This section is used to specify network settings such as network adapters, services, and protocols. If this section is not provided, networking will not be installed.	(Values: Yes | No Default: No)	The default networking configuration automatically installs the following: TCP/IP on all network adapters, File and Printer Sharing for Microsoft Networks, and Client for Microsoft Networks.

Creating Uniqueness Database Files

UDF files allow you to specify the unique settings associated with each computer in your environment. As shown in the previous section, UDF files can be created using the Setup Manager. You may, however, want to modify your UDF file to include additional configuration settings (above and beyond unique computer names).

UDF files contain two sections. One section of the file, indicated by the [UniqueIds] header, contains a listing of all Unique IDs referenced in the file and the sections associated with them. The second part of the file contains the actual sections that are to be used by each computer when it is installed.

When a UDF file is used in conjunction with an answer file, any configuration setting associated with a Unique ID is merged with the contents of the answer file.

The following is a listing of a standard UDF file:

```
;SetupMgrTag
[UniqueIds]
    Workstation1=UserData, Networking
    Workstation2=UserData
    Workstation3=UserData
    Workstation4=UserData

[Workstation1:UserData]
    ComputerName=Workstation1

[Workstation2:UserData]
    ComputerName=Workstation2

[Workstation3:UserData]
    ComputerName=Workstation3

[Workstation4:UserData]
    ComputerName=Workstation4

[Workstation1:Network]
    JoinDomain="DomainName"
```

Note the top header of this file. This UDF file is set up to configure four computers (Workstation1, Workstation2, Workstation3, and Workstation4). We see this from the [UniqueIds] section of the file. We can also see that Workstation1 will have a UserData and Network configuration stored in this file. Workstation2 through Workstation4 have UserData configurations stored. In this example, Workstation1 has a custom network configuration. Workstation2 through Workstation4 would receive the network configuration specified in the unattended answer file.

Using the Setup Manager

The Setup Manager is a powerful tool that assists in the creation of unattended answer and UDF files. The utility is part of the Windows 2000 Professional support tools and found in the zip file DEPLOY.ZIP in the \Support\Tools directory on the Windows 2000 Professional CD.

After you have extracted the files from the DEPLOY.ZIP file into a subdirectory, performing the steps in Step by Step 1.2 will run the Setup Manager.

STEP BY STEP

1.2 Running the Setup Manager

1. Go to the subdirectory into which you extracted the files from the DEPLOY.ZIP file. Double-click the SETUPMGR.EXE file to start the Setup Manager.

2. In the Welcome to the Windows 2000 Setup Manager Wizard window, click Next (as shown in Figure 1.1).

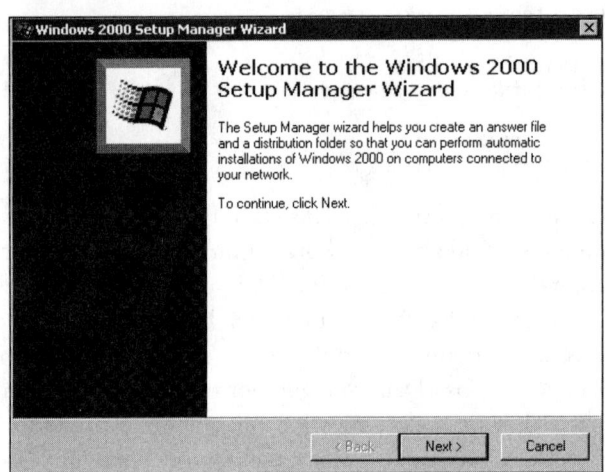

FIGURE 1.1
Windows 2000 Setup Manager welcome screen.

3. The New or Existing Answer File window will then be presented (see Figure 1.2). Your options are as follows:

   ◆ **Create a New Answer File.** This option will allow you to create a new answer file based on the information you supply. Use this option when you want to create a new answer file.

◆ **Create an Answer File that Duplicates this Computer Configuration.** This option will create a new answer file based on the existing configuration of the computer from which you are running Setup Manager. Use this option if the computer you are using is similar to the new computers you want to install.

◆ **Modify an Existing Answer File.** This option allows you to select an existing answer file so it can be edited. Use this option if you want to edit an existing configuration file.

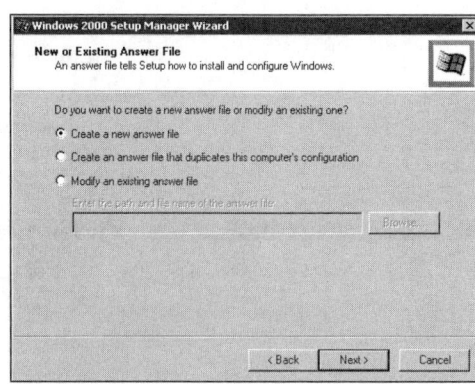

FIGURE 1.2
Setup Manager—New or Existing File Options.

Depending on the option you select, the Setup Wizard will walk you through the process of creating or editing an unattended text file.

Table 1.5 presents the major categories of information requested by the Setup Manager during the creation of a new answer file.

TABLE 1.5

WINDOWS 2000 SETUP WIZARD CONFIGURATION OPTIONS

Information Category	Options	Description
Product to Install (see Figure 1.3)	Windows 2000	Allows for the creation of an answer file for the installation of Windows 2000 (Professional or Server).
	RIS	Allows for the creation of an answer file for use with a Remote Installation Server.
	Sysprep	Allows for the creation of an answer file that can be used by the Sysprep mini installer program (see the section "The System Preparation (Sysprep) Tool" for details).

continues

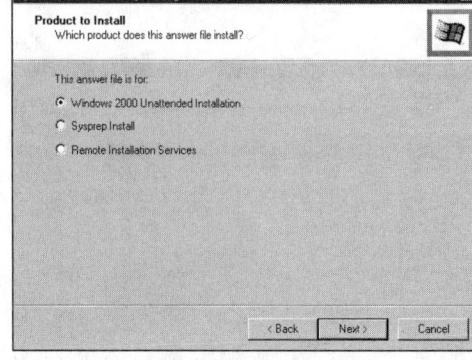

FIGURE 1.3
Setup Manager—Product to Install.

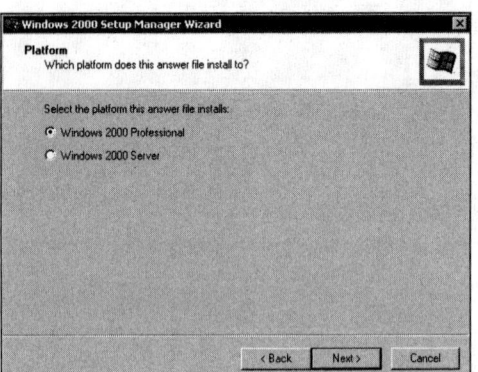

FIGURE 1.4
Setup Manager—Platform Installation Options.

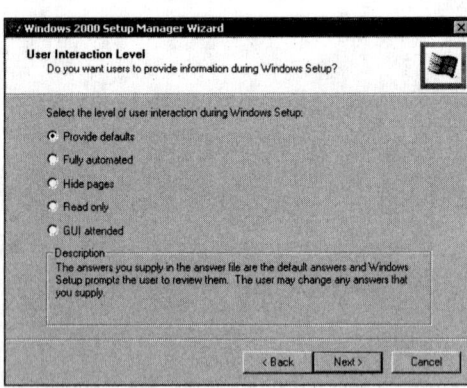

FIGURE 1.5
Setup Manager—User Interaction Level.

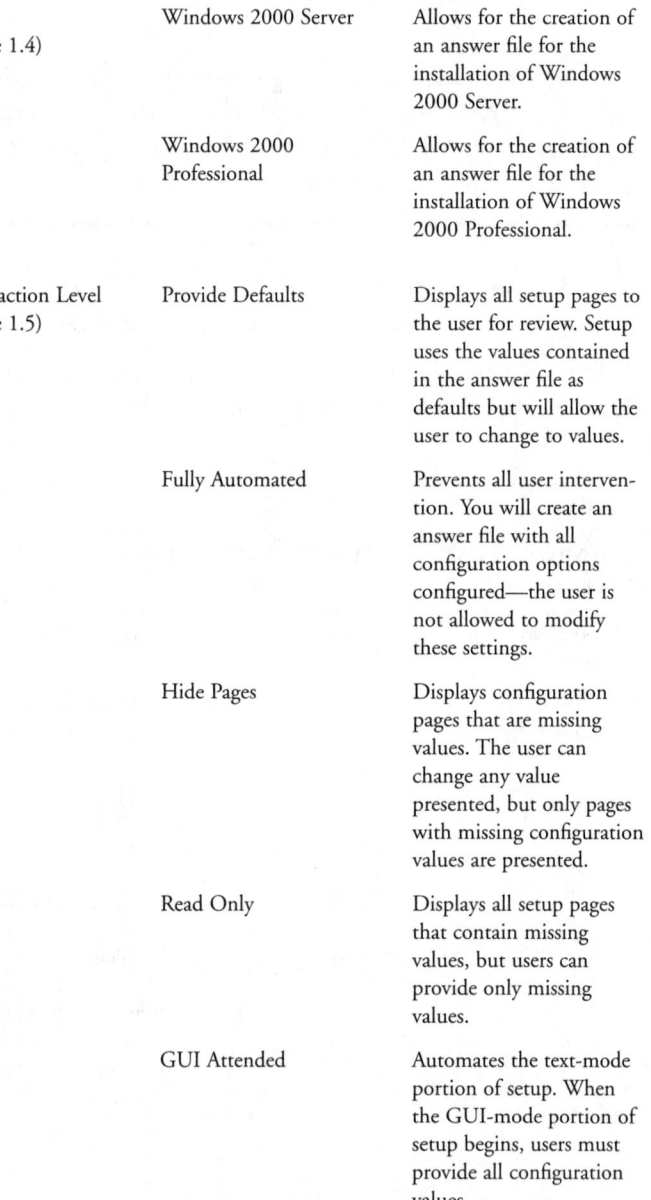

TABLE 1.5	*continued*

WINDOWS 2000 SETUP WIZARD CONFIGURATION OPTIONS

Information Category	Options	Description
Platform (see Figure 1.4)	Windows 2000 Server	Allows for the creation of an answer file for the installation of Windows 2000 Server.
	Windows 2000 Professional	Allows for the creation of an answer file for the installation of Windows 2000 Professional.
User Interaction Level (see Figure 1.5)	Provide Defaults	Displays all setup pages to the user for review. Setup uses the values contained in the answer file as defaults but will allow the user to change to values.
	Fully Automated	Prevents all user intervention. You will create an answer file with all configuration options configured—the user is not allowed to modify these settings.
	Hide Pages	Displays configuration pages that are missing values. The user can change any value presented, but only pages with missing configuration values are presented.
	Read Only	Displays all setup pages that contain missing values, but users can provide only missing values.
	GUI Attended	Automates the text-mode portion of setup. When the GUI-mode portion of setup begins, users must provide all configuration values.

Information Category	Options	Description	
Customize the Software (see Figure 1.6)	Name	Allows you to associate a name with this computer (usually a department name).	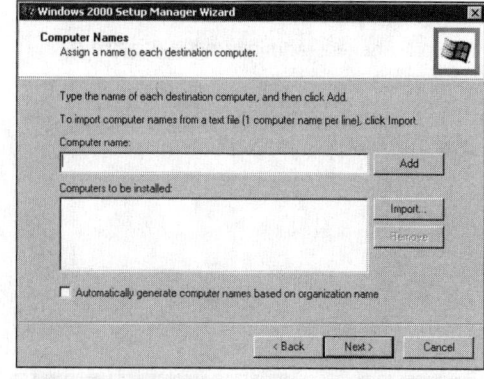
	Organization	Allows you to associate an organization with the computer (usually the company name).	
			FIGURE 1.6 Setup Manager—Customize the Software Options.
Computer Names (see Figure 1.7)	Computer Name/ Computers to Be Installed	Allows you to specify the name or names of the computers you want to install. If you specify multiple computer names, the Setup Wizard will automatically create a UDF file with the appropriate section headings to uniquely name each computer.	
		You also have the option to have the setup program automatically generate computer names (it uses part of the organization name and a random number to create unique computer names).	
Administrator Password (see Figure 1.8)	Prompt the User for an Administrator Password	During the GUI portion of the installation, the user is prompted for an Administrator password. This allows for some degree of security (because the Administrator's password is not written to the answer file), but the installation will not be fully automated because the user must provide the password during install.	**FIGURE 1.7** Setup Manager—Computer Names.

continues

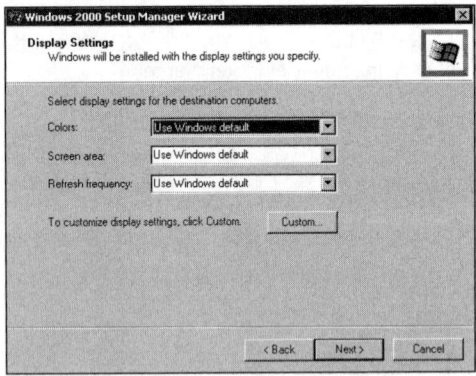

FIGURE 1.8
Setup Manager—Administrative Password
Options.

TABLE 1.5	*continued*

**WINDOWS 2000 SETUP WIZARD CONFIGURATION
OPTIONS**

Information Category	*Options*	*Description*
	Use the Following Administrator Password	This allows you to specify the Administrator's password. This might be considered a security risk. The password is written to the answer file (it is deleted once the installation is complete, however, so a copy is not left on the new computer), and all computers that use the answer file will have the same Administrator's password. This option does, however, allow for a completely unattended installation.
	When the Computer Starts, Automatically Log on as Administrator	This option will automatically log into the computer as Administrator after setup is complete. This option works only if the password has been left blank and therefore does not provide any security.
Display Settings (see Figure 1.9)	Colors	Allows you to set the color depth of your adapter.
	Screen Area	Allows you to set the horizontal and vertical screen area.
	Refresh Frequency	Allows you to set the video refresh rate.
	Custom Video Settings	This button will open a dialog box asking for the Color (in bits/pixel), Screen Area on the X (horizontal) axis, Screen Area on the Y (vertical) axis, and refresh frequency in Hertz.

FIGURE 1.9
Setup Manager—Display Settings.

Information Category	*Options*	*Description*
Network Settings (see Figure 1.10)	Typical Settings	The typical setting installs TCP/IP, enables the Dynamic Host Configuration Protocol (DHCP) client, and installs the Client for Microsoft Networks.
	Custom Settings	The custom setting allows you to select the number of network adapter cards and the network components you would like to install (such as TCP/IP or Client for Novell Networks).
Workgroup or Domain (see Figure 1.11)	Workgroup	Allows you to join a workgroup.
	Windows Server Domain	Allows you to join a Windows Server Domain. You can also provide the credentials required to create a computer account in the domain.
Time Zone (see Figure 1.12)	Time Zone	Allows you to set up your time zone and daylight savings configuration.

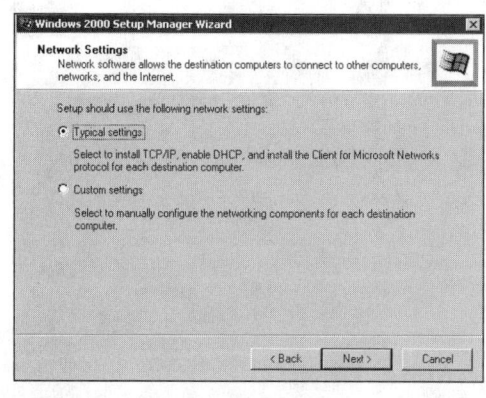

FIGURE 1.10
Setup Manager—Network Settings.

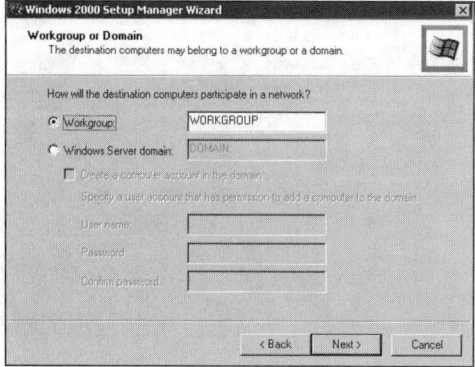

FIGURE 1.11
Setup Manager—Domain Configuration.

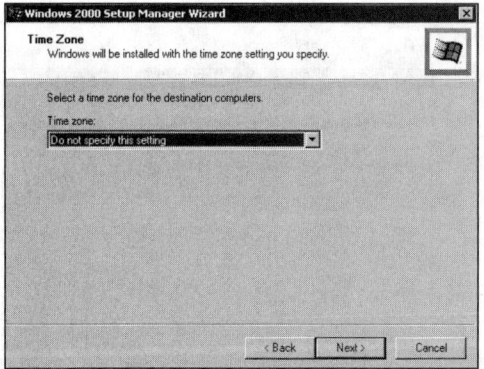

FIGURE 1.12
Setup Manager—Time Zone Configuration Options.

continues

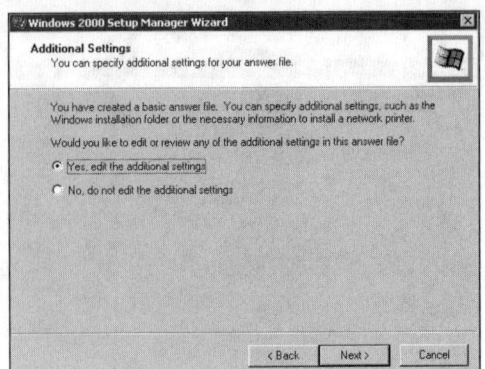

FIGURE 1.13
Setup Manager—Configure Additional Settings.

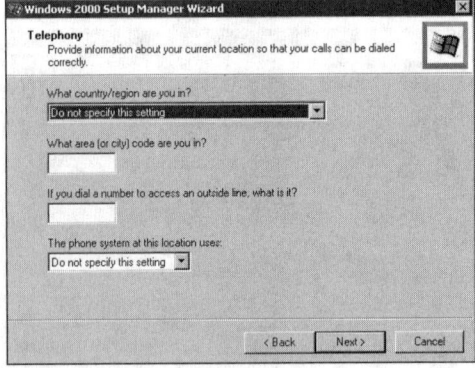

FIGURE 1.14
Setup Manager—Telephony Settings.

TABLE 1.5	*continued*

WINDOWS 2000 SETUP WIZARD CONFIGURATION OPTIONS

Information Category	*Options*	*Description*
Additional Settings (see Figure 1.13)	Telephony (see Figure 1.14)	Allows you to specify settings for telephony. This includes the country code, dialing type (tone or pulse), area code, and long distance access code.
	Regional Settings (see Figure 1.15)	Allows you to specify the regional preferences for dates, times, currency, numbers, and keyboard layout.
	Languages (see Figure 1.16)	Allows you to specify additional language character sets.
Browser and Shell Settings (see Figure 1.17)	Use Default Internet Explorer Settings	Allows the default configuration options associated with Internet Explorer to be used.

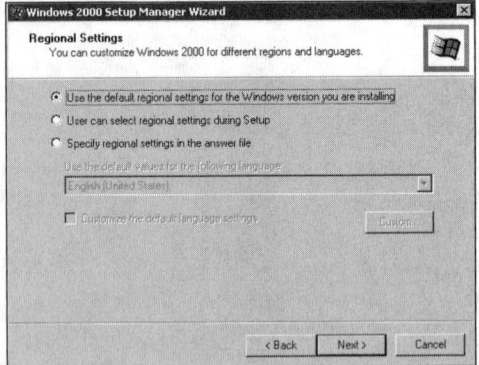

FIGURE 1.15
Setup Manager—Regional Settings.

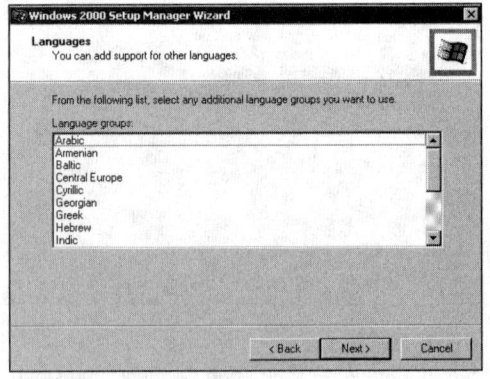

FIGURE 1.16
Setup Manager—Languages.

Information Category	Options	Description
	Use an Auto Configuration Script Created by the Internet Explorer Administration Kit to Configure Your Browser	Allows a PAC (Proxy Auto Configuration) file to be specified for the browser. PAC files are script files that tell the browser to work with proxy servers in your environment.
	Individually Specify Proxy and Default Home Page Settings	Allows individual configuration settings to be provided for the browser.
Installation Folder (see Figure 1.18)	Installation Folder	Allows you to specify the location where Windows 2000 will be installed.
Install Printers (see Figure 1.19)	Network Printer Name/ Install these Printers	Allows you to specify one or more printers to install as part of the automated installation. This allows you to have printers enabled as soon as the computer is installed. The first printer in the list of installed printers will be set as the default printer.
Run Once (see Figure 1.20)	Command to Run/ Run These Commands	The Run Once page allows you to specify commands that should be run upon first logon. The commands will be run in the user's security context, so you must ensure that the first user to log on has appropriate privileges to run the command. Any printers that you specified in the Printer Configuration page will be listed as part of the Run These Commands page.

continues

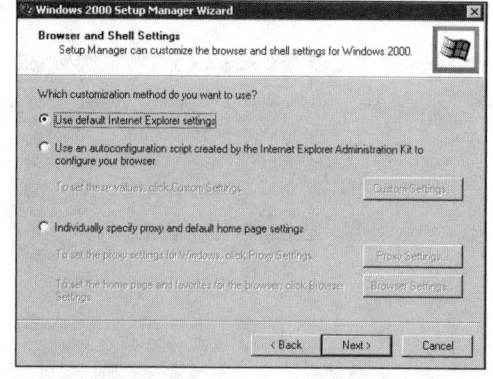

FIGURE 1.17
Setup Manager—Browser and Shell Settings.

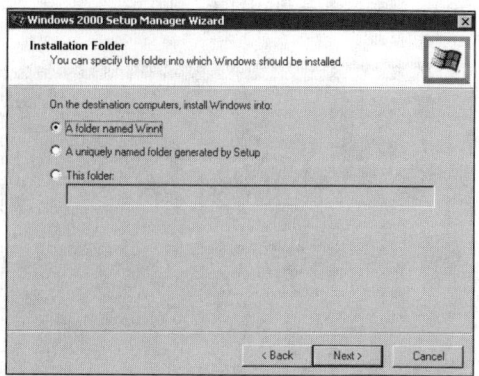

FIGURE 1.18
Setup Manager—Installation Folder.

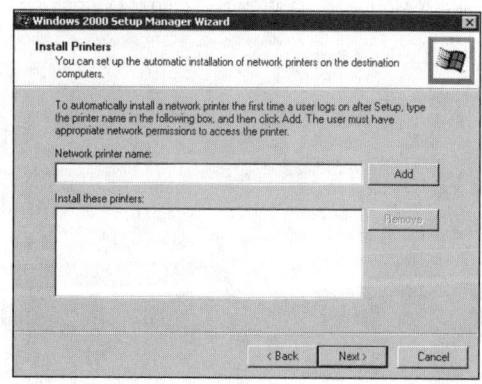

FIGURE 1.19
Setup Manager—Printer Installation Options.

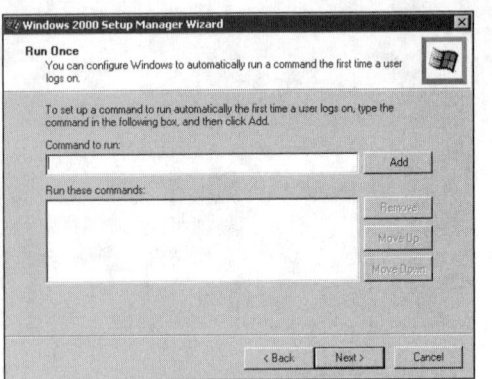

FIGURE 1.20
Setup Manager—Run Once Options.

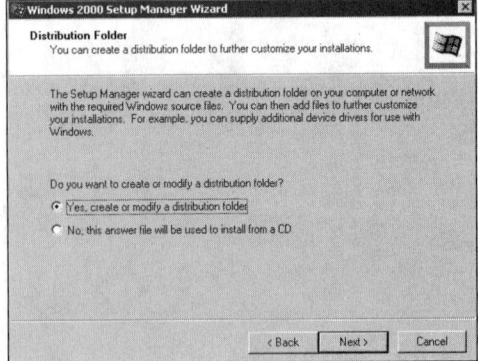

FIGURE 1.21
Setup Manager—Distribution Folder Options.

TABLE 1.5 *continued*

WINDOWS 2000 SETUP WIZARD CONFIGURATION OPTIONS

Information Category	Options	Description
Distribution Folder (see Figure 1.21)	Do You Want to Create or modify a Distribution Folder?	If you answer yes, the answer file will be added to a CD-based distribution folder.
		If you answer no, the files can be saved to disk and later associated with an installation image.
Distribution Folder Name/Answer File Name (see Figure 1.22)	If Yes above—Distribution Folder If No above—AnswerFile Name	Provides the location and file name of the file. If you save the answer file in a folder that contains a CD-based image, it will be made available to all users.
		If you save the file to a different folder, you will need to associate it with an existing CD-based image. Once associated, a copy will automatically be placed in the appropriate directory.

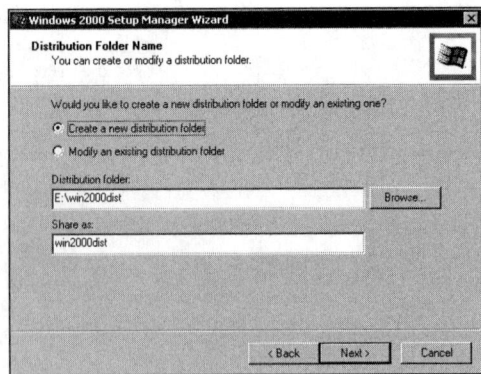

FIGURE 1.22
Setup Manager—Distribution Folder Name Options.

Information Category	*Options*	*Description*
Additional Mass Storage Drivers (see Figure 1.23) (Only available if the answer file is being used in conjunction with a distribution folder.)	Mass Storage Drivers	Allows you to specify additional mass storage drivers that are required to install your systems.
Hardware Abstraction Layer (HAL) (see Figure 1.24) (Only available if the answer file is being used in conjunction with a distribution folder.)	HAL	Allows you to replace the default HAL with one of your choice.
Additional Commands (see Figure 1.25) (Only available if the answer file is being used in conjunction with a distribution folder.)	Command to Run/ Command List	These options allow you to list a number of commands you want executed at the end of your unattended setup

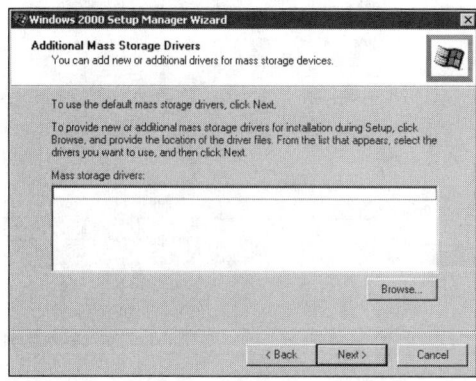

FIGURE 1.23

Setup Manager—Additional Mass Storage Drivers Options.

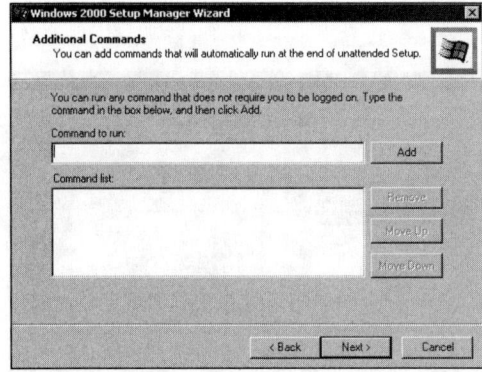

FIGURE 1.25

Setup Manager—Additional Commands Options.

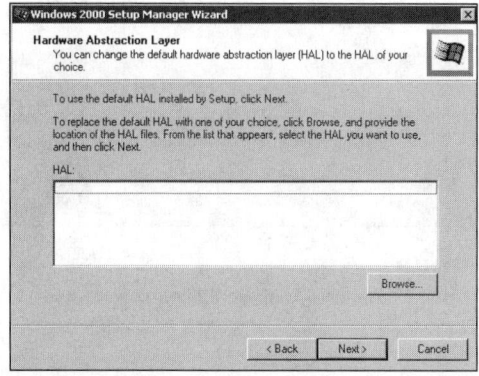

FIGURE 1.24

Setup Manager—HAL Options.

continues

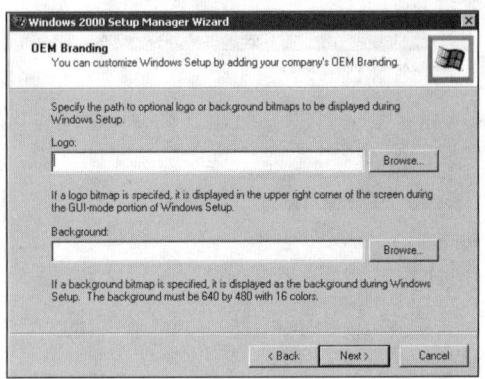

FIGURE 1.26
Setup Manager—OEM Branding Options.

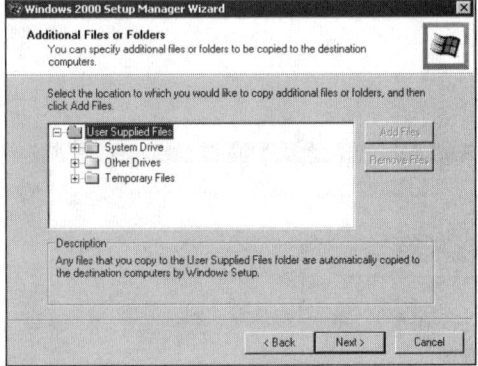

FIGURE 1.27
Setup Manager—Additional Files or Folders
Options.

TABLE 1.5   *continued*

WINDOWS 2000 SETUP WIZARD CONFIGURATION OPTIONS

Information Category	Options	Description
OEM Branding (see Figure 1.26) (Only available if the answer file is being used in conjunction with a distribution folder.)	Logo/Background	These options allow you to add a custom logo and background to the setup process.
Additional Files or Folders (see Figure 1.27) (Only available if the answer file is being used in conjunction with a distribution folder.)	File Location Window	Allows you to select the locations where you would like files to be copied during the installation process.
Answer File Name (see Figure 1.28)	Description String	Provides the text that describes the answer file. It is displayed to users when they run an install using the Client Installation Wizard.

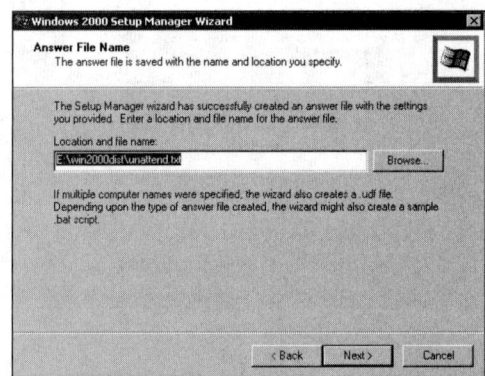

FIGURE 1.28
Setup Manager—Answer File Name.

Information Category	Options	Description
Location of Setup Files (see Figure 1.29)	Copy the Files from CD/Copy the Files from this Location	Allows you to specify the location where the Windows setup files can be found. This information is required so the Setup Manager can copy the files to the distribution folder.

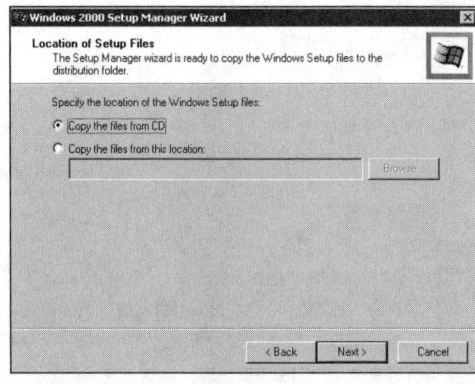

FIGURE 1.29
Setup Manager—Location of Setup Files.

When the Setup Wizard has finished, you will find it has created three files. The files are named as follows:

◆ Answer File Name.txt

◆ Answer File Name.udf

◆ Answer File Name.bat

The first file is the unattended answer file. The second file is the UDF file (if multiple computer names were specified during creation of the files). The third file is a batch file that will allow you to start your unattended installs from the command prompt without having to type the full syntax of the Winnt or Winnt32 commands.

The following is an example of this batch file:

```
@rem SetupMgrTag
@echo off

rem
rem This is a SAMPLE batch script generated by the Setup
rem Manager Wizard.
rem If this script is moved from the location where it was
rem generated, it may have
rem to be modified.
rem

set AnswerFile=.\unattend.txt
set UdfFile=.\unattend.udf
set ComputerName=%1
set SetupFiles=E:\i386

if "%ComputerName%" == "" goto USAGE
```

continues

continues

```
E:\i386\winnt32 /s:%SetupFiles% /unattend:%AnswerFile%
➥/udf:%ComputerName%,%UdfF
ile% /makelocalsource
goto DONE

:USAGE
echo.
echo Usage: unattend ^<computername^>
echo.
```

To use this file you will need to modify the set statements to point to your installation, unattend, and udf files. The syntax used to run the batch and install computer1 (for example) would be as follows:

```
unattend.bat computer1
```

> **EXAM TIP**
>
> **Remember the Syntax of the Files**
> The syntax of the unattended.txt and UDF files is complex. Create a sample using the Setup Manager and thoroughly review them before the exam. The code generated by the unattended.bat file is especially useful if you want to see the correct syntax associated with using the unattended text and UDF file together.

Remote Installation Services (RIS)

Windows 2000 Remote Installation Services (RIS) allow client computers to be installed throughout an enterprise from a central location. This service greatly reduces the effort required to manage the images that are being used throughout your environment because they are stored in and managed from a central location.

RIS provides the following benefits:

◆ Enables remote installation of Windows 2000 Professional

◆ Simplifies server image management

◆ Supports recovery of the operating system and computer if a system failure occurs during installation

RIS requires a Windows 2000 Active Directory infrastructure and has specific server and workstation requirements. The following sections discuss these requirements.

The RIS Process

Remote installation is the process of a RIS client connecting to a server running the Remote Installation Service (RIS) and then starting an automated installation of Windows 2000 Professional on a local computer.

> **NOTE**
>
> **RIS Images** Although referred to as images, RIS images are actual copies of the Windows 2000 installation files. When a client is installed using RIS, it actually runs the native Windows 2000 install process. For this reason the RIS process does not suffer from the difficulties that disk imaging can run into (such as hardware incompatibilities from computer to computer).

RIS Server Requirements

The RIS runs on a Windows 2000 server. RIS must be installed on the computer by running the Setup Wizard from the Add and Remove Programs icon of Control Panel. Once installed, the Windows 2000 Remote Installation Services Setup Wizard can be used to configure the RIS service.

The RIS server can be either a domain controller or a member server. The following network services do not have to be installed on the RIS server but must be available on the network:

◆ **DNS Server.** RIS uses DNS to resolve the IP addresses of directory servers and client computers on the network.

◆ **DHCP Server.** RIS clients need to obtain their network configurations from a DHCP server during the initial stages of the RIS installation procedure.

◆ **Active Directory.** RIS relies upon the Microsoft Active Directory service in Windows 2000 for locating existing client computers and RIS servers.

Remote installation also requires that RIS be installed on a partition that is formatted as NTFS and shared over the network. This partition must not be the boot partition for Windows 2000 (the drive where Windows 2000 Server is installed), but must be large enough to store the RIS images.

Once RIS is installed, it is ready to receive its first image. RIS can be configured to store multiple images on its local hard drive. Although referred to as images (which sometimes implies a single file that represents the contents of a hard drive), the files copied to the RIS server are actual copies of all the source files required to install Windows 2000 Professional.

After the first image is installed, the service can be authorized to respond to client requests. Once authorized, clients can download their operating system installation files from the RIS server.

RIS Client Requirements

Client computers that support remote installation must have one of the following configurations:

◆ A configuration meeting the Network PC (Net PC) specification

◆ A network adapter card configured to use the Pre-Boot Execution Environment (PXE) boot ROM

◆ A supported network adapter card and a remote installation boot disk

Computers that support one of these configurations can simply be plugged into the network and switched on. When they initialize, they will boot from the network and receive information regarding the location of the RIS server (most machines require the user to press F12 to indicate a network boot). The user is then prompted to log on. Once the user has logged on, a listing of the RIS installation images stored on the RIS server is displayed.

RIS servers can also be configured so that they respond only to computers that they are explicitly configured to service. This is called *prestaging* a client. During this process, a unique identifier for each workstation, the Media Access Control (MAC) address, is used to create a computer object in the active directory. The computer is assigned an RIS server and installation image. Under this configuration, when the client requests a configuration from the RIS server, the client is not presented a list of available installation images. The client is given its preconfigured image.

Using the Remote Image Preparation (Riprep) Tool

Remote Image Preparation (Riprep) is a utility that allows you to prepare a workstation image that can be loaded on the RIS server. The nice thing about Riprep images is that they can include Windows 2000 Professional and any applications you want included in your download image.

Two systems are required to create a Riprep image. The first system is the source computer (the computer that contains the base operating system and applications); the second is the RIS server.

NOTE

Booting from a Network Adapter Card You will need to configure your system to boot from the network adapter card. On most systems this is done through the system BIOS. Refer to your system documentation for details.

The steps in setting up the Riprep source computer are as follows:

1. Install Windows 2000 Professional.

2. Configure Windows 2000 components and settings to ensure that all settings are correct for your environment.

3. Install and configure all applications you want included in your image. You should verify all configuration settings for each application you install. During most of the configuration of the computer you will most likely be logged in as Administrator. When all configurations are complete, you should copy the Administrator profile over the Default User profile to ensure that the default user profile is updated to include all settings.

4. Test the source computer to ensure that it is configured properly. After you create the image, it cannot be changed.

Once the source computer is ready, you can run the Remote Installation Preparation Wizard. Type `\\RIS_SERVER_NAME\reminst\admin\i386\Riprep.exe` to run this wizard.

The wizard removes all unique information such as security identifier (SID) information, computer name, and registry settings from the computer. A RIPrep image is then transferred to a RIS server and an answer file is associated with the newly created image. At this point, the image is available for RIS clients.

Imaging Windows 2000 Professional Installs

Another popular option for installing Windows 2000 is to use third-party imaging tools to create installation images. This differs from a RIS image in that the Windows 2000 setup program is not being used to install Windows 2000 on the system. Instead, a duplicate copy of one computer's hard drive is transferred to other machines. This type of installation is very fast because the setup program does not need to be executed on the target system.

There are some issues associated with this type of installation, however. Because the hard disk is being duplicated, each system that is created using the image is an exact duplicate. For this reason, issues arise because computer names and security identifiers are duplicated across the network.

The System Preparation (Sysprep) Tool

Sysprep is a utility that gives users the ability to prepare a computer so it can be imaged. Disk duplication software can then be used to take a snapshot of the computer's hard drive so it can be transferred to another machine. Step by Step 1.3 illustrates the use of the Sysprep tool.

You can also use Sysprep as part of an audit process to verify the functionality of a computer before it is delivered. During the process you can, for example, check that the operating system loads and that applications launch properly. This allows you to examine each computer that has Windows 2000 preinstalled. You can examine the computer as it will exist at the user site and then use the Sysprep tool to return the computer to an end-user-ready state. Then, when the user receives the computer and turns it on for the first time, the computer runs Mini-Setup.

STEP BY STEP

1.3 The Sysprep Process

1. Install Windows 2000 Professional.

2. Configure Windows 2000 components and settings to ensure that all settings are correct for your environment.

3. Install and configure all applications you want included in your image. You should verify all configuration settings for each application you install.

4. Test the source computer to ensure that it is configured properly. After you create the image it cannot be changed.

5. Run Sysprep.exe on the computer from the Start menu. Sysprep will remove all unique configuration settings from the computer. Figure 1.30 shows the prompt that is displayed when Sysprep runs. You should only run Sysprep on a computer if you intend to image its hard drive.

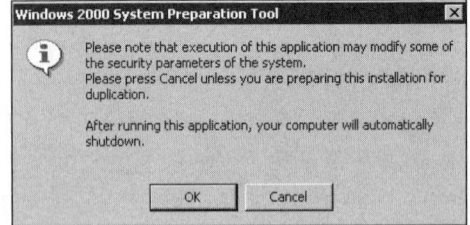

FIGURE 1.30
Sysprep warning screen.

6. Restart the computer and run a third-party disk image-copying tool to create a master image of the disk.

7. Save the new disk on a shared folder of a CD.

8. Copy the image to multiple destination computers.

9. When the new machines are started, you will be prompted for computer-specific variables, such as computer name and administrator password. If a Sysprep.inf file is provided, a mini-setup program will manage the install, and no user intervention is required.

Sysprep Command Options

To assist in the disk duplication process, the Sysprep utility supports a number of command options (as shown in Table 1.6).

TABLE 1.6

SYSPREP COMMAND OPTIONS

Option	Description
Sysprep.inf	A file created with Setup Manager to customize the Mini-Setup routine that will run the first time the target user reboots the computer.
-pnp	The Mini-Setup wizard that detects new or different Plug and Play devices on the destination computer and disables those that were used on the master computer but not found on the destination computer.
	You might want to use the -pnp switch to enable legacy device detection or to re-enumerate the devices on the destination computer. Using this switch adds a few extra minutes to the end-user's experience in order to do a complete hardware redetection.
-quiet	Suppresses confirmation dialogs displayed to the user.
-nosidgen	Informs the setup program not to generate new SIDs on the reboot.
-reboot	Forces the computer to reboot rather than shutting down.

USING A DUAL-BOOT SYSTEM

Dual-booting is a term used to describe a computer that has more than one operating system installed on it. When the computer starts, a boot manager presents the user a list of the installed operating systems so the user can choose the OS to be booted.

If you are in the process of transitioning your users to Windows 2000, users may want to configure their computers to dual-boot. Dual-booting your systems allows you to retain your original configuration (including software configurations) and still access the new operating system. In some environments this is useful, because it allows you to test new configurations and retain your original configuration.

When dual-booting a system, you need to be aware of incompatibilities that may arise between the different OSs you are installing. For example, if you were to dual-boot Windows 95 with Windows 2000 Professional, partitions formatted as NTFS under Windows 2000 Professional would not be accessible from Windows 95.

To create a dual-boot system, install Windows 2000 Professional over the top of the existing operating systems found on the computer. When the system reboots, the Windows boot manager will present you with a list of available operating systems.

> **WARNING**
>
> **Dual-booting is Not Recommended** Although it is possible to set up a dual-boot system with Windows 95/98, Windows NT, and Windows 2000, it is not recommended. Remember that you will need to install all applications multiple times (once for each OS supported) and no application/system settings are migrated or shared between the OSs.

UPGRADING TO WINDOWS 2000 PROFESSIONAL

Upgrade from a previous version of Windows to Windows 2000 Professional.

Windows 2000 offers a number of new technologies that help simplify network management. To take advantage of these features, network clients need to be upgraded to run Windows 2000 Professional. Upgrading clients also allows them to retain their software configurations and user preferences.

The following represents the basic upgrade process:

1. Verify the upgrade path.

2. Ensure hardware requirements are met.

3. Test compatibility with the Windows 2000 Compatibility Tool.

The following sections explore this process.

Verifying Upgrade Paths

You can upgrade earlier versions of Windows to Windows 2000. Table 1.7 presents the upgrade path for older Windows operating systems.

TABLE 1.7

WINDOWS 2000 PROFESSIONAL UPGRADE PATHS

Upgrade From:	*Upgrade To:*
Windows 3.x	Windows 95 or 98 and then upgrade to Windows 2000 Professional
Windows 95 and Windows 98	Windows 2000 Professional
Windows NT Workstation 3.51 or 4.0	Windows 2000 Professional
Windows NT Workstation 3.1 or 3.5	Windows NT Workstation 3.51 or 4.0 and then upgrade to Windows 2000 Professional

> **EXAM TIP**
>
> **Upgrade Paths** It is critical that you remember the upgrade paths that are available to you.

IN THE FIELD

UPGRADE VERSUS NEW INSTALL

Microsoft has noted a number of instances where the upgrade process from Windows 95/98 to Windows 2000 Professional does not always detect audio, printers, CD-RW drives, USB devices,

continues

continued

graphics cards, and software (especially if upgrading from Windows 98). Microsoft posted the following note regarding upgrading from Windows 95/98 to Windows 2000 on their Web site:

"In certain situations, even if you are currently running Windows 95 or Windows 98, you may prefer to do a new installation (or "clean install"), rather than an upgrade to Windows 2000. By installing the operating system from scratch, you place the operating system in a known state and avoid migrating any problems that may have existed in the previous configuration. However, a new installation requires reformatting your hard disk, so you must back up your data, install Windows 2000, reinstall your applications, and then reload your data from backup."

"You should upgrade if all of the following are true:

You're already using a previous version of Windows that supports upgrading.

You want to replace your previous Windows operating system with Windows 2000.

You want to maintain your existing user settings and files."

"You should perform a new installation if any of the following are true:

Your hard drive is blank (that is, you have no operating system installed on it).

Your current operating system does not support an upgrade to Windows 2000.

You have two partitions and want to create a dual-boot configuration with Windows 2000 and your current operating system. (Be sure to install Windows 2000 on a different partition than your current operating system.) Typically, dual-boot configurations are suitable for testing and evaluation; however, they are not recommended for long-term production use. "

(Microsoft Corporation: `http://www.microsoft.com/windows2000/ upgrade/path/win9x.asp`)

Client Hardware Requirements

Before you attempt to upgrade your system, you should ensure that it meets the minimum hardware requirements. Table 1.8 presents the minimum hardware requirements for Windows 2000 Professional.

TABLE 1.8

WINDOWS **2000** PROFESSIONAL HARDWARE REQUIREMENTS

Type of Hardware	*Requirement*
Processor	Pentium 133Mhz or higher
Memory	64MB (recommended minimum) for Intel-based computers
Hard Disk	2GB hard drive with 650MB of free space on the boot partition
Video	VGA or higher video card and monitor
CD/DVD	CD-ROM or DVD ROM for local CD-based installs
Networking	Network adapter and cables
Accessories	Keyboard and pointing device

Hardware Compatibility

During an upgrade, a hardware compatibility report is generated. This report shows you the hardware components that are not compatible with Windows 2000.

Microsoft recommends that you run the compatibility tools before you start your system upgrades. Knowledge of incompatibilities before you start your upgrades allows you to research new drivers or fixes that have been created for your specific incompatibility.

You can generate a compatibility report using the Windows 2000 Compatibility tools in two ways. This first involves running the WINNT32 setup program with the /checkupgradeonly command switch. This command switch starts the first part of the Windows 2000 installation program but checks only the hardware.

The second option is to run the Chkupgrd.exe utility. This utility can be downloaded from Microsoft (www.microsoft.com/downloads).

Both the WINNT32 /checkupgradeonly and the Chkupgrd.exe compatibility tools report the same information. The report is a simple text document that can be saved for future reference.

The report documents system hardware and software that is incompatible with Windows 2000 Professional. It will also identify if you need to obtain upgrades for software that is installed on your system.

Upgrading Compatible Windows 95/98 Clients

For Windows 95/98 clients that do not present any compatibility issues, you can run the Windows 2000 Professional setup program (WINNT32.EXE) to upgrade them to Windows 2000. Before you begin the upgrade process you should ensure that you have a recovery path if the upgrade fails (for example, back up your computer before you begin the upgrade process). Step by Step 1.4 illustrates the upgrade process.

STEP BY STEP

1.4 Upgrading Compatible Windows 95/98 Clients to Windows 2000

1. Make sure you have a current backup of your system before you begin this process. Run WINNT32.EXE.

2. Accept the license agreement.

3. If the computer you are upgrading is part of a domain, create a computer for the system in the domain (Windows 95/98 does not require computer accounts).

4. When prompted, load any upgrade packs required to bring your software up to be Windows 2000 compatible. You should be prepared for this based on the compatibility report generated prior to trying the upgrade.

5. When prompted, upgrade FAT and FAT32 partitions to NTFS.

6. The Windows 2000 Compatibility Tool runs and reports any compatibility issues that may exist. If the system is compatible, Windows 2000 will continue to upgrade the system. If an incompatibility exists, Windows 2000 Setup will terminate and the upgrade will stop.

Upgrading Compatible Windows NT Clients

For Windows NT clients that do not present any compatibility issues, you can run the Windows 2000 Professional setup program (WINNT32.EXE) to upgrade them to Windows 2000. Before you begin the upgrade process, you should ensure that you have a recovery path if the upgrade fails (again, back up your computer before you begin the upgrade process). Step by Step 1.5 leads you through the upgrade process.

STEP BY STEP

1.5 Upgrading Compatible Windows NT Clients to Windows 2000

1. Make sure you have a current backup of your system before you begin this process. Run WINNT32.EXE.

2. When prompted by the Windows 2000 Setup Wizard, specify whether this is a new install or an upgrade.

3. Accept the license agreement.

4. When prompted, upgrade FAT and FAT32 partitions to NTFS. You must also upgrade your existing NTFS (4.0) partitions to the Windows 2000 version of NTFS (5.0).

   Your system will now restart and setup will continue without user intervention.

NOTE **An Upgrade Is Different from a New Installation** If you select a new install you will need to reinstall all of your applications.

NOTE **Compatibility Reports** During the upgrade, the Setup Wizard will generate a compatibility report. The report is saved as %systemroot% \winnt32.log. If the upgrade fails, this is an excellent place to start your troubleshooting.

FIGURE 1.31
Directory Service Client Setup Wizard.

Incompatible Systems

Computers that do not meet the compatibility requirements of Windows 2000 can still participate, to a limited degree, in a Windows 2000 network.

Windows NT 3.51 or 4.0 clients that do not meet the hardware compatibility requirements can still log on to a Windows 2000 network. They cannot, however, utilize many of the advanced desktop management tools available in Windows 2000.

Windows 95/98 clients need a Windows 2000 Directory Service client installed on them to access Windows 2000 Fault-tolerant Distributed File Systems, search the active directory, and change passwords in the domain. To install the service, follow Step by Step 1.6.

FIGURE 1.32
Directory Service Client Setup Wizard—
Installation Completed.

STEP BY STEP

1.6 Installing the Windows 9x Directory Services Client

1. Run Dsclietn.exe from the Clients\Win9x directory of the Windows 2000 Server CD. You will see the Welcome to the Directory Service Client Setup Wizard (See Figure 1.31).

2. Click Next in the Directory Service Client Setup Wizard.

3. Accept the license agreement.

4. Click Finish to complete the installation (see Figure 1.32). Once the installation is complete, you will need to restart your computer.

5. Click OK to restart your computer.

SERVICE PACK DEPLOYMENT

Deploy service packs.

Once you have Windows 2000 installed and operational on your network, you will need to maintain it. The primary tool Microsoft uses to distribute updates to their operating systems is the Service Pack. Service packs contain more that just bug fixes. Microsoft uses the service packs as a vehicle to bring you the latest enhancements to its products.

It is in your best interest to monitor the current service packs available at Microsoft's Web site. As new service packs become available, you should thoroughly test them on your systems. It is also important that you read the release notes that ship with the service packs. Release notes provide important configuration information relating to compatibility issues and services you may be running on your systems.

Once you've tested them, service packs can be easily deployed to workstations and servers in your environment through Windows 2000 Group Policy objects or with products like Microsoft's System Management Server (SMS).

TROUBLESHOOTING THE INSTALLATION PROCESS

Troubleshoot a failed Windows 2000 installation.

The Windows 2000 installation process is relatively simple. There are, however, a number of common problems that you may experience. Table 1.9 presents a listing of common setup problems.

TABLE 1.9

COMMON SETUP PROBLEMS

Problem	Solution
Media errors	If your installation CD has been damaged, you will receive media errors. The only solution to this problem is to obtain a new copy of the installation CD.
Non-supported CD-ROM drive	If the Windows 2000 setup program reports that it cannot find or access the CD-ROM, you may need to replace the CD-ROM unit.
Non-supported mass storage device	You may experience the situation where the Windows 2000 setup program cannot access your hard disks. This is usually a problem with the drivers being used to access your hard drives. Remember that if you are running specialized RAID or SCSI controllers, you must specify (and provide) the appropriate drivers during installation.
Inability to connect to the domain controller	You should verify that the domain name is correct and that the domain controller is running. You should also verify that DNS is configured properly and is running.
Failure of Windows 2000 to install or start	Verify the Windows 2000 Compatibility report.

CASE STUDY: ABC COMPANY

ESSENCE OF THE CASE

Here are the essential elements in this case:

▶ Upgrading Windows 95/98/NT 4.0 to Windows 2000

▶ Upgrading Windows NT 3.5 to Windows 2000

▶ Automating the installation of new computers

ABC Company is in the process of installing Windows 2000 Professional on all desktop computers in their organization. Details of their environment are as follows:

▶ Existing Equipment:

  ▶ 200 Windows 95 Workstations

  ▶ 200 Windows 98 Workstations

  ▶ 150 Windows NT 4.0 Workstations

  ▶ 50 Windows NT 3.5 Workstations

CASE STUDY: ABC COMPANY

▶ New Equipment:

  ▶ 100 500Mhz Pentium III computers (new purchases) with 64MB of RAM and 6GB hard drives

Existing workstations need to be upgraded to support Windows 2000. New equipment must be installed to support Windows 2000. ABC Company uses a number of in-house applications and the standard MS Office products.

Before a budget approval can proceed on this project, a detailed rollout plan is required for the board of directors. The budget is tight for this project and it must be completed with the smallest amount of staff time as possible.

ANALYSIS

The information presented must be broken down into its individual components to fully analyze this scenario.

One of the first challenges for the installation team will be to fully inventory the existing equipment to determine if it meets the minimum hardware requirements for Windows 2000. Any equipment that does not meet the minimum requirements must be upgraded or replaced. From a budget perspective, it is critical that all upgrade/replacement costs are included in the implementation plan.

A standardized method of upgrading each machine should then be developed. Because each machine is currently in production use, you must include procedures to back up all data on the local machines before the upgrade occurs (to limit the possibility of data loss). Windows 95/98 machines can be upgraded directly to Windows 2000. You will, however, need to plan for the creation of computer accounts for computers being upgraded from Windows 95/98. Windows NT 3.5 machines must be upgraded to Windows NT 4.0 and then upgraded to Windows 2000 Professional.

New systems must have Windows 2000 Professional installed on them. You will need to test the fastest method of Installing Windows 2000 Professional (and required applications) on these machines. You should compare the installation technologies outlined in Table 1.10.

TABLE 1.10

INSTALLATION TECHNOLOGIES

Technology	Additional Considerations
RIS	Are Active Directory, DNS, DHCP, and a domain controller available?
Answer files	How many different common configurations are required?
Images	How well does a software image work on the new machines?

CHAPTER SUMMARY

KEY TERMS

- Boot partition
- Dual-boot
- System partition
- Primary partition
- Extended partition
- Logical drive
- Basic disks
- Dynamic disks
- NTFS
- FAT
- FAT32
- Bootable disk
- Remote Installation Services (RIS)
- Unattended text file
- Answer file
- Uniqueness definition file (UDF)

Microsoft has provided a number of excellent tools to aid in the installation of Windows 2000. This chapter has reviewed the Windows 2000 product line so that you are in a position to evaluate your business needs to determine the version of Windows 2000 that best meets those needs. After you determined the version of Windows 2000 you require, you were presented with the information you need before you start the installation of the product. Planning is a very important aspect of any installation. This chapter then reviewed the tools available to automate the installation process.

APPLY YOUR KNOWLEDGE

Exercises

1.1   Installing Windows 2000 Professional from a Local CD

This exercise demonstrates how to install Windows 2000 Professional from the local CD-ROM of your computer. It is assumed that your system meets the minimum system requirements discussed earlier in this chapter and that your hard disk is not currently partitioned.

Estimated Time: 50 Minutes

We will start this exercise by creating a Windows 2000 Professional installation disk. You will need four blank disks and access to any operating system that can access the Windows 2000 Professional installation CD.

1. Insert the Windows 2000 Professional Installation CD into the drive. Run MAKEDISK.EXE from the BOOTDISK directory.

2. You are prompted for the location of your floppy disk (usually A:). Press the letter that represents your local floppy drive. The first disk inserted will become the Windows 2000 Professional Setup Boot Disk. Follow the command prompts to complete the creation of the boot disks.

   You now have the boot disk available to start the installation process from your system's CD-ROM. Complete steps 3–12 to complete PHASE I ("Text Mode") of the installation of Windows 2000 Professional.

3. Boot the system from the first boot disk you created in the previous steps. Insert the remaining three disks as prompted.

4. Press Enter at the Setup Notification screen.

5. Press Enter at the Welcome to Setup screen.

6. The Windows 2000 Professional setup program reports whether your computer hard disk is new or has been erased. You are asked if you want to continue your installation. Press C to indicate that you want to continue.

7. Press F8 to accept the Windows 2000 Professional license agreement.

8. You are shown a list if existing partitions on your computer (it will be blank). Press C to create a new partition on disk 0.

9. You are prompted to enter the size of the new partition you want to create. Enter **2045** to create a 2GB partition.

10. Once again you are presented with a list of existing partitions. Press Enter to select the C: New (Unformatted) 2045 MB partition.

11. Setup displays a list of file systems that can be used to format the new partition. For this installation, select FAT. During an installation in a product environment, you would select the file system most appropriate for your environment.

    Setup now examines your hard disk and copies a number of files to the Windows 2000 installation folder.

APPLY YOUR KNOWLEDGE

12. Setup now reboots your computer. You should ensure that the Windows 2000 installation CD is still in the CD-ROM drive.

    PHASE II (GUI Mode) of the installation now begins. Complete steps 13–18 to complete this phase of the installation.

13. Click Next at the Windows 2000 Professional Setup Wizard window.

    An Installing Devices page appears. This window tells you that setup is detecting and installing devices.

14. The Regional Settings page then appears. You are prompted to customize your Regional Settings (time/date, currency, and so on) and Language. Click Next.

15. You are then prompted to personalize your software. Enter your name and organization in the prompt boxes.

16. At the next prompt, enter the product license key for your copy of Windows 2000 Professional.

17. You are then asked to provide a computer name and password for the local administrator account. Enter **TESTMACHINE** for your computer name and **password** for the administrator password. Click Next.

18. The Date/Time settings are now required. Adjust the date and time to your local time and click Next.

    PHASE III (Network Installation) of the installation now begins. Complete steps 19–20 to complete this phase of the installation.

19. The Network Settings page appears. Select Typical Settings and click Next.

20. You are now asked to join a workgroup or domain. Keep the default settings and join a workgroup named workgroup. Click Next.

    In step 21, PHASE IV (Final Installation) of the installation, you finish the installation.

21. Reboot the system. Once the system has restarted, log on to the system as Administrator with a password of password. This completes this exercise.

1.2 Verifying Windows NT 4.0 Compatibility with Windows 2000

In this exercise you will verify the compatibility of an existing Windows NT 4.0 Workstation with Windows 2000.

Estimated Time: 10 Minutes

Note: Completing the first part of this lab requires an existing computer running Windows NT 4.0 Workstation.

1. Insert the Windows 2000 Professional installation CD in the computer's CD-ROM.

2. From Start/Run/Open, execute d:\i386\ winnt32 /checkupgradeonly (where d: is your CD-ROM device).

3. From the Windows 2000 Professional Setup System Compatibility Check window, note whether any errors have been recorded.

4. Click the Save As button to save the report. Save the text file to your desktop.

5. Click Next. The Windows 2000 Professional Setup program should close.

6. Use Notepad to review the text file you generated in step 4. This ends this exercise.

APPLY YOUR KNOWLEDGE

1.3 Downloading Service Packs

In this exercise you search Microsoft's Web site for the latest service pack.

Note: This exercise is based on Microsoft's Web site as of Feb. 16, 2000. At the time of writing, no Windows 2000 Service Packs have been released. The exercise does, however, highlight how to find downloads on Microsoft's Web site.

Estimated Time: 10 Minutes

1. Start Internet Explorer.

2. Type **http://www.microsoft.com** in the location window. You will see Microsoft's Web site (as shown in Figure 1.33).

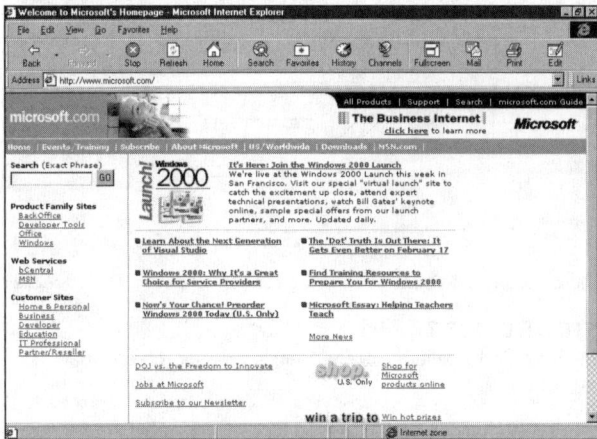

FIGURE 1.33
Microsoft's Web site.

3. Click the Download button. You will enter Microsoft's Download Center (as shown in Figure 1.34).

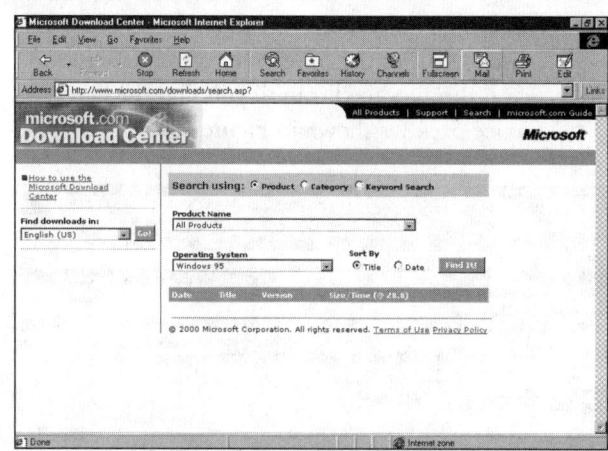

FIGURE 1.34
Microsoft's Download Center.

4. Select Keyword Search in the Search Using box.

5. Enter **Service Pack** as the keyword and select Windows 2000 as the operating system (see Figure 1.35).

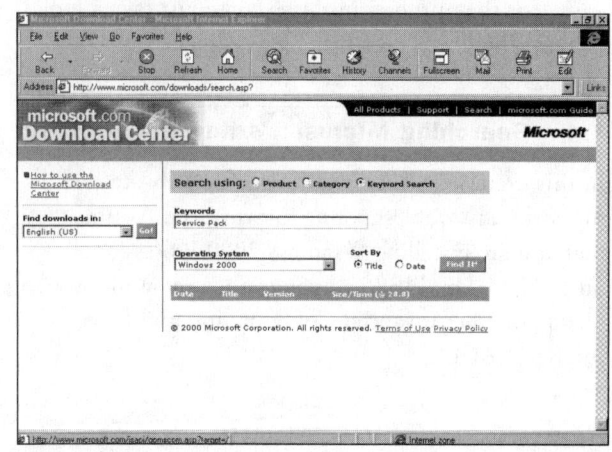

FIGURE 1.35
Keyword search.

APPLY YOUR KNOWLEDGE

6. Click the Find It button. You are presented with a listing of files that meet your search criteria. Scroll through the list until you find the latest service pack (as shown in Figure 1.36).

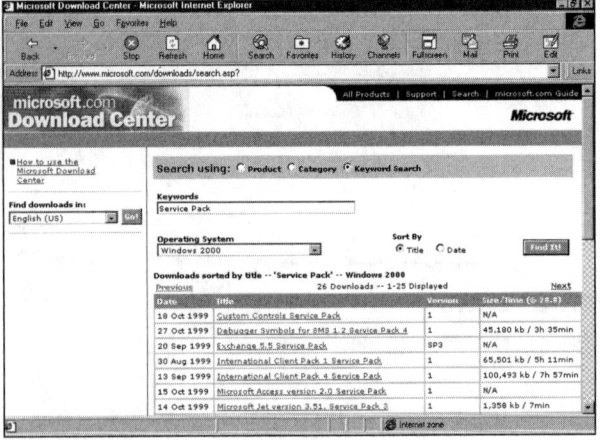

FIGURE 1.36
Search results.

7. For the purposes of this exercise just take a look at the downloads that are available.

1.4 Searching Microsoft's Knowledge Base

In this exercise you search Microsoft's Web site for support and troubleshooting information. Assume that you are installing Windows 2000 Professional on an IBM ThinkPad and you cannot get Windows to support the Advanced Configuration and Power Interface (ACPI).

Estimated Time: 10 Minutes

1. Start Internet Explorer.

2. Type `http://suppport.microsoft.com` in the location window. You will see Microsoft's Knowledge Base Web site.

3. Select Windows 2000 from the My Search Is About drop-down list. Leave the search type as Keyword. Enter `IBM ThinkPad` in the My Question Is field (your screen should look like Figure 1.37). Click the Go button.

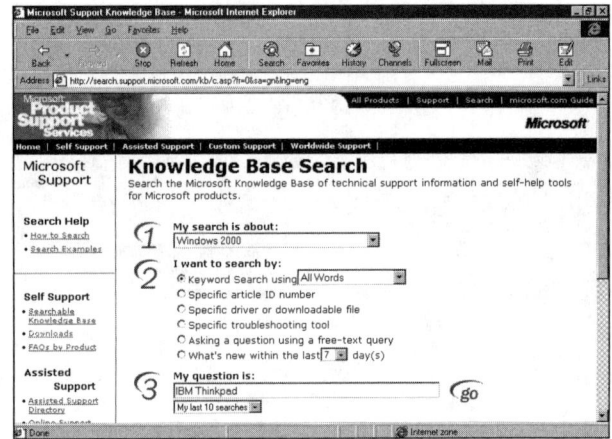

FIGURE 1.37
Microsoft's Knowledge Base Web site—search criteria.

The results of your search are displayed (as shown in Figure 1.38).

APPLY YOUR KNOWLEDGE

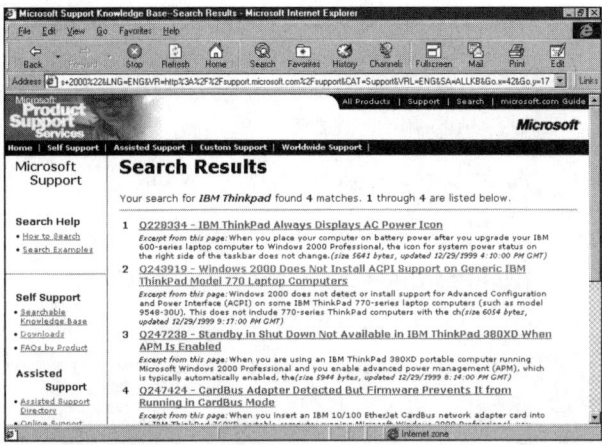

FIGURE 1.38
Search results.

4. Note the article regarding ACPI in the results list. To view the results, click the title.

Review Questions

1. What are the primary differences between Windows 2000 Professional, Server, Advanced Server, and Datacenter Server?

2. What are the minimum system requirements for Windows 2000 Professional?

3. What are the advantages and disadvantages of FAT/FAT32 versus NTFS?

4. What utility is used to generate unattended text files, and how is it installed?

5. What are the four phases of the Windows 2000 installation process?

6. What is the difference between a Local CD-based installation of Windows 2000 and a networked installation of Windows 2000?

7. What is the primary difference between a Sysprep and Riprep installation?

Exam Questions

1. You are the network administrator at a mid-size consulting firm. You are in the process of planning software requirements for next year because your corporate standard is moving from Windows NT 4.0 to Windows 2000. You currently have six computers running Windows NT Server 4.0 in your office. Three of the servers are acting as file and print servers. Each of these servers is running on a Quad Pentium II 300Mhz computer with 1GB of RAM. Two of the servers are dual Pentium III 500Mhz computers with 1GB of RAM and are currently configured as a cluster using Cluster Server. The last server supports a 6GB SQL database running on a server utilizing eight Pentium III 450 processors with 2GB of RAM.

What should you do to upgrade your servers in the most efficient manner?

A. Order six copies of Windows 2000 Server.

B. Order six copies of Windows 2000 Advanced Server.

C. Order six copies of Windows 2000 Datacenter Server.

D. Order four copies of Windows 2000 Server and two copies of Windows 2000 Advanced Server.

E. Order three copies of Windows 2000 Server, two copies of Windows 2000 Advanced Server, and one copy of Windows 2000 Datacenter Server.

2. Your company has experienced substantial growth over the past two years. Your network is currently running Windows NT Server 4.0 on a four-processor server. You are planning to purchase an additional six-processor system to ease the load on your existing equipment. You plan to run Windows 2000 on both servers. You purchase two copies of Windows 2000 Server and upgrade your existing server without incident. Windows 2000 will not install on your new server.

   What is the most likely source of the problem?

   A. The new server's CD-ROM is not compatible with Windows 2000.

   B. Windows 2000 Server supports up to four processors for new installations.

   C. Only Windows 2000 Datacenter Server supports SMP.

   D. Windows 2000 Server does not support SMP.

   E. Only Windows 2000 Advanced Server supports SMP.

3. As the network administrator for a large accounting firm, you are developing a Windows 2000 Professional deployment plan. During the planning process, you learn about dynamic disks and are not sure about the advantages of using them within your organization. In your plan, you document that you will revisit the issue of dynamic disks after the initial Windows 2000 Professional rollout is complete.

To ensure the greatest amount of flexibility in the future, what should you include in the Windows 2000 installation specifications for your environment?

   A. All partitions are formatted with NTFS.

   B. All partitions are formatted with FAT.

   C. All partitions are formatted with FAT32.

   D. 1MB of un-partitioned disk space must be left at the end of each physical drive.

   E. Planning for dynamic disks is not important; you can mix dynamic and basic disks on each physical hard disk.

4. You are the manager of the software-testing lab at your office. You are testing Windows 95/98, Windows NT 4.0, and Windows 2000. While testing a number of computers running Windows 2000 Professional and Windows 95, you convert the system partition to NTFS. Your Windows 95 installation will no longer boot.

   What should you do to fix this situation?

   A. Use the convert command to convert the partition from NTFS to FAT.

   B. Use a DOS boot disk to boot the computer and reinstall Windows 95.

   C. You will have to back up any data from the partition, reformat the partition, and reinstall both Windows 95 and Windows 2000.

   D. Look for a cause other than NTFS. Windows 95 supports NTFS, so the problem is not related to the partition.

5. You are a support technician for your company. You have been asked to set up a computer to dual-boot Windows NT 4.0 and Windows 2000 Professional. You have also been asked to install a new hard drive with a large 3GB partition formatted as FAT. You create the 3GB partition on the new drive during the installation of Windows 2000. You created the partition using the Windows 2000 Professional setup program. The user for whom you set up the computer is complaining that she cannot access the new 3GB partition from Windows NT 4.0.

   What is the most likely cause of the problem?

   A. Windows NT 4.0 is not able to read the file contained on a Windows 2000 formatted partition.

   B. Windows 2000 automatically formats FAT partitions greater than 2GB as FAT32. Windows NT 4.0 does not support FAT32.

   C. Windows 2000 and Windows NT 4.0 cannot be dual-booted.

   D. You cannot create a 3GB FAT partition on any Windows-based system.

6. As the network administrator for your company, you are planning the rollout of Windows 2000 Professional for 2,300 users at your company. You are evaluating the various options for deploying these computers.

   Your environment is as follows:

   ◆ Your company is divided into four divisions: Sales, Marketing, Operations, and Research and Development.

   ◆ Each division generally has three classes of computers (for example, R&D has a class of computers for its administrative staff, power users—in this case, AutoCAD operators—and traveling users).

   ◆ Each division has its own custom applications.

   ◆ You have multiple Windows NT 4.0 domains (and are not planning to introduce Windows 2000 Active Directory domains into the environment until next year).

   ◆ For security reasons, only one user has permission to create computer accounts (other than Administrator) in the Windows NT 4.0 domain. Access to this account cannot be given to the installation staff and cannot be added to unattended text files.

   ◆ The only protocol supported on your network is TCP/IP.

   ◆ The new computers you are purchasing are Pentium III 400s and 733s, depending on their job function.

   ◆ A small number of high-end dual Pentiums are arriving for the AutoCAD users.

   Your job is to determine the most effective installation method(s) for your environment.

   Required Result:

   Your plan should allow for the installation of all workstations with the least amount of user intervention possible.

APPLY YOUR KNOWLEDGE

Optional Desired Results:

You want to ensure that unskilled temporary staff can install all of the workstations.

You want to ensure that the proprietary company applications can be installed on the systems during the rollout.

Proposed Solution:

You propose to create 12 different unattended text files (one for each computer configuration within each of the four departments). The network administrator, in advance of the rollout, will create computer accounts for each computer to be installed. Installation staff will then use the unattended text files to install the computers. Script files will be created to automate the installation of proprietary company applications.

Which results does the proposed solution produce?

A. The proposed solution produces the required result and produces all of the optional results.

B. The proposed solution produces the required result and produces only one of the optional results.

C. The proposed solution produces the required result but does not produce any of the optional results.

D. The proposed solution does not produce the required result.

7. As the network administrator for your company, you are planning the rollout of Windows 2000 Professional for 2,300 users at your company. You are evaluating the various options for deploying these computers.

Your environment is as follows:

◆ Your company is divided into four divisions: Sales, Marketing, Operations, and Research and Development.

◆ Each division generally has three classes of computers (for example, R&D has a class of computer for its administrative staff, power users—in this case, AutoCAD operators—and traveling users).

◆ Each division has its own custom applications.

◆ You have multiple Windows NT 4.0 domains (and are not planning to introduce Windows 2000 Active Directory domains into the environment until next year).

◆ For security reasons, only one user has permissions to create computer accounts (other than Administrator) in the Windows NT 4.0 domain. Access to this account cannot be given to the installation staff and cannot be added to unattended text files.

◆ The only protocol supported on your network is TCP/IP.

◆ The new computers you are purchasing are Pentium III 400s and 733s, depending on their job function.

◆ A small number of high-end dual Pentiums are arriving for the AutoCAD users.

Your job is to determine the most effective installation method(s) for your environment.

Required Result:

Your plan should allow for the installation of all workstations with the least amount of user intervention possible.

Optional Desired Results:

> You want to ensure that unskilled temporary staff can install all of the workstations.

> You want to ensure that the proprietary company applications can be installed on the systems during the rollout.

Proposed Solution:

> You create 12 RIS images (one for each type of computer in each department). You then have the installation staff install each workstation from the RIS server.

Which results does the proposed solution produce?

A. The proposed solution produces the required result and produces all of the optional results.

B. The proposed solution produces the required result and produces only one of the optional results.

C. The proposed solution produces the required result but does not produce any of the optional results.

D. The proposed solution does not produce the required result.

8. As the network administrator for your company, you are planning the rollout of Windows 2000 Professional for 2,300 users at your company. You are evaluating the various options for deploying these computers.

   Your environment is as follows:

   ◆ Your company is divided into four divisions Sales, Marketing, Operations, and Research and Development.

   ◆ Each division generally has three classes of computers (for example, R&D has a class of computer for its administrative staff, power users—in this case, AutoCAD operators— and traveling users).

   ◆ Each division has its own custom applications.

   ◆ You have multiple Windows NT 4.0 domains (and are not planning to introduce Windows 2000 Active Directory domains into the environment until next year).

   ◆ For security reasons, only one user has permissions to create computer accounts (other than Administrator) in the Windows NT 4.0 domain. Access to this account cannot be given to the installation staff and cannot be added to unattended text files.

   ◆ The only protocol supported on your network is TCP/IP.

   ◆ The new computers you are purchasing are Pentium III 400s and 733s, depending on their job function.

   ◆ A small number of high-end dual Pentiums are arriving for the AutoCAD users.

   Your job is to determine the most effective installation method(s) for your environment.

Required Result:

> Your plan should allow for the installation of all workstations with the least amount of user intervention possible.

APPLY YOUR KNOWLEDGE

Optional Desired Results:

You want to ensure that unskilled temporary staff can install all of the workstations.

You want to ensure that the proprietary company applications can be installed on the systems during the rollout.

Proposed Solution:

You plan to use Sysprep to prepare installation images for your systems. You determine that you will need to develop approximately 12 different images (one image for each type of computer for each department type). You also determine that, depending on the hardware configuration of each computer, you may need additional images (such as for the dual-Pentium computers). To simplify the installation process you will create unattended text files to run with your Sysprep images.

To assist in the development of the images, you obtain samples of each type of equipment being used and a copy of each software application being used. The equipment and software is tested in your lab environment to ensure that it works without incident.

Which results does the proposed solution produce?

A. The proposed solution produces the required result and produces all of the optional results.

B. The proposed solution produces the required result and produces only one of the optional results.

C. The proposed solution produces the required result but does not produce any of the optional results.

D. The proposed solution does not produce the required result.

9. You are working the late shift at your company's help desk. A frustrated user contacts you and explains that he is trying to install four new workstations in his department. Each of the new workstations needs to be configured identically to his personal workstation (the workstation arrived configured with a default installation of Windows 95). Upon detailed questioning, the user explains that he ran Sysprep on his personal workstation to create an installation image. He is now very upset because setup runs whenever he reboots his computer. What should you tell the user? Select three.

A. Sysprep should be run only on a fresh installation of Windows so that a clean version of the operating system can be imaged.

B. Sysprep should be run only on an expendable (nonproduction) machine, because its Security Identifiers will be changed upon reboot (unless the -nosidgen option is used with Sysprep).

C. The user should have just installed the new workstation manually because the number of machines is very small.

D. The user should have considered using the Setup Manager to create an unattended text file based on the configuration of his computer.

APPLY YOUR KNOWLEDGE

E. The user should have installed Remote Installation Services and created a RIS image of the workstation to be installed.

F. The user should have upgraded the existing Windows 95 computers to Windows 2000 Professional.

10. You are installing a Windows 2000 Professional system over the network. The machine you are installing has the following specifications: Pentium 450Mhz CPU, 128MB RAM, 16MB SVGA video card, and a 14GB hard drive (currently unpartitioned). You boot from a disk that has the MS network client on it attached to the distribution server.

When you run WINNT, the install cannot complete. What is the most likely cause of the problem?

A. The system does not meet the minimum system requirements.

B. You cannot use WINNT to perform a networked installation of Windows 2000 Professional.

C. You must have a partition on the machine before you can perform a networked installation.

D. You do not have administrative privileges on the network.

11. You are in the process of installing Windows 2000 Professional on a new computer at your office. The computer you are working with does not support booting from the CD-ROM and you do not have a copy of the Windows 2000 setup disks. You need to install this machine as soon as possible.

What can you do to complete this installation?

A. From any system, access the Windows 2000 installation CD and run the MAKEBOOT command to create a system boot disk.

B. From an existing Windows 2000-based system, run the RDISK command to create a set of installation disks.

C. From an existing Windows 2000-based system, run the RIPrep utility to create a system boot disk.

D. From any system, access the Windows 2000 installation CD and run WINNT with the /ox option.

12. As network administrator at your company, you are required to install many Windows 2000 Professional workstations. Using the Setup Manager, you create an unattended text file that represents a standard configuration file called setup.txt for your environment. You have also shared a copy of the Windows 2000 source files on a server named dis_server in a share named I386.

What command will use your script file to install Windows 2000 Professional?

A. Sysprep - Sysprep.inf

B. WINNT32 /u:setup.txt /s:\\dis_server\
➥i386/b

C. WINNT32 /u:setup.txt /s:\\dis_server\i386
➥/b /udf:comp1,udf_file1.txt

D. WINNT /u:setup.txt /s:\\dis_server\i386

APPLY YOUR KNOWLEDGE

13. You are responsible for rolling out 600 computers with Windows 2000 Professional. Approximately 200 of the computers are brand new and will be shipped direct from the manufacturer. The remaining 400 are existing computers currently in use across your enterprise. Approximately half of these computers are running Windows NT Workstation 4.0, with the remaining running Windows 98. Many of the existing machines have software and data stored on them that will have to be preserved.

    Your manager suggests that all workstations be installed using a Sysprep image. As the person responsible for this rollout, what is your opinion of your manager's solution?

    A. You agree with your manager and support the suggested approach to the problem.

    B. You are concerned that data may be lost on the existing computers.

    C. You support the proposed solution for the new computers only.

    D. You support the proposed solution for the existing computers only.

    E. You do not agree with your manager and feel the plan should be redeveloped.

14. You are responsible for rolling out 600 computers with Windows 2000 Professional. Approximately 200 of the computers are brand new and will be shipped direct from the manufacturer. The remaining 400 are existing computers currently in use across your enterprise. Approximately half of these computers are running Windows NT 4.0 Workstation, with the remaining running Windows 98. Many of the existing computers have software and data stored on them that will have to be preserved.

    Your manager suggests that all new workstations be installed using a Sysprep image and that existing workstations be upgraded to Windows 2000 Professional using the setup program and an unattended text file. As the person responsible for this rollout, what is your opinion of your manager's solution?

    A. You agree with your manager and support the suggested approach to the problem.

    B. You are concerned that data may be lost on the existing computers.

    C. You support the proposed solution for the new computers only.

    D. You support the proposed solution for the existing computers only.

    E. You do not agree with your manager and feel the plan should be redeveloped.

15. You are in the process of setting up Remote Installation Services (RIS). Which of the following are required to support this service? Select three.

    A. Active Directory

    B. Sysprep

    C. DNS

    D. DHCP

    E. Riprep

Answers to Review Questions

1. Windows 2000 Server supports dual processors and is designed for workgroup environments. Advanced Server supports up to eight processors and includes cluster support. Datacenter Server

supports up to 32 processors and is designed for very large environments. See the section entitled "Windows 2000 Products" for details.

2. The minimum system requirements include a Pentium 133 with 64MB RAM and a 2GB hard drive with 650MB of free space. See the section entitled "Hardware Requirements" for details.

3. One of the primary advantages of FAT is that it is supported by almost every operating system on the market. On the downside, however, it lacks local security and is inefficient on large partitions.

   Windows 95 (OSR2), Windows 98, and Windows 2000 are the only operating systems that support FAT32. Like FAT, FAT32 lacks local security. FAT32, however, is more efficient than FAT for larger partitions.

   Windows 2000 and Windows NT (with SP3+) are the only operating systems that support the version of NTFS (5.0) that ships with Windows 2000. NTFS offers a number of advantages, such as local security, encryption, and compression. See the section entitled "Windows 2000 File Systems" for details.

4. Setup Manager is used to generate unattended text files. The Setup Manager utility ships with the Windows 2000 Resource Kit. See the section entitled "Automating the Installation Process" for details.

5. Phase I is the Text Mode of the installation. During this phase you will provide information regarding the installation partition, file format, and installation directory. Phase II, or GUI-mode setup, is when you configure the following: regional settings, name and organization, licensing mode (server only), computer name, and optional components to install. Phase III of

the installation involves setting up the network components on your system (network adapter cards and so on). The last phase of the installation copies the remaining files to your computer, applies configuration settings, removes temporary files, and restarts the computer. See the section entitled "Installing Windows 2000 Professional—An Overview" for details.

6. To complete a networked-based installation you must have the installation files copied to a distribution server, client software so you can attach to the distribution server, and a minimum of 685MB of free drive space on the local machine you want to install. See the section entitled "Installing Over a Network" for details.

7. RIPrep is used to create images (a copy of setup files and corresponding script files) that work in conjunction with the RIS server. Sysprep removes unique information from a computer so it can be "imaged" using third-party disk-imaging utilities. The key here is that Riprep works with RIS, and Sysprep works with third-party disk-imaging utilities. See the sections entitled "Using the Remote Image Preparation (RIPrep) Tool" and "Imaging Windows 2000 Professional Installs" for details.

Answers to Exam Questions

1. **E.** To fully answer this question, you must understand the base platform on which each version of Windows 2000 will run. You also need to be aware of the services that are provided with each server. Answer E is correct because the three file and print servers can run on Windows 2000 Server (remember that Windows 2000 Server

APPLY YOUR KNOWLEDGE

supports four processors). Two copies of Windows 2000 Advanced Server are required to support the two servers running as a clustered configuration. The database server requires a copy of Windows 2000 Data Center server. Answer A is incorrect because Windows 2000 Server does not support clustering or a platform with eight processors. Answer B is incorrect because Windows 2000 Advanced Server would be overkill for the file and print servers and is not the preferred OS for servers holding a large database. Answer C is incorrect because six copies of Windows 2000 Datacenter Server would be expensive to implement, and not all servers require it. See the section entitled "Windows 2000 Products" for details.

2. **B.** Windows 2000 Server supports up to four processors for new installations and upgrades. For this reason, the existing server can be upgraded without incident. The second new server has six CPUs and is not supported on a Windows 2000 server installation. Answer A is not likely because the CD is supported on the first server. Answers C, D, and E are incorrect because SMP is supported, to different degrees or levels, by all Windows 2000 platforms. See the section entitled "Windows 2000 Products" for details.

3. **D.** Dynamic disks are created by converting a basic disk to dynamic. The conversion process requires that a 1MB block of free space be available at the end of the hard drive. For this reason, D is the most appropriate answer. Since you are looking into the future, you must ensure that each hard drive has the ability to be converted if the need arises. Answers A, B, and C are incorrect because the file format does not affect drive types. Answer E is also incorrect because

dynamic disks and basic disks cannot coexist with each other at the drive level. See the section entitled "Disk and Partition Options" for details.

4. **C.** Windows 95 supports only FAT (and FAT32 if OSR2), Windows 98 supports FAT and FAT32, and Windows NT 4.0 supports FAT and NTFS. Windows 2000 supports FAT, FAT32, and NTFS. Because the Windows 95 operating system cannot support NFTS, you will need to reformat the drive and reinstall Windows 95 (and any other OS on the system). Answer A is incorrect because you cannot convert NTFS to FAT. Answer B is incorrect because DOS does not know how to access an NTFS formatted drive, so you would not be able to read the drive from DOS. Answer D is also incorrect because Windows 95 does not support NTFS. See the section entitled "Windows 2000 File Systems" for details.

5. **B.** Windows 2000 will, by default, format large FAT partitions with FAT32. FAT32 is not supported by Windows NT 4.0 and therefore cannot be run. Answer A is incorrect because Windows NT 4.0 and Windows 2000 are able to read information from the drive as long as the file system is supported. Answer C is incorrect because Windows 2000 and NT support dual booting. Answer D is incorrect because Windows has the ability to create larger drive partitions. See the section entitled "Windows 2000 File Systems" for details.

6. **A.** This type of question is very common on Microsoft tests. The key to answering these questions is to organize the information provided and draw a small table of the results. This will then assist you in selecting the most appropriate answer. You should also spend a few minutes

making sure you understand the question. Often you will find the same question is repeated multiple times with a different proposed solution each time. Table 1.11 summarizes the answer to question 6.

TABLE 1.11

SUMMARY OF EXAM QUESTION 6

Result	Result Met?	Rationale
Required Results		
Your plan should allow for the installation of all workstations with the least amount of user intervention possible.	Yes	Unattended installation files can be used to automate the installation of Windows 2000 Professional.
Desired Optional Results		
You want to ensure that unskilled temporary staff can install all the workstations.	Yes	Unattended installation files are very easy to use and can be run by unskilled staff.
You want to ensure that the proprietary company applications can be installed on the systems during the rollout.	Yes	Unattended text files can be used to install applications.

See the section entitled "Automating the Installation Process" for details.

7. **D.** Table 1.12 summarizes the answer to question 7.

TABLE 1.12

SUMMARY OF EXAM QUESTION 7

Result	Result Met?	Rationale
Required Results		
Your plan should allow for the installation of all workstations with the least amount of user intervention possible.	No	Using RIS is not an option in your environment. One of the requirements of RIS is Active Directory. Your organization is not planning to install Active Directory until next year.
Desired Optional Results		
You want to ensure that unskilled temporary staff can install all the workstations.	No	RIS installations are very easy to use and can be run by unskilled staff. In this case, however, RIS is not available because of how your environment is configured.
You want to ensure that the proprietary company applications can be installed on the systems during the rollout.	Yes	RIS, in conjunction with appropriate scripts, can be used to install applications.

See the section entitled "Remote Installation Services (RIS)" for details.

8. **A.** Table 1.13 summarizes the answer to question 8.

APPLY YOUR KNOWLEDGE

TABLE 1.13

SUMMARY OF EXAM QUESTION 8

Result	Result Met?	Rationale
Required Results		
Your plan should allow for the installation of all workstations with the least amount of user intervention possible.	Yes	Using a Sysprep image in conjunction with an unattended installation file makes the installation of Windows 2000 very easy. Once the installation is started no user intervention is required.
Desired Optional Results		
You want to ensure that unskilled temporary staff can install all the workstations.	Yes	Using a Sysprep image in conjunction with an unattended installation file makes the installation of Windows 2000 very easy.
You want to ensure that the proprietary company applications can be installed on the systems during the rollout.	Yes	Sysprep allows you to take an image of a working computer and transfer it to another. If your proprietary applications are working on the source computer, they should work on the new computers.

See the section entitled "Imaging Windows 2000 Professional Installs" for details.

9. **A, B, D.** This user assumed that he could simply copy his existing configuration to the rest of the computers. Remember that the Sysprep utility removes the security identifier (SID) from the machine on which it is being run so the hard disk can be imaged using a third-party utility.

Answer A is correct because any misconfigurations or errors on the workstation will be transferred to the new workstations. Answer B is correct because the Sysprep removes SID data from the local machine so it can be imaged to other computers.

Answers C and D are both correct, but you must choose only one (you were asked to select only three answers)—this is a classic Microsoft question. Technically, answer C is correct because the user could have installed all of the machines manually. Technically, answer D is also correct because Setup Manager can be used to create unattended text files based on the existing configuration of a computer. Some might argue that application configuration would not transfer using the Setup Manager method (which is true) and therefore answer C is more appropriate. In most cases, however, Microsoft wants you to be able to demonstrate that you know how all of their utilities work. For this reason, I would lean toward answer D because it emphasizes the fact that you understand the capabilities of Setup Manager.

Answer E is incorrect because the user most likely does not have rights to install RIS (remember that RIS requires Active Directory, DNS, and DHCP). This would also be a lot of work for such a small number of computers. Answer F is incorrect because the Windows 95 installation that shipped on the computers would not include all of the applications required. See the section entitled "Automating the Installation Process" for details.

10. **C.** To complete a network-based installation of Windows 2000, you must have a formatted partition with approximately 700MB of free space. This partition is required to hold the

APPLY YOUR KNOWLEDGE

temporary installation files that are pulled across the network before the installation starts. Answer A is incorrect because the system outlined does meet the minimum system requirements of Windows 2000. Answer B is incorrect because both WINNT and WINNT32 support network-based installations. Answer D is incorrect because you do not need administrative privileges to install a system. See the section entitled "Installing Over a Network" for details.

11. **A.** The Windows 2000 installation disks will allow you to access the local CD-ROM to run the Windows 2000 setup program. These disks are created using the MAKEBOOT utility found in the BOOT directory of the Windows 2000 installation CD. Answer B is incorrect because RDISK is not a valid utility under Windows 2000 (even under Windows NT 4.0, it would not allow for the creation of boot disks). Answer C is incorrect because Riprep is a utility that creates Remote Installation Server installation images. Answer D is incorrect because the /ox switch is no longer supported under Windows 2000. See the section entitled "Manually Installing Windows 2000 Professional" for details.

12. **D.** Answer D is the correct syntax for installing Windows 2000 with an unattended text file. Answer A is incorrect because Sysprep is not a valid command for installing Windows 2000. Answers B and C are incorrect because the /b switch is no longer supported under Windows 2000. See the section entitled "Automating the Installation Process" for details.

13. **B, C.** Using a Sysprep image to install the computer requires that data on existing hard drives be lost. If you used your manager's solution you would need to back up the data from each workstation before you installed the image. For this reason, the Sysprep installation is not the best method of installation for the existing workstation. Sysprep images are a very effective method of installing new workstations. See the section entitled "Imaging Windows 2000 Professional Installs" for details.

14. **A.** Your manager's plan is a sound one. Using a Sysprep image for the new machines will allow for a consistent and fast installation. Completing a scripted upgrade on the remaining machines should not affect existing data or applications. See the section entitled "Imaging Windows 2000 Professional Installs" for details.

15. **A, C, D.** Remote installation services require that Active Directory be present on the network. You must install the RIS server on a member server (or domain controller). DHCP and DNS are also required to support the RIS server. DHCP assigns IP Address configurations to RIS clients and DNS allows RIS Clients to find the Active Directory and RIS servers. See the section entitled "Remote Installation Services (RIS)" for details.

Suggested Readings and Resources

1. Web resources

- Deploying Windows 2000 Professional, available at `http://www.microsoft.com/windows2000/library/planning/client/deploy.asp`

- Step-by-Step Guide to a Common Infrastructure for Windows 2000 Server Deployment - Part 1: Installing a Windows 2000 Server as a domain controller, available at `http://www.microsoft.com/windows2000/library/planning/server/serversteps.asp`

- Step-by-Step Guide to a Common Infrastructure for Windows 2000 Server Deployment - Part 2: Installing a Windows 2000 Professional Workstation and Connecting it to a domain, available at `http://www.microsoft.com/windows2000/library/planning/server/prosteps.asp`

- Understanding the Value of IntelliMirror, Remote OS Installation, and Systems Management Server, available at `http://www.microsoft.com/windows2000/guide/server/solutions/valueim.asp`

- Microsoft Windows 2000 Unattended Setup Parameters Guide: Answer File Parameters for Unattended Installation of Microsoft Windows 2000, Microsoft Corporation, Revision 1.5 April 9, 1999, available at `http://www.microsoft.com/TechNet/win2000/win2ksrv/technote/unattend.asp`

- Step-by-Step Guide to Remote OS Installation, available at `http://www.microsoft.com/windows2000/library/planning/management/remotesteps.asp`

This chapter covers the following Microsoft-specified objectives for the Implementing and Conducting Administration of Resources section of the exam:

Monitor, manage, and troubleshoot access to files and folders.

- **Configure, manage, and troubleshoot file compression.**

- **Control access to files and folders by using permissions.**

- **Optimize access to files and folders.**

▶ File system resources represent one of the most important services used on networks today. As a network administrator, you must learn to balance the ease of networked access against security considerations. This objective also introduces the importance of designing an efficient directory structure so that access to folders and files is optimized for your environment.

Manage and troubleshoot access to shared folders.

- **Create and remove shared folders.**

- **Control access to shared folders by using permissions.**

- **Manage and troubleshoot Web server resources.**

▶ Shared folders allow users to gain access to folders and files remotely. As a network administrator you must gain a full appreciation of shared folders and shared folder security.

CHAPTER *2*

Implementing and Conducting Administration of Resources

Connect to local and network print devices.

- **Manage printers and print jobs.**
- **Control access to printers by using permissions.**
- **Connect to an Internet printer.**
- **Connect to a local print device.**

▶ The print environment is another heavily used network service. This objective ensures that, as a network administrator, you understand how to configure and manage the Windows 2000 printer environment. This objective includes print security, printer management, and print job management.

Configure and manage file systems.

- **Convert from one file system to another file system.**
- **Configure file systems by using NTFS, FAT32, or FAT.**

▶ The Windows 2000 file system offers network administrators a large number of configuration options. This objective ensures that you understand the implications of using one file system over another and that you have the skills required to manage the file system you use in your environment.

▶ The key to understanding the objectives for this chapter is your understanding of permissions. Permissions give users certain levels of rights to perform specific actions on resources on the network. If you understand how Microsoft applies permissions to the file system (the most complex of the permissions) you will find permissions, when applied to other services, very easy to understand. In short, focus your efforts on NTFS- and share-level permissions. Understanding these permissions makes working with printer permissions easy.

▶ You will need to understand the limitations of FAT and FAT32 with regard to security in the Windows 2000 environment. You also need to thoroughly understand how to manage these file systems (for example, what file system can be converted to one another versus a required re-format of the hard drive).

▶ Printing is a relatively easy section. I suggest you configure a few local printers and play for a couple of hours. I also suggest you focus on the Web-based printer management utilities (they are new to Windows 2000 and most likely to be hot exam topics).

INTRODUCTION

The primary focus of this chapter is the efficient management of network resources. Specifically, it takes a detailed look at the management of the network file and print environments.

The chapter starts with an overview of the challenges that face network administrators when it comes to the management of network resources. The issues associated with the management of a network file system are then covered. Specifically, shared folders are discussed to ensure that you have a thorough understanding of how shares and share security work. We then look at NTFS security and how it can be used, in conjunction with share level security, to secure a network file system. The second major service, printing, is then covered. These sections detail how a print environment is configured, secured, and then managed.

MANAGING NETWORK RESOURCES

Networks allow users to share resources. One of the primary goals of the network administrator is to control access to resources and ensure that a resource is accessible to authorized users and secured from unauthorized users. The following section focuses on the tools available to manage some of the most common networked resources.

Securing Network Resources

In the world of networks there are a number of different types of networked resources. Some of the most common networked resources include file systems, printers, and databases. Regardless of the service you are dealing with, network administrators typically use access rights (referred to as *permissions* in the world of Windows 2000) to control access to resources. Permissions define the level of access a user has to resources. Depending on the type of resources you are managing, different sets of permissions will be available to control different levels of access.

FILE RESOURCES

Monitor, manage and troubleshoot access to files and folders.

Manage and troubleshoot access to shared folders.

One of the most heavily used network services found in most environments is file system service. Microsoft Windows 2000 allows network administrators to "share" file system resources so that multiple users are accessing a file system remotely over the network. Windows 2000 also offers a very secure file system (NTFS) that gives an administrator the ability to secure a file system by giving a user permission to use the resource.

The following sections provide details on managing file system resources. Specifically, the skills required to manage and troubleshoot shared folders and NTFS permissions are presented.

File Shares

To allow remote access to resources you must make them available over the network. Once resources are available on the network, users with the appropriate permissions can access resources from computers found on the network. One of the challenges facing the network administrator is how to provide access to resources and still have a secure environment. Windows 2000 allows you to control the resources you want to make available over the network.

Sharing a folder in Windows 2000 means you are making a folder within a file system available to users on the network. Once you decide which file system resources you want to make available over the network, you will need to share them out and set user permissions. Shared folders are created at the folder (or directory) level for FAT, FAT32, and NTFS file systems. After a folder is shared, users with permissions to the share (and underlying file system if it is formatted with NTFS) have access to all of the files and subfolders beneath it.

Share Permissions

When sharing a folder you must determine the level of access you are going to assign to different users. Remember that managing access to a file system is a delicate balance of allowing access to appropriate resources for the appropriate users and protecting resources from unauthorized access. To assist in securing shared resources, Windows 2000 supports a number of share-level permissions. These permissions define the level of access a user will have when he/she accesses the file system resource over the network through the shared directory.

Table 2.1 presents a list of share permissions and the level of access associated with each.

TABLE 2.1

WINDOWS 2000 SHARE LEVEL PERMISSIONS

Share Permission	Definition
Read	The Read permission allows the user to display files and subfolders within the shared folder. The user is also allowed to execute programs that are contained in the directories.
Change	The Change permission gives the user all of the permissions associated with the Read permission and also allows him to add files or subfolders to the shared folder. The user is also allowed to append or delete the information from existing files and folders.
Full Control	The Full control permission gives the user all of the permissions associated with the Change permission and also allows him to change the file permissions or file system resources. The user is also allowed to take ownership of file resources (if he has the appropriate NTFS permissions).

> **WARNING**
>
> **Only Assign the Required Permissions to Users** You must be very careful when assigning share-level permissions. Do not give permissions to users who do not require them. Once you have access to a share, the permissions cannot be blocked unless you use NTFS file system permissions.

Multiple Share Permissions

Share-level permissions can be assigned to users and groups. Because of this, you may find that some users have multiple permissions assigned to them. For example, a user account named DougH is given the Read share permission to a shared folder. The user DougH is a member of the group called IT_Staff. The group IT_Staff is given Change permissions to the same shared folder. Because the user DougH is a member of the IT_Staff group, the effective permissions on the share are Read (received from assignment to the user account) and Change (received from assigned to the group). This means that the user has both Read and Change access to the share. When multiple permissions are assigned the least restrictive will be the final effective permission.

The only exception to the preceding rule is if the Deny permission is applied to a user. If you are denied permission to a share, this permission will override all other permissions you receive and you will not be given access to the resource. Specific permissions can be denied. If a user is denied Full Control, the user will have no access to the share. If the user is denied Change permission she is not able to have Full Control permissions but can still have Read permissions.

Creating Shared Folders

Shared folders can be created in two different ways. This section will provide detailed step-by-step instructions regarding the setup of shared folders.

Step by Step 2.1 shows how to share folders from your local hard drive. This means you have access to the local system. In this Step by Step, we will share a folder called DATA from the local C partition of your system to a local group called Accounts. The Accounts group needs Change permissions to this resource. The local Administrators group needs Full Control permissions to the share so the resource can be managed. This Step by Step assumes you have a directory called DATA on your local drive and a group called Accounts created on your local system.

STEP BY STEP

2.1 Sharing Folders on Local Drives

1. From the Explorer Window, find the DATA directory on the C partition.

2. Right-click the directory. From the secondary menu, select Properties.

3. From the Properties dialog box, click the Sharing tab (alternatively, you could have selected the Sharing option from the secondary menu in step 2).

4. The Sharing Properties tab is presented in Figure 2.1.

5. Select the Share This Folder option. Once this option has been selected, you will be able to provide a share name and description, and configure the share. The share name represents the name used when accessing the resource over the network. The Comment field is used to describe the resources being shared (some user interfaces show you the share description when accessing the share). For the share name enter **Accounting Data**.

6. Enter **Test of Account Data Share for the Comment**.

7. Leave the User Limit setting to Maximum Allowed. This setting allows you to limit the total number of users allowed to access this shared folder at any one time.

8. To set the share permissions, click the Permissions button. Figure 2.2 shows the share permissions assigned to the share.

9. Note the default permissions assigned to all new shares created in your environment. You should remove the default permissions of Everyone with Full Control permission by clicking the remove button. You can now add the Accounting group by clicking the Add button and selecting the Account group from the Select Computer, Users, Groups dialog box. Once you have found the group in the list, click the Add button and then click OK. You can now assign share permission to the accounting group. To do this, select the Accounting group and check the Allow box next to the Read permission. Repeat the same procedure to add the Administrator group to the list of users and groups with permission to use this share.

continues

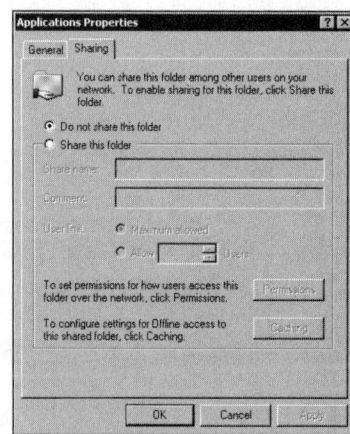

FIGURE 2.1
Windows 2000 Sharing Properties tab.

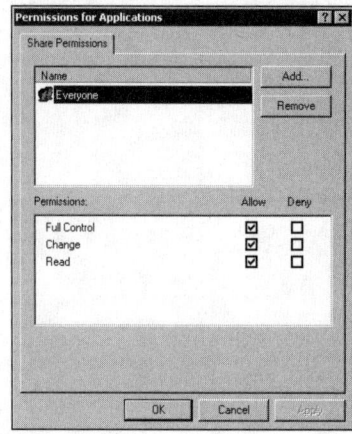

FIGURE 2.2
Windows 2000 Sharing Permissions Property page.

continued

10. The caching button allows you to control how the system will configure caching on the machines accessing data from the share—called making files and folder available "offline."

Offline files can be configured to store a version of themselves in a reserved portion of disk space on your computer called a *cache*. The computer can access this cache regardless of whether it is connected to the network. Table 2.2 shows the three configurations options available for a cache configuration.

TABLE 2.2

CACHE CONFIGURATION SETTINGS

Option	Description
Manual Caching for Documents	Provides offline access to only those files that someone using your shared folder specifically (or manually) identifies. This caching option is ideal for a shared network folder containing files that are to be accessed and modified by several people. This is the default option when you set up a shared folder to be used offline.
Automatic Caching for Documents	Makes every file that someone opens from your shared folder available to them offline. However, this setting does not make every file in your shared folder available to them offline, only those files that are opened. Files that are not opened are not available offline.
Automatic Caching for Programs	Provides offline access to shared folders containing files that are not to be changed. This caching option is ideal for making files available offline that are read, referenced, or run, but that are not changed in the process. This option reduces network traffic because offline files are opened directly, without accessing the network versions in any way, and generally start and run faster than the network versions.
	When you use this option, be sure to restrict permissions on the files contained in the shared folder to *read-only* access.

For this Step by Step, set the caching to Manual Caching for Documents.

11. Click the OK button to close the share property page. You should notice a small hand under the left corner of the C:\DATA folder to indicate that it is being shared.

The second method of creating shares can be performed on both local and remote computers. Step by Step 2.2 demonstrates how to create a share using the Computer Management Microsoft Management Snap-in.

STEP BY STEP

2.2 Creating Shares Using the Computer Management Snap-In

1. Click Start, Run. In the Open dialog box, type MMC and click OK.

2. From the Console menu, click the Add/Remove Snap-In menu.

3. From the Add/Remove Snap-In dialog box, click Add.

4. From the Add Standalone Snap-In window, highlight the Computer Management snap-in and click Add.

5. In the Computer Management dialog box, select either the local computer or a remote system. (If you select a remote system, you need to have permission to share resources on the remote system.) Click OK in the Computer Management window.

6. Close the Add Standalone Snap-In and Add/Remove Snap-In dialog boxes.

7. Open the Computer Management Snap-In by clicking the plus sign beside the snap-in. Open the Shared Folders node of the Computer Management Snap-In. From this location, you can create and manage shares on your system. Figure 2.3 shows the appropriate MMC screen.

continues

continued

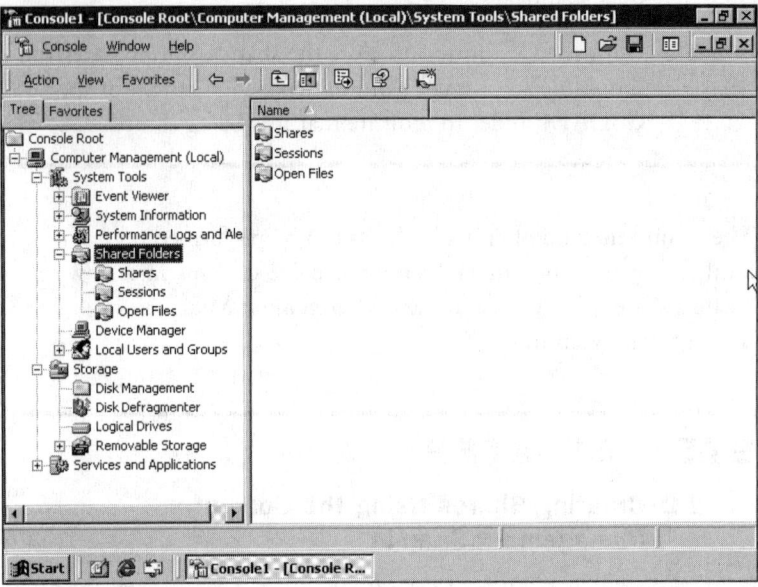

FIGURE 2.3
Computer Management Snap-In with Shared Folders Node

8. To create a new share, right-click the Shares folder in the Shared Folders node. From the secondary menu select New File Share. This action will launch the Create Share Folder Wizard.

9. The wizard will walk you through the process of creating the new share. At the first screen, you will need to indicate the physical path to the folder you want to share (browse is provided so you can find the folder you want). For this example, enter `C:\DATA`. You will also need to provide a share name and description. Click Next to continue.

10. You will now need to set the share permissions associated with the share. The wizard provides three common configurations and a custom option. In most cases, you will need to enter a custom configuration. Entering permissions is identical to the process documented in Step by Step 2.1. Click the Finish button to create your share.

Connecting to Shared Folders

Once shares have been created, users will need to connect to them. There are four common methods that can be used to connect to a share. Table 2.3 presents these methods.

TABLE 2.3

COMMON METHODS USED TO CONNECT TO FOLDER SHARES

Method	Description
Net Use Command	You can use the NET USE command to connect a share. At a command prompt type the following: **NET USE X: \\COMPUTERNAME\SHARE** In this command, COMPUTERNAME represents the name of the computer where the share physically resides; SHARE represents the name assigned to the share; and X: represents the local drive letter you can map to the shared location.
Map a network drive from the Tools menu in Windows Explorer	From the Tools menu of Windows Explorer, you can map network drives. This tool allows you to select a local drive letter and assign it to a network share location (either by typing the UNC path to the share or by browsing the network to find the path). This tool is also available if you right-click on the My Computer or My Network Places icons on your desktop.
My Network Places	By opening the computer icons found in My Network Places, you are able to see the shares available on each computer.
UNC Path	From the Windows Run menu, you can type the UNC path to a share (such as **\\COMPUTERNAME\SHARE**). This will cause a new window to be launched on your desktop displaying the contents of the share.

Administrative Shared Folders

Depending on the configuration of your computer, some or all of the following special shared folders are automatically created by Windows 2000 for administrative and system use. Figure 2.4 shows the default administrative shares found on a Windows 2000 Professional computer. In most cases, special shared folders should not be deleted or modified.

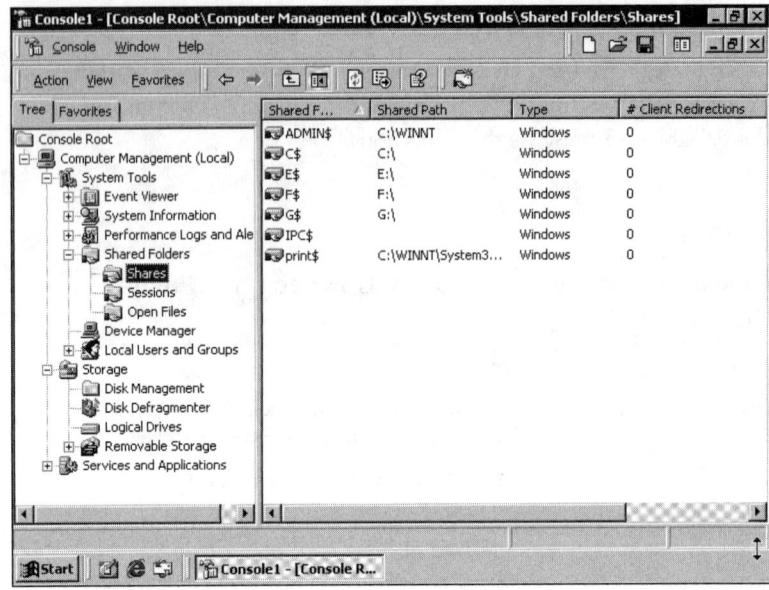

FIGURE 2.4
Windows 2000 default administrative shares.

Table 2.4 provides a definition for each of the administrative shares found.

TABLE 2.4

Types of Administrative Shares

Share Type	Description
DRIVELETTER$	A shared folder that allows administrative personnel to connect to the root directory of a drive. Shown as A$, B$, C$, D$, and so on. For example, D$ is a shared folder name by which drive D: might be accessed by an administrator over the network.
	For a Windows 2000 Professional computer, only members of the Administrators or Backup Operators group can connect to these shared folders. For a Windows 2000 Server computer, members of the Server Operators group can also connect to these shared folders.
ADMIN$	A resource used by the system during remote administration of a computer. The path of this resource is always the path to the Windows 2000 system root (the directory in which Windows 2000 is installed—for example, C:\Winnt).

Share Type	Description
IPC$	A resource sharing the resources essential for communication between programs. It is used during remote administration of a computer and when viewing a computer's shared resources.
PRINT$	The PRINT$ share will be found on any system that has a shared printer installed on it. This share is used for the remote administration of printers.

Web Server Resources

Another method of sharing information with users is through the Windows 2000 Internet Information Server (IIS) and the Internet Explorer (IE). You can make file resources available to users through their browsers through the click of a mouse button.

Accessing Information as a Web Page

To share a file system resource through IIS, you will need to access the Web Sharing tab of the property page for the folder (as shown in Figure 2.5). You can access this page by right-clicking the folder you want to share and selecting Properties from the secondary menu.

By selecting the Share This Folder option, you can enter the alias name you want to use to represent this folder on your Web site. For example, if you were to alias a folder as TEST it would be accessible through your browser at the following URL: HTTP://computer_name/ TEST. This allows you to access the information from the Web folder.

Web Folder Functionality

Web Folder Behaviors available in Microsoft Internet Explorer 5 allow users to navigate to a folder view. IE 5.0 also includes support for Distributed Authoring and Versioning (DAV) and Web Extender Client (WEC) protocols. DAV is a series of extensions to the Hypertext Transfer Protocol (HTTP) and defines how basic file functions, such as Copy, Move, Delete, and Create Folder, are performed across HTTP. WEC is a Microsoft FrontPage protocol that provides the same sort of functionality as DAV. Both protocols define how to send and retrieve properties on HTTP resources.

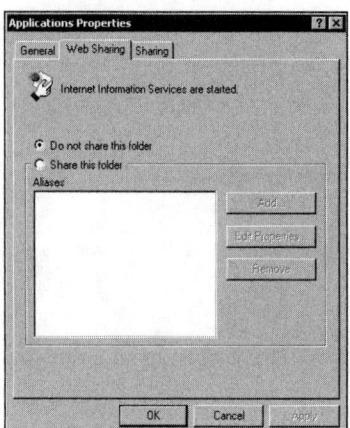

FIGURE 2.5
The Web Sharing tab.

The Web Folder Behaviors enable authors to view sites in a Web folder view, which is similar to the Microsoft Windows Explorer folder view. The DAV and WEC protocols add additional capabilities to the Web folder view. For example, using the Web Folder Behaviors and DAV makes it possible to perform the equivalent of a DIR command on an HTTP resource and retrieve all the information necessary to fill a Windows Explorer view. Internet Explorer 5 and later supports two Web Folder Behaviors that allow users to browse sites in a Web folder view.

A Web folder view maintains a consistent look and feel between navigating the local file system, a networked drive, and an Internet Web site. Although a Web folder is a part of the file system hierarchy, it does not necessarily represent anything in the file system.

To access a Web Folder click Open on the File menu of Internet Explorer 5.0. In the Open dialog box, enter the URL (**HTTP://** **computer_name/folder_name**) and click the Open as Web Folder option. By selecting the Open as Web Folder option, you will access the folder and acquire the ability to manage its contents as you would any file through Windows Explorer.

NTFS Permissions

Monitor, manage, and troubleshoot access to files and folders.

An optimal configuration for most Windows 2000 systems will include partitions formatted with NTFS. NTFS offers a number of advantages over FAT and FAT32—the most significant being folder and file security.

To secure folders and files on an NTFS partition, you assign NTFS permissions for each user or group that requires it. If a user does not have any permission assigned to his user account, or does not belong to a group with permissions assigned, the user will not be able to access the resource. By default, all users are given access to all file system resources on Windows 2000 NTFS partitions (the Everyone group is given the Full Control permission to all resources).

NTFS permissions can be assigned at both the file and folder level. You use NTFS folder permission to control access to a folder. You use NTFS file permissions to control access to specific files. Due to the nature of files and folders, the permissions assigned to files are different from the permissions assigned to folders. Folders are used to organize file resources and act as a container where files can be stored. Files, on the other hand, cannot contain other files. Because folders contain file permissions at the folder level, they give users the ability to create new files or list the files a folder contains. File permissions generally deal with the users' ability to manage the file itself (for example, to read or modify the file).

NTFS permissions can be assigned to both users and groups. Members of the Administrators group can assign NTFS permissions to files and folders on a system. The owner of a file or folder and users with Full Control permission can also assign permissions to a file or folder.

Folder Permissions

You assign folder permissions to control the access that users have to folders and the files contained within those folders. Table 2.5 lists the standard NTFS permissions that can be assigned to a folder and the level of access each provides.

TABLE 2.5

NTFS FOLDER PERMISSIONS

Permission	Description
Read	Allows a user to see the files and subfolders in a folder and view folder attributes, ownership, and permissions.
Write	Allows a user to create new files and subfolders with the folder, change folder attributes, and view folder ownership and permissions.
List Folder Contents	Allows a user to see the names of files and subfolders in the folder.
Read and Execute	Gives a user the rights assigned through the Read permission and the List Folder Contents permission. It also gives the user the ability to traverse folders. Traverse folders rights allow a user to reach files and folders located in subdirectories even if the user does not have permission to access portions of the directory path.

continues

TABLE 2.5 *continued*

NTFS FOLDER PERMISSIONS

Permission	Description
Modify	Gives a user the ability to delete the folder and perform the actions permitted by the Write and Read/Execute permissions.
Full Control	Allows a user to change permissions, take ownership, delete subfolders and files, and perform the actions granted by all other permissions.

File Permissions

You assign file permissions to control the access that users have to files. Table 2.6 lists the standard NTFS permissions that can be assigned to a file and the level of access it provides.

TABLE 2.6

NTFS FILE PERMISSIONS

Permission	Description
Read	Allows a user to read a file and view file attributes, ownership, and permissions.
Write	Allows a user to overwrite a file, change file attributes, and view file ownership and permissions.
Read and Execute	Gives a user the rights required to run applications and perform the actions permitted by the Read permission.
Modify	Gives a user the ability to modify and delete a file and perform the actions permitted by the Write and Read/Execute permissions.
Full Control	Allows a user to change permissions, take ownership, delete subfolders and files, and perform the actions granted by all other permissions.

Multiple NTFS Permissions

Permissions can be assigned to users and to groups. Because of this, it is possible for a user to be assigned permissions through multiple sources (for example you have membership in multiple groups each with permissions assigned). A user's effective permissions for a resource are the combination of the NTFS permissions that you assign to the individual user account and to all of the groups to which the user belongs.

Permissions can be denied. By denying permission to a folder or file you are denying a specific level of access regardless of the other permissions assigned to a user or group. Even if a user has access permissions to the file or folder as a member of a group, denying permission to the user blocks any other permissions the user has.

When determining a user's effective permissions, you must examine the permissions assigned at the specific resource. Remember that every file and folder on an NTFS partition has a list of permissions assigned to it. For this reason, permissions assigned at the file level will override permissions assigned at the folder level.

Permission Inheritance

By default, permissions assigned to a parent folder are inherited by and propagated to the subfolders and files that are contained in the parent folder. This default action, however, can be modified to meet the needs of specific environments. Figure 2.6 shows the folder permissions of a folder. Note the grayed-out permissions; this indicates that these permissions are being inherited from the parent.

You can prevent subfolders and files from inheriting permissions that are assigned to parent folders. By doing so, permission changes made to parent folders will not affect child folders and files.

When you prevent permission inheritance, you must choose one of the following options:

◆ Copy inherited permission from the parent folder.

◆ Remove the inherited permissions and retain only the permissions that were explicitly assigned.

Default NTFS Permissions

When you format an NTFS partition, Windows 2000 will assign a set of default permissions to the partition. You must understand the default assignments if you are to secure your environment. Table 2.7 lists the default NTFS permissions.

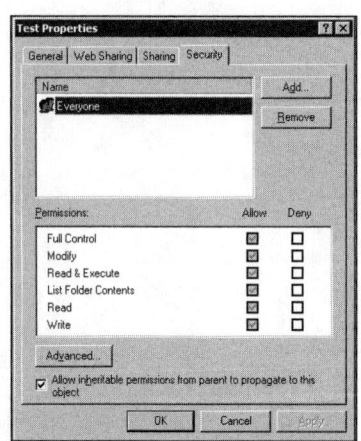

FIGURE 2.6
Folder permissions and inheritance.

TABLE 2.7

DEFAULT NTFS PERMISSION ASSIGNMENTS

Default Assignment	Description
For new NTFS partitions	When you format a partition with NTFS, Windows will automatically assign the Full Control permission for the root folder to the Everyone group.
For new folders or files	When you create a new folder or file on an NTFS partition, the folder or file inherits the permissions of its parent folder.
When a user or group is given access to a file or folder	When a user or group is given access to a folder, the default permissions assigned are Read & Execute, List Folder Contents, and Read.
	When a user or group is given access to a file, the default permissions assigned are Read & Execute and Read.

Assigning Permissions

Administrators, users with Full Control access, and the owner of a resource can grant permissions to a folder or file. The Security property page can be accessed by completing the following steps:

1. Right-click the file or folder you want to manage.

2. Select Properties from the drop-down menu.

3. Click the Security tab.

Table 2.8 presents the configuration options for NTFS security.

TABLE 2.8

NTFS SECURITY SETTINGS

Option	Description
Name	Lists the users and groups (also referred to as *security principals*) that have NTFS permissions assigned for this resource.
Permission	Lists the NTFS permissions assigned or denied for the security principal selected in the Name box.

Option	Description
Add	Opens the Select User, Groups, or Computers dialog box. This allows you to add new security principals to the Name box.
Remove	Removes the select security principal from the name box. By removing a security principal from the list, its associated permissions are also removed.

Special Permissions for Files and Folders

Standard permissions consist of a logical group of special permissions. Table 2.9 presents a listing of the special permissions supported on Windows 2000 NTFS partitions.

> **NOTE**
>
> **Owners of a Resource Can Manage Its Permissions**   Remember that if you own a resource you can manage its permissions. This is a very important concept because administrators always have the ability to take ownership of resources. Once you own the resource, you can then manage the permissions on the resource.
>
> You can view the ownership information associated with a resource by right-clicking the file or folder and selecting Properties from the secondary menu. From the Security tab, you can click the Advanced button to view the advanced security properties of the resource. To view the ownership information, click the Ownership tab.

TABLE 2.9

SPECIAL PERMISSIONS

Special Permission	Description
Traverse Folder/Execute File	Traverse Folder allows or denies moving through folders to reach other files or folders, even if the user has no permissions to the folders being traversed (the permission applies only to folders).
	Traverse Folder takes effect when a group or user is not granted the Bypass Traverse Checking user right in the Group Policy Snap-In. (By default, the Everyone group is given the Bypass Traverse Checking user right.)
	The Execute File permission allows or denies running program files (the permission applies only to files).
	Setting the Traverse Folder permission on a folder does not automatically set the Execute File permission on all files within that folder.
List Folder/Read Data	The List Folder permission allows or denies viewing filenames and subfolder names within the folder (the permission applies only to folders).
	The Read Data permission allows or denies viewing data in files (the permission applies only to files).

continues

| TABLE 2.9 | *continued* |

SPECIAL PERMISSIONS

Special Permission	*Description*
Read Attributes	The Read Attributes permission allows or denies viewing the attributes of a file or folder (for example, the read-only and hidden attributes). Attributes are defined by NTFS.
Read Extended Attributes	The Read Extended Attributes permission allows or denies viewing the extended attributes of a file or folder. Extended attributes are defined by programs and may vary by program.
Create Files/Write Data	The Create Files permission allows or denies creating files within the folder (the permission applies only to folders).
	The Write Data permission allows or denies making changes to the file and overwriting existing content (the permission applies only to files).
Create Folders/Append Data	The Create Folders permission allows or denies creating folders within the folder (the permission applies only to folders).
	The Append Data permission allows or denies making changes to the end of the file but not changing, deleting, or overwriting existing data (the permission applies only to files).
Write Attributes	The Write Attributes permission allows or denies changing the attributes of a file or folder.
Write Extended Attributes	The Write Extended Attributes permission allows or denies changing the extended attributes of a file or folder. Extended attributes are defined by programs and may vary by program.
Delete Subfolders and Files	The Delete Subfolders and Files permission allows or denies deleting subfolders and files, even if the Delete permission has not been granted on the subfolder or file.
Delete	The Delete permission allows or denies deleting the file or folder. If you don't have Delete permission on a file or folder, you can still delete it if you have been granted Delete Subfolders and Files permission on the parent folder.
Read Permissions	The Read Permissions permission allows or denies reading permissions of the file or folder, such as Full Control, Read, and Write.

Special Permission	Description
Change Permissions	The Change Permissions permission allows or denies changing permissions of the file or folder, such as Full Control, Read, and Write.
Take Ownership	The Take Ownership permission allows or denies taking ownership of the file or folder. The owner of a file or folder can always change permissions on it, regardless of any existing permissions that protect the file or folder.
Synchronize	The Synchronize permission allows or denies different threads to wait on the handle for the file or folder and synchronize with another thread that may signal it. This permission applies only to multithreaded, multiprocess programs.

File Permissions

File permissions include Full Control, Modify, Read & Execute, Read, and Write. Table 2.10 lists each file permission and specifies which special permissions are associated with that permission.

TABLE 2.10

SPECIAL FILE PERMISSIONS

Special Permissions	Full Control	Modify	Read & Execute	Read	Write
Traverse Folder/Execute File	x	x	x		
List Folder/Read Data	x	x	x	x	
Read Attributes	x	x	x	x	
Read Extended Attributes	x	x	x	x	
Create Files/Write Data	x	x			x
Create Folders/Append Data	x	x		x	
Write Attributes	x	x			x
Write Extended Attributes	x	x			x
Delete Subfolders and Files	x				
Delete	x	x			

continues

TABLE 2.10 | *continued*

SPECIAL FILE PERMISSIONS

Special Permissions	Full Control	Modify	Read & Execute	Read	Write
Read Permissions	x	x	x	x	x
Change Permissions	x				
Take Ownership	x				
Synchronize	x	x	x	x	x

Folder Permissions

Folder permissions include Full Control, Modify, Read & Execute, List Folder Contents, Read, and Write. Table 2.11 lists each folder permission and specifies which special permissions are associated with that permission.

TABLE 2.11

SPECIAL FOLDER PERMISSIONS

Special Permissions	Full Control	Modify	Read & Execute	List Folder Contents	Read	Write
Traverse Folder/ Execute File	x	x	x	x		
List Folder/Read Data	x	x	x	x	x	
Read Attributes	x	x	x	x	x	
Read Extended Attributes	x	x	x	x	x	
Create Files/ Write Data	x	x				x
Create Folders/ Append Data	x	x				x
Write Attributes	x	x				x
Write Extended Attributes	x	x				x
Delete Subfolders and Files	x					

Special Permissions	Full Control	Modify	Read & Execute	List Folder Contents	Read	Write
Delete	x	x				
Read Permissions	x	x	x	x	x	x
Change Permissions	x					
Take Ownership	x					
Synchronize	x	x	x	x	x	x

Special permission can be granted to users and groups from the Advanced button of the Security tab of a file or folder. The Permission Entry dialog box allows you to add, remove, and view/edit the special permissions assigned to users and groups. Figure 2.7 shows the special permissions assigned to the Everyone group on a folder (this dialog box is accessed by highlighting a user and group and clicking the View/Edit button).

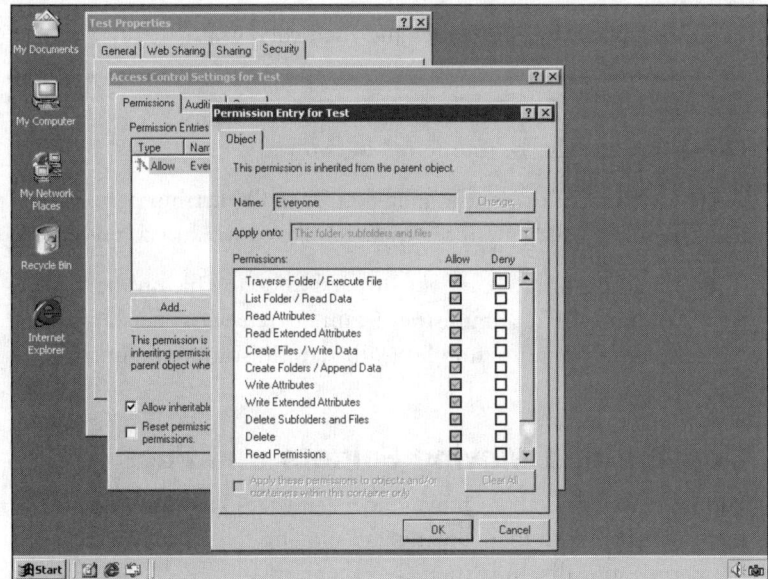

FIGURE 2.7
Special permissions configuration screen.

File/Folder Ownership

The owner of a resource can manage the permissions associated with it. As the administrator of a system, you can always take ownership of a file or folder and manage its permissions. This is helpful in instances where a deleted user is the only account with access to a file or folder.

Step by Step 2.3 shows how to take ownership of a file or folder.

STEP BY STEP

2.3 Taking Ownership of a File or Folder

1. Open Explorer and locate the file or folder of which you want to take ownership.

2. Right-click the file or folder, click Properties, and then click the Security tab.

3. Click Advanced, and then click the Owner tab.

4. Click the new owner and then click OK.

Ownership can also be transferred in two ways:

◆ The current owner can grant the Take Ownership permission to others, allowing those users to take ownership at any time.

◆ An administrator can take ownership of any file on the computer. The administrator cannot transfer ownership to others. This restriction keeps the administrator accountable.

Copying and Moving Folders and Files

You may need to copy or move folders and files in your environment. You will find that copying and moving folders may affect the permissions that are assigned to them.

Copying Folders and Files

When you copy files or folders from one folder to another folder, or from one partition to another, permissions may change. The following lists the results you can expect from various copy operations:

◆ When you copy a folder or file within a single NTFS partition, the copy of the folder or file inherits the permissions of the destination folder.

◆ When you copy a folder or file between NTFS partitions, the copy of the folder or file inherits the permissions of the destination folder.

◆ When you copy a folder or file to a non-NTFS partition, all permissions are lost (this is because non-NTFS partitions do not support NTFS permissions).

Moving Folders and Files

When you move files or folders from one folder to another, or from one partition to another, permissions may change. The following lists the results you can expect from various move operations:

◆ When you move a folder or file within a single NTFS partition, the folder or file retains its original permissions.

◆ When you move a folder or file between NTFS partitions, the folder or file inherits the permissions of the destination folder. When you move a folder or file between partitions, you are creating a new version of the resource and therefore it inherits permissions.

◆ When you move a folder or file to a non-NTFS partition, all permissions are lost (this is because non-NTFS partitions do not support NTFS permissions).

NTFS Permissions and Shared Folders

Shares represent the primary tool available for providing access to file resources over the network. In previous sections, we looked at shared folder permissions. Shared folder permissions provide very limited security; they only protect resources if they are accessed over the network. Shared folder permissions are also limited as they provide access to the entire directory structure from the share point down into the subdirectories. For these reasons, you will find that it is rare for shared folder permissions to be used in isolation from NTFS permissions. By combining both shared folder permission

---

EXAM TIP

Remember the Default NTFS Assignments   Remember that when a new file is created, it inherits the permissions from its parent. A Copy operation creates a new version of the resource you are copying; therefore, the permissions of the parent are inherited.

EXAM TIP

Again! Remember the Default NTFS Assignments   Remember that when a new file is created it inherits the permissions from its parent.

A Move operation creates a new version of the resource you are moving if you are moving the resource to a different partition—for this reason, permissions of the parent are inherited.

A Move operation does not create a new version of the resource if you are moving the resource to a different location on the same partition—for this reason, existing permissions are moved along with the resource.

and NTFS permissions, you have the greatest level of control and security. To effectively use shared folder and NTFS permissions together, you must understand how they interact with one another.

Combining NTFS and Shared Folder Permissions

When users gain access to a shared folder on a NTFS partition they need shared folder permissions and also the appropriate NTFS permission for each file and folder they access. This will require you to manage two sets of permissions for your environment.

Generally, you will use NTFS permissions to secure the resources in your file system. NTFS offers the greatest level of control and can be assigned to resources on an individual basis. You will then pick share points and create shares so users can access file resources over the network.

Users' effective permissions will be a combination of both the shared folder permissions and NTFS permissions. Unlike individual shared folder and NTFS permissions, however, the effective permissions will be the most restrictive permission assigned to the user.

Developing an Efficient Directory Structure

Network users will need resources on which to store their work. Where these resources are located is an important aspect of the planning process. A number of decisions will need to be made before users actually start creating documents. The following sections detail user home directories, shared data folders, and application folders.

Shared Home Directories

One of the first things that must be completed is an assessment of the types of information that users will be storing. As an organization, you must also decide if users are to have a private home directory that only they should have access to or a shared storage location the groups of users have access to. In most organizations, you will be required to plan for both private user directories and shared storage locations.

EXAM TIP

Permissions Remember that shared folder permissions and NTFS permissions represent two different security systems within Windows 2000.

NTFS on its own calculates effective permissions by adding all your permissions together (thereby granting you the least restrictive permission). Shared folder permissions are calculated the same way. You have two sets of permissions.

When the two security systems are used in combination, the most restrictive of your effective permissions (from each system) is applied.

Home directories are generally considered a location where users can store their own documents. No one, including the administrator, should have access to these private directories. In contrast, shared directories are locations where groups of users can share information.

When planning the structure of users' home directories, you must decide whether those directories should be on the users' local machine or on the network. Both of these options can be good depending on your organization's needs.

Table 2.12 compares storing users' home directories on local machines versus network servers.

TABLE 2.12

SERVER-BASED HOME DIRECTORIES VERSUS LOCAL HOME DIRECTORIES

Server-Based Directories	Local Home Directories
Are centrally located so that a user can access them from any location on the network.	Available only on the local machine. Users cannot retrieve their data if they are away from their computers unless a share is set up.
Backups of user data are much easier and can be centrally managed.	Backups are much more difficult to manage. Generally, users are left to complete their own backups (something that cannot be counted on). This situation is dangerous; a crashed hard drive will cause all user data to be lost.
Computer policies can be set to limit the amount of space a user has occupied on a server.	If a user stores a lot of information on his local computer, the only person who will notice will be that user.
If the server is down, the users will not have access to their data.	The user has access to his file regardless of whether the network is up or down because his files are stored locally.
Some network bandwidth is consumed due to the over-the-network access of data or files.	No network traffic is generated by users accessing data as it is stored locally.

Generally, when you are creating home directories on the server, it is best to centralize the directories under one directory (typically called USERS). An example of such a structure is shown in Figure 2.8.

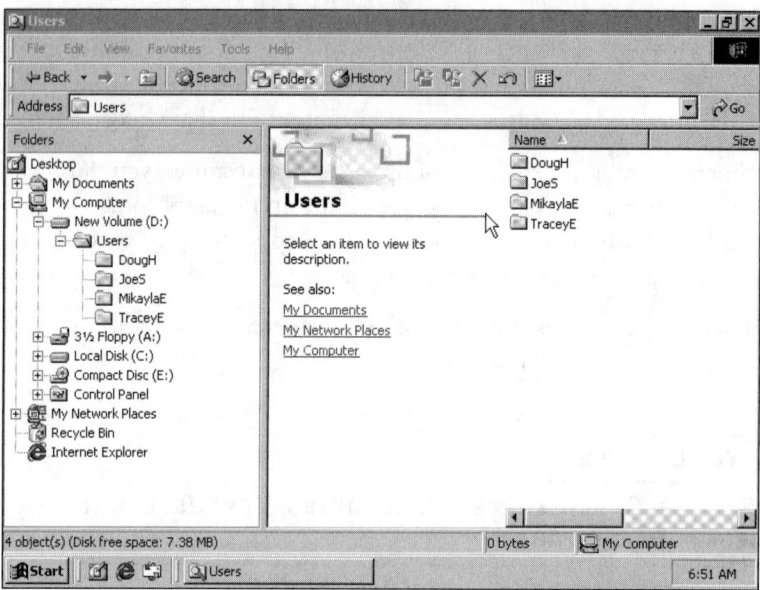

FIGURE 2.8
User home directory structure.

If your directory structure is on a non-NTFS formatted partition, you would have to share out each and every user directory separately. This is required because share level permissions are inherited to the lower-level directories. For example, if you shared at the USERS level and gave the Users group full control at the share, all users would be able to access anyone's user directories. For this reason, you would need to share each and every user directory separately.

If your directory structure is on a NTFS formatted partition, you would share out the structure at the USERS level and ensure that the NTFS permissions are set to allow users into their home directories but no one else's.

Sharing Common-Access Folders

Like users' home directories, which need to have very restricted access controls placed on them, common access or shared data folders will need to be planned carefully. Shared data folders are required on the network so that users or groups of users can exchange data. In many instances, this data also needs to be centrally managed. One of the biggest challenges in planning for shared data folders is to determine who needs to share what and the level of access everyone needs to the information.

Figure 2.9 represents a sample directory structure for a set of common access folders. Note that a top-level directory called DEPARTMENTS was created to act as a share point to the data. Each department (SALES, ACCOUNTING, HUMAN_RESOURCES, and FINANCE) has a subdirectory in which to store department-specific data.

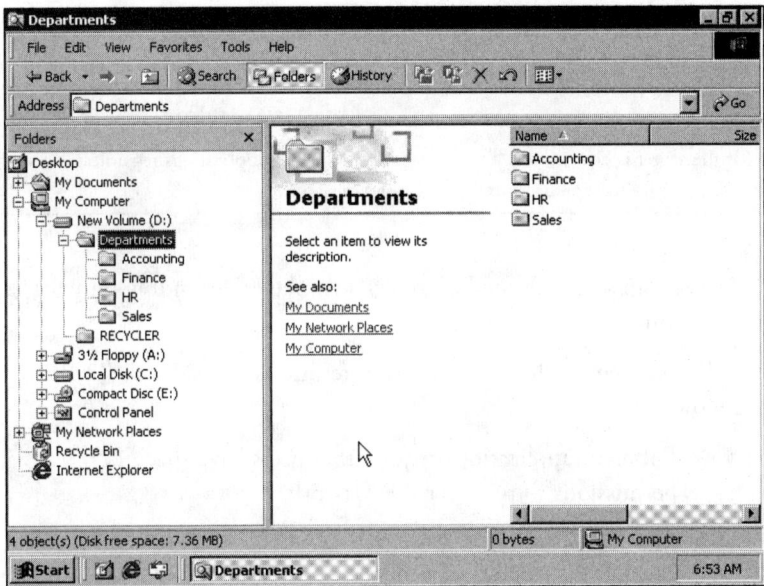

FIGURE 2.9
Shared departmental directory structure.

Sharing Application Folders

Another resource you will need to plan for is networked application folders. Shared application folders are typically used to give user access to applications that they will run from a network share point. Another option is to have users run applications locally from their own computer. Table 2.13 shows a comparison of these two options.

TABLE 2.13

NETWORKED APPLICATIONS VERSUS LOCALLY INSTALLED APPLICATIONS

Shared Network Applications	Locally Installed Applications
Takes up less disk space on the local workstation.	Uses more local disk space.
Easier to upgrade/control.	Upgrades require that staff visit each computer (although this is becoming less of an issue as Group Policy objects and products such as Microsoft System Management Server can assist in the delivery of applications to the desktop.
More bandwidth is used.	Little network bandwidth is used as applications are stored locally.
If the server is down, users cannot run their applications.	Users can run applications regardless of server status.

As you can see, each method offers advantages depending on your environment.

When setting up shared application resources, consider the following:

◆ Different applications require that users have specific permissions to run over the network.

◆ Many applications require that users have a location available to store their personal preferences or application settings.

◆ Staff will be required to upgrade and maintain application directories.

Based on the preceding considerations, a common approach to application directories is to create a structure similar to the one shown in Figure 2.10.

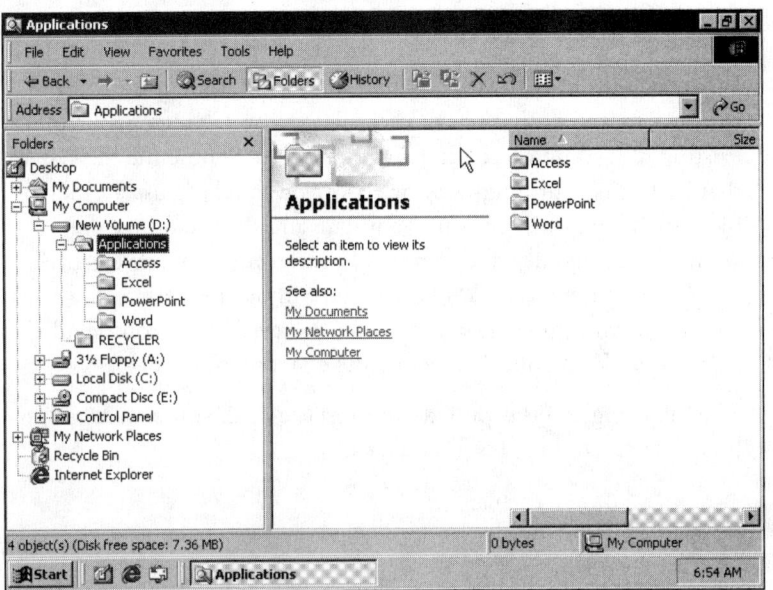

FIGURE 2.10
Shared application directory structure.

In this example you would share at the APPLICATIONS level and give users and administrators the appropriate NTFS permissions to the underlying applications. If you needed to restrict access to specific applications, you would share each application out separately, giving users share level permissions to only the applications they require access to.

MANAGING FILE RESOURCES

Configure and manage file systems.

As the administrator of a Windows 2000 system, you will need to understand how to manage file resources. The following section provides an overview of the NTFS, FAT, and FAT32 file systems and details common management tasks.

NTFS, FAT32, or FAT

Before you decide which file system to use, you should understand the benefits and limitations of each file system. Changing a volume's existing file system can be time consuming, so choose the file system that best suits your long-term needs. If you decide to use a different file system, you must back up your data and then reformat the volume using the new file system. However, you can convert a FAT or FAT32 volume to an NTFS volume without formatting the volume (as with most disk operations, however, it is recommended that you back up your data before the conversion).

The following sections provide an overview of the differences among FAT, FAT32, and NTFS file systems.

FAT

File Allocation Table (FAT) is a file system that has been around for a very long time and is currently supported by most operating systems.

The primary benefit of using FAT is that it is supported by Windows NT 3.5x/4.0, Windows 95/98, Windows 3.x, and DOS. For this reason, FAT is an exceptional choice for systems that are required to dual boot between Windows 2000 and one (or more) of the previously mentioned operating systems.

The version of FAT supported by Windows 2000 has a number of additional features that are not supported by systems running DOS. When used under Windows 2000, the FAT file system supports the following additional features:

◆ Long filenames up to 255 characters.

◆ Multiple spaces.

◆ Multiple periods.

◆ Filenames are not case sensitive but do preserve case.

The FAT file system is a logical choice for systems where dual-boot capabilities are required. FAT is also a logical choice for small partitions (less then 200MB) as it has very low system overhead.

For all of the benefits of FAT, it should be recognized that it has a number of major limitations that should make you stop and think before it becomes your file system of choice on your Windows 2000 system.

The primary limitations of FAT are as follows:

◆ FAT is inefficient for larger partitions. As files grow in size, they may become fragmented on the disk and cause slower access times. FAT also uses inefficient cluster sizes (a cluster is the smallest unit of storage on a partition). If the cluster size is too large, you can end up with lots of wasted space on the partition.

◆ The maximum size of a FAT partition is 2GB.

◆ No local security—the FAT file system does not support local security so there is no way to prevent a user from accessing a file if the user can log in to the local operating system.

◆ FAT does not support compression, encryption, or disk quotas under Windows 2000.

FAT32

The FAT32 file system is very similar to FAT. FAT32 was introduced in the Microsoft product line with Windows 95 OSR 2. The primary difference between FAT and FAT32 is that FAT32 supports a smaller cluster size so it does not have as much wasted space associated with larger partitions.

Like FAT, FAT32 supports long filenames, multiple spaces, multiple periods, and preserves case while not being case sensitive.

The primary limitations of FAT32 are as follows:

◆ No local security—FAT file system does not support local security so there is no way to prevent a user from accessing a file if the user can log in to the local operating system.

◆ The maximum size of a FAT32 partition is 2TB (a 32GB limit is imposed by the Windows 2000 format utility if you create the partition on a Windows 2000 system).

◆ Does not support compression, encryption, and disk quotas under Windows 2000.

◆ FAT32 is not support by all versions of Windows 95, and is not supported by DOS and Windows NT, so you need to be careful when deciding to use it. If you plan to dual-boot your system, ensure that all operating systems you are using support FAT32. If they do not, all FAT32 partitions will not be accessible.

NTFS

NTFS is the file system of choice on most systems running Windows 2000. NTFS offers the following benefits:

◆ **Support for long filenames.** NTFS supports long filenames up to 255 characters.

◆ **Preservation of case.** NTFS is not case sensitive, but it does have the capability to preserve case for POSIX compliance.

◆ **Recoverability.** NTFS is a recoverable file system. It uses transaction logging to automatically log all files and directory updates so that in the case of a system failure the operating system can redo failed operations.

◆ **Security.** NTFS provides folder- and file-level security for protecting files.

◆ **Compression.** NTFS supports compression of file and folders to help save disk space.

◆ **Encryption.** NTFS supports file-level encryption. This allows a user the ability to encrypt sensitive files so that no one else can read the files.

◆ **Disk quotas.** NTFS partitions support user-level disk quotas. This gives an administrator the ability to set an upper limit on the amount of space that a user can use on a partition. Once the user reaches her limit, she is not allowed to store any more information on the partition.

◆ **Size.** NTFS partitions can support much larger partition sizes than FAT. NTFS can support partitions up to 16 exabytes in size (this is equal to 16 billion gigabytes).

Using NTFS gives you enhanced functionality and scalability when compared to FAT and FAT32.

The main limitation of NTFS is that other operating systems do not support it and it has high system overhead. If you need to dual boot your system or have partitions less then 200 Meg in size it is recommended that you format your partitions with FAT or FAT32.

File Compression

NTFS compression is used to make more efficient use of the hard drive space available on your system. If you need more space on your system, you will most likely want to add an additional hard drive. In an emergency, however, you can always compress your existing drives to free up space.

Compression is implemented at the folder or file level on NTFS formatted partitions.

To compress a file or folder within Windows 2000 you can complete the following steps:

1. Right-click on the file or folder you want to compress.

2. Choose the Properties option for the secondary menu.

3. Click the Advanced button from the General tab.

4. Check the Compress Contents to Save Disk Space check box from the Compress or Encrypt Attributes section of the Advanced Attributes dialog box.

You can also manage the compression attributes associated with files and folders on your system from the command prompt. The Compact utility allows you to compress files and folders as well as check the compression statistics.

The syntax for the compact utility is as follows:

```
COMPACT [/C | /U] [/S[:dir]] [/A] [/I] [/F] [/Q]
➥[filename [...]]
```

/C compresses the specified files. Directories will be marked so that files added afterward will be compressed.

/U uncompresses the specified files. Directories will be marked so those files added afterward will not be compressed.

WARNING

NTFS 4.0 Versus NTFS 5.0 The version of NTFS used with Windows NT (NTFS 4.0) is different from the version used with Windows 2000 (NTFS 5.0). These two versions of NTFS are not compatible with one another so you cannot dual-boot a Windows NT 4.0 and Windows 2000 system unless your installation of Windows NT 4.0 is running SP 4 or higher. This is very important if installing Windows 2000 on a system with an existing installation of Windows NT 4.0 as the installation process will automatically upgrade NTFS 4.0 partitions to NTFS 5.0.

/S performs the specified operation on files in the given directory and all subdirectories. Default "dir" is the current directory.

/A displays files with the hidden or system attributes. These files are omitted by default.

/I continues performing the specified operation even after errors have occurred. By default, COMPACT stops when an error is encountered.

/F forces the compress operation on all specified files, even those which are already compressed. Already-compressed files are skipped by default.

/Q reports only the most essential information.

Filename specifies a pattern, file, or directory.

You may want to use the compact utility instead of the property tab of the files or folders as the compact command syntax can be included in batch files.

File Encryption

Encrypted File System (EFS) is a system service that allows the owner of a file system resource to encrypt it. The service is based on public/private key encryption technology and is managed by the Windows 2000 Public Key Infrastructure (PKI) services. Because EFS is an integrated service it is very easy to manage, difficult to break into, and transparent to the user.

A user who has ownership of a file system resource can either encrypt or decrypt the folder or file. If a user who does not own the resource attempts to access the resource he will receive an access denied message.

The technology is based on a public key-based structure. Each user has a public and private key. The keys were created in such a way that anything encrypted using the private key can only be decrypted using the public key, and anything encrypted using the public key can only by decrypted using the private key. As the names suggest, the public key is made available to any resource that requests it. The private key is kept secret and never exposed to non-authorized resources.

When the owner of a file encrypts a file system resource, a file encryption key is generated and used to encrypt the file. The file encryption keys are based on a fast symmetric key designed for bulk encryption. The file is encrypted in blocks with a different key for each block. All of the file encryption keys are then stored with the file (as part of the header of the file), in the Data Decryption Field (DDF) and the Data Recovery Field (DRF). Before the file encryption keys are stored, they are encrypted using the public key of the owner, in the case of the DDF keys, and a recovery agent, in the case of the DRF keys. Because the keys are stored with the file, the file can be moved or renamed and it will not impact on the recoverability of the file.

When a file is accessed, EFS detects the access attempt and locates the user's certificate, from the Windows 2000 PKI, and the user's associated private key. The private key is then used to decrypt the DDF to retrieve the file encryption keys used to encrypt each block of the file. The only key in existence with the ability to decrypt the information is that of the owner of the file. Access to the file is denied to anyone else, as they do not hold the private key required for decrypting the file encryption keys.

If the owner's private key is not available for some reason (for example, the user account was deleted), the recovery agent can open the file. The recovery agent decrypts the DRF to unlock the list of file encryption keys. The recovery agent must be configured as part of the security policies of the local computer.

To encrypt a file or folder within Windows 2000, you can complete the following steps:

STEP BY STEP

2.4 Encrypting a File or Folder

1. Right-click on the file or folder you want to compress.

2. Choose the Properties option from the secondary menu.

3. Click the Advanced button from the General tab.

4. Check the Encrypt Contents to Secure Data check box from the Compress or Encrypt Attributes section of the Advanced Attributes dialog box.

You can also manage the encryption attributes associated with files and folders on your system from the command prompt. The Cipher utility allows you to encrypt files and folders as well as check the encryption statistics.

The syntax for the encryption utility is as follows:

```
CIPHER [/e| /d] [/s:dir] [/i] [/f] [/q] [filename [...]]
```

/e encrypts the specified files or folders. Files added to the folder afterward will be encrypted.

/d decrypts the specified files or folders. Files added to the folder afterward will not be encrypted.

/s: *dir* performs the specified operation on files in the given directory and all subdirectories.

/i continues performing the specified operation even after errors have occurred. By default, Cipher stops when an error is encountered.

/f forces the encryption or decryption of all specified files. By default, files that have already been encrypted or decrypted are skipped.

/q reports only the most essential information.

filename specifies a pattern, file, or directory.

Converting File Systems

In many instances, you may find that you need to change the format of your partitions. Your options are to reformat the partition or convert it. If you chose to reformat your partition you will lose all data from the partition. Converting a partition allows you to change your file format without loosing your data. You can only convert from FAT to NTFS or from FAT32 to NTFS. You cannot convert from NTFS to FAT or from NTFS to FAT32.

If Convert cannot lock the drive, it will offer to convert it the next time the computer restarts. Locking the drive requires that the operating system gain exclusive access to all files and folders on the drive (data cannot be in use by other applications).

```
convert [drive:] /fs:ntfs [/v]
```

drive: specifies the drive to convert to NTFS.

> **WARNING**
>
> **Converting to NTFS Could Affect System Performance** Partitions and volumes that are converted from FAT/FAT32 to NTFS (rather than initially formatted with NTFS) may suffer from performance problems. There is a chance that the Master File Table (MFT) will be fragmented.

/fs:ntfs specifies that the volume be converted to NTFS.

/v specifies verbose mode. All messages will be displayed during conversion.

PRINT RESOURCES

Connect to local and network print devices.

Printers are a common resource shared by users on the network. As a network administrator you will need to be able manage the print environment. Management tasks include setting up printer resources, securing print resources, managing print jobs, and connecting to shared printers over the network. This section reviews each of these management tasks.

The Print Environment

Four primary components make up the Windows 2000 print environment. As a network administrator you should understand these components and how they interact with one another to create the print environment. The components are as follows:

◆ **Printer.** A printer is a software representation of a physical print device. You will find printers configured on computers so that print jobs can be sent to them. When a print job is sent to the printer, it is processed and forwarded to a physical print device (the process will vary depending on whether the physical print device is located on the network or attached directly to the computer generating the print job).

◆ **Print driver.** A print driver is used to convert print requests into a format understood by the physical print device being used in the environment.

◆ **Print server.** A printer server is a computer that receives and processes documents from client computers for processing.

◆ **Print device.** A print device is the physical device that produces the printed output.

The following represents how a print job is processed:

1. A user on a computer generates a print job by issuing a print command from a software application.

2. The print job is sent to a printer configured on the local machine (remember that the printer is a software representation of a physical print device).

3. The printer defines where the printer job will go to reach the physical print device and how the job should be managed during the printing process.

4. From the printer, the print job is sent to a print server for processing.

5. The print server then uses a printer driver to format the print job so that the physical print device can process it.

6. After the print driver has converted the print job into a specific printer language, it is forwarded to the physical print device.

7. When the physical print device receives the job it is printed.

Windows 2000 supports print devices that are either local or networked. As the name implies, local print devices are connected to a local computer (the same machine where the print job is generated). Network print devices are connected to a print server through the network.

Connecting to a Local Print Device

Installing printers in the Windows 2000 environment is accomplished with the aid of the Add Printer Wizard. The Add Printer Wizard is launched by double-clicking the Add Printer icon in the Printers folder of Control Panel. Step by Step 2.5 will walk you through the process of configuring a local printer.

STEP BY STEP

2.5 Installing a Local Printer

1. Double-click the Add Printer icon from the Printers folder of Control Panel.

---

2. At the Welcome to the Add Printer Wizard screen, click Next.

3. At the Local or Network Printer screen, click Local Printer. You may also want to check the Automatically Detect and Install My Plug and Play Printer box. (Most likely your Plug and Play-compatible printers would have been detected and installed at boot-up.)

4. You will then need to select the port where the printer is installed. Generally, you will select LPT1 or LPT2 for your printer. Some specialized print devices may require a COM port. You also have the option of creating your own port. This option is used for printer redirection and will be discussed later. For now, select LPT1.

5. Once you have indicated where the physical print device is located, you will need to indicate the print driver associated with your printer. You will find a large list of print drivers ship with Windows 2000. If your printer is not in the list, check with your printer's manufacturer, generally they have drivers available. If you do have drivers for your printer, you can select the Have Disk button to indicate a path where the drivers can be found. Select an appropriate driver for the printer you are installing (if you don't have a printer to install, pick any driver).

6. You will now name your printer. This is the software representation of your physical print device. The name you choose should be descriptive, but it can be no more then 32 characters in length. You will also need to indicate if the printer should be configured as the default Windows printer (if no other printers are currently installed on your computer this option will not be presented). Enter the name **Test Printer** for your printer's name.

7. One of the last steps in configuring a printer is deciding whether you want the printer shared. If you do not share the printer, it will not be available to users on the network. If you want to share the printer, you can select the Share As: option and provide the share name you want to use to represent the printer on the network. Enter **Test_Printer** as your share name. (Note: Because the

continues

continued

> share name is longer than 13 characters and has spaces in it, you will receive a warning that DOS-based workstations may not be able to access this resource. Keep the name short but descriptive and avoid spaces in the share name.)
>
> You will also be prompted to enter descriptive information describing the location and any other comments you add about the printer. Enter **Lab** as the location and **Test Printer** in the comment box.

8. You are then asked if you would like to print a test page. Indicating Yes will allow you to test your configuration. Select Yes to print a test page.

9. Once you have entered all of the required information, the Setup Wizard will provide a summary of the configuration you have requested. Click the Finish button to complete the installation.

You have now successfully installed a local printer.

Sharing a Local Printer

Sharing a local printer allows remote users to access it from across the network. This section describes how to share a local printer.

Creating a shared printer is very easy. It can be accomplished in one of two ways. The first method of creating a printer share was seen in Step by Step 2.4. During the installation of a local printer, the Printer Setup Wizard offers to automatically create a printer share for you. The other method involves viewing the properties of an existing printer object and selects the Sharing tab (you can access the property tab by right-clicking the printer object and selecting Properties from menu). Figure 2.11 shows the Sharing property tab from a local printer object.

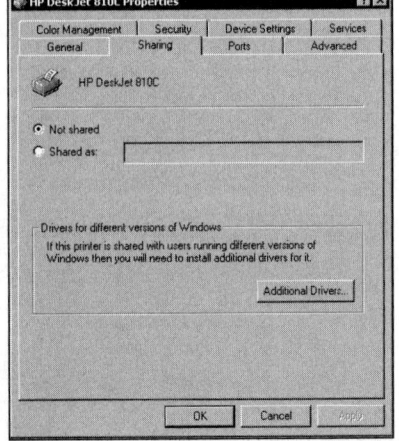

FIGURE 2.11
Sharing property tab for a local printer.

From this tab you can configure the share name you would like to use (or turn sharing off). You can also configure the print drivers associated with the printer. By clicking the Additional Drivers button, you can install additional print drivers. Figure 2.12 shows the Additional Drivers screen.

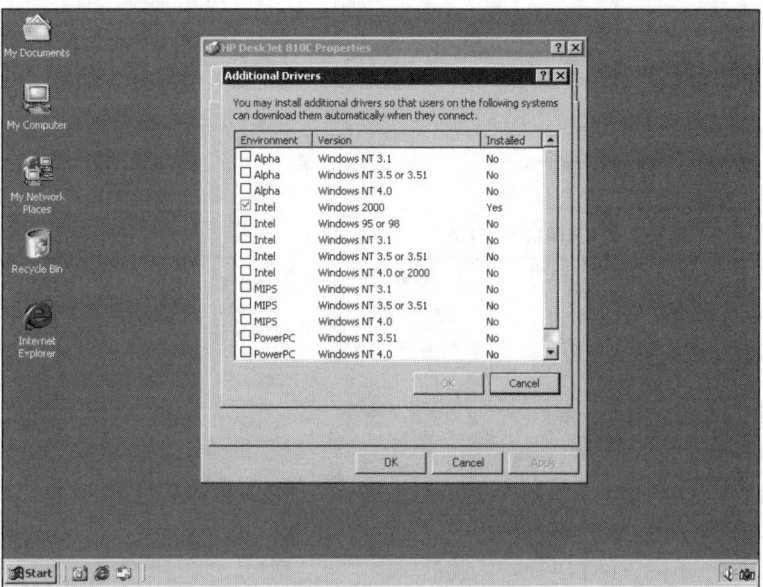

FIGURE 2.12
Additional Drivers screen of a shared printer.

If you select additional drivers to be installed, then Windows
will prompt you for the appropriate disk containing the drivers
requested. Once drivers are installed, additional types of workstation
clients will be able to connect to the share and have the drivers made
available to them without user intervention at the client side.

Printers Permissions

In many environments, printers are managed to ensure that only
certain users (or groups of users) can access specific print devices.
Access to the Windows 2000 print environment is managed through
printer permissions.

Like file system shares, printer shares allows users to access print
resources over the network. Printer shares have three different levels
of access that can be granted. Each printer permission allows users
to have a different level of access to the printer. For example, some
users may have print access, which allows them to submit print jobs
to the printer, whereas other users might have Manage Printers
permissions allowing them to manage the print device.

Table 2.14 presents a listing of common tasks associated with the print environment and the permissions required to perform each task.

TABLE 2.14

PRINTER PERMISSIONS

Capabilities	Print Permission	Manage Documents Permission	Manage Printer Permission
Print documents	Yes	Yes	Yes
Pause, resume, restart, and cancel the user's own print jobs	Yes	Yes	Yes
Connect to the shared printer	Yes	Yes	Yes
Control job settings for all print jobs	No	Yes	Yes
Pause, resume, restart, and cancel all users' print jobs	No	Yes	Yes
Cancel all print jobs	No	Yes	Yes
Pause and resume a printer, and take a printer offline	No	No	Yes
Share a printer	No	No	Yes
Change printer properties	No	No	Yes
Delete a printer	No	No	Yes
Change printer permissions	No	No	Yes

You can allow or deny printer permissions. Denying permissions always take precedence over all other permissions assigned to a user. Figure 2.13 shows the Printer Permission tab (Security tab) of printer properties. Right-clicking a printer object, selecting Properties from the secondary menu, and selecting the Security tab can access this screen.

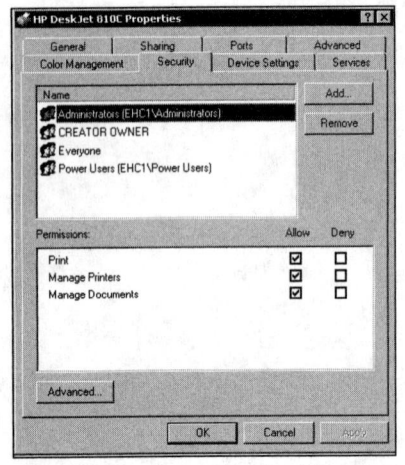

FIGURE 2.13
Printer permissions.

Connecting to a Shared Printer

Connecting to a shared printer (or a network print server) allows a user to print to a remote printer over the network. Connecting to a remote printer can be done in a number of different ways. The following section will explore each of these methods.

One of the easiest ways to connect to a remote printer is to run the Add Printer Wizard. This can be run by double-clicking the Add Printer icon in the Printers folder of Control Panel. After the initial welcome screen, you will be prompted to install a local or network printer; select network printer. You will then be asked to provide the UNC name for the printer you would like to attach to (for example, the printer installed in Step by Step 2.4 would be called \\WORKSTATION\Test_Printer).

You can also access the printer using an HTTP (hypertext transport protocol) request. In this case, the path to the printer would be HTTP://SERVER/printer_name.

You can also connect to a printer by dragging the printer from the Printers folder on the print server and dropping it into your Printers folder, or by simply right-clicking the icon and then clicking Connect from the secondary menu.

The last option you have for connecting to a printer involves the net use command. From the command prompt you can issue the following command to map a local LTP port to a network printer:

```
Net Use LPT1 \\servername\printer name
```

After you have connected to a shared printer over the network, you can use it as if it were attached to your computer.

Managing Printers

Once the print environment is set up, you will need to manage the printers. The Windows 2000 print environment is one of the easiest to use and manage. In the following sections you will explore many common printer management tasks.

Assigning Forms to Paper Trays

Many printers support multiple paper trays and paper sizes. You can assign various paper types and sizes to the specific trays installed on your printer. Once a form (or paper type/size) has been assigned to a specific tray, a user can select it from within her applications. When the user issues a print command, Windows 2000 automatically routes the print job to the paper tray with the correct form.

Figure 2.14 shows the device settings for an HP LaserJet printer. To assign forms to paper trays complete the following:

1. Open the Properties dialog box to the printer and click the Device Settings tab.

2. From the Form to Tray Assignment option, select a tray and assign a paper size to it (paper sizes are found in the drop-down lists).

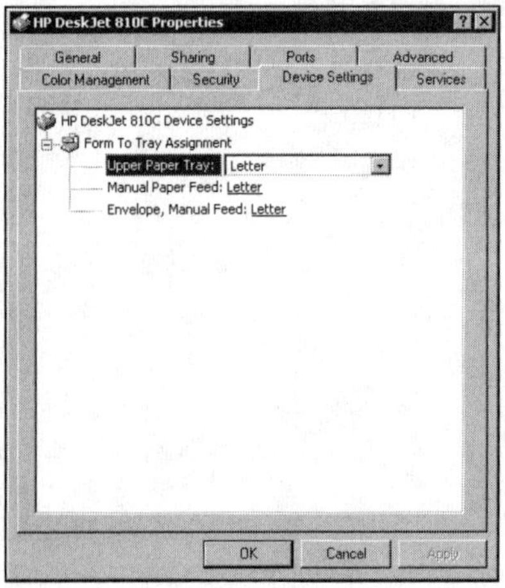

Setting Separator Pages

Most printers are able to operate in many different modes (for example PostScript or PCL [Printer Control Language]). Because different printers are configured to expect different print commands, you should be familiar with different types of separator pages and how they can be specified. A separator page is a file that contains the following commands:

◆ Identify each document that is being printed (also referred to as a banner page).

◆ Switch the print device between print modes (if supported by the physical printer). You could use a separator page to specify PostScript or PCL for a printer that is not able to automatically detect the type of print job it is processing.

Windows 2000 ships with four separator page files. They are located in the *systemroot\system32* directory. Table 2.15 presents the function of each file.

FIGURE 2.14
Device Settings tab of printer properties.

NOTE

The Printer Properties Tabs May Vary from Printer to Printer   Different printers offer many different features and options. For this reason, you may find that the Properties tab for your printer will not be the same as shown in this book.

TABLE 2.15

SEPARATOR PAGE FILES

Separator File	Function
Pcl.sep	Prints a page after switching the printer to PCL printing.
Sysprint.sep	Prints a page after switching the printer to PostScript printing.
Pscript.sep	Does not print a page after switching the printer to Postscript printing.
Sysprtj.sep	A Japanese version of the Sysprint.sep file.

The separator page can be changed from the Advanced tab of a printer property sheet. From the Advanced tab, you can click the Separator Page button and you will be presented with a dialog box prompting you to enter the name and path to a separator file. After the file is specified, click OK.

Pausing and Restarting Printers

As the administrator of a printer, you may find situations where the printer needs to be taken out of service for a period of time. Printers can be paused (or resumed if currently paused), or all print jobs can be cancelled. This can be accomplished by double-clicking a printer object from the Printers folder (found in the Control Panel). A window will open showing all pending print jobs for the printer. From the Printer menu you will find the Pause Printer and Cancel All Documents menu options.

Pausing a printer allows users to continue submitting print jobs to the printer even though the jobs will not print. This is useful in situations where you need to perform simple maintenance on the printer and do not want to disrupt the way users submit print jobs. Once the printer is fixed, unpause the printer and print jobs will begin to print.

Canceling all documents allows you to quickly clear a print queue that has a large number of documents waiting to print.

> **NOTE**
>
> **Restarting the Print Spooler Service**
> In some rare instances you may find that the Printer Spooler Service of your Windows 2000 system may need to be restarted to get printing to work properly. This service can be restarted from the Computer Management/ Service/Print Spooler of the MMC Computer Manager snap-in.

Setting Print Priority and Printer Availability

In many environments, management of printers involves being a traffic cop regarding whose print jobs get printed first. You may for example, want to ensure that print jobs submitted by the president and her assistant print before all other jobs. To this end, you can install two printers (the software representations of a printer) on a machine and point them to the same physical print device. You would then assign a higher priority to the printer used by the president and her staff.

Figure 2.15 shows the Advanced tab of the Printer Properties page. This is where printer priorities can be set.

Table 2.16 presents the configuration options available from this page.

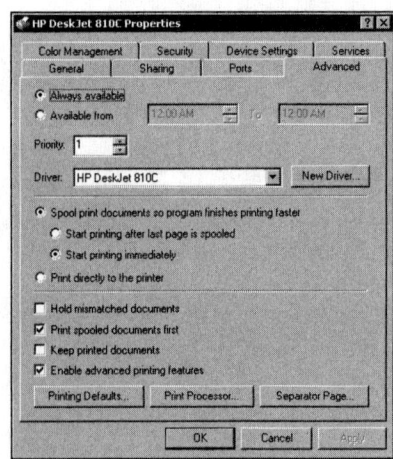

FIGURE 2.15
Printer Properties—Advanced tab.

TABLE 2.16

ADVANCED PRINTER SETTINGS

Option	Description
Availability	This option allows you to configure when this printer can be used.
Priority	Set this printer's priority relative to other printers configured to print to the same physical print device. The range is from 99 to 1 (99 being the highest priority).
Spool Print Documents so Programs Finish Printing Faster	Spooling is the process of writing the print job to the hard disk before it is sent to the physical print device. The theory is that writing to the hard disk is significantly faster than sending a job to the physical printer. Once the print job is written to disk, you can continue to work with the application and the spooler takes care of submitting the job to the physical printer in the background.
	Two options are associated with this configuration setting. The first, Start Printing After the Last Page Is Spooled, ensures that the entire print job has been completed before it is sent to the physical printer. This may require that the application participate in the print process longer because the entire job must be processed before it is printed.
	The second option, Start Printing Immediately, specifies that the print job be spooled and sent to the physical printer as soon as the spooler receives the job. This allows the print job to be processed faster.

Option	*Description*
Print Directly to the Printer	This option specifies that the print job should be sent directly to the printer and not spooled. This is a useful option if you are running low on disk space or if you have an application that requires a direct connection to the physical print device.
Hold Mismatched Documents	This option specifies that print jobs are checked to ensure the physical print device can print them (for example, the correct paper is loaded). Documents that cannot be printed are left in the spooler until the configuration of the printer is adjusted to accept the job. This setting allows mismatched jobs to sit in the spooler and still allow other (non-mismatched) jobs to print.
Print Spooled Documents First	When this option is enabled, the spooler chooses documents that have completed spooling to print first. This allows spooled documents to print first regardless of print priority.
Keep Printed Documents	This option instructs the print spooler not to delete jobs that have successfully printed. This allows jobs to be resubmitted if necessary.
Enable Advanced Printer Features	This option specifies whether the advanced printer features are enabled. When enabled, metafile spooling is turned on and options such as Page Order, Booklet Printing, and Pages Per Sheet are, as well.
Printing Defaults	Click this option to change the default document properties for all users of the selected printer. If you share your local printer, these settings will be the default document properties for each user.
Print Processing	Click this option to specify the data type used by this printer. In general, you should not need to change these settings. In some special instances, however, you may need to configure this setting for a few specialized programs.
Separator Page	As discussed previously, this option allows you to change the separator page used for this printer.

Printer Pooling

In very high-volume print environments, Windows 2000 offers a printer pooling option. Printer pooling allows a single printer to be directed to multiple physical printers.

Figure 2.16 shows the Ports tab of a Printer Property page.

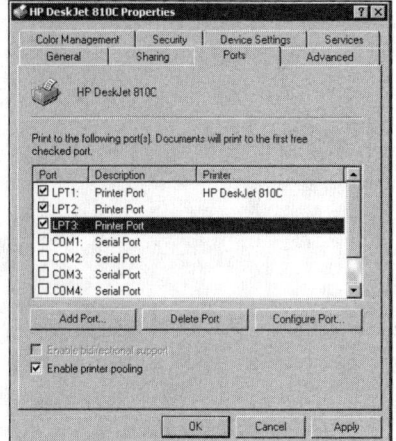

FIGURE 2.16
Printer Properties—Ports tab.

By checking the Enable Printer Pooling box on the bottom of the page, you are able to select multiple ports from the ports list shown in the figure. As shown in Figure 2.16, this printer will print to LPT1, LPT2, and LPT3, depending on which printer is ready to accept a job when the spooler receives this job.

You will need to ensure that all physical print devices use the same printer driver (are of the same type). It is also recommended that all of the printers are located in the same physical area (as users will not know which physical printer will be used to print their job).

Redirecting Printers

As the printer administrator in your environment, you may find it useful to redirect a printer. For example, if a printer fails and a large number of print jobs are currently spooled (and waiting to print), you can redirect the printer to another physical device so the jobs can print without needing to be resubmitted by the users who created them.

Step by Step 2.6 demonstrates the process of redirecting a printer. In this example, you will configure two local printers, pause the first printer (to simulate a printer failure), and submit a few print jobs to the printer. You will then redirect printer 1 to printer 2 and resume printing on printer 1. Through redirection, you will see the print jobs transfer from printer 1 to printer 2. In the real world, the printers would not be on the same machine, but for demonstration purposes this works well.

STEP BY STEP

2.6 Configuring Printer Redirection

1. Create two local printers based on the information in Table 2.17 (if you need assistance, refer to Step by Step 2.4).

2. You should now have two printers configured on your local system. Pause Printer1 (right-click Printer1 and select Pause Printer from the secondary menu).

TABLE 2.17

PRINTER CONFIGURATION FOR STEP BY STEP 2.6

Configuration	Printer 1	Printer 2
Location	Local	Local
Port	LPT1	LPT2
Driver	HP LaserJet 5Si	HP LaserJet 5Si
Name	Printer1	Printer2
Share	HP1	HP2
Local/Comment	N/A	N/A

3. Set Printer1 as the Default Windows printer (right-click Printer1 and select Set as Default Printer). This step ensures that print jobs submitted are sent to printer1.

4. Launch Notepad and submit a number of printer jobs. Double-click Printer1; you should see the print jobs sitting in the printer queue.

5. Now configure Printer1 so that it redirects its print jobs to Printer2. From the Printer menu of Printer1's print queue display, select Properties. Select the Ports tab. Note that LPT1 is the current port for Printer1. Click the Add Port button. In the Printer Ports dialog box, click New Port. In the Port Name dialog box enter \\`computer`\\`HP2` (where *computer* equals the name of your computer). Click OK. Click Close.

6. Notice that the new port you just created is now the port Printer1 will print to.

7. Double-click Printer2 to display the print jobs in the print queue (it should be empty). Position the print queue windows for Printer1 and Printer2 so you can view them both onscreen.

8. Resume printing for Printer1. The jobs from Printer1 should start showing up in Printer2's print queue.

Managing Print Jobs

In addition to managing the physical printers in your environment, you will need to become proficient at the management of print jobs. By default, users have the ability to manage their own print jobs. Users with Manage Printers or Manage Documents permissions have the ability to manage all print jobs received at the printer. It is important that you plan for print job management in your environment; jobs will sometimes get stuck in a print queue and hold up printing for everyone.

The next section provides an overview of document management activities.

Pausing, Restarting, and Canceling Print Jobs

By double-clicking on a printer icon, you can view the print jobs currently sitting in the print queue. If you have the appropriate permissions you can also manage print jobs.

You have the ability to pause, restart, or cancel jobs. Right-clicking on the job you would like to manage presents these options to you (as shown in Figure 2.17).

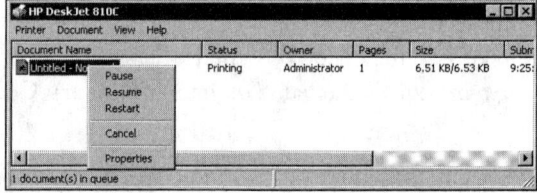

FIGURE 2.17
Print job management options.

By pausing a print job, you stop its printing. This will give you the opportunity to correct a problem with the job or allow other print jobs to print first. To resume the job, right-click the paused job and select Resume from the secondary menu.

Restarting a job allows you to restart a print job from the beginning. This is a useful option if a large job starts to print but is disrupted. It allows you to reprint the job without having to regenerate the job.

Canceling a print job causes the job to be removed from the print queue.

Setting Notifications and Priority Print Times

As a user with Manage Printer or Manage Documents permissions, you have the ability to set notification, priority, and printing time for individual print jobs (as the owner of a print job you can also modify these settings, but only for the print jobs you own).

Figure 2.18 shows the General tab of a print job (Double-click a job to access this tab).

The Notify option allows you to specify a user who should receive a notification when the print job completes. This is a useful option for users who submit jobs but want their assistants to pick them up from the printer.

The Priority option allows a job to be given priority relative to other jobs currently in the print queue. The value can range from 99 to 1 (with 99 being the highest priority).

The Schedule option allows you to specify when a specific job will be printed.

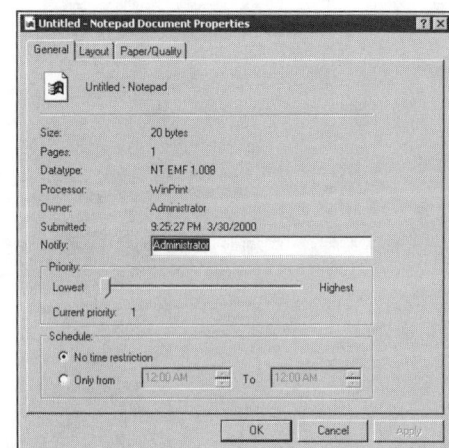

FIGURE 2.18
General tab of a print job.

Managing Printers Using a Web Browser

Windows 2000 enables you to manage printers from any computer running a Web browser. The computer acting as your print server must have Microsoft's Internet Information Server (IIS) installed on it (or Peer Web Services [PWS] on Windows 2000 Professional).

You can use your browser (you must be using Internet Explorer 4.0 or higher) to manage the printers installed on a remote machine by typing the following URL in the location box of your browser: `HTTP://printer_server_name/printers`. Figure 2.19 shows the resulting Web page that will be loaded.

FIGURE 2.19
Web-Based Printer Management screen.

By clicking on the name of a printer, you can view the details of the print jobs in the queue for that printer. Figure 2.20 shows the details of a specific printer. Note that on the left side of the Web page you have options that allow you to manage the printer and individual print jobs.

To manage a specific job, click the button beside the job you want to manage. You will find that the only limitation of this interface is that it does not allow you to manage advanced settings (such as notification, print time, or priority).

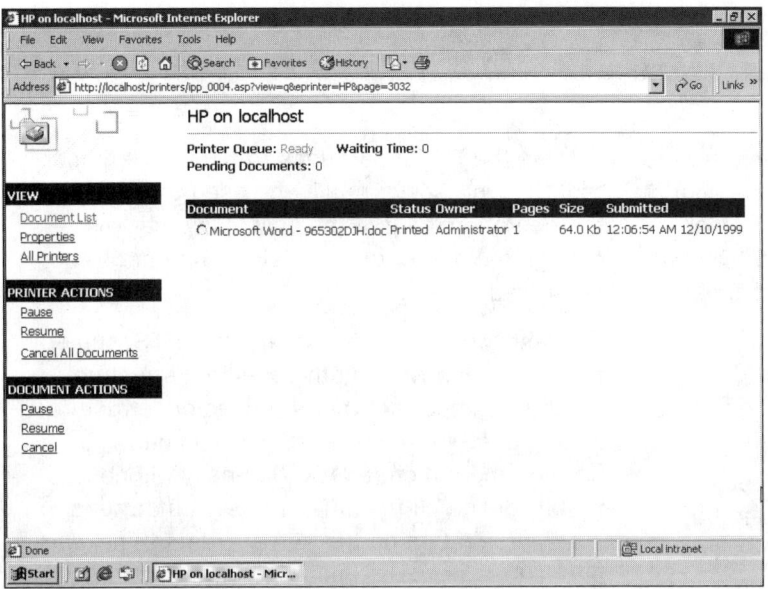

FIGURE 2.20
Web-Based Printer Details screen.

CASE STUDY: ABC COMPANY

ESSENCE OF THE CASE

Here are the essential elements in this case:

▶ File system security

▶ File system conversion

▶ Efficient directory structures

▶ Shared folder permissions

ABC Company is in the process of installing Windows 2000 Professional on all desktop computers in its organization. You want to ensure that you meet the following criteria with regard to the development of your file system and shared folder access plan.

· All resources must be secured.

· Only members of certain departments can gain access to department confidential data.

continues

CASE STUDY: ABC COMPANY

continued

A large number of workstations and servers were installed six months earlier as part of the pilot rollout, and have been in operation since then. These workstations and servers were configured with FAT32 partitions when they were installed. You need to make sure that data from these machines is not lost.

ANALYSIS

This case revolves around four main issues. The first is that all computers will need to be configured with NTFS. This is the case because NTFS is the only file system supported by Windows 2000 with folder and file level security. If security is a prime concern, NTFS is the only file system you can use to protect your equipment.

Second, for the workstations used during the pilot rollout of Windows 2000, you will need to convert the FAT32 partitions to NTFS. It is important that the Convert utility be used to perform the operation, as it is the only utility that will change the file system and allow the data to be preserved.

The last two issues revolve around NTFS/shared folder permissions and the directory structure used. It is important that the directory structure make sense for the users of the company. To develop the structure, ABC Company will need to fully define all the different users that need to store information on the servers, determine who needs to access the data, and determine what level of access each user needs. The directory structure created should optimize the assignment of permissions so that permissions assigned high in the directory structure do not give too many permissions to users who do not require them.

CHAPTER SUMMARY

Companies install networks so that resources can be shared between users. The challenge facing a network administrator is to ensure that users are given access to the resources they need and nothing more. This chapter presented how to manage, configure, and troubleshoot two of the most heavily used network services (file and print).

In the discussions relating to NTFS permissions, you also looked at the basic skills required to manage an NTFS file system. Specifically, the chapter covered NTFS permissions, compression, encryption, Web folders, and conversion.

The print environment was also covered. In these sections, printer permissions, printer configuration, and print job management were covered.

KEY TERMS

- Folder share
- Printer share
- NTFS permissions
- Printer permissions
- NTFS
- FAT
- FAT32
- Printer
- Print server
- Print driver
- Print device
- HyperText Transport Protocol (HTTP)

APPLY YOUR KNOWLEDGE

Exercises

2.1 Applying NTFS Permissions

In this exercise, you will assign permissions to a folder to test NTFS permissions. To test permissions, you will create a new folder on an NTFS partition and create a file in the folder. You will then create a new user account and assign the user account permission to the folder. You will then log on as the newly created user to test NTFS permissions.

Estimated Time: 10 Minutes

1. Log on to your system as Administrator.

2. From the Users and Password icon of Control Panel, create a new user called NTFSTest (create this user as a Standard User). Remember the password you assign to the user. (Note: These instructions assume that you are working on a Windows 2000 Professional computer that is part of a Workgroup. If your system is configured to be part of a Domain environment, you will need to use the Computer Manager snap-in to create and manage user accounts.)

3. Right-click on the Start button (start Explorer).

4. Scroll to an NTFS partition on your system.

5. Create a new Folder called NTFSData on the partition.

6. Right-click the new folder and select Properties from the secondary menu.

7. Click the Security tab. Uncheck the option Allow Inheritable Permission from Parent to Propagate to This Object and click the Remove button when prompted.

8. Click the Add button and select the NTFSTest user from the Select User, Groups, Computer dialog box. Click OK.

9. Verify the default permissions of Read & Execute, List Folder Contents, and Read.

10. Click the Add button and select the Users group from the Select User, Groups, Computer dialog box.

11. Verify that the Authenticated Users group has Read permissions.

12. Create a new folder under the NTFSData folder called Sub1.

13. Verify the default permissions inherited by the Sub1 folder when it was created. You should see the same permissions as assigned to NTFSData. The assignments will be grayed out to indicate that they are being inherited from the parent folders.

14. From the Security tab of the Sub1 folder, assign the NTFSTest user Full Control permissions.

15. Return to the partition you created NTFSData in, right-click the NTFSData Folder, and select Properties.

16. Uncheck the Allow Inheritable Permissions from Parent to Propagate to This Object option.

17. Click Copy when the Security screen pops up. (Either Copy or Remove will work for this example).

18. Highlight the Everyone group in the Name windows, click Remove, and then click OK.

19. Log on as the NTFSTest User.

APPLY YOUR KNOWLEDGE

20. Use Explorer to scroll to the NTFSData folder. Try to create a new text file in the folder. You should not be able to complete the operation, as you do not have the Write permission.

21. Try to create a new text file called TESTDATA.TXT in the Sub1 folder. You should be able to create new files at this location.

2.2   Applying the Deny NTFS Permission

In this exercise, you will use the Deny permission to limit the ability of a user from accessing a resource. In Exercise 2.1, you gave a user named NTFSTest the ability to write to a folder named x:\NTFSData\Sub1. To demonstrate the Deny permission, you will be assigning the Users group Deny Write permission Sub1. This will block the NTFSTest user's ability to write to the Sub1 folder.

Estimated Time: 5 Minutes.

1. Log on as Administrator.

2. From the Security tab of the Sub1 folder, assign the Users group the Deny Write permission.

3. Log on as NTFSUser.

4. Attempt to create a new file in the Sub1 folder. You are not able to, as you no longer have the Write permission. The Write permission is being denied due to your membership in the User group.

2.3   Taking Ownership of a File

In this exercise, you will delete the NTFSUser user account (this exercise assumes that you completed Exercise 2.1). Because the NTFSUser created a file called TESTDATA.TXT in the Sub1 folder, you will

need to manage the file. To do this, you must take ownership of the file and assign yourself permission to access it.

Estimated Time: 10 Minutes.

1. Log on to your system as Administrator.

2. From the Users and Password icon of Control Panel, delete the user called NTFSTest.

3. Using Windows Explorer, try to access the TESTDATA.TXT file in the Sub1 folder. You should be denied access.

4. Right-click the file and click the Security tab. Click the Advanced button, then click the Ownership tab.

5. In the Change Owner To dialog box, select Administrator from the list and click OK. The administrator is now the owner of the file.

6. Click OK to close the Property box for the file.

7. Right-click the file and click the Security tab. Notice that the Add button is now available. Assign the Full Control permissions to the Administrator.

8. You can now manage the file.

2.4   Applying Shared Folder Permissions

In this exercise, you will assign permissions to a folder to test NTFS permissions. To test permissions, you will create a new folder on an NTFS partition and create a file in the folder. You will then create a new user account and assign the user account permission to the folder. You will then log on as the newly created user to test NTFS permissions.

Estimated Time: 10 Minutes.

APPLY YOUR KNOWLEDGE

1. Log on to your system as Administrator.

2. From the Users and Password icon of Control Panel, create a new user called ShareTest (create this user as a Standard User). Remember the password you assign to the user. (Note: These instructions assume that you are working on a Windows 2000 Professional computer that is part of a workgroup. If your system is configured to be part of a Domain environment, you will need to use the Computer Manager snap-in to create and manage user accounts.)

3. Right-click on the Start button (start Explorer).

4. Scroll to an NTFS partition on your system.

5. Create a new Folder called SharedData on the partition.

6. Right-click the new folder and select Properties from the secondary menu.

7. Click the Sharing tab. Select Share This Folder. Enter SharedData as the share name.

8. Verify the default permissions of Name as Everyone and Permissions as Full Control, Change, and Read (you can view the permissions by clicking the Permissions button). Highlight the Everyone group and click Remove. Click Add and select the ShareTest user with Read permissions.

9. Log on as the ShareTest User.

10. Click Start, Run. In the Open dialog box, type *computername*\SHAREDATA (where *computername* is the name of your system). You should be attached to the shared directory.

11. Try to create a new text file called TESTDATA.TXT in the shared folder. You should not be able to create new files at this location because you have only Read access to the share.

2.5 Applying the Deny Shared Folder Permission

In this exercise, you will modify the Shared Folder permissions assigned in Exercise 2.4 so that the Users group will be denied access to the SharedData share. Because the ShareTest user is a member of this group, you will not be able to access the share.

Estimated Time: 10 Minutes

1. Log on to your system as Administrator.

2. View the permissions on the SharedData share (right-click the SharedData folder, click the Sharing tab, and click the Permissions button). Click Add and add the Users group to the permission list with Deny Full Control.

3. Logon as the ShareTest user account.

4. Click Start, Run. In the Open dialog box, type *computername*\SHARETEST (where *computername* is the name of your system). You should not be able to attach to the shared directory.

2.6 Applying Shared Folder and NTFS Permissions

In this exercise, you will combine NTFS and share-level permissions to secure a directory structure. In this exercise, you will give the user ShareTest full control permissions to a share and use NTFS permissions to limit the user's ability to write to the file system.

APPLY YOUR KNOWLEDGE

Estimated Time: 10 Minutes.

1. Log on to your system as Administrator.

2. View the permissions on the SharedData share (right-click the SharedData folder, click the Sharing tab, and click the Permissions button). Remove the Users group from the list of users with permissions to the resource. Verify that the ShareTest user has full control permissions to the folder.

3. Log on as the ShareTest user account.

4. Click Start, Run. In the Open dialog box. type `\\computername\SHARETEST` (where *computername* is the name of your system). You should be able to attach to the shared directory.

5. Create a new file in the directory. You should be able to create and access the file.

6. Log on as the Administrator.

7. Right-click the ShareData folder and click the Security tab. In the list of users with permissions, add the ShareTest user account with Deny Write permissions.

8. Log on as the ShareTest user account.

9. Click Start, Run. In the Open dialog box, type `\\computername\SHARETEST` (where *computername* is the name of your system). You should be able to attach to the shared directory.

10. Create a new file in the directory. You should not be able to create the file.

11. Try to edit the file you created in step 5. You should not be able to modify the file as you can no longer write to the directory.

Review Questions

1. How are effective NTFS permissions calculated for a user when he received rights from a number of groups?

2. A user leaves your company and her user account is deleted. You realize that company confidential data is still stored in that user's home directory. When you try to access the folder to retrieve the data (logged in as Administrator), you receive the message "`Access Denied.`" How can you fix this problem?

3. What are the default permissions used in the Windows 2000 environment?

4. You move a file from a folder on one partition to a folder on another partition. What permissions will the file have after the move?

5. You move a file from one folder to another folder (on the same partition). What permissions will the file have after the move?

6. You are in a high-volume print environment. What feature of Windows 2000 will you use to help support the large number of print jobs submitted in your environment?

7. What feature of the Windows 2000 environment allows you to remotely manage shared folders?

8. Your printer supports multiple paper trays. When you print, your jobs are put on the incorrect paper. How can you fix this problem?

9. What is the significance of the Deny permission?

10. In NTFS permissions, which permissions take precedence: folder or file level?

APPLY YOUR KNOWLEDGE

Exam Questions

1. You are working as a help desk operator in a large corporate environment. Sally calls to complain that she is not able to access all of the data on the \\NT4_CORP\SALES share. You check the share permissions on the share and determine that Sally has Full Control shared folder permissions assigned to her user account. Sally is also able to ping the \\NT4_CORP server. What is your next course of action to help Sally?

   A. Verify Sally's membership in other groups to determine whether she is denied access to the share.

   B. Verify Sally's NTFS permissions to the file system.

   C. Verify that Sally can connect to the \\NT4_CORP server over the network.

   D. Verify Sally's shared folder permissions and NTFS permissions.

2. You are conducting a security audit on your company's servers to ensure that all confidential data is secure. A consultant has conducted a preliminary review and determined that many of your critical data partitions are unsecured and at risk of being accessed by unauthorized personnel. The consultant has based this conclusion on your shared folder strategy. Your servers are all configured with NTFS, and NTFS permissions have been assigned to groups to control access to the data. Shared folders have been created at the root of each partition and the Domain Users group has been assigned Full Control. Is the poor review from your consultant cause for concern? (Choose the two best answers.)

   A. No; NTFS permissions are being used to control access to data.

   B. Yes; where NTFS and share permissions combine, the least restrictive permission is granted and therefore security will be breached.

   C. Yes; assigning the Domain Users group Full Control to the share is a security breach.

   D. No; the consultant you hired is incompetent and should be fired, as he does not understand Windows 2000 share security.

3. As the manager of a high-volume order-processing center, you need to optimize the print environment for your users. A large number of order-entry staff are inputting a high volume of orders. A copy of each order must be printed when the order is entered. All orders are collected in a central location to be filled. Problems arise when printers go off-line, as the entire staff cannot print. You need a solution that can handle the high volume of print jobs and will allow users to continue printing even if a printer is off-line. What should you suggest?

   A. Configure a number of printers to use printer redirection to print to a very fast and reliable printer.

   B. Buy a faster and more reliable printer.

   C. Set up a large number of network printers and configure the users' workstations to point to a number of the printers.

   D. Use printer pooling to create one printer with multiple physical devices.

4. You have configured your server with FAT partitions (the D: drive) and want to convert them to FAT32. You issue the following command, but find the system will not convert the drive.

   ```
   Convert d: /fs:fat32
   ```

   What is the cause of the problem? (Choose the two best answers.)

   A. The syntax for the command is Convert d: /fs:ntfs.

   B. You need to back up the FAT file system and reformat the drive as FAT32 and then restore from backup.

   C. You should use the Format command to convert the drive.

   D. You cannot convert from FAT to FAT32 in Windows 2000.

5. As the support technician for a large company, you are called in to fix the president's PC. The president read in a magazine that Windows 2000 computers are secure only if they are configured with NTFS-formatted partitions. He then proceeded to convert his hard drive from FAT to NTFS using the format utility. He is now very concerned that his PC will not boot. What should you tell him?

   A. The president should stop reading computer magazines.

   B. You will have to reinstall Windows to access the newly formatted drive to recover the data.

   C. The data is lost as the drive was formatted rather than converted.

   D. The president should have used the correct command switches with the format utility.

6. You are the network administrator for a large training company in Toronto, Canada. Your organization has a large number of administrative, sales, and order-processing personnel. You also have a large number of instructors.

   Your challenge is to secure data and applications so that only the people who require access to information are granted it. The following is a listing of the applications, secure data, and shared data requirements for your environments:

   • Sales and Administration need access to the Microsoft Office 2000 and the corporate administration system.

   • Order-processing staff need to access the corporate administration system.

   • Instructors need to access Microsoft Office 2000.

   • A common shared data folder is accessible to all users.

   • Sales, Administration, and Clerical all have separate areas to share data.

   • All data is stored on a single server with 32GB of drive space on a single NTFS-formatted partition.

   Required Result:

   All areas must be secured so only appropriate users can access designated data and applications.

   Optional Desired Results:

   Applications should be managed by a central team of network administrators.

APPLY YOUR KNOWLEDGE

The blocking of NTFS permissions inheritance should be minimized to simplify troubleshooting.

The total number of shares should be minimized.

Proposed Solution:

You create the directory structure presented in Figure 2.21. You then share out the Apps and Data folders and grant Domain Users Full Control permissions.

Next you make the NTFS permission assignments listed in Table 2.18.

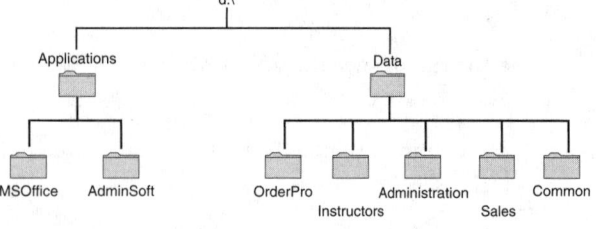

FIGURE 2.21
Figure for Exam Question 6.

TABLE 2.18

NTFS PERMISSIONS

Folder	NTFS Permission
Applications	Domain Administrator = Full Control
	Sales = Read
	Office Administration = Read
	Instructors = Read
Data	Sales = Full Control
	Office Administration = Full Conrol
	Instructors = Full Control

Which result(s) does the proposed solution produce?

A. The proposed solution produces the required result and produces all of the optional desired results.

B. The proposed solution produces the required result and produces only one of the optional desired results.

C. The proposed solution produces the required result but does not produce any of the optional desired results.

D. The proposed solution does not produce the required result.

APPLY YOUR KNOWLEDGE

7. You are the network administrator for a large training company in Toronto, Canada. Your organization has a large number of administrative, sales, and order-processing personnel. You also have a large number of instructors.

   Your challenge is to secure data and applications so that only the people who require access to information are granted it. The following is a listing of the applications, secure data, and shared data requirements for your environments:

   - Sales and Administration need access to the Microsoft Office 2000 and the corporate administration system.

   - Order-processing staff need to access the corporate administration system.

   - Instructors need to access Microsoft Office 2000.

   - A common shared data folder is accessible to all users.

   - Sales, Administration, and Clerical all have separate areas to share data.

   - All data is stored on a single server with 32 GB of drive space on a single NTFS-formatted partition.

   Required Result:

   All areas must be secured so only appropriate users can access designated data and applications.

   Optional Desired Results:

   Applications should be managed by a central team of network administrators.

   The blocking of NTFS permissions inheritance should be minimized to simplify troubleshooting.

   The total number of shares should be minimized.

   Proposed Solution:

   You create the directory structure presented in Figure 2.21. You then share out the Applications and Data folders and grant Domain Users Full Control permissions.

   Next you make the NTFS permission assignments listed in Table 2.19.

   TABLE 2.19

   NTFS PERMISSIONS

Folder	NTFS Permission
Applications	Domain Administrators = Full Control
	Authenticated Users = Read
Data	Domain Administrators = Full Control
Data\Data_pro	Data Processing = Full Control
Data\Instructors	Instructors = Full Control
Data\Sales	Sales = Full Control
Data\Office_Admin	Office Admin = Full Control
Data\Common	Domain Users = Full Control

   Which result(s) does the proposed solution produce?

   A. The proposed solution produces the required result and produces all of the optional desired results.

   B. The proposed solution produces the required result and produces only one of the optional desired results.

APPLY YOUR KNOWLEDGE

C. The proposed solution produces the required result but does not produce any of the optional desired results.

D. The proposed solution does not produce the required result.

8. As the network administrator of your company, you want to create a large number of user accounts with secure home directories. What is the most efficient way to secure these directories?

   A. Create a shared folder named Users on a FAT or FAT32 partition and create sub-folders for each user. You then share out the Users folders so all users can access it.

   B. Create a shared folder named Users on a NTFS partition and create sub-folders for each user (each user directory is secured so only one user can access it).

   C. Create a folder named Users on a NTFS partition and create sub-folders for each user. You then share each sub-folder so only one user can access it.

   D. Create a shared folder named Users on a FAT or FAT32 partition and create sub-folders for each user. You then share out each sub-folder so only one user can access it.

9. You are troubleshooting a resource access issue for a user on your network. Mikayla is not able to access data when accessing the shared data folder over the network. If Mikayla logs on locally at the computer where the shared data is stored, she can access the data directly from the file system. Where should you start troubleshooting her access problems?

A. Check the NTFS permissions assigned to Mikayla. She has been assigned No Access.

B. Check the NTFS permissions assigned to Mikayla. They are blocking her from accessing the resource when she attaches from the network.

C. Check the shared folder permissions assigned to Mikayla. She has been assigned No Access.

D. Mikayla needs to be a member of the Authenticated User group to access resources from over the network.

10. As the network administrator for a large accounting firm, you are developing a strategy to secure a shared data folder for the executives in your company. You created a folder called EXECDATA on a partition formatted with NTFS. Security is of prime concern, so you deny the Everyone group Full Control permissions to the folder. You then grant the Executives group Full Control permissions to the folder. To allow access to the resource over the network, you share the folder and grant Full Control access to the Executives group. Executives are not able to access the resource. What is the problem with your strategy?

   A. The Administrators group must be granted Full Control so that the resource can be managed properly.

   B. By denying full control to the Everyone group, all users are blocked from the resource regardless of group membership.

   C. The executives should be accessing all resources locally so shared permissions should not be assigned.

D. Future investigation is required to determine whether this is an NTFS or a shared folder issue.

11. As the network administrator of a large company, you create a shared folder with the permissions presented in Table 2.20.

TABLE 2.20

SHARED FOLDER PERMISSIONS

User/Group	Shared Folder Permission
Mikayla	Allow Change
Sales	Deny Full Control
Executives	Allow Full Control

Mikalya is a member of the Sales group and the Executives Group. What are Mikayla's effective permissions on the shared folder?

A. Full Control.

B. Change.

C. Read.

D. No Access will be allowed.

E. Not enough information is presented to calculate permissions.

12. As the network administrator of a large company, you create a shared folder with the permissions presented in Table 2.21. The shared resource is located on a partition formatted as NTFS.

TABLE 2.21

SHARED FOLDER PERMISSIONS

User/Group	Shared Folder Permission	NTFS Permissions
Mikayla	Allow Read	Allow Read
Sales	Allow Read	
Executives	Allow Full Control	

Mikalya and John are members of the Sales group and the Executives group. What are Mikayla's and John's effective permissions on the resource?

A. Mikayla has Read; John has Read.

B. Mikayla has Read; John has no access.

C. Mikayla has no access; John has Read.

D. Mikayla has Full Control; John has Full Control.

E. Mikayla has Full Control; John has no access.

F. Mikayla has no access; John has Full Control.

G. Not enough information is presented to calculate permissions.

13. You are working the help desk late one night when a user calls to complain that when she copies a file from one network share to another, the permissions are getting messed up. Table 2.22 presents the existing NTFS permissions on the file being moved. Table 2.23 presents the NTFS permissions on the target folder.

APPLY YOUR KNOWLEDGE

TABLE 2.22

SOURCE FILE NTFS PERMISSIONS

User/Group	NTFS Permission
Executives	Allow Full Control (inherited from the parent folder)
Sales	Deny Full Control

TABLE 2.23

TARGET FOLDER NTFS PERMISSIONS

User/Group	NTFS Permission
Sales	Allow Full Control

When the user copies the file to the target folder what will the effective permissions be on it?

A. Executives have Allow Full Control; Sales has Allow Full Control.

B. Executives have Deny Full Control; Sales has Deny Full Control.

C. Executives have Allow Full Control; Sales has Deny Full Control.

D. Executives have no permissions; Sales has Deny Full Control.

E. Executives have no permissions; Sales has Allow Full Control.

F. Executives have Deny Full Control; Sales has no permissions.

G. Executives have Allow Full Control; Sales has no permissions.

H. Not enough information is presented to calculate permissions.

14. You are working the help desk late one night when a user calls to complain that when she moves a file from one network share to another, the permissions are getting messed up (the shared folders are on separate partitions). Table 2.24 presents the existing NTFS permissions on the file being moved. Table 2.25 presents the NTFS permissions on the target folder.

TABLE 2.24

SOURCE FILE NTFS PERMISSIONS

User/Group	NTFS Permission
Executives	Allow Full Control (inherited from the parent folder)
Sales	Deny Full Control

TABLE 2.25

TARGET FOLDER NTFS PERMISSIONS

User/Group	NTFS Permission
Sales	Allow Full Control

When the user moves the file to the target folder, what will the effective permissions be on the file?

A. Executives have Allow Full Control; Sales has Allow Full Control.

B. Executives have Deny Full Control; Sales has Deny Full Control.

C. Executives have Allow Full Control; Sales has Deny Full Control.

D. Executives have no permissions; Sales has Deny Full Control.

E. Executives have no permissions; Sales has Allow Full Control.

F. Executives have Deny Full Control; Sales has no permissions.

G. Executives have Allow Full Control; Sales has no permissions.

H. Not enough information is presented to calculate permissions.

15. You are working the help desk late one night when a user calls to complain that when she moves a file from one folder to another folder (on the same partition) the permissions are getting messed up. Table 2.26 presents the existing NTFS permissions on the file being moved. Table 2.27 presents the NTFS permissions on the target folder.

TABLE 2.26

SOURCE FILE NTFS PERMISSIONS

User/Group	NTFS Permission
Executives	Allow Full Control (inherited from the parent folder)
Sales	Deny Full Control

TABLE 2.27

TARGET FOLDER NTFS PERMISSIONS

User/Group	NTFS Permission
Sales	Allow Full Control

When the user moves the file to the target folder, what will the effective permissions be on the file?

A. Executives have Allow Full Control; Sales has Allow Full Control.

B. Executives have Deny Full Control; Sales has Deny Full Control.

C. Executives have Allow Full Control; Sales has Deny Full Control.

D. Executives have no permissions; Sales has Deny Full Control.

E. Executives have no permissions; Sales has Allow Full Control.

F. Executives have Deny Full Control; Sales has no permissions.

G. Executives have Allow Full Control; Sales has no permissions.

H. Not enough information is presented to calculate permissions

Answers to Review Questions

1. Effective NTFS permissions are calculated as the least restrictive permission granted to the user account. For additional information see the section entitled "Multiple NTFS Permissions."

2. Because the user account has been deleted, no users have access to the home folder. When a user account is deleted, all references to the user account's Security Identifier (SID) are deleted from the operating system. The Administrator is not given access to the directory because the Administrator account does not have permissions to the NTFS folder. To fix this situation, the

Administrator will need to take ownership of the folder and give himself permission to access the folder. For additional information see the section entitled "Assigning Permissions."

3. The default permissions assigned in the Windows 2000 environment are as follows:

   - In new partitions, the Everyone group is given Full control.

   - New folders or files inherit permissions from their parent folders.

   For additional information see the section entitled "Default NTFS Permissions."

4. The file will inherit the permissions from the parent folder into which it is being moved. When a file is moved between physical partitions, a new copy of the file needs to be created on the target partition. The default NTFS permissions for a file are to inherent permissions from the parent. For additional information see the section entitled "Permission Inheritance."

5. The file will retain its existing permissions. Because you are moving a file within a partition, a new version of the file does not need to be created and therefore it can retain its permissions. For additional information see the section entitled "Copying and Moving Folders and Files."

6. The printer pool option would be best suited for this environment. Printer pooling allows all users in a high-volume print environment to print to the same printer. This printer is configured to send the print jobs to multiple printers. For additional information see the section entitled "Printer Pooling."

7. The Microsoft Management Console with the Computer Management snap-in allows you to manage remote shares. For additional information see the section entitled "Creating Shared Folders."

8. You will need to see how the paper sources have been configured for the printer on your system. This can be accomplished from the Device Setting tab of Printer properties. For additional information see the section entitled "Managing Printers."

9. The Deny permission will always override permissions that have been granted. For example, a user receives Full Control permissions to a folder from membership in Group1 and also receives Deny Full Control from membership in Group2. Since the user has been granted the Deny permission she is not given access to the resource. For additional information see the section entitled "File Permissions."

10. File-level permissions take precedence over folder permissions. In most environments, however, you will want to make sure you are managing access to your resources at the folder level (the higher up in the folder structure the better). For additional information see the section entitled "NTFS Permissions."

Answers to Exam Questions

1. **B.** Sally is able to connect to the share and access some of the data on it. Because of this, you can confirm that the shared folder is accessible. Remember that share permissions are assigned at the folder level and are then inherited from that point in the directory structure down. The only

reason why Sally would not be able to access all of the data in the share has to do with NTFS permissions. When NTFS and share permissions are combined the most restrictive permission applies. Answer A is incorrect, as Sally can access the share. Answer C is incorrect, as Sally can ping the server and can access some of the data from the share. Answer D is incorrect, as shared folder permissions are not the cause of Sally's difficulties. For additional information see the section entitled "NTFS Permissions and Shared Folders."

2. **A, D.** Answer A is correct; NTFS is being used to control access to resources. When NTFS and share permissions are combined, the most restrictive permission becomes the user's effective permissions. Answer D is also correct; the consultant you have hired is not qualified to conduct a security audit for your company. Answer B is incorrect, as NTFS and share permissions do not combine in the manner described. An argument could be made for Answer C, but technically it is not correct if NTFS permissions are being managed properly in your environment. For additional information see the section entitled "NTFS Permissions and Shared Folders."

3. **D.** Answer D is the best answer for this scenario. Printer pooling allows one printer to point to multiple physical print devices. This allows workstations to be configured so they point to one network printer. If a printer fails, the pooling function will allow jobs to be routed to another printer. Answer A is not correct, as redirection forwards jobs from one printer to another printer. Answer B would help, but is not the best solution. Answer C is incorrect, as the users would need to change their printer configuration

to print to a new printer if their current printer failed. For additional information see the section entitled "Managing Printers."

4. **B, D.** The Convert command only allows you to convert FAT or FAT32 to NTFS. If you would like to change a FAT partition to FAT32, you need to back up your data, reformat the drive, and then restore the data. Answer A is incorrect, as this command will convert the drive to NTFS. Answer C is incorrect, as formatting a drive is not the same as converting a drive. During a format all data is lost. Converting a drive will allow the data to be retained. For additional information see the section entitled "Converting File Systems."

5. **C.** Although answer A is tempting, it is not in your best interest to get the president upset. Technically, answer C is correct and the data is lost. Answers B and D are incorrect, as the format utility cannot be used to convert a drive under any circumstances. For additional information see the section entitled "Converting File Systems."

6. **D.** This type of question is very common in Microsoft tests. The key to answering these questions is to organize the information provided and draw a small table of the results. This will assist you in selecting the most appropriate answer. You should also spend a couple of minutes making sure you understand the question. Often you will find that the same question is repeated multiple times with a different proposed solution each time. Table 2.28 summarizes the answer to Exam Question 6.

APPLY YOUR KNOWLEDGE

<table>
<tr><td colspan="3">**TABLE 2.28**</td></tr>
<tr><td colspan="3">**SUMMARY OF EXAM QUESTION 6**</td></tr>
<tr><td>*Result*</td><td>*Result Met?*</td><td>*Rationale*</td></tr>
<tr><td colspan="3">**Required Results:**</td></tr>
<tr><td>All areas must be secured so only appropriate users can access designated data and applications.</td><td>No</td><td>The placement of the shares and the NTFS permissions assigned do not create a secure environment. All users have access to each other's applications and data.</td></tr>
<tr><td colspan="3">**Desired Optional Results:**</td></tr>
<tr><td>Applications should be managed by a central team of network administrators.</td><td>Yes</td><td>Domain Administrators have been granted Full Control permissions to the top of the Applications folder so they can manage its contents.</td></tr>
<tr><td>The blocking of NTFS Permissions inheritance should be minimized to simplify troubleshooting.</td><td>Yes</td><td>Based on the proposed directory structure and permissions, no inheritance will be blocked.</td></tr>
<tr><td>The total number of shares should be minimized.</td><td>Yes</td><td>Only two shares are created under this solution.</td></tr>
</table>

For additional information see the sections entitled "Developing an Efficient Directory Structure," "NTFS Permissions," and "Share Permissions."

7. **D.** Table 2.29 summarizes the answer to Exam Question 7.

<table>
<tr><td colspan="3">**TABLE 2.29**</td></tr>
<tr><td colspan="3">**SUMMARY OF EXAM QUESTION 7**</td></tr>
<tr><td>*Result*</td><td>*Result Met?*</td><td>*Rationale*</td></tr>
<tr><td colspan="3">**Required Results:**</td></tr>
<tr><td>All areas must be secured so only appropriate users can access designated data and applications.</td><td>No</td><td>Based on this solution, data resources are being secured by NTFS permissions. Applications, on the other hand, are accessible to all users. For this reason, they are not secure.</td></tr>
<tr><td colspan="3">**Desired Optional Results:**</td></tr>
<tr><td>Applications should be managed by a central team of network administrators.</td><td>Yes</td><td>The Domain Administrators group has been given full control permissions to the top level of the applications directory. Through inheritance the administrators would be able to manage all applications in the applications folder.</td></tr>
<tr><td>The blocking of NTFS Permissions inheritance should minimized to simplify troubleshooting.</td><td>Yes</td><td>Blocking of inheritance is not necessary under this solution.</td></tr>
<tr><td>The total number of shares should be minimized.</td><td>Yes</td><td>Only two shares are being used.</td></tr>
</table>

For additional information see the sections entitled "Developing an Efficient Directory Structure," "NTFS Permissions," and "Share Permissions."

8. **B.** The key to this question is understanding the limitations of FAT and FAT32 partitions. Remember that FAT and FAT32 do not support folder and file level security. For this reason, they are not very efficient for creating user home directories (as these directories are typically secure). Answer A is incorrect, as the user folders would not be secure. Answer C is incorrect, as this requires a large effort (creating all of the individual user shares). This effort is not required on NTFS partitions, where we can use file and folder security to secure the resource. To simplify the creating process, you can use the %Username% environment variable to create user home directories and assign NTFS permissions automatically when configuring the User home directory property of a user account. Answer D is incorrect, as this requires a large effort (creating all of the individual user shares). Answer B represents the most efficient answer. See the section entitled "Shared Home Directories" for more details.

9. **C.** You must remember how shared folder and NTFS permissions are applied when a user accesses a resource over the network. In this case, Mikalya can access a resource if she accesses the resource while logged on locally (she is accessing the resource directly from the file system), but cannot access the same resource from over the network. This situation points to a shared folder permission issue. When Mikalya is accessing the resource locally, shared folder permissions are not processed. You also know that Mikalya has NTFS permissions to the resource, as she can access it locally. For these reasons C is correct. Answer A is incorrect, as Mikalya can access the resource if logged on locally. Answer B is incorrect, as NTFS permissions cannot be applied for network access

vs. local access. Answer D is incorrect, as membership in Authenticated Users cannot be changed (it is a built-in group). See the section entitled "NTFS Permissions and Shared Folders" for details.

10. **B.** Expect a number of questions regarding troubleshooting permissions. The correct answer for this question revolves around the calculation of effective NTFS permissions. Remember that if a user is denied permission, it will override all other permissions granted to the user. In this case, denying Full Control to the Everyone group effectively denies access to all users on the network. Answer A is incorrect, as no such requirement exists in Windows 2000 (or any other version of Windows). Answer C is incorrect, as users need to be able to access resources from across the network. Answer D is incorrect, as the problem is an NTFS permission issue. See the section entitled "NTFS Permissions and Shared Folders" for details.

11. **D.** Remember that shared folder permissions will combine unless a Deny permission has been assigned. In this case, the Deny Full Control permission assigned to the Sales group will block Mikayla from this resource. Answers A, B, and C are incorrect, as the effective permissions are Deny Full Control. Answer E is incorrect, as the permission table and group member is provided. This is all the information you need to calculate effective permissions. See the section entitled "Multiple Share Permissions" for details.

12. **B.** When calculating effective permissions, you need to remember how both shared folder permissions and NTFS permissions work with one another. You also must remember that not being in the Access Control List of a resource is

APPLY YOUR KNOWLEDGE

the same as not having permissions to a resource. In this question, Mikayla and John both have the same effective shared folder permissions (Full Control). This is true, as shared folder permissions add up to give you the effective permissions (unless the Deny permission is assigned). The question, however, asks for Makayla and John's effective permissions on the resource. To calculate the overall effective permissions, you also need to look at the NTFS permissions assigned to the users. Mikayla has Read permissions explicitly assigned to her user account. John does not have any NTFS permissions at all. The overall effective permissions is the most restrictive of the shared folder and NTFS permissions combined. For this reason, Mikayla receives Full Control shared folder permissions plus Read NTFS permissions for a total effective permission of Read. John receives Full Control shared folder permission plus no NTFS permissions for a total effective permission of no access (or no permissions assigned). See the section entitled "NTFS Permissions and Shared Folders" for details.

13. **E.** Remember the rules when you copy files on NTFS partitions:

- When you copy a folder or file within a single NTFS partition, the copy of the folder or file inherits the permissions of the destination folder.

- When you copy a folder or file between NTFS partitions, the copy of the folder or file inherits the permissions of the destination folder.

- When you copy a folder or file to a non-NTFS partition, all permissions are lost (this is because non-NTFS partitions do not support NTFS permissions).

These questions will cause your mind to swim during an exam. You need to focus on each permission and determine how it will transfer. In this case, you are copying a file so you know the file inherits the permissions of the destination folder. For this reason, the answer is Sales will receive full control (the permissions currently on the target folder). See the section entitled "Copying and Moving Folders and Files" for details.

14. **E.** Again, recall the rules when you move files on NTFS partitions:

- When you move a folder or file within a single NTFS partition, the folder or file retains its original permissions.

- When you move a folder or file between NTFS partitions, the folder or file inherits the permissions of the destination folder. When you move a folder or file between partitions, you are creating a new version of the resource and therefore inherit permissions.

- When you move a folder or file to a non-NTFS partition, all permissions are lost (this is because non-NTFS partitions do not support NTFS permissions).

In this question we are moving a file between two different partitions, so the effective permissions on the target file are Sales Full Control. See the section entitled "Copying and Moving Folders and Files" for details.

15. **D.** Again, remember the rules when you move files on NTFS partitions:

- When you move a folder or file within a single NTFS partition, the folder or file retains its original permissions.

APPLY YOUR KNOWLEDGE

- When you move a folder or file between NTFS partitions, the folder or file inherits the permissions of the destination folder. When you move a folder or file between partitions, you are creating a new version of the resource and therefore inherit permissions.

- When you move a folder or file to a non-NTFS partition, all permissions are lost (this is because non-NTFS partitions do not support NTFS permissions).

In this question you are moving a file on the same partition, so the effective permissions on the target file are Sales Deny Full Control. In this case, you must also be aware of the fact that only explicitly assigned permissions carry over. See the section entitled "Copying and Moving Folders and Files" for details.

Suggested Readings and Resources

1. *Administering Microsoft Windows 2000.* Microsoft Official Curriculum (Course 1556A).

2. *Microsoft Windows 2000 Network and Operating System Essentials.* Microsoft Official Curriculum (Course 1251).

3. *Microsoft Windows 2000 Administrator's Pocket Consultant,* Microsoft Press, 2000.

4. *Microsoft Windows 2000 Professional Resource Kit,* Microsoft Press, 2000.

5. *MCSE Training Kit—Microsoft Windows 2000 Professional,* Microsoft Press, 2000.

Implement, manage, and troubleshoot disk devices.

▶ Disk technology is constantly evolving in capacity and available features. During the life of your computer you will probably add new functionality to your storage or playback devices. Windows 2000 provides advanced support for new devices like logical disk volumes and DVD playback.

Implement, manage, and troubleshoot display devices.

- **Configure multiple-display support.**

- **Install, configure, and troubleshoot a video adapter.**

▶ Windows 2000 provides support for multiple display devices as well as a wide range of video adapters. Being able to utilize these features will impact what you can do with your system.

Implement, manage, and troubleshoot mobile computer hardware.

- **Configure Advanced Power Management (APM).**

- **Configure and manage card services.**

▶ Laptops were once an expensive item with limited availability; however, that is changing. Mobile computing is becoming the rule rather than the exception. With that come requirements for preserving the limited resources available when running on battery as well as supporting PCMCIA and CardBus devices required to fit the slim laptop form.

CHAPTER 3

Implementing, Managing, and Troubleshooting Hardware Devices and Drivers

Implement, manage, and troubleshoot input and output (I/O) devices.

- **Monitor, configure, and troubleshoot I/O devices, such as printers, scanners, multimedia devices, mouse, keyboard, and smart card reader.**

- **Monitor, configure, and troubleshoot multimedia hardware, such as cameras.**

- **Install, configure, and manage modems.**

- **Install, configure, and manage Infrared Data Association (IrDA) devices.**

- **Install, configure, and manage wireless devices.**

- **Install, configure, and manage USB devices.**

▶ A Windows 2000 Professional computer system can have a variety of I/O devices connected to it, including printers, smart cards, cameras, and Infrared devices. Being able to manage a wide range of devices is important to getting the most out of your computer system.

Update drivers.

▶ Equipment manufacturers are constantly improving the drivers that support their devices. Unfortunately when you a buy a new device, the device driver may already be superceded by a better one. Windows 2000 Professional provides a way to automatically update the driver for a particular device either from a local source or over the Internet with a minimum of manual intervention.

Monitor and configure multiple processing units.

▶ If your processing requirements grow as you increasingly use a Windows 2000 Professional computer, there is the option of adding an additional processor. The ability to expand your computing power can have a significant impact on the workload your computer can manage.

Install, configure, and troubleshoot network adapters.

▶ Computers are attached to networks more often now than ever before. If your current computer is not attached to a network, there is a good chance that it soon will be. Additionally, network capacities are constantly improving. Being able to take full advantage of the network connections that you have will help you get the most out of your Windows 2000 Professional computer.

▶ Windows 2000 Professional supports more types of devices than any previous version of the OS. In addition to the range of devices supported, configuration is made automatic because of Plug and Play. You can expect a number of questions related to installing and supporting newer hardware devices on your Windows 2000 Professional computer. Many of these questions will be presented as scenarios in which the capabilities of these devices are used to solve problems.

▶ You should also expect to see questions dealing with new disk capabilities to provide fault tolerance as well as more options in configuring disk storage.

▶ Greater disk storage capacity creates a need for offline storage capabilities. Expect to see questions on Removable Storage Management (RSM) and the configuration of robotic libraries and media pools.

▶ Some new devices that you can expect to see questions on are support for Infrared (IrDA) and wireless support, plus support for Universal Serial Bus (USB) devices.

▶ Finally, Windows 2000 Professional can support the usage of an additional processor. You can expect to see some questions that focus on the impact of improving the CPU power of your Windows 2000 Professional computer and the impact that may have on other resources available within your system.

▶ In short, by focusing on the major areas just mentioned, you will be well-prepared for this portion of the exam.

INTRODUCTION

This chapter is mainly concerned with the hardware devices that can tailor the generalized personal computer into a device that does what you want. The extra pieces of hardware, from DVD devices to additional monitors, can greatly increase the functional value of the computer.

Understanding the available configuration options is key to arriving at solutions to problems likely to be presented in the exam. This chapter will examine the disk configurations and removable storage options that can provide solutions to disk storage problems. We will then look at I/O devices such as multiple displays, wireless I/O, cameras, scanners and printers, and USB devices, to name a few. Plug and Play features are fully supported in Windows 2000 Professional, so we will be looking at that feature as well.

We will round out the chapter with a look at the multiple CPU capability of Windows 2000 Professional and Network adapter configurations.

INSTALLING HARDWARE

The Windows 2000 Professional operating system includes many enhancements to simplify device management. Some of these include Advanced Power Management (APM), Advanced Configuration and Power Interface (ACPI), and Plug and Play (PnP).

Plug and Play is a combination of hardware and software that enables a computer to recognize and modify its hardware configuration changes with minimal intervention from the user. The hardware device that you are installing must support the Plug and Play initiative to be automatically configured correctly. You will find that some older devices that predate Plug and Play will not be recognized.

With Plug and Play, a user can add or remove a device dynamically without manual reconfiguration and without any intricate knowledge of the computer hardware. For example, you can have a laptop in a docking station that contains an Ethernet network connection and later use the same laptop connecting to the network using a built-in modem, without making any configuration changes.

With Plug and Play, you can make changes to the Windows 2000 Professional computer's configuration with the assurance that all devices will work and the computer will reboot correctly after the changes are made.

When you install a Plug and Play device, Windows 2000 Professional automatically configures the device to allow it to function properly with the other devices already installed in your computer. Windows 2000 Professional assigns system resources to the device, including the following:

- ◆ Interrupt request (IRQ) number
- ◆ Direct memory access (DMA) channel
- ◆ Input/Output (I/O) port address
- ◆ Memory address range

> **WARNING**
>
> **Manually Adjusting Resources**
> If you must manually configure a non-Plug and Play device, the resources assigned become fixed. This reduces the flexibility that Windows 2000 Professional has for allocating resources to other devices. If too many resources are manually configured, Windows 2000 Professional may not be able to install new Plug and Play devices.
>
> Resource settings should be changed only if you are certain that the new settings do not conflict with any other hardware, or if the hardware manufacturer has supplied a specific set of resource settings with the device.

Each resource must be unique, or the device will not function properly.

When the device you are installing is not Plug and Play-compatible, Windows 2000 Professional has no way of automatically configuring the device settings. You may have to manually configure the device driver or use the manufacturer-provided installation program.

You can configure devices using the Add/Remove Hardware applet in the Control Panel or by using the Device Manager, which is located in the Computer Management icon within the Administrative Tools folder in the Control Panel.

With most Plug and Play hardware, you simply connect the device to the computer and Windows 2000 Professional automatically configures the new settings. Plug and Play can be supported by devices and the drivers that control them. The possible combinations expand to four different support scenarios.

Full Plug and Play support is provided when the hardware and the device driver fully support Plug and Play.

If the hardware supports Plug and Play, but the device driver does not, Windows 2000 Professional will not support Plug and Play and the device will be treated as a legacy NT 4.0 device.

If the device driver supports Plug and Play, but the hardware does not, Windows 2000 can provide partial Plug and Play support. In this case, Windows 2000 will not be able to automatically configure the device drivers, but Plug and Play will be able to manage resource allocations and interface to the power management systems.

Windows 2000 will not provide support for Plug and Play if neither the device driver nor the hardware supports Plug and Play.

For hardware that cannot be automatically identified, the Add/Remove Hardware applet provides a method of manually configuring the device resources. Occasionally, you may need to initiate automatic installation even for some Plug and Play hardware.

Using the Add/Remove Hardware Wizard

The Add/Remove Hardware Wizard, started from the Control Panel, is used to initiate automatic hardware installation of both Plug and Play and non-Plug and Play hardware devices. The following steps will initiate a search for new Plug and Play hardware or, in its absence, present you with a screen to add a new device or troubleshoot an existing device.

STEP BY STEP

3.1 Searching for New Plug and Play Hardware

1. Click on Start, select Settings, and click on Control Panel.

2. Double-click the Add/Remove Hardware icon to start the wizard.

3. Click Next to close the Welcome page.

4. Select Add/Troubleshoot a Device and click Next to start the wizard.

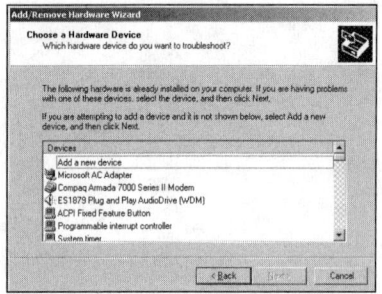

FIGURE 3.1
Troubleshooting devices.

Windows 2000 Professional will search for any new Plug and Play hardware and install any it finds. In the event that the wizard cannot detect any new hardware it will display a list of installed hardware for you to choose a device for troubleshooting (see Figure 3.1). The first entry on the hardware list is Add a New Device to provide the option of installing a new device.

Confirming Hardware Installation

After you have installed new hardware, you can confirm that the device is installed and functioning properly by using the Device Manager.

To start the Device Manager, double-click the System icon in the Control Panel. Select the Hardware tab and click the Device Manager button. This displays a list of installed hardware, as shown in Figure 3.2

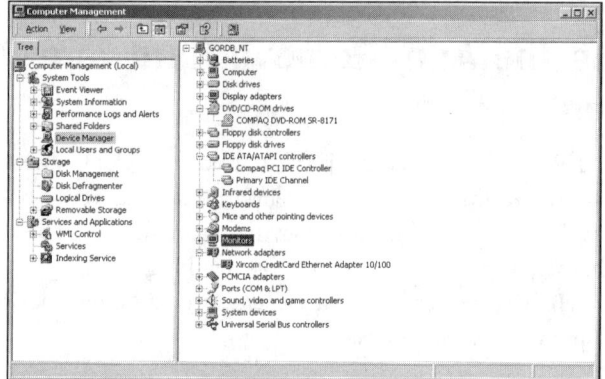

FIGURE 3.2
Installed devices listed by the Device Manager.

Expanding a device type displays all the specific devices of that type installed on the computer. The device icon will indicate if the device is functioning properly. You can use the information in Table 3.1 to determine the device status.

TABLE 3.1

DEVICE MANAGER HARDWARE STATUS

Device Icon	Device Status
Normal icon	The device is functioning normally.
Stop sign	Windows 2000 Professional has disabled the hardware due to resource conflicts. To correct this, right-click the device icon, click Properties, and set the resources manually according to what is available in the system.
Exclamation point	The device is not configured correctly or the device drivers are missing.

NOTE

Finding the Device Manager
You can access the Device Manager from a number of directions. It can be started using the Device Manager button from the Hardware tab in the System applet from the Control Panel. It can also be started from the Computer Management icon within the Administrative Tools folder in the Control Panel. Finally, it is available as a snap-in to the Microsoft Management Console (MMC).

Determining Required Resources

When you are manually installing and configuring non-Plug and Play hardware you need to understand the resources the hardware device expects to use. The manufacturer's product documentation will list the resources the device requires and you will have to determine how to fit them into your existing system. Table 3.2 describes the resources available in a Windows 2000 Professional computer system that hardware devices use to communicate with the operating system.

TABLE 3.2

HARDWARE DEVICE RESOURCES

Resource	Description
Interrupts	Hardware devices use interrupts to indicate to the processor that it needs attention. The processor uses this Interrupt Request (IRQ) as a way of determining which device is looking for service and what type of attention it needs. Windows 2000 provides interrupt numbers 0 through 15 to devices (IRQ 1 is always assigned to the keyboard).
Input/Output (I/O) port	I/O ports are areas of memory that the device uses to communicate with Windows 2000 Professional. When the processor sees an IRQ request, it checks the I/O port address to retrieve additional information about what the device wants.

continues

TABLE 3.2	*continued*

HARDWARE DEVICE RESOURCES

Resource	Description
Direct Memory Access (DMA)	DMAs are channels that allow the hardware device to access memory directly. This allows a device like a disk drive or floppy drive to write information into memory without interrupting the processor. Windows 2000 Professional provides DMA channels 0 through 7.
Memory	Many hardware devices have onboard memory or can reserve system memory for their use. Any reserved memory is not available for any other device or for Windows 2000 Professional.

IN THE FIELD

SHARABLE RESOURCES

Some of the resources used by device drives are reserved for specific devices and some can be shared between devices.

The Interrupt Request (IRQ) uses a Programmable Interrupt Controller (PIC) to request a service for the device. When a request is seen, the current operation is suspended and control given to the device drive associated with the IRQ number (1–15). This resource therefore cannot be shared between devices.

The Input/Output (I/O) port is a memory block used by the device to communicate the service it is requesting. This is tied to the IRQ number and therefore is dedicated to a device.

The Direct Memory Access (DMA) is a direct channel between the device and the computer's memory. The DMA controller supports a number of channels (usually seven) and they are shared between devices (one at a time).

A device memory block is a portion of system memory mapped to the internal memory of the device (usually). This is dedicated to the device and cannot be used by any other process (including Windows 2000 Professional).

Determining Available Resources

After you determine what resources your device requires, you can use Device Manager to display the resources available on your computer. To view the available resources list, double-click on the System icon in the Control Panel and select the Hardware tab. Click the Device Manager button and select the Resources by Connection entry in the View menu. Figure 3.3 shows the Device Manager view of resources and their availability.

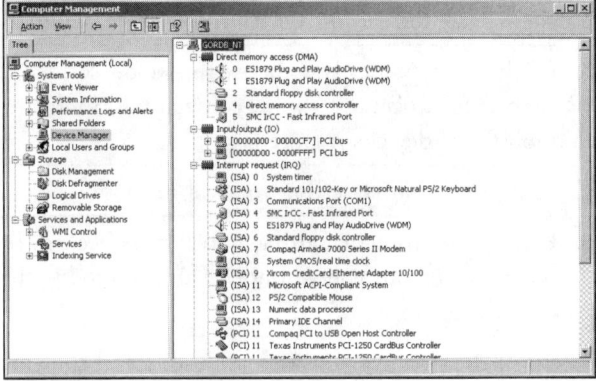

FIGURE 3.3
Hardware resources listed by connection.

Changing Resource Assignments

You might encounter two devices that request the same resources, resulting in a conflict. To change a resource setting use the Resources tab in the device's Properties information. The following procedure will allow you to modify a resource setting.

N O T E

Changing Resources for Non-Plug and Play Devices   Changing the resources assigned to a non-Plug and Play device will not actually change the resources the device uses. This only instructs the Windows 2000 Professional operating system what the device configuration is. You must consult the manufacturer's documentation on what jumpers or software switches to set on the device to conform to the resource assignment you have told Windows 2000 to expect.

STEP BY STEP

3.2 Modifying a Device's Resource Configuration

1. Click on Start, select Settings, and click on Control Panel.

2. Double-click on the System icon and select the Hardware tab.

3. Click on the Device Manager button.

4. Expand the device type that you wish to change.

5. Right-click the specific device you wish to modify.

6. Click on Properties and choose the Resources tab. If the Resources tab is not present, you will not be able to modify the device's resources.

7. Select the resource setting you will be modifying.

8. Clear the Automatic Settings box if it is checked. If this box is grayed out you will not be able to modify the device's resources.

9. Select the resource you wish to modify and click on the Change Setting button.

At this point you will be presented with a screen that will allow you to edit the value of the resource you have selected. Saving that new value will change what Windows 2000 Professional thinks the device will be using.

MEDIA DEVICES

Implement, manage, and troubleshoot disk devices.

The following sections address disk and other media devices.

CD-ROM and DVD Devices

Current CD-ROM and DVD devices support Plug and Play and therefore should be automatically configured when you install the devices.

Support for the CD-ROM File System (CDFS) is maintained in Windows 2000 Professional to support legacy applications and is used by RSM in storing CD-ROMs in Removable Storage libraries. CD-ROM devices support 650MB of storage per platter. Although this was once considered immense, it pales against the emerging standard of DVD, which currently can hold over 26 times as much data (up to 17GB of information).

DVD used to stand for Digital Versatile Disk. However, now it is recognized by the acronym alone. This line of devices is an enhancement of CD-ROM technology and is quickly replacing that as more multimedia technology is integrated into computer usage.

There are four primary types of DVD storage:

◆ **DVD-Video.** This is the actual technology usually referred to as *DVD*. This is a disk holding a video program such as a feature film that can be played back in either a DVD-Video player or a computer with a high-resolution display.

◆ **DVD-ROM.** This is the disk technology used to store computer data to be read by a DVD-ROM drive. All DVD devices should be able to read DVD disks, including double-sided, double-layered disks holding up to 17GB of data.

◆ **DVD-WO.** This is a variation of DVD-ROM that supports one-time recording capabilities like today's CD-R. The "WO" stands for Write Once.

◆ **DVD-RAM.** This is a variation of DVD-ROM supporting multiple recording capabilities similar to magneto-optical ("MO") disks.

Support for DVD in Windows 2000 Professional includes the following:

◆ **DVD-ROM driver.** The DVD-ROM industry standard command set (known as Mt. Fuji) is supported by the new Windows Driver Model (WDM) DVD-ROM device driver. Both Windows 2000 and Windows 98 can read data sectors from a DVD-ROM drive.

◆ **UDF file system.** The Universal Disk Format (UDF) provides support for UDF-formatted DVD disks.

◆ **WDM streaming class driver.** This is a driver written to follow the new Windows Driver Model (WDM) support. This driver supports MPEG-2 and AC-3 hardware decoders providing full-motion video and surround-sound capability.

◆ **DirectShow.** DirectShow is a replacement for ActiveMovie thats support DVD video and audio streams.

◆ **DirectDraw.** The video streams created by DVD devices can overwhelm a PCI bus on a computer. The solution to this is the creation of a dedicated bus to transfer decoded video streams from an MPEG-2 decoder to the display card.

◆ **Copyright protection.** DVD provides copyright protection by encrypting key sectors on a disk and then decrypting them prior to decoding.

◆ **Regionalization.** As part of the copyright protection scheme used for DVD, six worldwide regions have been defined by the DVD Consortiums. Disks are playable on DVD devices in some or all of the regions according to codes set by the creators of the content.

Monitoring CD-ROM and DVD Devices

The following procedure will allow you to view information about the device drivers controlling your CD-ROM and/or DVD devices.

STEP BY STEP

3.3 Displaying CD-ROM and DVD Device Information

1. Click Start and select Settings and click on the Control Panel.

2. Double-click on the System icon.

3. Select the Hardware tab and click on Device Manager.

4. Expand the CD-ROM/DVD device type.

5. Right-click the specific device to view and select Properties.

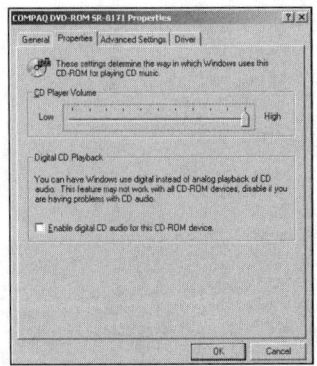

FIGURE 3.4
CD-ROM and DVD device properties.

A few properties can be manually adjusted, as shown in Figure 3.4.

Troubleshooting CD-ROM and DVD Devices

Most of these devices are now Plug and Play-compatible and therefore not prone to configuration errors. The CD-ROM and DVD devices are not immune to installation problems, however. These errors would be indicated by the tray door not opening, the usage light not being lit, or the device not showing up on your My Computer display. This type of problem (assuming the CD-ROM or DVD is not faulty) is probably caused by loose or badly installed power or data cables. To confirm this, you must physically open the computer case and examine the device connections. You may need the manufacturer's operator's guide information to correctly identify the data connections.

If the device is installed correctly but does not function correctly, follow the troubleshooting steps for these devices summarized in Table 3.3.

TABLE 3.3

TROUBLESHOOTING CD-ROM AND DVD DEVICES

Problem	Cause
The device reads data but not audio.	The audio drivers are incorrect or missing. You must update the device drivers to the latest available from Microsoft (see "Maintaining Updated Drivers" later in this chapter) or the manufacturer.
The audio drivers are installed but no audio is heard.	Audio cables are installed incorrectly. To check this, you must open the computer case and examine the audio cables. With some devices, it is possible to have the cable ends reversed.
Audio is heard over headphones but not the computer speakers.	Audio drivers or adapters are missing from the computer or are not configured correctly. You must install the latest available drivers from either Microsoft (see "Maintaining Updated Drivers" later in this chapter) or the manufacturer.
The computer plays audio but cannot be read.	The CD-ROM is faulty.
The CD-ROM can't be read or play audio.	Windows 2000 Professional is having difficulty detecting the hardware. The device driver or the hardware may not be Plug and Play-compatible. The next step would be to update the device drivers to the latest available.

Fixed Disks

Disk Management is a new graphical tool used in Windows 2000 Professional to manage disk and volumes. Disk Management can be started from within Computer Management or from inside Administrative Tools in the Control Panel, and can also be configured as an MMC snap-in.

Disk Management replaces the Disk Administrator in Windows NT and provides support for disk partitions, logical drives, and dynamic disks. Disk Management will do most of its support tasks dynamically without requiring a reboot of your computer. Disk Management also allows you to select the computer you are configuring, either the local machine or one on the network. In any case, you must have administrative rights on the computer you are configuring.

Once a new disk has been installed, Disk Management is used to rescan the drives. Normally you have to power off your computer hardware to install a new disk drive unless your system has support for hot-pluggable disk drive bays. When you rescan your disks, Disk Management will scan all attached disks looking for configuration changes, removable media, CD-ROM drives, basic volumes, file systems, and drive letters. If, however, the Rescan does not detect your new disk drive, it may be necessary to reboot your computer anyway.

Disk Storage is now configured as basic or dynamic. The terms basic disk and dynamic disk are not referring to a different type of disk, but rather the way the disk is configured. A disk can be configured as a basic disk and partitioned as you would have done in Windows NT 4.0 or configured as a dynamic disk and divided into volumes.

Basic Disk Storage

Basic storage supports partition-oriented disk configurations. A disk initialized for basic storage is called a basic disk. A basic disk can contain primary partitions, extended partitions, and logical drives. Basic disks can also contain volume sets, mirror sets, striped sets, and stripe sets with parity created by Windows NT 4.0 or earlier. Basic storage is supported by all versions of Microsoft Windows 3.x and Microsoft Windows 9x, and on Windows 2000 Professional and Server.

On a basic disk, a partition is a part of the disk that functions as a physically separate unit. A primary partition is reserved for use by an operating system. An active partition is a primary partition that contains the startup files for the operating system. Any disk can have up to four primary partitions (or three if there is an extended partition). An extended partition is created from free space and can be partitioned into logical drives. Only one extended partition is allowed per physical disk.

The following is a list of tasks that are supported on basic disks:

◆ The creation and deletion of primary and extended partitions and logical drives

◆ Marking a partition as active

◆ Deletion of volume sets, stripe sets, mirror sets, and stripe sets with parity

- ◆ Breaking a mirror from a mirrored volume

- ◆ Repair of a mirrored volume

- ◆ Repair of a RAID-5 volume

- ◆ Upgrading basic disks to dynamic disks

- ◆ Upgrading basic partitions and volumes to dynamic volumes

Disk Management will support existing mirror and RAID-5 configurations that were created under Windows NT 4.0; however, the creation of these configurations is restricted to dynamic disks only. The following is a list of tasks that are not supported on basic disks. These features are supported only on dynamic disks:

- ◆ Create simple, spanned, striped, mirrored, and RAID-5 volumes.

- ◆ Extend volumes and volume sets.

- ◆ Add a mirror to a simple volume.

- ◆ Remove a mirror from a mirrored volume.

Dynamic Storage

Dynamic storage is designed for new volume-oriented disk configurations. A disk initialized for dynamic storage is called a dynamic disk. Dynamic disks are physical disks that contain dynamic volumes created using Disk Management. Storage is divided into volumes instead of partitions. A volume consists of a part or parts of one or more physical disks laid out as a simple, spanned, mirrored, striped, or RAID-5 structure. Dynamic disks cannot contain partitions or logical drives and can be accessed only by computers running Windows 2000.

Dynamic disks can be reverted to basic disks using Disk Management; however, there is no procedure to convert dynamic volumes back to partitions. This limitation requires you to remove the volumes contained on a dynamic disk before reverting it to a basic disk.

Whereas basic disks use the partition table located in the Master Boot Record (MBR) to identify the start and end of partitions on the physical disk, dynamic disks do not follow the same format.

A dynamic disk still has a partition table, but it has only one entry that encompasses the entire disk. This allows the system to see a valid partition table when it is booting. A dynamic disk configuration stores the volume information on the physical disk in a small 1MB database at the end of the disk.

Each physical disk that has been initialized in a dynamic disk configuration contains a copy of this database replicated among each physical disk in the system. If one of the databases becomes corrupt, another copy is used and the corrupt one is refreshed with an uncorrupted copy.

Table 3.4 summarizes the major differences between basic disk configurations and dynamic disk configurations

NOTE

Converting Basic to Dynamic
For a basic disk to be upgraded to a dynamic configuration, enough space at the end of the disk must be available for this database. This space is automatically reserved when Disk Management creates partitions or volumes on a disk; however, a disk created by Windows NT 4.0 (for example) may not have the room available.

TABLE 3.4

DIFFERENCES BETWEEN BASIC AND DYNAMIC DISK CONFIGURATIONS

Basic Disks	*Dynamic Disks*
The configuration is stored in the partition table.	The configuration is stored in a 1MB database at the end of the disk.
There can be four primary partitions, or three primary partitions and one extended partition.	There can be an unlimited number of volumes.
Free space in an extended partition can be used to create multiple logical drives.	Logical drives are not supported.
Spanned, striped, mirrored, and RAID-5 configurations created by NT 4.0 are supported, but cannot be created.	Spanned, striped, mirrored, and RAID-5 configurations can be created.

In addition, mirrored and RAID-5 configurations are not supported on Windows 2000 Professional (only on Server); however, Windows 2000 Professional can create these configurations on a remote Windows 2000 Server system. Dynamic disk configurations are not supported on portable computers. If you are using Disk Management on a laptop, you will find that the options for converting a basic disk to a dynamic disk are not present.

Disk Management

The Disk Management utility (see Figure 3.5) graphically displays disks and volumes and allows a user with administrative rights to configure disks and volumes.

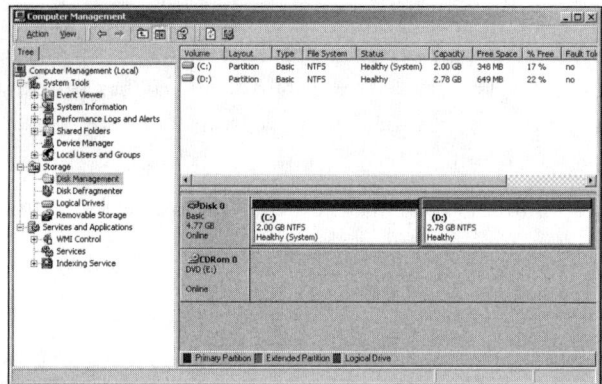

FIGURE 3.5
Disk management.

One of the most basic commands is to rescan the hardware. This allows you to update any hardware information if a new disk has been installed that Disk Management has not detected automatically.

To set up new disks, Disk Management provides wizards to help with the following tasks:

◆ Add disks for basic or dynamic storage.

◆ Create primary or extended partitions and logical disk drives (on basic disks only).

◆ Create simple, spanned, striped, mirrored, or RAID-5 volumes (on dynamic disks only).

◆ Format volumes in either File Allocation Table (FAT), FAT 32, or Windows NT File System (NTFS) format.

◆ Upgrade disks from basic to dynamic.

◆ Mount a local drive at any empty folder on an NTFS formatted volume.

The ability to mount a local drive to a folder rather than using a drive letter is an interesting feature. For example, you might have an NTFS volume that is disk C: and you have a CD-ROM drive currently known as disk D:. If you create an empty folder at C:\CD-ROM (the name is not important here—just that it is empty and on an NTFS disk), Disk Manager can mount the CD-ROM drive at that folder. Now you can access the information on the CD-ROM from the C: drive and reuse the D: drive letter for other devices.

Upgrading Basic Disks to Dynamic Disks

When a basic disk has been converted to dynamic, all existing partitions become simple dynamic volumes. This cannot be reversed. Any existing striped, mirrored, spanned, or RAID-5 partition becomes the equivalent volume.

Once upgraded, a dynamic disk cannot contain partitions or logical drives and cannot be accessed by MS-DOS or Windows operating systems other than Windows 2000.

If the basic disk contains a partition that resides on multiple disks (such as a spanned volume) all other disks that contain part of the volume must be upgraded as well. Volumes cannot be created on any removable media.

System and Boot Partitions

A basic disk that contains the system or active partitions can be upgraded to dynamic. These partitions become simple system or active volumes. An existing volume cannot be marked as active.

A basic disk that contains the boot partition can also be upgraded to a dynamic disk. The boot partition becomes a simple boot volume. A fresh installation of Windows 2000 Professional cannot be performed on an existing dynamic volume, but Windows 2000 can be upgraded on a dynamic boot volume. This limitation results from the Windows 2000 Professional setup only recognizing dynamic volumes that contain partition tables. Partition tables only occur in basic volumes and dynamic volumes that were upgraded from basic volumes. If you create a new dynamic volume on a dynamic disk, the new volume will not contain a partition table.

Once the disk containing the boot and system partitions has been upgraded to dynamic volumes, you can create a mirror set onto another disk. If one of the disks in the mirror set fails, you can restart your computer from the mirrored disk. This requires an entry in Boot.ini to reference the mirrored disk.

Troubleshooting Disk Problems

If a disk or volume fails, you will naturally want to repair the problem as quickly as possible. Disk Management displays the status of disks or volumes in both the text and graphical view. The Disk Management display can be customized by selecting the View tab and then Top or Bottom. This allows you to set the top or bottom frames of the display to disk, volume, or graphical display.

One of the disk statuses shown in Table 3.5 will appear in the Status column of the Disk List view and in the Graphical view. If there is a problem with a disk, this will help you to diagnose and correct the problem.

TABLE 3.5

DISK STATUS MEANINGS IN DISK MANAGEMENT

Disk Status	Meaning of Status
Online	The disk is accessible and has no detected problems.
Online (errors)	I/O errors have been detected. If the I/O errors are not permanent, you can reactivate the disk (using Reactivate Disk) to return it to Online status.
Offline	The disk is not accessible and may be powered down, disconnected, or corrupt.
Foreign	The disk has been moved to this computer from another Windows 2000 system. To set up this disk for use here, use the Import Foreign Disks task.
Unreadable	The disk cannot be accessed. It may have experienced hardware failure, corruption, or I/O errors. The 1MB database at the end of the physical disk may also be corrupted. Disks may be flagged as unreadable when they are spinning up or when Disk Management is rescanning all the disks in the system.

Disk Status	*Meaning of Status*
Unrecognized	The disk has a signature that Disk Management will not allow you to use. A disk from a UNIX system displays the Unrecognized status.
No Media	No media is in the CD-ROM or removable drive. This disk status changes when you insert the appropriate media into the device.

Volume Sets

Dynamic volumes are new in Windows 2000 and provide new disk storage strategies. There are five types of dynamic volumes:

- ◆ Simple

- ◆ Spanned

- ◆ Mirrored

- ◆ Striped

- ◆ RAID-5

Mirrored and RAID-5 volumes can be created only on systems running Windows 2000 Server. Because a system running Windows 2000 Professional can create mirrored and RAID-5 volumes remotely on servers, their definition is included in the following sections.

Simple Volumes

Simple volumes can be created only on dynamic disks. The number of volumes that can be created on a disk is limited only to the amount of free space available.

A simple volume can be extended to other regions on a disk or to other disks. When a simple volume extends to another disk it becomes a spanned volume. No portion of a spanned volume can be deleted without deleting the entire spanned volume. Extended volumes cannot be striped or mirrored.

NOTE

Performance Increases Using spanned volumes creates larger volumes and potentially improves system performance by spreading I/O across more drives, and it can reduce the number of drive letters used. Spanned volumes, however, are not fault-tolerant.

Spanned Volumes

A spanned volume is a mechanism for effectively using the free space on several disks. The disks used in a spanned volume can be dissimilar types like IDE and SCSI disk devices. Spanned volumes are created by combining the free space from one to 32 disks into one large volume. When the space on one disk is filled up, the system starts writing at the beginning of the next disk. This process continues in the same way up to a maximum of 32 disks.

Existing spanned volumes formatted with NTFS can be extended by adding free space. Disk Management formats the new area without affecting the existing files on the original volume or the spanned volume. Spanned volumes formatted with FAT cannot be extended.

Striped Volumes

NOTE

Improved Performance Striped volumes offer the best performance of all the Windows 2000 Professional disk management strategies, but, as with spanned volumes, striped volumes are not fault-tolerant. If a disk in a striped volume fails, the data in the entire volume is lost.

A striped volume is a mechanism for combining areas of free space from two to 32 disks into one logical volume. Data is divided into 64KB blocks and spread in a standard order among all the disks in the array.

With striped volumes, Windows 2000 Professional writes data to multiple disks such as spanned disks; however, the data is spread across all disks at the same rate.

Mirrored Volumes

A mirrored volume is a fault-tolerant volume that duplicates the data on two physical disks. It provides fault tolerance by using this copy to reduce the impact of a single disk failure. The mirror is always located on a different disk (locating it on the same disk is not only not fault-tolerant, it takes away needed bandwidth). If one disk in the mirror fails, the system continues to operate using its copy.

NOTE

Creating Mirrored Volumes When creating a mirrored volume, it is best to use disks of the same size, model, and manufacturer to minimize disk geometry compatibility issues.

A mirrored volume has better overall I/O performance than a RAID-5 volume (slower on read than a RAID-5 configuration but slightly faster on write). There is also no performance loss when a member disk in a volume fails. Mirrored volumes are more expensive because you are doubling the number of disks in your storage system; however, more disks can fail in a mirrored configuration before the data becomes inaccessible.

For example, a mirrored disk structure made of four disks actually has eight disks configured, each disk having its partner on the opposite side of the mirror. If, for example, disk3 fails on one side of the mirror, its counterpart will continue to function normally. If the remaining disk3 fails, the volume is unavailable until the hardware repaired. In this way, up to half of the disks can go offline before the mirror fails.

Mirrored drives perform write functions faster than RAID-5 and therefore might be considered for write-intensive functions.

RAID-5 Volumes

A RAID-5 volume is fault tolerant, with data and parity information striped intermittently across three to 32 disks. If a portion of a physical disk fails, the RAID-5 structure allows the hardware to re-create the lost data using the remaining parity information. RAID-5 is a good fault-tolerant solution in which the application mainly reads data. The RAID-5 configuration requires the equiva-lent of an additional disk to store parity information. In small configurations (three disks), that consumes 33% of the disk space (two drives going to the volume and one drive consumed for parity information). However, as the number of physical drives in the RAID-5 structure increases it becomes more efficient (a 10-drive RAID-5 structure has nine disks going to the volume and one being consumed for parity information).

When a member disk of a RAID-5 volume has failed, the read performance is degraded by the need to recover the data using only the parity information. RAID-5 was designed to protect against physical disk failure and therefore protects only against a single device failing in the volume. If a second device fails before the first is repaired, then the volume goes offline and the data is lost.

Troubleshooting Volume Problems

If a disk or volume fails, it is important to repair the problem as quickly as possible. Disk Management displays the status of disks or volumes in both the list and graphical view. The Disk Management display can be customized by selecting the View tab and then Top or Bottom. This allows you to set the top or bottom frames of the display to disk, volume, or graphical display.

One of the disk statuses shown in Table 3.6 will appear in the Status column of the Volume List view and in the Graphical view. If there is a problem with a volume, this will help you to diagnose and correct the problem.

TABLE 3.6

VOLUME STATUS DESCRIPTION IN DISK MANAGEMENT

Disk Status	Meaning of Status
Healthy	The volume is readable with no detected problems.
Healthy (at Risk)	The volume is currently readable, but I/O errors have been detected on one of the volume's physical disks. The disk view will show a disk that is Online (Errors). Use Reactivate Disk to return the disk to Online status, which will return the volume to Healthy status.
Initializing	The volume is being initialized. Only dynamic volumes display the Initializing status.
Resynching	The volume's mirrors are being resynchronized to contain identical data.
Regenerating	Data and parity are being regenerated for a RAID-5 volume. The RAID-5 volume can be accessed while regeneration is in progress.
Failed	The volume cannot be started automatically.
Failed Redundancy	The data on the volume is no longer fault-tolerant because one of the underlying physical disks is not online.
Failed Redundancy (At Risk)	The data on the volume is no longer protected by a fault-tolerant configuration, and I/O errors have been detected on the physical disk. The disk view will show a physical disk with Online (Errors) as the status. Returning the disk to Online status (using Reactivate Disk) will return the volume to Failed Redundancy status.

If the underlying disk is not online, but is successfully reactivated (using Reactivate Disk), the volume should automatically repair itself. A mirrored volume repairs itself by resynchronizing the data (sometimes called resilvering). A RAID-5 volume repairs itself by regenerating its parity and data.

If the disk returns to Online status but the volume does not, reactivate the volume manually using Reactivate Volume.

If the underlying disk will not reactivate, there is probably something wrong with the disk. Replace the disk and rebuild any mirror by using the Remove Mirror and Add Mirror commands. A RAID-5 volume can be rebuilt using the Repair Volume command.

Removable Media

Removable Storage Management (RSM) is the interface in Windows 2000 Professional for accessing removable media, including automated devices such as changers, jukeboxes, and libraries. RSM is installed by default to control most types of removable media, including CD-ROM, DVD-ROM, magneto-optical (MO), JAZ, and ZIP drives in both stand-alone and library configurations. RSM cannot manage the A: and B: drives.

RSM considers all device changes as a subset of an ideal standard. A given mini-driver tells RSM what functionality the actual changer implements, allowing RSM to treat it appropriately. This model is similar to the way Windows 2000 Professional treats network adapters and printers, each one having a slightly different way of doing common tasks, with an intermediate driver allowing client applications to access services in standard ways.

Client programs such as backup applications and Hierarchical Storage Management (HSM) systems use RSM to access their media. Once the media is available, the client applications use standard Windows 2000 API calls to read and write data.

This model provides the following benefits:

◆ **A common driver model.** The driver model allows a tape library to be used with any RSM-compatible application. An application written to use RSM can work with any device changer where the manufacturer has provided an RSM mini-driver.

◆ **Library sharing.** Multiple applications can now share a common library. Previously, if you wanted to use both a backup application and an HSM application supplied from two different vendors, you required two device changers. When using RSM, both applications can use the same changer.

NOTE

Legacy Applications   RSM will interfere with legacy applications because it controls all media changers on the system exclusively. This breaks applications that expect to access these changers directly. These applications must now access the changers via RSM.

The Windows 2000 Professional backup utility uses RSM for tape media but not for media with file systems (such as ZIP or JAZ drives).

◆ **Offline media.** A backup application does not need to know where the media is. It simply requests the media, and RSM loads it or asks the operator to mount it as required.

◆ **Media tracking.** RSM tracks all media that it recognizes in an internal database. Applications can register with RSM, allowing it to recognize its own media. Applications can also use RSM to search the database and load a particular media.

◆ **A common interface.** Backup applications that are RSM compatible work the same with a changer or with a stand-alone drive.

Windows 2000 Professional uses RSM to manage ATAPI CD-ROM changers and to mount and dismount all removable media. This includes disks contained in ATAPI CD-ROM changers that hold several CD-ROMs. This type of device receives only a single letter in Windows 2000.

Media Pools

RSM organizes removable media into media pools. RSM can then reassign media to different media pools to provide the amount of storage that different data management applications need.

A media pool is a logical collection of similar media with similar properties. All RSM media belongs to a media pool, and each media pool holds either tape or disk (but not both). Applications use media pools to gain access to specific types of media from a library.

RSM supports two classes of media pools:

◆ System, including unrecognized, import, and free

◆ Application, created for data management applications. There can be a number of application media pools created. Media reserved for an application (allocated) cannot be moved between media pools.

Unrecognized Media Pools

Unrecognized media pools contain new (blank) media. This should be immediately moved from the unrecognized media pool to the free media pool so it can be used by applications.

Import Media Pools

Import media pools contain media the RSM recognizes but has not catalogued in the RSM database. Media can be moved from import media pools to free or application media pools for reuse.

Free Media Pools

Free media pools contain media that is not currently allocated by an application and contains no current data. Media pools should be configured to draw from the free media pool when there is nothing available for a particular application.

Application Media Pools

Application media pools are created and used by data management applications. Media in an application pool is controlled by the management application or by the administrator. An application can use more than one media pool, and more than one application can share a media pool.

Library Types

Each media in RSM belongs to a library. There are two types of libraries, as described in the following sections.

Robotic Libraries

Robotic libraries are automated units (such as jukeboxes) that hold multiple tapes or disks and can have multiple drives.

Stand-Alone Libraries

Stand-alone libraries are single-slot CD-ROM or tape devices that hold a single piece of media.

RSM can also track offline media that is catalogued but not currently in a library. This media can be physically located elsewhere (for offsite storage supporting disaster recovery plans).

Media Resources

Before RSM can be set up and used, there must be removable media resources to manage. There are three types of removable media supported by RSM. They are described in the following sections.

Tape

The two major tape technologies in use today are Digital Audio Tape (DAT) and Digital Linear Tape (DLT).

Read-Only Optical Disk

Read-only optical media includes CD-ROM and DVD-ROM disks. These are written by the manufacturer and cannot be overwritten or erased. This type of media is most useful as reference material (such as online catalogues or documentation) or licenced software programs (such as applications and games).

Write-Able Optical Disk

Write-Able optical media includes Magneto-Optical (MO) devices, Phase Change (PC), Write Once Read Many (WORM), CD-Recordable (CD-R), and DVD-Recordable (DVD-R) disks. MO and PC media can be erased and overwritten, while WORM, CD-R, and DVD-R disks can be written to only once.

Operator Requests

An operator request is a message that requests a specific task. Operator requests are generated when offline media has been requested, or an application has requested media and none is available. An operator request will also be generated if a fault occurs in one of the libraries or a drive needs cleaning and no cleaner cartridges are available.

Troubleshooting RSM

Problems can occur when using RSM in either stand-alone configurations or with robotic libraries. To prevent problems, follow the guidelines in this list:

◆ Verify that the library is supported by Windows 2000. A good place to check is the Hardware Compatibility List (HCL) on the Microsoft Web site (www.microsoft.com/hcl).

◆ Verify that the library is properly connected. If the library uses a SCSI connection, make sure there are no SCSI ID conflicts with other devices in the computer, such as with hard drives or CD-ROMs. In addition, verify that all cables are installed and terminated properly and do not exceed the maximum length allowed.

◆ Use Device Manager to ensure that Windows 2000 has recognized the library and associated drives and has configured the device drivers correctly.

◆ If Removable Storage still cannot automatically configure the library correctly, it will need to be manually configured.

◆ If the library is configured correctly but begins malfunctioning, look at the Windows 2000 system event log. Many problems can be caused by device errors.

▶ Devices support Plug and Play to make their installation and configuration automatic and dynamic (without a reboot).

▶ The Device Manager can display the resources a device is using and allow you to edit and change any (not all will be available).

▶ Disk Management is the MMC snap-in GUI interface for managing disks, partitions, volumes, logical drives, and other configurations.

▶ Disks are either basic disks or dynamic disks.

▶ Basic disk configurations are stored in the partition table on each disk.

▶ Basic disks can have four primary partitions, or three primary partitions and one extended partition.

▶ A basic disk's extended partition can be divided into logical drives.

▶ Spanned, mirrored, striped, and RAID-5 configurations created under NT 4.0 can be maintained but not created on basic disks.

▶ Dynamic disk configurations are stored in a 1MB database at the end of the physical disk.

▶ Dynamic disks use volumes rather than partitions.

▶ Spanned, mirrored, striped, and RAID-5 configurations can be created on dynamic disks.

▶ Only Windows 2000 can access dynamic disks.

▶ Removable Storage manages access to stand-alone and robotic libraries and allows you to group disks and tapes into media pools.

▶ RSM keeps track of all catalogued media, even if it is currently not in a library device. Requesting the media will find the media or generate an operator message requesting the media be placed in a library.

DISPLAY DEVICES

Implement, manage, and troubleshoot display devices.

Windows 2000 Professional adds support for up to nine display adapters. This allows the desktop to extend to nine monitors supporting large graphical drawings (such as those produced by CAD systems). There are some important considerations to make if you're setting up a multiple display system.

Multiple Display Support

All of the video adapters used with multiple display units must be Peripheral Component Interconnect (PCI) or Accelerated Graphics Port (AGP) devices.

The hardware requirements for the primary video adapter (which drives the first screen of the multiple displays) are different from the requirements for the secondary video adapters. If the video adapter built into the motherboard is to be used as a secondary screen in a multiple display, it must be compatible with those requirements.

If you are using a video adapter built into the motherboard for a multiple display, you must first completely install Windows 2000 Professional before adding any other adapters. The Windows 2000 Professional setup program will disable an on-board video adapter if it sees an additional one. The BIOS in some systems will also shut down the on-board video adapter if an additional one is seen. If you can't defeat this detection, the built-in video adapter cannot be used in a multiple display.

One last consideration is to remember that the primary video adapter cannot be turned off. Since the multiple-display configuration uses the primary as the "anchor point" of the extended desktop, any system that shuts down the primary video adapter will not support multiple displays. Laptops that are placed in docking stations usually do just that and therefore will not function correctly in this configuration.

The Virtual Desktop

Windows 2000 Professional creates a virtual desktop when configuring multiple displays and uses this to determine the relationship of the displays to each other. The virtual desktop sets the coordinates of the top-left corner of the primary screen to (0,0). Additional screens are configured to exactly touch each other on the virtual desktop, allowing the mouse to move seamlessly from screen to screen; there are no spots not covered by a display.

The position of the displays on the virtual desktop can be viewed by clicking on the Display icon in the Control Panel. Select the Settings tab in the Control Panel to show the screen layout. Display positions are changed by dragging the icon representing the screen to its new location. There is also a check box to indicate which screen (and therefore video adapter) is going to be the primary monitor.

Configuring Multiple Display Adapters

Once the secondary adapter(s) are installed, the virtual desktop must be configured.

The following procedure is a configuration of a two-monitor system.

STEP BY STEP

3.4 Configuring Two Displays

1. Click Start, select Settings, and click Control Panel.

2. Double-click on Display.

3. Select the Settings tab. The numbers in the monitor representations indicate the displays. 1 is the primary display, and 2 through 9 are the secondary displays.

continues

continued

4. Select the primary display and click on the Use This Device as the primary monitor check box.

5. Select the video adapter for the primary display.

6. In the Colors box, select the color depth desired.

7. Move the screen area slider to select the resolution.

8. Select display number 2.

9. Select the Extend My Windows Desktop onto This Monitor check box.

10. Select the color depth desired.

11. Move the Screen Area slider to select the resolution.

This procedure is very similar to the one you would follow when configuring your display. In the case of multiple monitors, you must first choose the monitor you are configuring and then provide the same configuration for all the monitors in the system.

Troubleshooting Multiple Displays

Problems with multiple displays usually relate to the video adapter not initializing properly or not being supported as a secondary display. Table 3.7 indicates some typical symptoms and their solutions.

TABLE 3.7

PROBLEMS WITH MULTIPLE DISPLAYS

Symptom	Solution
There is no output on a secondary display.	Confirm that the device is activated in the Display Properties dialog box.
	Confirm that the correct video driver is installed.
	Confirm that the secondary display was initialized when the computer restarted. You can do this by checking Device Manager for the status of the video adapter.
	Physically switch the order of the adapters in the PCI slots. (This may require that the primary adapter also qualify as a secondary adapter.)

Symptom	*Solution*
The Extend My Windows Desktop onto This Monitor check box is unavailable.	Confirm that the secondary display is highlighted in the Display Properties dialog box.
	Confirm that the secondary display adapter is supported.
	Confirm that the secondary display is detected.
There are problems displaying an application on a multiple-display configuration.	Run the application on the primary display rather than on a secondary display, or on a window that spans more than one screen.
	Run the application on a full screen rather than on a window.
	Disable the secondary display and rerun the application to see whether the problem is specific to multiple-display support.

Video Adapters

Most computers are designed with a video adapter built into the motherboard, and generally this device will work best with most applications. With some new games, however, additional hardware acceleration is needed to power the effects.

Video adapters now support the Plug and Play standard and will be detected and installed by Windows 2000 Professional either during setup or when you reboot your computer after installing the device.

In the event that Plug and Play cannot detect the card directly, you can use the following procedure to install the new device.

STEP BY STEP

3.5 Installing a New Video Adapter

1. Click on Start, select Settings, and click on Control Panel.

2. Double-click on Add/Remove Hardware.

continues

continued

3. Click Next to close the Welcome page.

4. Select Add/Troubleshoot a Device and click Next.

5. After Windows searches for any new Plug and Play device, select Add New Device and click Next.

6. Select No, I Want to select the Hardware from a List and click Next.

7. Select Display Adapters and click Next.

8. Select the manufacturer and model of the display adapter you have installed and click Next. If the manufacturer or device model is not on the list of supported devices, click Have Disk. The Add/Remove Hardware Wizard will read the device information from the manufacturers disk.

9. Click Next to start the hardware installation.

10. Click Finish to complete the installation.

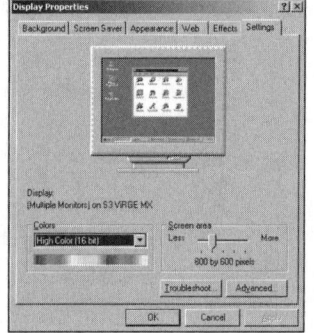

FIGURE 3.6
Display settings.

Once the new video adapter is installed, you can change the characteristics of your screen using the Display applet in the Control Panel. Figure 3.6 shows the Settings screen from the Display applet in Control Panel. From this point, you can vary the color depth and the screen resolution.

Table 3.8 lists the settings and advanced options for configuring your display.

TABLE 3.8

ADVANCED DISPLAY OPTIONS

Option	Description
Colors	Lists the color options for the display adapter.
Screen Area	Configures the screen area used by the display.
Font Size	Allows selection of a small or large font size.
Monitor Type	Allows selection of the monitor type the display adapter is using.

Option	Description
Refresh Frequency	Allows selection of the refresh frequency the display adapter will use with the monitor.
Hardware Acceleration	Allows setting the amount of hardware acceleration and performance supplied by the graphics hardware.
CRT Refresh Rate (Hz)	Allows choice of the refresh rate used to refresh information on your video screen. A higher rate (if supported by your video adapter) can produce a smoother, flicker-free display but can also change the size of the display area.

MOBILE COMPUTING

Implement, manage, and troubleshoot mobile computer hardware.

Being mobile with your computer is becoming the rule rather than the exception. Within corporations, a significant number of desktop systems are laptops in docking stations. Support for these devices requires special consideration compared to stationary desktop systems. Chiefly, this includes power management and support for PCMCIA cards.

Power Management

Advanced Power Management (APM) is the legacy power management scheme based on a BIOS approach that was first supported in Windows 95. Most of the interesting features of APM are in a machine-specific BIOS that is hidden from the Windows 2000 Professional operating system.

APM has been superseded by the Advanced Configuration and Power Interface (ACPI) standard. This is a more robust scheme for power management and system configuration supported in Windows 98 and Windows 2000 Professional.

Many laptop computers will have both ACPI and APM support, but some will have only APM support. Support for APM in Windows 2000 is mainly intended for laptops with limited support on desktop computers.

APM in Windows 2000 Professional is designed to support battery status, suspend and resume functions, and auto-off for hibernate. Functions such as wake on timed event, wake on LAN, and wake on ring are not supported.

When to Use APM

If the laptop has a supported ACPI BIOS, ACPI should be used for power management. Some functions, such as timed wakeups, are only available using ACPI under Windows 2000 Professional.

APM should not be used in the following circumstances:

◆ If the BIOS has been identified as incompatible with APM, the Windows 2000 Professional setup will not run APM on machines with these BIOSs.

◆ If the BIOS is not compliant with the APM standard, you shouldn't use APM. This results in an unstable system with the potential for data loss.

APM can be used in the following circumstances:

◆ There is no ACPI BIOS.

◆ The ACPI BIOS is not compliant or not implemented properly. However, APM may not work any better.

During installation, Windows 2000 Professional setup procedures use values in the Biosinfo.inf file (supplied on the Windows 2000 Professional CD-ROM) to determine whether the system is on the AutoEnable APM list or the Disable APM list.

If the system is on the AutoEnable list, setup will automatically install APM support. If the system is on the Disable APM list, setup will not install or enable APM support. It may still be necessary to disable the APM BIOS settings using the computer's BIOS setup routines.

If the system is not found on either list, the system is considered neutral. In this case, setup will install APM support but will leave it disabled. You can enable APM support by double-clicking the Power icon in the Control Panel and selecting the APM tab.

WARNING

Systems on the Disable APM List
You should never try to enable APM on a machine that is on the Disable APM list. This will generally produce erratic and undesirable results on an otherwise stable system.

You can determine whether APM support is configured for your system by clicking on Start and then selecting Shutdown. If APM support is running, the Stand-By entry appears in the list of choices.

Reboots May Be Necessary Turning the APM support off will require a reboot, but turning APM on does not.

Troubleshooting APM in Windows 2000 Professional

The following are items you should consider when using APM support in Windows 2000 Professional:

◆ **APM and multiprocessors.** Ensure that APM is turned off in the BIOS on multiprocessor systems. If possible, use ACPI (Advanced Configuration and Power Interface), which is supported with multiprocessor systems.

◆ **Desktop system.** APM support should be disabled on all desktop systems. The APM BIOS cannot correctly save most of the video displays on desktop systems, resulting in a vanished display after a Suspend and Resume. Occasionally, having APM turned off in the Windows 2000 Professional operating system but turned on in the BIOS will result in a timeout and powerdown even if the CPU is very busy.

◆ **Incompatible systems.** If APM support has been enabled on a system in the Disable APM list, use the Power applet in the Control Panel to disable APM support. Reboot the system in Safe Mode (F8) and delete the NTAPM.SYS file from \WINNT\System32\drivers.

◆ **Additional video adapter.** Using a video adapter other than the one included with the computer will change the system's APM configuration. If the adapter is not detected by the APM BIOS, suspend will not function properly.

◆ **Screen blanking.** If the video timeout is set in the BIOS and the screen blanks, moving a mouse will wake the system; however, an external USB mouse will not. To work around this, disable the BIOS timeout and use the Blank screen saver.

◆ **APM BIOS timeouts.** The BIOS should be configured to allow the Windows 2000 Professional operating system to blank the screen, turn off the disk, and so on. If APM is used to control these functions, the system will not always restore correctly on wake-up. BIOS timeouts should be set to none or for as long as possible.

Card Services

Windows 2000 Professional supports the connection of credit card-sized add-on devices through its card services.

Windows 2000 Professional supports PC Card socket controllers, 16-bit PC I/O cards (sometimes referred to as PCMCIA cards), and the newer 32-bit architecture that operates up to 33Mhz. Although PCMCIA cards were originally intended only as memory cards, the currently available cards are also used for many I/O devices, such as Global Positioning System (GPS) devices, modems, and network adapters. Windows 2000 Professional also supports power management and Plug and Play for PCMCIA cards.

If you are going to unplug a card device, it is important to allow Windows 2000 Professional to shut the device off prior to removing it from the computer.

The following procedure can be used to unplug a PC Card.

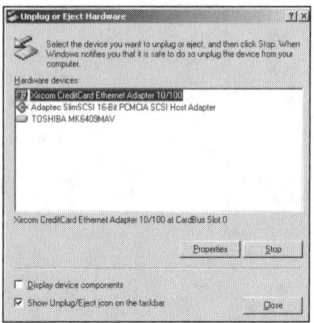

FIGURE 3.7
Ejecting a PC Card device.

STEP BY STEP

3.6 Unplugging or Ejecting a PC Card

1. Click Start, select Settings, and click Control Panel.

2. Double-click on the Add/Remove Hardware icon.

3. Click Next to close the Welcome page on the Add/Remove Hardware Wizard.

4. Select Uninstall/Unplug a Device and click Next.

5. Click Unplug/Eject a device and click Next.

6. Select the device you want to unplug or eject and click Next. See Figure 3.7 for an example of selecting a PC device to eject.

7. Click Next to confirm that you are ejecting the device you selected.

8. Click Finish to complete the task.

If you add and remove PC Cards frequently from your laptop computer, you may wish to add an Eject Device shortcut to your taskbar. The final screen of the Add/Remove hardware procedure outlined previously contains a check box that will add the Eject Device icon to your taskbar (see Figure 3.8).

INPUT AND OUTPUT (I/O) DEVICES

Implement, manage, and troubleshoot input and output (I/O) devices.

Since their introduction, personal computers have always been generalized in design. Additional functionality and personalizing features were provided by manufacturers of add-on cards and adapters. With many different manufacturers all providing different approaches to installing and configuring their devices, using PC add-ons was often confusing and contradictory.

Windows 2000 Professional supports the Plug and Play standard. Most new devices use this to standardize their installation steps.

Configuring Input and Output (I/O) Devices

Devices such as printers, image capturing devices, multimedia, pointing and input devices, and now smart cards form a class of device that works more at the Human Machine interface than other devices (such as display adapters or network cards). This means that there are more features combined into these devices, giving them more than a single-purpose device. The installation and configuration of these devices are therefore discussed separately.

Printers

The printing system is modular and works hand in hand with other systems to provide printing services. When a printer is a local printer and a print job is specified by an application, data is sent to the

FIGURE 3.8
Adding Eject Device to your taskbar.

NOTE · **Stop the Device First**   It is important to use the Add/Remove Hardware Wizard or the Eject Device taskbar icon to stop a PC Card device that you are about to unplug or eject. Doing so prevents data loss or other serious malfunction to the device.

Graphics Device Interface (GDI). The GDI calls the printer driver
for print device information useful in rendering the print job into
the printer language of the print device. The GDI is therefore the
main interface between the application and the printing system.
The print job is passed to the spooler and is written to disk as a
temporary file so it can survive a power outage or system shutdown.
Print jobs can be spooled in either the RAW or Enhanced Meta
File (EMF) printer language. Figure 3.9 shows the layout of the
components of the Windows 2000 Professional printing subsystem.

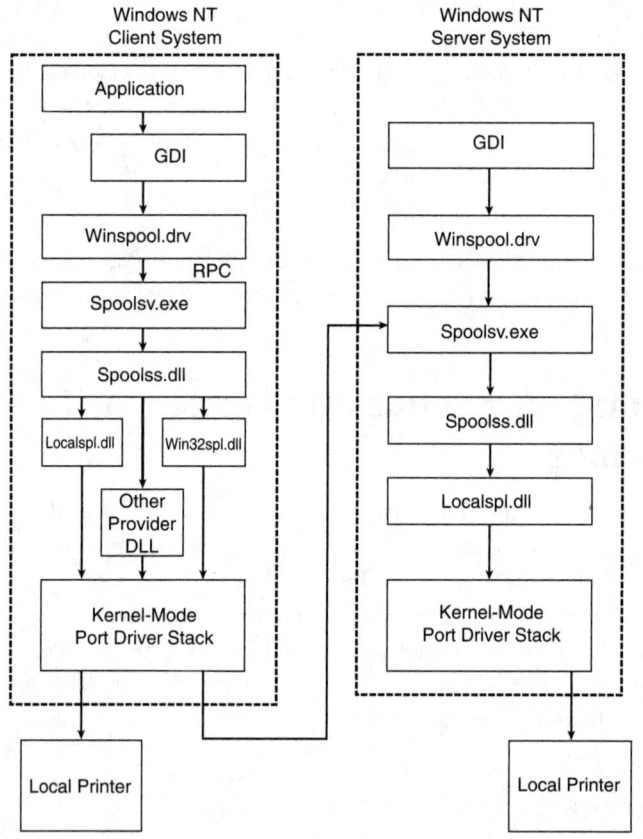

FIGURE 3.9
Components of the Windows printing subsystem.

The client side of the print spooler is winspool.drv, and that driver makes an RPC call to the spoolsv.exe server side of the spooler. This split in functionality is what allows print devices to be local to your computer or remotely installed on a print server and still function the same. Clients for spoolsv.exe include winspool.drv for handling locally created print jobs and win32spl.dll for print jobs created on remote machines.

If the printer is located on a different Windows 2000 or Windows NT server, the network provider win32spl.dll is used. This module uses RPC calls to redirect the print jobs from the client's computer to the server's spoolsv.exe process. Once there, the server's local print provider will handle the print job.

You generally install printers using the Add Printer Wizard that you find in the Printers folder in Control Panel. After you step through the wizard you will have created a local printer with the name you provided. You can create other local printers for the same physical printer configured to print differently, have different security schemes, or provide different access times. You can manipulate printers by performing the following actions:

◆ Double-click on the printer to see any spooled jobs, provided you have the privilege to do so.

◆ Right-click on the printer to view a shortcut menu that provides several options. You can delete a printer that no longer exists or use the Default Printer command to set this printer as the default one for your Windows 2000 Professional computer.

◆ Right-click on a printer and select the Properties command from the shortcut menu to access the Printer Properties and control any number of settings.

Using a Basic Error Checklist

Any number of things can go wrong when you attempt to print to a printer. In many cases, Windows 2000 Professional alerts you to an error and in some cases will actually tell you what the error type is.

Here is a standard checklist of the most common solutions to print problems.

If your print job spools but does not print, try the following:

◆ Check that the printer is turned on and all the connections are secure.

◆ Check that the paper tray is full and no paper is jammed inside the printer.

◆ Verify that the printer is operational. If the printer is a shared resource and other users can print, the problem is not with the printer or the print server.

◆ Verify that the printer does not have any outstanding error conditions set.

◆ If there is a job currently printing that is hung up (looking for paper that is not loaded on the printer, for example), you can delete it by pausing the printer and deleting the stopped print job. Restarting the printer will allow other spooled jobs to complete.

The preceding problems are so simple that it is easy to waste time and overlook them. A large percentage of printer problems will disappear when you restart your printer. If that fails, restart your Windows 2000 computer.

If none of these solutions seems to work, try the following:

◆ Verify that the printer is using the correct printer driver. If the printer is a shared resource and other users have operating systems other than Windows 2000 Professional, make sure you install all the drivers necessary.

◆ Verify that the printer you attempted to print to is either the default printer for your system, or the printer you selected from your application.

◆ Verify that you can access the printer you are attempting to use. Select the Printers item from the Settings submenu on the Start menu. Right-click on the printer icon and select Open. If the printer control panel does not open correctly and the status persists at Opening or Unable to Connect, there could be a permissions problem.

◆ Verify that there is enough hard disk space to create the temporary spool file.

◆ Try printing a smaller page of text from Notepad. This will often confirm that the print problem is application-specific.

◆ Print to a file and copy the file to the printer port being used either locally or on the printer server. If you can print in this manner, there could be a spooler or data-transmission error.

IN THE FIELD

UPDATE YOUR PRINT DRIVERS

At the very worst, you can try reinstalling the printer and supplying a new or updated printer driver.

There are a number of places to find updated printer drivers, including the following:

· The Windows 2000 Professional distribution disks

· The setup disks that come with the printer

· The printer manufacturer's Web site

· The Microsoft Web site. Use the Search button to search for the particular model of printer

Scanners

Scanners are added by using the Scanners and Cameras Wizard found in the Control Panel.

After installing the scanner and connecting any cables required to your Windows 2000 Professional computer, you can use the following procedure to install a scanner.

STEP BY STEP

3.7 Installing a Scanner

1. Click Start, select Settings, and click Control Panel.

2. Double-click the Scanners and Cameras icon.

3. Click the Add button to start the Scanners and Cameras Installation Wizard.

4. Click Next to close the Welcome screen.

5. Select the manufacturer and device model that you are installing and click Next.

6. Select the port that you have installed your scanner on and click Next.

7. Provide a name for the device and click Next.

8. Click Finish to complete the installation.

> **NOTE**
>
> **Administrator Privileges** You must be logged on with a user ID that has administrator privileges to complete the procedure for installing a scanner. If your scanner supports Plug and Play, Windows 2000 Professional will detect it and install the correct drivers automatically.

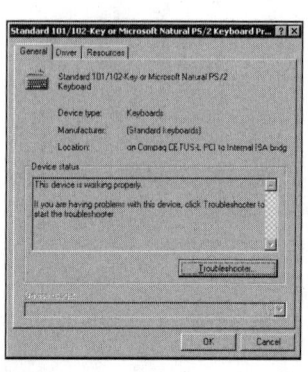

FIGURE 3.10
General information on a working keyboard.

Keyboards

Keyboards can be built in, connected with a specific device port, or operate as a USB device connected directly or via a USB hub.

Windows 2000 Professional will detect a new keyboard if it is Plug and Play-compatible. If it is not, you will have to use the Add/Remove Hardware Wizard and use the manufacturer's setup disks to install the device manually. Figure 3.10 shows the hardware properties of a typical keyboard.

Once the keyboard is installed, you can change the characteristics of the device to meet your personal requirements. Figure 3.11 shows the Speed tab on the Keyboard Properties page.

Keyboard Customizations

The Accessibility Options applet in the Control Panel also provides a number of ways to customize how your keyboard functions. The following features allow you to customize your keyboard functions:

◆ **StickyKeys.** This option allows you to press a modifier key such as Ctrl, Alt, Shift, or the Windows Logo key and have it remain in effect until a non-modifier key is pressed.

◆ **FilterKeys.** This option allows you to ignore brief or repeated keystrokes.

◆ **ToggleKeys.** This option emits a sound when locking keys are pressed.

To enable any of these functions, double-click on the Accessibility applet in the Control Panel and select the Keyboard tab.

Shortcut Key Combinations

For those who are keyboard wizards and who like to use shortcuts rather than the mouse to find and select certain options, Windows 2000 Professional provides shortcuts to well-known tasks. See Table 3.9.

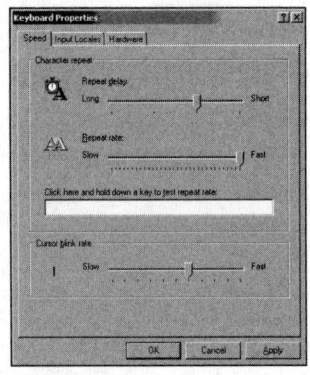

FIGURE 3.11
Adjusting speed characteristics of a keyboard.

TABLE 3.9

WINDOWS 2000 PROFESSIONAL KEYBOARD SHORTCUTS

Shortcut	Function
Ctrl+C	Copy
Ctrl+X	Cut
Ctrl+V	Paste
Ctrl+Z	Undo
Delete	Delete
Shift+Delete	Delete selected item permanently without placing the item in the Recycle Bin
Ctrl while dragging an item	Copy selected item
Ctrl+Shift while dragging an item	Create shortcut to selected item

continues

TABLE 3.9	*continued*

WINDOWS 2000 PROFESSIONAL KEYBOARD SHORTCUTS

Shortcut	*Function*
F2	Rename selected item
Ctrl+right arrow	Move the insertion point to the beginning of the next word
Ctrl+left arrow	Move the insertion point to the beginning of the previous word
Ctrl+down arrow	Move the insertion point to the beginning of the next paragraph
Ctrl+up arrow	Move the insertion point to the beginning of the previous paragraph
Ctrl+Shift with any of the arrow keys	Highlight a block of text
Shift with any of the arrow keys	Select more than one item in a window or on the desktop, or select text within a document
Ctrl+A	Select all
F3	Search for a file or folder
Ctrl+O	Open an item
Alt+Enter	View properties for the selected item
Alt+F4	Close the active item, or quit the active program
Ctrl+F4	Close the active document in programs that allow you to have multiple documents open simultaneously
Alt+Tab key	Switch between open items
Alt+Esc	Cycle through items in the order in which they were opened
F6	Cycle through screen elements in a window or on the desktop
F4	Display the Address bar list in My Computer or Windows Explorer
Shift+F10	Display the shortcut menu for the selected item
Alt+spacebar	Display the System menu for the active window
Ctrl+Esc	Display the Start menu
Alt+underlined letter in a menu name	Display the corresponding menu

Shortcut	*Function*
Underlined letter in a command name on an open menu	Carry out the corresponding command
F10	Activate the menu bar in the active program
Right arrow	Open the next menu to the right, or open a submenu
Left arrow	Open the next menu to the left, or close a submenu
F5	Refresh the active window
Backspace	View the folder one level up in My Computer or Windows Explorer
Esc	Cancel the current task
Shift when you insert a CD into the CD-ROM drive	Prevent the CD from automatically playing

Mouse

Like keyboards, the mouse can be directly connected to a mouse port, built into the keyboard as a piezoelectric control, or connected to the serial port or device on a USB port or hub.

After the mouse has been installed, you can adjust the characteristics of its action by changing the configuration on the Properties page of the Mouse applet in the Control Panel. Figure 3.12 shows a typical Mouse Properties page.

Using the Mouse applet you can select the mouse to be left-handed or right-handed, select double- or single-click to select objects, and set the speed at which a double-click is recognized.

You can also have the mouse pointer jump to the default dialog box or button, thereby requiring fewer mouse movements to make a selection. You can configure the mouse pointer to accelerate if you move the mouse faster. This results in the mouse pointer moving a longer distance with a quicker mouse movement than it would if you moved the mouse over the same distance but at a slower rate.

Windows 2000 Professional does not support the Intellipoint software because of conflicts with the new Power Management features. Windows 2000 Professional does, however, fully support

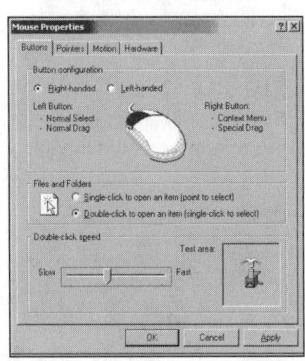

FIGURE 3.12
Setting mouse properties.

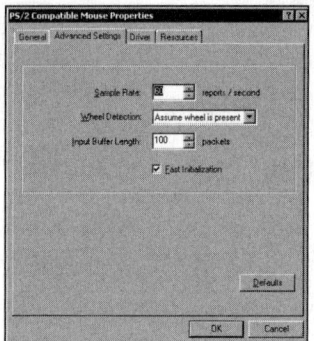

FIGURE 3.13
Advanced mouse properties.

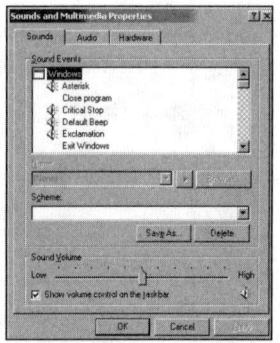

FIGURE 3.14
Sound configuration options in Sounds and Multimedia.

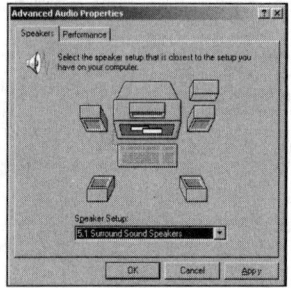

FIGURE 3.15
A complex speaker system setup.

the IntelliMouse wheel without any additional software. Windows 2000 Professional natively supports the positioning wheel found in many mouse devices. Figure 3.13 shows the Advanced Settings screen from the Mouse applet in Control Panel, showing the detection of a positioning wheel.

Multimedia

Categories of multimedia devices in Windows 2000 Professional include audio, video, and MIDI. In addition, the Microsoft Media Player can use the Web to access music files and radio stations that broadcast programming. The CD Player can be used to control the playback of music CDs from the system's CD-ROM drive.

Figure 3.14 shows the Sounds configuration page from the Sounds and Multimedia folder in the Control Panel.

This provides a mechanism to control the sounds used for specific events within Windows 2000 and many of its installed services (such as Netmeeting, MSN messaging, and Active Sync). You can also customize the sounds used for these events and save the configuration as a sound scheme.

The Speakers tab also allows you to specify the type of speaker system you have attached to your Windows 2000 Professional computer. This can vary from the simple to a five-speaker surround-sound setup (see Figure 3.15).

Smart Cards

Smart cards are programmable computing devices that are usually credit card-sized. Applications and data can be downloaded onto these cards for a variety of uses, including authentication, certificate storage, record keeping, and so on.

Although the processor included in the card can give it great capability, a smart card is not a stand-alone computer. It must be connected to other computers to be useful. Smart cards today contain an 8-bit micro-controller with 16KB or more of memory.

In the Windows 2000 operating system, smart cards and certificate-based logon are fully supported. In this architecture, the smart card contains the certificate and associated private key. When you are logging on to your Windows 2000 Professional computer, a challenge is sent to the smart card. The smart card signs the challenge with the private key, and the result, along with the certificate, is submitted to the authentication service. The authentication service verifies the signature and permits or denies the logon request.

To communicate with its host computer, a smart card must be placed in a smart card reader. The following procedure describes how to connect a smart card reader to your Windows 2000 Professional computer.

STEP BY STEP

3.8 Installing a Smart Card Reader

1. Shut down and turn off your computer.

2. Attach the smart card reader to an available serial port or insert it into an available PCMCIA slot.

3. If you are installing a serial reader and it has a supplemental cable, attach your keyboard or mouse connector to it and then connect the smart card reader to your keyboard or mouse port. Newer smart card readers use power from the keyboard or mouse port.

4. Boot your machine and log on.

5. If your smart card reader is a Plug and Play-compliant device, Windows 2000 Professional will automatically detect it and install the correct device drivers.

6. If your device is not Plug and Play-compliant, you will require a setup disk from the manufacturer and possibly the Windows 2000 Professional CDs to load the correct device drivers.

7. Click on Start, select Settings, and click on Control Panel.

8. Double-click on Administrative Tools.

9. Double-click on Computer Management.

10. Expand Services and Applications and click on Services.

continues

continued

11. Right-click on Smart Cards Resource Manager, select Properties, and choose Automatic from the Startup Option.

12. Click Start to start the Smart Card Resource Manager and click OK.

Cameras

Cameras are added by using the Scanners and Cameras Wizard found in the Control Panel. After installing the camera and connecting any cables required to your Windows 2000 Professional computer, you can use the following procedure to install a camera.

STEP BY STEP

3.9 Installing a Camera

1. Click Start, select Settings, and click Control Panel.

2. Double-click the Scanners and Cameras icon.

3. Click the Add button to start the Scanners and Cameras Installation Wizard.

4. Click Next to close the Welcome screen.

5. Select the manufacturer and device model that you are installing and click Next.

6. Select the port that you have installed your camera on and click Next.

7. Provide a name for the device and click Next.

8. Click Finish to complete the installation.

NOTE

Administrator Privileges You must be logged on with a user ID that has administrator privileges to complete the camera installation. If your camera supports Plug and Play, Windows 2000 Professional will detect it and install the correct drivers automatically.

Modems

Windows 2000 Professional supports many different brands of modems. To check whether the modem you are installing is supported, you can review the Hardware Compatibility list (HCL) on the Microsoft Web site (www.microsoft.com/hcl).

Modems are most commonly used to dial up remote systems or Internet service providers using speeds up to 56Kb over analog phone lines. Modems from different manufacturers achieve high-speed transmission by using a variety of techniques (some of which are proprietary to that company). Compatibility problems between these different methods can cause your modem to drop to a lower speed in search of a compatible transmission technique.

Installing Modems

The following procedure will allow you to install a new modem into your Windows 2000 Professional computer.

STEP BY STEP

3.10 Installing a Modem

1. Click Start, select Settings, and click Control Panel.

2. Click Phone and Modem options and select the Modems tab.

3. Click Add to start the Add/Remove Hardware Wizard.

4. If your modem supports Plug and Play click Next to allow Windows 2000 Professional to detect any new hardware.

5. If your modem is not detected automatically, click on Don't Detect My Modem and click Next.

6. Select the manufacturer and model of modem you have installed and click Next.

7. Select the port you have installed your modem on and click Next to start the modem installation.

8. Click Finish to complete the modem setup.

Troubleshooting Modem Installations

The following are some troubleshooting suggestions when you run into problems while installing a new modem:

◆ **Turn on external modems.** Plug and Play-compliant devices may not be detected correctly if they are not powered on.

◆ **Check the manufacturer's Web site.** The modem manufacturer may have new installation files (.INF files) available online.

◆ **Use diagnostics.** By selecting your new modem (after installation and setup), clicking on Properties, and selecting the Diagnostics tab, you can query the modem and view log files.

◆ **Check hardware settings.** Typical settings for a modem are 8 data bits, no parity, and 1 stop bit. An alternate (and older) configuration is 7 bits, even parity, and 1 stop bit.

◆ **Use the Add/Remove Hardware Wizard.** If you install an internal modem card or PCMCIA modem card that is not Plug and Play-compatible, you may need to configure its internal COM port using the Add/Remove Hardware Wizard in the Control Panel.

Infrared Data Association (IrDA) Devices

Windows 2000 Professional supports the IrDA protocols enabling data transfer over infrared connections. The Windows 2000 Professional Plug and Play architecture will automatically detect and install the IrDA components for computers with built-in IrDA hardware (most laptops, for example, will have an infrared port somewhere). For computers that do not have built-in infrared ports, you can attach a serial IrDA device to a COM port or connect one using a USB port or hub.

Most laptops now ship with IrDA ports that provide either 115Kbps or 4Mbps transmission speeds. Figure 3.16 shows the properties page of the IrDA port where the maximum speed of the port is configured.

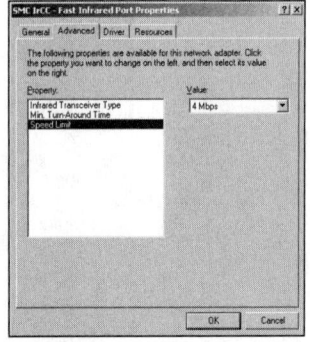

FIGURE 3.16
The Infrared device property page.

The most common implementation of the infrared ports on portable computers is the Serial IrDA (SIR) standard. This is a half-duplex system with a maximum transmission speed of 115Kbps. It will adjust to accommodate lower speed devices. This standard provides short-range infrared asynchronous serial connections with 8 bits of data, no parity, and 1 stop bit.

There is a high-speed extension (FIR) that supports half-duplex connections at 4Mbps. This standard is commonly installed on new devices and can communicate with existing lower-speed devices. In a device that is half-duplex, communications cannot go in both directions at once. Access to the line is signaled, and control of the communications link will flip back and forth between one device and the other. This turnaround does take some time to happen, so if many small messages are being sent, full duplex (even at a slower speed) may be more efficient. The high-speed half-duplex connections are best for devices that are transmitting data in bulk (such as cameras or scanners).

Installing Infrared Devices

Most internal IrDA devices will be installed automatically by Windows 2000 Professional setup or when you reboot your computer after adding an IrDA device.

The following procedure shows you how to install a new infrared serial transceiver.

STEP BY STEP

3.11 Installing an Infrared Device

1. Click on Start, select Settings, and click on Control Panel.

2. Double-click on the Add/Remove Hardware icon.

3. Click Next to close the Welcome page.

4. Select the Add/Troubleshoot a Device option and click Next.

continues

continued

5. In the Choose a Hardware Device window, select Add a New Device and click Next.

6. Select No, I Want to Select the Hardware from a List option and click Next.

7. In the Hardware Types window, select Infrared Devices and click Next.

8. Select the manufacturer and model of the device you are installing and click Next.

9. Click Finish to complete the installation.

> **N O T E**
>
> **Configuring IrDA Devices** You can change the infrared device properties by using Device Manager. Select the General tab to determine whether the device is working correctly. The Advanced tab will display other properties, including maximum transmission speed, that you can view or change.

Wireless Devices

The Wireless Link file transfer program, infrared printing functions, and image transfer capability are installed by default with your Windows 2000 Professional operating system. In addition, IrDA supports Winsock API calls to support programs created by other software and hardware manufacturers. The Winsock API calls can be used to provide infrared connections to printers, modems, pagers, PDAs, electronic cameras, cell phones, and handheld computers.

In addition to sending or printing files, you can also set up network connections between two computers using the infrared port. This capability can be used to set up shared drives and work with files and folders from your laptop to a host computer.

If your computer comes with an infrared port or you have installed an infrared transceiver, Windows 2000 Professional will include an infrared port as a local port in the Add Printer Wizard dialog box. If you associate a printer with this port, Windows 2000 Professional will use the IrDA port (using a protocol called IrLPT) to transmit output to the printer. Figure 3.17 shows the point in the Add Printer Wizard dialog box where the infrared printer port can be selected.

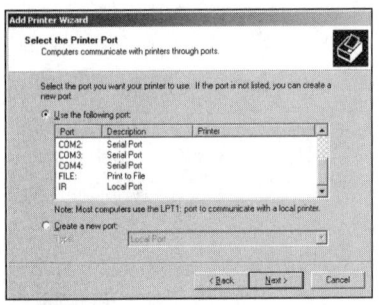

FIGURE 3.17
The infrared port is available for printing.

Linking Infrared Devices

Infrared links are established between two infrared devices. In any link, one device is considered to be primary and one secondary. This role is determined dynamically when the link is established and continues until the link is broken. Normally, any station can assume any role, so data transfer can be initiated from either side.

When communications are first established, the commanding station sends out a connection request at 9600bps. The responding station assumes the secondary role and returns information listing its capabilities. Both the primary and secondary stations then change the connection rate and link parameters to the common set established by this initial negotiation. With the connection established, data transfer is put under the control of the primary device.

A single IrDA device cannot link to more than one other IrDA device at a time. You can, however, install multiple IrDA devices to COM ports or USB hubs to provide simultaneous links to multiple remote devices. For example, you can have a desktop computer connect to a notebook and a digital camera simultaneously using two IrDA transceivers.

The Winsock API does support multiple simultaneous connections over a single IrDA device. This allows different programs to use the infrared device to perform many tasks with the remote device. For example, your laptop can connect to a desktop device, share files, synchronize offline folders, and send and receive mail. Each task is controlled by a different program on the laptop; however, they all use the single connection over an IrDA device.

Printing to an Infrared Printer

Printing to an infrared-connected printer is much the same as printing to a locally connected printer. After you establish an infrared connection to the printer, Windows 2000 Professional automatically installs the printer onto your system. You may need to install the printer manually using the Add Printer Wizard if Plug and Play does not detect or install the new printer, or if you have installed the infrared transceiver to the COM port.

Infrared Network Connections

If your computer has a built-in infrared port or you have installed an infrared transceiver, you can create a direct connection to another computer using the infrared port. When Windows 2000 Professional detects an infrared port, it includes that information as an available connection using Network and Dial-up Connections. This enables you to map shared drives on your network (through a host computer) to your laptop.

> **NOTE**
>
> **Establish a Connection** Before printing to the infrared attached printer, you must always establish a connection first. You do that by aligning the IR "eyes" until the InfraRed connection icon appears in the taskbar.

To connect two computers using the infrared port, you must first create an infrared network connection on both computers. When you use the Network and Dial-Up Connections Wizard to create a network connection, you specify a local connection using the infrared port.

The following procedure can be used to create an infrared network connection.

STEP BY STEP

3.12 Creating an Infrared Network Connection

1. Click on Start, select Settings, and click on Control Panel.

2. Double-click on Network and Dial-Up Connections.

3. Double-click on Make New Connection.

4. Click Next to close the Network Connection Wizard Welcome page.

5. Select Connect Directly to Another Computer and click Next.

6. Select Host if this computer will receive dial-up connections, or Guest if it will be dialing out.

7. Click Next.

8. Under Select a Device, select Infrared Port and click Next.

9. To make this connection available for all profiles, select For All Users and click Next.

10. Enter the name of the connection and click Finish.

Universal Serial Bus (USB) Devices

The Universal Serial Bus (USB) is an external polled serial bus deployed in a star topology that allows you to connect high-speed, low-latency devices to your computer. The USB protocol runs at 1 to 12Mb/sec, and supports Plug and Play and power management. USB devices are hot-pluggable to allow you to add or change devices without restarting your Windows 2000 Professional computer. The higher speed and polling rate that USB performs provides better support for games, and the higher bandwidth provides better support for multimedia devices.

USB is a token-based protocol that Windows 2000 Professional polls to detect changes to the number and type of devices connected. A computer equipped with a USB port can support up to 127 devices attached simultaneously. This means you can have a scanner, printer, camera, mouse, keyboard, game controller, and speakers running simultaneously. Connecting this many devices to the USB port is accomplished using a USB hub (or set of USB hubs).

Hubs can be self-powered with an external power source or they can be bus-powered and get their power from the bus itself. The USB definition allows for a total of five tiers (that is, hubs attached to hubs) in a USB network. With the Windows 2000 Professional computer acting as the USB host, that leaves a total of four tiers (or network segments) for actual devices.

Figure 3.18 is a representation of the way that USB connections are depicted.

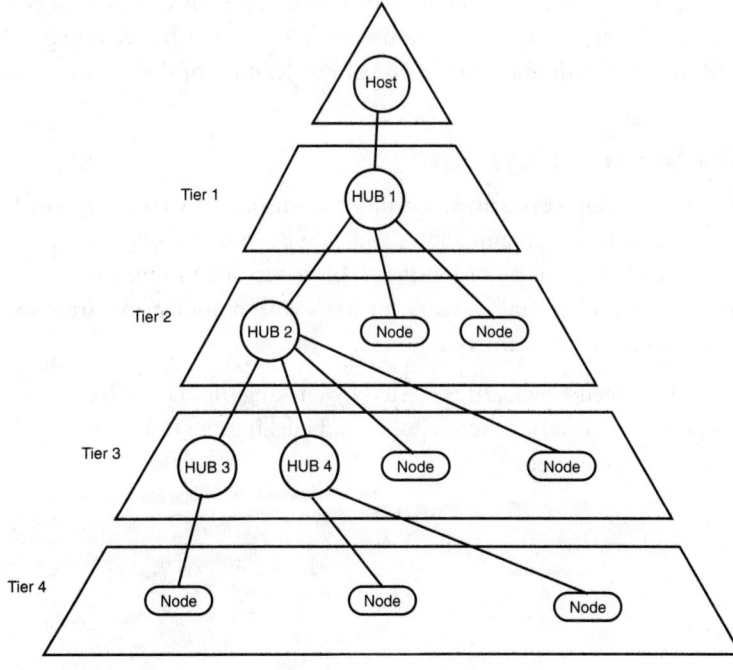

FIGURE 3.18
USB architecture.

There are a few restrictions on using a multi-tiered architecture. The following is a list of restrictions:

◆ Bus-powered hubs cannot be plugged into bus-powered hubs if a device is connected after the second hub that uses the full bandwidth of 12Mb/sec.

◆ Bus-powered hubs cannot have more than four downstream ports.

◆ Bus-powered hubs cannot support bus-powered devices that use more than 100 milliamps. Bus-powered hubs will, however, support self-powered devices.

◆ The hub cascade depth including the host computer cannot exceed five tiers.

Configuring Accessibility Options

If you have a motion-related disability, you can use Windows 2000 Professional to configure the keyboard and mouse to provide a more comfortable environment. The Keyboard applet in Control Panel contains configurations for people who use alternate keyboard layouts or type with one hand. The Mouse applet in Control Panel can be used to configure the mouse for left- or right-handed usage and to vary the double-click speed or acceleration of the pointer.

On Screen Keyboard

The On Screen Keyboard is a utility that displays a virtual keyboard on the display screen and allows you to type in data using a pointing device such as a mouse or joystick. This is intended to provide a minimum level of functionality for users with mobility impairments. It also works if you can't type.

The On Screen Keyboard is started by clicking on Start, selecting Programs, Accessories, Accessibility and clicking the On Screen Keyboard menu item.

The On Screen Keyboard has the following three modes for typing:

◆ **Clicking mode.** You click the onscreen keys to type in text.

◆ **Scanning mode.** The On Screen Keyboards continually scan the keyboard and highlight areas where you can type by pressing a hot key or using a joystick.

◆ **Hover mode.** You use a mouse or joystick to point to a key for a predefined period of time, and the selected character is automatically typed.

MouseKeys

Through the Accessibility Options applet in the Control Panel and by selecting the Mouse tab you can enable MouseKeys. This allows the numeric keyboard to move the cursor and provides for left- and right-clicking plus dragging and dropping. To perform these actions, try one of the following:

◆ To click, press 5 on your numeric keypad.

◆ To double-click, press the plus sign (+) on your numeric keypad.

◆ To right-click, press the minus sign (-) on your numeric keypad, and then press 5 to click, or press the plus sign (+) to double-click.

◆ To click as if you were using both mouse buttons at once, press the asterisk (*) on your numeric keypad, and then press 5 to click or use the plus sign (+) to double-click.

◆ To switch back to standard clicking, press slash (/) on your numeric keypad.

The mouse is also used in an additional accessibility option called Magnifier. This is a utility that makes the screen more readable if you have low vision. Magnifier creates a separate window that displays a magnified portion of your screen. The magnifier will track the mouse pointer as it moves on the screen, follow the keyboard focus, and follow text editing. Magnifier also provides the following functionality:

◆ You can change the magnification level.

◆ You can change the size of the magnification windows.

◆ You can change the position of the magnification windows on your desktop.

◆ You can invert the screen colors.

◆ You can set the contrast high.

MAINTAINING UPDATED DRIVERS

Update drivers.

Windows 2000 Professional provides a mechanism to automatically update device drives on your computer. The following procedure can be used to update a single device driver.

STEP BY STEP

3.13 Updating a Device Driver

1. Click Start, select Settings, and click Control Panel.

2. Double-click the System icon and select the Hardware tab.

3. Click the Device Manager button to display the list of devices by type.

4. Expand a device type to show the specific devices installed.

5. Right-click a specific device and select Properties.

6. Select the Driver tab and click the Update Driver button.

7. Click Next to close the Welcome page of the Update Device Driver Wizard.

8. Select the Search for a Suitable Driver for My Device button and click Next.

9. Click Next to start a search for an updated driver for this device. The search will be made on disk, on CD (if available), or at the Windows Update Web site.

Windows 2000 Professional provides an additional mechanism for updating all device drivers and software at once, rather than by individually addressing each device on your computer.

When using Windows Update, the hardware IDs for the devices installed are compared to what the Microsoft Web site has to offer. If an exact match is made, the new driver is downloaded and installed. If an update to an existing driver is found, the new software components will be listed in the Web site and a download button will load the updated drivers onto your Windows 2000 Professional computer into a temporary directory for installation.

The following procedure will update all the device drivers on your computer.

NOTE **Administrative Privileges** You must be logged in with a user ID that has administrative privileges to update device drivers. The permissions that your user ID requires will allow you to load and unload a driver, copy files to the system32\drivers directory, and write settings to the registry.

STEP BY STEP

3.14 Using Windows Update

1. Click Start and select Windows Update.

2. Click Products Updates on the Microsoft Windows Update Web page.

3. Select the components to download and click on the Download icon.

NOTE **Administrative Privileges** You must be logged in with a user ID that has administrative privileges. Your computer must also be connected to a network with access to the Internet. The first time you visit the Product Updates page you may be required to install additional software or controls.

MULTIPLE PROCESSOR MACHINES

Monitor and configure multiple processing units.

Windows 2000 Professional is designed to run uniformly on uniprocessors and symmetric multiprocessor platforms.

Windows 2000 Professional supports the addition of a second CPU. Support for multiprocessors has the following conditions:

◆ Both CPUs are identical and either have identical coprocessors or no coprocessors.

◆ Both CPUs can share memory and have uniform access to memory.

◆ Both CPUs can access memory, process interrupts, and access I/O devices.

Although the Windows 2000 Professional operating system has been designed for both uniprocessor and multiprocessor operations, if you originally installed Windows 2000 Professional on a computer with a single CPU, the Hardware Abstraction Layer (HAL) must be updated to use the additional CPU.

The following procedure will install support for multiple CPUs.

STEP BY STEP

3.15 Supporting Multiple CPUs

1. Click Start, select Settings, and click on Control Panel.

2. Double-click on the System icon and select the Hardware tab.

3. Click on the Device Manager button.

4. Expand the Computer item. Make note of the current CPU support.

5. Double-click on the computer type listed and select the Drivers table.

6. Click the Update Driver button and then click Next to close the Welcome screen of the Update Driver Wizard.

7. Select Display a List of Known Drivers for This Device and click on Show All Hardware of This Device Class.

8. Click on Next and then click Finish.

Monitoring Multiple CPUs

Scaling is the process of adding processors to your system to achieve greater throughput. CPU-intensive applications such as database servers, Web servers, and file and print servers will benefit from multiple CPUs. Applications such as scientific, financial, or CAD systems may also demand the power of multiple CPUs.

You can monitor the activity of your multiprocessor system by using the Performance Monitor counters and charts. The following factors are important when looking at the performance of multiple CPUs:

◆ **Processor utilization and queue length.** Your workload may be structured such that one CPU is overloaded.

◆ **Processor data.** Context switches and interrupts, for example, can provide information on the workload your system is handling.

◆ **Resource utilization information.** Disk, memory, and network components, for example, may indicate that your system requires an increase in the capacity of these resources.

Impact on Resources

Increasing the performance power of your computer will place additional strain on system resources. For example, sharing resources will increase memory latency. A multiprocessor system needs to lock out shared data to ensure data integrity, and locked shared data may result in contention for shared data structures. The synchronization mechanism used to lock shared structures increases the processor code path. As a rule of thumb, it may be necessary to increase other resources when adding additional processor resources.

Memory

It is recommended that you scale the amount of memory with the number of CPUs. For example, if your uniprocessor system required 64MB of memory, a dual-processor system will require 128MB of memory.

Disk and Networking

When adding processors to your system, it is generally necessary to increase the disk capacity and network capacity. This can mean replacing your disks with disks of higher rotational speed or by striping or mirroring some data disks. Networking components can be upgraded to intelligent interrupt pooling adapters that reduce the processor workload. Table 3.10 contains the Performance Monitor objects that are most useful in monitoring a system with multiple CPUs.

TABLE 3.10

PERFORMANCE MONITOR COUNTERS FOR MULTIPLE-CPU SYSTEMS

Counter	Description
Process: Thread Count	Shows the instantaneous value, not the average. You need to monitor this counter at various times to get an accurate picture of activity.
Processor: % DPC Time	Determines how much time the processor is spending processing Deferred Procedure Calls (DPCs). DPCs originate when the processor performs tasks requiring immediate attention (such as answering an interrupt request), and then defers the remainder of the task to be handled at lower priority. DPCs represent further processing of client requests.
Processor: % Interrupt Time	Determines how much time the processor is spending processing interrupts.
	If processor time is more than 90 percent and this value is greater than 15 percent, the processor is probably overloaded with interrupts.
Processor: DPCs Queued/Sec	Monitors the rate at which DPCs are queued on a particular processor.
Processor: Interrupts/Sec	Reflects the rate at which the processor is handling interrupts.

Counter	*Description*
System: Context Switches/Sec	Indicates that the kernel has switched the thread it is running on a processor. A context switch occurs each time a new thread runs or takes over from another. A large number of threads is likely to increase the number of context switches. Context switches allow multiple threads to share time slices on the processors, but they also interrupt the processor and might reduce overall system performance, especially on a multiprocessor. You should also observe the level of context switching over time.
System: System Calls/Sec	Monitors the frequency of calls to Windows 2000 Professional system service routines. These are the services exported to applications from the kernel.
Thread: % Processor Time	Monitors processor time usage by threads on the system.
Thread: Context Switches/Sec	Monitors context switches generated by individual threads.

NETWORK ADAPTERS

Install, configure, and troubleshoot network adapters.

If you install a new network adapter in your computer, the next time you start Windows 2000 Professional, a new local area connection icon appears in the Network and Dial-Up Connections folder. Plug and Play functionality finds the network adapter and creates a local area connection for it. By default, the local area connection is always activated. If your computer has more than one network adapter, a local area connection icon is displayed for each adapter in the Network and Dial-Up Connections folder.

The new network adapter is linked into the operating system by using Bindings. Windows 2000 Professional divides networks into several layers, each acting independently of the other. The bottom layer is the network adapter card and driver.

A binding is the process that links the network components on different layers. A component in a layer can be linked to multiple components in the layer just above or below. Figure 3.19 is an example of the network architecture and how bindings connect different components in different layers.

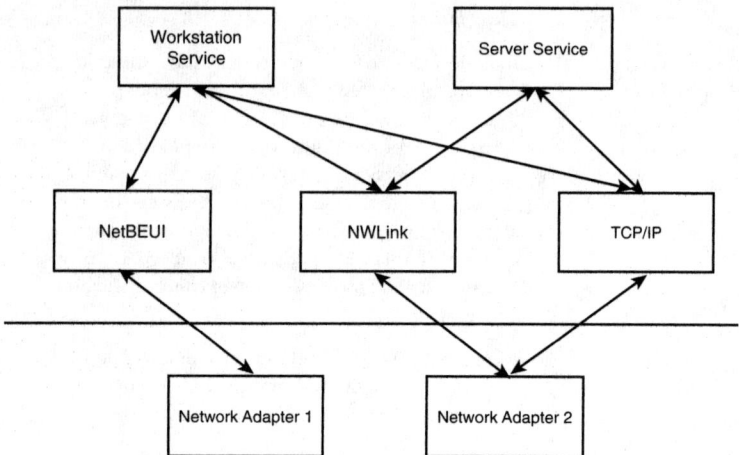

FIGURE 3.19
Network bindings.

In this example, the workstation service is bound to all possible protocols; however, the server service is only bound to the routable protocols (NWLink and TCP/IP). When configuring a network card, you assign protocols to it. The order in which these protocols are assigned can significantly improve the response you get from your network. If you have NWLink and TCP/IP traffic on your network, but your computer usually uses TCP/IP, moving that binding to the top of the list will provide better response overall. If you are connecting to a server, the server does not need to have the protocols ordered, just the Windows 2000 Professional workstation.

The following procedure allows you to modify the Network Binding order.

STEP BY STEP

3.16 Modifying the Network Binding Order

1. Click Start, select Settings, and click Control Panel.

2. Double-click Networking and Dial-Up Connections.

3. Select the Advanced tab and click on Advanced Settings.

4. Under Client for Microsoft Networks, click one of the protocols listed.

5. Click the Up Arrow or Down Arrow button.

6. Click OK and then close the Network and Dial-Up Connections window.

Installing a Network Adapter

In addition to checking the connection into the operating system, you can also view and change the characteristics of a network card itself from the Device Manager screen.

The following procedure allows you to view and modify Network Adapter options.

STEP BY STEP

3.17 Modifying Network Adapter Options

1. Click on Start, select Settings, and click on Control Panel.

2. Double-click on System.

3. Select the Hardware tab and click the Device Manager button.

4. Expand the Network Adapters entry and select a specific network adapter.

5. Right-click the network adapter and select Properties.

6. Select the Advanced tab to display the options available for your network adapter.

If you disconnect your local area connection, the connection will not be automatically activated. Because your hardware profile saves this setting, it can accommodate your requirement for differing devices at different locations. For example, if you travel to a remote sales office and use a separate hardware profile for that location that does not enable your local area connection, you do not waste time waiting for your network adapter to time out. The network adapter does not even try to connect.

By selecting the Advanced tab in Network and Dial-Up Connections and clicking on Advanced Settings, you can modify the order in which adapters are used by a connection and the associated clients, services, and protocols for the adapter.

Managing Network Adapters

Windows 2000 Professional creates a local area connection in the Network and Dial-Up Connections folder for each network adapter installed in your computer. You can eliminate possible confusion by renaming each local area connection to reflect the network it is connected to.

You must enable the network clients, services, and protocols that are required for your local area connections. When you do so, the client, service, or protocol is enabled in all other network and dial-up connections automatically.

You can create multiple dial-up, VPN, or direct connections by creating new ones with the wizard or by copying them in the Network and Dial-Up Connections folder. After you copy the connections, you can rename them and modify the connection settings.

CASE STUDY: THE AMARANTH ENGINEERING COMPANY

ESSENCE OF THE CASE

The following points summarize the essence of the case study:

▶ The back-end database has all the important files on one disk.

▶ The disk failed with no recent backup.

▶ Recovery to the previous night required the next day's data to be reentered.

SCENARIO

Although you work at an engineering company, your responsibility is to oversee the computer systems that support the company's work. In this case, you are analyzing the recent events of the company's accounting system. The company uses a commercial accounting system that uses a single server for a back-end database. This was installed over a year ago and has been working well. However, the database was installed with all the default settings, and a single large database file holding indexes and data was created. The transaction log files are also held on this main disk, and full backups are done each night. The incident you are reviewing involves a disk failure on the database disk late one afternoon last week. The disk was replaced, but the database needed to be recovered from the previous backup. No transaction logs are available to apply, and the entire day's work needs to be reentered. Your task is to prevent this from happening again.

ANALYSIS

This situation is quite a common one. An application system (in this case, an accounting application) uses a back-end database to store data and produce invoices and reports. Once all this is set up, there is a tendency to not revisit the initial configuration again until there is a problem.

Having the database tables and indexes on one disk is generally considered a potential disk performance bottleneck; however, the real problem comes when the previous night's backup

continues

CASE STUDY: THE AMARANTH ENGINEERING COMPANY

continued

is restored to disk. There are no transaction logs left to apply to the database in order to bring it up to the current time. With the database recovered to the previous night, all the day's transactions are lost.

The solution to this problem lies in using the disk management features of Windows 2000 Professional to create a fault-tolerant disk structure on the Windows 2000 Server to house the database and transaction logs. First, transaction logs should always be separated from the database tables since they are written sequentially and the database is accessed randomly. Because the transaction logs are usually only written and not read, they are best on mirrored volumes that are not striped. Striping divides the data across multiple spindles so that reading can proceed in a parallel fashion. If you are only writing to a file, this is not important.

The database tables, however, are read and written randomly. In an accounting application, it may seem that you are entering a great deal of data, but almost every field must be validated against existing data (customer name, address, existing invoice number, and so on); therefore, the database is read from much more than it is written to. Because of this, the database tables should be striped (to allow parallel reads) but configured as a striped mirror or RAID-5 structure to provide redundancy.

The combination of separating the transaction logs onto a mirrored set of disks, and the database files to a mirrored striped set of disks or a RAID-5 structure, reduces your system's vulnerability to single device failures in the future.

CHAPTER SUMMARY

This chapter focused on devices and drivers that you can add to your computer to customize it for your needs.

First, the Windows 2000 Professional implementation of Plug and Play was discussed, along with resources available in Windows 2000 Professional and ways of assigning them to devices. The new dynamic disk structures available were discussed, along with CD-ROM technology and removable storage.

Second, the new Windows 2000 Professional feature allowing multiple video displays was discussed, along with the procedures for configuring your virtual desktop.

Third, to support mobile computing, the card services and APM/ACPI features of Windows 2000 Professional were discussed, along with problems associated with these devices.

Fourth, the general I/O devices available for both the desktop and laptop computer were discussed. This includes keyboards, the mouse, printers, scanners, and cameras.

Fifth, the procedures for automatically updating device drivers on Windows 2000 Professional were discussed, along with the procedure for installing multiple CPUs into your computer and the performance characteristics you should measure when you do this.

Finally, the installation and troubleshooting of network adapters was discussed.

KEY TERMS

- Plug and Play
- Dynamic disks
- Simple volumes
- Spanned
- Striped
- RAID-5
- Mirrored
- Media pools
- Libraries
- Advanced Power Management (APM)
- Advanced Configuration and Power Interface (ACPI)
- IrDA devices
- USB devices

APPLY YOUR KNOWLEDGE

Exercises

3.1 Upgrading a Basic Disk to Dynamic

This exercise will go through the steps necessary to convert a basic disk with enough free space to support the dynamic volume database to a simple volume on a dynamic disk.

Estimated Time: 10 Minutes

1. Open Disk Management by clicking on Start, selecting Settings, Control Panel, Administrative Tools, Computer Management, and clicking on Disk Management.

2. Right-click on the disk you wish to convert to dynamic and select the Upgrade to Dynamic Disk menu option (see Figure 3.20).

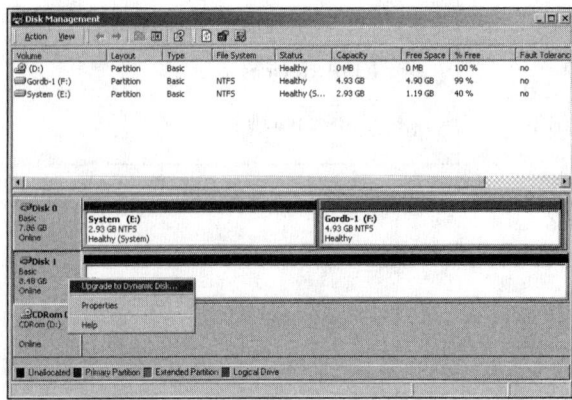

FIGURE 3.20
Selecting a basic disk for upgrade to dynamic.

3. Select the disk drive to upgrade and click OK.

4. Right-click the unallocated space on the new dynamic disk and select Create Volume.

5. Click Next to close the Welcome screen of the Create Volume Wizard.

6. Select the Simple Volume button and click Next.

7. Set the size of the volume to approximately one half of the available space on the dynamic disk and click Next.

8. Select Don't Assign a Drive Letter or Drive Path and click Next.

9. Check off Perform a Quick Format (for brevity) and click Next.

10. Click Finish to start the volume creation process.

3.2 Extending a Volume

This exercise will extend the volume created in the previous exercise to use the remaining disk space on the dynamic disk.

Estimated Time: 10 Minutes

1. Open Disk Management by clicking on Start, selecting Settings, Control Panel, Administrative Tools, Computer Management, and clicking on Disk Management.

2. Right-click on the disk volume you wish to expand and select Extend Volume.

3. Click Next to close the Welcome screen on the Extend Volume Wizard.

4. Select the amount of disk to use in extending the existing volume and click Next.

5. Click Finish to start the extension process.

APPLY YOUR KNOWLEDGE

3.3   Placing a Volume Under a Folder

This exercise will create an empty folder and then mount the volume created in the preceding exercises under that volume.

Estimated Time: 10 Minutes

1. Open Windows Explorer and create an empty folder under the system drive (C:).

2. Open Disk Management by clicking on Start, selecting Settings, Control Panel, Administrative Tools, Computer Management, and clicking on Disk Management.

3. Right-click on the volume to mount under the empty folder and select Change Drive Letter and Path.

4. Click on the Add button and choose the Mount in the NTFS Folder button.

5. Enter the path of the empty folder created in step 1 (or use Browse to locate it) and click Next.

6. Return to the Windows Explorer screen to see that the new folder is now associated with a disk icon.

3.4   Creating an RSM Media Pool

This exercise will walk through the steps to create a media pool using an Iomega ZIP device and two removable disk media.

Estimated Time: 20 Minutes

1. Open the Computer Management folder in Control Panel by clicking on Start, selecting Settings, Control Panel, Administrative Tools, and clicking on Computer Management.

2. Expand the Removable Storage item.

3. Insert the first blank disk into the Iomega ZIP device.

4. Right-click the physical device in Removable Storage and select Inject.

5. Select Next to close the Welcome screen of the Media Inject Wizard.

6. Wait for the inject process to finish and click on Finish.

7. Select the Iomega ZIP icon in the Import Media pool.

8. Right-click the new disk icon and select Properties.

9. Change the name of the disk to "Disk1" and click OK.

10. Right-click the Disk1 icon and select Prepare. (The disk will move from the Import Media pool to the Free Media pool.)

11. Right-click the Disk1 icon in the Free Media pool and select Eject. (Disk1 should now be part of the Offline Media Pool as well.)

12. Repeat steps 3–11 for a second disk, labeling it Disk2.

13. Right-click the Media Pool icon in Removable Storage of Computer Management and select Create Media Pool.

14. Name the new pool "Test" and select IOMega ZIP as the media type it contains.

15. Check the Draw Media from Free Media Pool and Return Media to Free Media Pool boxes and click OK.

APPLY YOUR KNOWLEDGE

16. Start a command prompt window and enter the command `RSM ALLOCATE /Mtest /Onew /LNBack1`.

17. Click OK on the Messenger Service window.

18. Load Disk1 into the Iomega ZIP device. (Disk1 will have moved from the Free Media pool to the Test Media pool.)

19. The disk can now be formatted using the sample command `format g:/FS:NTFS/V:Disk1` and mounted and dismounted using the commands `RSM MOUNT/LFBack1/Owrite` and `RSM DISMOUNT /LFBack1`. The device can be ejected using the command `RSM EJECT/PFDisk1/ASTART`.

3.5 Enabling Hibernation

This exercise will enable your system to go into hibernation depending on conditions within your computer.

Estimated Time: 5 Minutes

1. Open Power Options in Control Panel by clicking on Start, selecting Settings, Control Panel, and clicking on Power Options.

2. Select the Hibernate tab and select the Enable Hibernate Support check box.

3. Click Apply to set up Hibernation. (If Enable Hibernate is not available, your system does not support hibernation or there is not enough disk space available to support the process.)

4. Selecting the Power Schemes tab will allow you to set the time delays for blanking the monitor, spinning down hard drives, and putting the system on standby when under battery power.

3.6 Installing a USB Device and Measuring Power Used

This exercise will go through the steps to install a bus-powered USB device (a Microsoft IntelliMouse Optical) and then cover how to measure the power consumed.

Estimated Time: 10 Minutes

1. Unplug any existing mouse currently connected to your Windows 2000 Professional computer.

2. Plug in the Microsoft IntelliMouse Optical mouse to a USB port on your computer.

3. Wait until the Found New Hardware window closes (it should find a Microsoft IntelliMouse Optical and a USB Human Interface Device). The new optical mouse should now function.

4. Click on Start, select Settings, and click on Control Panel.

5. Double-click on Administrative Tools.

6. Double-click on Computer Management, then click on Device Manager.

7. In the right window expand the Universal Serial Bus Controllers item.

8. Right-click on USB Root Hub and select Properties.

9. Select the Power tab. You should see a device on the hub identified as an HID-compliant mouse using a total of 100mA.

APPLY YOUR KNOWLEDGE

3.7 Transferring Files Using a Wireless Connection

This exercise will walk through the steps necessary to set up a connection and transfer files between computers using a wireless (IrDA) connection.

Estimated Time: 10 Minutes

1. Click Start, select Settings, Control Panel, and double-click on Wireless Link.

2. Select the File Transfer tab and check the Display an Icon on the Taskbar Indicating Infrared Activity check box.

3. Click OK to close the Wireless Link window.

4. Reposition the two infrared transceiver windows until the Infrared icon appears on the taskbar.

5. Click on the Infrared icon on the taskbar.

6. In the Wireless Link dialog box, select the files you want to send and click Send.

7. You can also send files using the IRFTP program started from Start/Run or any command prompt.

Review Questions

1. After you change the resources your non-Plug and Play video adapter uses in Device Manager, the system will not boot correctly. What is wrong?

2. Your application currently uses logical disks on which to store some of its data. The application needs to reference these logical devices using drive letters. You have converted your system to use dynamic disks and would like to organize these files into a subdirectory. Will your application be able to read its data? Why or why not?

3. What devices does RSM manage on a typical desktop computer?

4. You have a laptop that you have configured with multiple display adapters while it is in its docking bay. When you boot your laptop, the multiple displays do not work correctly. What is the reason?

5. When you installed Windows 2000 Professional, you noticed that Advanced Power Management (APM) was not enabled. After you enable APM, you find that your system will not boot correctly. What is the reason?

6. You install a new high-speed modem that the salesman said would run at 56Kb. When you dial up to your Internet Service Provider (ISP), you find you can't get as much speed as you expected. What is the reason?

7. You have just purchased a new desktop computer that has Windows 2000 Professional already installed on it. You want to ensure that the latest device drivers available are installed and the drivers are all signed. What is your most efficient course of action?

8. You are using Performance Monitoring to display how busy your computer is. You note that the CPU is at 100% utilized for extended periods of time. What other performance variable should you chart to help you decide if adding an additional CPU would help the throughput of your system?

APPLY YOUR KNOWLEDGE

9. Your business has a network that uses both IPX and IP for data communications, but your Windows 2000 Professional computer uses IP almost exclusively. How should you configure your network connections to reflect this usage?

Exam Questions

1. You are the system administrator with a small engineering firm. You look after all the application and database systems.

   You have three applications that all share a common database server. The database supports many transactional systems for the company. The server is running Windows 2000 Advanced Server and has five large disk drives.

   You have been tasked with the job of recommending a new configuration to minimize system downtime in case of disk hardware failure.

   Required Result:

   You must protect the application data from loss when a disk fails.

   Optional Desired Results:

   You should configure the disks to give the best performance.

   You should allow the disk system to grow with additional activity.

Proposed Solution:

Split the disk structure into two logical sections: a basic disk system for the Windows 2000 operating system and a dynamic disk supporting the database tables and logs. You make the dynamic disks part of a RAID-5 structure.

Which result(s) does the proposed solution produce?

A. The proposed solution produces the required result and produces all of the optional desired results.

B. The proposed solution produces the required result and produces only one of the optional desired results.

C. The proposed solution produces the required result but does not produce any of the optional desired results.

D. The proposed solution does not produce the required result.

2. You are the system administrator with a small engineering firm. You look after all the application and database systems.

   You have three applications that all share a common database server. The database supports many transactional systems for the company. The server is running Windows 2000 Advanced Server and has five large disk drives.

   You have been tasked with the job of recommending a new configuration to minimize system downtime in case of disk hardware failure.

APPLY YOUR KNOWLEDGE

Required Result:

You must protect the application data from loss when a disk fails.

Optional Desired Results:

You should configure the disks to give the best performance.

You should allow the disk system to grow with additional activity.

Proposed Solution:

Split the disk structure into three logical sections: a basic disk system for the Windows 2000 operating system, a dynamic disk supporting the database tables, and a separate dynamic disk supporting the transaction logs. You make the dynamic disks supporting the database files part of a RAID-5 structure and the dynamic disk supporting the transaction logs part of a mirrored disk structure.

Which result(s) does the proposed solution produce?

A. The proposed solution produces the required result and produces all of the optional desired results.

B. The proposed solution produces the required result and produces only one of the optional desired results.

C. The proposed solution produces the required result but does not produce any of the optional desired results.

D. The proposed solution does not produce the required result.

3. You are responsible for maintaining online copies of graphical images used by an application program. These images need to be available all the time; however, you have no idea how much storage space will be needed. How should you configure storage on your computer?

A. Connect a tape drive to your computer and save the image files to tape when your disk fills.

B. Add additional disks to your computer when storage space runs low and use Disk Management to create a spanned volume.

C. Compress the images and place them in .ZIP files.

D. Create a RAID-5 disk structure on a Windows 2000 Server and store the images there.

4. You are the applications expert at an engineering firm.

You are attempting to install multiple display adapters to your Windows 2000 Professional workstation to enhance your CAD application.

You are at the point in the process when you are about to extend the virtual desktop to the new display, but Windows 2000 Professional has grayed out the check box, indicating that it cannot use the device.

What should be your first debugging step?

A. Run the application full screen.

B. Confirm that the video adapter is supported as a secondary display.

APPLY YOUR KNOWLEDGE

C. Confirm that the secondary display is detected.

D. Run the application on the primary screen.

5. You have an application that performs an analysis of statistical data captured by your engineering firm. To do this analysis, your application reads and writes a large number of temporary files to disk. You wish to provide the best throughput possible for this temporary information, but you do not need to provide any fault tolerance. What should you do?

A. Create a spanned volume across several disks.

B. Create a striped volume across several disks.

C. Create a RAID-5 structure on a Windows 2000 Server and store the temporary files there.

D. Create a single large volume named \TEMP and direct your application to store its temporary files there.

6. You are the local business lead for your department and are considered the local IT expert and the person people go to for help before involving the company's help desk.

Your new desktop standard includes APM support in the BIOS.

You have enabled APM on several pilot machines in your department to see what the effect is on the systems and applications your group runs. You configure APM and try a suspend and resume. The video display does not restart after the resume.

What is the problem?

A. The BIOS timeout for video blanking is enabled and resume does not restore the video configuration correctly.

B. The timeout value for the screen saver to blank the video elapsed while the suspend was in place. When resume restarts the system, the screen immediately will blank out until a mouse movement or keyboard entry restarts it.

C. The video adapters found in the desktop system cannot normally be corrected by suspend. When resume restores the system, the video is not restarted.

D. Suspend will save the video configuration correctly, but resume will not restore it if the APM is enabled in the BIOS.

7. You are visiting one of your company's remote customer offices and need to transfer some files from your laptop to a local machine. For security reasons you do not want to join your customer's domain, but you still need to transfer the files. What should you do?

A. Create a null modem cable and transfer the files via FTP.

B. Create a crossover network cable and copy the files via command line or Windows Explorer drag and drop.

C. Align the machines' IrDA ports and copy the files using the wireless link.

D. Connect to your ISP host and copy the files to the customer's Web site using FTP.

APPLY YOUR KNOWLEDGE

8. You have a small network installed at your home office and are installing a new printer.

   The printer is attached to a Windows 2000 Server on your network.

   You wish to share the printer with the other systems you use. You have installed the printer with the driver provided by the manufacturer, but you can't get anything to print from the other Windows 2000 Professional workstations you use.

   When you open the Printer icon on the task bar you see Opening as the status but nothing is ever printed.

   What is the first thing you need to check?

   A. The share permissions are not correct for this printer.

   B. The server does not have enough disk space for the spooling operation and the printer will not initialize.

   C. The driver is incorrect or out of date and should be updated.

   D. The printer is jammed and will not initialize until the problem is cleared and the printer comes back online.

9. As the system administrator, you set the policy on the configuration of new computer hardware purchased for the company. You decide that, for flexibility, you will have all the disk storage devices for new Windows 2000 Professional computers configured as simple volumes. When you configure this on a new laptop you find that the option to do the conversion from basic to dynamic disks is not present. What is your course of action?

   A. Make sure you purchase disk drives that support being dynamic disks.

   B. Amend your policy to allow laptops to remain configured with basic disks.

   C. Manually fix the DMA, I/O, and IRQ resources used by the disk drive rather than letting Plug and Play choose them.

   D. The disk drives cannot be made dynamic until a small partition is created at the end of the device.

10. You are setting up a computer system to be used in displaying CAD output in a lecture theater. You have already set up the nine display devices and are now ready to install the computer system to drive them. What is your course of action?

    A. Install Windows 2000 Professional and then install the display adapters.

    B. Install the display adapters and then install Windows 2000 Professional.

    C. Disable the built-in AGP-compliant video adapter.

    D. Turn off the built-in video adapter after the system is set up.

11. You are a local expert in a department of financial analysts.

    Some of the financial models you and your staff run are very computer-intensive. They use a common network server for the model. You have several machines in your group that are running at 100% CPU usage for extended periods of time.

APPLY YOUR KNOWLEDGE

Required Result:

You need to increase the amount of CPU available for these systems.

Optional Desired Results:

You should ensure that the system does not develop any other bottlenecks.

You should ensure that the workload is utilizing the system resources correctly.

Proposed Solution:

You add a CPU to the system.

You replace the network adapter with an intelligent device that supports interrupt pooling.

Which result(s) does the proposed solution produce?

A. The proposed solution produces the required result and produces all of the optional desired results.

B. The proposed solution produces the required result and produces only one of the optional desired results.

C. The proposed solution produces the required result but does not produce any of the optional desired results.

D. The proposed solution does not produce the required result.

12. You are a local expert in a department of financial analysts.

Some of the financial models you and your staff run are very computer-intensive. They use a common network server for the model. The machines in your group are running at 100% CPU usage for extended periods of time.

Required Result:

You need to increase the amount of CPU available for these systems.

Optional Desired Results:

You should ensure that the system does not develop any other bottlenecks.

You should ensure that the workload is utilizing the system resources correctly.

Proposed Solution:

You add a CPU to the system.

You replace the disk subsystem with devices that have a higher rotational speed.

You replace the network card with an intelligent device that supports interrupt pooling.

You monitor the processor queue length in the Performance Monitor to make sure your workload does not overwork one of the CPUs.

Which result(s) does the proposed solution produce?

A. The proposed solution produces the required result and produces all of the optional desired results.

B. The proposed solution produces the required result and produces only one of the optional desired results.

C. The proposed solution produces the required result but does not produce any of the optional desired results.

D. The proposed solution does not produce the required result.

APPLY YOUR KNOWLEDGE

13. You have installed an infrared printer on your desktop for use with your laptop. When you first go to use the printer you find that you cannot connect to it. What is your first step in troubleshooting this problem?

    A. You should manually adjust the speed of the ports to the manufacturer's specifications.

    B. Check that the Infrared ports are aligned and you have a connection icon on the taskbar.

    C. The device driver must be verified and upgraded to the latest available.

    D. Check to make sure you have administrative privileges; you must have them the first time you access the printer in order to correctly install the printer driver.

14. You are an analyst working with the desktop support group. You are responsible for configuring new desktop machines according to the company standards.

    You install all protocols used in the company and bind them to all adapters.

    Several Windows 2000 Professional users have complained that their machines do not connect to network resources very quickly. You want to improve access to network resources with the minimum reconfiguration necessary.

    Required Result:

    You must improve the performance of the network configuration for the new machines.

    Optional Desired Results:

    You should ensure that the system is using the network resources efficiently.

You should ensure that the system does not develop any other bottlenecks.

Proposed Solution:

You review the binding order and make the most common connections first in the list.

Which result(s) does the proposed solution produce?

A. The proposed solution produces the required result and produces all of the optional desired results.

B. The proposed solution produces the required result and produces only one of the optional desired results.

C. The proposed solution produces the required result but does not produce any of the optional desired results.

D. The proposed solution does not produce the required result.

15. You are an analyst working with the desktop support group. You are responsible for configuring new desktop machines according to the company standards.

    You install all protocols used in the company and bind them to all adapters.

    Several Windows 2000 Professional users have complained that their machines do not connect to network resources very quickly. You want to improve access to network resources with the minimum reconfiguration necessary.

    Required Result:

    You must improve the performance of the network configuration for the new machines.

APPLY YOUR KNOWLEDGE

Optional Desired Results:

You should ensure that the system is using the network resources efficiently.

You should ensure that the system does not develop any other bottlenecks.

Proposed Solution:

You review the binding order and make the most common connections first in the list.

You run Performance Monitoring to see if the network device is causing a high rate of interrupts to the CPU. If it is, you plan to replace the adapter with an intelligent network adapter that supports interrupt pooling.

You run Performance Monitoring to baseline the performance characteristics of the system to track the impact that any networking changes have on the rest of the system.

Which result(s) does the proposed solution produce?

A. The proposed solution produces the required result and produces all of the optional desired results.

B. The proposed solution produces the required result and produces only one of the optional desired results.

C. The proposed solution produces the required result but does not produce any of the optional desired results.

D. The proposed solution does not produce the required result.

Answers to Review Questions

1. Non-Plug and Play devices are not detected by Windows 2000 Professional and therefore their requirements as far as the Device Manager are concerned are unknown. By manually configuring the resources used, you have told Windows 2000 Professional which resources to reserve for your device. You now need to reconfigure the device by using the manufacturer-supplied configuration program or by manually selecting onboard switches or jumpers. See "Implementing, Managing, and Troubleshooting Hardware Devices and Drivers."

2. Dynamic disks can be accessed using an assigned drive letter as well as a path. If, however, you are going to reorganize your files into subdirectories, your only access is via the path. Your application that expects to use drive letters will not be able to access its data. See "Fixed Disks."

3. Removable Storage Manager (RSM) manages all devices that can be removed or replaced with other media. This includes tape drives, CD-ROM and DVD-ROM drives, and JAZ and ZIP drives. RSM can handle any removable device except A: and B:. See "Removable Media."

4. One of the rules for using multiple displays on your Windows 2000 Professional computer is that the primary display cannot be turned off. When you insert a laptop into its docking station, the display is usually disabled. This prevents the multiple display system from functioning. See "Troubleshooting Multiple Displays."

APPLY YOUR KNOWLEDGE

5. If APM was installed but not enabled, Windows 2000 Professional has not found your system in its list of systems on which APM is unsafe to run. It also has not found your system in its list of APM safe systems. Thus, it considers your system to be APM-neutral. When you enabled APM, you discovered that your system should have been placed on the APM unsafe list since it has destabilized your computer. See "When to Use APM."

6. Modems get their speed from various compression techniques. The faster the modem, the more elaborate the compression techniques. Unfortunately, these methods are not always compatible and, when connecting to an ISP, your system has negotiated a lower speed to where both devices agree on the compression methods being used. See "Modems."

7. The most efficient way to ensure that you have the latest device drivers installed on your system and that these drivers have been signed is to use the Windows Update option directly from the Start menu. This will canvas the Microsoft Web site for the latest signed version of drivers for your system and allow you to download them for installation. See "Maintaining Updated Drivers."

8. The other variable to chart would be the Processor Queue Length. A busy processor may be handling the workload very efficiently, or it could be overwhelmed by the workload. In that case, the backlog of work waiting to be done by the CPU would be building. This situation is identified by the processor queue length, or the number of tasks that are ready to execute if there were enough CPU resources available. See "Monitoring Multiple CPUs."

9. The priority of the protocols used by your Windows 2000 Professional computer is reflected in the binding order. By moving TCP/IP to the top of the list and lowering IPX below it, you can significantly improve the response you get from your network. See "Managing Network Adapters."

Answers to Exam Questions

1. **B.** The solution provides for fault tolerance when one disk drive fails. RAID-5 will protect you from a single device failure. (Mirrors allow 50% of the devices to fail provided that the two disks that make up the mirror do not fail together.) The dynamic disks that make up a RAID-5 structure allow additional disks to be added without interrupting the application. Earlier versions of RAID-5 required you to unload and restructure the disks, and reload the data; however, newer hardware-enabled RAID-5 does not require it. The system is still not optimal because both the applications data and the transaction logs are on the same disk. This reduces the fault tolerance and does not give the best performance possible because transaction logs are only written sequentially. Writing to a RAID-5 device is slower than other fault-tolerant solutions. See "RAID-5 Volumes."

2. **A.** The solution provides for fault tolerance when one disk drive fails. RAID-5 protects you from a single device failure. (Mirrors allow 50% of the devices to fail provided that the two disks that make up the mirror do not fail together.) The dynamic disks that make up a RAID-5 structure allow additional disks to be added without interrupting the application. Earlier versions of

APPLY YOUR KNOWLEDGE

RAID-5 required you to unload and restructure the disks and reload the data; however, newer hardware-enabled RAID-5 does not require it. Separating the transaction logs to a mirrored disk structure provides additional fault tolerance and provides the best performance. Transaction logs are only written sequentially and would benefit best from a mirrored fault-tolerant disk structure over other fault-tolerant configurations. See "Raid-5 Volumes."

3. **B.** The solution calls for online storage but there is no performance requirement mentioned. The application that uses the image files will not be able to find them if the images are rolled out to tape. Although this solution provides for all the images to be available, manual intervention would be required to load needed images back to disk. Likewise, most applications would not be able to extract a file from a ZIP library, and creating a RAID-5 structure provides more fault tolerance and I/O performance than is requested. The most efficient solution would be to create a dynamic disk with a simple volume and span that volume to additional disk devices when space runs low. This allows the images to appear to be available from one location even though that may span several disks. See "Spanned Volumes."

4. **B.** The first thing to check is whether the device to which you are trying to extend is actually supported as a secondary display. You can assume that if the display adapter is listed in Device Manager, it has been detected successfully. Running the application in full-screen mode or on the primary display are steps that you would take if you were having problems running the application on multiple screens. In this case, you have not gotten that far in the process yet. See "Multiple Display Support."

5. **B.** The problem requires better throughput on disk for data that is not going to be stored. There is no requirement for a fault-redundant RAID-5 configuration. Likewise, providing a single large volume or a spanned volume would not give the same performance as a striped volume. A striped volume will write 64KB blocks to each disk in rotation. This will have the effect of spreading the I/O load across all drives evenly. See "Striped Volumes."

6. **C.** The problem with using APM on the desktop is that most video adapters used here are not expecting to be powered down (since that is more often a requirement of mobile systems). Suspend cannot correctly save the configuration, and therefore resume has nothing to reload and restart. See "Power Management."

7. **C.** The easiest solution uses the built-in capabilities of Windows 2000 Professional. The built-in IrDA ports can transfer data at a rate up to 4Mb per second. This would be far faster and easier than using the COM port or built-in modem. See "Infrared Network Connections."

8. **A.** A problem that shows up as Opening or Unable to Connect is probably a permissions problem. This would be caused by not configuring the share permissions on the server or by not having access to the server. See "Printers."

9. **B.** Windows 2000 does not support dynamic disks on laptops, so your policy must be changed to reflect that. Neither Plug and Play nor the type of disk defines whether it can be dynamic. The "dynamic" part of dynamic disks refers to the storage structures created on the device, not the device itself. Finally, the Disk Management application will automatically reserve space at the end of the disk for its

APPLY YOUR KNOWLEDGE

database when converting a basic disk to dynamic. See "Upgrading Basic Disks to Dynamic Disks."

10. **A.** Windows 2000 Professional must be completely installed before you add any additional devices for a virtual desktop. There would be no reason to disable a built-in adapter that is AGP-compliant because that is one of the accepted standards for multiple displays on Windows 2000 Professional. Once the virtual desktop has been established, you cannot turn off the first adapter since it forms the anchor point for the displays. See "Multiple Display Support."

11. **C.** Adding a CPU to the overloaded systems will improve response in that area. Changing one component always has some impact on the rest of the resource usage in the system. Improving the network resource and reducing the number of interrupts it generates will reduce bottlenecks on the network; however, the CPU also consumes memory and disk resources that have not been addressed. See "Monitoring Multiple CPUs."

12. **A.** Adding an additional CPU provides more computing power but it will have an impact on other resources in the system. By providing reduced network interrupts, higher rotational speed disks, and, most importantly, additional physical memory, you have guaranteed that by adding a CPU you have not just shifted the bottleneck to the next most scarce resource. See "Monitoring Multiple CPUs."

13. **B.** The most obvious problem is misalignment of the IR eyes. To print to an infrared printer, you must first establish a connection. As soon as this is done, the printer should start to install (if it supports Plug and Play). User privilege is enough to install printer devices. The protocol used to connect to IR devices will automatically negotiate the correct speed during initialization. See "Printing to an Infrared Printer."

14. **C.** The Windows 2000 Professional workstation will attempt to access a network resource in the order the bindings appear. The solution, however, does not address any performance problem within the network devices themselves and does not address any system bottlenecks created by networking. See "Managing Network Adapters."

15. **A.** The Windows 2000 Professional workstation will attempt to access a network resource in the order in which the bindings appear. By charting the performance of the network components, you can address any system slowdown caused by network-generated interrupts. Changing the network adapter to a newer intelligent adapter that supports interrupt pooling will alleviate some performance problems if they occur, and baselining the performance of the entire system will allow you to track the impact of the configuration changes you are making. See "Managing Network Adapters."

APPLY YOUR KNOWLEDGE

Suggested Readings and Resources

1. *MCSE Training Kit: Upgrading to Windows 2000.* Microsoft Press, 2000.

2. *Microsoft Windows 2000 Professional: Step by Step.* Microsoft Press, 2000.

3. Joyce, Jerry, and Marianne Moon. *Microsoft Windows 2000 Professional at a Glance.* Microsoft Press, 2000.

This chapter helps you prepare for the MCSE Windows 2000 Professional exam by covering the following objectives:

Manage and troubleshoot driver signing.

▶ One of the areas in earlier versions of Windows that has caused support problems is the area of device drivers. To that end Microsoft has developed a rigorous driver testing program to ensure that device drivers function correctly. Providing digital signatures of the binary code being installed guarantees that it has passed these tests. Managing the policy that governs these checks can have significant impact on the stability of your system.

Configure, manage, and troubleshoot the Task Scheduler.

▶ The Windows 2000 Task Scheduler can be used to schedule programs and batch files to run at regular intervals or specific times. You can also have Task Scheduler execute programs or scripts when certain operating system events occur. Using Task Scheduler to periodically run maintenance tasks or when some problem occurs can improve your system's stability.

Manage and troubleshoot the use and synchronization of offline files.

▶ The increase in the use of laptop computers indicates the need for access to information when you are traveling and without a network connection. With offline files, you can continue to access network files and programs when you are not connected to the network, and automatically save the changes you make to your files the next time you reconnect to your network.

CHAPTER 4

Monitoring and Optimizing System Performance and Reliability

Optimize and troubleshoot performance of the Windows 2000 Professional desktop.

- **Optimize and troubleshoot memory performance.**

- **Optimize and troubleshoot processor utilization.**

- **Optimize and troubleshoot disk performance.**

- **Optimize and troubleshoot network performance.**

- **Optimize and troubleshoot application performance.**

▶ The performance monitoring subsystem in Windows 2000 provides a comprehensive array of indicators from within various areas of the operating system. Monitoring disk performance, memory usage, application-assigned resources, and network activity can enhance the performance of your system.

Manage hardware profiles.

▶ Hardware profiles allow you to tailor the devices that start up when you power on your computer based on the configuration you have available. This is particularly useful when your system is a laptop and may have a docked configuration that includes other external devices and network adapters. Being able to configure and invoke various hardware configurations will optimize the system based on use.

Recover systems and user data.

- **Recover systems and user data by using Windows Backup.**

- **Troubleshoot system restoration by using Safe Mode.**

- **Recover systems and user data by using the Recovery Console.**

▶ The ultimate goal of backing up your system and data files is the recovery of all your data in the event of a hardware or software failure. Your system may contain company-specific information and/or personal information. In either case, the data may not be reproducible without a good backup/restore procedure. Being able to recover your system regardless of the type and extent of the failure will significantly improve the reliability of your computer.

► You can expect a number of questions related to maintaining or increasing the performance of the disk, memory, and network subsystems of your Windows 2000 Professional computer. Many of these will be in scenario format, where the causes of a performance problem will be related to more than one factor. The author's suggestion is to first understand the important counters maintained within the Performance Monitor system and be able to relate changes in those counters to events happening in the computer. Once you have a solid understanding of the theory presented here, you should work with your Windows 2000 Professional system to see firsthand the impact of varying the availability of resources on system response. Look to the resource kits to provide tools to strain the resources of your computer at various points (high memory consumption, memory leaks, high CPU usage, excessive network activity) that will allow you to gain some practical experience with reading performance data.

► You should also expect scenario questions on both recovering a system using some options from the safe boot menu (Recovery Console and using the last known good configuration) and saving and restoring data using backup. In the latter, you can expect questions where the backup method is not wisely chosen and can be optimized to better suit the users' needs. Understanding the options available and the impact that one style of backup over another would have on the availability of your computer system in the event of a failure will allow you to address this type of exam question well.

► In short, by focusing on the two major areas mentioned here, you will be well prepared for this portion of the exam.

INTRODUCTION

This chapter is mainly concerned with the performance and reliability of your computer. The techniques available in Windows 2000 range from digital signing of device drivers and operating system files to running a command-based Recovery Console in the event the system will not even boot.

To make the most of the hardware you have available, you need to take steps to optimize its use and to prevent the operating system from being modified without your consent. Finally, you need to be able to recover the system in the case of a catastrophic failure.

MANAGING AND TROUBLESHOOTING DRIVER SIGNING

Manage and troubleshoot driver signing.

A new feature in Windows 2000 Professional is the ability to digitally sign both drivers and operating system files. This is the assurance that a particular file has met a certain level of testing and that the file has not been overwritten by the installation program of another application. The application of driver signing is governed by a policy set using the System program in the Control Panel.

Digitally Signing a File

Digitally signing a file is the process by which you can guarantee that a particular file comes from the source that it claims to. Since any file can be signed, it is necessary to be able to handle all formats of files, including binary files. A technique called catalog file signing is used to provide digital signing information about files without modifying the file itself.

In catalog file signing, a CAT file is created for each driver or operating system file that is being signed. The CAT file includes a hash of the binary file. A hash is the result of a mathematical operation on some data (in this case, the binary file) that is sensitive to any changes made in the source data. In this way, any change to the binary file can be detected because the hash procedure will produce a different value. Other information like filename and version number is also added to the file. A certificate from the publisher along with a Microsoft digital signature is included in the catalog file to complete the signing process.

The relationship between the catalog file and the driver binary is contained in the information file (.INF) that is maintained by the system after the driver is installed.

The Windows 2000 Professional system provides you with three choices when installing a new device driver. The first is to disable signature checking and install all new device drivers regardless of the file signature. The second choice is to check for driver signatures before installing them and display a warning if the signature verification fails. The third choice is to check for driver signatures and block any installation if the signature verification fails.

Figure 4.1 shows an example of the options available in enforcing device signing.

When a driver is being added to the system, the Microsoft certificate in the CAT file indicates that it has passed a strenuous testing routine. The hash of the driver code is compared to the contents of the CAT file to ensure the binary is correct. The certificates indicate that the driver has been certified, and the system policy is examined to see if driver signing is to be ignored, a warning is to be issued when unsigned files are installed, or unsigned files are to be blocked from installation.

Step by Step 4.1 shows how to configure driver signing.

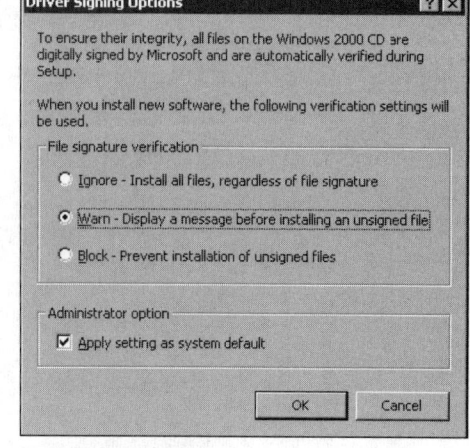

FIGURE 4.1
Driver signing options.

STEP BY STEP

4.1 Configuring Driver Signing

1. Double-click on the System application in the Control Panel.

2. Select the Hardware tab and click on Driver Signing.

3. At this point there are three options from which to select:

• Ignore will allow all device drivers to be installed whether they are digitally signed or not.

continues

continued

> **N O T E**
> **Configuring Driver Settings** If you have administrator rights, selecting Apply Setting as System Default will apply the configured driver signing level for all users who log on to the computer.

•Warn will display a warning message when an installation is attempted on a device driver without a digital signature.

• Block will prevent an installation of an unsigned device driver.

System File Checker

There is a command-line utility that scans and verifies the versions of all protected system files. System file checker (sfc.exe) will discover that a protected file has been overwritten and replace it with the correct version of the file from the %systemroot%\system32\dllcache folder.

The command to start the system file checker program is:

```
sfc [/scannow] [/scanonce] [/scanboot] [/cancel] [/quiet]
➥[/enable] [/purgecache] [/cachesize=x]
```

System file checker parameters are outlined in Table 4.1.

TABLE 4.1

SYSTEM FILE CHECKER PARAMETERS

Parameter	Action
scannow	Scans all protected files immediately.
scanonce	Scans all protected system files once at the next boot.
scanboot	Scans all protected system files every time the computer is rebooted.
cancel	Cancels all pending scans.
quiet	Replaces all altered system files without prompting the user.
enable	Turns prompting back on.
purgecache	Purges the file cache and rescans all protected files immediately.
cachesize=x	Sets the cache size (in MB).

CONFIGURING, MANAGING, AND TROUBLESHOOTING THE TASK SCHEDULER

Configure, manage, and troubleshoot the Task Scheduler.

The Task Scheduler is a graphical utility that allows you to schedule programs or batch files to run at specific times or when specific events occur. The Task Scheduler runs as a wizard when creating a task and provides a graphical means of altering the properties of a scheduled task from the Scheduled Tasks folder in the Control Panel. Tasks scheduled are saved as files (with a .JOB extension) in the Winnt\Tasks folder.

Task Scheduler and the AT Command

Earlier versions of Windows provided the AT command to schedule programs or scripts to run at specific times. Windows 2000 introduces a graphical utility called the Task Scheduler that enhances this scheduling capability.

The Task Scheduler is not the same as the AT command. However, they share many common characteristics. When a task is scheduled by AT, an entry for it appears in the Task Scheduler task window.

With the Task Scheduler you can specify the user account to run a task (even if scheduled with the AT command). Whenever you use Task Scheduler to modify an AT task, you can no longer use AT to modify any characteristics of the job.

Creating a Scheduled Task

When you open the Scheduled Tasks folder from the Control Panel and double-click on Add Scheduled Task, you start a wizard that will create the job file that represents the task to run (see Figure 4.2). The file contains userid and password information to allow the job to be copied from one machine to another.

> **NOTE**
>
> **Running SFC**   You must have administrator rights to run the system file checker. If for some reason the dllcache folder becomes corrupt or unusable, the scannow, scanonce, or scanboot options will repair the contents of the dllcache directory.

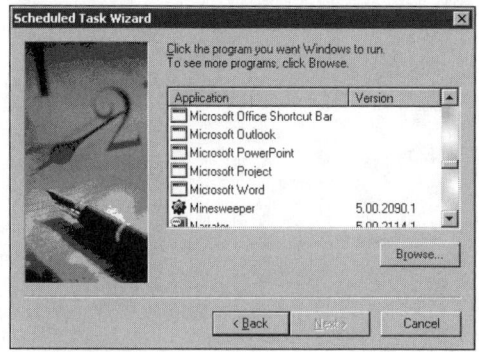

FIGURE 4.2
Selecting programs to run with the Scheduled Task Wizard.

The wizard allows you to customize the information shown in Table 4.2.

TABLE 4.2

SCHEDULED TASK WIZARD OPTIONS

Option	Description
Program to Run	The application to schedule. This can be an entry from the supplied list or a batch file or other program selected using the Browse command.
Task Name	A local name for the scheduled task.
Frequency	How often the task will be executed. You can select daily, weekly, monthly, once only, when the computer starts, or when you log in.
Time and Date	The start time and date the task file executes on. Depending on the frequency, you can also specify the month and/or the day of the week to run the job.
User Name and Password	You can specify the user ID that is used to execute this job. If your user ID does not have the security rights required by the scheduled task, you can specify a different user ID.
Advanced Properties	This checkbox will cause the properties page for the scheduled task to display after the Finish button is clicked. Advanced properties include editing the command line to run, the starting directory, and the userid and password to execute the task with. You can also modify the jobs schedule and some system environmental factors such as not running the job if the computer is on battery power.

Step by Step 4.2 shows how to create a Scheduled Task.

STEP BY STEP

4.2 Creating a Scheduled Task

1. Open the Control Panel and double-click on Scheduled Tasks.

2. Double-click the Add Scheduled Task icon.

3. Click Next to continue the Add Scheduled Task Wizard.

4. Click Browse to start a task not on the default list.

5. Enter the string **c:\winnt\system32\notepad.exe** in the File window and click Open.

6. Provide a name for the scheduled task, select the Daily option, and click Next.

7. Choose a time and date for the job to run and click Next.

8. Enter the password to your account in both the Password and Confirm windows and click Next.

9. Click Finish to complete the task creation.

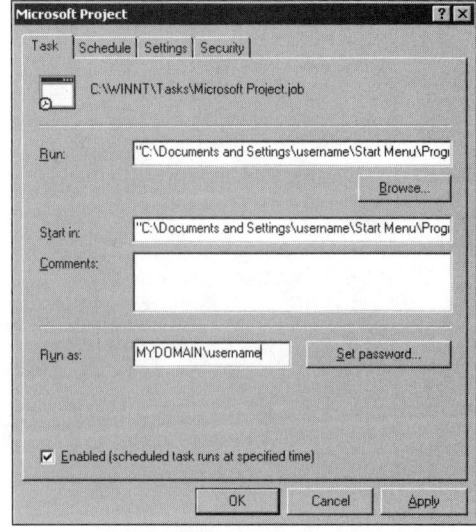

There will now be a file in the Winnt\Tasks folder with a JOB extension that represents the task you just created. Right-clicking the task icon and selecting the Properties menu item will display the parameters used to run this job. Figure 4.3 shows the properties sheet.

FIGURE 4.3
Properties of a sample job in Scheduled Tasks.

MANAGING AND TROUBLESHOOTING THE USE AND SYNCHRONIZATION OF OFFLINE FILES

Manage and troubleshoot the use and synchronization of offline files.

Network connections are becoming more common, and it is often assumed that your computer always has network access. If, however, you are offline either because you are disconnected from the network or because you have undocked your laptop, you can still access files and folders to which you have configured offline access. Using Offline Files, you can navigate the shared folders and files as if you were connected to the network.

NOTE **Support for Offline Files** Any shared file or folder can be configured as offline. Any computer that supports Server and Message Block (SMB) File and Printer Sharing can be the source of offline files. Computers running Windows 95, Windows 98, and Windows NT 4.0 all support Offline Files. Offline Files is not supported for computers running Novell NetWare.

Offline Files and Mobile Users

If you travel frequently and use your laptop for most of your work, offline files provides a way to ensure that the network files you are working with are the most current versions and that changes you make when offline will be synchronized when you reconnect to the network.

When you undock your laptop, the shared network files that were configured as available offline remain just as they were when you were connected. You continue to work with them normally with the same access permission as the original network files. For example, a read-only document on a mapped network drive would remain read-only if you were disconnected from the network.

Selecting Items to Be Available Offline

The first step is to enable your Windows 2000 Professional computer to use offline files. Open My Computer on your desktop and select Folder Options from the Tools drop-down menu. Selecting the Offline Files tab will allow you to set synchronization events and enable offline file usage.

You must now indicate which folders or files are to be accessed when your computer is disconnected from the network. This flag is part of the menu list (right-click) for files and folders.

Step by Step 4.3 shows how to select a folder for offline access.

STEP BY STEP

4.3 Selecting a Folder for Offline Access

1. Start Windows Explorer and expand the My Computer entries.

2. Expand your network shares to locate a folder to make available offline.

3. Right-click on the folder and select Make Available Offline. A display window will open, indicating the progression of the synchronization. When the synchronization window disappears, the file or folder is available offline.

> **NOTE**
> **Selecting Folders** If you make a folder available offline, all the files within the folder are also available offline and the menu option for each of them is grayed out.

Synchronizing

When you reconnect to the network (perhaps by docking your portable computer), changes that you have made to the offline files are synchronized back to their original network files. If someone else has made changes to the same file, you have the option of saving your version of the file, keeping the other version, or saving them both.

Synchronization can be started manually or by using the Synchronization Manager when you want to control what files are synchronized and when it occurs. Figure 4.4 shows the settings to synchronize a file when logging on or off a network.

Step by Step 4.4 describes how to use the Sychronization Manager.

STEP BY STEP

4.4 Using the Synchronization Manager

1. From the Start menu select Programs and then Accessories.

2. Select the Synchronize item to start the Synchronize Manager.

3. The display will list all the folders selected for offline availability. Double-click on an entry to see the Offline File folder.

4. Close the Offline File folder display and return to the Items to Synchronize window. Click the Setup button.

5. You can select each item in the window to be synchronized when you log on or log off, when the computer is idle, or at some scheduled time for each connection configured on your computer.

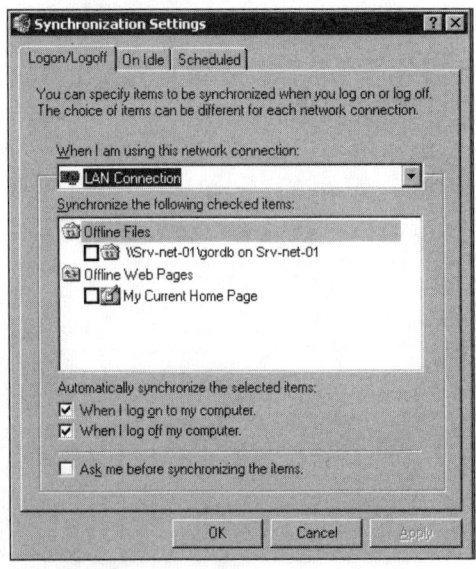

FIGURE 4.4
Setup options for synchronization.

> **NOTE**
>
> **Managing Your Workload** By choosing when to synchronize items, you can manage the workload placed on your computer and the network. For example, if you are connected to the network by modem, you can minimize synchronization time by clearing the automatic synchronization flags and manually synchronizing individual files.
>
> When using offline files, you should always synchronize at logon. This will ensure that changes made on your computer are synchronized with changes made to the network files while you were disconnected.

File Conflicts

When you synchronize files, the files that you modified while disconnected from the network are compared to the version saved on the network. If the network versions have not been changed by someone else, your changes will be copied to the network.

If someone else has updated the network versions of your offline files, you are given a choice of keeping your version, keeping the version currently on the network, or keeping both. To keep both versions, you have to give your version a different filename, and then both files will appear on the network and in your offline files folder.

If you delete a network file on your computer while working offline but someone else on the network makes changes to that file, the file is deleted from your computer but not from the network.

If you change a network file while working offline but someone else on the network deletes that file, you can choose to save your version onto the network or delete it from your computer.

If you are disconnected from the network when a new file is added to a shared network folder that you have made available offline, that new file will be added to your computer when you reconnect and synchronize.

OPTIMIZING AND TROUBLESHOOTING PERFORMANCE OF THE WINDOWS 2000 PROFESSIONAL DESKTOP

Optimize and troubleshoot performance of the Windows 2000 Professional desktop.

In general, performance monitoring addresses how the operating system and any applications or services use the resources of the system, including disks, memory, processors, and network components. The statistics measured are usually throughput, queues, and response times that represent resource usage.

Windows 2000 Professional defines performance data in terms of objects, counters, and instances. An object is any resource, application, or service that you can measure.

Table 4.3 is a partial list of the objects on which Performance Monitor can display statistics.

TABLE 4.3

OBJECTS ON WHICH PERFORMANCE MONITOR CAN DISPLAY STATISTICS

Object	*Description*
Cache	Reports activity for the file system cache.
IP	Reports activity on the Internet Protocol (IP) traffic.
Network Interface	Reports rates at which bytes and packets are sent or received over a network connection.
Paging File	Reports activity to the paging file used to back up virtual memory allocations.
System	Reports statistics for system-wide counters that reflect file operations and processor usage.

Each object has counters that are used to measure various aspects of performance, such as transfer rates for disks, packet transmit rates for networks, or memory and processor time consumed by applications or services.

Each object will have at least one counter, although most have many different counters available. Each counter will have at least one instance (usually Total or Average), although some objects (like Process) will have an instance for each process currently active on the computer.

The tool used to display performance statistics is the Performance Monitor. The Performance Monitor provides a graphical interface to the counters maintained by the operating system in the registry or using Windows Management Interface (WMI) and provides ways to capture or log the output or to display it graphically on the screen.

To view the Performance Monitor system, double-click on the Administrative Tools applet in the Control Panel, then double-click on the Performance applet. Maximize the display and click on the plus sign on the chart menu bar. The Add Counters display has a window called Performance Object. This drop-down list will show all the areas in the operating system where performance counters are kept.

Optimizing and Troubleshooting Memory Performance

Memory availability is one of the most important factors in managing the performance of your Windows 2000 Professional computer. Knowing the amount of memory you have configured and understanding how Windows 2000 will use that memory is one of the first steps to take in understanding your system's performance.

Determining the Physical Memory Available

You can identify the amount of physical memory configured by running the System applet from the Control Panel and selecting the General tab. The physical memory available is under the Computer section of the display. Figure 4.5 shows the General display of the System applet.

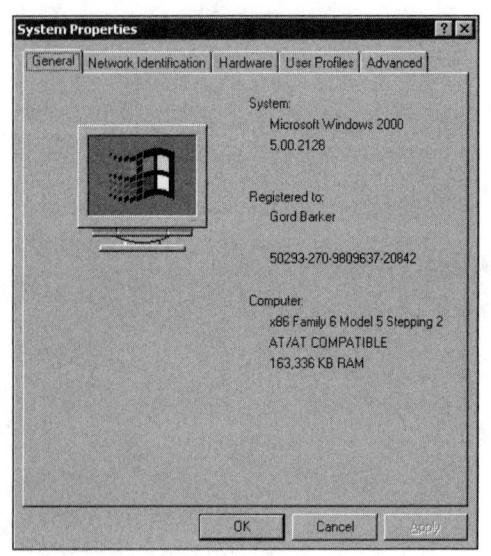

FIGURE 4.5
Determining physical memory.

The Windows 2000 Professional operating system distinguishes memory usage depending on whether it is part of the paged pool or the non-paged pool. The paged pool contains memory that can be paged to disk; memory in the non-paged pool cannot. The size of each pool is based on the amount of physical memory available.

The paging file (also called the swap file) is a file on the hard disk that serves as a temporary virtual memory space. By utilizing the paging file, Windows 2000 Professional can allocate virtual memory space that exceeds the amount of physical memory. Two important measurements of the paging file are the amount of space allocated to a process and the amount of available space that is not in use by any processes.

A portion of memory in your Windows 2000 Professional system is reserved as a file system cache. This is a subset of memory that contains recently used information for quick access. The size of the file system cache depends on the amount of physical memory installed and the amount of memory required for applications.

File System Cache

Memory that is not used for the working sets of processes is available for the file system cache. The Windows 2000 Professional operating system will dynamically adjust the size of cache as needed. It is more appropriate, when monitoring cache, to measure its effectiveness (hit ratio) rather than its absolute size. When data is found in the cache, the performance system registers a hit. If the cache size is too small and data is not found, the performance system registers a miss. A high rate of data misses, therefore, indicates a low physical memory situation.

You can determine the amount of cache being used by starting the Task Manager and selecting the Performance tab. The value for System Cache reflects only the currently mapped pages; it does not reflect any cache pages currently swapped to the paging file. Figure 4.6 shows the System Cache information available from the Task Manager.

The Paging File

Windows 2000 creates one paging file (Pagefile.sys) on the hard drive on which the operating system is installed. The default size is the amount of physical memory plus 12MB. If the paging file is too small, you will exhaust the amount of virtual memory available for applications. If the amount of physical memory is too low, it will generate excessive activity on the paging file disk, slowing response time for the system.

Setting the paging file's initial size and maximum size to the same value increases efficiency because the operating system does not need to expand the file during processing. Setting different values for initial and maximum size can contribute to disk fragmentation. Care must be taken not to consume all the free space on the system disk. The Windows 2000 Professional operating system requires a minimum of 5MB free space to operate.

Expanding the initial size of the paging file can increase performance if applications are consuming virtual memory and the full capacity of the existing file is being used.

Creating a large paging file on a disk that is very active or has limited space will impact system performance. Changing the file size gradually will allow you to optimize the size of the paging file without consuming too much free space.

If disk space is limited or the system disk is very active, you can improve the performance of your system by moving the paging file to another volume.

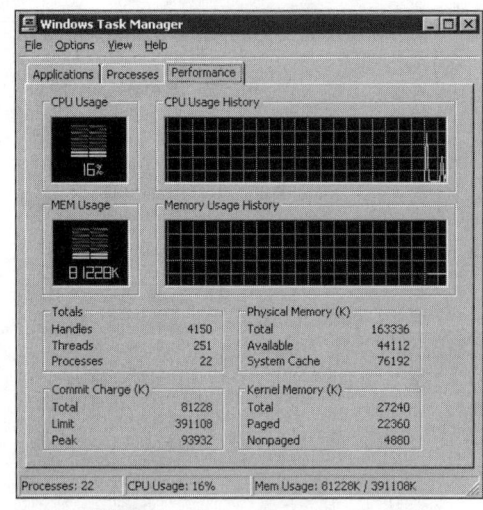

FIGURE 4.6
Determining system cache size.

N O T E **Sizing the Paging File**   You can use two counters from the Memory object in the Performance Monitor application to determine the best size of the paging file.

To determine how large your paging file should be based on your system workload, monitor the Process (_Total)/Page File Bytes counter. This indicates, in bytes, how much of the paging file is being used.

You can also determine the appropriate size of a paging file by multiplying the Paging File/% Usage Peak counter value by the size of Pagefile.sys. The % Usage Peak counter indicates how much of the paging file is being used.

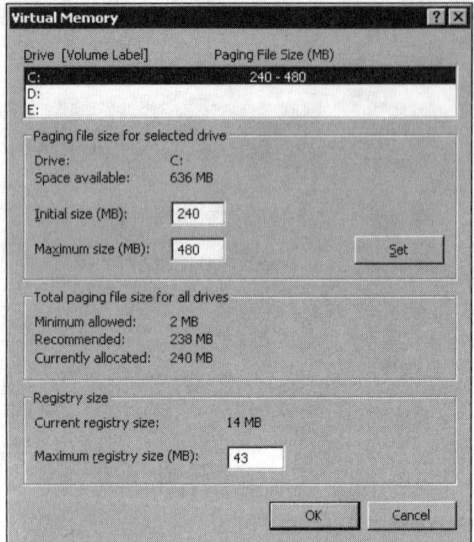

FIGURE 4.7
Paging file properties.

Figure 4.7 shows the current and maximum size of the paging file as well as the current and maximum size of the registry.

The system requires a 2MB file on the system disk to write events to the system log, automatically restart the system after a system failure, or send an administrative alert.

If you want to be able to write debugging information to a file, the system requires a file that is equal to the size of RAM plus 12MB on the system root directory. If performance is more critical than recoverability, you can put the paging file on a volume separate from the operating system.

Although Windows 2000 limits the size of each paging file to 4GB, you can supply more virtual memory to applications by spreading paging files across multiple disks. Creating multiple paging files on a single physical disk will provide more space but not improve performance.

Memory Shortages

Your Windows 2000 Professional computer can develop memory shortages if processes demand much more memory than what is available or the applications you are running leak memory. To identify a memory shortage situation you can watch the counters displayed in Table 4.4.

TABLE 4.4

IMPORTANT MEMORY COUNTERS

Counter	Description
Available Bytes	The amount of physical memory available to processes. Indicates the amount of physical memory that remains after the working sets of running processes and the cache have been served.
Cache Bytes	The number of bytes currently being used for the file system cache.
Commit Limit	The amount of virtual memory that can be committed without expanding the paging file.
Committed Bytes	The amount of committed virtual memory.

Counter	Description
Page Faults/Sec	The overall rate of page faults per second including hard page faults (the page is on disk) and soft page faults (the page is elsewhere in memory).
Pages/Sec	The number of pages read from or written to disk to resolve hard page faults.
Pool Non-Paged Bytes	The amount of space in the non-paged pool of memory. These pages must remain in physical memory.
Pool Paged Bytes	The amount of space in the paged memory pool. These pages can be written to disk when they are not being used.

Available Bytes in the Memory object indicates the amount of physical memory remaining after all the processes and cache requirements are met.

Working Set in the Process area indicates the amount of memory used by one or more processes when there is abundant memory. When memory is in short supply, the working sets of some processes are reduced to allow other processes to expand. This results in an increase in page faults.

Pages per Second in the Memory object indicates the number of pages that were not immediately available in memory and had to be read in from disk, or were in memory and had to be written to disk to make way for other information. This value will be high if there are too many hard page faults.

Disk Activity to the Paging File

Memory shortages can lead to paging activity that results in a disk bottleneck. If hard page faults are occurring, it is important to understand how the disk is performing during this paging.

Acceptable rates for the Memory counter Pages per Second range from 40 per second on older computers to 150 per second for the newest disk systems. When looking at paging activity, it is appropriate to have the scan rate as low as once every second, since paging will appear as a burst of activity. A scan rate that is too long will show only the average usage and not activity spikes.

NOTE **Enabling the LogicalDisk Counters** The LogicalDisk object counters are not available by default. If you want to monitor the values for these counters, you must first activate the counters by typing `diskperf -yv` at the Windows command prompt.

The Memory objects Pages Input per Second and Pages Output per Second indicate the rate at which pages were read from disk or written to disk to provide room in physical memory for other pages. A high value here can indicate low physical memory. Figure 4.8 shows the effect of low physical memory on the paging rate.

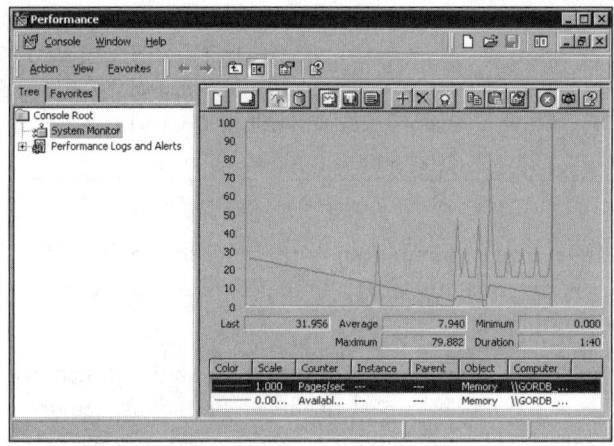

FIGURE 4.8
The effect of low memory on paging rate.

The other Memory object, Pages Output per Second, indicates the rate at which pages were written back to the disk. This activity does not generate hard page faults but can indicate a memory shortage and does result in additional disk activity. Pages are written back to disk when the Virtual Memory Manager needs to reduce pages from a working set of a process and it finds that some data pages contain changes. The changed data must be written back to the paging file rather than just being discarded, and this generates disk activity.

To understand what impact paging is having on your system you must first understand if paging is dominating your disks' workload.

The Memory counter Page Reads per Second indicates the number of read operations required to retrieve pages referenced by page faults. If you compare this number to the number of pages faulted you will be able to determine how many pages are retrieved per read. A high ratio means a large number of faulted pages are not found in physical memory and must be retrieved from disk. This will create a disk bottleneck. Figure 4.9 shows the effects of a high paging rate on disk activity.

Although the effect of this paging rate is on disk activity, it may also indicate that the physical memory available is not large enough to hold the working set for the active applications. This constraint can be alleviated by adding additional physical memory.

To determine what portion of your disk's work this paging activity occupies, you can compare the page reads versus disk reads. These are found in the Memory counter Page Reads per Second and the LogicalDisk counter Disk Reads per Second. If there is a correlation between these two counters then it is likely that paging activity makes up most of your disk activity and you could have a disk bottleneck and memory constraint.

Another way of looking at this is to compare the LogicalDisk counter Average Disk Read Bytes per Second to the Memory counter Page Reads per Second. The Average Disk Read Bytes indicates the rate at which the disk is transferring data during reads (don't forget to convert bytes to pages by dividing by 4096).

If the result is about equal to the Memory counter Page Reads per Second then the majority of the disk activity is caused by paging and any memory shortage that results in a high paging rate will result in a disk bottleneck. Exactly how much of a disk bottleneck will result depends on the disk and the number of I/O transactions per second it will be able to sustain.

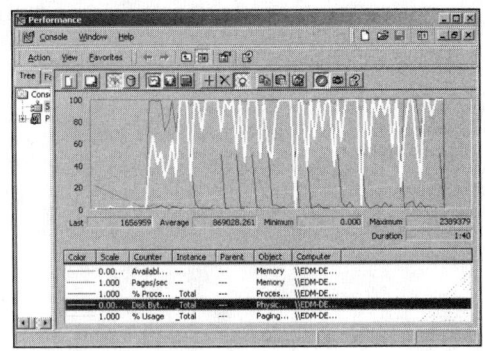

FIGURE 4.9
Disk I/O caused by paging.

Monitoring the Cache

The Windows 2000 file system cache is an area of memory into which the I/O system keeps a copy of recently used data from disk. If a process needs to read from or write to disk and the I/O Manager has the data still in cache, the data can be copied much quicker than if it must be retrieved from disk.

The file system cache can't be a bottleneck since it is just a part of physical memory. However, if there is not enough memory to make an effective cache area, the result is increased disk activity and perhaps a disk bottleneck. Table 4.5 shows important file cache counters.

TABLE 4.5

IMPORTANT FILE CACHE COUNTERS

Counter	Description
Copy Read Hits %	A value over 80% indicates that the cache is very efficient.
Copy Reads/Sec	The rate at which the file system attempts to find data in cache.
Data Flush Pages/Sec	The rate at which applications are changing cached pages and the pages are written back to disk.
Data Flushes/Sec	The rate at which cache data is written to disk.
Data Maps/Sec	The rate at which file data pages are copied into cache.
Fast Reads/Sec	The rate at which the data is found in cache rather than on disk.
Lazy Write Flushes/Sec	The rate at which applications change data, causing the cache to write back to disk.
Lazy Write Pages/Sec	The rate at which pages are changed by applications and written back to disk.
Read Aheads/Sec	The rate at which the Cache Manager detects a file being read sequentially.
Cache Bytes (Memory object)	This counter indicates the growth or shrinking of the cache.
Cache Faults/Sec (Memory object)	The rate at which cache pages were sought but not found and had to be retrieved from disk.

Resolving Memory Bottlenecks

Adding memory to a computer is an easy solution but not always cost-effective. Prior to purchasing more memory you can try some of the following:

◆ Correct any applications that may have memory leaks.

◆ Increase the size of the paging file. Generally, the bigger file you can make, the better performance will be. You can also make multiple files on different disks to increase performance. Striped volumes can also be used to spread the work of accessing the paging file over many disks.

◆ Check for available space on the disk with the paging file(s). Low disk space can manifest itself as memory problems.

◆ Avoid using some display and sound features. Features that consume memory are animated cursors, desktop icons, large bitmap wallpaper, and some screen saver programs.

◆ Remove unused protocols and drivers. Idle protocols still use space from both paged and non-paged memory.

◆ Replace 16-bit systems with 32-bit systems for better performance.

Optimizing and Troubleshooting Processor Performance

After memory consumption, processor activity is the most important thing to monitor in your system. A busy processor might be efficiently handling all the work on your computer, or it might be overwhelmed. The following factors provide an indication as to the workload on your Windows 2000 Professional computer:

◆ The processor queue length and processor utilization together indicate the overall processor usage.

◆ Interrupt activity and context switches are activities that can significantly add to the processor workload.

◆ Individual processes can monopolize the available CPU resources.

◆ Threads within the active processes can sometimes have their priorities changed to improve performance.

Processor Counters

The System, Processor, Process, and Thread objects contain counters that provide useful information about the work of your processor. Examine the thread counters shown in Table 4.6 for details about computer processes.

TABLE 4.6

IMPORTANT COUNTERS FOR PROCESSOR ACTIVITY

Counter	Description
System: Context Switches/Sec	The average rate per second at which context switches among threads on the computer. High activity rates can indicate inefficient hardware or poorly designed applications.
Processor: Interrupts/Sec	The average rate per second at which the processor handles interrupts.
System: Processor Queue Length	The number of threads that are in the processor queue.
Processor: % Processor Time	The percentage of time the processor was busy during the sampling interval.
Process: % Privileged Time	The percentage of time a process was running in privileged mode. Privileged or kernel mode is the processing mode that allows code to have direct access to all hardware and memory in the system.
Process: % Processor Time	The percentage of time the processor was busy servicing a specific process.
Process: % User Time	The percentage of time a process was running in user mode.
Thread: Context Switches/Sec	The average rate per second at which the processor switches context among threads. A high rate can indicate that many threads are contending for processor time.
Thread: % Privileged Time	The percentage of time a thread was running in privileged mode.
Thread: % User Time	The percentage of time a thread was running in user mode. User mode is the processing mode in which applications run.

Because System Monitor samples processor time, the values for processor time counters reported by the Processor, Process, and Thread objects might underestimate or overestimate activity on your system that occurs before or after collection of the sample.

Processor Bottlenecks

A processor bottleneck will occur when the processor is so busy that it cannot respond to an application that is requesting time. High activity may indicate that a processor is either handling the work adequately or it is a bottleneck and slowing down the system. Looking for a sustained processor queue is a better indicator of a bottlenecked processor. The following counters can help in identifying processor bottlenecks:

◆ The % Processor Time counter in the Processor object, with its value often exceeding 80%

◆ The Processor Queue Length in the System object, with its value often greater than 2, in a single CPU system

◆ Unusually high values for context switches/sec or interrupt switches/sec

> **Normal Workloads**   Some normal activities within Windows 2000 Professional will generate interrupts. For example, the processor's timer ticks occur every 15 milliseconds (or about 66 per second), at which point the processor hardware timer is updated. Interrupt rates that fall outside of the normal range (between 200 and 300 per second on Windows 2000 Professional) can be an indication of excessive activity.

Processor Time Counter

The Processor object counter % Processor Time determines the percentage of time the processor is busy. It does this by measuring the amount of time the Idle process is running and subtracting that from 100 percent.

What would appear as high values (70% or greater) on this counter may not in fact indicate a problem. High processor time situations will always occur when a process is starting up, although this is not usually a concern. Values that exceed 70% for extended periods of time, however, may indicate a problem, and additional counters can be monitored to provide more information.

If the Processor Time counter is consistently high, you need to determine if a processor queue is causing a bottleneck and preventing important work from being done.

Processor Queue Length

A collection of threads that are ready to run, but that are not able to because of an active thread currently using the processor, is a *processor queue*. A sustained queue of more than two threads is a sign of a processor bottleneck. Although queues are most often seen when the processor is very busy, they can develop with any utilization rate.

If the Processor Queue Length counter shows that many threads are ready to use the processor, you can identify which threads are using processor time by displaying the processes that appear in the Instance windows on the % Processor Time counter in the Process object.

Figure 4.10 shows the effects of a busy processor on the Processor Queue Length counter.

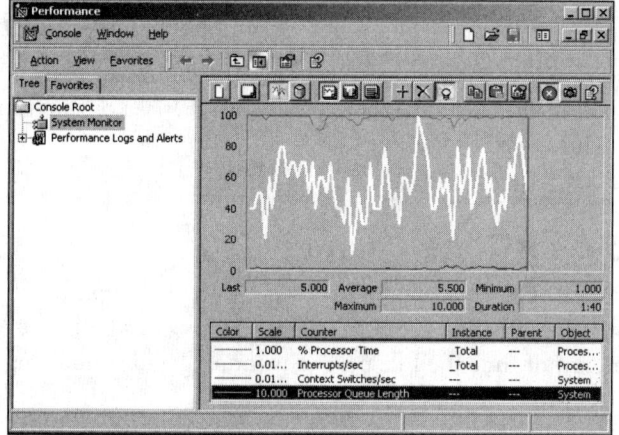

FIGURE 4.10
Processor queue length on a busy system.

Interrupts

The Interrupts/Sec counter in the Processor object reports the number of interrupts the processor is servicing from applications or hardware devices. The value of this counter should be 100 per second, or more for computers running Windows 2000 Professional.

If you are connected to a network, you may want to upgrade your Windows 2000 Professional computer to include a driver that supports interrupt moderation or avoidance. Interrupt moderation allows for several interrupts to be grouped into one hardware interrupt. This provides for greater efficiency in servicing the interrupt. Interrupt avoidance allows the processor to continue processing interrupts without new ones being queued until pending interrupts are complete. High values for % Processor Time for threads of the system process can also indicate a problem with a device driver.

Context Switches

When the kernel switches the processor from running one thread to another (for example, a thread with a higher priority), a context switch occurs. The Context Switches/Sec counter can indicate that a thread is monopolizing the processor. If the rate of context switches is low, the processor is spending all its time with one process. If the rate of context switches is high, then the processor is being shared between many processes all at the same priority. A rate of 150 context switches per second is moderate but a rate of 500 or more context switches per second is high and might indicate a problem.

Context switches can be displayed using the Context Switches/Sec counter in the System object.

Processes Causing a Bottleneck

If you have decided that your processor is overloaded and that it is the cause of your computer's performance problem, the next step is to investigate whether there is a single process that is monopolizing your CPU, or if it is being consumed by running many processes. You can display the percentage of the processor time that each process is consuming by using the following procedure.

STEP BY STEP

4.5 Process Usage of the CPU

1. Start the Performance Monitor program.

2. Right-click the plus sign to add some counters.

3. Select the Process object.

4. Select the % Processor Time counter.

5. Select each process instance. You can do this quickly by selecting the first counter (after the _Total instance) and then selecting the last counter while holding down the Shift key.

6. Click on Add and then Close to display the counters.

N O T E

> **Avoiding Processor Bottlenecks**
> Some device driver problems can
> cause high % Processor Time values
> for the System process. Additionally,
> if you are using a screen saver,
> particularly one that uses OpenGL,
> you will find that it can consume
> large amounts of processor time. If
> possible, change to a screen saver
> that uses less processor time.

If a single process is monopolizing the processor, the chart for that process will be higher than all the rest. If the cause of your processor performance problems is a specific application, your options include moving it to a different computer, perhaps running it on a larger Windows 2000 Server system, or running it at times when you are not trying to use the Windows 2000 Processional computer at the same time.

Eliminating a Processor Bottleneck

If you determine that you do have a processor bottleneck, some of the following steps might shorten the processor queue and reduce the burden on your processor:

◆ Delete memory bottlenecks that might be consuming the processor. Memory bottlenecks are far more common than processor bottlenecks and severely degrade processor performance.

◆ Upgrade your network or disk adapters to intelligent 32-bit adapters. Intelligent adapters provide better overall system performance because they allow interrupts to be processed on the adapter itself, relieving the processor of this work.

◆ Try to obtain adapters that have optimization features such as interrupt moderation and features for networking, such as card-based TCP/IP checksum support.

◆ Upgrade to a faster processor. A faster processor improves response time and throughput for any type of workload.

◆ Add another processor. If the process you are running has multiple active threads that are processor-intensive, then it is a prime candidate for a multiprocessor computer.

Examining and Tuning Disk Performance

The disk system handles the storage of programs and data as well as the movement of these between disk and memory. Since disk transfers run many hundreds of times slower than memory transfers, the overall influence of disk problems on your system will be great.

Disk Monitoring Concepts

There are many factors that you need to consider in determining whether the disk system is impacting the performance of your Windows 2000 Professional computer. The level of utilization, the rate of throughput, and the development of a queue are all important factors. Other types of activity may arise from disk operations, such as interrupts and paging activity.

Many of these factors are interrelated. For example, if disk utilization is high, then an I/O queue may form. If, at this time, memory utilization also peaks and paging increases, the overall performance of the computer will suffer.

Enabling Disk Counters

Windows 2000 Professional includes counters that monitor the activity of physical disks. The PhysicalDisk object provides counters that report physical disk activity; the LogicalDisk object provides counters that report statistics for logical disks and storage volumes. Both these objects measure disk throughput, queue length usage, and other data, but from different points of view. It is often beneficial to monitor them simultaneously. The Windows 2000 Professional operating system automatically enables PhysicalDisk counters. However, you must manually enable the LogicalDisk counters using the following command:

```
diskperf -yv
```

After the next reboot of your computer, the LogicalDisk object counters will be available to the Performance Monitor.

Diskperf has a number of command-line switches that are used to modify the availability of performance monitoring counters:

◆ -y will enable both physical and logical disk performance counters.

◆ -yd will enable physical disk performance counters.

◆ -yv will enable logical disk performance counters.

◆ -n will disable all disk performance counters.

◆ -nd will disable physical disk performance counters.

◆ -nv will disable logical disk performance counters.

Any change in the availability of performance monitoring counters set by diskperf will be made when the system is restarted.

When you are looking at logical volumes, remember that they might share a physical disk and your data might represent contention between the logical volumes trying to share a single resource. If you have a spanned, striped, or mirrored volume supported by disk controllers that provide a hardware-enabled redundant array of independent disks (RAID) volume, then the counters for physical disk data for all disks in the stripe or mirror act as if they are representing a single disk. If you have a RAID array that is supported by software, the counters will report data for each physical disk separately. Table 4.7 lists important physical disk performance counters.

TABLE 4.7

IMPORTANT PHYSICAL DISK PERFORMANCE COUNTERS

Counter	Description
Avg. Disk Bytes/ Transfer	This counter measures the size of I/O operations. If disk accesses are efficient then larger amounts of data will be transferred.
Avg. Disk/Sec Transfer	This counter measures the average time for each transfer regardless of the size. A high rate for this counter might mean the system is retrying requests due to disk queuing.
Avg. Disk Queue Length	This is the total number of requests waiting as well as the requests in service. If there are more than two requests continually waiting, then the disk might be a bottleneck.
Current Disk Queue Length	This counter reports the number of I/O requests waiting as well as those being serviced. This is an instantaneous snapshot of the disk queue rather than an average.
Disk Bytes/Sec	This is the rate at which data is being transferred to the disk. This is the primary measure of disk throughput.
Disk Transfers/Sec	This is the number of reads and writes completed per second, regardless of the amount of data involved. This is the primary measure of disk utilization.
Split IO/Sec	This is the rate at which the operating system divides I/O requests into multiple requests. This might indicate a fragmented disk.

Counter	*Description*
% Disk Time	This is the percentage of time the selected disk drive is busy reading or writing. This counter can span more than one sample period and therefore overstate the disk utilization. Compare this against % Idle Time for a more accurate picture.
% Disk Write Time	The percentage of time the selected drive was busy servicing write requests.
% Disk Read Time	The percentage of time the selected drive was busy servicing read requests.
% Idle Time	The percentage of time the disk subsystem was not processing requests and no I/O requests were queued.

Monitoring Disk Space

It is important to monitor the amount of available storage space on your disks because a shortage of disk space can adversely affect the paging file and as the disk space diminishes, disk fragmentation usually increases.

The % Free Space and Free Megabytes counters in the LogicalDisk object allow you to monitor the amount of available disk space. If the amount of available space is becoming low, then you may want to move some files to other disks if available, compress the disk, and remove temporary files to free up some disk space.

Disk fragmentation can slow the transfer rate and increase the seek time of your disk system. On a single-disk system, the Split IO/Sec counter in the Physical Disk object will indicate the degree of fragmentation. If this counter increases, run the Disk Defragmenter to help keep disk storage organized for the best performance.

Investigating Disk Performance Problems

Several factors must exist simultaneously for your Windows 2000 Professional computer to have a disk bottleneck. These factors include a high and sustained rate of disk activity, disk queues longer than two for extended periods of time, and an absence of significant amounts of paging. Without these conditions, it is unlikely that you have a disk bottleneck. Figure 4.11 shows the effects of a high I/O load on Disk Queue Length.

NOTE

Watch for Exaggerated Rates The % Disk Read Time and % Disk Write Time counters can exaggerate disk time. They report busy time based on the duration of the I/O request, which includes time spent on activities other than actually reading or writing to the disk. All the busy times are summed and divided by the duration of the sample interval. If multiple requests were in process, this can result in a number greater than 100%.

If your Windows 2000 Professional computer has more than one disk installed, the _Total instance for % Disk Time, for example, reports the value totaled for all disks but does not divide by the number of disks sampled. Therefore, a system with one idle disk and one busy disk appears to have all disks busy.

NOTE

Free Space on DFS Volumes Free space on a Distributed File System (DFS) share will change as you move from one directory to another. Do not assume that the amount of free space you see at the root of the DFS share is the actual space available throughout the entire tree. DFS volumes may be partially or completely replicated from one site to another and span many computers. A number that represents the total free space would not be very meaningful.

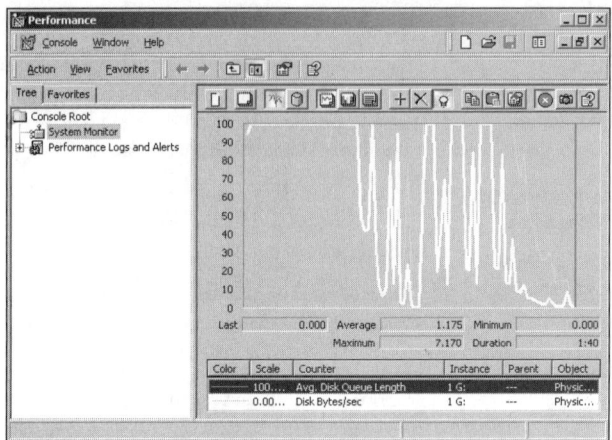

FIGURE 4.11
Disk queue length on an I/O-bottlenecked system.

Processors Can Be Impacted by Disk Hardware The rate of interrupts generated by your disk hardware can have a performance impact. If there is a significant number of interrupts generated, the result will be a slowed processor. Although this is not strictly a disk bottleneck, it is a processor bottleneck caused by the disk system.

If these conditions do exist and you think there is a disk bottleneck, then the following counters will be useful during analysis of the problem:

◆ Paging counters (found in the Memory object): Pages/Sec, Page Reads/Sec, Page Writes/Sec

◆ Usage counters: % Disk Time, % Disk Read Time, % Disk Write Time, % Idle Time, Disk Reads/Sec, Disk Writes/Sec, Disk Transfers/Sec

◆ Queue-length counters: Avg. Disk Queue Length, Avg. Disk Read Queue Length, Avg. Disk Write Queue Length, Current Disk Queue Length

◆ Throughput counters: Disk Bytes/Sec, Disk Read Bytes/Sec, Disk Write Bytes/Sec

Paging

The symptoms of a memory shortage are similar to a disk bottleneck. When physical memory is scarce, the system starts writing to the paging file and reading smaller blocks more frequently. The less physical memory available, the more disk spaced used and the greater the load on the disk system.

It is important, therefore, to monitor memory counters along with disk counters when you suspect a performance problem with your disk system.

Usage

A high-performance disk is capable of at least 50 random I/O operations per second. Some newer disks with faster rotation speeds can handle up to 100 I/O operations per second. The actual capacity of the disk is decided by factors other than the actual disk components, including bus speed and I/O request size.

Sustained values at 70 to 85 percent of the maximum capacity of the disk are a definite cause for concern. If a queue is developing at lower usage rates, it may indicate that the disk might be unable to handle the load.

Queue Length

To determine whether there is a queue developing for service on your disk system, examine the value of the Avg. Disk Queue Length. If it exceeds twice the number of physical disks configured in your system, you probably have a disk bottleneck.

Resolving Disk Bottlenecks

A disk bottleneck may cause the entire system to slow down. If you have determined that disk availability or capacity is responsible for your performance problem, you should consider taking one or more of the following actions:

◆ Add an additional disk if you can move some files to it, if you can create a stripe set, or if you are out of space. For disk space problems only, you can consider compressing the disk if your processor has enough power to handle the compression activity.

◆ Add memory if the disk activity you have measured is related to the paging file.

◆ Defragment the disk.

◆ Use stripe sets to spread the I/O requests across a number of disks simultaneously. If your applications are read-intensive and require fault tolerance, consider a hardware level Raid 5 volume. Use mirrored volumes for fault tolerance and good overall I/O performance. If you can live without fault tolerance, then a stripe set will provide fast reading and writing and, usually, higher storage capacity.

◆ If there is no throughput improvement seen with additional disk capacity or the addition of a stripe set, the bottleneck could be caused by contention between disks for the disk adapter. You should consider adding an adapter to distribute the load.

◆ Distribute the workload across multiple drives. For example, a database application may have the transaction logs on separate disks from the data. Writing to a transaction log is sequential and performs better on a physical disk than the random operations against the data, which perform better on striped volumes.

◆ Limit the use of file compression or encryption. These features add overhead to disk I/O and should only be used if performance is not critical.

◆ When purchasing disk systems, use the most intelligent and efficient components available. Upgrading to faster controllers with wider bandwidth access will generally improve throughput.

Monitoring Network Performance

Most workstations now require some communications over a network. The behavior of the network components of your Windows 2000 Professional computer has a direct impact on the performance your system can deliver.

Windows 2000 Professional provides two mechanisms for monitoring network performance: Performance Monitor network objects and the Network Monitor. The Performance Monitor network counters track resource utilization and throughput, while the Network Monitor tracks packets in and out of the network adapter.

The Performance Monitor contains several objects that reflect different layers of the OSI networking model. Table 4.8 describes the objects and the layer with which they are most closely associated.

TABLE 4.8

PERFORMANCE OBJECT BY OSI LAYER

OSI Layer	Performance Object
Application or Presentation	Browser, Server, Redirector, and Server Work Queues
Session	NBT Connection
Transport	TCP, IP, UDP, NetBEUI, NWLink IPX/SPX, AppleTalk (installed with the protocol)
Network	Network Segment (installed when you install the Network Monitor Driver)
Data Link and Physical	Network Interface

As with other resources, when analyzing the performance of your Windows 2000 Professional computer network components it is always best to establish a baseline for comparison. When performance data varies from your established baseline there may be a network resource bottleneck or a performance problem with some other resource that is having an impact on network performance. For that reason network counters should be viewed in conjunction with the % Processor Time (in the Processor object), the % Disk Time (in the PhysicalDisk object) and Pages/Sec (in the Memory object).

For example, if an increase in the Memory counter Pages/Sec is accompanied by a decrease in the Network counter Bytes Total/Sec, the computer is probably running short of physical memory for network operations. Most network resources, including network adapters and protocol software, use non-paged memory. If your computer is paging excessively, it could be that most of its physical memory has been allocated to network activities, leaving a small amount for applications that use paged memory. If this is the case, the system event log will indicate that the operating system has run out of non-paged memory. Also, the memory counter for non-paged pool memory and overall memory availability will indicate a shift from paged to non-paged memory.

Network Counters

The best approach for understanding the performance characteristics of your Windows 2000 Professional computer is to look at the Network performance objects from the Physical layer to the Application layer.

Network Interface Object

The Network Interface object monitors transmissions starting at the Physical layer. The Network Interface object is installed with the TCP/IP protocol and monitors activity of the IP protocol. There are no other separate objects to monitor the adapters for other networking protocols. Counters are shown in Table 4.9. Figure 4.12 shows typical network activity and its impact on interrupt rates.

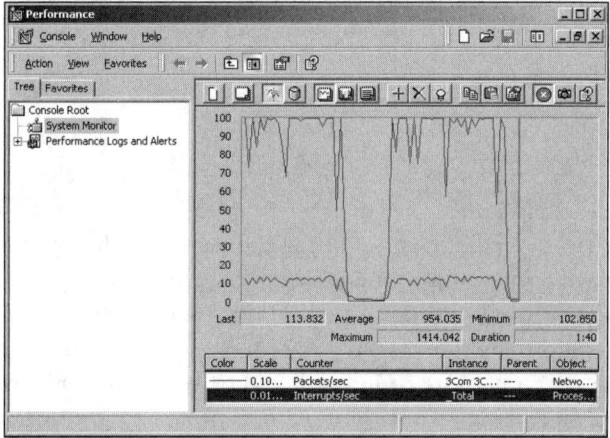

FIGURE 4.12
Network activity with normal interrupt activity.

The instances always list the loopback address (127.0.0.1) first, followed by the instances matching the binding order of the TCP/IP protocol. To view the binding order of TCP/IP, open up the Network and Dial-up connections folder from the Control Panel, select the Advanced Settings item on the Advanced tab, and select the Adapters and Bindings tab.

TABLE 4.9

NETWORK INTERFACE COUNTERS

Counter	Description
Output Queue Length	The length of the Output Packet queue. This value should be 0 or 1. Queue lengths of 2 or more mean the adapter cannot keep pace with server requests.
Packets Outbound Discarded	The number of packets discarded although there were no errors. If this number is incrementing continuously, it might indicate that the network is so busy that the network buffers cannot keep up with the outbound flow of packets.
Bytes Total/Sec	This indicates the rate at which data is sent and received by the adapter.

Network Segment Object

The Network Segment object is installed as part of the Network Monitor driver and reports throughput statistics for the local network segment. Important network segment counters are listed in Table 4.10.

TABLE 4.10

IMPORTANT NETWORK SEGMENT COUNTERS

Counter	Description
Broadcast Frames Received/Sec	Your computer processes every broadcast received. A high broadcast level means lower performance. This counter is good for establishing a baseline of network workload.
% Network Utilization	This reflects the percentage of network bandwidth used for the local segment. A low value is preferred. For a TCP/IP network, this value should not exceed 30%. If the value is above 40%, then collisions can cause performance problems.
Total Frames Received/Sec	This counter reflects the number of frames received on a network adapter. This counter can indicate when bridges and routers might be saturated. If network traffic exceeds the local network capacity, network performance suffers.

Network Protocol Objects

The Network Protocol objects contain counters for the installed protocols on your Windows 2000 Professional computer. These are mostly used to monitor transmission rates with counters such as Bytes/Sec, Datagrams Received/Sec, and Frames Sent/Sec.

For the TCP/IP protocol, use the TCP, IP, UDP, and ICMP objects. The IP objects provide statistics on the Network layer with counters on datagram throughput. To monitor traffic at the Transport layer, use the TCP object counters Segments Received/Sec and Segments Sent/Sec. The ICMP counters are used to maintain route tables and diagnosing problems, and UDP is used for NetBIOS name resolution by WINS and for DNS host name lookup.

If the retransmission rates are high, there could be hardware problems with your network adapter. If the Segments Sent and Received counters are not high, the network bandwidth could be consumed by broadcasts.

For the NWLink protocol, there are three objects available for monitoring throughput: NWLink IPX, NWLink NetBIOS, and NWLink SPX. Each object contains counters for Bytes Total/Sec and Frame Bytes Sent, Received, and Rejected.

Bytes Total/Sec should be high on an active network. Frames Rejected/Sec should be low.

For the NetBEUI protocol, use the NetBEUI and NetBEUI resource objects. Monitor Bytes Total/Sec and other transmission counters such as Frame Bytes Received/Sec and Frame Bytes Sent/Sec. In addition, track Frames Rejected/Sec for increasing values. Also include Times Exhausted, which can indicate whether resource buffers are being consumed. Information about the resource objects is also recorded in the Event log.

NBT Connection Object

The NBT connection object collects statistics on NetBIOS over TCP/IP session level communications between computers. These counters are used to monitor routed servers that use NetBIOS name resolution.

Application-Layer Objects

Finally, you should monitor services or applications at the Presentation or Application layers. By default, Setup installs the Browser, Redirector, Server, and Server Work Queues objects on computers running Windows 2000. These objects describe the performance of file and print services using the Server Message Block (SMB) protocol.

Browser Object

The Browser object maintains statistics on the Browser server in Windows 2000. The main function of the Browser service is to provide a list of computers sharing resources in the client's domain along with a list of other domains and workgroup names available on the wide-area network (WAN). This list is provided in the Network Neighborhood or through the NET VIEW command. The Active Directory replaces the browser service from previous versions of Windows NT but the interface is provided for backwards compatibility.

One of the communication methods used by the Browser service is the Mailslot. Mailslots are message structures on client machines that receive connectionless communications from other networked computers. The Mailslot service supported by Windows 2000 Professional is most useful in managing the broadcast messages used for identifying other computers or services on the network.

The Browser object collects statistics on the rate of announcements, enumerations, and other browser transmissions. Table 4.11 is a list of important Browser performance counters.

TABLE 4.11

IMPORTANT BROWSER COUNTERS

Counter	Description
Mailslot Allocation Failed	The number of times the datagram receiver has failed to allocate a buffer
Mailslot Opens Failed/Sec	The rate of mailslot messages received that were not delivered
Mailslot Received	The number of mailslot messages that could not be

continues

| TABLE 4.11 | *continued* |

IMPORTANT BROWSER COUNTERS

Counter	Description
Failed	received due to transport failures
Mailslot Writes Failed	The number of mailslot messages that were successfully received but could not be written to the mailslot
Missed Mailslot Datagrams	The number of datagrams discarded due to allocation limits
Missed Server Announcements	The number of server announcements missed due to allocation limits
Missed Server List Requests	The number of requests to retrieve a list of browser servers that were received but could not be processed
Server Announce Allocations Failed/Sec	The rate of server announcements that have failed due to lack of memory

Redirector Object

The redirector object supplies statistics for the Workstation service. The counters for this object describe activity at the Presentation layer of the networking architecture. Important redirector counters are shown in Table 4.12.

| TABLE 4.12 |

IMPORTANT REDIRECTOR COUNTERS

Counter	Description
Bytes Total/Sec	The rate at which the Redirector is processing data.
Current Commands	The number of requests to the Redirector that are currently queued for service. This number should not be much larger than the number of network adapter cards.
Network Errors/Sec	The number of serious unexpected errors indicating communication difficulties, usually resulting in an event log entry.
Reads Denied/Sec	The rate at which the server is unable to accommodate read requests. This usually indicates that the server is overloaded.

Counter	Description
Server Sessions Hung	The number of active sessions that have timed out due to lack of response.
Writes Denied/Sec	The rate at which the server is unable to accommodate write requests. This usually indicates that the server is overloaded.

Server Object

The Server object provides statistics for the Server service as it provides support for file and print sharing. Because many services run on top of the Server service, it is important to identify problems with this network service. Important server counters are listed in Table 4.13.

TABLE 4.13

IMPORTANT SERVER COUNTERS

Counter	Description
Blocking Requests Rejected	The number of times the server has rejected blocking SMBs due to lack of resources
Bytes Total/Sec	An overall indication of the throughput of the Server service
Context Blocks Queued/Sec	The rate at which requests are placed in the server's queue
Errors System	The number of times an internal Server error was detected
Pool Non-Paged Failures	The number of times non-paged memory could not be allocated
Pool Non-Paged Peak	The maximum number of bytes of non-paged memory the server has used
Pool Paged Failures	The number of times paged memory could not be allocated
Pool Paged Peak	The maximum number of bytes of paged memory the server has used
Sessions Errored Out	The number of auto-disconnects detected
Work Item Shortages	The number of times the work item (where the server stores an SMB) resource was not available

Server Work Queues Object

The Server Work Queues performance object consists of counters that monitor the length of queues and objects in the queues. Important server work queue counters are listed in Table 4.14.

TABLE 4.14

IMPORTANT SERVER WORK QUEUE COUNTERS

Counter	Description
Bytes Transferred/Sec	The rate at which the server is sending and receiving data.
Queue Length	The current length of the server work queue. A sustained queue length greater than 4 indicates a processor bottleneck.
Total Bytes/Sec	The rate at which the server is reading and writing data to and from files.
Total Operations/Sec	The rate at which the server is accommodating file read and write requests.

Resolving Network Bottlenecks

Network bottlenecks are typically caused by an overloaded processor, an overloaded network, or a problem on the network itself. Some of the approaches you can take to resolving network bottlenecks include the following:

◆ Use adapters with the highest bandwidth available for the best performance. Don't forget that increasing the bandwidth will mean more transmissions per second, which in turn will translate into more work to do and more interrupts to answer.

◆ Remove unused network adapters to reduce overhead.

◆ If your network uses multiple protocols, place each protocol on a different adapter. If you can, use protocols that minimize broadcasts.

◆ Use network adapters that support interrupt moderation to improve performance.

◆ Modify the protocol binding order on your Windows 2000 Professional computer to reflect the amount of use each protocols gets. If TCP/IP is the protocol used most often, it should be first in the binding order.

◆ Use offline files to work on network applications without being connected to the network to help reduce network traffic.

Optimizing and Troubleshooting Application Performance

Applications are not developed in a vacuum. They are driven by a business case and have requirements they must meet to be considered successful. One requirement is achieving the necessary performance. Other factors that are just as important, or even more so, are ease of development and maintenance, time to develop, availability of good programming tools, and developer expertise. Very few applications require high performance as a top priority. One example would be real-time data collection or a transaction system with a potentially unlimited load (like the stock market).

For everyone else, it becomes important to define what the required performance level is and to determine a way to measure it.

Application performance can be described from three points of view:

◆ **The real performance.** This is how fast the application actually performs its work.

◆ **The perceived performance.** This is how fast the application looks and feels to the user. This is often related to real performance. However, if there is a long initial startup sequence or heavy network traffic at some point in the processing, the user may consider the application to be slow despite its actual level of performance.

◆ **The consistency of the application's response.** This aspect of performance can be characterized in terms of the stability, scalability, and availability of the application. As the workload increases, the application will scale gracefully and still continue to perform well.

The application that satisfies all three views will always be considered successful.

If you are the application developer, there are usually tools available within the development environment to aid in understanding the performance of your application as it scales up. For example, if you are developing within Visual Studio, you can use the Application Performance Explorer to create run-time scenarios to stress all the application infrastructure. APE is configurable to show the performance implications of client loads, network bandwidth, machine boundaries, transfer methods, and other factors that impact performance in the real world.

Once the application has been deployed, an important step is to define a baseline of expected performance. This involves stressing the application to real load and measuring how it responds and what resources it consumes. You first have to realize that in any system there will always be bottlenecks. There is no point in looking for them before you have a performance problem to solve.

If the performance "out of the box" is not acceptable or if over time the performance of the application, as compared to the baseline performance, degrades, then the performance-monitoring tools can be used to pinpoint the bottleneck.

Memory Bottlenecks

Application consumption of memory can create a bottleneck on your Windows 2000 Professional computer when it is added to an existing workload. For example, if an application accesses a database and opens a large client-side cursor with the intent to speed later processing, it will do so by consuming memory (and network bandwidth). If physical memory is scarce this may cause an increase in paging and appear outwardly to be a disk system bottleneck.

Because of that, it is important to view a number of performance counters in comparison to each other.

The Process object in Performance Monitor supplies statistics about active processes. Important Application counters are listed in Table 4.15.

TABLE 4.15

IMPORTANT APPLICATION COUNTERS

Resource	*Counter*
Memory	Pool Paged Bytes, Pool Non-Paged Bytes, Working Set, Working Set Peak
Processor	% Privilege Time, % User Time, % Processor Time
I/O	Read Bytes/Sec, Read Operations/Sec, Write Bytes/Sec, Write Operation/Sec

In conjunction with the Processor counters, the Network Interface counters for Bytes Read, Bytes Sent, Output Queue Length, and the System counter Process Queue Length are useful in assessing impact on other parts of your Windows 2000 Professional computer.

Application Disk Space

Even if you are not currently short on disk space, you need to be aware of the storage requirements for applications you are running. To evaluate if the existing capacity of your computer's disk system is enough for your application requirements, estimate the expected disk usage, as in the following steps:

1. For best results, start with 1GB even though the minimum disk size required to install the operating system might be lower.

2. Add the total size of all applications.

3. Add the size of the paging file (this depends on the amount of memory; this size should be at least twice that of system memory).

4. Add the amount of disk space budgeted per user (if this is a multiuser system).

5. Multiply by the number of users.

6. Multiply by 110 percent to allow room for expansion (this percentage can vary based on your expected growth).

The result is the size of disk you need.

Disk Usage by Applications

How an application uses the disk will often have a major impact on the performance seen by the end user.

Applications can access data sequentially or randomly. Sequential access is faster than random access because of the way that disk hardware works. The seek operation that must occur when the disk head is repositioned takes more time than any other part of the I/O operation. Because random I/O involves a number of seeks, the overall throughput of data to and from the disk will be lower. The same is true for random writes. If you find that disk activity is predominantly random, you might consider positioning the application's disk files on a stripe set. This allows the I/O access to be spread over many spindles, providing some parallel access.

For any type of I/O the best solution involves using drives with the fastest rotational speeds and the fastest seek times for random I/O.

If your application has a high I/O rate, a stripe set will improve performance since the increased number of disk spindles provides for concurrent access. Hardware-enabled RAID sets provide better performance than stripe sets enabled by software.

For workloads of either random or sequential I/O, use drives with faster rotational speeds. For workloads that are predominantly random I/O, use a drive with a faster seek time.

N O T E

Fragmentation Can Impact Performance Even if an application reads and writes data sequentially, if the file is fragmented the I/O will not be sequential. If the disk transfer rate deteriorates over time in comparison to the baseline performance, you should run Disk Defragmenter.

MANAGING HARDWARE PROFILES

Manage hardware profiles.

Hardware profiles tell your Windows 2000 Professional computer which devices to start and what setting to use for each device.

When you first install Windows 2000 Professional, a hardware profile called Profile 1 (or, for laptops, Docked Profile or Undocked Profile) is created. By default, this profile contains every device that is installed on your computer at the time you install Windows 2000 Professional.

Hardware profiles are useful if you have a portable computer and use it in a variety of locations. Most people who have laptops use them in locations other than where the docking station is (at home or in the office). Because of that, network adapters, CD-ROM devices, and perhaps floppy disk drives that are part of the docking station are not available when you are staying in a hotel. You may want to use a modem and a portable printer when you are away that you would not use when in the office. Hardware profiles allow you to maintain different configurations of available peripherals.

Creating a New Hardware Profile

You create hardware profiles from the System applet in the Control Panel. If there is more than one hardware profile, you can designate one as the default that will be loaded when you start your Windows 2000 Professional computer (assuming you don't make a choice manually). Once you create a hardware profile, you can use Device Manager to enable or disable devices in the profile. When you disable a device while a hardware profile is selected, that device will no longer be available and will not be loaded the next time you start your computer. Figure 4.13 shows the making of a new hardware profile by copying the original.

Step by Step 4.6 shows how to create a hardware profile.

STEP BY STEP

4.6 Creating a Hardware Profile

1. Click Start, then point to Settings and then Control Panel.

2. Double-click on System.

3. Select the Hardware tab and click on Hardware Profiles.

4. Under Available Hardware Profiles click on Profile 1 (or Docked Profile if it is the default).

5. Click Copy and then OK.

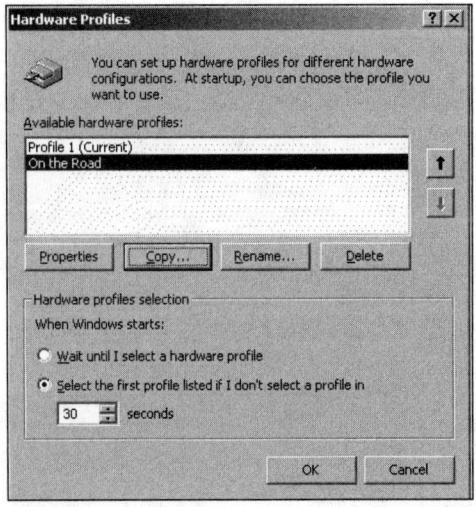

FIGURE 4.13
Making a new hardware profile from the original.

Once a profile has been created, reboot your computer and select it during the boot process. After the computer boot has completed and you have logged in as an administrator, you can modify the devices available when using this profile, as described in Step by Step 4.7.

NOTE
Administrator Rights You must be logged on as the administrator to copy or create hardware profiles.

STEP BY STEP

4.7 Changing Devices in a Profile

1. Click on Start, then point to Settings and then Control Panel.

2. Double-click System and select the Hardware tab.

3. Click Device Manager.

4. To disable a specific device driver, expand the section that pertains to that device. For example, to disable a network card, expand Network Adapters.

5. Highlight the driver to disable, and right-click. Select the Disable menu item and close the window.

When you next reboot the system and select the hardware profile you have modified, the driver you disabled will not be loaded.

RECOVERING SYSTEM AND USER DATA

Recover systems and user data.

This section addresses the recovery of system and user data through the use of Windows Backup, Safe Mode, and the Recovery Console.

Recovering System and User Data by Using Windows Backup

Information is the most important resource on your computer. Programs and services can often be easily reinstalled in the event of a hardware problem. However, the data is often irreplaceable. The best mechanism to back up your Windows 2000 Professional computer is to copy important data to a tape drive attached directly to your computer.

Backing up your computer to tape is safer than making copies to disk (and it's cheaper), and it allows you to keep versions of your data over time. The capability to keep backup copies for an extended period of time (for example, a 12-week rotation of tapes) can be used to provide protection against virus infections (you can retrieve a file from an earlier time) or from problems that may occur but not be fatal until later (for example, from a corrupted file).

A tested backup and recovery procedure is one of the most important administrative tasks to perform. When you are creating your backup policy you must consider the following issues:

◆ How often should a backup be done?

◆ What type of backup is the most appropriate?

◆ How long should backup tapes be stored?

◆ How long will the recovery of lost data take?

Naturally, as you use your Windows 2000 Professional computer over time, the location and importance of the data you back up will vary. An occasional reassessment of risk will help to keep your backup policy relevant and minimize your exposure to loss.

Backup Types

There are five types of backups available through the Windows 2000 Backup utility:

◆ A normal backup copies all selected files and marks each as being backed up. With normal backups you can restore files quickly because the files on tape are the most current.

◆ A copy backup copies all the selected files but does not mark them as backed up. This is useful if you want to make a backup copy of some of your files between scheduled backups without altering your backup operations.

◆ An incremental backup copies only those files created or changed since the last normal or incremental backup. It marks the files as having been backed up. If you use a combination of normal and incremental backups, then a system restore would require a restore of the last normal backup and then all the incremental backups done since.

◆ A differential backup copies those files created or changed since the last normal backup. It does not mark the files as having been backed up. If you are using a combination of normal and differential backups, then a system restore would require a restore of the last normal backup and then the last differential backup.

◆ A daily backup copies those files that have been modified the day the daily backup is performed. The files are not marked as backed up. This is useful if you want to take work home and need a quick way to select the files you have just recently been working on.

Each type of backup has its advantages and disadvantages when it comes to recovering data from your backup tape set. Table 4.16 lists the advantages and disadvantages of each type.

TABLE 4.16

ADVANTAGES AND DISADVANTAGES OF BACKUP TYPES

Backup Type	Advantages	Disadvantages
Normal	Files are easy to find because they are always on the current backup tape. Recovery requires only one set of tapes.	This is the most time-consuming backup process. If your files do not change frequently, the backups are redundant.
Incremental	This uses the least amount of tape storage and takes the least amount of time.	Files are more difficult to find because they are on several tapes.
Differential	This is less time-consuming than a normal backup.	If most of your files backed up change every day, this begins to resemble a normal backup.

Although it is best to have at least three copies of your data, the frequency at which you create these backups depends on how often your data changes and its value to you.

Backing Up Your Data

Windows 2000 Professional provides two ways to create backup jobs using the Windows Backup utility: a wizard to walk you through the steps involved and a graphical interface to allow you to define the backup job manually. Figure 4.14 shows the Backup Wizard screen for selecting files to back up.

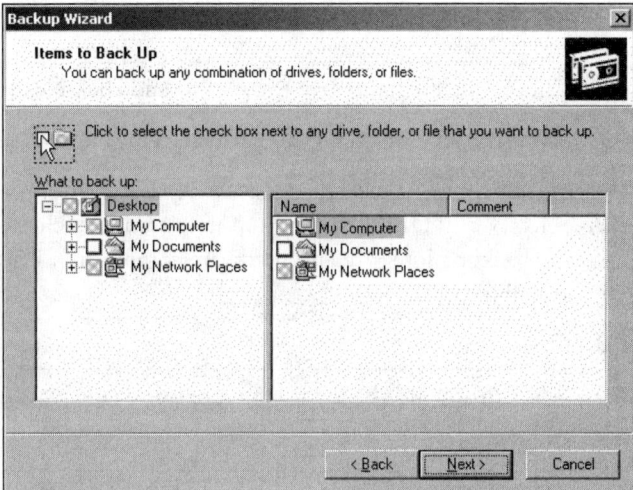

FIGURE 4.14
Selecting files to back up.

To define the files to back up and the tape drive to write to, use the following procedure.

STEP BY STEP

4.8 Creating a Sample Backup Job

1. Click on Start and select Programs, Accessories, System Tools, Backup.

2. Select the Schedule Job tab and click on Add Job.

3. On the Backup Wizard window, click Next.

continues

continued

4. Select the type of data you would like to back up.

If you are backing up selected files, the Backup Wizard will display a tree diagram of the files on your computer.

Selecting a file or directory will mark it and anything below it for backup.

5. Click Next.

6. Choose the media to save the files to and click Next.

7. Select the type of backup to perform (Normal to Daily) and click Next.

8. Select Verify Data After Backup if you want to check the backup's integrity and hardware compression if it is available.

9. Click Next.

10. Select to append the data if you are using tape storage.

11. Click Next.

12. Change the backup labels if you are following a standard.

13. Click Next.

14. Provide a job name and click Set Schedule.

15. Select the schedule on which to run the backup job and click OK.

16. Click Next.

17. Click Finish to create the scheduled job.

When you finish creating this job, you will find that the Microsoft Backup utility has created a job that you can now review using the Task Scheduler.

Restoring Your Data

Windows 2000 Professional provides two ways to restore files using the Windows Backup utility: a wizard to walk you through the steps involved and a graphical interface to allow you to define the restore job manually.

When you wish to recover some or all of the files stored during a backup job, you must select the backup set to restore from and then the specific files (or all files) to restore. The backup catalogs are stored by the name of the media (see Figure 4.15). You can also restore the files to their original location or to an alternate location if you want to copy the recovered files by hand.

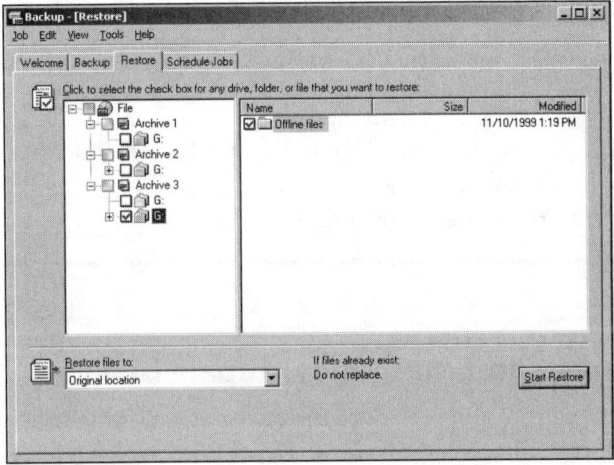

FIGURE 4.15
Backup catalogs are stored by media name.

The following procedure is an example of restoring some selected files from a previous backup.

STEP BY STEP

4.9 Restoring Files from a Normal Backup

1. Click on Start and select Programs, Accessories, System Tools, Backup.

2. Select the Restore tab.

3. In the left frame, select the backup set you would like to restore from and expand the file listings.

4. Use the Restore Files drop-down menu to select either the original location or an alternate.

continues

continued

5. Click on Start Restore.

6. From the Confirm Restore window, click on Advanced.

7. Set any options regarding removable storage or security and click OK.

8. Click OK to start the restore.

9. Enter the path of the backup set if it has changed (been moved) and click OK.

10. When the restore is complete, the Restore Progress window will allow you to view a report of the restore's actions or close the utility.

Creating an Emergency Repair Disk

The Backup tool also provides a mechanism to create an Emergency Repair Disk. The wizard for this is started from the main backup screen and requires a blank 1.44MB floppy disk. Choosing to also back up the registry will save the current registry files in a folder within the %systemroot$\repair directory. This will be useful if you need to recover your system in the event of a hard disk failure. The Emergency Repair process relies on information that is saved in the %systemroot$\repair folder.

Troubleshooting System Restoration Using Safe Mode

If at some point you reboot your Windows 2000 Professional computer and it fails before Windows 2000 is started, then you could have a problem somewhere in the boot process. The key to solving this type of problem is to understand the sequence of events that occurs in the computer as it is starting up. Windows 2000 shows you various boot sequence errors, the meaning of which should help you diagnose the problem with your system. You can also diagnose problems in the boot.ini file, apply your Emergency Repair Disk to fix your system, and have Windows 2000 automatically attempt to repair the process.

A boot error is a very obvious problem. When you can't start your computer system, you know you have a problem. It's also the kind of problem that forces you to stop what you are doing and fix it before you go on.

The Boot Process

The boot process occurs in stages. The first stage is preboot, in which the system is checked and the boot information located.

Preboot

The computer runs a power-on self-test (POST) to determine the amount of memory and what hardware components are present. The hardware devices are enumerated and configured during pre-boot. The system may display a series of messages indicating that the mouse is detected, that certain IDE or SCSI adapters are detected, responses from devices on the SCSI chain, and so forth. Failure at this stage represents a hardware concern and is not really a boot sequence error.

If all the hardware components are present and working, the computer BIOS locates the boot device and loads the Master Boot Record (MBR) into memory and executes it. The MBR scans the partition table to locate the active partition and loads the boot sector from the active partition into memory and executes it.

The computer finds and loads the file NTLDR from the active partition. NTLDR is a hidden system file located in the root folder of your system partition.

Initial Boot Phase

Once NTLDR is executing it does the following:

◆ Switches the processor from real mode into a 32-bit flat memory mode that NTLDR requires to complete its function.

◆ Starts the appropriate minifile system drivers, which are built into NTLDR to find and load Windows NT from different file system formats (File Allocation Table (FAT)) or Windows NT File System (NTFS)).

> **NOTE**
>
> **When Boot.ini Is Missing** If the Boot.ini file is not present, NTLDR attempts to load Windows NT from \Winnt on the first partition of the first disk.

> **NOTE**
>
> **On Dual-Boot Systems** If you select another operating system such as Microsoft Windows 98, NTLDR loads and executes BOOTSECT.DOS. This is a copy of the boot sector that was on the system partition at the time that Windows 2000 Professional was installed and executing. It begins the boot process for the selected operating system.

> **NOTE**
>
> **Automatically Choosing the Default Profile** If you do not press the spacebar, or if there is only a single hardware profile, NTLDR will load Windows 2000 Professional using the default hardware profile configuration.

◆ Displays the Boot Loader Operating System Selection menu from the boot.ini file. This provides you a selection of the operating system to use. If you do not select an entry before the timer reaches zero, NTLDR will load the operating system specified by the default parameter in boot.ini. The default parameter is the more recent operating system installed.

◆ After you select the operating system, a hardware detection routine is initiated. For Windows 2000 and Windows NT this is NTDETECT.COM and NTOSKRNL.EXE.

NTDETECT.COM collects a list of the hardware components currently installed and returns this list to NTLDR for inclusion in the registry under HKEY_LOCAL_MACHINE/HARDWARE.

NTDETECT.COM will detect the following components:

◆ Computer ID

◆ Keyboard

◆ Communications ports

◆ Mouse/pointing devices

◆ Floating-point coprocessor

◆ Floppy disks

◆ Bus/adapter type

◆ Parallel ports

◆ Small Computer Standard Interface (SCSI) adapters

◆ Video adapters

Configuration Selection

After NTLDR starts loading Windows 2000 and collects hardware information, OS Loader presents you with the option of selecting a hardware profile to use.

Kernel Load Phase

After the configuration has been selected, the Windows kernel (NTOSKRNL.EXE) loads and initializes. NTOSKRNL.EXE also loads and initializes device drivers and services. During this phase of the boot procedure, the screen clears and a bar graph appears at the bottom of the screen.

During the kernel load phase, NTLDR performs the following:

◆ Loads Ntoskrnl.exe but does not initialize it.

◆ Loads the hardware abstraction layer file (HAL.DLL).

◆ Loads the HKEY_LOCAL_MACHINE\SYSTEM registry key from %systemroot%\System32\Config\System.

◆ Selects a configuration. The first hardware profile is high-lighted by default. If you have created other hardware profiles, use the down arrow key to select the one that you want to use.

◆ Selects the control set it will use to initialize the computer.

◆ Loads the low-level hardware device drivers (for example, hard disk device drivers).

NTLDR now initializes the kernel and passes control to it. The kernel uses the data collected during hardware detection to create the HKEY_LOCAL_MACHINE\HARDWARE key. This key contains information about the hardware components and interrupts used.

When the kernel load phase is complete, the kernel initializes, and then NTLDR passes control to the kernel. At this point, the system displays a graphical screen with a status bar indicating load status.

The kernel initializes the low-level device drivers that were loaded during the kernel load phase. If an error occurs while loading or initializing a device driver, the boot process may do any of the following:

◆ Ignore the error and proceed without issuing an error message.

◆ Display an error message and proceed.

◆ Restart using the Last Known Good control set or ignore the error if the Last Known Good control set is causing the error. This option can be picked from the menu that is displayed after pressing F8 during the initial boot process. The Last Known Good control set represents the registry configuration that was used the last time the computer was successfully logged onto. This configuration will not be replaced until the next successful logon.

◆ Restart using the Last Known Good control set or halt if the Last Known Good control set is causing the error.

NOTE **Debugging the Boot Process** By entering the /SOS switch in the boot.ini file, Windows 2000 Professional will list the drivers' name on the screen as the system starts up.

NOTE **Loading the Device Drivers** A *control set* contains configuration data used to control the system, such as a list of the device drivers and services to load and start.

NOTE **Specifying Driver Order** The value of the LIST entry specified in the HKEY_LOCAL_MACHINE\SYSTEM\ CurrentControlSet\Control\ ServiceGroupOrder subkey defines the order in which NTLDR loads the device drivers.

A RISC (reduced instruction set computing) computer contains the NTLDR software as part of its BIOS. Therefore, the boot phase of a RISC-based computer is both simpler and faster than the boot phase of an Intel-based computer. A RISC computer keeps its hardware configuration in its BIOS, which obviates the need for the NTDETECT.COM program. Another item kept in firmware is the list of any valid operating systems and how to access them. This means that a RISC computer does not use a boot.ini file as well.

A RISC computer boots by loading a file called OSLOADER.EXE. After reading the hardware configuration from the BIOS and executing, OSLOADER.EXE passes control of the boot process to NTOSKRNL.EXE. After this HAL.DLL is loaded, followed by the system file.

Advanced Boot Options

Pressing F8 during the operating system selection phase displays a screen with advanced options for booting Windows 2000. Table 4.17 lists the Windows 2000 advanced boot options and their functions.

TABLE 4.17

ADVANCED BOOT OPTIONS

Option	Function
Safe Mode	Loads only the basic devices and drivers required to start the system. This includes the mouse, keyboard, mass storage, base video, and the default set of system services.
Safe Mode with Networking	This performs a Safe Load with the drivers and services necessary for networking.
Safe Mode with Command Prompt	This performs a Safe Load but launches a command prompt rather than Windows Explorer.
Enable Boot Logging	Logs the loading and initialization of drivers and services.
Enable VGA Mode	Restricts the startup to use only the base video.
Last Known Good Configuration	Uses the Last Known Good configuration to boot the system.
Directory Services Restore Mode	Allows the restoration of the Active Directory (on Domain Controllers only).
Debugging Mode	Turns on debugging.

When logging is enabled, the boot process writes the log information to \%systemroot%\NTBTLOG.TXT.

When you use one of the Safe Boot options, an environmental variable is created, Safeboot_Option, which is set to either Network or Minimal.

Understanding the BOOT.INI File

The Boot.ini file includes two sections, [boot loader] and [operating systems], that contain information that NTLDR uses to create the Boot Loader Operating System Selection menu.

During installation, Windows NT generates the Boot.ini file, which contains Advanced RISC Computing (ARC) paths pointing to the computer's boot partition. The following is an example of an ARC path:

```
multi(0)disk(0)rdisk(1)partition(2)
```

Table 4.18 describes the naming conventions for ARC paths.

TABLE 4.18

ARC FIELD DEFINITIONS

Convention	*Description*
Multi (*x*) or scsi (*x*)	The adapter/disk controller. Use scsi to indicate a SCSI controller on which SCSI BIOS is *not* enabled. For all other adapter/disk controllers, use multi, including SCSI disk controllers with the BIOS enabled.
	The *x* field represents a number that indicates the load order of the hardware adapter. For example, if you have two SCSI adapters in a computer, the first to load and initialize receives number 0, and the next SCSI adapter, number 1.
disk(*y*)	The SCSI ID. For multi, this value is always 0.
rdisk(*z*)	A number that identifies the disk. This is not used with SCSI controllers.
partition(*a*)	A number that identifies the partition.

In both multi and scsi conventions, multi, scsi, disk, and rdisk numbers are assigned starting with (0). Partition numbers start with (1). All nonextended partitions are assigned numbers first, followed by logical drives in extended partitions.

You can add a variety of switches to the entries in the [operating systems] section of the Boot.ini file to provide additional functionality. Table 4.19 describes optional switches that you can use for entries in the Boot.ini file.

TABLE 4.19

BOOT.INI SWITCHES

Switch	*Description*
/basevideo	Boots the computer using the standard VGA video driver. If a new video driver is not working properly, this switch will allow Windows 2000 to load.
/baudrate=*n*	Uses a baudrate different from the default (19200).
/crashdebug	Sends debug information only on a fatal system error.
/debug	Always sends debug information.
/debugport=com*x*	Uses serial port *x* instead of the default.
/maxmem:n	Specifies the amount of RAM that Windows 2000 uses. This switch is used if you suspect a memory chip is bad.
/nodebug	Does not send debug information.
/noserialmice=com*x*	Disables the serial mouse connected on port *x*.
/sos	Displays the device driver names as they are loaded. This switch is used when startup fails while loading drivers.

The following is an example of the output produced when the /sos switch is included in the Boot.ini file on an Intel processor. The `multi(0)disk(0)rdisk(0)partition(1)` refers to the system disk. This is followed by the path (usually \WINNT\System32) and then the file, dll, or system driver that is being loaded.

```
multi(0)disk(0)rdisk(0)partition(1)\WINNT\System32\
➥ntoskrnl.exe
multi(0)disk(0)rdisk(0)partition(1)\WINNT\System32\hal.dll
multi(0)disk(0)rdisk(0)partition(1)\WINNT\System32\
➥BOOTVID.DLL
multi(0)disk(0)rdisk(0)partition(1)\WINNT\System32\config\
➥system
multi(0)disk(0)rdisk(0)partition(1)\WINNT\System32\
➥c_1252.nls
multi(0)disk(0)rdisk(0)partition(1)\WINNT\System32\
➥c_850.nls
multi(0)disk(0)rdisk(0)partition(1)\WINNT\System32\
➥l-intl.nls
```

```
multi(0)disk(0)rdisk(0)partition(1)\WINNT\FONTS\vgaoem.fon
multi(0)disk(0)rdisk(0)partition(1)\WINNT\System32\DRIVERS\
➥pci.sys
multi(0)disk(0)rdisk(0)partition(1)\WINNT\System32\DRIVERS\
➥isapnp.sys
multi(0)disk(0)rdisk(0)partition(1)\WINNT\System32\DRIVERS\
➥pciide.sys
multi(0)disk(0)rdisk(0)partition(1)\WINNT\System32\DRIVERS\
➥PCIIDEX.SYS
multi(0)disk(0)rdisk(0)partition(1)\WINNT\System32\DRIVERS\
➥MountMgr.sys
multi(0)disk(0)rdisk(0)partition(1)\WINNT\System32\DRIVERS\
➥ftdisk.sys
multi(0)disk(0)rdisk(0)partition(1)\WINNT\System32\DRIVERS\
➥Diskperf.sys
multi(0)disk(0)rdisk(0)partition(1)\WINNT\System32\DRIVERS\
➥WMILIB.sys
multi(0)disk(0)rdisk(0)partition(1)\WINNT\System32\DRIVERS\
➥dmload.sys
multi(0)disk(0)rdisk(0)partition(1)\WINNT\System32\DRIVERS\
➥dmio.sys
multi(0)disk(0)rdisk(0)partition(1)\WINNT\System32\DRIVERS\
➥PartMgr.sys
multi(0)disk(0)rdisk(0)partition(1)\WINNT\System32\DRIVERS\
➥atai.sys
multi(0)disk(0)rdisk(0)partition(1)\WINNT\System32\DRIVERS\
➥disk.sys
multi(0)disk(0)rdisk(0)partition(1)\WINNT\System32\DRIVERS\
➥CLASSPNP.sys
multi(0)disk(0)rdisk(0)partition(1)\WINNT\System32\DRIVERS\
➥KsecDD.sys
multi(0)disk(0)rdisk(0)partition(1)\WINNT\System32\DRIVERS\
➥ntfs.sys
multi(0)disk(0)rdisk(0)partition(1)\WINNT\System32\DRIVERS\
➥ndis.sys
multi(0)disk(0)rdisk(0)partition(1)\WINNT\System32\DRIVERS\
➥Mup.sys
```

You can modify the timeout and default parameter values in the Boot.ini file by using System Properties in the Control Panel. In addition, you can edit these and other parameter values in the Boot.ini file manually. You might want to modify the Boot.ini file to add more descriptive entries for the Boot Loader Operating System Selection menu or to include various switches to aid in troubleshooting the boot process.

Last Known Good Configuration

Configuration information in Windows 2000 Professional is kept in a control set subkey. A typical Windows 2000 installation would have subkeys like ControlSet001, ControlSet002, and

CurrentControlSet. The CurrentControlSet is a pointer to one of the ControlSet*xxx* subkeys. There is another control set named Clone that is used to initialize the computer (either the Default or LastKnownGood). It is re-created by the kernel initialization process each time the computer starts.

The key HKEY_LOCAL_MACHINE\SYSTEM\Select contains subkeys named Current, Default, Failed, and LastKnownGood, which are described in the following list:

◆ **Current.** This value identifies which control set is the CurrentControlSet.

◆ **Default.** This value identifies the control set to use the next time Windows 2000 starts (unless you choose the Last Known Good configuration during the boot process).

◆ **Failed.** This value identifies the control set that was the cause of a boot failure the last time the computer started.

◆ **LastKnownGood.** This value identifies the control set that was used the last time Windows 2000 was started successfully. After a successful logon, the Clone control set is copied to the LastKnownGood control set.

When you log on to a Windows 2000 Professional computer and modify its configuration by adding or removing drivers, the changes are saved in the Current control set. The next time the computer is booted, the kernel copies the information in the Current control set to the Clone control set. After the next successful logon to Windows 2000, the information in the Clone control set is copied to LastKnownGood.

If you experience problems starting the computer that you think might be related to Windows 2000 configuration changes that you just made, restart the computer with logging on and press F8 during the initial boot phase. Selecting the Last Known Good configuration will restore the system configuration to the last one that Windows 2000 used to start successfully.

Using the Last Known Good configuration does not help in the following situations:

◆ If the problem is not related to the Windows 2000 configuration, such as problems with a user profile or with file permissions.

◆ If you complete the boot process and log on to the Windows 2000 system, the information in the LastKnownGood control set is updated.

◆ If the startup problem is related to hardware failures or missing or corrupted files.

Using the Emergency Repair Disk (ERD)

The Emergency Repair Disk (ERD) can be used to repair problems with the boot sector on your system's disk. The ERD is usually created immediately after installing Windows 2000 Professional for the first time.

Step by Step 4.10 shows how to create an Emergency Repair Disk.

NOTE **The ERD References the Original Registry** You should not use the ERD to repair a registry problem. The copy of the registry used by the ERD is the original one created during the setup of Windows 2000 Professional, or the registry that was in place the last time the ERD was re-created.

STEP BY STEP

4.10 Creating an Emergency Repair Disk (ERD)

1. Log on to your computer as administrator.

2. Click on Start, point to Programs, Accessories, and click on Backup.

3. Select the Emergency Repair Disk icon or select the Tools menu item and click on Create an Emergency Repair Disk.

4. Insert a blank, formatted 1.44MB disk in drive A: and click OK.

5. When the process is complete, remove the disk and label it appropriately.

You should re-create the ERD on a scheduled basis to reflect any changes made to the configuration of the computer.

To restore your settings from the Emergency Repair Disk you will need the Windows 2000 Professional CD or the Windows 2000 Professional setup disks, as described in Step by Step 4.11.

STEP BY STEP

4.11 Restoring Your System Using the ERD

1. Start your computer with the Windows 2000 Professional CD or with the Windows 2000 Professional setup disk number 1 in the floppy disk drive.

2. After Setup copies files from the CD or disk, the system will start the operating system installation.

3. At the Welcome to Setup screen, select the R option to repair or recover a Windows 2000 installation.

4. Select the R option to repair a damaged Windows 2000 installation.

5. Select the manual repair if you don't want to repair the registry and want to selectively repair the system files, partition boot sector, or the startup environment.

6. Select the fast repair if you want to repair the system files, the boot sector, startup environment, and the system registry.

7. The Manual repair option allows you to select the tasks to perform. The tasks you can select are 1) check the startup environment for missing or corrupt files, 2) verify the Windows 2000 system files are installed, and 3) verify the boot sector references the correct boot loader.

8. The repair option will request the ERD disk in Drive A: or will attempt to locate Windows 2000 automatically if one is not available.

9. If you have the Windows 2000 Professional CD, you can choose to have Setup verify your installation against corruption.

10. When the repair process completes, the computer will automatically reboot and Windows 2000 will load.

Missing or corrupted files are reloaded from the original media. This means that any changes made, software installed, or service packs applied will be lost.

Saving and Restoring System State Data

The Backup utility can save and restore system state data. For Windows 2000 Professional, system state data refers to the registry, the COM+ Class Registration database, and boot files. When you choose to back up system state data, all system state data is saved (it is not possible to save components of the system state data).

If you use Backup to restore the saved system state data, it will erase the system state data currently on your computer and replace it with the system state data that you are restoring.

This is a method of saving registry data on a regular basis to have a recent copy available for restoration in the event of corruption or loss of the registry information.

Using the Windows 2000 Recovery Console

If your computer will not start due to a corrupted or missing file, you can use the Windows 2000 Recovery Console to gain access to the disk without starting Windows 2000. This will provide you with a command prompt from which you can perform limited administrative tasks. The following is a list of some of the tasks you can perform from the Recovery Console:

◆ Start and stop services.

◆ Copy data from a floppy disk or a CD.

◆ Read or write data on a local drive.

◆ Format a disk drive.

◆ Repair the boot sector or boot record.

If you get an error message when booting your computer that indicates that a system file is missing, you can use the Recovery Console to start the system and copy a new version of the file from the CD to the system drive.

The Recovery Console does have some limitations, however:

◆ You cannot copy files from the hard drive to a floppy disk.

◆ You can view only the %windir% directory (usually C:\Winnt) and its subdirectories.

◆ You need to identify yourself by logging in as the Administrator. If the Security Accounts Manager (SAM) hive is corrupt or missing, you will not be able to use the Recovery Console.

Configuring the Windows 2000 Recovery Console

To use the Recovery Console, you must first install it from the Windows 2000 CD. The Installation Wizard will create all the files necessary and modify Boot.ini to provide an additional boot menu item that will allow you to select the Recovery Console while starting your system.

Installing the Recovery Console

The Recovery Console Wizard is started with the following command:

```
path_to_executable\WINNT32 /cmdcons
```

path_to_executable refers to the \I386 subdirectory on the Windows 2000 CD. For example, if you have two hard drives and your CD-ROM drive is E:, then the command to start the Recovery Console Installation Wizard would look like the following:

```
E:\I386\winnt32 /cmdcons
```

Using the Recovery Console

The following procedure can be used to start your computer with the Windows 2000 Recovery Console.

STEP BY STEP

4.12 Starting the Windows 2000 Recovery Console

1. Start your computer and select the Windows 2000 Recovery Console boot menu item.

2. Enter the number of the Windows 2000 installation you want to log on to (there may be more than one if there are multiple operating systems loaded on your computer).

3. Enter the administrator password when prompted.

4. Make any required changes to the system.

5. Type **Exit** to restart your computer.

The Windows 2000 Recovery Console gives you a command prompt in the %windir% directory, usually c:\Winnt.

Table 4.20 lists the commands available to you when running the Windows 2000 Recovery Console.

TABLE 4.20

WINDOWS 2000 RECOVERY CONSOLE COMMANDS

Command	Description
Disable *servicename*	Disables a service or driver.
Enable *servicename*	Enables a service or driver.
DiskPart [/add|/delete] [*device\drive\partition*] [*size*]	Adds or deletes a disk partition. If the partition is being added, *size* specifies the size of the new partition.
FixBoot [*driveletter*]	Replaces the Windows 2000 boot sector in the system partition or on the disk specified by *driveletter* (if specified).
FixMBR *devicename*	Repairs the master boot record (MBR) of the boot partition. This is used if the MBR has become corrupted and Windows 2000 cannot start.
ListSVC	Lists the services and whether they are automatically or manually started.

continues

TABLE 4.20	*continued*

WINDOWS 2000 RECOVERY CONSOLE COMMANDS

Command	*Description*
Logon	Lists the available system to log on to, requests the administrative password, and then logs you on to a Windows 2000 installation.
Map arc	Lists all connected drives. The arc command will list them in ARC paths instead of drive letters. ARC paths are used in the Boot.ini file to specify the local drives to boot from.
SystemRoot	Sets the current directory to systemroot.

The Windows 2000 Recovery Console also supports a number of DOS commands, such as Attrib, Cd, Cls, Copy, Delete, Dir, Extract, Format, Md, More, Rd, Rename, and Type.

Troubleshooting Stop Errors

If a Stop error screen appears, it could be a transient problem that will not reoccur if you restart, or it could signify a more serious or permanent error occurring in your computer. If the Stop screen reoccurs, use the following steps to identify the problem:

1. Verify that any recently installed hardware or software is properly installed.

2. Disable or remove any newly installed hardware (such as RAM, network adapters, or modems), drivers, or software.

3. If you can start Windows 2000, check the Event Viewer for additional error messages that might help identify the cause of your problem. To open the Event Viewer, click Start, point to Settings, click Control Panel, double-click Administrative Tools, double-click Event Viewer, and click System Log.

4. If you cannot start Windows 2000, try to start the computer in Safe Mode. From here you should be able to disable or remove any added drivers or programs. To start your computer in Safe Mode, press F8 during the initial boot screen and select Safe Mode.

5. Verify that you have the latest drivers for any hardware devices and that you have the most recent system BIOS. Check with your hardware manufacturer for this information (often available freely over the Internet).

6. Disable any BIOS memory options like caching or shadowing.

7. Check for viruses on your computer, using a recent version of your virus-protection software.

8. Verify that all the hardware and drivers installed in your computer are on the Microsoft Hardware Compatibility list for Windows 2000.

9. Run any system diagnostic programs that were included when you purchased the computer. Especially important will be any memory checks.

10. Revert to the Last Known Good Configuration.

CASE STUDY: PERFORMANCE PROBLEMS WITH A NEW PROCESS

ESSENCE OF THE CASE

The following points summarize the essence of the case study:

▶ The system has just had a new application installed.

▶ The application runs continually as a service to local and remote users.

▶ After a number of days of continual running, the system performance degrades.

▶ Rebooting the system temporarily resolves the problem. However, it eventually returns.

▶ Available memory is consumed and paging activity increases.

SCENARIO

You have installed a new locally developed service program. This service runs in the background continually. You and a number of remote users who are accessing data on your system use it. When you first install it, you run the Performance Monitor on your system to establish a baseline of performance during normal working conditions. A few days later, your system becomes sluggish and noticeably slower in all functions. You reboot your system and it appears to be working normally again. A few days later the same performance problems occur again. You run the Performance Monitor and discover that the amount of available memory has dropped to almost zero and the paging file is active.

continues

CASE STUDY: PERFORMANCE PROBLEMS WITH A NEW PROCESS

continued

ANALYSIS

When dealing with performance problems, it is important to remember that almost everything is interrelated with everything else. Memory problems can cause disk activity, which can manifest itself as a processor bottleneck. In this case, because the problem was apparently solved when the system was restarted, the problem is likely related to consumption of a resource rather than an elevated rate of activity. When the problem occurred again days later, the Performance Monitor showed higher-than-expected paging activity and almost no available memory. That combination would normally indicate a system that is underconfigured in memory for the process running. Since this situation did not exist when the new application was brought on line, the conclusion is that the new background service leaks memory. In this situation, memory acquired by the service during normal processing is not returned to the system. Over time, the amount of working memory assigned to the service would exceed the amount available, and the Windows 2000 Professional operating system would begin to page to meet the needs of its normal workload. The recommendation would be to send the new service back to the developers for analysis.

CHAPTER SUMMARY

This chapter focused on actions you can take and procedures you can use to increase the reliability and performance of your Windows 2000 Professional computer system. Knowing how your system functions and the workload under which you normally expect to see it perform is vital to being able to recover your data in the event that something catastrophic occurs. Planning how to recover your system is not a task that can occur after the problem happens.

The processes built into Windows 2000 Professional to assist in protecting your currently well-running system from being corrupted by the addition of an incompatible driver or a driver not certified as working with Windows 2000 Professional were covered first.

Next, additional built-in processes to assist in running daily or routine tasks using the Task Scheduler were discussed. Additionally, offline files and synchronization were shown to allow mobile users to function off the network as well as they could when on the network and to allow them to reintegrate changes made when reconnected.

The third topic of performance monitoring was discussed from the point of view of memory usage, processor resource utilization, and network and disk activity, as well as how all those factors combine to influence how user applications run.

Finally, this chapter addressed the topics of backup and restore, booting options available when problems arise during startup, and the added functionality of the Recovery Console.

KEY TERMS
- Performance Monitor
- Hardware profiles
- Task Scheduler
- Offline files
- Synchronization
- Performance Counter
- LastKnownGood configuration
- Recovery Console

Exercises

4.1 Configuring Driver Signing

This exercise will help you explore the steps necessary to configure device driver signing—a built-in mechanism to prevent uncertified device drivers from being installed accidentally.

Estimated Time: 10 Minutes

1. Click on Start.

2. Select Settings and select Control Panel.

3. Double-click on System.

4. Select the Hardware tab.

5. Click the Driver Signing button.

6. Select an option.

7. Click OK.

4.2 Scheduling a Task

This exercise will help you explore the Task Scheduler by having it schedule a batch job. An important part of managing your Windows 2000 Professional computer is having it automatically run jobs that you create.

Estimated Time: 10 Minutes

1. Open a command window and create a batch job with the command net send *machine_name* Hi There. Substitute the word machine_name with the name of your Windows 2000 Professional computer.

2. Click on Start.

3. Select Settings and select Control Panel.

4. Double-click on Scheduled Tasks.

5. Double-click on Add a Scheduled Task.

6. In the Scheduled Task Wizard, click Next.

7. Click Browse.

8. Highlight the test batch job created for this exercise and click Open.

9. Select the option One Time Only and click Next.

10. Select a time one or two minutes into the future and click Next.

11. Enter the userid and password under which the job should run and click Next.

12. Click Finish to create the job. At the time selected, a popup window should appear with the message Hi There.

4.3 Configuring Synchronization of Offline Files

This exercise explores the Synchronization Manager to configure and schedule jobs to synchronize offline files—one of the ways to maintain access to networked files even if you are on the road or just disconnected from your network.

Estimated Time: 10 Minutes

1. Click on Start.

2. Select Programs, Accessories, and click on Synchronize.

3. Click Properties to see the status of the contents of the offline file folder.

4. Close the offline file folder window.

5. Click on Setup.

6. Select the Logon/Logoff tab.

APPLY YOUR KNOWLEDGE

7. Select the network connection that synchronization will use.

8. Select the files to synchronize the time (logon or logoff) to do the synchronization.

9. Select the On Idle tab.

10. Ensure that the Idle Synchronization box is checked and click on Advanced.

11. Set the amount of time your Windows 2000 Professional computer must be idle before synchronization is performed.

12. Click OK to close the window.

13. Select the Scheduled tab and click the Add button to start a new scheduled task.

14. Click Next to start the wizard.

15. Select a network connection and file to synchronize and click Next.

16. Enter the schedule information for automatically synchronizing the offline files.

17. Click OK to close the window.

18. Click Synchronize to start a manual synchronization or click Close if a scheduled task was created.

4.4 Watch Memory Usage Using Performance Manager

This exercise explores using the Performance Manager to watch typical memory counters on your Windows 2000 Professional system. The techniques used here are applicable to all the other performance objects available through the Performance Manager. Performance Manager is an important tool in understanding the workload on your system.

Estimated Time: 15 Minutes

1. Click on Start and select Programs.

2. Select Administrative Tools.

3. Select Performance.

4. Expand the Performance Monitor to full screen size and click on the plus (+) button.

5. In the Performance Object drop-down list, select the Memory entry.

6. Select and add the counters Available Bytes, Cache Bytes, Pages/Sec, Non-Paged Bytes, and Paged Bytes.

7. Select the performance object Cache.

8. Select and add the counter Copy Read Hits %.

9. Close the Add Counters window.

4.5 Create a New Hardware Profile

This exercise explores creating a new hardware profile and modifying it to disable drivers not used in the new profile. This is a method that Windows 2000 Professional provides to allow mobile users to have hardware configurations other than the complete configuration usually available at the docking station.

Estimated Time: 10 Minutes

1. Click on Start.

2. Select Settings and click Control Panel.

3. Double-click System.

4. Select the Hardware tab.

5. Click Hardware Profiles.

6. Select a profile to copy (either Profile 1 or Docked Profile).

APPLY YOUR KNOWLEDGE

7. Click Copy.

8. Name the new profile and click OK.

9. Click OK twice and close the Control Panel.

10. Restart your computer and select the new profile when prompted.

11. After the system restarts, click Start.

12. Select Settings and click Control Panel.

13. Double-click on System.

14. Select the Hardware tab.

15. Click Device Driver.

16. Select the devices to disable when using this profile by expanding a device type (such as Network Adapters), right-clicking a device, and selecting Disable.

17. Click OK to close the system applet and close the Control Panel.

4.6   Install the Recovery Console

This exercise explores the steps to install and then run the Recovery Console. This feature of Windows 2000 Professional provides an additional mechanism for repairing your system in the event of a problem at boot time.

Estimated Time: 15 Minutes

1. Insert the Windows 2000 Professional disc in the CD-ROM device.

2. Open a command window and change drives to the CD-ROM.

3. Change directory to the I386 subdirectory.

4. Enter the command `winnt32 /cmdcons`.

5. Answer Yes at the installation window. (Note that installation of the Recovery Console takes about 7MB of disk space.)

6. Wait until the necessary files are copied to disk and answer OK to finish when prompted.

7. Restart your Windows 2000 Professional computer.

8. Select the Recovery Console boot option when prompted.

9. Wait for the installation process to complete.

10. Select the Windows installation to log in to (choose your normal boot system).

11. Enter the Administrator password when prompted.

12. At the command prompt, enter the `DIR` command. You should be in the C:\WINNT directory.

13. Enter `HELP` to see the commands available.

14. Enter `EXIT` to exit the Recovery Console and automatically reboot your computer.

4.7   Recovering Files to an Alternate Location

This exercise uses a set of previously backed-up files to explore reloading to an alternate location. This technique is very useful in restoring either data or programs without impacting other information contained in the folder.

Estimated Time: 15 Minutes

1. Click Start.

2. Select Programs, Accessories, System and click on Backup.

APPLY YOUR KNOWLEDGE

3. Click on the Restore Wizard.

4. In the Restore Wizard window, click Next to start the process.

5. The catalog of files to restore is sorted by the media name given during the backup procedure. Expand a media entry and select the folder or files to restore.

6. Click Next and then click the Advanced button to change the location of the restore.

7. In the Restore File To drop-down window, select Alternate Location and enter a new location in the provided window.

8. Select how you want to restore the files (do not overwrite, overwrite only older files, always overwrite) and click Next.

9. Ensure that security is restored and click Next.

10. Click Finish to start the process.

11. Enter the path of the media file to restore from and click OK.

12. Click Close when the process is complete and close the Backup window.

Review Questions

1. Where is the digital signature kept for a signed device driver?

2. How do you run a job under administrative rights with Task Scheduler?

3. If memory is in short supply, what does the Windows 2000 Professional operating system rely on?

4. What is the best indicator to look at when judging a processor to be overloaded?

5. How do you enable logical disk counters?

6. If you have copied Profile 1 to a new hardware profile, how do you disable devices you don't want to load?

7. If you want to reload some files by using only two sets of backup tapes, what backup method should you use?

8. If you load a new device driver and your Windows 2000 Professional computer will not boot, what safe boot option should you use to recover?

Exam Questions

1. You are a user with administrative rights on your Windows 2000 Professional computer. You download a new driver for your video card over the Internet and update your system to include it. When you restart your computer, you find that it halts partway through the boot sequence. What action should you take first to diagnose the problem?

   A. Reboot your computer, start the Recovery Console, and remove the new driver from your system.

   B. Use the Emergency Repair Disk feature to restore the system.

   C. Use the Recovery Console to start a restore of the system from your last backup.

   D. Reboot using the LastKnownGood option and enable driver signing as soon as possible.

APPLY YOUR KNOWLEDGE

2. You are an SMS administrator and you need to run a set of customized reports on the status of jobs in the SMS system every Wednesday morning. The reports take some time to complete, but you would like them to be done by the time you get to the office.

Required Result:

You need to run the reports on a scheduled basis.

Optional Desired Results:

The reports should be run using the SMS administrator account.

You would like to be notified when the reports finish.

Proposed Solution:

You implement a scheduled task to run a batch job you have created to produce the reports from SMS. You include a Net Send command at the end to send a message to your Windows 2000 Professional workstation when the job completes all the reports. You also configure the Scheduled Task to run the batch job under the SMS administrator account and password.

Which result(s) does the proposed solution produce?

A. The proposed solution produces the required result and produces all of the optional desired results.

B. The proposed solution produces the required result and produces only one of the optional desired results.

C. The proposed solution produces the required result but does not produce any of the optional desired results.

D. The proposed solution does not produce the required result.

3. You are an IT specialist with a large courier company. It seems that you are on the road making presentations more now than ever before. Normally, when you are working in your office, you share information with your group using a set of shared folders on one of the networked servers. You would like to take your files and some other common ones with you when you travel and then be able to update changes you have made when you return.

Required Result:

You must be able to copy selected folders and/or files onto your computer prior to leaving.

Optional Desired Results:

You would like to have the system automatically return changed files to the network share when you reconnect.

You would like to maintain security access settings while the folders and files are on your computer.

Proposed Solution:

You flag the networked files as being available offline and set the Synchronization Manager to resynchronize the files when you log off.

Which result(s) does the proposed solution produce?

A. The proposed solution produces the required result and produces all of the optional desired results.

B. The proposed solution produces the required result and produces only one of the optional desired results.

C. The proposed solution produces the required result but does not produce any of the optional desired results.

D. The proposed solution does not produce the required result.

4. You are an IT specialist for a small engineering firm. You have added a new application to your system and have upgraded the memory to support it. When you run the new application you find that your system runs a little slower and the new application does not run as well as expected. In addition, the system disk seems to be on more often and you occasionally get a message about being low on virtual memory. You know that your system is almost out of disk space on the system drive with less than 50MB left. You review the Performance Monitor counters and see that paging activity is up but the processor is not particularly busy.

Required Result:

You must resolve the virtual memory problems and increase the performance of the system overall.

Optional Desired Results:

The paging activity would be reduced.

The configuration would support a workload that will expand over time.

Proposed Solution:

You use the remaining space on the system drive to expand the paging file.

Which result(s) does the proposed solution produce?

A. The proposed solution produces the required result and produces all of the optional desired results.

B. The proposed solution produces the required result and produces only one of the optional desired results.

C. The proposed solution produces the required result but does not produce any of the optional desired results.

D. The proposed solution does not produce the required result.

5. You are an IT specialist for a small engineering firm. You have added a new application to your system and have upgraded the memory to support it. When you run the new application you find that your system runs a little slower and the new application does not run as well as expected. In addition, the system disk seems to be on more often and you occasionally get a message about being low on virtual memory. You know that your system is almost out of disk space on the system drive with less than 50MB left. You review the Performance Monitor counters and see that paging activity is up but the processor is not particularly busy.

Required Result:

You must resolve the virtual memory problems and increase the performance of the system overall.

Optional Desired Results:

The paging activity would be reduced.

The configuration would support a workload that will expand over time.

APPLY YOUR KNOWLEDGE

Proposed Solution:

You leave a 2MB paging file on the system disk and add new paging files on other disks. If necessary, you may have to add disk space to your computer's configuration to have enough free disk space available to allow you to supply a paging file at least twice the size of physical memory.

Which result(s) does the proposed solution produce?

A. The proposed solution produces the required result and produces all of the optional desired results.

B. The proposed solution produces the required result and produces only one of the optional desired results.

C. The proposed solution produces the required result but does not produce any of the optional desired results.

D. The proposed solution does not produce the required result.

6. You are an IT specialist with a large courier company. It seems that you are on the road making presentations more now than ever before. Normally, when you are working in your office, you share information with your group using a set of shared folders on one of the networked servers. You would like to take your files and some other common ones with you when you travel and then be able to update changes you have made when you return.

Required Result:

You must be able to copy selected folders and/or files onto your computer prior to leaving.

Optional Desired Results:

You would like to have the system automatically return changed files to the network share when you reconnect.

You would like to maintain security access settings while the folders and files are on your computer.

Proposed Solution:

You flag the networked files as being available offline and set the Synchronization Manager to resynchronize the files when you log off. You also configure the Synchronization Manager to resynchronize the files back to the network shares when you log on again.

Which result(s) does the proposed solution produce?

A. The proposed solution produces the required result and produces all of the optional desired results.

B. The proposed solution produces the required result and produces only one of the optional desired results.

C. The proposed solution produces the required result but does not produce any of the optional desired results.

D. The proposed solution does not produce the required result.

7. You are a salesman with a large insurance company. You maintain a home office and travel extensively on job-related business. You have a variety of ways to connect to your corporate

network, including ISDN from the office, a cable modem from your home office, and modem lines to the company RAS server when you are on the road.

Required Result:

You need to supply the network connection options necessary for each location.

Optional Desired Results:

You would like to minimize the overhead of maintaining drivers and protocols that are not in use at a location.

You would like the Home Office profile to be the default since you work at home more often than you visit the corporate office.

Proposed Solution:

You make two copies of the default (docked) profile and call them *Home Office* and *On the Road*, respectively. You modify each profile to have the ISDN driver (docked), TCP/IP only (Home Office), and modem only (On the Road). You also use the Hardware section of the System applet in the Control Panel to move the Home Office hardware profile to the top of the list, making it the default profile.

Which result(s) does the proposed solution produce?

A. The proposed solution produces the required result and produces all of the optional desired results.

B. The proposed solution produces the required result and produces only one of the optional desired results.

C. The proposed solution produces the required result but does not produce any of the optional desired results.

D. The proposed solution does not produce the required result.

8. You are a business lead in a user department in a large telco. As a business lead you are the local IT expert that your users go to first for advice. Your company has just upgraded the network in your department, so you decide to try a larger bandwidth adapter in your computer to see what difference the network changes make. You add a faster network adapter but find that your computer seems a little sluggish. You check the Performance Monitor and see that the CPU is very busy, interrupts are way up, and there is a little paging.

What change should you make to your system to compensate?

A. Get a faster processor.

B. Replace the network adapter with one that supports interrupt avoidance or moderation.

C. Balance the disk activity to reduce the overall interrupt activity.

D. Add memory to reduce the paging activity.

9. You are a financial analyst in the accounting department of a manufacturing firm. You have developed a set of financial models that you run every day to help you in your work. The models change greatly during processing and have become very important to your department. The data and the programs are all kept in a folder that you back up once a week completely

APPLY YOUR KNOWLEDGE

and incrementally every day. Somehow the application has gotten corrupted partway through the day and will no longer start.

Required Result:

Get the application running again without losing any data.

Optional Desired Results:

Since the financial models are so important and they change considerably during the day, you should protect the data more often than with just daily backups.

Reduce the amount of time necessary to restore the data in the event this occurs again.

Proposed Solution:

You copy all the data your models use to another disk or file folder not in the path that you have backed up.

You reload the files using the full backup and then each of the incremental backups.

You copy all the data for your models back to the application folder.

Which result(s) does the proposed solution produce?

A. The proposed solution produces the required result and produces all of the optional desired results.

B. The proposed solution produces the required result and produces only one of the optional desired results.

C. The proposed solution produces the required result but does not produce any of the optional desired results.

D. The proposed solution does not produce the required result.

10. You are a financial analyst in the accounting department of a manufacturing firm. You have developed a set of financial models that you run every day to help you in your work. The models change greatly during processing and have become very important to your department. The data and the programs are all kept in a folder that you back up once a week completely and incrementally every day. Somehow the application has gotten corrupted partway through the day and will no longer start.

Required Results:

Get the application running again without losing any data.

Optional Desired Results:

Since the financial models are so important and they change considerably during the day, you should protect the data more often than with just daily backups.

Reduce the amount of time necessary to restore the data in the event this occurs again.

Proposed Solution:

You copy all the data your models use to another disk or file folder not in the path that you have backed up.

You reload the files using the full backup and then each of the incremental backups.

You copy all the data for your models back to the application folder.

APPLY YOUR KNOWLEDGE

You alter the backups to be differential rather than incremental, which will mean a restore will use only two tape sets (the full backup and the last differential).

You create a scheduled backup job to copy the data files from your financial model to another disk every weekday at noon.

Which result(s) does the proposed solution produce?

A. The proposed solution produces the required result and produces all of the optional desired results.

B. The proposed solution produces the required result and produces only one of the optional desired results.

C. The proposed solution produces the required result but does not produce any of the optional desired results.

D. The proposed solution does not produce the required result.

11. You are a database specialist working for a software company. You are building an application that uses a COM object to extract employee changes from your company's financial system and saves them in a database that is referenced by the company's internal home page as an employee directory listing. Your company has recently merged with another of about the same size and has reorganized. This has resulted in a large number of changes every day. You notice that retrieving data takes longer now than you expect even after examining the indexes on the database. You examine your system and find that memory is not in short supply and the paging activity is normal. The disk subsystem the database is on is only performing about 15 I/O operations per second and the CPU is not busy. You suspect the database has been configured to grow its datafiles in too small an increment, resulting in disk fragmentation.

You need to return the performance to its previous levels. What should you do? Choose the most correct answer.

A. Defragment the disk the database data files are on.

B. Resize the database, defragment the disk, save and reload the database, and rebuild the indexes.

C. Replace the disk holding the database with one that has a higher rotational speed.

D. Replace the disk holding the database with a hardware-enabled RAID-5 structure.

12. You are a financial analyst in a large insurance firm that is using Windows 2000 Professional to run a number of financial models daily. The financial model uses some locally written processes in its execution. As your model has grown in complexity, you notice that the length of time taken to run the model once has increased sharply. You use the Task Manager to observe the amount of CPU used and find that it is at 100% during most of the execution of the financial model. Upon further investigation with Performance Monitor, you find that one process (part of your customization of the model) is monopolizing the CPU resource and that disk activity to the paging file has increased. Access to network shares while the model is running is also noticeably slower than at other times.

APPLY YOUR KNOWLEDGE

Required Result:

Improve the execution time of the financial model.

Optional Desired Results:

The disk activity to the paging file would be reduced.

Network access would be increased.

Proposed Solution:

You add an additional CPU to your Windows 2000 Professional computer to provide additional processing power.

Which result(s) does the proposed solution produce?

A. The proposed solution produces the required result and produces all of the optional desired results.

B. The proposed solution produces the required result and produces only one of the optional desired results.

C. The proposed solution produces the required result but does not produce any of the optional desired results.

D. The proposed solution does not produce the required result.

13. You are a financial analyst in a large insurance firm that is using Windows 2000 Professional to run a number of financial models daily. As your model has grown in complexity, you notice that the length of time taken to run the model once has increased sharply. You use the Task Manager to observe the amount of CPU used and find that it is at 100% during most of the execution of the financial model. Upon further investigation with Performance Monitor, you find that one process (part of your model) is monopolizing the CPU resource and that disk activity to the paging file has increased. Access to network shares while the model is running is also noticeably slower than at other times.

Required Result:

Improve the execution time of the financial model.

Optional Desired Results:

The disk activity to the paging file would be reduced.

Network access would be increased.

Proposed Solution:

You replace your existing CPU with the fastest speed available to your computer. In addition, you add physical memory and increase the size of the paging file appropriately.

Which result(s) does the proposed solution produce?

A. The proposed solution produces the required result and produces all of the optional desired results.

B. The proposed solution produces the required result and produces only one of the optional desired results.

C. The proposed solution produces the required result but does not produce any of the optional desired results.

D. The proposed solution does not produce the required result.

14. You are a database analyst in a small engineering firm. You are running a SQLServer database from a Windows 2000 Professional desktop and providing access to this database to others in your workgroup. Your coworkers complain that after a few minutes, response on the database drops off. You open up the performance monitoring system on the desktop and notice that CPU usage and disk activity appear normal. During this time the performance of the database also appears normal. When you close the screen the problem returns after a delay. You suspect that some task is consuming all the available CPU but you can't identify it.

    You need to have the system respond better with greater predictability. What should you do? Pick the most correct answer.

    A. Remove any scheduled tasks that are executing in the background.

    B. Remove any screen saver being used on the desktop.

    C. Increase the amount of physical memory available to SQLServer.

    D. Increase the performance of the disks on which the database resides.

15. You are a database administrator in a centralized database administration group with a large utility company. You are assisting a development group by managing their test database server that you are running on a Windows 2000 Professional desktop. This is a test system, so database files and log files reside on the main system disk partition. The development group is complaining that the database is responding more slowly than

their project will allow and asks you to resolve the problem. You run the Performance applet from the control page and track CPU usage, disk, and memory activity. You discover that the CPU is not very busy, but there is a large number of disk I/Os to the disk subsystem that seem to be correlated to memory page faults.

Required Result:

Improve the response of the database.

Optional Desired Results:

The disk activity to the paging file would be reduced.

The amount of memory page faults would be reduced.

Proposed Solution:

You move the database and log file to a separate disk drive, increase the amount of physical memory available, and increase the size of the paging file appropriately.

Which result(s) does the proposed solution produce?

A. The proposed solution produces the required result and produces all of the optional desired results.

B. The proposed solution produces the required result and produces only one of the optional desired results.

C. The proposed solution produces the required result but does not produce any of the optional desired results.

D. The proposed solution does not produce the required result.

APPLY YOUR KNOWLEDGE

Answers to Review Questions

1. Digital signing is not strictly limited to device drivers and can be applied to any type of file. Because of this, the file itself cannot be modified (since each type would require a separate mechanism to accommodate the signature information). The digital signatures are kept in an associated file with a .CAT extension. The link between the .CAT file and the device driver is in the .INF file for the driver. See "Managing and Troubleshooting Driver Signing."

2. Part of the information required by the Task Scheduler's Add a New Task Wizard is the inclusion of a domain/userid and password to run the job under. This allows the user to schedule a job with a userid that has privileges other than the one currently logged in. See "Configuring, Managing, and Troubleshooting the Task Scheduler."

3. The Windows 2000 Professional operating system uses the paging file as the extension to physical memory. It is used as a backup to allocated virtual memory and to provide a place to contain memory dumps of the system in case of a failure. The paging file is normally 12MB larger than physical memory, but that can vary depending on the processes run on the system. The paging file can be moved, added to, or split across a number of disks and controllers to increase performance. See "Optimizing and Troubleshooting Memory Performance."

4. The best indicators are those that show that a queue is forming to access the resource. This is true for other resources (like disk and network interfaces) as well. If there is a processor-bound task running, the Windows 2000 Professional operating system will allocate all of it to that task. The CPU will appear to be 100% busy. However, it is not a bottleneck until some other task needs it but the processor is not available because it is being monopolized or is busy doing other administrative tasks such as paging or seeking disk sectors. See "Optimizing and Troubleshooting Processor Performance."

5. Normally, Windows 2000 Professional enables physical disk counters when it starts. This can be verified by running the DISKPERF command, which will show the status of both physical and logical disk counters. To enable the logical disk counter, the command is DISKPERF –YV. After the system is restarted, the logical counters will be available. See "Examining and Tuning Disk Performance."

6. The process to modify a hardware profile is to reboot the system under that hardware profile and then, by using an account with administrative privileges on the local computer, start the System application from the Control Panel, access the Device Manager, and disable those devices that are not needed. By copying the original hardware profile, you will be starting with all the devices you have configured on your computer. See "Managing Hardware Profiles."

7. Planning your backup strategy is important and of course dependent on how you want to perform any recover actions. In this case, the choice is a normal backup at some time interval and differential backups in between. The timing between normal backups will depend on how long you want to maintain those tapes and also how much the system is changing. If the number of files chosen by the differential backup become a significant portion of the normal backup, then

APPLY YOUR KNOWLEDGE

the differential backup becomes wasteful of both time and tape resources. See "Recovering System and User Data by Using Windows Backup."

8. The best option is to reboot your computer and press F8 during the boot process to access the Last Known Good configuration. When a change is made to the registry to include a new driver, that change is not made permanent until after a successful logon. If you are having problems getting past that point, you still have the last working copy of the registry to fall back on. Rebooting with the Last Known Good option will throw away the changes and revert to a working environment. See "Troubleshooting System Restoration Using Safe Mode."

Answers to Exam Questions

1. **D.** The new device driver has been installed in the system but the changes are not permanent until a successful boot has completed. No matter how many times you try to get through a boot, if it fails, the last changes made can still be rolled back. The way to recover the last working configuration is to reboot the computer and press F8 to access the Safe Boot menu and select the LastKnownGood configuration option. This will load the working copy of the registry and the system will restart with the old video driver in place. Using the Recovery Console is primarily for repairing disk damage and file corruption and is not appropriate for reloading the system or manually configuring device drivers. The ERD contains the configuration of the system at the point the ERD was created, and although this would work, it would also wipe out any changes made since that time. See "Troubleshooting System Restoration Using Safe Mode."

2. **A.** The Task Scheduler allows you to run known system programs like Word or Excel, but it also allows you to execute batch jobs or programs that you have prepared. The Task Scheduler provides a mechanism to run the job using the rights of a different userid. The NET SEND command can be included in the report job to provide a pop-up window on your workstation when the reports are either completed or have passed some known point in the processing. See "Configuring, Managing, and Troubleshooting the Task Scheduler."

3. **B.** Offline files provides an automatic way of copying files from network shares to your computer for access when you are disconnected from the network and/or away from the office. The Synchronization Manager can be configured to synchronize when the system is idle, at select times, or at logon/logoff. The Synchronization Manager automatically maintains the security setting for offline folders. Since the solution as presented only synchronizes at logoff point, the optional results are not addressed. See "Managing and Troubleshooting the Use and Synchronization of Offline Files."

4. **D.** This is a system that has had the workload increased and the available memory increased without resizing the paging file. In this case, consuming all the available space on the system drive may help the availability of virtual memory, but the Windows 2000 Professional operating system requires at least 5MB of free space to function properly. Without that, it will be spending its time looking for free space and not processing data. You will have shifted from one bottleneck to another. See "Optimizing and Troubleshooting Memory Performance."

5. **A.** This is a system that has had the workload increased and the available memory increased without resizing the paging file. In this case, reducing the paging file to 2MB on the system drive (the minimum recommended), moving the paging file to other disks (adding them if necessary), and expanding the paging file to at least twice physical memory will reduce the paging activity, solve the virtual memory problems (there will be space in the paging file to allocate to processes), and provide some growth for the workload the system is capable of taking on. See "Optimizing and Troubleshooting Memory Performance."

6. **A.** The Synchronization Manager maintains the same security setting offline as the folders and files have when they are on their network share. Likewise, the times to synchronize the files are also configurable. The best solution here is to synchronize the file when you log off, providing you with the latest copies before you disconnect, and synchronize again when you log on, providing the network shares with any changes you have made. See "Managing and Troubleshooting the Use and Synchronization of Offline Files."

7. **A.** Hardware profiles are the built-in method of loading different device drivers when your Windows 2000 Professional system loads. By making copies of the Docked profile (assuming this is a laptop since the user travels) you are getting a copy of all the devices installed when the Windows 2000 Professional operating system was installed. You can then adjust these copies to load only the drivers you want when using that configuration. The Available Profiles window allows you to position the profiles in any order,

with the top one being the default to choose when booting. See "Managing Hardware Profiles."

8. **B.** This is a case of a problem manifesting itself in many areas of the system. The new network adapter provides greater bandwidth and therefore a larger workload to the processor. The amount of memory it reserves from the non-paged pool will be greater (because of the faster packet I/O rate) and the increased memory has triggered an increase in paging. These events combine to slow the system down. Adding a faster processor can address some of the symptoms but does not attack the bottleneck directly. Likewise, working with the disks to even out the interrupt rate does not deal with the problem directly. Adding memory is always a good idea, but the real solution is to replace the network adapter with one that does not interrupt the system as much. See "Monitoring Network Performance."

9. **C.** This solution will meet the primary requirement, which is to recover the application without losing any data. Since the application will not start, the problem is in an initialization file, the registry, or the program files themselves. Recovering the directory will repair it. However, it will also reload the model data files from last night. Without saving today's changes, you run the risk of wiping out the morning's work. The solution does not address any of the optional requirements of increasing the frequency of backups (perhaps by using scheduled tasks to back up the data during the day) or reducing the amount of time the restore takes (perhaps by changing the backup from a daily increment to a full or differential backup). See "Recovering System and User Data by Using Windows Backup."

10. **A.** This solution not only repairs the application by reloading the copy from last night's backup without losing this morning's work with the financial model, but it addresses the problem of reducing the recovery time by using differential backups. Since the application does not change (or not very often) the differential backup will focus on the data only. Then any restore procedure will require reading only two tape sets. By using backup to copy the data models to disk every noon, you provide for a fast restore from noon in the event of a disk failure or other program file corruption. See "Recovering System and User Data by Using Windows Backup."

11. **B.** The problem here is the incremental growth the database would experience because the workload has changed in the way described. As an expert analyzing the impact an application has on the use of system resources, you must take into account the behavior of the application as well. A database system uses disk space at two levels. The first is as a normal application writing to a system file. The second is as a database system using that system file space as its own complicated storage mechanism that it allocates to tables, indexes, and logs. Both these structures can fragment when many small increments are made over time. Just defragmenting the disk space at the system file level will not gain you the performance you want. Reloading the data will allow you to load the data back into the database tables contiguously for best performance. Replacing the disk drive with a faster rotating one will help reads since a database does its I/O randomly, and reducing the seek time will make the system faster; however, it does not address the root problem, which is a fragmented database structure. Similarly, adding a hardware-enabled RAID 5 disk system for the database will provide multiple disk drive for each read request, which will speed up response, but does not address the root problem. See "Examining and Tuning Disk Performance."

12. **D.** One of the processes in the financial model that you are running is consuming all the available CPU resources. The fact that the CPU is constantly at 100% utilization would not increase the activity to the paging file, so that must indicate that the amount of memory required by the application has also increased recently. Since the process using the CPU is written by an in-house programmer, it will probably not be using the multiprocessor capabilities of the operating system. Adding an additional CPU will therefore not allow the application to split its functions in half and utilize the other CPU. If the high CPU utilization rate is slowing network performance, then adding an additional CPU may well facilitate that requirement, but without solving the core problem. Without addressing the additional memory requirements as indicated by an increase in paging activity, you have not provided the remaining optional result. See "Optimizing and Troubleshooting Memory Performance."

13. **A.** The process that is consuming all the available CPU resources is a locally written extension to a financial modeling package. That process would not be multiprocessor-safe and therefore would not be able to take advantage of an additional CPU. It would benefit, however, from a faster CPU. Replacing the CPU on your computer's motherboard with the fastest one available would help return the performance of your computer to acceptable levels. Adding additional memory and resizing the paging file will solve the memory

APPLY YOUR KNOWLEDGE

restrictions implied by an increase in paging file activity. Solving both the CPU bottleneck and any memory shortage will solve the slowdown on network response as well. See "Optimizing and Troubleshooting Processor Performance" and "Optimizing and Troubleshooting Memory Performance."

14. **B.** The key to the solution here is the timing of the performance problems. In this case, the database performance is unacceptable when the system is running by itself. When you begin to examine performance counters on the display, the performance returns to acceptable levels. The correct answer lies in removing a screen saver that is starting up a length of time after the keyboard and mouse go inactive, and is probably building a complex screen (like Pipes) and consuming too much CPU in the execution. See " Optimizing and Troubleshooting Processor Performance."

15. **A.** The database file and transaction log exist on the same partition (and physical disk) as the operating system (and therefore the paging file). Your correlation between memory paging activity and a large I/O load indicates that the majority of the disk activity is probably paging file I/O. This indicates that the amount of physical memory is not great enough to support the requirements of the database activity. Increasing the amount of physical memory available will lower the amount of paging I/O, which will leave more time for database activity. Moving the database and transaction log files to a separate spindle will also isolate them from other system activity, which will increase response as well. See "Optimizing and Troubleshooting Memory Performance" and "Examining and Tuning Disk Performance."

Suggested Readings and Resources

1. Stanek, William R. *Microsoft Windows 2000 Administrator's Pocket Consultant.* Microsoft Press, 2000.

2. Joyce, Jerry and Marianne Moon. *Microsoft Windows 2000 Professional at a Glance.* Microsoft Press, 2000.

3. *Microsoft Windows 2000 Professional Step by Step.* Microsoft Press, 2000.

This chapter will help you prepare for the "Configuring and Troubleshooting the Desktop Environment" section of the exam.

Configure and manage user profiles.

▶ All users logging on to a local computer running Windows 2000 or a Windows 2000 domain receive a user profile. There are two types of user profiles, local and roaming. As the administrator, you can specify the type of user profile that the user receives and whether the user is able to make changes to the profile that persist after the user logs off.

Configure support for multiple languages or multiple locations.

- **Enable multiple-language support.**
- **Configure multiple-language support for users.**
- **Configure local settings.**
- **Configure Windows 2000 Professional for multiple locations.**

▶ In multinational organizations it is common to see the use of different versions (linguistically) of the Windows 2000 operating system in different countries. To accommodate users who travel between countries it may be necessary to enable and configure different regional settings that allow a user to easily switch between languages. We will look at how to configure regional options and explain input locales.

Install applications via Windows Installer packages.

▶ The Windows Installer service is a component of the Intellimirror Management Technologies. Intellimirror can be broken into three core areas: User Data Management, User Settings Management, and Sofware Installation and Maintenance. The Windows Installer service falls

CHAPTER 5

Configuring and Troubleshooting the Desktop Environment

within the Software Installation and Maintenance component of Intellimirror. Two goals of Intellimirror and, subsequently, the Windows Installer Service are to reduce total cost of ownership and provide all users with a truly roaming desktop wherein a user's desktop area and applications are always available. It achieves this lofty goal through a new file type known as an .msi file that allows applications to be rolled out to users and computers through application packages. The cost reduction is achieved through rollout benefits and through application self-repair features that we will examine. By providing a more stable desktop environment to your users for a longer period of time and reducing the time it takes to correct desktop problems, the cost of ownership can be reduced.

Configure and troubleshoot desktop settings.

▶ A user's desktop settings are the personal settings that a user is sometimes able to configure himself to personalize his computer's desktop. Users tend to like to create work environments that are comfortable to them. In their offices or cubicles, they might hang family pictures or certificates displaying their achievements. Computer desktop settings offer much the same type of personalization to users. We will look at how a user can configure his personal local profile to include his desired desktop settings.

Unfortunately, not all jobs can offer the ability to customize the work environment. For example, a construction worker does not have the luxury of customizing every work site with his personal effects because it just wouldn't be efficient. We will look at ways to limit or entirely remove the ability of the user to make changes to his profile by using roaming mandatory profiles.

Configure and troubleshoot fax support.

▶ Fax support has been incorporated into Windows 2000 to provide organizations with the ability to send, receive, and store faxes for users in your network. We will look at the steps involved in setting up fax support and troubleshooting some of the more common fax problems.

Configure and troubleshoot accessibility services.

▶ In today's work environment, most individuals are required to work at a computer in some capacity throughout the day. To allow individuals with special needs to interact more effectively, Microsoft has improved upon the accessibility features in Windows 2000. We will examine the configuration of these services for our users and troubleshoot some common problems.

- ▶ The concept of local and roaming profiles has not changed from Windows NT 4.0 Workstation to Windows 2000 Professional. You need to understand how to configure both local and roaming profiles as well as personal and mandatory profiles.

- ▶ Know how to analyze and configure a local security policy through the Security Configuration and Analysis snap-in.

- ▶ Know how to set up and configure a local group policy and the order in which multiple policies get applied.

- ▶ Have an understanding of the types of IPSec Policies available and what each one does.

- ▶ Make sure you are comfortable with the theory and application of the Windows Installer service in Windows 2000 Professional and the available options for software installation.

- ▶ Know the available Internet Explorer options that allow you to configure your Internet settings in Windows 2000 Professional.

INTRODUCTION

In this chapter we will explore how to configure and troubleshoot the Windows 2000 desktop environment. Knowing how to configure the Windows 2000 desktop environment is critical for systems administrators; this skill will be a key component of their management responsibilities. We will cover creation and configuration of local and roaming profiles, use of Windows Installer, and configuration of desktop and Internet options.

CONFIGURING USER PROFILES

Configure and manage user profiles.

User profiles define a specific user's desktop settings, printer and drive mappings, background color, wallpaper, and display options. A user's personal profile defines his own unique settings on the computer. Your personal local user profile could be compared to your office or cubicle in your department (assuming you are not working in an "open concept" environment). You hang your own pictures on the wall, and put your family photos on the desk. Every day, you come in to work and your office is the same as you left it the day before. The way in which you set up your office could be correlated to your profile. It is "local" in the sense that if you went to another geographical location where your company had offices, your office would not be there. Your office does not roam or travel with you. In the context of user profiles, this means that your local user profile is stored on one computer, the computer that it was originally created on by you as a user logging on to that computer. The path to this profile is %systemdrive%\Documents and Settings*Username*, where *Username* is the user's logon name.

User profiles contain all of the user-specific settings and are saved in the user's profile directory. If the only location of this directory is the local hard disk in the path C:\Documents and Settings, then the profile is known as a local user profile. In this directory, there are a series of subdirectories, as shown in Figure 5.1 for the user fsmith. As you can see from Figure 5.1, some of the subdirectories appear shaded, which denotes a hidden directory. To see these directories, you must change your view settings in Windows Explorer to Show

All Files. In addition to the directories in each user's profile folder is a file called NTUSER.DAT. When a user logs on, his configuration settings in his profile directory and the settings in the NTUSER.DAT file are loaded. The user's profile settings found within the user's directory are used to make changes to the desktop, and the contents of the NTUSER.DAT are loaded into the HKEY_CURRENT_USER portion of the registry of the local computer. It is the NTUSER.DAT file that is used to maintain the user's environment preferences during his logon session. The settings that combine to make up the NTUSER.DAT file are outlined in Table 5.1. Table 5.2 defines the settings that are included in the user's profile directory.

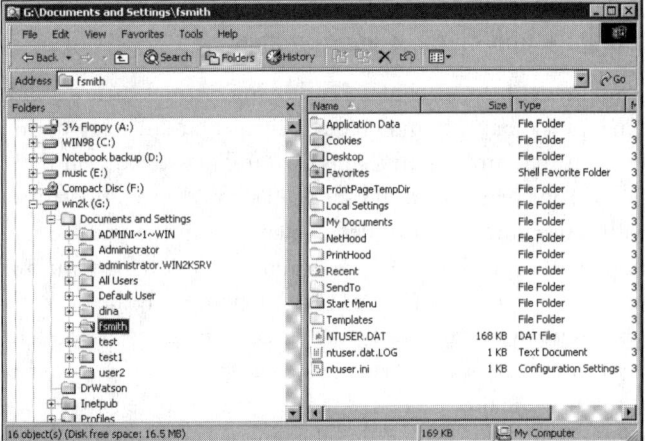

FIGURE 5.1
Local profile directory structure.

TABLE 5.1

NTUSER.DAT SETTINGS

Setting	Definition
Windows Explorer	Any persistent connections and user-defined Windows Explorer settings.
Taskbar	Taskbar settings, personal program groups and associated settings, and program items and associated properties.

Setting	*Definition*
Printer Settings	All the user's network printer settings.
Control Panel	Any user settings made in Control Panel.
Accessories	All Windows 2000 application settings for applications like Notepad, Paint, Calculator, Clock, and Hyperterminal.
Help Favorites	Any user-defined Help favorites.

TABLE 5.2

USER PROFILE COMPONENTS

Component	*Contents*
Application Data	Application-specific data. The contents of the data stored in this directory are determined by the software vendor.
Cookies	User preferences and information, most commonly used on the Web to track site visits and areas of interest.
Desktop	The desktop layout and content, including program shortcuts, files, and folders.
Favorites	Shortcuts to your favorite sites on the Internet or intranet.
Local Settings	Application data, temporary files, and the history of sites on the Web you have visited recently.
My Documents	The default location where you store your data.
My Pictures	A subdirectory of My Documents created to save your personal pictures.
NetHood	Shortcuts to My Network Places.
PrintHood	Printer shortcuts.
Recent	Shortcuts to your most recently accessed documents.
SendTo	Configuration of the SendTo menu. Applications or storage locations to which to send a document (such as Notepad, 3 1/2-inch Floppy, Mail Recipient, and so on).
Start Menu	User's personal Start menu configuration. All common Start menu shortcuts are found in the All Users profile directory in %systemdrive%\Documents and Settings\All Users.
Templates	User templates.

User Profile Types

Going back to the example we discussed earlier, if you wanted to have your office environment travel with you between geographical locations, a great deal of work would be involved. Having your user profile travel with you is not as much work. To have your user profile travel with you, it must be changed from a local user profile to a roaming user profile. This would not change your user profile settings; only the location of your user profile would be changed. The user profile would have to be moved to a network share where it could be accessed from anywhere in the network.

This brings us to the two types of profiles that exist in Windows 2000: local and roaming. Each of these types can be further divided into two subtypes: personal and mandatory. In other words, a local profile could be either a local personal profile that allows a user to make changes, or a local mandatory profile that does not allow a user's changes to be saved. Likewise, a roaming personal profile allows a user to make changes to her profile that travels or roams with her. A mandatory roaming user profile does not allow a user to make changes that persist, but it does roam or travel with the user.

> **EXAM TIP**
>
> **Local Mandatory Profiles** Although the creation of local mandatory profiles is possible, their use is very limited and therefore should not be a focus of the exam.

Local User Profiles

A local user profile is created automatically when a user logs on to a computer running Windows 2000, and it is stored locally on that machine. This makes the local user profile available to the user only when logging on to the same machine. A local user profile is configurable by the user and the changes made to that profile get saved when the user logs off the computer.

Every user who logs on locally to a computer running Windows 2000 Professional receives a local user profile. There are two default profile folders that are used in the creation of all new local user profiles and are installed with Windows 2000. These two default profile folders are known as the Default User profile and the All Users profile.

The Default Users profile acts as a template for all local user profiles. The contents of the Default User profile are copied to a folder named after the username of the user logging on. Every user's initial local profile begins as a simple copy of the Default User profile. This

copy gets stored on the local machine in the path %systemdrive%\
Documents and Settings*Username.* This local storage location
means that this profile is only available on the machine on which it
is stored; therefore, it is a local user profile.

The All Users profile contains settings that apply to every user
logging on locally to the computer. These settings are appended to
the user's own profile settings. An example of the types of settings
contained in the All Users profile are program shortcuts that appear
on every user's Start menu. These shortcuts for tools or applications
like Solitare, Calculator, and Paint are stored in the All Users profile.
The reasoning behind this is as follows: If every user is going to use
the same shortcuts, why store the same set of shortcuts for each
user? Rather, it makes more sense to store them once in a central
profile (All Users) and link to that central profile. This being
said, Microsoft, for some reason that defines rational logic, has
chosen again not to be consistent in how they do things. I am
referring to the fact that other application shortcuts like
Command Prompt, Imaging, Notepad, Synchronize, and
Windows Explorer are included in each user's profile directory
in the path %systemdrive%\Documents and Settings*Username*\
Start Menu\Programs\Accessories.

Step by Step 5.1 demonstrates the automatic creation of a local
user profile.

> **N O T E**   **Location of Local Profiles**   The local
> profiles location may vary depending
> on how Windows 2000 was installed.
> If you upgraded to Windows 2000
> from Windows NT Workstation 4.0,
> local profiles will still be located in
> their NT 4.0 location (%windir%\
> profiles*user_name,* where *user_name*
> represents the user's logon name).
> If a clean installation of Windows
> 2000 Professional was performed,
> the local profiles will be stored in
> the path %systemdrive%\Documents
> and Settings*user_name.*

STEP BY STEP

5.1 Creating a Local Profile

1. Log on to a computer running Windows 2000
   Professional as the Administrator. Open Computer
   Management in the Administrative Tools menu.

2. Under System Tools, expand Local Users and Groups
   and right-click on the Users folder. Select New User from
   the context menu. Figure 5.2 shows the New User dialog
   box. In the User Name box enter **user1** and remove the
   check mark from the box titled User Must Change
   Password at Next Logon. Click Create and click Close.
   Close Computer Management. User1 is the user account
   that you will use to log on locally and for which a local
   user profile will be created automatically.

continues

continued

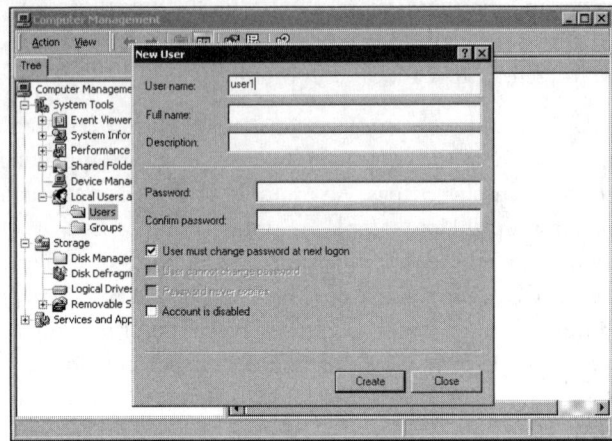

FIGURE 5.2
Creating a new local user account in Computer Management.

Changing Your View Settings in Windows Explorer If you do not see the Default User folder you may have to change your view. The Default User folder is a hidden folder and cannot be seen with the default view settings. Select Tools from the menu bar followed by Folder Options. Select the View tab and select Show Hidden Files and Folders. Click OK, and the Default User folder should appear. If the folder still does not appear, select View on the menu followed by Refresh.

N O T E

3. To verify that user1 does not have a local user profile, double-click on My Computer and then double-click on the drive that contains the Windows 2000 Professional system files. Double-click on the Documents and Settings folder and verify that no folder for User1 exists. Also confirm that there are folders named Administrator, All Users, and Default User.

4. Close My Computer and log off as Administrator.

5. Log on as User1.

6. To see the newly created local user profile, double-click on My Computer, double-click on the drive that contains the Windows 2000 Professional system files, and double-click on the Documents and Settings folder. A folder named user1 should now appear. This is the folder that contains the local user profile for user1.

Now we know how local user profiles are created and where they are stored when a user logs on locally to a computer running Windows 2000 Professional. Unfortunately, having a local profile on one computer doesn't help us if we want to log on to another computer. To solve this dilemma we need to configure the second type of user profile: a roaming profile.

Roaming User Profiles

A roaming user profile is stored on a network share and can be accessed from any computer across the network. Like local user profiles, roaming user profiles can be either personal or mandatory. We will start our discussion looking at the concept of a roaming profile and then look at the difference in both personal and mandatory profiles.

A roaming user profile is very similar to a local user profile; the difference is that a roaming user profile can be accessed from any computer on the network. If changes to the profile are permitted, they are saved to a network location as opposed to the local hard disk when the user logs off, and are applied again when the user logs back on by accessing the network location.

To configure a roaming user profile, we must edit the user's properties and enter the path to the network share that contains the user's profile. Step by Step 5.2 demonstrates how to enable a roaming user profile.

> **NOTE**
>
> **Personal Local User Profiles** Local user profiles are personal by default. In other words, when a user logs on to a computer for the first time a local personal profile is created and that user is able to make changes and personalize that profile. Although it is possible to create a mandatory local user profile, the use of these profiles is very limited and will not be a focus of the exam, nor will they normally be used in your administration.

STEP BY STEP

5.2 Creating a Roaming User Profile

1. Log on as Administrator to the local machine.

2. To enable access to a roaming profile, a network share must exist in which to store the profiles. To create a network share, double-click on My Computer, and double-click on the C: drive. From the menu bar select File, New Folder. Enter **Profiles** as the name of the new folder and press Enter. Right-click on the Profiles folder and select Sharing. Select Share This Folder and in the Share Name box, Profiles will appear. Click OK to create the network share. Close My Computer.

3. In Administrative Tools, select Computer Management. Expand System Tools and Expand Local Users and Groups. Right-click the Users folder and select New User. In the User name box enter **user2**. Clear the check mark in the box titled User Must Change Password at Next Logon, and click Create, followed by Close.

continues

continued

4. Click once on the Users folder. In the list of users on the right side, double-click on user2. The user2 Properties dialog box appears. Select the Profile tab, as shown in Figure 5.3. In the Profile Path box, type the Universal Naming Convention (UNC) path to the profiles share on your computer. Enter **computer_name****profiles**\ **%username%** (where *computer_name* is the name of your computer, *profiles* is the name of the network share you created in step 2, and %*username*% is a variable that will be replaced with the user's logon name). Click OK and close Computer Management.

IN THE FIELD

USING ENVIRONMENT VARIABLES

The variable %*username*% is an environment variable that tells the operating system to replace that variable with the user account ID of a particular user. Using the variable is this situation will create a sub-directory in the profiles network share named user2 (the user's logon name) and will store user2's roaming profile within that folder. An alternative would be to enter **computer_name****profiles** **user2** but this is more likely to result in spelling or typing mistakes.

This environment variable can be especially useful when creating multiple user accounts. A template account can be created by the administrator that is configured with all the settings required by all the users in a particular department, perhaps Sales, and named #SalesTemplate. The reason for the # symbol is that it will be listed at the top of your list of users, making it easier to find in Active Directory Users and Computers or Computer Management. This template account can then be set to use the profile path *computername**profiles*\%*username*%. When the template account is copied, the variable is renamed to that of the username and a roaming profile is automatically configured. One restriction to be aware of is that you can only copy in Active Directory Users and Computers, so this only applies to domain user accounts.

5. Log off as administrator and log on as user2.

6. Double-click on My Computer, double-click on the drive that contains the Profiles network share, and double-click on the Profiles shared folder. You should see a folder named user2. This folder will contain user2's roaming personal profile. If you double-click on the user2 folder, it will currently be empty. The reason for that is that user2 must log off first before the profile is saved to the network share. To prove this, log off user2.

7. Log on again as user2. Double-click My Computer, double-click the drive containing the Profiles shared folder, and double-click the Profiles shared folder. Double-click the user2 folder. The user2 folder now contains the contents of user2's roaming profile. This roaming profile gets updated with the changes user2 makes during his current session when he logs off.

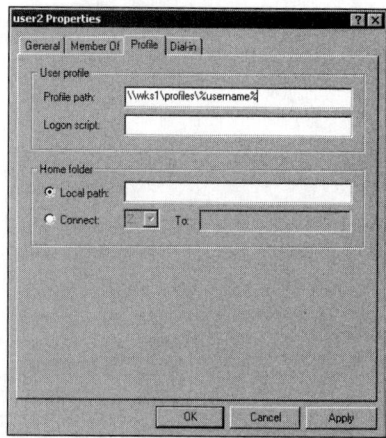

FIGURE 5.3
User Properties dialog box.

Personal User Profiles

Roaming personal user profiles can be configured on a number of individual Windows 2000 Professional computers and set to direct the user to a network share, but this would be a very tedious and highly inefficient process. The recommended approach would be to configure a domain environment and create accounts in the domain. Then configure the profile path of each user account to point to the shared network location. Step by Step 5.3 walks through an alternate method of changing a user's profile from local to roaming that involves using the User Profiles tab in the System applet in Control Panel.

STEP BY STEP

5.3 Changing a Local User Profile to a Roaming User Profile Through the System Applet in Control Panel

We will start this Step by Step by creating a local user account and local profile by logging on as the newly created user.

1. Log on as Administrator.

2. Open Computer Management in Administrative Tools. Expand Local Users and Computers and right-click on the Users folder.

3. Select New User from the Context menu and enter the Username **Bill**. Clear the check mark next to User Must Change Password at Next Logon and click Create followed by Close.

4. Close Computer Management and log off.

5. Log on as Bill with a blank password. This will create the local user profile for the user Bill.

6. Log off and log back on as Administrator.

7. Open Control Panel and double-click on the System applet. Select the User Profiles tab and select the user Bill.

8. With the user Bill selected, click on the Copy To button in the bottom-right corner of the dialog box.

9. In the Copy To dialog box, enter the path to the network location where your roaming profiles are to be stored. Sticking with the location we used in Step by Step 5.2, enter *computername**profiles**Bill* in the Copy Profile To box.

10. In the Permitted to Use section of the Copy To dialog box, make sure that the user Bill is listed. The Change button allows you to change the user or group of users permitted to use this profile. In this case we only want Bill to use it so we will leave it as is. Changing who could

use the profile will change the NTFS permissions on the directory to which we have selected to copy this profile if the directory is located on an NTFS volume or partition.

11. At this point we have changed the location of the local user profile from %systemdrive%\Documents and Settings\Bill to the shared network path of *computername**profiles*\Bill but the profile is still not a roaming profile. To configure it as a roaming profile we must complete the remaining steps.

12. Open Computer Management and expand Local Users and Computers. Click on the Users folder and then double-click on the Bill user.

13. The Bill Properties dialog box appears. Select the Profile tab and in the Profile Path box enter the path to the network share where the profile has been copied to (*computername**profiles*\Bill) and click OK.

14. Close Computer Management. Log off as Administrator. Log on as Bill. This will force the change from a local user profile to a roaming user profile to occur. Log off as Bill.

15. Log on as Administrator to confirm the change has taken place.

16. In Control Panel, double-click on the System applet and select the User Profiles tab. The Bill profile should now appear under the Type column as Roaming, not Local any longer.

Mandatory User Profiles

A mandatory user profile can be configured to be either local or roaming. As a local mandatory profile, it is available only on the computer on which it is stored and is applied only when the user logs on to that one specific computer.

A roaming mandatory user profile travels with the user regardless of the computer the user is logging on to. Any changes that the user makes during his logon session do not get saved when he logs off. Mandatory roaming user profiles are useful in environments where you want a group of users to always have the same profile regardless of the computer they log on to. An example of this might be for bank tellers. Suppose a bank has 14 different teller windows, each equipped with a computer, and you would like every teller to get the same settings regardless of which teller window at which they are working. To accomplish this, you could create a mandatory roaming user profile and configure each of your teller accounts to use that profile.

Think of a mandatory profile as a hotel room. While you are checked into the hotel, you can hang your own pictures on the wall and change the layout of the room, but when you check out the staff will change everything back to the way it was when you originally checked in. In this case, the changes you made do not persist once you check out or log off in the case of a mandatory profile.

Creating a roaming mandatory user profile is not very different from creating a roaming personal user profile, except we must ensure that any changes the user makes to the profile are not saved. The key to not allowing the user to maintain changes is to rename the NTUSER.DAT file to NTUSER.MAN. The NTUSER.DAT file can be found in the user's profile folder and renamed from there.

Step by Step 5.4 walks you through the process of changing user2's roaming personal profile to a roaming mandatory profile.

STEP BY STEP

5.4 Changing a Roaming Personal User Profile to a Roaming Mandatory User Profile

1. Log on as Administrator. Double-click My Computer, and double-click the drive on which the profiles shared folder is located. Double-click on the profiles shared folder and double-click on the user2 folder.

2. Rename the file ntuser.dat to ntuser.man and close My Computer.

3. Log off as Administrator and log on as user2. Right-click the desktop and select Properties from the context menu. On the Appearance tab, change the background color to Black, as shown in Figure 5.4, and click OK.

4. Log off and log back on as user2.

5. When you log back on, the desktop color is the default rather than black, confirming that you have configured a roaming mandatory user profile for user2.

Before we move on, we should discuss one of the potential troubleshooting issues with mandatory profiles that might arise. When configuring a roaming mandatory profile, the user's properties must be changed to indicate the network share in which the profile is located. This folder should not include an extension (such as *computername**profiles*\Bill.man) because this will prevent the user from logging on. Be careful with mandatory profiles and do not name folders with extensions.

In this section, we have learned about the two types of user profiles: local and roaming. We discussed the process that the operating system uses to create a local user profile from the Default User and All Users profiles. We have also learned the two types of roaming profiles—personal and mandatory—and walked through how to create all types. In the next section, we will look at what is involved in configuring your desktop environment.

The facts on profiles can be summarized as follows:

▶ The two types of profiles are local and roaming. Both of these types can be either personal or mandatory.

▶ Changes made during a logon session to a mandatory profile do not get saved.

▶ Changes made during a logon session to a personal profile do get saved.

▶ Local profiles are available only on the computer on which they are stored.

▶ Roaming profiles are stored on a shared network location, making them available from anywhere across the network.

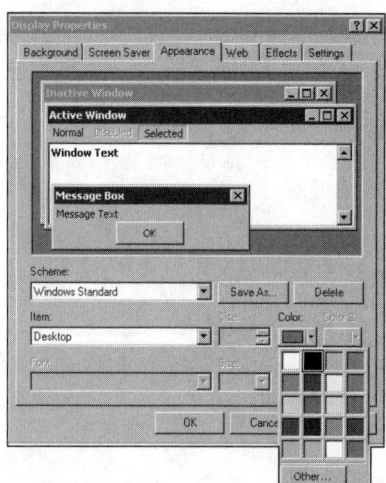

FIGURE 5.4
Display Properties dialog box.

REVIEW BREAK

CONFIGURING THE DESKTOP ENVIRONMENT

Configure and troubleshoot desktop settings.

Understanding that not all users are the same is the first step in configuring the desktop environment. Some of the users that we as administrators are responsible for supporting have special needs. The Windows 2000 operating system offers us a number of options to address the needs of our users.

In this section we will look at the available regional and accessibility options in Windows 2000 Professional.

Configuring Regional Options

Configure support for multiple languages or multiple locations.

With the globalization of the world economy, the requirements for business travel and language diversity are also increasing. More than ever before, we need to be able to access documents in multiple languages. Windows 2000 offers users the ability to switch between various regional settings to change the display format of numerical data or the keyboard layout.

The Regional Options applet in Control Panel allows you to switch between units of measurement or change the way the time, date, currency amounts, and numbers with decimals or fractions are displayed to the user. It also allows you to add support for multiple input locales so that a user visiting a United States office from your Paris office could switch to the French keyboard layout from the current default U.S. keyboard layout. Step by Step 5.5 walks you through the setup of multiple input locales in the Regional Options utility.

STEP BY STEP

5.5 Configuring Multiple Input Locales

1. Log on as Administrator.

2. Open Regional Options in Control Panel and select the Input Locales tab in the Regional Options dialog box.

3. Click the Add button in the Installed Input Locales section of the dialog box. From the Input Locale drop-down list, select the locale you would like to add and the keyboard layout and click OK. Repeat this step until you have added all the input locales that you require.

4. Select one of the input locales from the Input Language box and click the Set as Default button to establish the default locale, as shown in Figure 5.5.

5. Ensure that the Enable Indicator on Taskbar check box is selected and click OK.

6. In Accessories on the Start menu, open Wordpad. Type the sentence **My dog is fast**. and press Enter to start a new line of text. Hold down the left Alt key on the keyboard and press Shift and then type the same sentence again.

You should notice that the text is different. This is because you have switched between the two input locales with the Alt+Shift key sequence. Switching between input locales changes the keyboard layout to the format associated with that language.

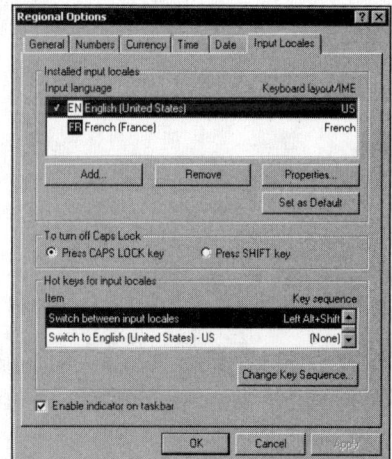

FIGURE 5.5
Establishing a default locale.

This exercise was meant to demonstrate to you how easy it is within the Windows 2000 desktop to switch between two different input locales in the very same document.

Another potential need in multinational organizations is to switch between languages and language settings on the desktop. The Windows 2000 operating system comes in a number of localized versions that are language-specific, as well as a language-independent version that allows you to install multiple languages. To take advantage of the different input locales that were discussed earlier it may be necessary to install additional languages first. Step by Step 5.6 looks at how to install multiple languages.

STEP BY STEP

5.6 Installing Multiple Languages

1. Logged on as Administrator, open Control Panel and double-click on the Regional Options applet.

2. On the General tab, select the languages that you are interested in installing and supporting by placing a check mark in the box next to the language. When you have selected all of the languages you require, click OK.

3. Insert the Windows 2000 CD or browse to a network path that contains the installation files and click OK.

4. Restart your computer for the settings to take effect.

Another component of the Windows 2000 desktop environment is the support for accessibility options, which we will explore next.

Configuring Accessibility Options

Configure and troubleshoot accessibility services.

Accessibility options can be configured within Windows 2000 to assist users with special needs or disabilities and help those users to more effectively interact with the operating system. Table 5.3 outlines the accessibility options available in Windows 2000.

TABLE 5.3

ACCESSIBILITY OPTIONS

Tool	*Function*
StickyKeys	Allows you to press key sequences such as Ctrl+Alt+Delete individually in sequential order instead of all at once for users with limited hand dexterity.
FilterKeys	Alerts Windows 2000 to ignore brief or repeated keystrokes.
ToggleKeys	Allows you to configure sounds for certain locking keys such as Caps Lock, Num Lock, and Scroll Lock.
SoundSentry	Provides visual warnings when your system makes a sound (for the hearing impaired).
ShowSounds	Displays captions for speech and sound made by your applications.
High Contrast	Configures Windows 2000 to use colors and fonts designed for easier reading.
MouseKeys	Allows the mouse pointer to be controlled by the numeric keypad.
SerialKey Devices	Allows support for serial key devices.

Using Control Panel is not the only way to enable the accessibility options; they can also be enabled by a hot key. Holding down the right Shift key for more than eight seconds will prompt you with the FilterKeys dialog box which contains a settings button that opens up the Accessibility Options applet. Step by Step 5.7 walks through how to configure and enable FilterKeys.

STEP BY STEP

5.7 Configuring and Enabling FilterKeys Options

1. Hold down the right Shift key on the keyboard until the FilterKeys dialog box pops up.

2. Click the Settings button on the FilterKeys dialog box.

continues

continued

3. To enable FilterKeys, place a check mark in the box to the left of Use FilterKeys. Click Apply. You should notice the FilterKeys icon appear in the bottom-right corner of the screen in the System Tray.

4. To change the settings of the FilterKeys, click on the Settings button in the FilterKeys section of the dialog box. Make your changes and click OK when you are finished.

In addition to the accessibility options enabled through Control Panel, Windows 2000 also ships with accessibility programs. The accessibility programs can be found in Accessories area on the Start menu. These programs are described in Table 5.4.

TABLE 5.4

ACCESSIBILITY PROGRAMS

Program	Function
Magnifier	Allows a portion of the screen to be magnified for easier viewing.
Narrator	Reads the contents of the screen aloud, assisting people with limited vision or a vision impairment.
On-Screen Keyboard	Allows users the ability to type on-screen with a pointing device.
Utility Manager	Enables administrative users to define the startup properties of accessibility programs and to start and stop individual accessibility programs.

The accessibility options included with Windows 2000 are not all-encompassing; many users with special needs will require additional applications that address their special requirements. To find out more about available accessibility programs, visit the Microsoft Accessibility section of the Microsoft Web site at http://www.microsoft.com/enable. Microsoft also has a catalog of accessibility aids that can be used with the Windows operating system. It's available by phone at 1-800-426-9400, via fax-back at 1-800-727-3351, or by writing Microsoft Sales Information Center, One Microsoft Way, Redmond, Washington 98052-6393.

Now that we have examined how to configure and optimize the Windows 2000 desktop to meet our regional and accessibility requirements, we will explore the management and configuration of applications. The Windows 2000 operating system will rarely be configured without applications. Normally, a user will require multiple applications to be installed on the computer to allow him to do his work. In the next section, we will look at the options available to install and configure applications on Windows 2000 Professional.

INSTALLING AND CONFIGURING APPLICATIONS

Install applications via Windows Installer packages.

The ongoing management and administration involved with desktop applications is generally one of the highest contributors to the cost of ownership of desktop computers. Microsoft has realized this and integrated technologies into the Windows 2000 operating system to reduce these associated costs.

The Windows 2000 operating system offers a number of options to install and configure applications on computers running Windows 2000 Professional. One of the options available to install applications is the Add/Remove Programs utility in Control Panel. This utility is not new to Windows operating systems and exists in many of Microsoft's previous GUI-based operating systems. Another option that is new to Windows 2000 is the Windows Installer service. The Windows Installer service allows application packages to be assigned or published to users or computers running Windows 2000 Professional and offers some additional features that help to reduce total cost of ownership.

The first step in managing applications in the Windows 2000 environment is to ensure that the application is supported. Microsoft has established an online Directory of Windows 2000 Applications that classifies applications into four categories, as shown in Table 5.5. The online directory can be found on the Web at http://www.microsoft.com/windows2000/upgrade/compat/search/ CompatApps.asp.

TABLE 5.5	
APPLICATION CATEGORIES	
Category	*Definition*
Certified	The highest level of certification. Applications have been tested by both the Independent Software Vendor (ISV) and VeriTest, and meet all standards.
Ready	The ISV has approved the application as compatible for Windows 2000 and provides product support for the application.
Planned	The ISV has committed to providing a Windows 2000-compatible version at the Ready or Certified levels at some later point in time.
Caution	Before upgrading to Windows 2000 Professional, read the important information about the application.

Once you have identified that the application you are about to install is supported, you can proceed by following the setup instructions that come with the application or by using Add/Remove Programs in Control Panel.

Add/Remove Programs

The Add/Remove Programs utility found in Control Panel in Windows 2000 uses the Windows Installer service to simplify the installation, removal, configuration, and repair of applications.

The Windows Installer Service is a client-side service that is installed with Windows 2000 Professional in the same way that other services like Alerter or Plug and Play are installed. The Windows Installer service manages the installation of applications and their associated system files, including .dlls, so that the applications can be efficiently removed if that need arises. Step by Step 5.8 walks through the process of removing an installed application.

STEP BY STEP

5.8 Removing an Installed Application Through Add/Remove Programs

1. Click Start, Settings, Control Panel.

2. Double-click on the Add/Remove Programs icon.

3. Select the program that you would like to remove. Examine the Size and Last Used On properties of the application.

4. Click the Remove button.

5. Respond to any application-specific questions pertaining to the removal.

Add/Remove Programs has been enhanced in Windows 2000 and now includes three sections, as shown in Figure 5.6.

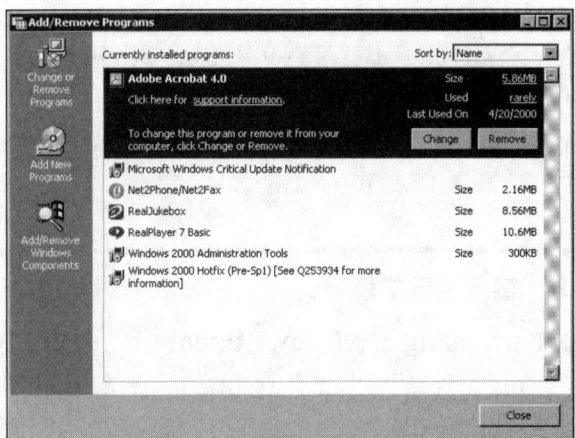

FIGURE 5.6
Add/Remove Programs applet.

The Change or Remove Programs section lists all of your currently installed programs by name and indicates their respective size. By clicking on one of the installed applications, as shown in Figure 5.6, you receive more information about the application and are able to change or remove it. Other very useful information from an administrative perspective includes the date when the application was last used. This can be helpful when deciding on an application to remove if disk space is filling up. If you ask a user which applications he would like removed, he might say, "Not that one; I use it all the time." This is a great way of seeing if that statement is entirely true.

Additionally, if you would like to sort the installed applications by size or date last used, you can use the Sort By option at the top-left corner of the Add/Remove Programs dialog box.

The second section is Add New Programs, which allows you to install an application from floppy disk, CD, the hard drive, or across the network. It also allows you to activate a Windows Update. Windows Update is a Web extension to the operating system that allows you to connect to the Microsoft Web site and download critical or optional updates, fixes, and device drivers. Clicking on the Windows Update button launches Internet Explorer and takes you to `http://windowsupdate.microsoft.com`. Step by Step 5.9 demonstrates how to perform a Windows Update.

This step-by-step tutorial will require Internet access in order to work.

STEP BY STEP

5.9 Performing a Windows Update

1. Click on Start, Settings, Control Panel.

2. Double-click on the Add/Remove Programs applet and select Add New Programs, and then click on the Windows Update button.

3. Internet Explorer will launch and take you to the Windows Update site at Microsoft.

4. Click on the Product Updates link in the top-left corner of the screen to get a list of critical updates, picks of the month, recommended updates, additional Windows features, preview versions, and device drivers. Select the update(s) that are of interest to you and proceed by clicking the Download link at the top of the right frame.

The third section of Add/Remove Programs is Add/Remove Windows Components. This is where new or additional services and accessories such as games are added or removed. Previously, in Windows NT 4.0, services were added and removed through the Network icon in Control Panel and accessories were added or removed through Add/Remove Programs.

Windows Installer

The Windows Installer service does not exist in isolation. With the introduction of the Windows Installer service comes Windows Installer files, which end with the extensions .msi and .mst. All applications and service packs released from Microsoft will now be released with Windows Installer files. Windows 2000 also comes with an application called WinInstall LE that allows for the creation of Windows Installer package files if an application does not come with one. A Windows Installer file is an alternative to or a replacement for your application's setup.exe or install.exe files and offers some enhanced functionality.

An example of a Windows Installer file can be found in the Winnt\System32 directory and is called adminpak.msi. This Windows Installer file gets added to the system32 directory during the installation of Windows 2000 Professional and is used to install the Windows 2000 Administrative Tools. Some of the functionality provided by Windows Installer files can be seen by right-clicking on the file to bring up the context menu shown in Figure 5.7.

NOTE

Disabling Windows Update As a network or systems administrator in a corporate setting, you may not want your users to have the ability to access Windows Update. It is possible to disable access to Windows Update for all users. To do this, at the Run command type **mmc**, and from the Console menu select Add/Remove Snap-in. Click Add, and choose Group Policy from the list of available snap-ins. Click Add again, followed by Finish, Close, and OK. Expand the Local Computer Policy, and then expand User Configuration, Administrative Tools and select the Start Menu & Taskbar folder. Double-click the Disable and Remove Links to Windows Update and select the Enabled option. Click OK, and close the mmc. Select No to save the console settings when prompted. These steps may differ slightly depending on the operating system you are working with (for example, Server or Professional).

It is also possible to disable the use of Windows Update for users in a domain by configuring a Group Policy with Active Directory Users and Computers.

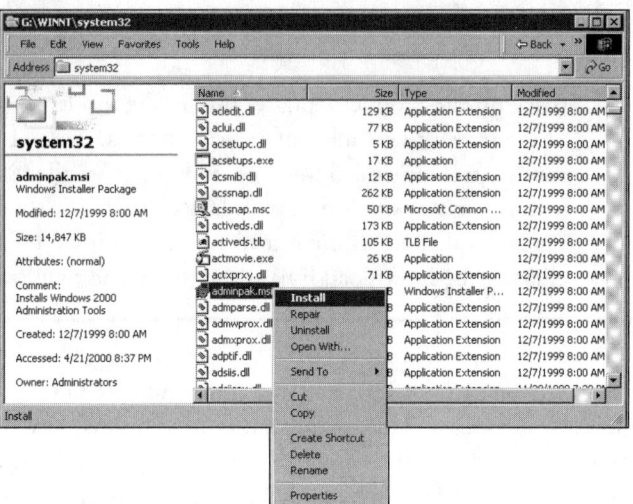

FIGURE 5.7
Context menu of an .msi (Windows Installer) file.

The context menu includes a number of choices, including Install, Repair, and Uninstall. These options do not require a great deal of additional explanation except to note that total cost of ownership can be greatly reduced by their use. This is particularly true of the Repair option. The Repair option is designed to eliminate the need for a technical support call at the user's desktop. If a user accidentally or intentionally deletes a system file or executable associated with an application and then tries to launch that application, with any previous Windows operating system the application would fail. Now in Windows 2000, by right-clicking on the .msi file that was used to install the application and selecting Repair, the required system files are reinstalled and the application can launch without error.

Support for the Windows Installer service and Windows Installer files can also be incorporated into Windows 9x and Windows NT 4.0 by downloading and installing the self-extracting executable from the Microsoft site at

http://msdn.microsoft.com/downloads/sdks/platform/WinInst.asp.

In a corporate environment with an Active Directory domain structure it is possible to roll out software through Windows Installer packages to either users or computers. Windows Installer packages can be either assigned or published. The configuration of Group Policy is broken into two different configurations much like System Policy in NT 4.0: User Configuration and Computer Configuration. The creation of the Windows Installer packages, although important, will not be a focus of this exam, but an understanding of how the packages could affect the Windows 2000 Professional desktop environment is important, so that is where we will focus our attention.

Assigning Windows Installer Packages

A Windows Installer package file can be assigned to either a user or a computer. When a package is assigned to a user, the application's shortcuts will be created on the Start menu and desktop the next time the user logs on. The application is not installed at logon—only the shortcuts are created and the file associations made within the registry. The application is installed the first time the user starts the application via the shortcuts or by double-clicking on a file with an extension associated with the assigned application. This allows a user's applications to roam with him in the same way his profile can roam with him. This gives the user access to the applications he requires regardless of the computer running Windows 2000 that he logs on to, but installs the application only if the user needs to work with it.

A Windows Installer package can also be assigned to a computer. Assigning a package to a computer launches the installation of the application the next time the computer is turned on. This is a useful approach if the assigned application is required by all users of that computer. This ensures that the application is available to all users of the computer and is not tied to a specific user.

The assignment of applications through Windows Installer packages has an additional benefit: resilience through self-repair. If a system file or executable is accidentally or maliciously deleted but was originally assigned to either a user or computer, it will repair itself the next time it is started. The application will use the Windows Installer service to reconnect to the original distribution point and copy the required files back to the computer running Windows 2000 Professional and reinstall them. Following that, the application will launch and a technical support call will be averted.

> **WARNING**
>
> **Planning and Testing When Using Windows Installer** Caution and testing should be the rule of thumb with Windows Installer files and the Windows Installer service. Although it is not well documented, Windows Installer files that were installed manually have been known to be resilient in some cases. It appears that the MSI installs remember the original installation location and try to go back to that location for self repair. Oftentimes the location will no longer contain the installation files, particularly in the case of a CD drive where the CD has been removed, but the point is that it does seem to try. Planning and testing the use of Windows Installer files is highly recommended.

Publishing Windows Installer Packages

Windows Installer packages can also be published but the publishing support is limited to users only. Publishing a Windows Installer package to a user makes that application available through Add/Remove Programs the next time the user logs on. The application can be installed one of two ways when it is published to a user. The first way involves the user installing the application through Add/Remove Programs. The second way is through document invocation. By double-clicking on a file with an extension that is associated with the published application, the installation will begin.

Windows Installer packages cannot be published to a computer. The reason for this is that a computer will never invoke an application nor will a computer ever know to install an application through Add/Remove Programs.

One of the key differences between publishing and assigning Windows Installer packages is that published packages are not resilient. If a published package is accidently deleted, it will not automatically install or repair itself.

Publishing ZAP files

An alternative to publishing Windows Installer files is to use .zap files. A .zap file is a text file that can be read and used to execute software installation. These files come with some restrictions and offer a lot less functionality than Windows Installer files, so it should be stressed that the use of Windows Installer files is recommended whenever possible.

The limitations of .zap files include the following:

◆ .zap files can only be published. They cannot be assigned to users or computers.

◆ .zap files offer no resiliency and do not attempt to repair themselves if files are deleted or become corrupted.

◆ The majority of .zap files will require user intervention during the installation.

◆ .zap files do not have the ability to install with elevated privileges, which means that users must have the ability to install software on their local computers.

Any text editor can be used to create a .zap file. Each file has two primary sections: the Application section and the File Extensions section.

The Application section includes information that will be displayed to users in Add/Remove Programs and must include two tags: FriendlyName and SetupCommand. The Application section is mandatory.

The FriendlyName tag is the name that will be used in Add/Remove Programs.

The SetupCommand tag is the name of the executable or command to install the application. The path to this command should be relative to the .zap file itself, meaning that if the setup command is in the same folder as the .zap file only the name of the setup file needs to be entered.

The second section of the .zap file is the File Extensions section. This section is used to associate the application with file extensions saved in Active Directory. This section is optional. A sample .zap file looks something like the following:

```
[Application]
FriendlyName = Microsoft Office 2000
SetupCommand = setup.exe /unattend
[Ext]
DOC=
DOT=
```

SECURING THE DESKTOP USING SECURITY POLICIES

Security policies are a means of enforcing security in a corporate network. A security policy should define your corporate computer usage policy and prevent inappropriate access. Security policies can also be used to prevent users from damaging a computer's configuration or limit a particular user's or group's access to specific computers or applications running on those computers. The use of security templates is the most efficient way to implement security policies. A security template contains configurable security settings and is saved as a text file.

Security settings can be applied through either a local security policy on each individual computer or through a group policy in a domain, which could be configured to apply to all computers in the domain. The application of security policy at the domain level via a group policy is beyond the scope of this book. Chapter 6, "Using Group Policy to Manage Users," in New Riders' *MCSE Training Guide: Windows 2000 Directory Services Infrastructure* discusses the use of Group Policy to manage users in great depth. Here, we will endeavor to explain the use of local security policy settings applied to a single computer.

Before we look at the different available local security options, it should be made clear that if both local security and domain security policies exist for the same computer, the local security policy will be overwritten by the domain policy. The order in which security policy is applied is local policy first followed by site, domain, and organizational unit policies. Figure 5.8 is a snapshot of the Local Security Policy snap-in and illustrates this concept. Looking at the Local Security Policy snap-in, you will notice that the settings in the right frame are divided into two categories: Local Settings and Effective Settings. What is important to understand here is that the effective setting could be different from the local setting if both a local and domain security policy exist. The local security policy will be applied first, but the domain policy will overwrite the local policy because it takes precedence.

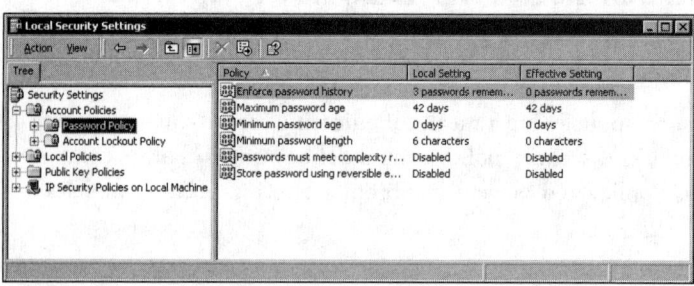

FIGURE 5.8
Local Security Settings dialog box.

Implementing Security on a Local Computer

Security can be set on a local computer using Administrative Tools, Local Security Policy. Table 5.6 outlines the available security settings and their respective definitions.

TABLE 5.6

SECURITY SETTINGS

Policy	Description
Account Policy	Used to set password and account policies.
Local Policy	Used to configure auditing, user rights, and security options.
Public Key Policy	Used to configure data recovery agents, domain roots, and trusted certificate authorities.
IPSec Policy	Used to configure IP Security on a network.

Security settings can be individually defined for each computer in your workgroup, but this would not be the most efficient use of your administrative time. If your goal is to configure all workstations in the workgroup with the same security settings it would be much more efficient to use security templates. Windows 2000 comes with a set of predefined templates, which are defined in Table 5.7. Any of the predefined templates can be imported and applied to a local computer or they can be modified to meet your own unique requirements and then applied to the local computer. The predefined security templates are stored in the path Winnt\security\templates. Step by Step 5.10 walks through the steps involved in setting up a password policy on a local computer running Windows 2000 Professional.

STEP BY STEP

5.10 Setting Up a Local Account Security Policy

1. Click Start, Programs, Administrative Tools, Local Security Policy and expand Account Policies. Select Password Policy.

continues

continued

2. Double-click Minimum Password Length and set the minimum length to 6 characters.

3. Double-click on Enforce Password History and set the number of passwords to be remembered to 3. The dialog box should now look like Figure 5.8.

4. Close the local security settings.

5. Press Ctrl+Alt+Delete and select to change the password. Enter your current password and leave the New Password and Confirm New Password boxes empty. Click OK.

6. After you receive a warning message indicating that the password must be at least 6 characters in length, type a new password that is 6 characters in length into the New Password and Confirm New Password boxes.

TABLE 5.7

SECURITY TEMPLATES

Template Name	*Definition*
Basicwk.inf	Default workstation security template.
Basicsv.inf	Default server security template.
Basicdc.inf	Default domain controller security template.
Compatws.inf	Compatible workstation or server; provides a higher level of security than the basic templates but still ensures that all applications will run.
Securews.inf	Secure workstation or server; provides increased security but does not guarantee that all applications will function.
Securedc.inf	Secure domain controller; provides increased security for domain controllers but does not guarantee that all applications will function.
Hisecws.inf	Highly secure workstation or server; enforces the maximum security regardless of the functionality of applications.
Hisecdc.inf	Highly secure domain controller; enforces the maximum security regardless of the functionality of applications.
Dedicadc.inf	Implements security setting ideal for local users on a Windows 2000 domain controller (not recommended).

Step by Step 5.11 shows you how to compare your computer's local security configuration to that of a predefined template using Security Configuration and Analysis. This is useful in determining how secure your computer is compared to the predefined template. Once you analyze the differences you can decide whether to import the predefined security template into the local workstation to increase or decrease the existing level of security.

STEP BY STEP

5.11 Comparing Your Local Computer's Security Against a Predefined Template

1. At the Run command type `mmc`.

2. From the console menu, select Add/Remove Snap-In and click Add. Select Security Configuration and Analysis from the list of available snap-ins and click Add, Close, OK.

3. Right-click Security Configuration and Analysis, select Open Database, and type a filename in the filename box. (The filename can be anything you like. This example uses test.sdb.)

4. When the Import Template dialog box appears, choose a template against which to compare the local security setting. In this case, choose compatws.inf if your computer is currently running Windows 2000 Professional. Click Open.

5. Right-click Security Configuration and Analysis and select Analyze Computer Now. Agree to the default log file path or enter an alternate path and click OK.

6. Expand Security Configuration and Analysis, Account Policies, and click on Password Policy.

7. Notice that two settings in the right frame have a red X through them, as shown in Figure 5.9. These settings are depicted this way to indicate that they are different from the database settings. To compare the database and computer settings, look in the right frame rather than at the differences in values in the two columns.

continues

continued

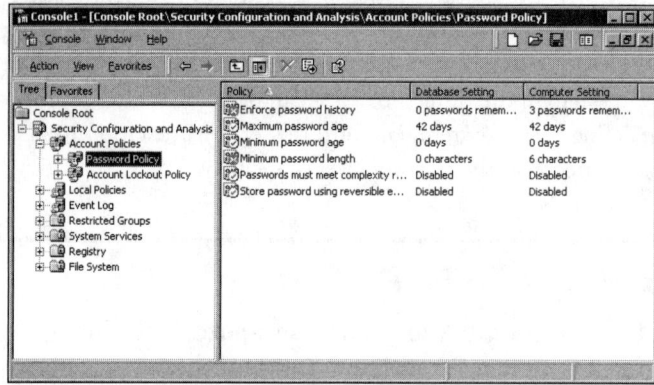

FIGURE 5.9
Analyzed comparison of local security policy to security template.

8. Leave the console open for Step by Step 5.12.

Step by Step 5.12 covers how to configure the local computer with the policy in the predefined template and overwrite all existing local settings.

STEP BY STEP

5.12 Apply a Security Template to the Local Computer

1. In the Security Configuration and Analysis snap-in that you left open from Step by Step 5.11, right-click Security Configuration and Analysis, Configure Computer Now.

2. Agree to the default log file path or specify an alternative and click OK.

3. Once the configuration is complete, right-click on Security Configuration and Analysis and select Analyze Computer Now. Agree to the default log location, and click OK.

4. Expand Account Policies, and select Password Policy. There should no longer be any settings conflicts; what you see should look like the window in Figure 5.10.

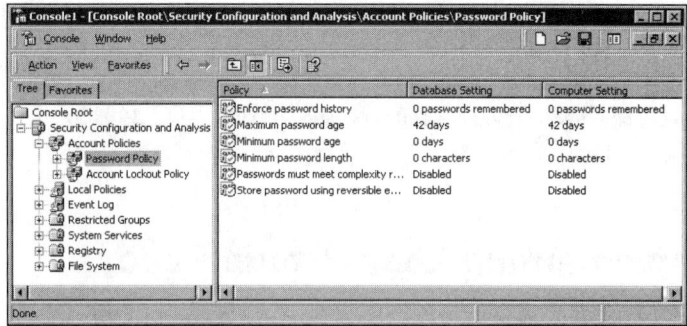

FIGURE 5.10
Imported security template.

IP Security Policy

Table 5.6 described one of the local security features known as IP Security. IP Security is new to Windows 2000 and deserves a look at the types of IP Security policies that can be set. Table 5.8 lists and describes the three different IP Security settings available in Windows 2000 Professional.

TABLE 5.8

IP SECURITY POLICIES

Policy Name	Description
Client	Allows for IPSec negotiations with other computers requesting IPSec. Only the requested protocol and port traffic is secured.
Secure	Requires secure communications all the time.
Server	Allows for security most of the time. The computer is able to accept unsecured communications but will always attempt to secure any additional communications.

IP Security is currently an Internet Engineering Task Force (IETF) proposal. This simply means that it is not proprietary to Microsoft but rather on its way to becoming an open standard.

Internet Protocol Security (IPSec) allows computers to authenticate and encrypt data for transmission between other computers in a network. Currently, Windows 2000 is the only Microsoft operating system to support IPSec. To learn more about IPSec, read the whitepaper available at www.microsoft.com/windows2000/library/howitworks/security/ip_security.asp, or read RFC 2401, which can be found at http://www.ietf.org/rfc/rfc2401.txt.

Implementing Local Group Policy

Local group policy is another way to enforce security settings on a local computer. Every computer running Windows 2000 has one local group policy object. Again, like local security policy, a local group policy will be overwritten by site, domain, or organizational unit group policy objects. Therefore, use of local group policy will be minimal in a domain environment.

Local group policy objects are stored in the path Winnt\System32\GroupPolicy and can be edited with gpedit.msc, also known as the Group Policy snap-in. The Group Policy snap-in is not one of the default administrative tools. To access the Group Policy snap-in, type **gpedit.msc** at the Run command. The other alternative is to add it to an empty Microsoft Management Console. Step by Step 5.13 walks through the process of adding the Group Policy snap-in to a new Microsoft Management Console.

STEP BY STEP

5.13 Adding the Group Policy Snap-In to a New Microsoft Management Console

1. Click on Start, Run and type **mmc**, and then click OK.

2. On the Console menu, select Add/Remove Snap-In and click Add.

3. Select the Group Policy snap-in from the list and click Add. Choose the Local Computer as the focus and click Finish.

4. Click Close and OK.

5. On the Console menu, select Save As and enter the filename **Gpconsole.msc** in the filename box. Click Save.

At this point you should see the Group Policy window. It should look similar to Figure 5.11.

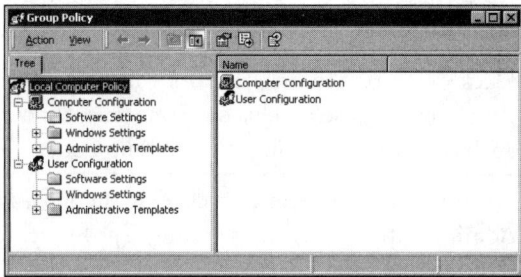

FIGURE 5.11
Group Policy dialog box.

Group policy replaces system policy in Windows 2000 as a means of establishing a set of rules in your environment. Like system policy in Windows NT 4.0, group policy is divided into two configurations: computer configuration and user configuration.

Computer configuration settings set through local group policy will apply to the local computer. User configuration settings set through local group policy will apply to the local user logging on to the computer. Both user and computer configurations are subdivided into three sections: Software Settings, Windows Settings, and Administrative Templates.

Software settings are not configurable through local group policy.

The Windows settings found within the computer configuration section are identical to the settings we examined earlier in the Local Security Settings snap-in with the exception of the scripts settings for Startup and Shutdown scripts. The Windows settings found within the user configuration are unique to this snap-in.

The Administrative Templates section of both user and computer configurations have some similiarities between them and allow you to define a set of rules or restrictions on either a user or computer basis. Step by Step 5.14 walks through the creation of a local group policy used to disable the Control Panel. For this step-by-step tutorial, you will need to have completed Step by Step 5.13, which created the Group Policy snap-in.

STEP BY STEP

5.14 Disabling the Control Panel Through a Local Group Policy

1. Click on Start, Settings, Control Panel. Once the Control Panel opens, close it. This confirms that it is currently enabled before enforcing a local group policy.

2. Open up Gpconsole.msc by clicking on Start, Programs, Administrative Tools and selecting Gpconsole.msc.

3. Expand Local Computer Policy, User Configuration, Administrative Templates and select Control Panel.

4. Double-click on Disable Control Panel and select Enabled. Click OK.

5. Close Gpconsole.msc and click Yes to save the changes.

6. At the Run command type **cmd**.

7. At the command prompt, type **secedit /refreshpolicy user_policy**. This automatically refreshes the user policy on the local computer.

8. Close the command prompt.

9. Click on Start, Settings to verify that the Control Panel option has been disabled.

The list of settings available for configuration in the Group Policy snap-in is quite exhaustive; because the individual settings will probably not be a focus of the exam, they will not be covered here individually. However, two nice features of group policy that will help to define the individual settings are the Explain tab and the Help button. To find out more about a specific policy in Windows 2000, double-click on that policy setting. Its dialog box will appear, similar to the explanation dialog box shown in Figure 5.12.

On the Explain tab, you will find an explanation of the policy setting to help you decide whether you would like to use it. Some policy settings do not come with an Explain tab but rather offer a Help button to provide an explanation of what the setting is meant to do.

Other sources of information on group policy settings include the group policy help file (gp.chm) in the Microsoft Windows 2000 Server documentation and the Windows 2000 Group Policy whitepaper available at the Microsoft Web site at `http://www.microsoft.com/windows2000/library/planning/ management/groupsteps.asp`.

CONFIGURING FAX SUPPORT

Configure and troubleshoot fax support.

Windows 2000 ships with built-in fax support that gives you the ability to fax a document as easily as you could print the document and receive incoming faxes. Single-user fax support is integrated into Windows 2000 and configured in the Printers dialog box, as shown in Figure 5.13.

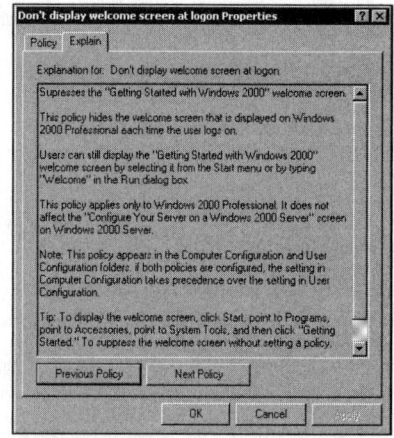

FIGURE 5.12
Explain tab for group policy settings.

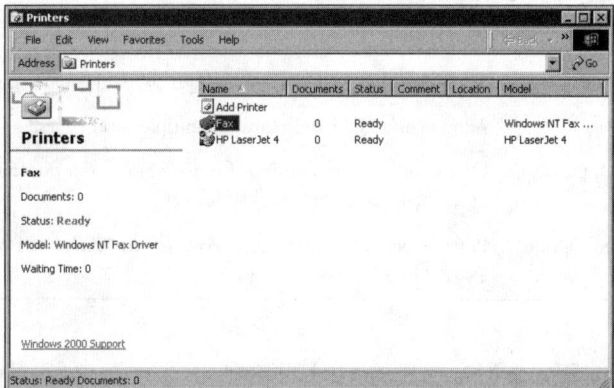

FIGURE 5.13
The Printers dialog box.

Installing fax support is a two-step process; if your hardware is Plug and Play, both steps could be performed automatically by the operating system.

As with any hardware installation, the first step is to install the physical device after confirming that it is included on the Hardware Compatibility List. The second second step is to configure the device within the Printers dialog box and through the Fax Service Management tool.

If Windows 2000 detects your new hardware when you reboot the computer, it will install the device and add a default fax icon within the Printers dialog box. Fax support in Windows 2000 is single user because an installed fax device does not support sharing with other network users.

Fax Service Management is the tool that is installed when a fax device is added to the computer. The Fax Service Management tool can be found in Start, Programs, Accessories, Communications, Fax or can be launched from the Advanced Options tab in the Fax icon in Control Panel.

The Fax icon in Control Panel consists of four tabs that allow you to accomplish a number of administrative tasks; these are explained in Table 5.9.

TABLE 5.9

FAX OPTIONS IN CONTROL PANEL

Option	*Definition*
User Information	Allows for the configuration of cover page information.
Cover Pages	Allows you to add and manage multiple cover pages.
Status Monitor	Offers configuration options for notification and the enabling of manual answer for the first device.
Advanced Options	Provides access to Fax Service Management, Help, and Adding a Fax Printer.

The Fax Service Management tool allows for a number of device-specific settings to be configured, including the options to send and receive, and the receive options. The receive options include the ability to print to a print device, save in a folder, or send to a local email inbox. The option to receive is not enabled by default. Logging of Initialization/Termination, Outbound, Inbound, and Unknown can also be configured within Fax Service Management.

Step by Step 5.15 assumes that you already have a fax device installed in your computer. Based on this assumption, this tutorial walks through the steps involved in setting up a fax device to receive incoming faxes on a shared voice/data line, similar to a home-based business setup.

STEP BY STEP

5.15 Setting Up a Fax Device to Receive Incoming Faxes

1. Click Start, Programs, Accessories, Communications, Fax, Fax Service Management.

2. In Fax Service Management, click on Devices, right-click on your fax device in the list of installed devices, and select Properties.

3. Select the Received Faxes tab and select the Enable Receive check box. Click OK.

4. Close Fax Service Management.

5. Click on Start, Settings, Control Panel and double-click on the Fax icon.

6. Select the Static Monitor tab and select Enable Manual Answer for the First Device. Click OK.

Step by Step 5.16 walks you through the process of viewing and printing a received fax.

STEP BY STEP

5.16 Viewing and Printing a Received Fax

1. Click on Start, Programs, Accessories, Communications, Fax, and select My Faxes.

2. To view a fax, in the My Faxes folder, double-click the Received Faxes folder and double-click the fax that you would like to view.

3. The fax is displayed in the Imaging Preview viewer. To print the fax, select File from the menu bar, and then select the Print option.

Troubleshooting Fax Problems

There are a number of possible reasons why faxing might not function properly. In this section we will focus on some good first steps to take when troubleshooting fax problems.

Troubleshooting should be approached very methodically in all instances where it is required. Troubleshooting is very similar to solving a crossword puzzle. Chances are that you will not know all of the answers immediately, but as you fill in the answers you do know, you will begin to get clues to the ones you don't. When troubleshooting any problem, approach it with a "process of elimination" mindset. As you begin to eliminate potential causes, your focus will start to become more defined.

With respect to fax problems, the first thing to check is that a fax device is installed. Without a hardware fax device installed in the computer, none of the previously discussed fax options will be available.

If faxes are not being sent, check that the user sending the fax has the required permissions. Fax permissions can be viewed by right-clicking on the Fax icon found in Start, Settings, Printers and selecting Properties from the context menu. In the Fax Properties dialog box, select the Security tab to display the permissions for the fax. Also ensure that the fax device has not been configured to fax only during specific times of day.

If faxes are not being received, ensure that the feature to Enable Receive has been enabled. If the fax server is connected to a dedicated line for faxing, ensure that the feature to Enable Manual Answer for the First Device is *not* selected; otherwise, someone will have to phyically answer the call.

There are a number of possible scenarios that could be preventing a fax device from working properly. Use your common sense and the process of elimination to troubleshoot the problem.

The next section discusses the configuration of Internet options and how they can be used to ensure that specific settings, such as proxy settings, are configured for all users.

CONFIGURING INTERNET OPTIONS

The configuration of Internet options is becoming increasingly important as more and more companies have integrated Internet access into their network architecture. We will look at some of the settings that can be configured for Internet Explorer that can simplify administration and streamline Internet access.

One of the most basic choices that we can configure for individual users is the default home page. The default home page is defined in the properties of Internet Explorer but can also be assigned through a group policy. Step by Step 5.17 walks through the steps of setting up the default home page individually.

STEP BY STEP

5.17 Setting the Default Home Page

1. Right-click on Internet Explorer on the desktop and select Properties.

2. On the General tab, in the Address box of the Home Page section, type the URL of the Internet or intranet site that you would like to have as your default home page.

The location and size of temporary Internet files is also an important setting to govern, particularly if the amount of available disk space on a client computer is limited. Step by Step 5.18 walks through how to set the size and location of temporary Internet files.

STEP BY STEP

5.18 Setting the Size and Location of Temporary Internet Files

1. Right-click on Internet Explorer on the desktop and select Properties.

2. On the General tab, click the Settings button in the Temporary Internet files section.

continues

continued

3. Select a setting from the list at the top of the dialog box that will determine when newer versions of stored pages are checked for.

4. In the Temporary Internet Files Folder section, use the sliderule or the size box to allocate how much disk space is reserved for temporary Internet files.

5. To move the temporary Internet files folder's location, click the Move Folder button and browse the directory structure to indicate where you would like the temporary Internet files to be stored.

Proxy settings can be set by connection rather than at a single place for the entire system. Proxy settings can also be set within the properties of Internet Explorer for users who access the Internet through a proxy server. Internet Explorer can be set up to automatically detect settings, use an automatic configuration script, or use a static proxy server address. The benefit of the automatic configuration script is that a number of settings can be provided through the automatic configuration script as opposed to a simple proxy address. The automatic configuration script also centralizes administration by allowing the administrator to create one script for all users; by directing users to that script, all users are identically configured. Step by Step 5.19 addresses the process of configuring proxy settings.

STEP BY STEP

5.19 Configuring Proxy Settings

1. Right-click Internet Explorer and select Properties.

2. Select the Connections tab and the LAN Settings button.

3. To configure your client for automatic configuration, select one of the automatic configuration settings. To specify a single, static proxy server, enable the Use a Proxy Server box and enter an address and port number for the proxy server.

4. To enable the Bypass Proxy Server for Local Addresses option, select that box.

Many companies have or are beginning to establish a set of Internet User guidelines that restrict users to viewing only certain material or surfing only to specific sites using the corporation's Internet access. These types of restrictive options are available within Internet Explorer but are by no means all-encompassing. Third-party products are generally used in most corporate environments where there is interest in filtering or blocking access to certain Internet sites. We will examine the options available in Internet Explorer.

Internet Explorer offers the ability to control security through Authenticode publishers, security zones, and content ratings.

Security zones enable you to assign specific Web sites to specific security zones, of which there are five defaults to choose from. The five different zones are explained in Table 5.10.

TABLE 5.10

INTERNET EXPLORER SECURITY ZONES

Zone	Description
Internet	Contains all Internet sites.
Local Intranet	Used for computers connected to the local intranet.
Trusted Sites	Allows for the assignment of sites you trust.
Restricted Sites	Allows for the assignment of sites you do *not* trust.
My Computer	Contains the files on the local computer; configurable only through the Internet Explorer Administration Kit or from Group Policy.

Adding sites to which you are interested in preventing access can be accomplished by adding those particular sites to the Restricted Sites zone. Step by Step 5.20 details the process of adding sites to the Restricted Sites zone.

STEP BY STEP

5.20 Configuring a Restricted Zone

1. Right-click Internet Explorer and select Properties.

2. Select the Security tab. In the list of zones at the top, select the Restricted Sites zone.

3. Click the Sites button and add one or more URLs of sites that you want to define as restricted. Click OK.

4. Again on the Security tab, select the security level for the restricted zone via the sliderule or click the Custom Level button to define your own security settings for the zone.

In this section, we have looked at how to configure a number of different Internet Explorer settings for a Windows 2000 Professional client. These settings are useful in defining a common Internet environment for a number of clients. Although setting the properties locally is not the most efficient way to define these settings, it is an available option when only a few computers need configuring. Alternatively, these settings could be applied through a group policy to all computers or users within a site, domain, or organizational unit.

CHAPTER SUMMARY

Summarized briefly, this chapter covered the following main points:

◆ **Understanding profiles.** This section defined the two types of profiles (local and roaming) and the differences between personal and mandatory profiles.

◆ **Understanding the Windows Installer Service.** This new service in Windows 2000 helps to reduce the total cost of ownership through both application self-repair and making applications available to users from any Windows 2000 computer they log on to.

◆ **Configuring the desktop.** We broke this section into local security policy and local group policy and examined the similarities and differences between the two. We also discussed the application of local policy and the order in which it is applied—first. In addition to security, we also looked at setting up and configuring both fax and accessibility options to meet the needs of our user community.

◆ **Configuring Internet options.** This section looked at the options available in Internet Explorer and how to configure the home page, proxy settings, temporary Internet file size and location, and the setting of security zones.

KEY TERMS

- Accessibility options
- Group policy
- Local profile
- Roaming profile
- Mandatory profile
- Windows Installer
- IP Security

APPLY YOUR KNOWLEDGE

Exercises

5.1 Remove a Program

In this exercise, you've run out of disk space. To recover some space until your request for a new hard drive is approved, you've decided to remove your least-used programs.

Estimated Time: 10 minutes

1. Click the Start button; select Settings, Control Panel.

2. Double-click the Add/Remove Programs applet.

3. Click on each program in the installed programs list, looking at Used and Last Used On, as well as the size of the application to determine which application is the least-used and the largest in size.

4. Click the Change/Remove button.

5. Follow the program-specific instructions for removing the program.

5.2 Send a Fax

In this exercise, you will simply send a fax with a cover sheet.

Estimated Time: 2 minutes

1. Open Wordpad.

2. Type a funny letter to your best friend.

3. Select File, Print.

4. Select the Fax Printer and click Print.

5. Click the Next button in the Send a Fax Wizard dialog box.

6. Enter the name of your friend and her fax number, and click the Add button. Repeat this step for any additional friends that you would like to see the fax, and then click the Next button.

7. Click the Include a Cover Page check box, and then select the cover page to use from the Cover Page Template combo box.

8. Type in the subject line and notes for the cover page.

9. Click the Next button to show the delivery time page.

10. Click the Next button to show the finalization page.

11. Click Finish to send your fax.

Review Questions

1. What are the two different types of user profiles?

2. What feature allows Windows Installer to dynamically install applications?

3. What are the two sections of a .zap file?

4. What is the purpose of accessibility options?

Exam Questions

1. Which solution is best suited to an environment where you need to control the changes that are made to a profile?

   A. Mandatory profiles

   B. Group policies

APPLY YOUR KNOWLEDGE

C. Accessibility options

D. Mandatory profiles and group policies

2. You need to develop a standard desktop operating environment for your data entry staff. They all do the same data entry into the same system. There is no need for them to be able to change their environment. In fact, the company doesn't want them to change their environment at all. What should you use?

A. Mandatory profiles

B. Group policies

C. Accessibility options

D. Mandatory profiles and group policies

3. Your environment has three general-purpose workstations that are shared between 200 employees and used as kiosk computers for customizing employee health benefits. Each employee needs access to a workstation for only a short period of time, and doesn't necessarily always use the same one. Which setup is best?

A. Local user profiles on each machine

B. Roaming profiles on the network

C. Mandatory profiles on the network

D. Group policies and roaming profiles on the network

4. The display of numbers, dates, and times is strange. You notice that commas and periods are transposed, and that other punctuation appears to be transposed. What is the most likely cause?

A. Your display font is corrupted; restart the computer.

B. Your display font is corrupted; reinstall the font.

C. Your regional options are not correct.

D. You have the wrong time zone set in the Time/Date applet.

5. You're running out of hard disk space and need to generate space quickly. What should you do?

A. Delete old Word documents that you don't need anymore.

B. Write a purchase order to get a new, larger hard drive.

C. Remove unneeded applications by using the Add/Remove Programs applet.

D. Clear the event logs.

6. You need to remove a program that you installed. The application uses the Windows Installer technology. What is the best way to remove the program?

A. Delete the directory in which the program was installed.

B. Reinstall Windows 2000 Professional.

C. Run the Add/Remove Programs applet.

D. Run a third-party uninstallation program.

7. You tried changing the resolution and color depth of your display and now your monitor is making a very nasty screech. What should you do?

A. Reboot the PC immediately.

B. Reinstall Windows 2000 Professional.

C. Turn off the monitor and wait 20 seconds.

D. Press Ctrl+Alt+Delete.

APPLY YOUR KNOWLEDGE

8. You need to get a document to a business associate, but she doesn't have email. You're in a hurry, because it's critical information. How should you proceed?

   A. Print a copy of the document and deliver it to the business associate.

   B. Print a copy of the document and fax it to the business associate.

   C. Use Microsoft Fax Services to send the document to your business associate.

   D. Save the document to a TIFF file and use Microsoft Fax Services to send the fax.

9. Your company has just hired a new employee whose vision is impaired to the point where he is legally blind even with glasses. You've given him a 20-inch monitor but he is still having trouble reading the company's documents on the computer screen. What should you do?

   A. Buy a serial input device and enable serial input from Accessibility Options.

   B. Turn on the narrator service.

   C. Turn on the magnifier service.

   D. Turn on the on-screen keyboard.

10. You have a user who logs in to several computers. However, changes that he makes on these computers don't seem to stick. What is the most likely reason for this?

    A. The user has a local profile.

    B. The user has a mandatory profile.

    C. The group policies are set to disallow changes.

D. The user has selected the Don't Save Changes at Exit checkbox.

11. Joe, the president of your company, normally uses his notebook to log on to the network, but occasionally he logs in from the plant floor. He keeps complaining that his desktop isn't the same on the plant floor as it is on his notebook. What is the most likely cause?

    A. The machine on the plant floor is configured for local profiles.

    B. The machine on the plant floor is configured for roaming profiles.

    C. Joe is configured for local profiles.

    D. Joe is configured for roaming profiles.

12. Your shop floor is very noisy, but your primary software vendor has provided software that rings a bell when there's a problem. However, there's no visual identification that there's a problem from the main screen that the employees use. What action should you take to improve the chances that they will notice the bell?

    A. Install louder speakers.

    B. Turn the volume control all the way up in the Sounds and Multimedia applet.

    C. Turn on Sound Sentry.

    D. Turn on Show Sounds.

13. You need the ability to enter documents in multiple languages but there's no locale item on the task bar. What are the potential causes? (Choose two.)

    A. The program you're using to enter the information doesn't support input locales.

APPLY YOUR KNOWLEDGE

B. The input locales feature isn't installed.

C. There is only one input locale installed.

D. Display of the icon isn't enabled.

14. You have configured a local security policy on one of the workstations in your network. The workstation you configured is part of a domain. You confirm that the local security policy is set using the Local Security Policy snap-in but notice that the effective setting is different. What would cause the effective setting to differ from the local setting?

    A. Another administrator made changes to the local computer's security policy and didn't tell you.

    B. The administrator of the domain has configured a domain policy that is overriding the local policy.

    C. The user of the workstation has made changes to the local security policy.

    D. The local security policy has not been enabled on the computer by running secedit /refreshpolicy machine_policy.

Answers to Review Questions

1. The two different types of user profiles are local and roaming. Local and roaming profiles can be further divided into personal (which allow the user's changes to be saved) and mandatory (which do not save the user's changes). See the section "User Profile Types."

2. Advertising an application allows it to be installed automatically and with elevated privileges by the Windows Installer Service. An application can be assigned to either a user or a computer. Assigning an application to a user creates the program shortcuts and file associations in the registry but does not install the application until it is invoked. Assigning an application to a computer forces the install to take place at the next reboot. See the section " Assigning Windows Installer Packages."

3. The two sections of a .zap file are the Application section and the File Extensions sections. The Application section is mandatory within a .zap file but the File Extensions section is not. See the section "Publishing ZAP Files."

4. The purpose of accessibility options is to make Windows 2000 Professional usable to a wider audience. In addition to the accessibility features included with the operating system, there are a number of additional add-on programs and products to assist people with disabilities. See the section "Configuring Accessibility Options."

Answers to Exam Questions

1. **B.** The solution best suited to an environment in which you need to control the changes that are made to a profile is a group policy. Group policy would allow you to enforce the level of control you require. Mandatory profiles allow control of an environment, but only absolute control, and only prevent changes from being saved. Accessibility options are methods for improving a user's ability to use the operating system and are not a valid option in this case. The use of mandatory profiles in conjunction with group

APPLY YOUR KNOWLEDGE

policies is not an option; you don't want to prevent profile changes—only limit them. See the sections "Mandatory User Profiles" and "Implementing Local Group Policy."

2. **D.** The correct answer in this case is the use of both group policies and mandatory user profiles. This way you can govern what the users have access to and not allow them to make changes to their profiles that get saved. Mandatory profiles could be used in this case by multiple users, and would prevent changes from being saved, but group policies will further restrict the user of the desktop. Accessibility options don't solve the problem and group policies alone are not enough. See the sections "Mandatory User Profiles" and "Implementing Local Group Policy."

3. **D.** Group policies and roaming user profiles on the network is the correct answer. Group policies can be used to restrict access to the three machines and allow users limited access to only the Human Resource information they require. Roaming profiles could be used as well to ensure that all 200 users still get their unique profiles when logging on to the kiosk computers. See the sections "Roaming User Profiles" and "Implementing Local Group Policy."

4. **C.** Regional options control the display of dates, times, and numbers. Many other locales use different punctuation for these types of information than we do in the United States. Although it's possible that a display font was corrupted, it's unlikely because the effect is only on the punctuation. An incorrect time zone won't cause the punctuation of a time or date to change. See the section "Configuring Regional Options."

5. **C.** The key here is to free up space quickly. The fastest way to accomplish this is to remove large applications that have not been used for a period of time. Space can be recouped by deleting Word documents but they are generally so small that it will have little impact. Writing a request for a new hard drive is a good solution but not an immediate one in most cases. Lastly, cleaning out the event logs will have little or no effect on the amount of disk space in use. See the section "Add/Remove Programs."

6. **C.** Running the Add/Remove Programs applet ensures that all of the components of the application that were installed will be removed. Deleting the application directory is the wrong way to remove an application; this action won't remove any shared files or registry settings. Reinstalling Windows 2000 isn't practical and could be very time-consuming. The third-party uninstallation program may or may not get all of the changes unapplied, depending upon its ability to effectively monitor all changes. See the section "Add/Remove Programs."

7. **C.** When you change your display settings, Windows 2000 Professional tests those settings for 15 seconds. If you don't confirm the change, Windows will revert to the old settings. Rebooting the PC is an option but will take a long time. Reinstalling Windows 2000 is an even longer process. Finally, pressing Ctrl+Alt+Delete isn't a bad answer, other than it presumes that the monitor can handle the input it's getting from the video card. It's important to not expose the monitor to the incorrect settings. If it does happen, you want to make sure it is for as little time as possible. See the section "Configuring the Desktop Environment."

8. **C.** Using the fax capabilities of Windows 2000 would allow you to get the document to your associate quickly. While it's possible to print it and drive it to the business associate, it's not as efficient. Likewise, you could print the document and manually fax it, but that is repetitious and uses extra paper. See the section "Configuring Fax Support."

9. **C.** Because the person is legally blind, a new input device wouldn't be of much use, but the magnifier service might help. Many legally blind individuals are able to read if the print is large enough. Turning on the narrator service may seem, at first glance, to be the perfect solution, but the narrator service only reads dialog boxes and controls; it doesn't read the text in the application itself. See the section "Configuring Accessibility Options."

10. **B.** If changes do not persist, it could be that the user has been assigned a mandatory profile. Mandatory profiles prevent changes made by a user during his logon session from being saved. If the user had a local profile it should persist as long as it wasn't a local mandatory profile. A group policy would prevent the change from occurring, not discard the change after logoff. There is no Don't Save Changes at Exit checkbox in Windows 2000. See the section "Mandatory User Profiles."

11. **C.** The most likely cause is that Joe's user account is configured for local profiles. Machines cannot be configured for profiles—only users—so both answers A and B are incorrect. If Joe's user account were configured with a roaming profile, the problem wouldn't occur, thus eliminating that answer. See the section "Local User Profiles."

12. **C.** The best solution here would be to enable Sound Sentry, which would indicate on the screen that a sound has occurred. Turning up the volume or installing new, louder speakers might help, but would probably just lead to the generation of more noise. Show Sounds might also work, but it depends on support from the software vendor, which isn't very likely at this time. See the section "Configuring Accessibility Options."

13. **C, D.** If no input locales are installed, the icon certainly will not be there. Even when additional input locales are installed, the icon must still be enabled to be seen. Input locales are not an optional part of the operating system, making this an invalid option. Applications do need to support the use of input locales but this would not prevent the icon from appearing—only the application from using them. See the section "Configuring Regional Options."

14. **B.** Domain security policies override local security policies if both exist. This allows a centralized policy to be maintained and effective. Only the administrator is able to make changes to the local security policy, eliminating answer C. Another administrator changing the local security policy would not make a difference here, either; the domain policy would override any local policy. Lastly, running secedit only refreshes a policy change and is not used to enable local policies. See the section "Securing the Desktop Using Security Policies."

APPLY YOUR KNOWLEDGE

Suggested Readings and Resources

1. Web sites
   - `http://www.microsoft.com/windows2000/professional/`
   - `http://www.microsoft.com/train_cert/`
   - `http://www.labmice.net/`
   - `http://activewin.com/win2000/`
   - `http://www.prometric.com/testingcandidates/assessment/chosetest.html` (to take online assessment tests)
   - `http://www.microsoft.com/windows2000/library/resources/reskit/dpg/default.asp` (Deployment Planning Guide)
   - `http://www.microsoft.com/enable` (Accessibility section)
   - `http://www.microsoft.com/windows2000/library/planning/management/groupsteps.asp` (Group Policy Whitepaper)

   - `http://www.microsoft.com/windows/professional/deploy/compatible/default.asp` (Hardware and Software Compatibility List)
   - `http://windowsupdate.microsoft.com/` (Windows Update)
   - `http://www.microsoft.com/windows2000/library/howitworks/security/ip_security.asp`
   - `http://www.ietf.org/rfc/rfc2401.txt`

2. MOC 1560B *Updating Support Skills from Microsoft Windows NT to Microsoft Windows 2000.*

3. MOC 2152A *Supporting Microsoft Windows 2000 Professional.*

4. *Windows 2000 Group Policy Technical Paper*, Version 2.0 (May 1999).

5. *Microsoft Windows 2000 Professional Support and Management Improvements* whitepaper.

6. *Microsoft Windows NT Server Guide to Microsoft Windows NT Profiles and Policies* whitepaper.

This chapter helps you prepare for the MCSE Windows 2000 Professional exam by covering the following objectives:

Configure and troubleshoot the TCP/IP protocol.

▶ The de facto standard for networking on the Internet is TCP/IP. It is also a very common protocol found in many business networks and has been adapted to support many different kinds of media. To effectively access network resources, you must understand how to install and configure the TCP/IP client and utilize the services available on TCP/IP networks.

Connect to computers by using dial-up networking.

- **Connect to computers by using a virtual private network (VPN) connection.**

- **Create a dial-up connection to connect to a remote access server.**

- **Connect to the Internet by using dial-up networking.**

- **Configure and troubleshoot Internet Connection Sharing.**

▶ Connectivity between LANs where a persistent connection is not needed can be provided by Dial-Up network connections. To accomplish this, you must be able to install and configure Dial-Up components in various configurations.

Connect to shared resources on a Microsoft network.

▶ The availability of networking technology means resources need not be centralized into a few large servers. File shares and printers can be distributed across the entire network and applications can involve many remote computers as system components. To accomplish this task, you must be able to find and access resources on the network.

CHAPTER 6

Implementing, Managing, and Troubleshooting Network Protocols and Services

STUDY STRATEGIES

▶ Exam questions on TCP/IP and networking will focus on a number of separate areas. The first is the configuration of network components and where they fit within the Windows 2000 Professional structure. You should also expect exam questions to focus on the configuration of the TCP/IP components, including addressing, subnet masking, and gateway addressing. This is an area that is fundamental to understanding how TCP/IP functions in finding resources on the network and how it responds to requests from other computers. You should expect to find scenario questions on the exam that will require you to know addressing, subnet masking, and routing to troubleshoot a problem. The exam will also have scenario questions that will test your understanding of how DHCP works and how DNS is used for name resolution.

▶ An important part of Windows 2000 Professional, and an area the exam will cover, is Dial-Up connection configurations and troubleshooting. It is important to understand how PPTP and VPN services and Internet Connection sharing work. You should also expect scenario questions that address finding and connecting to resources on the network both by browsing and using the Net commands.

▶ Finally, you should expect scenario questions that focus on your skills in troubleshooting network connectivity.

▶ If you focus on these areas you will be well prepared for this portion of the exam.

INTRODUCTION

A *local area network (LAN)* is a collection of computers in a specific area that are connected by a communications network. This can range from just two computers to hundreds or thousands. LANs are considered to be computers that all share high-speed network access. LANs in geographically separate areas can be connected into a *wide area network (WAN)*. Generally, the speed at which computers connect within a LAN is greater than what is available between LANs (across the WAN). It is also common for computer networks, even if primarily composed of Windows 2000 Professional and Server computers, to also include diverse operating systems such as UNIX, Novell, or Apple Macintosh. Interoperability between these systems is important. Connectivity with the Internet is also important, and its availability can be a part of the design of distributed applications. For Windows 2000 Professional to participate as a desktop or Network Operating System (NOS) in various LAN and WAN configurations, you must be able to properly configure its network components.

THE WINDOWS 2000 PROFESSIONAL NETWORKING MODEL

Before reviewing how to configure the networking components of Windows 2000 Professional, it is important to examine the underlying components that make up the network architecture. These components are put together as layers from interfacing with an application program down to interfacing with the physical connection to the network. Each layer interacts only with the layers directly above and directly below through a well-defined interface. Knowledge of how the different layers interact is important in understanding how the Windows 2000 network architecture enables computers in a network to communicate.

All the networking components in Windows 2000 Professional are built into the operating system, although some of them are not automatically installed. Any Windows 2000 computer can participate as the following:

- ◆ A client or a server in a distributed application environment
- ◆ A client in a peer-to-peer networking environment

To participate with distributed applications or peer-to-peer network applications, you must ensure that the proper client software is installed on your Windows 2000 Professional computer.

The built-in networking components allow Windows 2000 Professional systems to share printers, files, and applications with other networked computers (including other computers not based on Windows NT or Windows 2000).

WINDOWS 2000 NETWORKING VERSUS THE OSI REFERENCE MODEL

The Open Systems Interconnection (OSI) model is one system that can help you to understand the networking architecture used in Windows 2000 Professional. The OSI model was developed by the International Standards Organization (ISO) and is a layered model that standardizes how computers participating in a network should communicate and how the network data is exchanged between layers from the application to the network media.

The OSI model divides the network protocol stack into seven layers to which software systems must adhere to communicate over the network. In the case of Windows 2000, the system does not implement each layer separately; however, the end result complies with the overall OSI model.

NOTE **Distributed Applications** A distributed application is also referred to as a client/server application. Component pieces of the application are run on both the client system of the user and the (usually) centralized server. Many client systems (running the front-end process) can share the resources of the server (running the back-end processes).

NOTE **Peer-to-Peer Networking** A peer-to-peer network enables any computer to connect to shares and direct output to printers on any other computer in the network (not just to a specialized server).

The advantage of this modular design is the increase in flexibility and reliability. Each layer communicates only with the layers directly above and below with clearly defined interfaces between each layer. It is much easier to test and change a module of code rather than the entire block of network software. With each layer interfacing only with its neighbor, new capabilities can be added much more easily. Figure 6.1 compares the Windows 2000 network architecture with the OSI network model.

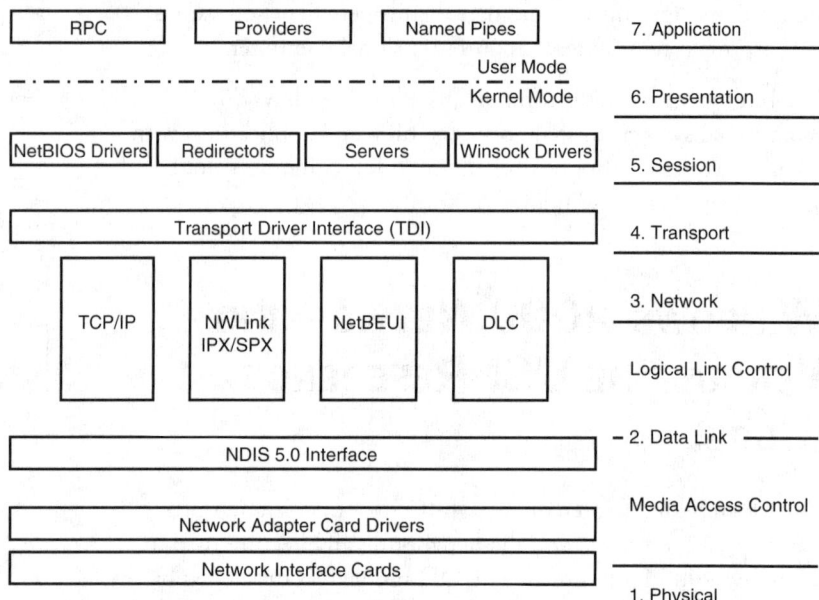

FIGURE 6.1
Windows 2000 networking architecture versus the OSI model.

NDIS-Compatible Network Adapter Card Drivers

The bottom layers of the Windows 2000 network architecture include the network adapter card driver and the network interface card (NIC). These must be 32-bit and compliant with the Network Device Interface Specification (NDIS) 3.0, 4.0, or 5.0. NDIS supports both connection-oriented protocols such as ATM and ISDN, as well as the traditional connectionless protocols such as Ethernet, Token Ring, and Fiber Distributed Data Interface (FDDI).

The mechanism that NDIS uses to bridge these two layers is the miniport driver specification. The miniport drivers directly access the network adapters while providing common code where possible. Hardware vendors therefore do not have to write complete Media Access Control (MAC) drivers, and protocols can be substituted without changing network adapter card drivers.

NDIS 5.0

NDIS 5.0 extends the previous versions of NDIS that define the interaction of network protocols and network card adapters.

The initial connection made between each protocol being used and the network card driver is referred to as a *network binding*. The actual set of network components is called a *protocol stack*. If you have more than one network adapter in your computer, each adapter card's protocol stack can be configured individually. The only limit on the number of network adapter cards you can install is the capacity of your computer hardware. Figure 6.2 shows two protocols binding to two network adapter cards using NDIS 5.0.

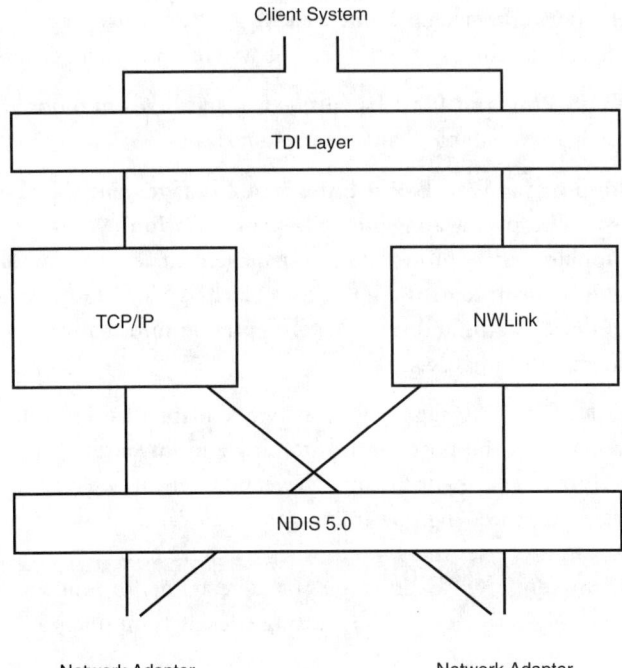

FIGURE 6.2

Two protocols binding to two network adapter cards.

NDIS 4.0 added the following new features to earlier NDIS specifications:

- ◆ Out of band data support (for Broadcast PC)
- ◆ Wireless WAN Media Extensions
- ◆ High-speed packet transmit (for performance)
- ◆ Fast IrDA (infrared) Media Extensions

Windows 2000 Professional and NDIS 5.0 provide the following new features in addition to those of the NDIS 4.0 specification:

- ◆ **Power management and network wake-up.** NDIS power management can power down network adapters at the request of the user or the system. For example, the user might want to put the system in sleep mode, or the system might request this based on keyboard/mouse inactivity. A power-down request can also be caused by disconnecting the network cable (if supported by the NIC). The system can also be awakened from a lower power state based on network events. A wakeup signal can be caused by the detection of a change in the network link state (for example, cable reconnect) or the receipt of a network wakeup frame or a Magic Packet packet (16 contiguous copies of the receiving system's Ethernet address).

- ◆ **NDIS Plug and Play.** Installs, loads, and binds miniports when a new adapter card is introduced.

- ◆ **Support for Web-Based Enterprise Management (WBEM) and Windows Management Instrumentation (WMI).** Supplies device information to management services. WMI is used by management applications (such as SMS) to query and set device status and retrieve configuration information directly from hardware devices.

- ◆ **Task offload.** Available if the network adapter card has the capability to support check-summing and forwarding for performance enhancements. Newer adapter cards have onboard processing power and can take over the tasks of certain processes that would otherwise have to be performed by the central CPU. Examples of these are performing check-summing activities and forwarding packets from one port to another without using the CPU. This would be a common task if your Windows 2000 Professional computer were acting as a router.

◆ **Support for Quality of Service (QoS) and connection-oriented media like ATM and ISDN.** These improvements extend the functionality of Windows 2000 Professional even further.

Most of the new features in NDIS 5.0 are accessible only by using the miniport driver model and are therefore not supported for MAC drivers or older miniport drivers.

> **NOTE**
>
> **Backward Compatibility** Windows 2000 Professional can also use drivers written to be compliant with the NDIS 3.0 and 4.0 specifications that were used by Windows NT 3.x and Windows 4.0. Windows 2000 uses Windows 95/98 INFs with extensions to allow for a common declarative INF between the operating systems. However, Windows 2000 uses drivers and Windows 9x uses VxDs, so some porting by the manufacturer is required.

Network Protocols

The network protocols referred to earlier in Figure 6.1 control the communications between computers on the network. Different network protocols provide varying communications services and capabilities.

TCP/IP

Transmission Control Protocol/Internet Protocol (TCP/IP) is the default protocol for Windows 2000 Professional and is an industry standard suite of protocols available for wide area networks (WAN) and the Internet. The TCP/IP suite for Windows 2000 is designed to make it easy to integrate Microsoft systems into large-scale networks and to provide the ability to operate over those networks in a secure manner.

Microsoft's implementation of TCP/IP provides a number of standard features, including the following:

◆ Ability to bind to multiple network adapters with different media types

◆ Logical and physical multi-homing

◆ Internal IP routing capability

◆ Internet Group Management Protocol (IGMP) version 2 (IP Multicasting)

◆ Duplicate IP address detection

◆ Multiple default gateways

◆ Dead gateway detection

◆ Automatic Path Maximum Transmission Unit (PMTU) discovery

◆ IP Security (IPSec)

◆ Quality of Service (QoS)

◆ Virtual Private Networks (VPNs)

In addition, Windows 2000 includes the following performance enhancements:

◆ **Internet Router Discovery Protocol (IRDP).** Windows 2000 performs router discovery through an improved method of configuring and detecting default gateways. Instead of manually configuring default gateways or using DHCP to set them, hosts can dynamically discover routers on their subnet and can automatically switch to a backup router if the primary router fails or the network administrators change router preferences.

◆ **TCP scalable window sizes.** The TCP receive window size is the amount of receive data (in bytes) that can be buffered at one time on a connection. The sending host can send only that amount of data before waiting for an acknowledgment and window update from the receiving host. The Windows 2000 TCP/IP stack will tune itself and use a larger default window size than earlier versions. Rather than using a hard-coded default receive window size, TCP adjusts in even increments of the maximum segment size (MSS).

◆ **Selective acknowledgments (SACK).** Windows 2000 introduces support for an important performance feature known as *Selective Acknowledgement* (SACK). SACK is especially important for connections using large TCP window sizes. With SACK enabled, the receiver continues to use the ACK number to acknowledge the left edge of the receive window, but it can also acknowledge other blocks of received data individually.

◆ **TCP Fast Retransmit.** There are some circumstances under which TCP retransmits data prior to the time that the retransmission timer expires. The most common of these occurs due to a feature known as *fast retransmit*. When a receiver that supports fast retransmit receives data with a sequence number beyond the current expected one, it is likely that some data was dropped. To help make the sender aware of this event, the receiver immediately sends an ACK, with the ACK number set to the sequence number that it was expecting. The receiver continues to do this for each additional TCP segment that arrives containing data after the missing data. When the sender starts to receive a stream of ACKs that are acknowledging the same sequence number, and that sequence number is earlier than the current sequence number being sent, the sender infers that a segment (or more) must have been dropped and immediately resends the segment that the receiver is expecting to fill in the gap in the data.

Windows 2000 TCP/IP also provides a number of services, including the following:

◆ Dynamic Host Configuration Protocol (DHCP) client and server

◆ Windows Internet Name Service (WINS), a NetBIOS name resolution client and server

◆ Domain Name Server (DNS)

◆ Dial-up (PPP/SLIP) support

◆ Point-to-Point Tunneling Protocol (PPTP), used for virtual private remote networks

◆ TCP/IP network printing (lpr/lpd)

◆ SNMP agent

◆ NetBIOS interface

◆ Windows Sockets version 2 (Winsock2) interface

◆ Remote Procedure Call (RPC) support

◆ Network Dynamic Data Exchange (NetDDE)

◆ Wide Area Network (WAN) browsing support

NWLink IPX/SPX Compatible Transport

NWLink is an NDIS-compliant, native 32-bit implementation of Novell's IPX/SPX protocol. NWLink supports two networking Application Programming Interfaces (APIs): NetBIOS and Windows Sockets. These APIs allow communication among computers running Windows 2000 and between computers running Windows 2000 and NetWare servers.

The NWLink transport driver is an implementation of the lower-level NetWare protocols, which include IPX, SPX, Routing Information Protocol over IPX (RIPX), and NetBIOS over IPX (NBIPX). IPX controls addressing and routing of packets of data within and between networks. SPX provides reliable delivery through sequencing and acknowledgments. NWLink provides NetBIOS compatibility with NetBIOS layer over IPX.

When used in conjunction with a redirector such as Client Service for NetWare (CSNW), NWLink allows a computer running Windows 2000 to access files or printers shared on a NetWare server. Non-NetWare computers on a network that are not running NWLink or another IPX/SPX transport can access NetWare file and print resources through a computer running Windows 2000 Server that has been configured with Gateway Services for NetWare and NWLink. For a NetWare client to access print and file services on a computer running Windows 2000, File and Print Services for NetWare and NWLink must be installed on the Windows 2000 system. The Interoperability between NetWare and Windows 2000 is summarized in Table 6.1.

TABLE 6.1

WINDOWS 2000 INTEROPERABILITY WITH NETWARE

Platform	Running	Can Connect To
Windows 2000	NWLink	Client/server application running on a NetWare server
Windows 2000	NWLink and CSNW, or NWLink and GSNW	NetWare servers for file and print services
NetWare Client	IPX with NetBIOS, Named Pipes, or Windows Sockets	Computers running Windows 2000 (with NWLink) running IPX-aware applications (such as SQL Server)

Platform	Running	Can Connect To
NetWare Client	IPX	Computers running Windows 2000 Server (with NWLink and File and Print services for NetWare) for file and print services

NWLink can be used if there are NetWare client/server applications running that use Sockets or NetBIOS over the IPX/SPX protocol. The client component of the application can be run on a Windows 2000 Professional system to access the server portion on a NetWare server, and vice versa. The NWLink component is used to format NetBIOS-level requests and pass them to the NWLink component for transmission on the network.

NetBIOS Extended User Interface (NetBEUI)

NetBEUI is a simple non-routable protocol designed for Peer-to-Peer Networks that takes little memory overhead. All hosts are considered to be on the same logical network and all resources are considered to be local. Other machines on the network are located via their NetBIOS computer name. This name is resolved to a MAC address mapping via the use of broadcast messages. This makes NetBEUI unsuitable for large networks (because the overhead added by broadcasts can eventually consume all of the network bandwidth), but it is ideal for small networks. Without the added complexity of other protocols, more of the packet is used to transport data, making NetBEUI faster than TCP/IP and IPX/SPX in a small network (fewer than 50 computers).

In the Windows 2000 operating system implementation, the programming interface (NetBIOS) has been separated from the protocol (NetBEUI) to increase flexibility in the layered architecture. The difference between these two can be kept straight if you remember that NetBEUI is a protocol and NetBIOS is a programming interface.

Transport Driver Interface

The Transport Driver Interface (TDI) is a common interface for drivers (such as the Windows 2000 redirector and server) to use to communicate with the various network transport protocols allowing services to remain independent of transport protocols. Unlike NDIS, there is no driver for TDI, which is just a specification for passing messages between two layers in the network architecture.

TDI provides greater flexibility and functionality than existing interfaces (such as Winsock and NetBIOS) and all Windows 2000 transport providers directly interface with the Transport Driver Interface. The TDI specification describes the set of functions and call mechanisms by which transport drivers and TDI clients communicate.

Network Application Programming Interfaces

An Application Programming Interface (API) is a set of routines that an application program uses to request and carry out lower-level services performed by the operating system. Windows 2000 network APIs include those outlined in the following sections.

Winsock API

Winsock is an API that allows Windows-based applications to access the transport protocols. Winsock in Windows 2000 is a protocol-independent implementation of the widely used Sockets API and is the standard for accessing datagram and session services over TCP/IP, NWLink IPX/SPX NetBIOS, and AppleTalk. Applications written to the Winsock interface include File Transfer Protocol (FTP) and Simple Network Management Protocol (SNMP).

NetBIOS API

NetBIOS is a standard application programming interface used for developing client/server applications. NetBIOS has been used as an interprocess communication (IPC) mechanism since its introduction and is included with Windows 2000 to support legacy applications.

Telephony API

Telephony is a technology that integrates computers with telephone networks. Telephony API (TAPI) supports both speech and data transmission and allows for a variety of terminals.

TAPI allows programmers to develop applications that provide support for call management, call conferencing, call waiting, and voice mail.

Messaging API

The Messaging Application Programming Interface (MAPI) is an API that allows developers to write messaging applications and back-end services that can be connected in a distributed computing environment. MAPI is part of WOSA (Windows Open Services Architecture) and includes a *messaging subsystem* that provides various services such as common UI for messaging apps, message stores, and address books.

WNet API

WNet APIs provide Windows networking (WNet) capabilities that extend networking functionality to applications. This set of APIs is also known as the Win32 APIs and allows applications to access networking functions while remaining independent of the network over which they communicate.

Network services are one of many categories of services that the Win32 APIs can provide. Requests for network services are provided by the Multiple Provider Router (MPR), which, after receiving the network command, determines the appropriate redirector and passes the command to it. The Multiple Provider Router then routes the requests for network service to the appropriate provider for transmission over the network.

Interprocess Communication

Interprocess communication (IPC) allows bidirectional communication between clients and multiuser servers working on different computer systems. IPCs can also be used as an intertask communication system on a local computer as well as between a local computer and a remote one.

Applications that split processing between networked computers are referred to as *distributed* applications. The two or more portions of a distributed application can be located on the same machine or on separate machines. A client/server application uses distributed processing, in which processing is divided between a workstation (the client) and a more powerful server. The client portion is sometimes referred to as the *front end* and the server portion is referred to as the *back end.* The client portion of a client/server application can consist of just the user interface to the application. However, there are no hard and fast rules, and the application can actually be split at various places with the client end handling only the screen drawings, keyboard entry, and movement of the mouse.

Multitier applications (often called three-tier) are an extension of the basic client/server model with an additional application-specific component between the client and the backend server. It is common for this type of application to be split between a user interface on the client, the application code or business rules in the middle tier, and data services interacting with a large shared database server on the back end.

There are a number of ways in which the Windows 2000 operating system implements Interprocess Communication (IPC) mechanisms.

Distributed Component Object Model

Windows 2000 supports the distributed component object model (DCOM). DCOM allows components to be efficiently invoked on multiple computers so that the application can take advantage of the most optimal resources on the network. Processing occurs transparently to the user because DCOM handles the function of locating the called component.

Remote Procedure Call

Remote Procedure Calls are another mechanism that allows client and server software to communicate. The Microsoft RPC facility is compatible with the Open Group's Distributed Computing Environment (DCE) specification for remote procedure calls and is interoperable with other DCE-based RPC systems, such as those for HP-UX and IBM AIX UNIX–based operating systems.

The Microsoft RPC mechanism uses other IPC mechanisms such as named pipes, NetBIOS, or Winsock to establish communications between the client and the server with the program logic and related procedure code existing on different computers.

Named Pipes

Named pipes provide connection-oriented messaging by using a portion of memory called a pipe. A *pipe* connects two processes such that the output of one process is used as the input to the other. Named pipes are based on OS/2 API calls that have been added to the WNet API's. Named pipes are included to provide backward compatibility with Microsoft LAN Manager and related applications.

The Windows 2000 operating system provides special APIs that increase security for named pipes called impersonation. With impersonation, the server can change its security identity to that of the client at the other end of the message. A server typically has more permissions to access databases on the server than a client requesting services. When the request is delivered to the server through a named pipe, the server changes its security identity to the security identity of the client limiting the permissions granted to the client rather than the server.

Common Internet File System

The Common Internet File System (CIFS) is the standard way that computer users share files across corporate intranets and the Internet. It is an enhancement to the cross-platform Server Message Block (SMB) protocol that defines a series of commands used to pass information between networked computers. The CIFS messages can be broadly classified as follows:

- ◆ Connection establishment messages that start and end a redirector connection to a shared resource

- ◆ Namespace and File Manipulation messages used by the redirector to gain access to files

- ◆ Printer messages used by the redirector to retrieve information and send data to a print queue

- ◆ Miscellaneous messages used by the redirector to write to mailslots and named pipes

CIFS supports most common operating systems such as Windows or Windows 9x through Windows 2000, UNIX, VMS, and Macintosh.

CIFS complements Hypertext Transfer Protocol (HTTP) while providing more sophisticated file sharing and file transfer than older protocols, such as FTP. CIFS works at the application level of the Windows 2000 network architecture and services user requests, selecting the correct redirector and protocol for transport. For NetBIOS requests, NetBIOS is encapsulated in the IP protocol and transported over the network to the appropriate server. The request is passed up to the server, which sends data back to satisfy the request.

There is a mini-redirector for the Network File System (NFS), Mrxnfs.sys, providing support for NFS. Mrxnfs.sys is included in Services for UNIX (SFU).

Basic Network Services

Network services support application programs and provide the components and APIs necessary to access files on networked computers. Both the server service and the workstation service also assist in accessing I/O requests.

Server Service

The server service is located above the TDI and is implemented as a file system driver. The CIFS server service interacts directly with other file-system drivers to satisfy I/O requests, such as reading or writing to a file. The server service supplies the connection requested by client-side redirectors and provides them with access to the resources they request.

When the server service receives a request from a remote computer asking to read a file that resides on the local hard drive, the following steps occur:

1. The low-level network drivers receive the request and pass it to the server driver.

NOTE

Ports Previously in Windows NT 4.0, Windows Internet Name Service (WINS) and Domain Name System (DNS) name resolution was accomplished by using TCP port 134. Extensions to CIFS and NetBT now allow connections directly over TCP/IP with the use of TCP port 445. Both means of resolution are still available in Windows 2000. It is possible to disable either or both of these services in the registry.

2. The server service passes the request to the appropriate local file-system driver.

3. The local file-system driver calls lower-level disk-device drivers to access the file.

4. The data is passed back to the local file-system driver.

5. The local file-system driver passes the data back to the server service.

6. The server service passes the data to the lower-level network drivers for transmission back to the remote computer.

The server service is composed of two parts. Services.exe is the Service Control Manager where all services start. Srv.sys is a file system driver that handles the interaction with the lower levels of the protocol stack and directly interacts with various file system devices to satisfy command requests, such as file read and write.

Workstation Service

All user requests from the Multiple Uniform Naming Convention Provider (Multi-UNC Provider) go through the workstation service. This service consists of two components: the user interface, which resides in Services.exe in Windows 2000, and the redirector (Mrxsmb.sys), which is a file-system driver that interacts with the lower-level network drivers by means of the TDI interface.

The workstation service receives the user request and passes it to the kernel redirector.

Windows 2000 Redirectors

The *redirector* is a component that resides above TDI and is the mechanism through which one computer gains access to another computer. The Windows 2000 operating system redirector allows connection to Windows 9x, Windows for Workgroups, LAN Manager, LAN Server, and other CIFS servers. The redirector communicates with the protocols using the TDI specifications.

The redirector is implemented as a Windows 2000 file system driver. This provides several benefits:

◆ It allows applications to call a single API (the Windows 2000 I/O API) to access files on local and remote computers. From the I/O manager perspective, there is no difference between accessing files stored on a remote computer on the network and accessing those stored locally on a hard disk.

◆ It runs in kernel mode and can directly call other drivers and other kernel-mode components, such as cache manager. This improves the performance of the redirector.

◆ It can be dynamically loaded and unloaded, like any other file-system driver.

◆ It can easily coexist with other redirectors.

Interoperating with Other Networks

Besides allowing connections to Windows 9x, peer-to-peer networks, LAN Manager, LAN Server, and MS-Net servers, the Windows 2000 redirector can coexist with redirectors for other networks, such as Novell NetWare and UNIX networks.

Providers and the Provider-Interface Layer

For each additional type of network, such as NetWare or UNIX, you must install a provider. The provider is the component that allows a computer running Windows 2000 Professional to communicate with the lower levels of the network. Client Services for NetWare and Gateway Services for NetWare are two such providers.

Client Services for NetWare is included with Windows 2000 Professional and allows the computer to connect as a client to the NetWare network. The Gateway service, included with Windows 2000 Server, provides gateway services between Microsoft network-based clients and Novell NetWare servers.

When a process on a Windows 2000 computer tries to open a file that resides on a remote computer, the following steps occur:

1. The process calls the I/O manager to request that the file be opened.

2. The I/O manager recognizes that the request is for a file on a remote computer, and passes the request to the redirector file-system driver.

3. The redirector passes the request to lower-level network drivers that transmit it to the remote server for processing.

Network Resource Access

Applications have a unified interface for accessing network resources, independent of any redirectors installed on the system. Access to resources is provided through the Multiple Uniform Naming Convention Provider (Multi-UNC Provider) and the Multi-Provider Router (MPR).

Multiple Universal Naming Convention Provider

When applications make I/O calls containing Uniform Naming Convention (UNC) names, these requests are passed to the Multiple UNC (Multi-UNC) Provider. The Multi-UNC Provider is implemented as a driver, unlike the TDI, which is only a specification defining the way one network layer talks to another.

The Multi-UNC Provider allows multiple redirectors to coexist in the computer. However, if there are multiple redirectors present, there must be a means of deciding which one to use. One of the Multi-UNC Provider's functions, then, is to act as an arbitrator to decide the most appropriate redirector to use.

Universal Naming Convention Names

UNC is a naming convention for describing network servers and the share points on those servers. UNC names start with two back-slashes followed by the server name. All other fields in the name are separated by a single backslash. A typical UNC name appears as follows:

`\\server\share\subdirectory\filename.`

Not all of the components of the UNC name need to be present with each command; only the share component is required. For example, the following command can be used to obtain a directory of the root of a specified share:

`dir \\server_name\share_name`

I/O requests from applications that contain UNC names are received by the I/O manager, which passes the requests to the Multi-UNC Provider. If the Multi-UNC Provider has not seen the UNC name during the previous 15 minutes (approximately), the Multi-UNC Provider sends the name to each of the UNC providers registered with it.

When the Multi-UNC Provider receives a request containing a UNC name, it checks with each redirector to find out which one can process the request. It then looks for the redirector with the highest registered-priority response that claims it can establish a connection to the UNC. This connection remains as long as there is activity. If there has been no request for approximately 15 minutes on the UNC name, then the Multi-UNC Provider negotiates to find another appropriate redirector.

> **NOTE**
>
> **MPR Versus MPR** The acronym MPR is also used for the Multi-Protocol Router, a series of routing components supplied with Windows NT 4. In Windows 2000, the Multi-Protocol Router has become the Routing and Remote Access Service.

Multi-Provider Router

Not all programs use UNC names in their I/O requests. Some applications use WNet APIs, which are the Win32 network APIs. The Multi-Provider Router (MPR) supports these applications.

MPR is similar to Multi-UNC Provider. MPR receives WNet commands, determines the appropriate redirector, and passes the command to that redirector.

ADDING AND CONFIGURING THE NETWORK COMPONENTS OF WINDOWS 2000

You can configure all your network components when you first install Windows 2000 Professional. If you want to examine how your network components are configured or make changes to your network identification, double-click the System applet in the Control Panel and select the Network Identification tab (see Figure 6.3).

To view and configure the other aspects of your network configuration (Services, Clients, and Protocols), identify the appropriate connection to configure using Settings, Network and Dial-Up Connections from the Start pop-up menu, or from the Control Panel (see Figure 6.4).

Identification Options

Use the Network Identification option in the System applet to view your computer name and your workgroup or domain information. Click on the Network ID button to start the Network Identification Wizard, which will walk you through the process of joining a workgroup or domain. Windows 2000 can support both the Active Directory and the NT 4 domain structures. If you are joining an NT 4 domain, the domain name you can enter must have 15 or fewer characters. If the domain you are joining is a Window 2000 domain, the domain structure will resemble an Internet domain address (such as ntdev.microsoft.com). Figure 6.5 shows a typical logon screen showing the user ID, password, and account domain.

The Windows 2000 security system requires that all Windows 2000 Professional computers joining a domain first have a machine account. Only domain administrators or people who have been delegated the right to create user and machine accounts can create computer accounts. By default, in a Windows 2000 domain, each authenticated user has the right to create computer accounts for workstations (unless disabled by a domain administrator).

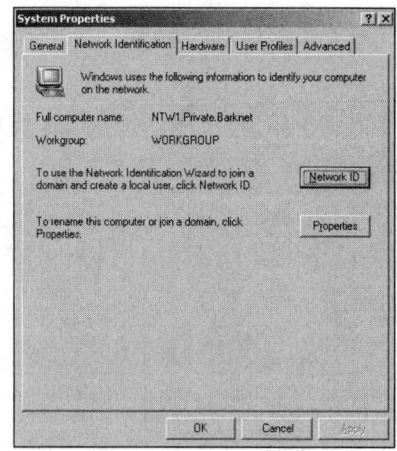

FIGURE 6.3
Network Identification tab in the System applet.

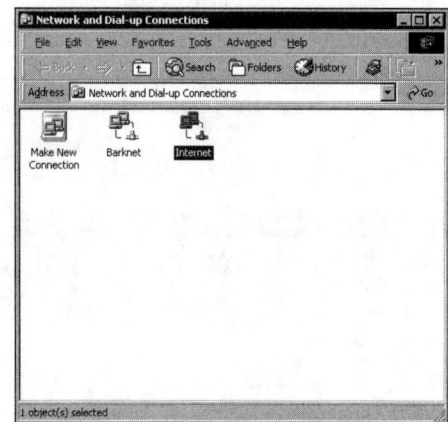

FIGURE 6.4
Selecting a network connection.

> **N O T E**
>
> **Role** You must be a local administrator to make any changes to the network settings of your computer.

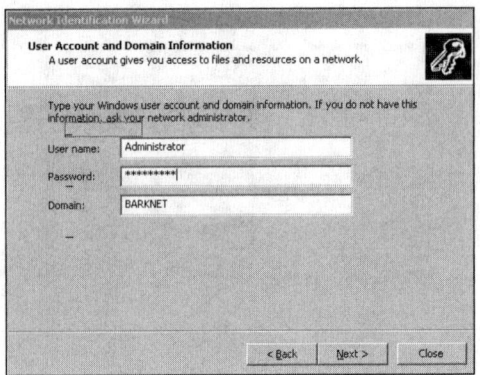

FIGURE 6.5
Joining a domain.

> **N O T E**
>
> **Joining a Domain** To join a domain, you must have already established network connectivity to a domain controller in the domain that you wish to join.

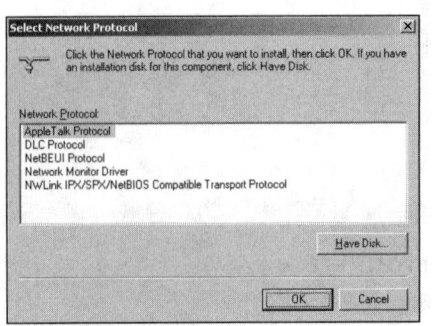

FIGURE 6.6
Protocols available to install.

To join a domain, you must be a local administrator on your computer. If the userid that you logged on with does not have administrative privileges, the Network ID and Properties buttons will be grayed out.

Clicking the Network ID button will start the Network Identification Wizard. You will need to provide your domain userid and password and know the account domain you are joining. If there is a computer account already set up in the domain by a domain administrator, you will be able to join the domain directly. If the computer account has not been set up, you can create an account by using a valid userid for the domain. The computer will need to be rebooted to complete the process of joining the domain.

To view or modify the protocols, services, and clients available to your computer, select Network and Dial-up Connections from the Control Panel. In that display, right-click on the local area network connection for the adapter you wish to view or modify and select the Properties entry. The Properties window will display all the clients, services, and protocols currently configured for that adapter. Selecting an entry in the components window and clicking on the Uninstall button will remove that component.

Protocol Options

To configure Protocols, click the Install button. This will bring up the Select Network Component Type button. Highlight the Protocol entry and click the Add button. This will show the protocols that are available to install on your computer (see Figure 6.6).

You might want to add some of the following network transport protocols to a Windows 2000 Professional workstation:

- ◆ **Internet Protocol (TCP/IP).** This is the default protocol for Windows 2000 Professional. It is required for Internet connectivity.

- ◆ **NWLINK IPX/SPX/NetBIOS Compatible Transport Protocol.** This is Microsoft's implementation of IPX and SPX used by NetWare networks; it allows NetBIOS packets to be interchanged between Windows 2000 computers and NetWare servers running Novell NetBIOS.

- ◆ **NetBEUI Protocol.** This is a non-routable protocol used to connect a small number of Microsoft-based computers.

- ◆ **DLC Protocol.** This is a protocol to enable IBM mainframes to connect to Microsoft-based computers (with additional software), and to set up printers attached directly to the network.

- ◆ **AppleTalk Protocol.** This protocol allows other computers to communicate with your computer and printers via the AppleTalk protocol. This is also used in Windows 2000 Server to provide network routing services.

- ◆ **Network Monitor Driver.** This driver allows the Network Monitoring system (NetMon) to acquire packets from the network.

Service Options

Clicking on the Install button and selecting a service to add will display all the available services not currently installed (see Figure 6.7).

You might want to add some of the following network services to a Windows 2000 Professional workstation:

- ◆ **File and Printer Sharing for Microsoft Networks.** This allows other computers to access resources on your computer.

- ◆ **SAP Agent.** This is a NetWare service that advertises servers and addresses on a network

- ◆ **QOS Packet Scheduler.** This service provides network traffic control, rate control, and prioritization.

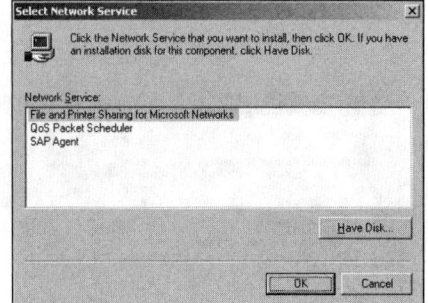

FIGURE 6.7
Services available to install.

Client Options

Selecting the Client entry and clicking the Add button will show the clients available to install on your computer (see Figure 6.8).

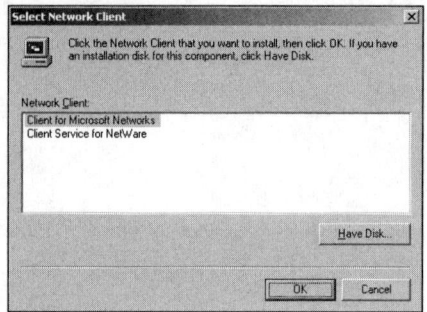

FIGURE 6.8
Clients available to install.

You might want to add some of the following network clients to a Windows 2000 Professional workstation:

◆ **Client for Microsoft Network.** Allows your computer to communicate on Microsoft networks.

◆ **Client Service for NetWare.** Allows your computer to access resources on NetWare networks.

Advanced Options

The advanced options provide you a place to improve the performance of your computer on networks that contain more than one protocol.

Two options are available from the Network and Dial-Up Communications applet in the Control Panel. Select the Advanced tab from the menu bar and Advanced Settings within the drop-down list.

Provider Order

This tab allows you to choose the order in which network providers (such as Microsoft networks and NetWare networks) are accessed (see Figure 6.9).

If your network connection accesses both Microsoft and NetWare networks using both IPX/SPX and TCP/IP, but your primary interface is the Microsoft Network, move the Microsoft Windows Network to the top for best performance.

Adapters and Bindings

This tab allows you to choose the order in which protocols (such as IPX/SPX and TCP/IP) are accessed (see Figure 6.10).

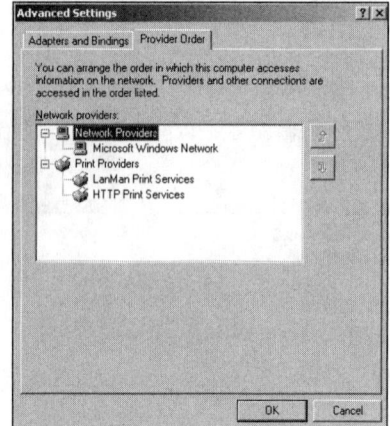

FIGURE 6.9
Typical providers available.

Suppose your network connection supports both IPX/SPX and TCP/IP protocols; however, your primary interface is using TCP/IP. In that case, you would move that protocol to the top for best performance. When connecting to a server, the client defines the protocol being used. Setting the order of the protocols on a server therefore does not enhance performance, whereas changing the order of the protocols on your Windows 2000 Professional client will impact performance. Deselecting a network protocol will make it temporarily unavailable without uninstalling it.

CONFIGURING THE **TCP/IP** PROTOCOL

Configure and troubleshoot the TCP/IP protocol.

TCP/IP is the default protocol for Windows 2000 Professional and is supported by most common operating systems. TCP/IP is a suite of protocols used to provide connectivity within an enterprise network (LAN) in addition to providing connectivity to the Internet. When you manually configure a computer with a TCP/IP network adapter, you must enter the appropriate settings for connectivity with your network.

IP Addressing

Before delving into IP addressing schemes, it is appropriate to review binary-to-decimal conversions. IP addresses are 32-bit integers that are usually depicted as four 8-bit numbers. This can be thought of as a series of 1s or 0s, with eight taken together to be a number. Each position in the 8 bits (from right to left) is twice the value of the field before it. (In decimal notation, the same rule would state that each column is worth 10 times the value of the previous column—100s versus 10s versus 1s.) The smallest integer number that can be represented with 8 bits is 0 0 0 0 0 0 0 0 (2^0-1), or 0. The largest integer that can be represented by 8 bits is 1 1 1 1 1 1 1 1 (2^8-1), or 255. Because of this, you will always see IP addresses as four numbers ranging from 0 to 255.

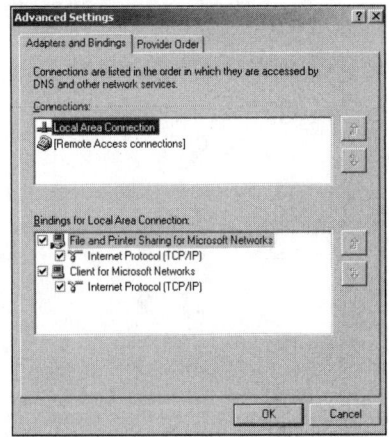

FIGURE 6.10
Typical protocols available.

> **N O T E**
>
> **Unnecessary Protocols** For maximum performance, remove any unnecessary protocols and always make sure that your most frequently used protocol is configured to be the first one accessed.

Each TCP/IP connection must be identified by an address. The address is a 32-bit number that is used to uniquely identify a host on a network. The TCP/IP address has no dependence on the Data-Link layer address such as the MAC address of a Network adapter.

Although the IP address is 32 bits, it is customary to break it into four 8-bit numbers expressed in decimal and separated by dots. This can be referred to in dotted decimal format and is expressed as *w.x.y.z*. The value of breaking down this address into four 8-bit values can be seen in the following example. Suppose you have an address that is 192.168.8.4. If you had to remember that as a binary 32-bit number it would be 11000000101010000000100000000100 or, converted to a decimal number, it would be the sum of $2^3 + 2^{12} + 2^{20} + 2^{22} + 2^{24} + 2^{31} + 2^{32}$, which is 8+4,096+1,048,576+4,194,304 +16,777,216+2,147,483,648+4,294,967,296, or 6,464,475,144. 192.168.8.4 is definitely easier to remember.

This addressing scheme is again broken down into two halves: a network ID (also known as the network address) and the host ID (also known as the host address). The network ID must be unique in the Internet or intranet, and the host ID must be unique to the network ID. The network portion of the *w.x.y.z* notation is separated from the host through the use of the subnet mask. See the section entitled "Subnet Mask" later in this chapter.

The Internet community was originally divided into five address classes. Microsoft TCP/IP supports class A, B, and C addresses assigned to hosts.

The class of address defines which bits are used for the network ID and which bits are used for the host ID. It also defines the possible number of networks and the number of hosts per network. Here is a rundown of the five classes:

◆ **Class A addresses.** The high-order bit is always binary 0 and the next seven bits complete the network ID. The next three octets define the host ID. This represents 126 networks with 16,777,214 hosts per network.

◆ **Class B addresses.** The top two bits in a class B address are always set to binary 1 0. The next 14 bits complete the network ID. The remaining two octets define the host ID. This represents 16,384 networks with 65,534 hosts per network.

◆ **Class C addresses.** The top three bits in a class C address are always set to binary 1 1 0. The next 21 bits define the network ID. The remaining octet defines the host ID. This represents 2,097,152 networks with 254 hosts per network.

◆ **Class D addresses.** Class D addresses are used for multicasting to a number of hosts. Packets are passed to a selected subset of hosts on a network. Only those hosts registered for the multicast address accept the packet. The four high-order bits in a class D address are always set to binary 1 1 1 0. The remaining bits are for the address that interested hosts will recognize.

◆ **Class E addresses.** Class E is an experimental address that is reserved for future use. The high-order bits in a class E address are set to 1 1 1 1.

Table 6.2 indicates how the three classes supported by Microsoft TCP/IP divide up network IDs and host IDs.

TABLE 6.2

CLASS ADDRESS RANGES

Class	Network ID	Network Portion	Host Portion	Number of Networks	Number of Hosts
A	1.126	w.	x.y.z	126	16,777,214
B	128.191	w.x	y.z	16,384	65,534
C	192.223	w.x.y	z	2,097,152	254

Subnet Mask

Once an IP address from a particular class has been decided upon, it is possible to divide it into smaller segments to better utilize the addresses available. Each segment is bounded by an IP router and assigned a new subnetted network ID that is a subset of the original class-based network ID.

A subnet mask (also known as an address mask) is defined as a 32-bit value that is used to distinguish the network ID from the host ID in an IP address. The bits of the subnet mask are defined as follows:

◆ All bits that correspond to the network ID are set to 1.

◆ All bits that correspond to the host ID are set to 0.

The subnet mask is broken down into four 8-bit octets in the same fashion as the class addresses.

Table 6.3 lists the default subnet masks using dotted decimal notation.

TABLE 6.3

DEFAULT SUBNET MASKS

Address Class	Bits for Subnet Mask	Subnet Mask
Class A	11111111 00000000 00000000 00000000	255.0.0.0
Class B	11111111 11111111 00000000 00000000	255.255.0.0
Class C	11111111 11111111 11111111 00000000	255.255.255.0

> **NOTE**
>
> **Hosts Need a Subnet Mask**   Each host on a TCP/IP network requires a subnet mask even if it is on a single-segment network. Although the subnet mask is expressed in dotted decimal notation, a subnet mask is not an IP address.

Default Gateway (Router)

This optional setting is the IP address of the router for this subnet segment. Each subnet segment is bounded by a router that will direct packets destined for segments outside the local one to the correct segment or to another router that can complete the connection. Routers, therefore, have connections to more than one network segment, and this address points to the router's network adapter on the same segment as your computer. If this address is left blank, this computer will only be able to communicate with other computers on the same network segment.

Figure 6.11 shows a hypothetical network that is using a subnet mask of 255.255.224.0. This provides for a maximum of six subnets of 8,190 hosts each; however, in this example only three connections are being used. The hosts on the subnet 192.168.32.0 would each have the default gateway address set to the address of the router port connecting that subnet, 192.168.32.1. The IP address of each router connection is local to the subnet it serves, allowing the hosts on that subnet to communicate with it directly.

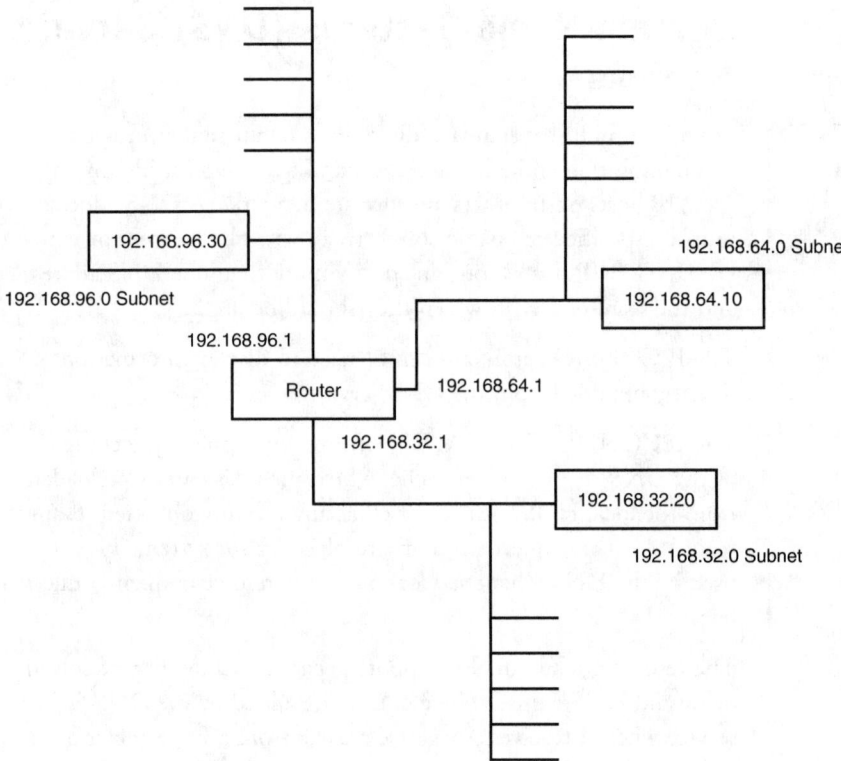

FIGURE 6.11
Default gateways on a subnetted network.

Windows Internet Name Service (WINS)

Computers may use IP addresses to identify one another, but users generally prefer to use computer names. Windows 2000 Professional allows Windows 9x and Windows NT 4 clients to use NetBIOS names to communicate and therefore requires a means to resolve

N O T E

The Dynamic Nature of WINS   WINS eliminates the need for an LMHOSTS file, which is a static alternative to WINS. Maintaining an LMHOSTS file requires much more administrative overhead than using WINS.

N O T E

Name Resolution   Name resolution is the process of translating fully qualified domain names (FQDN) to IP addresses.

W A R N I N G

TCP/IP Setting   If the settings for the TCP/IP protocol are incorrectly specified, you will experience problems that may keep your computer from establishing communications with other TCP/IP hosts in your network. In extreme cases, communications on your entire subnet can be disrupted.

NetBIOS names to IP addresses. The Windows Internet Name Service is an enhanced NetBIOS name server that registers NetBIOS computer names and resolves them to IP addresses. WINS provides a dynamic database that maintains mappings of computer names to IP addresses.

Domain Name Systems (DNS) Server Address

DNS is an industry-standard distributed database that provides name resolution and a hierarchical naming system for identifying TCP/IP hosts on Internets and private networks. A DNS address must be specified to enable connectivity with the Internet or with UNIX TCP/IP hosts. You can specify more than one DNS address and the search order in which they should be used.

The IPCONFIG command can be used to display information recently obtained from the DNS service.

The IPCONFIG /DISPLAYDNS command displays the contents of the DNS client resolver cache, which includes entries preloaded from the local HOSTS file, as well as any recently obtained resource records for name queries recently resolved by the system. This is used by the DNS Client service to quickly resolve frequently queried names.

The resolver cache can also support negative caching of unresolved or invalid DNS names. These entries are added by the DNS Client service when it receives a negative answer from a DNS server for a queried name. The negative result is then cached for a brief period of time so that this name is not queried repeatedly by the system.

The IPCONFIG /FLUSHDNS command will flush and reset the DNS resolver cache. Once this option is used, the computer must query DNS servers again for any names previously used on the computer.

Windows 2000 Server contains a dynamically updated DNS service. This service is updated with records obtained from either a DHCP server or the DHCP client service on a Windows 2000 Professional workstation. Normally, this is done when the DHCP address is assigned to the Windows 2000 Professional workstation. The IPCONFIG /REGISTERDNS command provides a mechanism to manually initiate dynamic registration for the DNS names and IP addresses configured at a computer. This option would normally only be used in troubleshooting DNS name resolution problems.

By default, the IPCONFIG /REGISTERDNS command refreshes all DHCP address leases and registers all related DNS names configured and used by the client computer.

You can specify all the settings for the TCP/IP protocol manually, or they can be automatically configured through a network service called *Dynamic Host Configuration Protocol* (DHCP).

Understanding DHCP

One way to avoid the possible problems of administrative overhead and incorrect settings for the TCP/IP protocol (which are usually caused by manual configurations) is to set up your network so that all your clients receive their TCP/IP configuration information automatically through DHCP. DHCP centralizes and manages the allocation of the TCP/IP settings required for proper network functionality for computers that have been configured as DHCP clients. One major advantage of DHCP is that most of the configuration of your network settings need happen only once, at the DHCP server. Also, the TCP/IP settings that the DHCP client receives from the *DHCP server* are only leased, and must be periodically renewed. This lease and renewal sequence enables a network administrator to change client TCP/IP settings, if needed.

Using DHCP

To configure a computer as a DHCP client, all you must do is to specify an IP address automatically in the TCP/IP properties box (see Figure 6.12). Exercise 6.2 at the end of the chapter contains complete instructions.

Testing DHCP

To determine the network settings that a DHCP server has leased to your computer, type the following command at a command prompt:

```
IPCONFIG /all
```

> **NOTE**
>
> **Dynamic DNS Only** The registerdns option on IPCONFIG will function correctly only if the DNS allows the client to register directly (it is configurable by the Network Administrator) or if the DNS can accept configuration records. This is only true with the Microsoft DNS service and recent version of BIND.

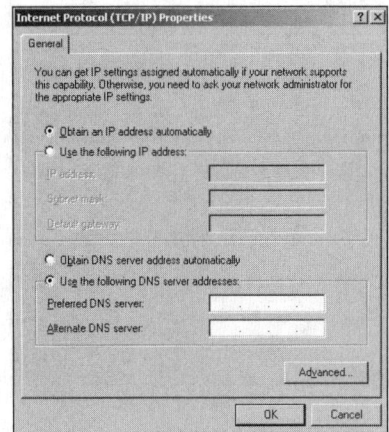

FIGURE 6.12
Specifying that TCP/IP configuration comes from a DHCP server.

The following is a sample output from the IPCONFIG command.

```
Windows 2000 IP Configuration
        Host Name . . . . . . . . . . . . : NTW1
        Primary DNS Suffix  . . . . . . . : Private.Barknet
        Node Type . . . . . . . . . . . . : Mixed
        IP Routing Enabled. . . . . . . . : No
        WINS Proxy Enabled. . . . . . . . : No
        DNS Suffix Search List. . . . . . : Private.Barknet
        Ethernet adapter Local Area Connection:
        Connection-specific DNS Suffix  . :
        Description . . . . . . . . . . . : NE2000
➟Compatible
        Physical Address. . . . . . . . . : 00-40-05-3E-C7-
➟BF
        DHCP Enabled. . . . . . . . . . . : Yes
        Autoconfiguration Enabled . . . . : Yes
        IP Address. . . . . . . . . . . . : 192.168.0.113
        Subnet Mask . . . . . . . . . . . : 255.255.255.0
        Default Gateway . . . . . . . . . : 192.168.0.1
        DHCP Server . . . . . . . . . . . : 192.168.0.1
        DNS Servers . . . . . . . . . . . : 192.168.0.1
        Lease Obtained. . . . . . . . . . : June 4, 1999
➟11:40:48 PM
        Lease Expires . . . . . . . . . . : June 12, 1999
➟11:40:48 PM
```

Note that IPCONFIG also gives you full details on the duration of your current lease. You can verify whether a DHCP client has connectivity to a DHCP server by releasing the IP address and requesting a new lease. You can conduct this test by typing the following commands in a command window:

```
IPCONFIG /release
IPCONFIG /renew
```

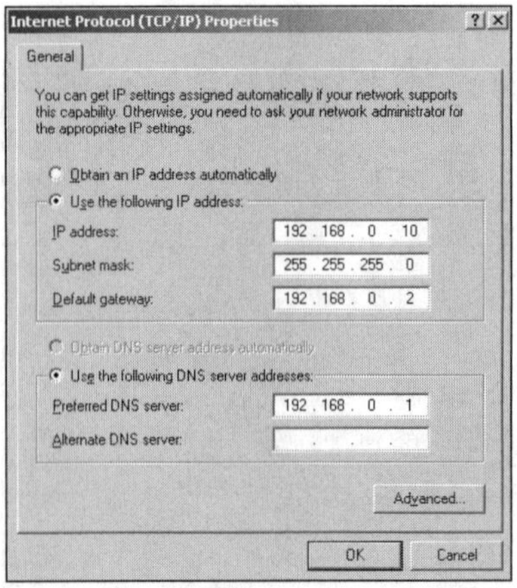

Manually Configuring TCP/IP

You can manually configure your TCP/IP settings by entering the required values into the TCP/IP properties sheet (see Figure 6.13). For complete details, see Exercise 6.1 at the end of the chapter.

Name Resolution with TCP/IP

DNS and WINS are not the only name resolution methods available for Windows 2000 TCP/IP hosts. Microsoft also provides two different lookup files: LMHOSTS and HOSTS. You can find samples of these files in the *winnt_root*\SYSTEM32\DRIVERS\ETC folder. Read the contents of each sample file for instructions on how to use them.

FIGURE 6.13
Manual configuration of a TCP/IP host.

> **NOTE**
>
> **LMHOSTS File** Although the sample LMHOSTS file in the *winnt_root*\SYSTEM32\DRIVERS\ETC folder is named LMHOSTS.SAM, it must be renamed LMHOSTS with no file extension. Otherwise, it will not be used for name resolution.

Advanced TCP/IP Configuration

As the complexity of networks grows, the requirement for more sophisticated access and control of information flowing over the networks grows as well. Two recent additions to the TCP/IP configuration options in Windows 2000 are Virtual Private Networks (VPN) and IP Security (IPSec). These automatic methods encrypt the information flowing between two computer systems even if it is using the public Internet network.

Virtual Private Networks (VPN)

A *Virtual Private Network (VPN)* allows the computers in one network to connect to the computers in another network by the use of a tunnel through the Internet or other public network. The VPN provides the same security and features formerly available only in private networks.

A VPN connection allows you to connect to a server on your corporate network from home or when traveling using the routing facilities of the Internet. The connection appears to be a private point-to-point network connection between your computer and the corporate server.

Additionally, VPNs can be used to connect remote office LANs to the corporate LAN or to other remote LANs to share resources and information using direct connect of dial-up access.

The basic functions managed by VPNs are the following:

- ◆ **User authentication.** Verifies the user's identity and restricts VPN access to authorized users only.

- ◆ **Address management.** Assigns the client's address on the private net and ensures that private addresses are kept private.

- ◆ **Data encryption.** Data carried on the public network must be unreadable to unauthorized clients on the network.

- ◆ **Key management.** Encryption keys must be refreshed for both the client and the server.

- ◆ **Multiprotocol support.** The most common protocols used in the public network are supported.

A VPN is not a protocol in itself, but rather the encapsulation of existing protocols and the encryption of the data being transmitted.

Windows 2000 Professional provides two encapsulation methods for creating VPN connections.

Point-to-Point Tunneling Protocol (PPTP)

This protocol enables the secure transfer of data from your computer to a remote computer on TCP/IP networks. PPTP tunnels, or encapsulates, IP, IPX, or NetBEUI protocols inside PPP datagrams. PPTP can work over dedicated Internet connections or over dial-up connections; however, it does require IP connectivity between your computer and the server to which it is authenticating before the tunnel can be established.

In Point-to-Point Tunneling, a PPP frame (containing an IP datagram or an IPX datagram) is wrapped with a Generic Routing Encapsulation (GRE) header and an IP header. In the IP header are the source and destination IP address that correspond to the VPN client and VPN server.

Figure 6.14 shows the PPTP encapsulation of a PPP payload.

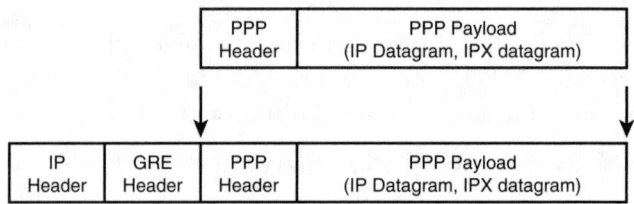

FIGURE 6.14
PPTP encapsulation of an encrypted datagram.

PPTP Encryption

The PPP frame is encrypted with Microsoft Point-to-Point Encryption (MPPE) by using encryption keys generated from the MS-CHAP or EAP-TLS authentication process. Virtual private networking clients must use either the MS-CHAP or EAP-TLS authentication protocol in order to encrypt PPP payloads. PPTP does not provide encryption services. PPTP encapsulates a previously encrypted PPP frame.

Layer 2 Tunneling Protocol (L2TP)

L2TP is an Internet tunneling protocol with roughly the same functionality as PPTP. The Windows 2000 implementation of L2TP is designed to run natively over IP networks.

Encapsulation for L2TP consists of two separate layers:

◆ A PPP frame (containing an IP datagram or an IPX datagram) is wrapped with an L2TP header and a UDP header.

◆ The resulting L2TP message is then wrapped with an IPSec Encapsulating Security Payload (ESP) header and trailer, an IPSec Authentication trailer that provides message integrity and authentication, and a final IP header. In the IP header are the source and destination IP addresses that correspond to the VPN client and VPN server.

Figure 6.15 shows the L2TP encapsulation of a PPP payload.

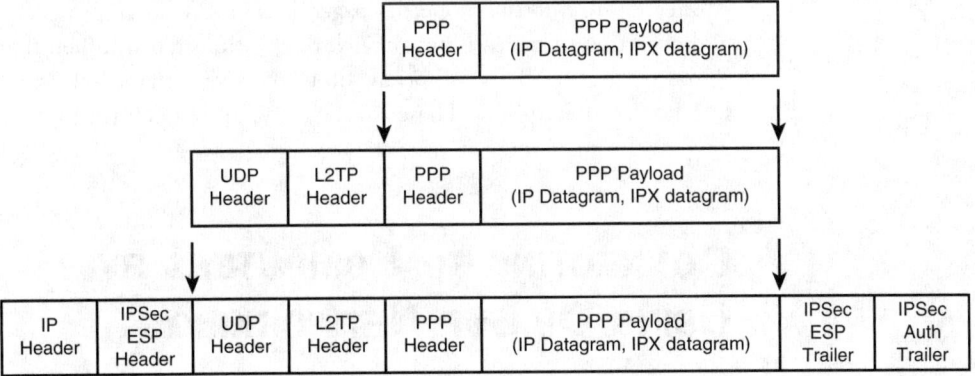

FIGURE 6.15
L2TP encapsulation of an encrypted PPP payload.

Encryption

The L2TP message is encrypted with IPSec encryption mechanisms by using encryption keys generated from the IPSec authentication process. The portion of the packet from the UDP header to the IPSec ESP Trailer inclusive is encrypted by IPSec.

N O T E **Non-Encrypted L2TP packets** It is possible to have a non-IPSec-based (non-encrypted) L2TP connection, where the PPP payload is sent in plain text. However, a non-encrypted L2TP connection is not recommended for virtual private network connections over the Internet because communications of this type are not secure.

Installing VPN Connections

A VPN connection is configured running the Network Connection Wizard (Make New Connection) in the Network and Dial-Up Connection applet in the Control Panel. A VPN is created by selecting the option Connects to a Private Network Through the Internet. The connection can be configured to dial to an Internet Service Provider (ISP) or to connect directly to a VPN server if your computer is directly connected to the Internet.

The type of connection (PPTP or L2TP) is defined by the server you are connecting to. In any case, the connection and security are negotiated automatically.

Configuring IPSec

IPSec is applied according to a global policy. Select Network and Dial-Up Connections from the Control Panel and right-click a connection to find the properties page. Select the TCP/IP protocol and click the Advanced button. Click the Options tab and then the Properties button. This will bring you to the screen that allows you to select an IPSec policy. These are system-wide and defined by the system administrator.

CONNECTING TO COMPUTERS BY USING DIAL-UP NETWORKING

Connect to computers by using dial-up networking.

Dial-Up Networking enables you to extend your network to unlimited locations. A dial-up connection connects your computer to a private network or the Internet (through an Internet Service Provider), to a private network through the public Internet using a secure Virtual Private Network (VPN) connection, or to a RAS server using the Microsoft RAS Protocol. The Microsoft RAS protocol is a proprietary protocol that supports the NetBIOS standard.

The dial-up connection can be made by a modem over the public switched network (also known as the Plain Old Telephone System, or POTS), or through a cable modem, xDSL service, X.25

interface, or high-speed ISDN line. The incoming connections can also be made by Point-to-Point (PPP) or Serial Line Internet Protocol (SLIP) to support dial-up connections to SLIP servers.

After a client connects to a Remote Access Server (RAS), it is registered into the local network and can take advantage of the same network services and data that it could if it were actually connected to the local network. The only difference that clients would notice is that WAN connections are much slower than direct physical connections to their LAN.

Line Protocols

The network transport protocols (TCP/IP, NWLink, and NetBEUI) were designed for the characteristics of LANs and are not suitable for use in phone-based connections. To make the network transport protocols function properly over phone-based connections, it is necessary to encapsulate them in a line protocol. Windows 2000 Professional supports two different line protocols: SLIP and PPP.

Serial Line Internet Protocol (SLIP)

SLIP is an industry-standard line protocol that supports TCP/IP connections made over serial lines. SLIP is a very simple protocol designed when networks were simpler. Because of this, SLIP implementations have several limitations:

◆ SLIP supports TCP/IP only. SLIP does not include support for IPX or NetBEUI, and because there is no mechanism in the SLIP definition to identify other protocols, TCP/IP is assumed.

◆ SLIP requires that both computers understand the other's IP address for routing purposes. SLIP provides no mechanism for hosts to communicate addressing information over a SLIP connection, and there is no support for DHCP.

◆ SLIP has no error detection, so noisy phone lines will corrupt packets in transit. When SLIP was created, phone line speeds were quite low (remember 2400 baud?) and network applications usually detect a checksum error in the encapsulated TCP/IP packet. Some applications, like NFS, however, usually ignore checksums.

NOTE
Limits on SLIP Support Windows 2000 Professional supports only SLIP client functionality. A Windows 2000 computer can't act as a SLIP server.

◆ SLIP does not support any encryption and therefore passwords are sent as clear text.

◆ To log on to a SLIP server, it is usually necessary to include some scripting or manual intervention to complete the connection.

Point-to-Point Protocol (PPP)

The limitations of SLIP prompted the development of a newer industry-standard protocol: Point-to-Point Protocol (PPP). Some of the advantages of PPP include the following:

◆ Supports TCP/IP, IPX, NetBEUI, and other protocols

◆ Supports both static IP addresses and DHCP

◆ Supports encryption for authentication

◆ Scripting and other manual interventions not required to complete the logon process

NOTE
Multilink Connections PPP includes support for multilink dialing. This feature allows you to combine multiple physical links into one logical connection. A client with multiple ISDN, X.25, and modem lines can establish a multilink connection that transmits data at a rate equal to the sum of the physical connections. For example, if a computer has two phone lines at 28.8Kb, a PPP multilink connection over these two physical connections would result in logical connections of 56Kb.

Multiple links can also be allocated only as they are required, thereby eliminating excess bandwidth.

Point-to-Point Tunneling Protocol (PPTP)

Point-to-Point Tunneling Protocol (PPTP) is an extension to PPP. PPTP can be used to create secure connections (VPNs) on LAN connections and it can be used with Dial-Up Networking. In this configuration, a dial-up connection is established with a RAS server (through an Internet Access Provider or a RAS server in a private network). PPTP will use this connection to establish a secure tunnel from your computer to the remote network you are connecting to.

Installing a Dial-Up Networking Connection

The wizard for installing a Dial-Up Networking connection is started when you double-click on the Make New Connection icon in the Network and Dial-Up Connections Control Panel applet. The wizard automatically creates outgoing connections to other networks or incoming connections from remote computers.

The wizard allows the creation of five types of connections (see Figure 6.16); these are discussed in the following sections.

Dial-Up to Private Network

This option is used to connect to a RAS server on a private network (such as a RAS server connected to a corporate network). If the remote network supports X.25 access, then it can be reached by establishing a connection to an X.25 PAD (Packet Assembler/Disassembler) provided by a network provider.

Handshaking between the client and the remote RAS server sets the parameters of the connection.

Dial-Up to the Internet

This option is used to connect to an Internet Service Provider (ISP). Configuration options include the following:

◆ Phone number of the ISP to connect to

◆ PPP/SLIP/C-SLIP connectivity

◆ Logon scripts if required by the ISP

◆ IP addressing configured or supplied by the ISP

◆ DNS addresses

◆ User ID and password

The Internet Connection Wizard will also allow you to enter email configuration information to allow Outlook Express to connect to an Internet mail service. Outlook Express is configured when Windows 2000 Professional is installed and can be used to connect to POP3, IMAP4, or HTTP mail servers. To successfully connect to your Internet mail service, you must have already obtained an email account from your local Internet Service Provider and obtained the configuration information, including your email account name, the mail sending and receiving server names, connection type (POP3, IMAP4, or HTTP), and the email address that friends will use to correctly send email to your account.

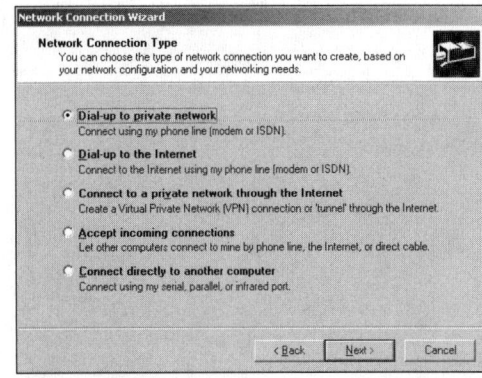

FIGURE 6.16
Dial-up connection types available.

Security is a major consideration when connecting to a public network. As shown in Figure 6.17, you can choose from several different security settings, including the following:

◆ **Password Authentication Protocol (PAP).** This uses clear text passwords and is the least sophisticated authentication protocol.

◆ **Challenge Handshake Authentication Protocol (CHAP).** This uses a secure encryption authentication technique based on Message Digest 5 (MD5) encryption. CHAP uses challenge-response with one-way MD5 hashing on the response. In this way, you can prove to the server that you know your password without actually sending the password over the network. By supporting CHAP and MD5, Network and Dial-Up Connections is able to securely connect to almost all third-party PPP servers. When you connect to a remote server, however, it may negotiate clear text authentication if it does not support MD5 hashing.

◆ **Microsoft Challenge Handshake Authentication Protocol (MS-CHAP).** This is a variation on CHAP authentication that does not require the use of clear text or reversibly encrypted passwords.

◆ **Shiva Password Authentication Protocol (SPAP).** This allows Shiva clients to dial in to computers running Windows 2000 server.

◆ **Extensible Authentication Protocol (EAP).** This is an extension to PPP that provides a standard method for supporting additional authentication methods such as smart cards and certificates. EAP provides greater security against attacks, such as password guessing or dictionary attacks, than other methods, such as CHAP.

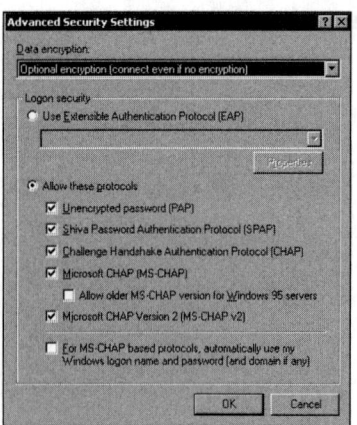

FIGURE 6.17
Encrypted authentication options.

Connect to a Private Network Through the Internet

This option provides for a secure Virtual Private Network (VPN) connection over the public Internet. This type of network connection allows you to select a dial-up connection to establish first; or, if you already have a persistent connection to the Internet through

a LAN connection (for example, a cable modem), the VPN can
be established using the local connection. The remote VPN
server computer's name or IP address is added to complete the
configuration.

Accept Incoming Connections

This option allows you to configure your Windows 2000 computer
to accept connections from phone lines, from the Internet, or via
direct cable. Configuration options include the following:

◆ The device (modem or serial port) to answer

◆ Whether to allow VPN connections

◆ Users allowed to connect to your computer

◆ Network components available to incoming users

Connect Directly to Another Computer

This option allows you to configure your Windows 2000 computer
with a direct connection to another computer. The configuration
options include the following:

◆ Whether to be the host of the connection or a guest on
another computer

◆ The port to use (Infrared, direct connection, or a COM port)

◆ Users allowed to connect to your computer

Internet Connection Sharing

With the Internet connection-sharing feature of Network and Dial-
Up Connections, you can use Windows 2000 to connect your home
network or small office network to the Internet. If you have a home
network and you connect to the Internet using a dial-up connection,
by enabling connection sharing you provide network address translation, addressing, and name resolution for all the other computers on
your home network.

The Internet connection-sharing feature is intended for use in a small office or home office in which network configuration and the Internet connection are managed by the computer running Windows 2000 where the shared connection resides. It is assumed that on its network, this computer is the only Internet connection, is the only gateway to the Internet, and sets up all internal network addresses.

A computer with Internet connection sharing needs two connections: one to the internal LAN and one to the Internet. Internet connection sharing is enabled on the Internet connection. This shared connection will allow your internal network to receive its addresses using DHCP, provide a DNS service to resolve names, and provide a gateway service to access computer systems outside your home network. The network address translation (NAT) service allows your home network to use any addressing scheme you want because the internal addresses are not broadcast onto the Internet.

The NAT is transparent to both the client and server. The client appears to be talking directly with the external server and the external server believes the NAT is the end client. To the client, the NAT may be its default gateway (as is the case with Internet connection sharing) or, in a larger network, the router that connects to the Internet.

When the NAT is doing address and port translation, all internal addresses will be mapped to the single IP address of the NAT's external network card or dial-up interface. Ports will be mapped so that they remain unique. For example, if two Windows 2000 Professional computers on the internal network are running an application that uses TCP port 1025 as a source, after translation, the clients will have the same IP address but will need unique ports to identify their applications.

When the NAT receives a packet, it checks the packet's internal tables to see if there is already a mapping. If there is a mapping, it will be used; if not, a new one is created.

- ◆ In an outgoing packet, the NAT modifies the source IP address and port number.

- ◆ In an incoming packet, the NAT modifies the destination IP address and port number.

The computer on which Internet connection sharing is enabled becomes a DHCP allocator for the home network. DHCP dynamically distributes TCP/IP addresses to users as they start up.

You cannot modify the default configuration created by enabling Internet connection sharing. This includes items such as disabling the DHCP allocator or modifying the range of private IP addresses that are handed out, disabling the DNS proxy, configuring a range of public IP addresses, or configuring inbound mappings. If you want to modify any of these items, you must use network address translation.

Internet connection sharing supports usage of virtual private networking (VPN) tunnels from corporate servers on the Internet back to your home network. The VPN connection is authenticated and secure, and creating the tunneled connection allocates proper IP addresses, DNS server addresses, and WINS server addresses for the corporate network.

Internet Connection Sharing Settings

When you enable Internet connection sharing, certain protocols, services, interfaces, and routes are configured automatically. Table 6.4 describes the settings used when Internet connection sharing is enabled.

TABLE 6.4

INTERNET CONNECTION SHARING SETTINGS

Configured Item	Action
IP address 192.168.0.1	Configured with a subnet mask of 255.255.255.0 on the LAN adapter that is connected to the small office or home office network
Autodial feature	Enabled
Static default IP route	Created when the dial-up connection is established
Internet connection sharing service	Started
DHCP allocator	Enabled with the default range of 192.168.0.2 to 192.168.0.254 and a subnet mask of 255.255.255.0
DNS proxy	Enabled

NOTE **Persistence of Information** By default, an idle TCP session will remain in the NAT table for 24 hours and a UDP mapping will remain for one minute.

WARNING **Internal Versus External Connection Sharing** Enabling the Internet connection sharing on the internal network connection rather than the external one can cause DHCP to grant TCP/IP addresses to users outside your home network, causing network problems on their computers.

NOTE **Role** You must be a member of the Administrators group to configure Internet connection sharing.

If you are using Internet connection sharing, it should be on a network with no other Windows 2000 domain controllers, DNS servers, gateways, DHCP servers, or computers using static IP addressing. The server that is sharing the Internet connection assumes the role of gateway and DHCP allocator. The DHCP allocator provides IP addresses and gateway configurations to all computers on the local network that require an Internet connection. Problems will arise if there are other servers providing the same service.

Internet Connection Sharing for Applications

If you have applications that interact with services on the Internet (usually games), then you will need to configure the application in the Internet connection sharing service (see Step by Step 6.1). In addition, if you wish to provide services to users on the Internet (for example, you are hosting a Web site), then you must configure the Web server service.

STEP BY STEP

6.1 Configure Internet Connection Sharing for Applications and Services

1. Select Network and Dial-Up Connections.

2. Right-click the shared connection and select Properties.

3. Select the Sharing tab and verify that Enable Internet Connection Sharing for This Connection is selected. Then click Settings.

4. To configure a network application, select the Applications tab and click Add.

5. Enter the name of the application and the remote server port number, and select UDP or TCP or both. Enter the Incoming Response Port numbers.

6. To configure a service to provide to remote users select the Services tab and click Add.

7. Enter the name of the service, the service port number, and the name or IP address of the server on your home network that is providing the service.

CONNECTING TO SHARED RESOURCES ON A MICROSOFT NETWORK

Connect to shared resources on a Microsoft network.

Windows 2000 provides different methods to work with network resources and to determine what network resources are available.

Browsing

Users on a Windows 2000 network often need to know what domains and computers are accessible from their local computer. Viewing all the network resources available is called *browsing*. The Windows 2000 Browser service maintains a list (called the *browse list*) of all available domains and servers. This list can be viewed using Windows NT Explorer and is provided by a browser in the local computer's domain.

Windows NT assigns browser tasks to specific computers on the network. They work together to provide a centralized list of shared resources, eliminating the need for all machines to maintain their own lists.

The Windows NT browser system consists of a Master Browser, Backup Browsers, and Browser Clients. The computer that is the Master Browser maintains the browse list and periodically sends copies to the Backup Browsers. When a Browser Client needs information, it obtains the current browse list by remotely sending a request to either the Master Browser or a Backup Browser.

Browsing Other Domains

Users need to be able to retrieve lists of servers within their domain and also a list of other workgroups and domains. Upon becoming a Master Browser, each Master Browser in each domain will broadcast an announcement every minute for the first five minutes and once every 15 minutes thereafter. If a domain has not announced itself for a period equaling 45 minutes, it is removed from the master browse list.

It is the responsibility of the Master Browser in each domain to build a list of available domains and to replicate them to the Backup Browsers every 15 minutes.

Browsing a Wide Area Network (WAN)

When using domains that are split across routers, each network segment functions as an independent browsing entity with its own Master Browser and Backup Browsers. Therefore, browser elections occur within each network segment.

Domain Master Browsers are responsible for spanning the network segments to collect computer name information for maintaining a domain-wide browse list of available computers in the domain.

Universal Naming Convention

The *Universal Naming Convention (UNC)* was introduced earlier in this chapter as a network provider service. This is a standardized way of specifying a share name on a specific computer. The share name can refer to folders or printers. The UNC path takes the form of *computer_name\share_name*.

You can also use UNC paths to refer to network printers. For example, \\ACCTSERVER\ACCTPRINT refers to the printer named ACCTPRINT on the server named ACCTSERVER.

My Network Places

The icon for My Network Places appears on your desktop. When you double-click on this icon a number of pieces of information are displayed. If there is more than one network provider available on your computer (perhaps NetWare networks as well as Microsoft Networks), those providers will be shown as available networks to explore.

By double-clicking on the Entire Network icon, you can display either the entire network or alternatively decide to view only printers, computers, people, or files and folders.

Clicking on one of these entries will allow you to search for a particular object in the Active Directory based on its characteristics.

You can see computers in your local workgroup by selecting Computer Near Me or all the computers in your organization's network by selecting the globe icon. If you have recently worked with network shares, they will also be shown as objects you can browse.

NOTE

UNC Connections Connections made via UNC paths take place immediately and do not require the use of a drive letter.

WARNING

UNC Paths and 16-Bit Applications Many 16-bit applications do not work with UNC paths. If you need to work with a 16-bit application, you may have to map a drive letter to the shared folder or connect a port to the network printer.

If your Windows 2000 Professional computer is attached to a network that has a domain controller that is a Windows 2000 Server, viewing the entire contents of the network will then display an Active Directory icon as well. Double-click this icon to explore the Active Directory namespace created by the system administrators for your site.

Net View Command

You can also access the list of computers in your workgroup by using the NET VIEW command. A sample list looks like this:

```
C:\Net View
Server Name              Remark------------------------------
-----
\\TEST1
\\TEST2
\\NTW1
The command completed successfully.
```

Net Use Command

You can assign network resources to drive letters from the command prompt as well as from the Tools menu from Windows Explorer. To connect drive letter X: to a share called GoodStuff on a server named SERVER1, for example, you would type the following command at the command prompt:

```
C:\Net Use X: \\SERVER1\GoodStuff
```

You can also use the Net Use command to connect clients to network printers. If you want to connect port LPT1: to a network printer named HP5 on a server named SERVER1, use the following command:

```
Net Use LPT1: \\SERVER1\HP5
```

To disconnect the network resources for these two, use the following two commands:

```
Net Use X: /d
```

```
Net Use LPT1: /d
```

TROUBLESHOOTING TCP/IP CONNECTIONS

There are a large number of network troubleshooting tools available for TCP/IP and the Windows 2000 platform. Some of these are included in the Windows 2000 release and some are part of the resource kits and SMS (NetMon). However, the best approach for troubleshooting network connections is to work from the bottom up, eliminating configuration issues first before checking basic connectivity and then advancing to higher functions and services.

Configuration Errors

The first thing to check when troubleshooting TCP/IP networking connections is the local TCP/IP configuration.

The IPCONFIG /all command is used to get a detailed listing of the host computer configuration information, including the IP address, subnet mask, and default gateway.

Typical problems found in the configuration are duplicate IP addresses with other computers on the network, or a subnet mask of 0.0.0.0.

The following example is the result of an IPCONFIG /all command on a computer system that is configured to have DHCP supply the TCP/IP configuration values, including IP address and WINS, and the DNS name resolution server addresses:

```
        Host Name . . . . . . . . . : NTW1.Barknet.Private
        Node Type . . . . . . . . . : Hybrid
        IP Routing Enabled. . . . . : No
        WINS Proxy Enabled. . . . . : No

Ethernet adapter Local Area Connection:
        Adapter Domain Name . . . . : Barknet.Private
        DNS Servers . . . . . . . . : 192.168.0.1
        Description . . . . . . . . : Xircom CreditCard
Ethernet Adapter 10/100
        Physical Address. . . . . . : 00-80-C7-BA-DF-9E
        DHCP Enabled. . . . . . . . : Yes
        IP Address. . . . . . . . . : 192.168.0.10
        Subnet Mask . . . . . . . . : 255.255.255.0
        Default Gateway . . . . . . : 192.168.0.1
        DHCP Server . . . . . . . . : 192.168.0.1
        Primary WINS Server . . . . : 192.168.0.2
```

```
        Secondary WINS Server . . . : 192.168.0.3
        Lease Obtained. . . . . . . : Sunday, October 17,
➡1999 11:43:01 PM
        Lease Expires . . . . . . . : Wednesday, May 20,
➡1999 11:43:01 PM
```

If your local address is returned as 169.254.y.z, you have been assigned an IP address by the Automatic Private IP Addressing (APIA) feature of Windows 2000. This means that the local DHCP server is not configured properly or cannot be reached from your computer, and an IP address has been assigned automatically with a subnet mask of 255.255.0.0.

If your local address is returned as 0.0.0.0, the Microsoft MediaSense software detects that the network adapter is not connected to a network. If the connection is solid and the problem persists, you may have to update the network adapter drivers to the latest revision.

Checking Basic Connectivity

If the computer system appears to be configured correctly, the next step is to try to connect to other hosts on the TCP/IP network.

Using PING

PING is a tool that will help to verify connectivity at the IP level. The PING command will send out an ICMP Echo request to the target host name or IP address. This does not always work because some servers will not respond to echo requests as a security measure. However, you will find that most workstations automatically enable it.

The best process to follow when using PING to detect network problems is to use IP addresses only (so as not to confuse name resolution errors with network errors) and to ping progressively more remote computers.

The first interface to check is the loopback address. The following command will verify that TCP/IP is installed correctly:

```
Ping 127.0.0.1
```

If this fails, the TCP/IP drivers are corrupted, the network adapter is not working, or some other service is interfering with TCP/IP.

Next, ping the IP address of the local computer using the following command:

```
Ping <ip address of local host>
```

If the routing table is correct, this will simply be forwarded to the loopback address.

Next, ping the default gateway:

```
Ping <ip address of gateway>
```

This command will determine that the default gateway is functioning and that you can communicate with a local host on the local network.

Next, ping a remote host to verify that you can access a remote network through a router:

```
ping <IP address of remote host>
```

PING uses host name resolution (via DNS or WINS or the static name configuration files). If you can access a remote system using its IP address but not its host name, then the problem is in name resolution, not network connectivity.

Using Tracert

The Tracert diagnostic utility determines the route taken to a destination by sending Internet Control Message Protocol (ICMP) echo packets with varying IP Time-to-Live (TTL) values to the destination. Each router along the path is required to decrement the TTL on a packet by at least 1 before forwarding it. When the TTL on a packet reaches 0, the router should send an "ICMP Time Exceeded" message back to the source computer.

Tracert determines the route by sending the first echo packet with a TTL of 1 and incrementing the TTL by 1 on each subsequent transmission until the target responds or the maximum TTL is reached. The route is determined by examining the "ICMP Time Exceeded" messages sent back by intermediate routers. Some routers silently drop packets with expired TTLs and are invisible to the Tracert utility.

Tracert cannot record the path the packet takes in returning. However, it will show if the destination was reachable. If this is not the case, the remote computer might be off the network, behind a firewall, or behind a router that filters ICMP packets.

Using ARP

Windows 2000 TCP/IP will communicate with remote computers over a network using an IP address, a NetBIOS name, or a host name. Regardless of what naming convention is used, eventually the address must be resolved to a MAC address (for shared access media such as Ethernet and Token Ring).

Troubleshooting the ARP cache is one of the more difficult tasks because the problems are often intermittent.

For example, if two computers are using the same IP address on a network, you may see an intermittent problem in accessing the correct one because the most recent ARP table entry is always the one from the host that responded more quickly to any ARP request.

IP addresses assigned by DHCP do not cause duplicate IP conflicts (unless, of course, DHCP is configured with overlapping ranges), so most conflicts are due to static IP addresses. Examining a list of static IP addresses and their corresponding MAC address will help you track down the problem.

If you do not have a record of all IP and MAC address pairs on your network, you can still get some information from the manufacturer bytes of the MAC addresses for inconsistencies. These 3-byte numbers are called Organizationally Unique Identifiers (OUIs) and are assigned by the Institute of Electrical and Electronics Engineers (IEEE). The first 3 bytes of each MAC address identify the card's manufacturer. Knowing what equipment you installed and comparing that with the values returned by ARP might allow you to determine which static address was entered in error.

The following is an example of the ARP –a command that is used to display current cache of IP addresses and the MAC addresses associated with them:

```
Arp -a
Interface: 157.57.18.16 on Interface 0x1000003
  Internet Address      Physical Address     Type
  157.57.18.1           00-d0-ba-09-9c-d6    dynamic
  157.57.18.26          00-a0-c9-96-03-7f    dynamic
```

This output indicates that the current IP address is 157.57.18.16 and that two addresses have been recently used: 157.57.18.1 and 157.57.18.26. Check the output of the ipconfig command to see if either or both of the addresses are part of the IP configuration (such as the default gateway) or use tracert <ip address> to resolve the name.

If the problem still persists and no obvious error is apparent, then check the Event Viewer for additional clues. For example, DHCP might have detected a duplicate card on the network and denied the computer's request to join.

Verify Server Services

Sometimes a system configured as a remote gateway or router is not functioning as a router. To confirm that the remote computer you want to contact is set up to forward packets, you can either examine it with a remote administration tool (assuming that it is a computer you administer) or you can attempt to contact the person who maintains the computer.

Check IPSec Configuration

IPSec can increase the defenses of a network, but it can also make changing network configurations or troubleshooting problems more difficult. In some cases, IPSec running on the initiating host of a computer under investigation can create difficulties in connecting to a remote host. To determine whether this is a source of problems, turn off IPSec and attempt to run the requested network service or function.

If the problem disappears when IPSec policies are turned off, you know that the additional IPSec processing burden or its packet filtering is responsible for the problem.

Resolving Host Names in TCP/IP

The process for two computers to communicate using TCP/IP involves four distinct steps:

1. Resolve the host name or NetBIOS name to an IP address.

2. Use the IP address and the routing table to determine the interface to use and the forwarding IP address.

3. Use ARP to resolve the forwarding IP address to a MAC address.

4. Use the MAC address to send the IP datagram.

If the computer to be reached is a host name or a NetBIOS name, then the name must be resolved to an IP address before any data can be sent. Host names and NetBIOS names are resolved in different ways.

Resolve a NetBIOS Name to an IP Address

Resolving a NetBIOS name means successfully mapping a 16-byte NetBIOS name to an IP address. The File and Printer Sharing for the Microsoft Networks service in Windows 2000 Professional uses NetBIOS name resolution. When your computer starts up, this service registers a unique NetBIOS name based on the name of your computer (padded out to 15 characters if it is shorter than that) with 0x20 as the 16th character.

When you attempt to make a file-sharing connection to a computer running Windows 2000 by name, the File and Printer Sharing for Microsoft Networks service on the file server you specify corresponds to a specific NetBIOS name. For example, when you attempt to connect to a computer called COMMONSERVER, the NetBIOS name corresponding to the File and Printer Sharing for Microsoft Networks service on that computer is as follows:

COMMONSERVER   [20]

Note that the name of the server is padded out to 15 characters.

To actually use the file server, its IP address must be established.

The exact mechanism by which NetBIOS names are resolved to IP addresses depends on the NetBIOS node type that is configured for the node. Table 6.5 covers the various node types and the associated resolution mechanism.

TABLE 6.5

NODE TYPES AND RESOLUTION MECHANISMS

Node Type	Description
B-node (broadcast)	B-node uses broadcast NetBIOS name queries for name registration and resolution. B-node has two major problems: (1) Broadcasts disturb every node on the network, and (2) routers typically do not forward broadcasts, so only NetBIOS names on the local network can be resolved.

continues

TABLE 6.5 | *continued*

NODE TYPES AND RESOLUTION MECHANISMS

Node Type	Description
P-node (peer-peer)	P-node uses a NetBIOS name server (NBNS), such as a WINS server, to resolve NetBIOS names. P-node does not use broadcasts; instead, it queries the name server directly.
M-node (mixed)	M-node is a combination of B-node and P-node. By default, an M-node functions as a B-node. If an M-node is unable to resolve a name by broadcast, it queries an NBNS using P-node.
H-node (hybrid)	H-node is a combination of P-node and B-node. By default, an H-node functions as a P-node. If an H-node is unable to resolve a name through the NBNS, it uses a broadcast to resolve the name.

NOTE

NetBIOS Nodes   Computers running Windows 2000 are B-node by default and become H-node when they are configured with a WINS server.

Windows 2000 can also use a local database file called LMHOSTS to resolve remote NetBIOS names. The LMHOSTS file is stored in the *systemroot*\System32\Drivers\Etc folder.

NetBIOS names are resolved to an IP address by the NetBIOS session service through the following sequence:

◆ Consults the NetBIOS cache

◆ Broadcasts a request for the computer to identify itself

◆ Consults the LMHOSTS file directly for an address assigned to the computer name

◆ Queries a WINS server if it is configured

The NetBIOS cache is always checked first. The next step taken in resolving a name depends on the node type.

A B-node will broadcast locally only. A P-node will query the WINS server to resolve the name only. An M-node will broadcast locally first and then query the WINS server to resolve the name. The default node (H-node) will query the WINS server and then broadcast locally to resolve the name.

If these methods fail the following methods are attempted:

◆ Query the HOSTS file.

◆ Query the DNS server if it is configured.

The Nbtstat utility and the NET USE command can be used to diagnose NetBIOS name resolution problems.

Resolve a Host or Domain Name to an IP Address

Host names are resolved by using the HOSTS file or by querying a DNS server. Problems in the HOSTS file usually involve spelling errors and duplicate entries.

The Nslookup utility or the Netdiag resource kit utility can be used to diagnose host name resolution problems.

Nslookup.exe is a command-line administrative tool for testing and troubleshooting DNS servers and it can be run in both interactive and noninteractive modes. Noninteractive mode is useful when only a single piece of data needs to be returned. The syntax for noninteractive mode is as follows:

```
nslookup [-option] [hostname] [server]
```

To start Nslookup.exe in interactive mode, simply type **nslookup** at the command prompt:

```
C:\> nslookup
Default Server:  nameserver1.domain.com
Address:  10.0.0.1
>
```

Typing **help** or **?** at the command prompt will generate a list of available commands. Anything typed at the command prompt that is not recognized as a valid command is assumed to be a host name and an attempt is made to resolve it using the default server. To interrupt interactive commands, press Ctrl+C. To exit interactive mode and return to the command prompt, type **exit** at the command prompt.

What follows is the help output. It contains the complete list of options. The general syntax is given first:

Commands (identifiers are shown in uppercase; [] means optional):

```
NAME                - print info about the host/domain NAME
                    - using default server
NAME1 NAME2         - as above, but use NAME2 as server
help or ?           - print info on common commands
set OPTION          - set an option
    all                 - print options, current server and
                        - host
    [no]debug           - print debugging information
    [no]d2              - print exhaustive debugging
```

continues

NOTE

NetBIOS Name Resolution Problem
If the problem accessing the remote computer is related to the NetBIOS name resolution, the computer can still be reached by using the IP address.

continued

```
information
    [no]defname         - append domain name to each query
    [no]recurse         - ask for recursive answer to query
    [no]search          - use domain search list
    [no]vc              - always use a virtual circuit
    domain=NAME         - set default domain name to NAME
    srchlist=N1[/N2/.../N6] - set domain to N1 and search
                            - list to N1,N2, etc.
    root=NAME           - set root server to NAME
    retry=X             - set number of retries to X
    timeout=X           - set initial time-out interval to
                        - X seconds
    type=X              - set query type (ex.
                        - A,ANY,CNAME,MX,NS,PTR,SOA,SRV)
    querytype=X         - same as type
    class=X             - set query class (ex. IN
                        - (Internet), ANY)
    [no]msxfr           - use MS fast zone transfer
    ixfrver=X           - current version to use in IXFR
                        - transfer request
server NAME         - set default server to NAME, using current
                    - default server
lserver NAME        - set default server to NAME, using initial
                    - server
finger [USER]       - finger the optional NAME at the current
                    - default host
root                - set current default server to the root
ls [opt] DOMAIN [> FILE] - list addresses in DOMAIN
(optional: output to FILE)
    -a              - list canonical names and aliases
    -d              - list all records
    -t TYPE         - list records of the given type (e.g.
                    - A,CNAME,MX,NS,PTR etc.)
view FILE           - sort an 'ls' output file and view it
                    - with pg
exit                - exit the program
```

Determine Whether the Address Is Local

The subnet mask along with the IP address are used to determine whether the IP address is local or on a remote subnet.

A misconfigured subnet mask can result in the system's inability to access any other system on the local subnet while still being able to communicate with remote systems.

If the IP address is local, ARP is used to identify the destination MAC address.

Problems at this point are usually related to an invalid ARP cache (such as a duplicate address) or an invalid subnet mask. The utilities ARP and IPCONFIG can be used to solve local address resolution problems.

Determine the Correct Gateway

If the IP address is remote from the local subnet, the gateway to use to reach the remote address must be determined. If the network has a single router, this problem is straightforward. In a network with more than one router connected, additional steps must be taken.

To solve this problem, the system uses the routing table. The entries in the routing table enable IP to determine which gateway to send outgoing traffic through. The routing table has many entries for individual routes, each one consisting of a destination, network mask, gateway interface, and hop count (metric).

The Route utility can be used to diagnose problems with accessing the gateway.

The Route program is a utility that is called from the command line to manipulate network routing tables. Most of the routing information that your system uses is maintained automatically by Windows 2000 Professional. However, in the event that you need to add a static route from your system to a remote network, the key to remember is to route to the network you cannot see by using the nearest gateway that you can see. Because that gateway is also a router (by definition) it will be able to access networks to which you have no direct access.

The structure of the command line is as follows:

```
ROUTE [-F] [-P] [COMMAND [destination] [MASK subnetmask]
➥[gateway] [METRIC costmetric]]
```

The -F parameter clears the routing tables of all gateway entries. If this is used in conjunction with one of the commands, the tables are cleared prior to running the command.

The -P parameter when used with the add command, makes a route persistent across boots of the system. By default, routes are not preserved when the system is restarted. When used with the print command, -P displays the list of registered persistent routes. It is ignored for all other commands, which always affect the appropriate persistent routes.

The following is the definition of the command-line arguments for ROUTE:

◆ COMMAND. Specifies one of the following commands:

PRINT	Prints a route.
ADD	Adds a route.
DELETE	Deletes a route.
CHANGE	Modifies an existing route.

◆ destination. Specifies the computer to send the command to.

◆ MASK subnetmask. Specifies a subnet mask to be associated with this route entry. If not specified, 255.255.255.255 is used.

◆ gateway. Specifies the gateway.

◆ METRIC costmetric. Assigns an integer cost metric (ranging from 1 to 9999) to be used in calculating the fastest, most reliable, and/or least expensive routes.

The following is an example of the output derived from the print command in the route utility.

```
===========================================================
Interface List
0x1 ......................... MS TCP Loopback interface
0x1000003 ...00 80 c7 ba df 9e ...... Xircom Ethernet
10/100 PC Card
===========================================================
Active Routes:
Network Destination        Netmask          Gateway
Interface  Metric
         0.0.0.0          0.0.0.0        157.57.18.1
157.57.18.16     1
       127.0.0.0        255.0.0.0        127.0.0.1
127.0.0.1        1
     157.57.18.0  255.255.255.192      157.57.18.16
157.57.18.16     1
     157.57.18.16  255.255.255.255        127.0.0.1
127.0.0.1        1
   157.57.255.255  255.255.255.255      157.57.18.16
157.57.18.16     1
         224.0.0.0        224.0.0.0      157.57.18.16
157.57.18.16     1
   255.255.255.255  255.255.255.255      157.57.18.16
157.57.18.16     1
```

```
Default Gateway:        157.57.18.1
===============================================================
Persistent Routes:
  None
```

The IP routing table for this Windows 2000 computer contains the following routes:

◆ **Default route.** The route with the network destination of 0.0.0.0 and the netmask of 0.0.0.0 is the default route. Any destination IP address ANDed with 0.0.0.0 results in 0.0.0.0. Therefore, for any IP address, the default route produces a match. If the default route is chosen because no better routes are found, the IP datagram is forwarded to the IP address in the Gateway column using the interface corresponding to the IP address in the Interface column.

◆ **Loopback network.** The route with the network destination of 127.0.0.0 and the netmask of 255.0.0.0 is a route designed to take any IP address of the form 127.$x.y.z$ and forward it to the special loopback address of 127.0.0.1.

◆ **Directly attached network.** The route with the network destination of 157.57.18.0 and the netmask of 255.255.255.192 is a route for the directly attached network. IP packets destined for the directly attached network are not forwarded to a router but sent directly to the destination. Note that the gateway address and interface are the IP address of the node. This indicates that the packet is sent from the network adapter corresponding to the node's IP address.

◆ **Local host.** The route with the network destination of 157.57.18.16 and the netmask of 255.255.255.255 is a host route corresponding to the IP address of the host. All IP datagrams to the IP address of the host are forwarded to the loopback address.

◆ **All-subnets directed broadcast.** The route with the network destination of 157.57.255.255 and the netmask of 255.255.255.255 is a host route for the all-subnets directed broadcast address for the class B network ID 157.57.0.0. The all-subnets directed broadcast address is designed to reach all subnets of class-based network ID. Packets addressed to the all-subnets directed broadcast are sent out of the network adapter corresponding to the node's IP address. A host route for the all-subnets directed broadcast is only present for network IDs that are subnets of a class-based network ID.

◆ **Multicast address.** The route with the network destination of 224.0.0.0 and the netmask of 240.0.0.0 is a route for all class D multicast addresses. An IP datagram matching this route is sent from the network adapter corresponding to the node's IP address.

◆ **Limited broadcast.** The route with the network destination of 255.255.255.255 and the netmask of 255.255.255.255 is a host route for the limited broadcast address. Packets addressed to the limited broadcast are sent out of the network adapter corresponding to the node's IP address.

For example, when the Windows 2000 computer sends traffic to 157.57.18.60, the route determination process matches two routes: the default route and the directly attached network route. The directly attached network route is the closest matching route. Because the gateway address and the interface address for the directly attached network route are the same, the forwarding IP address is set to the destination address 157.57.18.60. The interface on which to forward the IP datagram is identified by the IP address in the Interface column. In this case, the interface is the Xircom Ethernet 10/100 PC Card, which is assigned the IP address 157.57.18.16.

When the Windows 2000 computer sends traffic to 204.71.200.68, the route determination process matches the default route (the default route will always match the destination IP address). Because the gateway address and the interface address for the directly attached network route are different, the forwarding IP address is set to the IP address in the Gateway column (157.57.18.1). The interface on which to forward the IP datagram is identified by the IP address in the Interface column. In this case, the interface is the Xircom Ethernet 10/100 PC Card, which is assigned the IP address 157.57.18.16.

Determine the Gateway Address

By definition, the gateway address is local to the computer system. The ARP process is used to determine its MAC address in the same manner that a local address is found. The IP datagram can then be sent to the gateway for further routing.

Identifying Name Resolution Problems

To determine why a remote host name cannot be resolved, you must first distinguish whether the remote computer is being addressed using NetBIOS or Sockets. If the application uses the NET commands or is an NT 4.0 version administrator tool, it is a NetBIOS problem. If the application uses WinSock like Telnet, FTP, and the Web browsers, the problem will lie with DNS or the HOSTS file.

Net View Errors

If the Net View utility returns an Error 53 message, the problem is most commonly a NetBIOS name resolution error or an error in establishing a NetBIOS session. The distinction between these two situations can be determined by entering the following command, where *<hostname>* is a remote computer you are sure is active:

```
net view \\<hostname>
```

If this works, name resolution is not the source of the problem. To confirm this, check the status of the temporary session that NetBIOS creates for the Net View command by entering the following command, where *<ip address>* is the same remote computer used in the previous procedure.

```
net view \\<ip address>
```

If this also fails, the problem is in establishing a session.

If the NET VIEW command fails with a "System Error 53 has occurred" message, the computer running Windows 2000 is not running the File and Printer Sharing for Microsoft Networks service.

Socket Connection Errors

If the problem is not NetBIOS, the name resolution problem is related to either a HOSTS file or a DNS configuration error.

If you can ping the remote IP address but not the host name, there is a problem in the HOSTS file or the DNS entries in the TCP/IP configuration on the computer.

Step by Step 6.2 shows how to check the host name resolution configuration.

STEP BY STEP

6.2   Check the Host Name Resolution Configuration

1. In the Control Panel, click the Network and Dial-Up Connection icon.

2. Right-click Local Area Connections, and then select Properties.

3. Click on Internet Protocol (TCP/IP), and then click Properties.

4. Click the Advanced button in the Microsoft TCP/IP Properties dialog box.

5. Click the DNS tab.

6. Confirm that DNS is configured properly. If the DNS server IP address is missing, add it to the list of DNS server addresses.

NOTE

DNS Configuration   If the IP addresses are supplied by DHCP, there will not be any DNS entries; these entries are supplied when the IP address is obtained. Check the DNS configuration for your subnet with the system administrator.

Check the HOSTS file

If you are having trouble connecting to a remote system using a host name and are using a HOSTS file for name resolution, the problem may be with the contents of that file. Make sure the name of the remote computer is spelled correctly in the HOSTS file and by the application using it.

The HOSTS file or a DNS server is used to resolve host names to IP addresses whenever you use TCP/IP utilities such as PING. You can find the HOSTS file in the following directory:

```
\\%systemroot%\system32\drivers\etc
```

This file is not dynamic, so all entries must be made manually.

Host Name Resolution Using DNS

The DNS system is a worldwide distributed database that replaces the HOSTS file with a hierarchical domain name system that maps names to IP addresses.

If you are trying to contact a computer with the name testcomp .microsoft.com, for example, the following steps would be performed in using DNS to resolve this:

1. The client contacts the DNS name server with a recursive query for testcomp.microsoft.com. The server must now return the answer or an error message.

2. The DNS name server checks its cache and zone files for the answer, but doesn't find it. It contacts a server at the root of the Internet (a root DNS server) with an iterative query for testcomp.microsoft.com.

3. The root server doesn't know the answer, so it responds with a referral to an authoritative server in the .com domain.

4. The DNS name server contacts a server in the .com domain with an iterative query for testcomp.microsoft.com.

5. The server in the .com domain does not know the exact answer, so it responds with a referral to an authoritative server in the Microsoft.com domain.

6. The DNS name server contacts the server in the microsoft .com domain with an iterative query for testcomp .microsoft.com.

7. The server in the microsoft.com domain does know the answer. It responds with the correct IP address to the preferred client's DNS server.

8. The DNS name server responds to the client query with the IP address for testcomp.microsoft.com.

DNS Error Messages

Errors in name resolution can occur if the entries in a DNS server or client are not configured correctly, if the DNS server is not running, or if there is a problem with network connectivity. To determine the cause of any name resolution problem, you can use the Nslookup utility.

Queries that cannot be answered will fail with a number of different error messages depending on the actual problem encountered. For example, Nslookup replies that a name cannot be found if the name can't be resolved, or with a timeout message if the DNS server doesn't reply within the expected time. The actual problem could be that the server is down or the network access to the server is interrupted somewhere.

LMHOSTS File Errors

The LMHOSTS file is scanned from the top down. If there is more than one address listed for the same hostname, TCP/IP uses the first value it encounters.

Long Connect Times Using LMHOSTS

To determine the cause of long connect times after adding an entry to LMHOSTS, take a look at the order of the entries in the LMHOSTS file. Delays in resolving names when using an LMHOSTS file can be minimized by using the #PRE tag to preload an entry and placing often-used entries at the top of the file.

WINS Configuration Errors

To examine your computer's WINS configuration, follow Step by Step 6.3:

STEP BY STEP

6.3 Examine Your WINS Configuration

1. In the Control Panel, select Network and Dial-Up Connections.

2. Right-click on the Local Area connection and select Properties.

3. Select the Internet Protocol (TCP/IP) and select Properties.

4. Click on Advanced and select the WINS tab.

The WINS server IP address should be listed in the Configuration box, unless the address is obtained from a DHCP server. This is also the place that LMHOSTS lookup is enabled and NetBIOS over TCP/IP is selected as well.

A number of diagnostic utilities are included with Windows 2000 Professional. These utilities are useful in identifying and resolving TCP/IP networking problems. They are listed in Table 6.6.

TABLE 6.6

TCP/IP DIAGNOSTIC UTILITIES

Utility	*Function*
ARP	View the ARP (Address Resolution Protocol) cache on the interface of the local computer to detect invalid entries.
Hostname	Display the host name of the computer.
Ipconfig	Display current TCP/IP network configuration values, update or release Dynamic Host Configuration Protocol (DHCP) allocated leases, and display, register, or flush Domain Name System (DNS) names.
Nbtstat	Check the state of current NetBIOS over TCP/IP connections, update the NetBIOS name cache, and determine the registered names and scope ID.
Netdiag	Check all aspects of the network connection.
Netstat	Display statistics for current TCP/IP connections.
Nslookup	Check records, domain host aliases, domain host services, and operating system information by querying Internet domain name servers.
Pathping	Trace a path to a remote system and report packet losses at each router along the way.
Ping	Send ICMP Echo Requests to verify that TCP/IP is configured correctly and that a remote TCP/IP system is available.
Route	Display the IP routing table, and add or delete IP routes.
Tracert	Trace a path to a remote system.

There are also some Windows 2000 tools that can be used to aid in TCP/IP network troubleshooting.

◆ Microsoft SNMP service provides statistical information to SNMP management systems.

◆ Event Viewer tracks errors and events.

◆ Microsoft Network Monitor performs in-depth network traces. The full version is part of the Systems Management Server (SMS) product, and a limited version is included with Windows 2000 Server.

◆ Performance Monitor analyzes TCP/IP network performance.

◆ Registry editors Regedit.exe and Regedt32.exe allow viewing and editing of Registry parameters.

CASE STUDY: HOME OFFICE

ESSENCE OF THE CASE

▶ There is an internal TCP/IP network.

▶ There is a Windows 2000 Server sharing a connection with the Internet.

▶ There is a VPN connection to a corporate server.

▶ Access to hosts on the Internet is failing.

SCENARIO

Like everyone else, you work too much and have set up an office in your home. There is a TCP/IP network internal to your house that connects all the PCs and laptops you have as one network. You are running Windows 2000 Server on one of the systems that acts as a gateway and it is sharing a connection to the Internet through a local cable company. Your laptop is running Windows 2000 Professional with TCP/IP configured by DHCP. You normally connect to your company VPN server via the cable modem and from there, the Internet in general. Today you find that you cannot access your favorite search engine Web page.

CASE STUDY: HOME OFFICE

ANALYSIS

There are a number of network interfaces that are being used in this case study. The first is the TCP/IP configuration of the Windows 2000 Professional computer that is trying to access the search engine home page. The TCP/IP configuration for this computer will be DHCP-enabled and will point to the internal domain hosted by the Windows 2000 Server system. The IPCONFIG /ALL display should show a DHCP-enabled connection with the IP address in the range 192.168.0.x (the default address assigned by the server) with a gateway address that points to the Windows 2000 server computer. In addition, the domain name should be the domain that was set up when the Windows 2000 server was installed. If any of these values are missing or incorrect, the following command will refresh the configuration:

```
Ipconfig /release
Ipconfig /renew
```

The second network interface is on the Windows 2000 server. This system will have two network adapters: one on the inside network and one on the outside. When this system was installed, that distinction was made and connection sharing was enabled on the outside connection. The IPCONFIG /ALL display should show two connections: an inside connection that has a static IP address (usually 192.168.0.1) and an outside address that is usually configured as DHCP-supplied. The local cable company would normally supply the outside address when the cable modem became active on their network.

As with the Windows 2000 Professional system, the following commands will refresh the configuration provided by the cable company:

```
Ipconfig /release
Ipconfig /renew
```

The third network interface is the VPN connection between the Windows 2000 Professional computer and the VPN server in your corporation. That connection is established on the Windows 2000 Professional machine through the gateway server (the gateway server does not need a connection itself). This will appear as a new network entry on your Windows 2000 Professional computer with an IP address from your corporate network. In addition, DNS and WINS entries will be assigned from your corporate network and they should be displayed by the IPCONFIG /ALL command.

The first thing to try after reviewing all the configurations is to ping your gateway. From the Windows 2000 Professional computer, that would be the Windows 2000 server system. If that works, try to ping an outside host (such as your search engine home page) from the Windows 2000 Server. If that works, but it does not work from the Windows 2000 Professional computer, the problem is in the connection sharing setup. Unconfiguring it and reinstalling it on the server will correct any problem.

continues

CASE STUDY: HOME OFFICE

continued

The next thing to try is to trace the route that packets take to a known outside host (the search engine home page again). From the Windows 2000 Professional computer, enter the following command, where <host name> is the search engine host name:

```
Tracert <host name>
```

Tracert will trace the hops (routers) that a packet must take to get to the destination. If it gets to the destination, your problems are solved. If it can't display a router name and shows only IP addresses, the problem is in the DNS servers provided by your cable company. If you get to your corporate network routers (as identified by the IP address ranges) but you don't get from there to the destination, the problem is in your corporate DNS servers or gateway, or the configuration provided when you logged in to the VPN server. Logging out and logging back in will refresh this configuration and solve the problem. If the problem persists, the error is likely on your corporate network, and a call to tech support is in order.

CHAPTER SUMMARY

KEY TERMS

- TCP/IP
- IPX/SPX
- NetBEUI
- DNS
- WINS
- DHCP
- VPN
- IPSEC
- UNC

This chapter discussed the main topics of implementing, managing, and troubleshooting network protocols and services.

The essence of these topics is to understand the components of networking with emphasis on TCP/IP and the role that each component plays in successfully connecting to a network. In addition, the chapter also highlighted two other points not addressed by the objectives, but which may be tested on:

◆ Access to IPX/SPX and NetBEUI protocols to access legacy applications

◆ The steps taken to perform name resolution in TCP/IP (primarily to help you analyze the problem occurring when all you have to work with is a null response)

Also covered were the various configurations available for accessing outside networks, including ISDN multilink, access to private RAS servers, connections to the Internet, and VPN connections through the Internet to secure servers on your corporate network.

APPLY YOUR KNOWLEDGE	

Exercises

6.1 Add the TCP/IP Protocol

This exercise shows you the steps to add and configure the TCP/IP protocols.

Estimated Time: 10 Minutes

1. Double-click on the Network and Dial-Up Connections applet in the Control Panel.

2. Right-click on the connection to which you want to add TCP/IP, and select Properties.

3. Click the Install button, select Protocol, and click the Add button.

4. Select the TCP/IP protocol and click OK.

5. When the Properties page is redisplayed, the TCP/IP protocol will have been installed. If it has a check mark associated with it, it is available to use.

6. Select the TCP/IP entry in the Properties page and click the Properties button.

7. Click on Use the Following IP Address and enter **10.100.5.27** in the IP Address field.

8. Enter **255.255.255.0** in the Subnet Mask field and click OK.

9. Click OK to close the Properties page.

6.2 Change the TCP/IP Properties to Use DHCP

This exercise shows you how to change the properties of the TCP/IP protocol from a static IP to that of a DHCP client.

Estimated Time: 10 Minutes

1. Double-click on the Network and Dial-Up Connections applet in the Control Panel.

2. Right-click on the connection you wish to modify TCP/IP for and select Properties.

3. Select Obtain an IP Address Automatically and click OK.

4. Click OK to close the Properties page.

5. Open a command window and enter the command **IPCONFIG/RELEASE** and then **IPCONFIG/RENEW.**

6. To verify that DHCP is supplying your computer with configuration information, enter the command **IPCONFIG/ALL.**

7. If you don't see a valid IP address with lease information, verify that the DHCP server is functioning and reboot your computer.

6.3 Change the Protocol Binding Order

This exercise shows you how to change the order in which connections are attempted.

Estimated Time: 10 Minutes

1. Click on Start, select Settings, and click on Control Panel.

2. Double-click on the Network and Dial-Up Connections applet in the Control Panel.

3. Select the Advanced menu from the menu bar.

4. Select the Advanced Settings entry.

5. Select one of the connections displayed in the Connections windows.

APPLY YOUR KNOWLEDGE

6. Select one of the entries below File and Print Sharing for Microsoft Networks or Client for Microsoft Networks and move it to the top of the list.

7. Click on OK.

6.4 Install a Dial-Up Connection to a Private Network

This exercise shows you how to set up your computer to access a private network via a modem.

Estimated Time: 10 Minutes

1. Click on Start, select Settings, and click on Control Panel.

2. Double-click on the Network and Dial-Up Connections applet in the Control Panel.

3. Double-click on the Make New Connection icon and click Next.

4. Select Dial Up to My Private Network and click Next.

5. Enter the phone number **555-5555** and click Next.

6. In the connection availability screen, select For All Users and click Next.

7. Enter a name for the connection and click Finish.

6.5 Install a Dial-Up Connection to the Internet

This exercise shows you how to set up your computer to access the Internet via a modem.

Estimated Time: 10 Minutes

1. Click on Start, select Settings, and click on Control Panel.

2. Double-click on the Network and Dial-Up Connections applet in the Control Panel.

3. Double-click on the Make New Connection icon and click Next.

4. Select Dial Up to the Internet and click Next.

5. On the Internet Connection Wizard screen, select Connect Using My Phone Line and click Next.

6. On the Dial-Up Connection screen, select Create a New Dial-Up Connection and click Next.

7. Enter **555** for the area code and **555-5555** for the phone number. Select United States of America (1) for the Country/Region and click on the Advanced button.

8. Ensure that the PPP option is selected and None is selected for the Logon procedure.

9. Select the Addressing tab.

10. Ensure that the IP address and the DNS server address are automatically provided by the ISP and click OK.

11. Click Next.

12. Enter your user name and password needed to log on to your ISP. (The Internet Service Provider usually provides this information when your account is first set up.)

13. Enter a recognizable name for this connection to your ISP and click Next.

14. Click Finish to complete the configuration.

APPLY YOUR KNOWLEDGE

6.6 Install a Dial-Up Connection to a VPN Server

This exercise shows you how to connect you computer to a VPN server via a LAN connection like a cable modem service.

Estimated Time: 10 Minutes

1. Click on Start, select Settings, and click on Control Panel.

2. Double-click on the Network and Dial-Up Connections applet in the Control Panel.

3. Double-click on the Make New Connection icon and click Next.

4. Select Connect to a Private Network Through the Internet and click Next.

5. Select Do Not Dial the Initial Connection and click Next.

6. Enter the host name of `cxn-vpn.company.com` and click Next.

7. Select For All Users and click Next.

8. Enter the name `VPN for Company` and click Finish.

9. Dial the connection if you want, or click on Cancel. The named connection will be available on the Network and Dial-Up Connections screen.

6.7 Configure a Connection to Use Connection Sharing

This exercise shows you how to take an existing connection and reconfigure it to share the connection with other computers on your private TCP/IP network.

Estimated Time: 10 Minutes

1. Double-click on the Network and Dial-Up Connection icon in the Control Panel.

2. Highlight the connection to share. This connection should be on the Internet or some external private network.

3. Right-click the connection icon and select Properties.

4. Select the Sharing tab.

5. Select the Enable Internet Connection Sharing box.

6. Clear the Enable On-Demand Dialing box unless you want this connection to be made whenever a computer on your local network requests an external address.

7. Click on Settings.

8. Select the Applications tab.

9. Enter any application that needs to know the external network connection. These could be network-aware application like network games.

10. Click OK.

11. Select the Services tab.

12. Add any service that you are providing to external users. This could be a Web service.

13. Click OK.

14. Click OK.

APPLY YOUR KNOWLEDGE

6.8 Connect to a Share Using the Active Directory

This exercise shows you how to locate a server in the Active Directory and how to connect to a share on that server.

Estimated Time: 10 Minutes

1. From the Desktop, double-click on My Network Places.

2. Double-click on Add Network Place.

3. Click the Browse button on the Add Network Place Wizard.

4. Expand the display to locate the computer and shared folder to access.

5. Click OK to return to the wizard.

6. Enter a local name for the share.

7. Click on Final to display the contents of the share and to add a new icon to the My Network Places display.

6.9 Map a Drive Letter to a Share

This exercise shows you how to associate a drive letter to a network share.

Estimated Time: 10 Minutes

1. Start Windows Explorer.

2. Select the Tools menu bar option and select Map Network Drive.

3. Expand the display to locate the computer and shared folder to access.

4. Click OK to return to the wizard.

5. Enter a local name for the share.

6. Click on Final to display the contents of the share and to add a new icon to the My Network Places display.

6.10 Locate and Install a Network Printer

This exercise shows you how to find a printer using the Active Directory and how to install it as a print device on your computer.

Estimated Time: 10 Minutes

1. Double-click on the Printer icon in the Control Panel.

2. Double-click on Add Printer.

3. Click Next on the Add Printer Wizard.

4. Select Network Printer and click Next.

5. Select Find a Printer in the Directory and click Next.

6. At this point you can perform the following actions:

   - Browse for a location of a printer.

   - Search for a printer at a specific location.

   - Search for a particular model of printer.

   - Browse the entire network for a computer and printer.

7. Highlight one of the printers returned from the search.

8. Click OK to return to the Add Printer Wizard.

APPLY YOUR KNOWLEDGE

9. Ensure that the printer is selected as the default printer.

10. Click Finish to add the printer to the Printers display.

Review Questions

1. You have two networks that use the NetBEUI protocol. You connect the two networks with a router, but the computers on the different networks can't connect to one another. What is wrong?

2. You have installed NWLink IPX/SPX Compatible Transport protocol on your computer, but you can't establish a session with the NetWare file server. What other component do you need to install?

3. What command should you use to redirect port LPT1: to a printer named HP5 on a server named PRINTSERVE?

4. When do you need to install a default gateway on a computer configured with TCP/IP?

5. You have a computer configured for IPX and you can't make a connection to a UNIX computer running SLIP. What is the problem?

6. You have an older network adapter card that only has drivers for Windows for Workgroups. Can you use it with Windows 2000 Professional?

7. What are network bindings?

8. How many network adapter cards can you put into a single Windows 2000 Professional computer?

9. You have manually configured a TCP/IP connection with a subnet mask of 255.255.255.252 but find that you can't connect to any other computers on your network. What is the problem?

Exam Questions

1. You are the network administrator for a small but rapidly growing company.

   When first installed, your network consisted of only 10 computers running Windows NT Workstation 4, and one computer running Windows NT Server 4. Since then, the network has grown to over 100 computers running Windows 2000 Professional and eight computers running Windows 2000 Advanced Server. Your old method of using manually assigned IP numbers has become too clumsy and you need a more flexible way to handle addresses.

   Required Results:

   Allow new machines to obtain their IP addresses automatically.

   Facilitate the growth of the network into subnets.

   Eliminate any mistakes that would cause network problems.

   Optional Desired Result:

   Provide some redundancy in the event of a failure in the addressing mechanism.

APPLY YOUR KNOWLEDGE

Proposed Solution:

You create a DHCP server, provide the servers a range of leased addresses, and then provide the workstations a range of dynamically assigned addresses. You specify that any router installed to facilitate subnetting must also be configured as a DHCP relay agent.

Which results does the proposed solution produce?

A. The proposed solution produces the required results and the optional desired result.

B. The proposed solution produces one of the required results and the optional desired result.

C. The proposed solution produces the required results but not the optional desired result.

D. The proposed solution does not produce the required results.

2. You are the network administrator for a small but rapidly growing company.

When first installed, your network consisted of 10 computers running Windows NT Workstation 4 and one computer running Windows NT Server 4. Since then, the network has grown to over 100 computers running Windows 2000 Professional and eight computers running Windows 2000 Advanced Server. Your old method of using manually assigned IP numbers has become too clumsy and you need a more flexible way to handle addresses.

Required Results:

Allow new machines to obtain their IP addresses automatically.

Facilitate the growth of the network into subnets.

Eliminate any mistakes that would cause network problems.

Optional Desired Result:

Provide some redundancy in the event of a failure in the addressing mechanism.

Proposed Solution:

You create a DHCP server and provide an excluded range of addresses that you supply manually to the servers and provide the workstations with a range of dynamically assigned addresses. The addresses you supply to the workstations are only half of the ranges possibly allowed by the subnet mask. You then create a duplicate DHCP server as the first DHCP server and supply it with the same excluded list of addresses for the servers. Then you provide the workstations with the other half of the addresses allowed by the subnet mask. You specify that any router installed to facilitate subnetting must also be configured as a DHCP relay agent.

Which result does the proposed solution produce?

A. The proposed solution produces the required results and the optional desired result.

B. The proposed solution produces one of the required results and the optional desired result.

C. The proposed solution produces the required results but not the optional desired result.

D. The proposed solution does not produce the required results.

APPLY YOUR KNOWLEDGE

3. Carlos is an administrator of a TCP/IP network similar to the network shown in Figure 6.18.

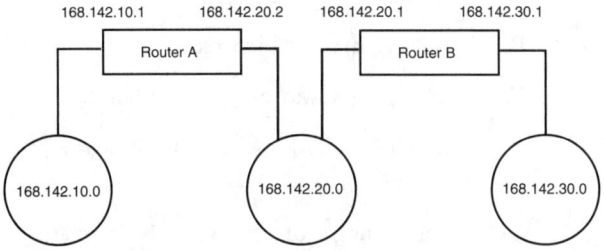

FIGURE 6.18
The TCP/IP network.

Windows 2000 Professional computers can act as routers if they have more than one network adapter card installed (dual-homed). In this configuration, both Router A and Router B are dual-homed Windows 2000 computers.

What should Carlos do to these servers to add a static route that would allow all three networks to communicate?

A. On Router A execute the command ROUTE ADD 168.142.30.0 MASK 255.255.255.0 168.142.20.1.

On Router B execute the command ROUTE ADD 168.142.10.0 MASK 255.255.255.0 168.142.20.2.

B. On Router B execute the command ROUTE ADD 168.142.30.0 MASK 255.255.255.0 168.142.20.1.

On Router A execute the command ROUTE ADD 168.142.10.0 MASK 255.255.255.0 168.142.20.2.

C. On Router A execute the command ROUTE ADD 168.142.20.1 MASK 255.255.255.0 168.142.30.0.

On Router B execute the command ROUTE ADD 168.142.20.2 MASK 255.255.255.0 168.142.10.0.

D. On Router A execute the command ROUTE ADD 168.142.10.0 168.142.20.1.

On Router B execute the command ROUTE ADD 168.142.30.0 168.142.20.2.

4. You work on the help desk for the city's transportation department. The building in which you work occupies three floors, with one subnet for each floor. For the network layout, refer to Figure 6.18.

A user who is on a Windows 2000 Professional workstation with an IP address of 168.142.10.12 reports that she cannot reach a server that you identify as having an IP address of 168.142.30.15. She also reports that she is having no problem assigning a drive letter to a server that you identify as being on the same subnet as she is.

You have tried to ping the server directly but you receive a timeout error from PING.

What address should you attempt to reach next?

A. 127.0.0.1

B. 168.142.20.2

C. 168.142.20.1

D. 168.142.30.1

APPLY YOUR KNOWLEDGE

5. Darrell is a member of the network group at a large company. The network uses TCP/IP exclusively and is made up of several subnets, each of which has servers used by the users in that subnet. He receives a report from a user who says he cannot reach any servers in his local group. Using the NetMon utility, Darrell notices that every time the user tries to connect to a server, his workstation sends out an ARP request for the address of the local gateway.

   Which of the following should Darrell identify as the most likely problem? (Choose one.)

   A. The DNS information is not configured properly.

   B. The WINS addresses are missing.

   C. The subnet mask is incorrect.

   D. The IP address is a duplicate of one on the local subnet.

6. Kevin is part of the networking group at a large metropolitan utility. He has been part of a project that involves moving several computers from one subnet to another. The next day one user complains that he can connect to local servers but cannot connect to any remote server. Other users on the same subnet do not have this problem. The IPCONFIG output from the user's computer contains the following information:

IP Address	168.142.66.31
Subnet Mask	255.255.224.0
Default Gateway	168.142.32.1

   What should Kevin identify as the most likely cause of the problem?

   A. The IP address is incorrect.

   B. The subnet mask is incorrect.

   C. The default gateway address is incorrect.

   D. There is a problem in the user's network connection.

7. You are the manager of a network that is made up of several subnets. You have a mixture of computers running Windows 2000 Server and Windows NT 4 Server in your pool of domain controllers. A user whose computer is running Windows NT Workstation 4 on one subnet reports that she can browse servers on her local network but nothing remote. You try to map a drive to the server and are successful.

   What is most likely the problem?

   A. The default gateway on the client's computer is incorrect.

   B. The DNS server is not available.

   C. The router for this subnet is not functioning.

   D. The domain controller is unavailable.

8. Sparky is the network administrator at a large company in the energy sector. The network carries TCP/IP packets the majority of the time, but there is also NetBIOS traffic as well as some AppleTalk. During a capacity planning study, Sparky discovers that most computer protocol bindings show TCP/IP at the lowest priority. He decides to modify them.

APPLY YOUR KNOWLEDGE

What should Sparky do?

A. Change the protocol binding order on the domain controllers.

B. Change the protocol binding order on the member servers.

C. Change the protocol binding order on the workstations.

D. Change the protocol binding order on the servers and workstations together.

9. Dave is part of the server services group at a large telco. One of the services offered is a RAS server for after-hours access to make repairs to server problems from home. To increase the security of the connection, several authentication methods are available. Dave is charged with picking the most secure authentication method.

What should Dave do? (Choose one.)

A. Use Password Authentication Protocol (PAP).

B. Use Challenge Handshake Authentication Protocol (CHAP).

C. Use Microsoft Challenge Handshake Authentication Protocol (MS-CHAP).

D. Use Microsoft Point-to-Point Encryption (MPPE).

10. Jeff is the local administrator at a remote office of a large insurance corporation. He has 60 computers running Windows 2000 Professional to manage and is concerned about losing connection back to the home office. He installs an additional router for redundancy. When the first router fails, users on his network complain that they can't reach any servers on the network.

What action should Jeff take to stop this problem from reoccurring?

A. Add a second IP address to each workstation.

B. Enter each router into WINS as a unique address.

C. Add an additional default gateway to each workstation.

D. Set up a WINS proxy on the subnet.

11. Patricia is a network administrator working for a large outsourcing company that provides network services to several departments in municipal government. The network is comprised of eight computers running Windows NT 4 Server, 14 computers running Windows 2000 Server, 100 computers running Windows 2000 Professional, 80 computers running Windows 98, and 13 computers running UNIX as servers. The Windows 2000 domain controllers are configured to run the Dynamic DNS service to support the active directory. The UNIX servers transmit data to the Windows NT servers using FTP and the Windows 2000 Professional workstations access a legacy application on the UNIX servers that uses Telnet. The network uses TCP/IP as its primary protocol. Because the city is accustomed to reorganizing itself frequently, Patricia finds that she must physically move computers between subnets. Only the UNIX computers never seem to move. To facilitate this Patricia has the following requirements.

Required Results:

Each Windows computer must be able to access the Windows 2000 servers by name.

APPLY YOUR KNOWLEDGE

Each Windows 2000 Professional computer must receive its IP address and TCP/IP configuration from a DHCP server.

Optional Desired Results:

Each UNIX server must be able to reach the Windows 2000 server via FTP.

The DHCP service must be able to survive a failure of the DHCP server.

Proposed Solution:

Configure all the network routers to forward DHCP broadcasts to all subnets.

Install a WINS server on the network.

Configure DHCP to supply WINS and the DNS address to clients.

On the DHCP server, exclude the address ranges used by the UNIX servers and create a client reservation for the WINS server.

What results does the proposed solution produce?

A. The proposed solution produces the required results and all of the optional desired results.

B. The proposed solution produces the required results and one of the optional desired results.

C. The proposed solution produces the required results and none of the optional desired results.

D. The proposed solution does not produce the required results.

12. Patricia is a network administrator working for a large outsourcing company that provides network services to several departments in municipal government. The network is comprised of eight computers running Windows NT 4 Server, 14 computers running Windows 2000 Server, 100 computers running Windows 2000 Professional, 80 computers running Windows 98, and 13 computers running UNIX as servers. The Windows 2000 domain controllers are configured to run the Dynamic DNS service to support the active directory. The UNIX servers transmit data to the NT servers using FTP and the Windows 2000 Professional workstations access a legacy application on the UNIX servers that uses Telnet. The network uses TCP/IP as its primary protocol. Because the city is accustomed to reorganizing itself frequently, Patricia finds that she must physically move computers between subnets. Only the UNIX computers never seem to move. To facilitate this Patricia has the following requirements.

Required Results:

Each Windows 2000 Professional computer must be able to access the Windows 2000 servers by name.

Each Windows 2000 Professional computer must receive its IP address and TCP/IP configuration from a DHCP server.

Optional Desired Results:

Each UNIX server must be able to reach the Windows 2000 server via FTP.

The DHCP service must be able to survive a failure of the DHCP server.

Proposed Solution:

Configure all the network routers to forward DHCP broadcasts to all subnets.

Install a WINS server on the network.

Configure DHCP to supply WINS and the DNS address to clients.

APPLY YOUR KNOWLEDGE

On the WINS server, enter static mapping entries for the UNIX computers.

On the DHCP server, exclude the address ranges used by the UNIX servers and create a client reservation for the WINS server.

What results does the proposed solution produce?

A. The proposed solution produces the required results and all of the optional desired results.

B. The proposed solution produces the required results and one of the optional desired results.

C. The proposed solution produces the required results and none of the optional desired results.

D. The proposed solution does not produce the required results.

13. Patricia is a network administrator working for a large outsourcing company that provides network services to several departments in municipal government. The network is comprised of eight computers running Windows NT 4 Server, 14 computers running Windows 2000 Server, 100 computers running Windows 2000 Professional, 80 computers running Windows 98, and 13 computers running UNIX as servers. The Windows 2000 domain controllers are configured to run the Dynamic DNS service to support the active directory. The UNIX servers transmit data to the NT servers using FTP and the Windows 2000 Professional workstations access a legacy application on the UNIX servers that uses Telnet. The network uses TCP/IP as its primary protocol. Because the city is accustomed to reorganizing itself frequently, Patricia finds that she must physically move computers between subnets. Only the UNIX computers never seem to move. To facilitate this Patricia has the following requirements.

Required Results:

Each Windows 2000 Professional computer must be able to access the Windows 2000 servers by name.

Each Windows 2000 Professional computer must receive its IP address and TCP/IP configuration from a DHCP server.

Optional Desired Results:

Each UNIX server must be able to reach the Windows 2000 server via FTP.

The DHCP service must be able to survive a failure of the DHCP server.

Proposed Solution:

Configure all the network routers to forward DHCP broadcasts to all subnets.

Install a WINS server on the network.

Add the Windows 2000 server IP addresses to the UNIX server HOSTS file.

Configure DHCP to supply WINS and the DNS address to clients.

On the WINS server enter static mapping addresses for the UNIX servers.

Add an additional DHCP server and duplicate the subnets and split the address ranges evenly between the two servers.

On the DHCP server, exclude the address ranges used by the UNIX servers and create a client reservation for the WINS server.

What results does the proposed solution produce?

A. The proposed solution produces the required results and all of the optional desired results.

APPLY YOUR KNOWLEDGE

B. The proposed solution produces the required results and one of the optional desired results.

C. The proposed solution produces the required results and none of the optional desired results.

D. The proposed solution does not produce the required results.

14. You are the manager of a small company that does research for clients. Your network is made up of computers running Windows 2000 Professional and Windows 98 with an existing DHCP server to provide address configuration. Occasionally, it is necessary for an employee to search for information on the Internet and to facilitate the process of adding a dial-out port for those people who have asked for one. With your company growing, it is becoming expensive and more troublesome to maintain good service. Your local cable company has suggested that they install a cable modem into your office and provide some IP addresses using DHCP. The problem is that you have more employees wanting Internet access than the cable company will provide addresses for.

Required Results:

Computers will still get their TCP/IP configuration from DHCP.

The number of addresses provided by the cable company will not be exceeded.

All your employees' computers will have access to the Internet.

Optional Desired Results:

The internal network should be protected from outside access.

The employee workstations should be able to resolve Internet names without further configuration changes.

Proposed Solution:

Add an additional NIC card to a Windows 2000 server.

Configure the outside connection (the new NIC card) as a shared connection.

Which results does the proposed solution produce?

A. The proposed solution produces the required results and the optional desired results.

B. The proposed solution produces the required results but only one of the optional desired results.

C. The proposed solution produces the required results and none of the optional desired results.

D. The proposed solution does not produce the required results.

15. You are the manager of a small company that does research for clients. Your network is made up of computers running Windows 2000 Professional and Windows 98 with an existing DHCP server to provide address configuration. Occasionally, it is necessary for an employee to search for information on the Internet and to facilitate the process of adding a dial-out port for those people who have asked for one. With your company growing, it is becoming expensive and more troublesome to maintain good service. Your local cable company has suggested that they install a cable modem into your office and provide some IP addresses using DHCP. The

APPLY YOUR KNOWLEDGE

problem is that you have more employees wanting Internet access than the cable company will provide addresses for.

Required Results:

Computers will still get their TCP/IP configuration from DHCP.

The number of addresses provided by the cable company will not be exceeded.

All your employees' computers will have access to the Internet.

Optional Desired Results:

The internal network should be protected from outside access.

The employee workstations should be able to resolve Internet names without further configuration changes.

Proposed Solution:

Add an addition NIC card to a Windows 2000 server.

Configure the outside connection (the new NIC card) as a shared connection.

Delete your existing DHCP service.

Which results does the proposed solution produce?

A. The proposed solution produces the required results and the optional results.

B. The proposed solution produces the required results but only one of the optional results.

C. The proposed solution produces the required results and none of the optional results.

D. The proposed solution does not produce the required results.

Review Answers

1. NetBEUI is not normally supported by routers. Either configure your router to support NetBEUI or switch your network protocol to IPX or TCP/IP. See "NetBIOS Extended User Interface (NetBEUI)."

2. NWLink is not sufficient to access file shares and print services on a NetWare server. You must also install CSNW. See "NWLINK IPX/SPX Compatible Transport."

3. Net Use LPT1: \\PRINTSERVE\HP5. See "Net Use Command."

4. You need to install a default gateway when your TCP/IP-configured computer needs to communicate with a computer located on a different physical network or subnetwork. See "Default Gateway (Router)."

5. SLIP does not support IPX or NetBEUI. SLIP stands for Serial Line Internet Protocol and only supports encapsulating TCP/IP. See "Serial Line Internet Protocol (SLIP)."

6. Windows 2000 Professional does not support any 16-bit devices. You must use a device driver written to support Windows NT or Windows 2000. See "NDIS-Compatible Network Adapter Card Drivers."

7. Network binding is the association of a network adapter card to a protocol being used. See "NDIS 5.0."

8. Windows 2000 Professional supports an unlimited number of network adapters. The number of network adapter cards that you can install in your computer, however, will be the limiting factor. See "NDIS 5.0."

APPLY YOUR KNOWLEDGE

9. The subnet specified has only two nodes on it. With such a restricted subnet, every address other than the one remaining address on your subnet would be considered remote. The other local address must therefore be a router if you are to communicate with any remote systems at all. This configuration is usually used for router connections, however, and is not very useful when connecting computers. See "Subnet Mask."

Answers to Exam Questions

1. **C.** Adding a DHCP server to the network would allow any Windows workstation to acquire its IP address and other TCP/IP configuration information automatically and stop mistakes that would cause network problems (such as duplicate IP addresses) by automating the configuration tasks previously handled manually. Adding the support for DHCP broadcasts at any router in the network would extend the DHCP service to new subnets as they are created. The solution does not, however, address the lack of redundancy of the DHCP service itself. See "Understanding DCHP."

2. **A.** Adding a DHCP server to the network would allow any Windows workstation to acquire its IP address and other TCP/IP configuration infor-mation automatically and stop mistakes that would cause network problems (such as duplicate IP addresses) by automating the configuration tasks previously handled manually. Adding the support for DHCP broadcasts at any router in the network would extend the DHCP service to new subnets as they are created. The second DHCP server contains all the scope (subnet) definitions but half the address space. The

original DHCP server contains the other half of the addresses. When one server fails or is taken offline, the other can continue to dispense address information. See "Understanding DHCP."

3. **A.** The correct syntax for a route command is `ROUTE ADD [destination network] [subnet mask] [gateway address]`. The mask argument is required only when subnet masking is being used, as is the case here (class B addresses subnet-ted at the third octet). The rule for adding static routes is to bind the subnet you cannot reach through the gateway that you can reach. In this case, the system acting as Router A has two NIC cards—one on the first subnet and one on the middle subnet. Access from the first subnet is the directed through the gateway to the system acting as Router B (which can be reached by Router A since they share access to the middle subnet). See "Determine the Correct Gateway."

4. **B.** The problem with using PING as a diagnostic tool is that the problem in reaching an IP address could be caused at any node along the way. The problem is to determine by the most direct method where on the network the problem occurs. The first address to check is 127.0.0.1 (the loopback address) and then your IP address. A reply from both of these tests will indicate that the network adapter is working and is configured correctly. The next step would be to ping the far side of the server acting as Router A. The next step would be to ping the near side of the server acting as Router B and then the far side of the same system. See "Using PING."

5. **C.** IP must first resolve the MAC address of the destination IP. At this point, WINS, DNS, and any static files (HOSTS and LMHOSTS) are not

used. IP compares its IP address with its subnet mask and then inspects the destination address. If the destination address is remote (on a different subnet), IP will use the local gateway to help determine the destination MAC address. If the address is local (on the same subnet as defined by IP current address and the subnet mask), then IP will use ARP to return the MAC address directly. If the subnet mask is incorrect, then local addresses could look remote and remote addresses look like they are local. If the IP address is duplicated, TCP/IP notifies the user with a dialog box repeatedly, until the problem is fixed. See "Determine Whether the Address Is Local."

6. **C.** The default gateway for a computer must be in the same subnet. The gateway is used by IP on the local computer to help determine the MAC address of the destination IP address. If the default gateway is already remote, it can't be used to locate remote addresses. The class B address 168.142.0.0 with a subnet mask of 255.255.224.0 divides into six usable subnets with the following addresses:

168.142.32.1	168.142.63.254
168.142.64.1	168.142.95.254
168.142.96.1	168.142.127.254
168.142.128.1	168.142.159.254
168.142.160.1	168.142.191.254
168.142.192.1	168.142.223.254

Note that the first and last subnets are not included because they have illegal addresses.

The IP of the computer is on the second subnet; however, the gateway address is on the first subnet and therefore cannot be reached to help

resolve remote addresses. If the host address were incorrect and the gateway address were correct, then no local addresses would be reachable. See "Determine the Correct Gateway."

7. **D.** In a Windows 2000 environment, browsing is still available for those clients that are using Windows 95/98 or Windows NT. Browsing is concerned with keeping a list of named computers and not Name to IP address resolution. In the case where you are mapping a drive to a computer on a remote subnet and are successful, the router, the default gateway address, and the name resolution service must all be working correctly. Browsing across subnets relies on the Master Browser, which will be one of the domain controllers. The Master Browser merges all the computer lists from the browsers on each subnet to produce one global list. Local browsers rely on this list when looking for remote machines. If this list is not available (meaning that you can't browse) but you can map to a specific share on a named system, then the Master Browser service or domain controller is not available. See "Browsing Other Domains."

8. **C.** A connection initiated by a Windows 2000 Professional client will define the protocol used. The server can have many different protocols set and the binding order is irrelevant. Modifying the binding order at the client side, however, can improve performance. See "Adapters and Bindings."

9. **C.** The MS-CHAP authentication protocol does not require the use of clear text or encrypted passwords. It can be configured to refuse any connection that cannot be made in a secure manner. PAP is a very unsophisticated technique that will send clear text passwords, and CHAP

APPLY YOUR KNOWLEDGE

will negotiate down to clear text if the server you are connecting to does not support MD5 hashing. MPPE is the data encryption technique used to secure PPTP connections. See "Dial-Up to the Internet."

10. **C.** The Microsoft TCP/IP implementation allows for multiple gateway addresses (currently five) to be configured for a network. Only one address is in use as the default gateway at any time. However, the other addresses can act as backup. If the router that is the current default gateway fails to respond, TCP/IP automatically makes the next gateway address in the list the current default gateway. See "TCP/IP."

11. **C.** The solution solves the NetBIOS naming issues but does not address any of the UNIX network integration issues and the requirement for redundancy of the DHCP service. Configuring all routers to forward all DHCP broadcasts to all subnets will allow the DHCP server to answer requests from any subnet defined. Installing a WINS server will allow the Windows NT and Windows 95/98 workstations to access any server by name. The DHCP service can provide IP addresses and other configuration information to client computers, and excluding the UNIX computers' IP addresses will prevent them from being leased out to other clients. See "Windows Internet Name Service (WINS)" and "Understanding DHCP."

12. **C.** The solution solves the NetBIOS naming issues but does not address any of the UNIX network integration issues and the requirement for redundancy of the DHCP service. Configuring all routers to forward all DHCP broadcasts to all subnets will allow the DHCP server to answer requests from any

subnet defined. Installing a WINS server will allow the Windows NT and Windows 95/98 workstations to access any server by name. The DHCP service can provide IP addresses and other configuration information to client computers. The UNIX computers cannot participate in WINS so their IP addresses must be entered as static WINS entries to allow WINS clients to find them. Excluding the UNIX computers' IP addresses will prevent them from being leased out to other clients. See "Windows Internet Name Service (WINS)" and "Understanding DHCP."

13. **A.** The solution solves the NetBIOS naming issues and addresses the UNIX network integration issues and the requirement for redundancy of the DHCP service. Configuring all routers to forward all DHCP broadcasts to all subnets will allow the DHCP server to answer requests from any subnet defined. Installing a WINS server will allow the Windows NT and Windows 95/98 workstations to access any server by name. The DHCP service can provide IP addresses and other configuration information to client computers. The UNIX computers cannot participate in WINS so their IP addresses must be entered as static WINS entries to allow WINS clients to find them. Excluding the UNIX computers' IP addresses will prevent them from being leased out to other clients. Adding the Windows 2000 server IP addresses to the UNIX HOSTS file will allow the UNIX computers to FTP data directly. The addition of a second DHCP server with all the scopes (subnets) defined but the addresses evenly split between the two servers will provide a backup service for the DHCP clients on the network in the event that one DHCP server fails or is taken

APPLY YOUR KNOWLEDGE

offline. See "Windows Internet Name Service (WINS)" and "Understanding DHCP."

14. **D.** The solution here is to provide a server that has two NIC cards: one on the inside network and one on the network provided by the cable company. The selection of Connection Sharing on the outside network will normally start up several services on the Windows 2000 computer to enable Connection Sharing, including a DHCP service with a single scope and a DNS proxy service to provide name resolution using the cable company's ISP service. When the client computers obtain their IP address leases, they will have this information sent to them along with the gateway server address set as the default

gateway. However, this plan is derailed because there is an existing DHCP service on the network. The Connection Sharing DHCP service will not run properly with any other competing service running. See "Internet Connection Sharing."

15. **A.** The selection of Connection Sharing will start a DHCP service with a single scope and a DNS proxy service to provide name resolution using the cable company's ISP service. When the client computers renew their DHCP address leases, they will receive this information along with the gateway server's IP address as the default gateway. See "Internet Connection Sharing."

Suggested Readings and Resources

1. *Optimize Network Traffic (Notes from the Field).* Microsoft Press, 2000.

2. Lee, Thomas and Joseph Davies. *Microsoft Windows 2000 TCP/IP Protocol and Services Technical Reference.* Microsoft Press, 2000.

3. Stanek, William R. *Microsoft Windows 2000 Administrator's Pocket Consultant.* Microsoft Press, 2000.

4. Joyce, Jerry and Marianne Moon. *Microsoft Windows 2000 Professional at a Glance.* Microsoft Press, 2000.

This chapter covers topics associated with Windows 2000 security. It helps you prepare for the exam by addressing the following exam objectives:

Encrypt data on a hard disk by using Encrypting File System (EFS).

▶ Encrypting File System is a new service supported in the Windows 2000 environment. It is important that network administrators understand how EFS can be used to secure file resources. It is also important that administrators understand how encrypted files can be recovered if a user is not available to decrypt the file.

Implement, configure, manage, and troubleshoot local Group Policy.

▶ Group Policy is a very powerful tool built into Windows 2000. Group Policy gives an administrator the ability to secure a computer's local settings.

Implement, configure, manage, and troubleshoot local user accounts.

- **Implement, configure, manage, and troubleshoot auditing.**

- **Implement, configure, manage, and troubleshoot account settings.**

- **Implement, configure, manage, and troubleshoot account policy.**

- **Create and manage local users and groups.**

- **Implement, configure, manage, and troubleshoot user rights.**

CHAPTER 7

Implementing, Monitoring, and Troubleshooting Security

▶ The efficient management of user accounts is critical to the overall management of a network. Administrators must understand the tools that are available to them to manage user accounts in the Windows 2000 environment.

Implement, configure, manage, and troubleshoot local user authentication.

- **Configure and troubleshoot local user accounts.**

- **Configure and troubleshoot domain user accounts.**

▶ Administrators must be able to distinguish between local and domain-based users. They also must understand how to manage each type of account.

Implement, configure, manage, and troubleshoot a security configuration.

▶ A new tool introduced to the Windows 2000 environment is a security template. Administrators will find that security templates are a powerful feature of Windows 2000 that can make the overall administration of computers in their environment easier.

STUDY STRATEGIES

▶ This chapter presents a number of concepts related to securing your environment. It is important for you to remember that securing your environment is a process of setting many different features and services. Each feature/service works in conjunction with the others to provide a secure environment. If one security feature fails, then the remaining features will present a new line of defense.

▶ As you review the material in this chapter always try to distinguish whether the topic is related to the workgroup or domain environment.

INTRODUCTION

This chapter provides an overview of Windows 2000 security. The chapter presents a number of different topics that relate to securing your environment. We start with a discussion of the workgroup and domain models and user/group management. Effectively managing your users and groups will make or break the security plans for your organization. During this discussion we specifically look at creating and managing users and groups in both the workgroup and domain environments and the type of groups supported by Windows 2000. We also look at the account settings at our disposal to assist in the management of the accounts.

Other security technologies also are covered in this chapter. We look at the use of local policies for securing the local desktop environment and for managing passwords. The last three topics in this chapter look at the use of Encrypted File System, audit policies, and security templates to assist in securing your environment.

USER AND GROUP MANAGEMENT

Implement, configure, manage, and troubleshoot local user authentication.

User accounts are used to represent people in your networked environment. A user account contains information about a person who can gain access to your network. Information stored in a user account includes the user's name and password, as well as other information that describes the configuration of the user. Accounts enable users to identify themselves when they log on to the local computer or domain. Users accounts also are used to grant (or deny) access to resources. Through user accounts, you can control how a user gains access to a resource.

User accounts are stored in a protected database on Windows 2000 systems. When a user logs on to a system, the Security Accounts Manager (SAM) will compare the user's name and password against the data stored in the database. If these credentials are correct, the user can gain access to the computer or network. If the credentials are incorrect, the user is denied access to the system or network.

Windows 2000 supports two user account models: the workgroup model and the domain model. The following sections provide a brief overview of these models.

The Workgroup Model

Under the workgroup model each computer in your environment is responsible for the management of its own local account database. Local user accounts contain information that defines users for the local computer. With a local user account, a user can log on to the local computer and gain access to local resources. To gain access to resources on another computer, a user must use an account on the other computer.

The workgroup model is meant for small environments. This model has a very high administrative cost, as user accounts must be managed on each computer in your environment. For example, if you have five computers on your network and you require access to resources on each computer, you need to physically create a user account on each computer. If you change the password on one computer, you also need to change the password on the remaining four computers. The workgroup model is very simple to implement, however, and does not require specialized computers to manage a shared account database.

The workgroup model is also useful for temporary environments. If, for example, a team of people needs to share resources for a short period of time, the workgroup model makes sense. For longer-term projects, however, the team would most likely benefit from the centralized database of account information provided by the domain model.

The Domain Model

Under the domain model, a centralized database of user accounts is managed for a grouping (or domain) of computers. Domain user accounts contain information that defines users within the domain.

In Windows 2000, all user account information for the domain is stored in the Active Directory database. The Active Directory is stored on a special computer called a domain controller. With a single domain user account, a user can log on to the network and gain access to resources on any computer in the Active Directory environment (referred to as an Active Directory tree or forest), provided they have the correct permissions. The primary benefit of the domain model is that account management is simplified, as each user in your environment will have only a single user account defined. This model, however, is much more complex to set up, design, and configure.

Although a detailed discussion of the Active Directory is beyond the scope of this course, it is useful to note the following features of Active Directory:

◆ Active Directory stores network resource information as objects in a centralized database. Objects represent resources (i.e., users, printers, shared folders, etc.).

◆ Each object contains a number of attributes. Attributes contain values. Attributes are used to store information about objects (for example a user's name, password, etc.).

◆ Users and administrators can search the Active Directory to locate objects. Searches are based on the attributes of objects.

◆ All object information is stored centrally. Administrators can centrally organize, manage, and control access to network resources through the directory.

◆ Administrators can delegate authority to users to administer portions of the Active Directory. This enables the administrative activities to be distributed to select users.

The basic building blocks of the Active Directory are domains. Active Directory organizes domains into a hierarchical structure, based on Domain Name Service (DNS) naming conventions.

The primary characteristic of an Active Directory tree is that the domain names used fall with a contiguous DNS name space (i.e., a parent/child relationship is created between domains, based on a contiguous name space). Figure 7.1 shows a sample of an Active Directory Tree.

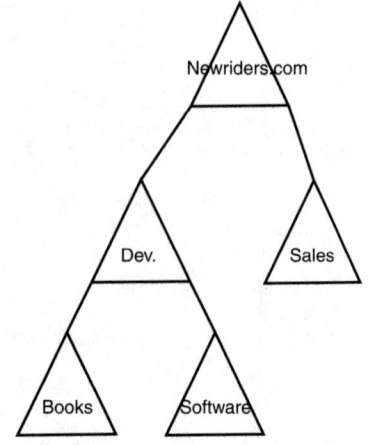

FIGURE 7.1
Sample Active Directory tree.

Active Directory also enables the creation of forests. A forest is a collection of domains that do not share a common DNS name space. Figure 7.2 shows a sample of an Active Directory forest.

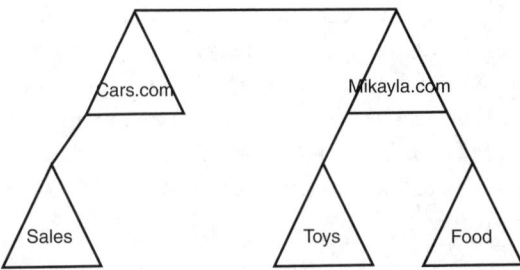

FIGURE 7.2
Sample Active Directory forest.

All domains within an Active Directory tree or forest share the following three things in common:

◆ **Common database schema.** The database schema defines the database objects and the attributes that can be stored about each object.

◆ **Two-way transitive trust relationships.** Two-way transitive trusts enable users from any domain to access resources in any other domain (if they have the appropriate permissions).

◆ **A Global Catalog (GC).** The GC is a service that runs on selected domain controllers within the Active Directory forest. The GC contains data about every object in the forest. (Only a select number of attributes about each object are stored in the GC to limit the total amount of data that needs to be replicated and stored on the GC servers.)

Active Directory is a very powerful tool that can be used to manage your environment. Active Directory is designed to support very large environments. The directory database in Active Directory also can be modified to support new objects and attributes. In the future we will see new Active Directory-aware applications (MS Exchange 2000, for example) that can access the data stored in Active Directory. The benefits of this environment are significant, as all data is stored in one secure and manageable location.

NOTE

Windows NT versus Windows 2000—Can They Play with One Another? You can add a Windows 2000-based computer to a Windows NT 4.0 domain and receive all of the benefits of centralized user accounts.

You also can add a Windows NT-based computer to a Windows 2000 domain. In this case, however, you will find that not all of the functionality of Active Directory is available.

Accounts and Security Identifiers

Every account with Windows 2000 that can be assigned permission to a resource is considered a Security Principal within Windows 2000. A unique security identifier, or SID, identifies Security Principals on the network. This is a very important concept, as a SID is unique to each Security Principal and will never be modified for the life of the account (unless it is migrated to another domain). In addition, SIDs are never reused when new objects are created. If an account is deleted, all references to the object's SID are removed from the network.

Renaming a user account enables an account to receive a new name and retain its security assignments and group membership (as the SID is not changed). This is a very useful option if a user leaves the company and is replaced. Instead of creating a new user account for the new staff member, you can rename the old staff member's account so that the new staff member can use it.

User Accounts

As a network administrator in the Windows 2000 environment, you need to learn the skills required to manage users and groups. The following sections demonstrate how to manage and create users (in both the workgroup and domain environments).

Windows 2000 automatically creates two user accounts, called built-in accounts, when it is installed. The Administrator account is the account that is used to manage the configuration of the computer and users stored on the computer. The Administrator account has the capability of managing all aspects of the computer, so access to this account must be protected. You can rename the Administrator account, but it cannot be deleted. Guest is the second built-in account created when Windows 2000 is installed. The Guest account can be used to grant occasional users access to resources. The Guest account is disabled by default.

Regardless of whether you are managing a workgroup or domain environment, you need to plan for user accounts. Details that you should consider are listed in Table 7.1.

TABLE 7.1

USER ACCOUNT PLANNING CONSIDERATIONS

Planning Consideration	Topic	Details
Naming Conventions	User logon name and full names must be unique	Domain user accounts must be unique to the Domain. Local user accounts must be unique to the local machine.
	User logon name can contain up to 20 characters	User logon names can contain up to 20 uppercase or lowercase characters. The field will allow for additional characters, but Windows 2000 only uses the first 20 entered. Logon names can contain up to 20 characters of uppercase or lowercase characters. Windows recognizes any alpha-numeric character except for "/\[];:ll=.+*?<>.
	Naming convention must accommodate duplicate employee names	You should develop a naming convention that will accommodate duplicate employee names—for example, two users named Sally Smith. Your naming convention should accommodate both users.
Secure Passwords	Assign passwords to administrator accounts	The administrator (and all accounts with administrator privileges) should have a password assigned. Access to the Administrator account must be closely guarded or you will not be able to secure your systems.

continues

TABLE 7.1 *continued*		
USER ACCOUNT PLANNING CONSIDERATIONS		
Planning Consideration	*Topic*	*Details*
	Password management	You should determine whether the administrator or the users will control passwords. You can assign passwords for the users accounts and prevent users from changing them, or you can allow users to enter their own passwords and manage them afterward.
	User education	Users need to understand that passwords are there to protect them (and you, as administrator). If a user uses an obvious password, it can compromise network security. Generally users should avoid passwords such as family names or a pet's name; Use long passwords (passwords can be up to 128 characters long); password are case-sensitive; a mix of upper and lowercase can help secure passwords.

Creating Local User Accounts

Local user accounts are typically associated with the workgroup model previously discussed. Local user accounts can be used to access the computer on which the account physically resides and resources on the local machine. Local user accounts are limited to local resources.

Local user accounts are managed from the Computer Management Microsoft Management Console (MMC) snap-in. The Computer Management snap-in can be accessed by clicking the Start\Programs\ Administrative Tools\Computer Management menu options. Alternatively you can add the Computer Management snap-in to the MMC. Step by Step 7.1 demonstrates how to view the Computer Management snap-in from a custom MMC and how to create a new local user account.

STEP BY STEP

7.1 Creating Local User Accounts by Using the Computer Management Snap-in

This Step by Step assumes that your computer is running Windows 2000 Professional or Windows 2000 Server (configured as a member server in a domain or workgroup).

1. Click Start/Run. In the Open dialog box, type MMC and click OK.

2. From the Console menu, click the Add/Remove Snap-in menu.

3. In the Add/Remove Snap-in window, click Add.

4. In the Add Standalone Snap-in window, highlight the Computer Management snap-in and click Add.

5. In the Computer Management window, select either the local computer or a remote system (if you select a remote system you need to have permission to create user accounts on the remote system). Click Finish in the Computer Management window.

6. Close the Add Standalone Snap-in and Add/Remove Snap-in windows by clicking OK.

7. Open the Computer Management snap-in by clicking the plus sign beside the snap-in.

8. Open the System Tools node of the Computer Management snap-in by clicking the plus sign beside the node.

9. Open the Local Users and Groups node of the Computer Management snap-in. From this location, you can create and manage users on the system. Figure 7.3 shows the appropriate MMC screen.

continues

NOTE

Users and Passwords Applet If you are working with Windows 2000 Professional systems configured as part of a workgroup, you also can use the Users and Passwords applet to create user accounts. The applet is found under Control Panel.

continued

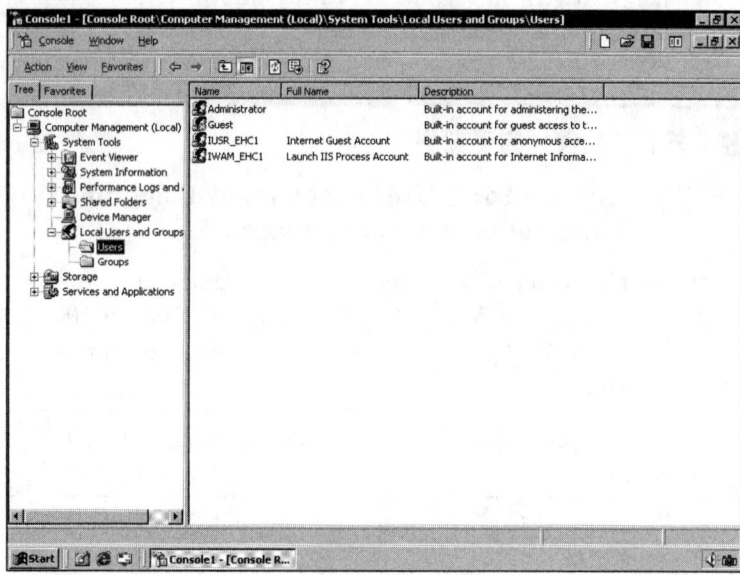

FIGURE 7.3
Computer Management snap-in Local Users and Groups node.

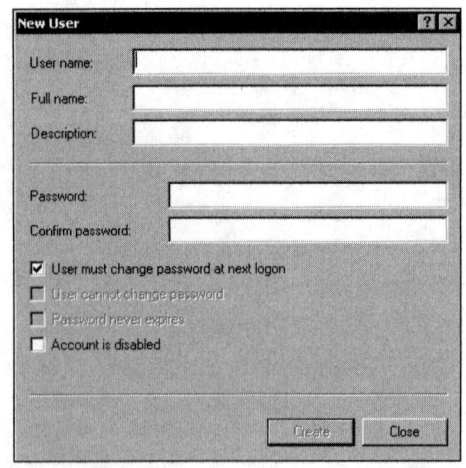

FIGURE 7.4
Create a new user in the New User dialog box.

10. To create a new Local User, right-click the "Users" folder in the Local Users and Groups node. From the secondary menu, select New User. This action will launch the New User dialog box (see Figure 7.4).

11. You need to enter the information for the user account. Table 7.2 defines the information required and the values used for this walkthrough.

TABLE 7.2

NEW USER CONFIGURATION OPTIONS

Configuration Setting	Description	Value for this Walkthrough
User name	The user's unique logon name.	DougH
Full name	The user's full name (this is a required field).	Doug Harrison
Description	This option is for information purposes and gives you the option to describe the purpose of the account.	Local User for Doug Harrison
Password/Confirm password	To ensure that you type the password correctly, you must enter the password in the "Password" and "Confirm password" fields. Be careful typing, as passwords are case-sensitive.	MyDogsNameIsSpot
User must change password at next logon	Select this checkbox if you want the user to change his password the first time he logs on. This ensures that the user is the only person who knows the password. Note: This option is disabled if the User cannot change password or the Password never expires options are checked	Checked
User cannot change password	Select this checkbox if you never want the password to be changed for this user. This is a great option if multiple users use this account to access the system (and you don't want one of them to change the password so the rest can't log on). Note: This option is disabled if you select the User must change the password at next logon option.	N/A

continues

TABLE 7.2 *continued*

NEW USER CONFIGURATION OPTIONS

Configuration Setting	Description	Value for this Walkthrough
Password never expires	Select this check box if you never want the password to change. This setting will override policies that indicate passwords must be changed. Note: This option is disabled if you select the User must change the password at next logon option.	N/A
Account is disabled	Select this checkbox to prevent use of this user account.	Unchecked

12. After you have entered the user configuration, click Create. The user will be created, and the dialog box will be cleared so that you can create additional users. After all user accounts have been created, click Close to return to the MMC.

13. Log off of your workstation and log on as the DougH account. Note that you will be required to enter a new password (and confirm it) when you log on—you have verified that the account is opperational. Log off the DougH account and log on as your Administrator account (or an account with Administrative privileges).

Every user in your environment should have his or her own user account. For security reasons, users should not share user accounts. You should also ensure that users protect their passwords. Users need to understand that passwords protect their identities on the network. System administrators rely on passwords to ensure that user accounts are not used inappropriately (i.e., by someone other than the appropriate user). If system administrators cannot rely on users to protect their passwords, many audit and security functions on the network are defeated.

In some special instances, groups of users might share user accounts. For example, your company might have a large team of users acting as order-desk representatives who require the same access to network resources. In instances such as these, all users can share the same user account. If all users do share the same account you should ensure that the "User cannot change password" option is set for the account. This will limit an individual's ability to change the password and lock out all of the other users.

Network administrators also will want to ensure that users change their passwords often. This can be accomplished through group and local policies. Again, it is important that users understand the importance of their passwords. You might have noticed that administrators have the ability to set a user account so that passwords never expire. This option is useful for system and service accounts. If this option is not set for system and service accounts, you might find that the services relying on the accounts stop operating correctly if their password expires.

After the user account is created, you might need to manage the account. Common management tasks are as follows:

◆ Resetting passwords

◆ Renaming accounts

◆ Deleting accounts

◆ Enabling accounts

◆ Unlocking accounts

◆ Changing group membership

◆ Modifying profile paths

◆ Modifying user home directory paths

All of these tasks are completed from the Computer Management snap-in of the MMC. Passwords can be reset for a user account by right-clicking on the user account and selecting Set Password from the secondary menu. You also will find the Rename account and Delete account options from the user account secondary menu.

Deleting a user account will permanently remove the account from the system.

The remaining configuration options can be accessed by double-clicking the user account (or right-clicking the account and selecting Properties from the secondary menu).

> **NOTE**
>
> **User Accounts and Windows 2000 Server** You will find that user accounts created on Windows 2000 Server (configured as a domain controller) will not be able to log on locally to a server unless they are members of the Administrators, Account Operators, Backup Operators, Print Operators, or Server Operators groups. Users need the user right called Log on Locally to enable them to log on to a system from the console (i.e., the computer's keyboard).

Figure 7.5 shows the Test User Properties page. From this page, you can modify the full name and description of the account. You also have the ability to configure how passwords should be managed for the user and disable the account (as discussed in Step by Step 7.1).

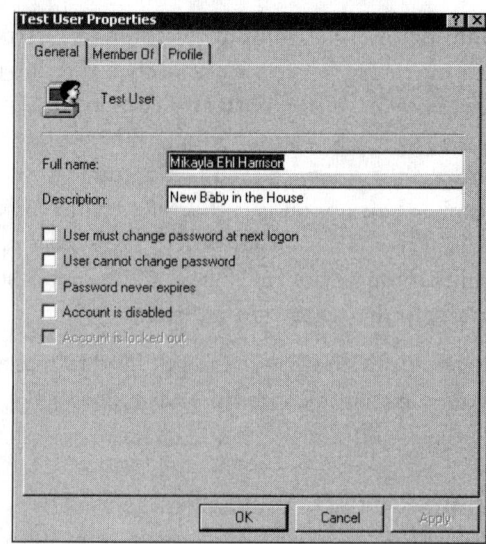

FIGURE 7.5
Test User Property page—General tab.

Groups are used to simplify resource access (groups will be discussed in greater detail later in this chapter). The Member Of tab enables you to manage the group membership of a user account. From this tab, you can click the Add or Remove buttons to modify group membership (see Figure 7.6).

The Profile tab enables you to configure the User profile (profile path and logon script) and home folder location (see Figure 7.7).

Creating Domain User Accounts

Domain user accounts are very similar to local user accounts. The primary difference between a local user account and a domain user account is that a domain account can be used to gain access to resources throughout a domain or within an Active Directory environment.

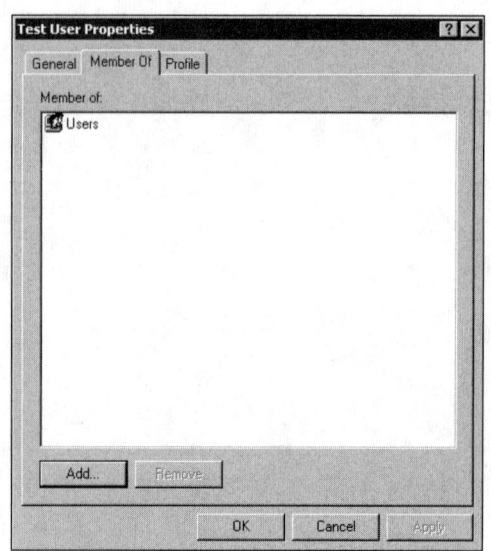

FIGURE 7.6
Test User Property page—Member Of tab.

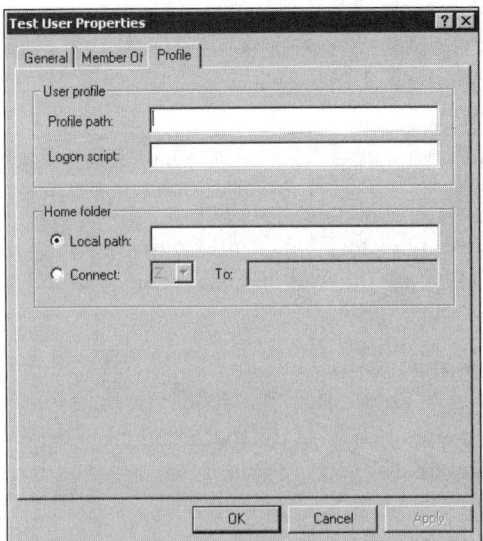

FIGURE 7.7
Test User Property page—Profile tab.

NOTE **%username%** When setting up a user's home directory you can use the following syntax to reference the location of his or her folder:

\\servername\sharename\ %username%

Using this syntax the system will automatically substitute the user's user name in place of the variable %username%.

Domain user accounts are created and managed through the Active Directory User and Computers snap-in of the MMC. The Active Directory Users and Computers snap-in can be accessed by clicking Start\Programs\Administrative Tools\Active Directory Users and Computers. You also can add the Active Directory Users and Computers snap-in to the MMC manually. Step by Step 7.2 demonstrates how to view the Active Directory Users and Computers snap-in from a custom MMC and create a new domain user account.

STEP BY STEP

7.2 Creating Domain User Accounts by Using the Active Directory Users and Computers Snap-in

This Step By Step assumes that your computer is running Windows 2000 Server configured as a domain controller.

1. Click Start/Run. In the Open dialog box, type **MMC** and click OK.

NOTE **Administration Snap-ins** Many administration snap-ins are available only if you install the services that they manage. For example, if you want to manage domain user accounts from a Windows 2000 Professional system, you need to install the Windows 2000 administration pack to the system. This can be found on the Windows 2000 installation CD in the \I386 folder. The administration pack is installed from a file named AdminPak.msi.

By default, this file is copied to the %winnt%\system32 directory on Windows 2000 Servers.

continues

continued

2. From the Console menu, click the Add/Remove Snap-in menu.

3. In the Add/Remove Snap-in window, click Add.

4. In the Add Standalone Snap-in window, highlight the Active Directory Users and Computers snap-in and click Add. Close the Add Standalone Snap-in and Add/Remove Snap-in window.

5. Open the Active Directory Users and Computers snap-in by clicking the plus sign beside the snap-in. Open the domain by clicking the plus sign beside the domain. Figure 7.8 shows the appropriate MMC screen.

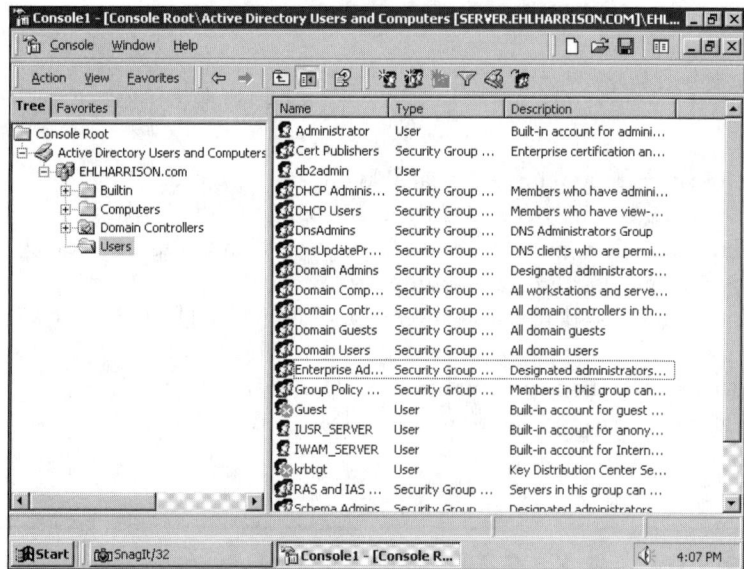

FIGURE 7.8
Active Directory Users and Computers snap-in.

6. To create a new domain user, right-click the "Users" folder. From the secondary menu, select New. When the mouse is over the New menu option, another menu will open with all of the different objects that you can create in the domain. Select User. This action will launch the New Object - User dialog box (see Figure 7.9).

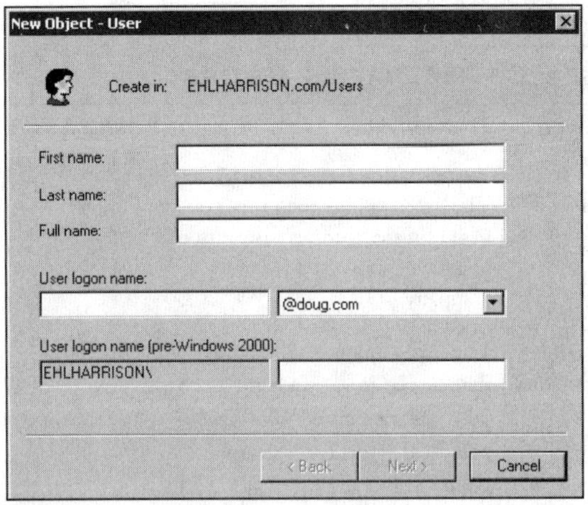

FIGURE 7.9
New Object - User dialog box—user name settings.

7. You need to enter the information for the user account.
Table 7.3 defines the information required and the values
used for this walkthrough.

TABLE 7.3

NEW USER CONFIGURATION OPTIONS

Configuration Setting	Description	Value for this Walkthrough
First name	The user's first name.	Doug
Last name	The user's last name.	Harrison
Full name	The user's complete name. This name must be unique within the folder in which you create the user account. Windows 2000 completes the option if you enter the first and last name. Windows 2000 displays this name in the folders in which the user account is located in Active Directory.	N/A (this should be filled in automatically)

continues

TABLE 7.3		*continued*
NEW USER CONFIGURATION OPTIONS		
Configuration Setting	*Description*	*Value for this Walkthrough*
User logon name	The user's unique logon name, based on the naming conventions you have established for your company.	DougH
User logon name (pre-Windows 2000)	The user's unique logon name that is used to log on from previous versions of Windows NT. By default this is set to the same value as the user logon name. (You will also hear this name referred to as a downlevel logon name.)	DougH

8. Once you have entered the user name options, click the Next button. You will now be required to specify password settings, as shown in Figure 7.10. Table 7.4 presents a list of the password options.

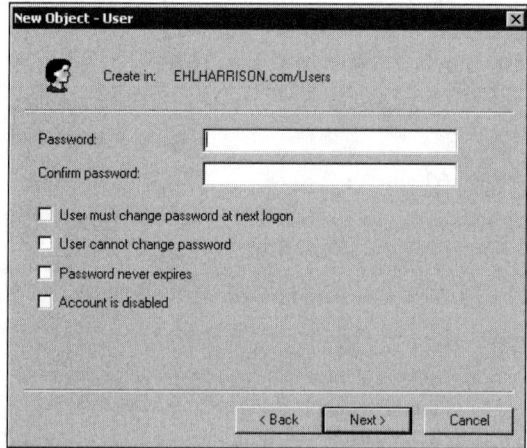

FIGURE 7.10
New Object - User dialog box—password settings.

TABLE 7.4

Password Configuration Options

Configuration Setting	Description	Value for this Walkthrough
Password/Confirm password	To ensure that you type the password correctly, you must enter the password in the "Password" and "Confirm password" fields. Be careful typing, as passwords are case-sensitive.	MyDogsNameIsSpot
User must change password at next logon	Select this checkbox if you want the user to change his password the first time he logs on. This ensures that the user is the only person who knows the password. Note: This option is disabled if the User cannot change password or the Password never expires options are checked.	Checked
User cannot change password	Select this checkbox if you never want the password to be changed for this user. This is a great option if multiple users use this account to access the system (and you don't want one of them to change the password so that the rest can't log on). Note: This option is disabled if you select the User must change the password at next logon option.	N/A
Password never expires	Select this checkbox if you never want the password to change. This setting will override policies that indicate passwords must be changed. Note: This option is disabled if you select the User must change the password at next logon option.	N/A
Account is disabled	Select this checkbox to prevent use of this user account.	Unchecked

continues

continued

9. After you enter the user password configuration, click Next. Windows 2000 will then confirm that you want to create the user. Click Finish to create the account.

After the user account is created, you might need to manage the account. Common management tasks are as follows:

◆ Resetting passwords

◆ Renaming accounts

◆ Deleting accounts

◆ Enabling accounts

◆ Unlocking accounts

◆ Changing group membership

◆ Modifying profile paths

◆ Modifying user home directory paths

All of these tasks are completed from the Active Directory Users and Computers snap-in of the MMC. Passwords can be reset for a user account by right-clicking on the user account and selecting Set Password from the secondary menu. You will also find the Rename and Delete options from the user account secondary menu, as shown in Figure 7.11.

Like local user accounts, renaming a user account enables an account to receive a new name and retain its security assignments and group membership. Deleting a user account will permanently remove the account from the system.

The remaining configuration options can be accessed by double-clicking the user account (or right-clicking the account and selecting Properties from the secondary menu). Domain user accounts have a large number of configuration options associated with them. The following section will review common configuration options.

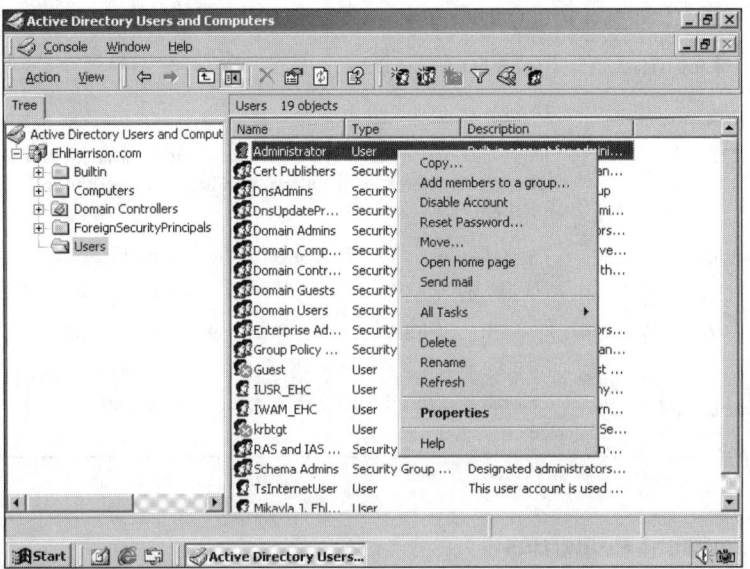

FIGURE 7.11
User account secondary menu.

Account Settings

A set of default properties is associated with each domain user account that you create. You can use these properties to define how users can access the network. After you create a domain user account, you need to configure the account.

Personal Properties

The most common tabs in the Properties dialog box that contain personal information about each user account are the General, Address, Telephones, and Organization tabs (note the tabs at the top of the user account Properties page in Figure 7.12).

Table 7.5 describes these four tabs.

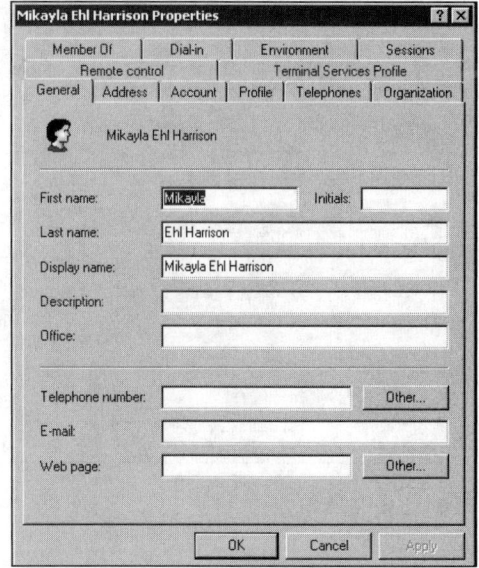

FIGURE 7.12
Domain user account Properties page—General tab.

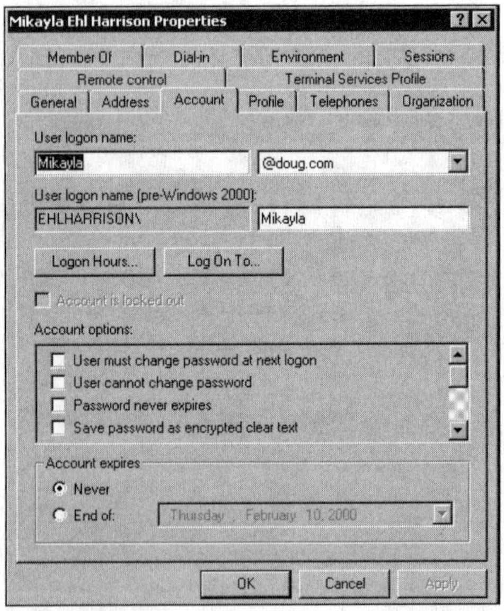

FIGURE 7.13
The Account tab.

TABLE 7.5

PERSONAL PROPERTIES TABS

Tab	Description
General	This tab contains the User's name, description, office location, telephone number, email address, web page, and telephone number(s).
Address	This tab contains the User's street address, post office box, city, state, postal code, and country.
Telephones	This tab contains telephone numbers (home, office, pager, etc.).
Organization	This tab contains the user's title, department, company, manager, and direct reports.

Account Properties

Figure 7.13 shows the Account tab of a user account Properties page.

From this tab you can manage a user's logon name, password settings, the hours during which the user can log on, and the computers from which the user can log on.

Setting logon hours gives administrators the ability to control when a user account is allowed to log on to the network. For example, if you know a user is going to access the network only during business hours, the account can be set to allow logon only during those hours.

Clicking the Logon Hours button launches the Logon Hours dialog box, as shown in Figure 7.14. In this dialog box you can set the hours when logon is allowed or denied.

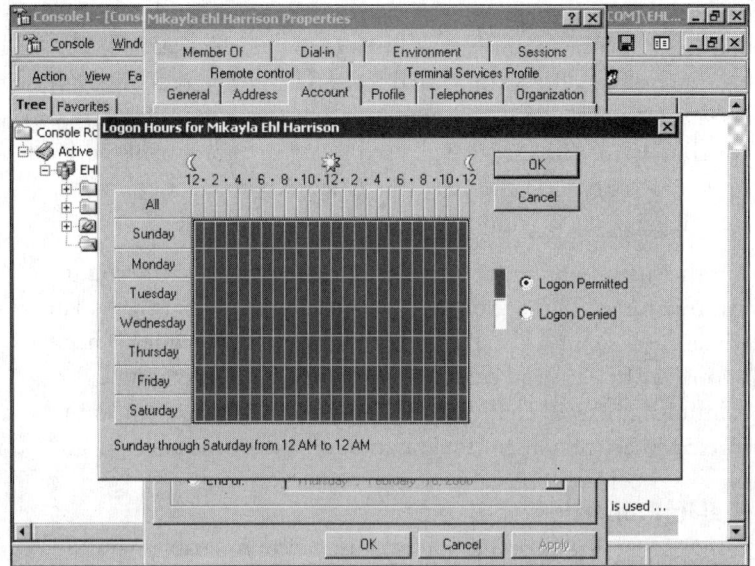

Logon Hours A security policy can be configured to automatically log users off when logon hours expire. This option is set through a Local or Group Policy.

The alternative is to allow connections to network resources on the domain to remain but to not allow new connections to be established.

FIGURE 7.14
The Logon Hours dialog box.

You also can restrict the computers from which users can log on. By clicking the Log On To button, you launch the dialog box shown in Figure 7.15.

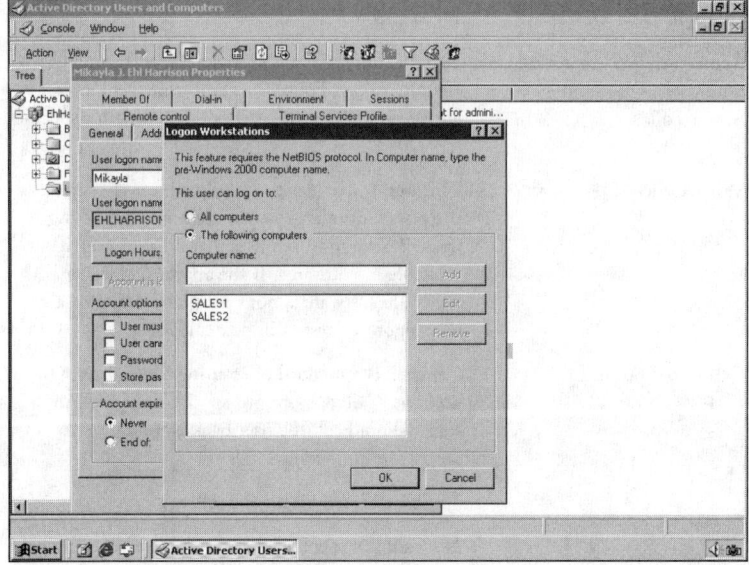

FIGURE 7.15
The Logon Workstations dialog box.

This enables you to list all of the computers from which a user is allowed to log on. As presented in Figure 7.15, the user Mikayla can log on from the SALES1 and SALES2 computers. This is an extremely powerful option if you have areas of your building from which only specific users are allowed to log on. You can also use this option to restrict specific users (the Guest account, for example) from logging on at stations throughout your network.

Another useful option found on the Account tab is the Account expires option. This option enables the administrator to set a date when the account will expire and no longer accept logons. This option is often used in environments that have contract staff. Administrators will configure the contractor's user account so that it remains active only for the duration of the contract.

Dial-in Properties

Configuring dial-in properties for a user account enables you to control how a user can connect to a network through a remote access server (i.e., a dial-up). Configuration settings can be managed from the Dial-in tab of a user account. Figure 7.16 shows the Dial-in properties tab, and Table 7.6 describes the setup options.

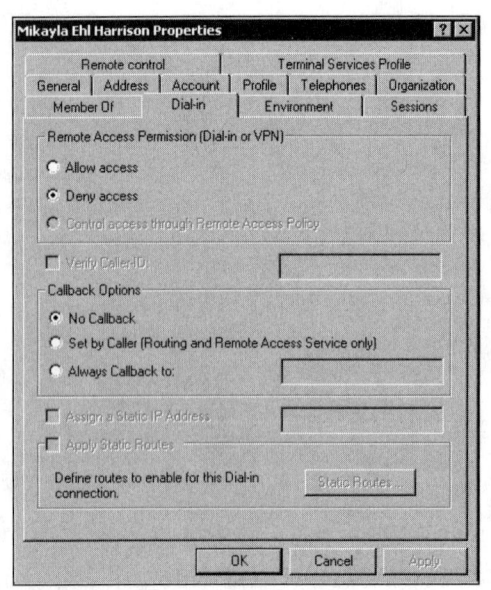

FIGURE 7.16
The Dial-in tab of the Properties dialog box.

TABLE 7.6

DIAL-IN PROPERTIES CONFIGURATION OPTIONS

Configuration Option	Description
Allow/Deny/or Control access through Remote Access Policy	The Default setting is Control Access through Remote Access Policy. The Allow or Deny options enable you to override the policy setting for specific users.
Verify Caller-ID	This option enables the administrator to specify the phone number that the user must be calling from. This option requires that caller ID service is available in your area. If the appropriate caller ID hardware/software is not configured properly, all user logon requests will be denied access.
Callback Options	Callback is a method of securing the dial-up account. Callback options specify that the RAS server should call the user back at a number to accept the connection.
	You have three options for callback.
	No Callback specifies that the RAS server will not call the user back at a specific number.

Configuration Option	*Description*
	Set by Caller specifies that the user will provide their phone number when they dial into the network. The RAS server will then call the user back at the number provided.
	Always Callback to specifies that the user will only be allowed to dial in from a specific phone number.
	Callback is an effective form of security, as the user must provide callback information (and, therefore, leave a paper trail as to the location they called from), or the user must be calling from a pre-determined phone number.
Assign a Static IP Address	If this property is enabled, you can assign a specific IP address to a user when a connection is made.
	This option is helpful if you track the activities of users when they dial into your network. Because you know the IP address of the user, you can track the systems and services that they access.
Apply Static Routes	With this property, you can restrict users to specific areas of your network (i.e., if you don't know routes to certain networks, you cannot request access to services on those networks).
	You can also define a series of static routes that are added to the routing table of remote access servers when a connection is made. This setting is designed for user accounts that Windows 2000 routers use for demand-dial routing.

Group Membership

Groups are used to simplify resource access. The Member Of tab enables you to manage the group membership of a user account. From this tab, you can click the Add or Remove buttons to modify group membership (see Figure 7.17).

Profile

The Profile tab enables you to configure the user profile (profile path and logon script) and home folder location (see Figure 7.18). User profiles and logon scripts are covered in Chapter 5, "Configuring and Troubleshooting the Desktop Environment" and user home directories are covered in Chapter 2 "Implementing and Conducting Administration of Resources."

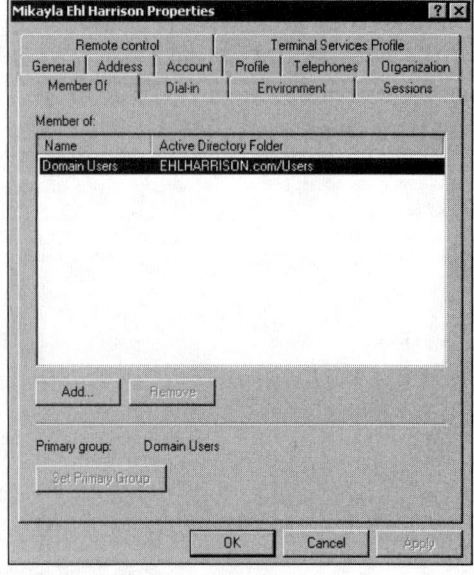

FIGURE 7.17
User account Properties page—Member Of tab.

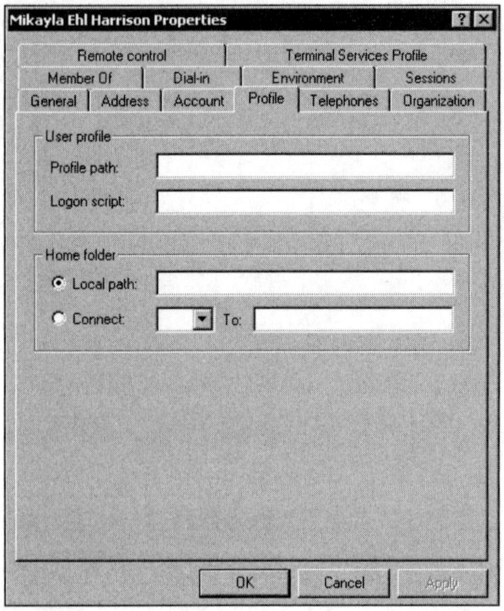

FIGURE 7.18
User account Properties page—Profile tab.

Groups

Groups are used to simplify the overall management of accounts in your environment. In most environments, users can be grouped into categories of user account (accountants, sales people, etc.). These categories of user account generally define common access needs for groups of users in your environment. To assist in the management of access needs for these users, Windows 2000 supports the creation of groups within its account database. Group objects can then be granted access to resources. Being a member of a group automatically grants you the same rights as the group object. If you have memberships in multiple groups, the rights associated with each group will be combined (how your effective rights are calculated depends on the type of rights being combined). Depending on the type of group, you also can make groups members of other groups.

Group Types

In the Windows 2000 domain environment, two types of groups are supported. The group type determines the tasks that you manage with the group. Both types of groups are stored in the Active Directory database, so they can be accessed from anywhere on the network.

The first group type is called a Security group. Security groups are used to organize user accounts so that the group of users can be given permission to the resource.

The second group type is called a Distribution group. Distribution groups are used to organize users into groups for non-security related purposes. For example, if a group of users needs to have email messages sent to them, a Distribution group is appropriate. In this example, an Active Directory-aware email package would be used to send a message to all users in the Distribution group. Security groups can be used for this purpose, as well.

The main difference between a Security group and a Distribution group is that membership in a Distribution group is not added to a user's access token when he or she logs into the network. The goal of Distribution groups is to make the logon token of users as small (and efficient) as possible.

Distribution groups do not exist on a member server or workstations. Groups created on these machines are Security groups by default.

Group Scope

The scope of a group controls where a group can be used within your environment. Specifically, group scope defines the following characteristics of a group:

◆ The domains in which you can use the group to grant permissions

◆ The domains from which you can add members to the group

◆ The domains in which you can nest the groups within other groups

The following sections examine the three elements of the different groups. During this discussion, we need to distinguish between Windows 2000 domains that are in mixed or native mode. Active Directory has been designed to support a phased implementation. Active Directory domains can be configured to support a mixed mode or native mode. In mixed mode, domains can emulate a Windows NT environment so you can synchronize the directory database with legacy Windows NT Backup domain controllers. This enables you to install Windows 2000 Active Directory and slowly install the complete Windows 2000 with minimal disruption to your users. Native mode domains support only Windows 2000-based domain controllers.

Because mixed mode environments must be compatible with Windows NT domains, the groups act the same as in Windows NT. In native mode, however, Windows 2000 supports new groups (Domain Local and Universal groups) and supports greater nesting of groups. The following section assumes that you are working in a Windows 2000 domain environment configured in native mode.

Global Groups

Table 7.7 presents the characteristics of a Global group. The most common use of Global groups is to organize users who share similar network access requirements.

TABLE 7.7

CHARACTERISTICS OF A GLOBAL GROUP

Characteristic	How a Global Group Can Be Used
The domains in which you can use the group to grant permissions.	You can use Global groups to assign permission to gain access to resources that are located in any domain.
The domains from which you can add members to the group.	You can add user accounts and Global groups only from the domain in which you create the Global group.
The domains in which you can nest the groups within other groups.	You can add Global groups to another Global group within the same domain or to Universal groups and Domain Local groups in the same domain or other domains.

Domain Local Groups

Table 7.8 presents the characteristics of a Domain Local group. The most common use of a Domain Local group is to assign permissions to resources. Resources can be located anywhere in the domain.

TABLE 7.8

CHARACTERISTICS OF A DOMAIN LOCAL GROUP

Characteristic	How a Domain Local Group Can Be Used
The domains in which you can use the group to grant permissions.	You can use a Domain Local group to assign permissions to gain access to resources that are located in the same domain in which you create the Domain Local group.
The domains from which you can add members to the group.	You can add user accounts, Universal groups, and Global groups from any domain.
The domains in which you can nest the groups within other groups.	You cannot add a Domain Local group to any group in any other domain.

Local Groups

Table 7.9 presents the characteristics of a Local group. The most common use of a Local group is to assign permissions to resources on a workstation or member server.

TABLE 7.9

CHARACTERISTICS OF A LOCAL GROUP

Characteristic	How a Domain Local Group Can Be Used
The domains in which you can use the group to grant permissions.	You can use a Local group only to assign permissions to gain access to resources located on the physical system on which the group has been created.
The domains from which you can add members to the group.	You can add user accounts, Universal groups, and Global groups from any domain.
The domains in which you can nest the groups within other groups.	You cannot add a Local group to any group in any domain.

Microsoft does not recommend using Local groups if you are in a domain environment. You should use Domain Local groups instead. Domain Local groups enable centralized management of the group; therefore, you should limit the use of Local groups to systems in a workgroup environment.

Universal Groups

Table 7.10 presents the characteristics of a Universal group. The most common use of a Universal group is to assign permissions to resources in multiple domains.

TABLE 7.10

CHARACTERISTICS OF A UNIVERSAL GROUP

Characteristic	How a Universal Group Can Be Used
The domains in which you can use the group to grant permissions.	You can use a Universal group to assign permissions to gain access to resources that are located in any domain.
The domains from which you can add members to the group.	You can add user accounts, Universal groups, and Global groups from any domain.
The domains in which you can nest the groups within other groups.	You can add a Universal group to Domain Local or Universal groups in any domain.

After you create your groups, you can convert them if necessary. The trick to converting groups is to evaluate whether or not the target group you want to convert to supports the current members of your group. In many instances, you might find that a group currently has members that are not compatible with the type of group that you want to convert to. To convert a group's type, you need to access the properties of the group and change the type from the General tab.

Implementation Strategies

Windows 2000 groups give network administrators a large number of options regarding the use of groups. You need to assess your environment to determine the most effective strategy for you.

If you are in a single domain environment, for example, you can use Global groups to organize your users into logical groupings and then create Local groups to provide access to resources (i.e., assign permissions to the Domain Local groups). You would then make the appropriate Global groups members in the Domain Local group with access to required resources.

In multi-domain environments, you might find that Universal groups also can be used. Under this scenario, you would create Global groups in each domain to organize users into logical groupings. You would then make the Global group from each domain a member of the Universal group. Domain Local groups would then be created in each location in which resources exist and the Local group would be given permission to the resource. The Universal group would then be made a member of the Local group.

When determining your approach to groups, the following strategy will simplify things:

1. Organize users based on administrative needs, such as job responsibilities. Create a Global group for each grouping of users. Add the users to the appropriate Global group(s).

2. Identify the resources to which users need to gain access. Create a Domain Local group for each resource. Assign the appropriate permission to each Domain Local group.

3. Make all Global groups that require access to a resource a member of the appropriate Domain Local group.

4. If a resource is spread over a number of domains, consider using a Universal group. Follow steps 1 through 3 but instead of making the Global group a member of the Domain Local

group, make it a member of a Universal group. Then make the Universal group a member of the Domain Local groups with permission to the resources.

Microsoft uses the acronym A-G-DL-P to describe the Windows 2000 group strategy. The acronym states that accounts (A) should be organized into Global (G) groups, Global groups are placed in Domain Local (DL) groups, and Domain Local groups are given permission (P) to resources.

Creating Local Groups

Local groups are managed from the Computer Management Microsoft Management Console (MMC) snap-in. The Computer Management snap-in can be started by clicking Start\Programs\Administrative Tools\Computer Management. You also can add the Computer Management snap-in to the MMC. Step by Step 7.3 demonstrates how to view the Computer Management snap-in from a custom MMC, and create a new local group.

STEP BY STEP

7.3 Creating Local Groups by Using the Computer Management Snap-in

1. Click Start/Run. In the Open dialog box, type MMC and click OK.

2. From the Console menu, click the Add/Remove Snap-in menu.

3. In the Add/Remove Snap-in window, click Add.

4. In the Add Standalone Snap-in window, highlight the Computer Management snap-in and click Add.

5. In the Computer Management window, select either the local computer or a remote system (if you select a remote system, you need to have permission to share resources on the remote system). Remember that Local groups need to be created on the system where the resources reside. Click OK in the Computer Management window.

continues

EXAM TIP

Remember the AGDLP Strategy for Groups Expect questions regarding the use of groups in the Windows 2000 environment.

NOTE

Universal Group Membership Do not make users members of a Universal group directly. Membership in Universal groups is tracked in the Active Directory Global Catalog server(s). Assigning membership directly to users can generate excess Active Directory replication traffic.

NOTE

Limit the Use of Universal Groups Microsoft suggests that you limit the use of Universal groups, as they potentially can generate a great deal of replication and query traffic to the Global Catalog server(s).

continued

6. Close the Add Standalone Snap-in and Add/Remove Snap-in windows.

7. Open the Computer Management snap-in by clicking the plus sign beside the snap-in. Open the Local Users and Groups node of the Computer Management snap-in. From this location, you can create and manage groups on your system. Figure 7.19 shows the appropriate MMC screen.

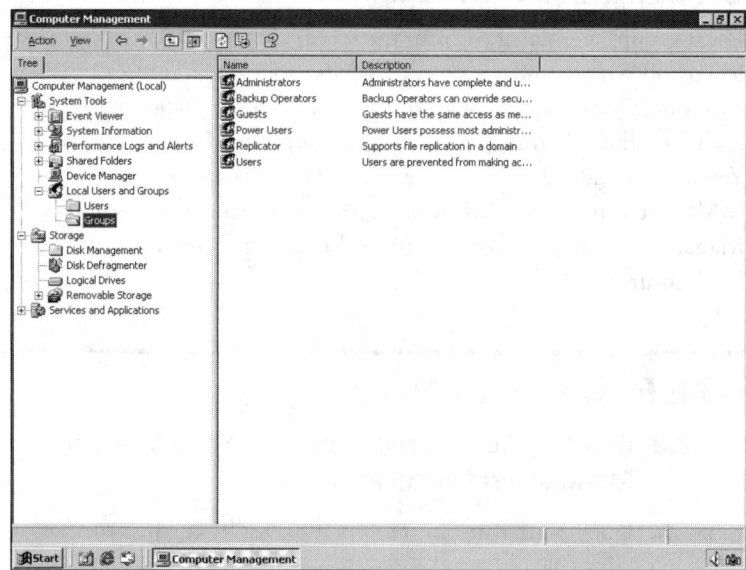

FIGURE 7.19
Computer Management snap-in—Local Users and Groups.

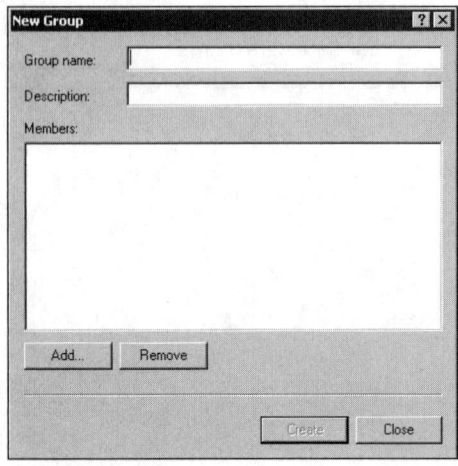

FIGURE 7.20
The New Group dialog box.

8. To create a new Local group, right-click the "Groups" folder in the Local Users and Groups node. From the secondary menu, select New Group. This action launches the New Group dialog box (see Figure 7.20).

9. Enter the name of the group (call the group TEST for the purposes of this walkthrough); enter a brief description.

10. Click the Add button to add users to the group. In the Select Users or Groups dialog box, select the Administrator user account and click Add. Then select the Authenticated Users group and click Add. This will add the Administrator user account and Authenticated Users group to the membership list of the new group. Click OK to close the Select Users or Groups dialog box.

11. After you enter the group configuration, click Create. The New Group dialog box will reappear so that you can create another group. Click Close to close the dialog box.

To add additional members, you can right-click the group and select Add to Group from the secondary menu.

You can rename and delete a group by right-clicking it and selecting the appropriate option from the secondary menu. If you rename a group, the name of the group is changed and the security assignments will be retained. If you delete a group, all references to it will be deleted and its security assignments will be lost (the objects that represent the members of the group will not be deleted).

Creating Domain Local, Global, and Universal Groups

Domain Local groups are very similar to Local groups. The primary difference between a Local group and a Domain group is that a Domain group can be used to gain access to resources throughout a domain environment.

Domain groups are created and managed through the Active Directory User and Computers snap-in of the MMC. The Active Directory Users and Computers snap-in can be accessed by clicking Start\Programs\Administrative Tools\Active Directory Users and Computers. You also can add the Active Directory Users and Computers snap-in to the MMC manually. Step by Step 7.4 demonstrates how to view the Active Directory Users and Computers snap-in and create a new Domain group account.

STEP BY STEP

7.4 Creating Group Accounts by Using the Active Directory Users and Computers Snap-in

1. Click Start/Run. In the Open dialog box, type MMC and click OK.

2. From the Console menu, click the Add/Remove Snap-in menu.

3. In the Add/Remove Snap-in window, click Add.

4. In the Add Standalone Snap-in window, highlight the Active Directory Users and Computers snap-in and click Add. Close the Add Standalone Snap-in and Add/Remove Snap-in windows.

5. Open the Active Directory Users and Computers snap-in by clicking the plus sign beside the snap-in. Open the domain by clicking the plus sign beside the domain. Figure 7.21 shows the appropriate MMC screen.

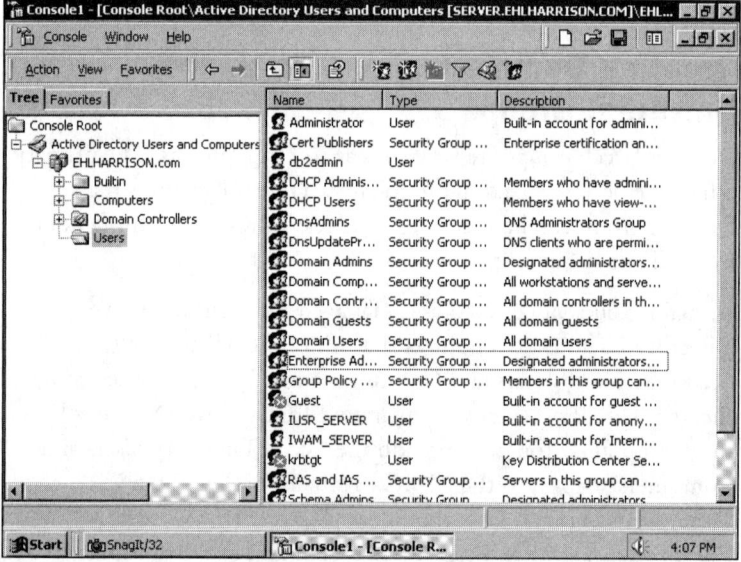

FIGURE 7.21
Active Directory Users and Computers snap-in.

6. To create a new group, right-click the "Users" folder. From the secondary menu, select New. When the mouse is over the New menu option, another menu will open, showing you all of the different objects that you can create in the domain. Select Group. This action will launch the New Object-Group dialog box (see Figure 7.22).

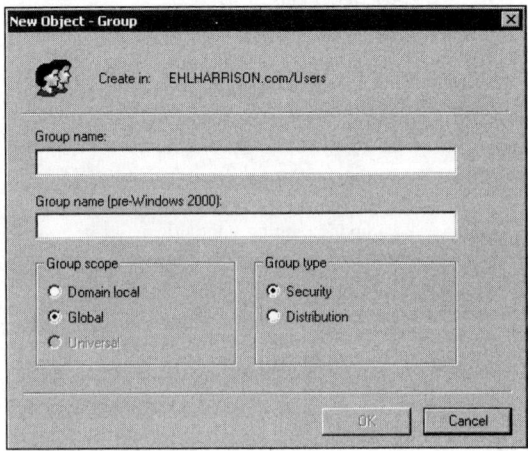

FIGURE 7.22
New Object-Group dialog box.

7. You need to enter the information for the group account. Table 7.11 defines the information required and the values used for this walkthrough.

TABLE 7.11

NEW GROUP CONFIGURATION OPTIONS

Configuration Setting	Description	Value for this Walkthrough
Group name	The name of the Group.	DL1-Security

continues

TABLE 7.11 *continued*		
NEW GROUP CONFIGURATION OPTIONS		
Configuration Setting	*Description*	*Value for this Walkthrough*
Group name (pre-Windows 2000)	A pre-Windows 2000 group name. This option is used for compatibility with legacy Windows NT environments. By default the pre-Windows 2000 name will be the same as the Windows 2000 group name. In some instances, however, you might want to configure it as a different name (e.g., if you are changing your company naming standards while moving from Windows NT to Windows 2000).	This option will be filled out automatically
Group scope	You can set up the group as a Domain Local, Global, or Universal group. The Universal group option will not be available if the domain is in mixed mode.	Select Domain local
Group type	You can configure the group as a Security or Distribution group.	Select Security

8. After you enter the options listed in Table 7.11, click OK to create the group.

9. Repeat steps 6-8 to create the following groups:

◆ Group name = G1-Security; Group scope = Global; Group type = Security

◆ Group name = U1-Security; Group scope = Universal; Group type = Security

◆ Group name = DL1-Distribution; Group scope = Domain Local; Group type = Distribution

◆ Group name = G1-Distribution; Group scope = Global; Group type = Distribution

◆ Group name = U1-Distribution; Group scope = Universal; Group type = Distribution

To manage groups after they have been created, right-click the group and select Properties from the secondary menu. From the Members and Member Of tabs, you can manage who is a member of the group and what groups the group is a member of.

From the secondary menu, you can also rename and delete a group. If you rename the group, it retains its security assignments on the network. If you delete a group, all references to the group will be deleted from the network. Deleting a group will not affect the members of the group (i.e., if you delete a group that has a user named Sally as one of its members, Sally's user account is not affected if the group is deleted).

Built-in Groups

Windows 2000 systems have a number of built-in groups associated with them. These groups provide a powerful tool for the management of resources on the local system/domain. Membership in one (or more) of these groups gives users rights to access (and manage) the local operating system, depending on the group. Each group is, by default, assigned a useful collection of rights and privileges.

User rights are rules that determine the actions a user can perform on a computer (user rights are discussed in detail in later sections). In addition, user rights control whether a user can log on to a computer directly (locally) or over the network, add users to local groups, delete users, and so on. Built-in groups have sets of user rights already assigned. Administrators usually assign user rights by adding a user account to one of the built-in groups or by creating a new group and assigning specific user rights to that group. Users who are subsequently added to a group are automatically granted all user rights assigned to the group account. User rights are managed by using Group Policy.

To gain an understanding of how groups and user rights relate, the following section provides a review of the privileges that have been assigned to each built-in group. We will then look at where the built-in groups receive their default configuration.

Built-in Local Groups

Built-in Local groups are used to manage Windows 2000 Professional workstation and Windows 2000 Servers (configured as a member server). The six built-in Local groups added during installation are as follows:

◆ Administrators

◆ Backup Operators

◆ Guests

◆ Power Users

◆ Replicator

◆ Users

Each of the following sections describes the built-in Local groups.

Administrators Group

Membership in the Administrators groups enables a user to manage all aspects of the local operating system. Members of this group have the ability to manage user accounts, load and unload system drivers, and perform backups and restores of file systems.

Users with administrative authority have a great deal of privilege on a system. Membership does not, however, give the user automatic access to all resources on the system. If a user with administrative rights tries to access a resource that he or she does not have permission to use he or she will receive an access denied message. The user, however, does have the ability to take ownership of any resource, if the need arises. Once the user owns a resource he or she can change the permissions on the resource to allow access.

Membership in the Administrators groups should be managed very closely. Administrator access to the system should be limited to individuals who perform the following types of tasks:

◆ Install the operating system and components (such as hardware drivers, system services, and so on)

◆ Install Service Packs and Windows Packs

◆ Upgrade the operating system

◆ Repair the operating system

◆ Configure critical operating system parameters (such as password policy, access control, audit policy, kernel mode driver configuration, and so on)

Backup Operators Group

Regular users have the ability to back up and restore files that they have permission to access without being part of this group. In most environments, however, backups are managed centrally so that they can be completed at set intervals with a high degree of reliability.

Membership in the Backup Operators group enables a user to back up and restore file systems regardless of permissions, ownership, encryption settings, or audit settings. Membership in this group enables you to assign users the authority to back up file systems without having to assign the users specific permissions to access the resources.

Guests

The Guests group is used to give someone limited access to resources on the system. The Guest account is automatically added to this group. The Guest account can be removed from the Guests group if you want.

Two additional Guest accounts are added if you have installed the Internet Information Server (IIS) on your system (ISUR_computername and IWAM_computername). These accounts are used to support anonymous access to the IIS content.

Power Users Group

Members of the Power Users group have more permission than members of the Users group and less permission than members of the Administrators group. Power Users can perform most operating system tasks.

Members of the Power Users group can perform the following tasks:

◆ Install and remove applications that can be run by all users (except for the software that can be removed only by an administrator).

NOTE

The Administrator User Account and the Administrators Group
The Administrator user account is automatically made a member of the Administrators group. The Administrator user account cannot be removed from this group.

You also should note that if the computer is a member of a domain, the Domain Admins group is automatically added to the local Administrators group.

◆ Customize system-wide resources, including printers, date/time, power options, and other Control Panel resources.

◆ Share resources on the local system.

Members of the Powers Users group do not have permission to add themselves to the Administrators group, and they do not have access to the data of other users on a NTFS volume.

In addition, members of the Power Users group have the ability to create and administer user accounts and groups. Power Users are limited to managing the accounts they have created and, therefore, cannot manage the Administrators group or Administrator user account. Power Users can, however, manage membership of the Power Users group.

Replicator

The Replicator group is a group used by the Windows 2000 Directory Replication Service to replicate content between domain controllers.

Users

By default all users (with the exception of the built-in Administrator and Guest accounts) created on the local system are made members of the Users group. The Users group provides the user with all of the necessary rights to run the computer as an end user.

If the computer is a member of a domain, the domain user and interactive users will be members of this group as well. These built-in groups will be discussed later in this chapter.

Ideally, all users will be able to run applications that have been installed on the local system by the administrator or by the members of the Power Users group. Users will not be able to run applications that have been installed on the local system by other users.

In addition, on volumes formatted with NTFS, members of the Users group are only able to access files that they have permission to use. For this reason, users are not able to see one another's files and folders. The default security configuration of Windows 2000 limits the ability of a user to modify operating system files (i.e., a user cannot modify system critical files and configuration settings).

N O T E **Legacy Applications and the Power Users Group** Power Users might not be able to install some applications written for previous versions of Windows, as these applications do not utilize the Windows 2000 installer service and, therefore, do not operate from within its security context.

N O T E **Legacy Application Support** Users will not be able to run some applications written for previous versions of Windows because most of these applications were not designed with knowledge of Windows 2000 security. Members of the Power Users group should be able to run applications written for previous versions of Windows.

Built-in Domain Local Groups

Built-in Domain Local groups are used to provide users with rights and permissions to perform tasks on domain controllers in a domain environment. The nine built-in local groups added during installation are as follows:

◆ Account Operators

◆ Server Operators

◆ Print Operators

◆ Administrators

◆ Backup Operators

◆ Replicator

◆ Pre-Windows 2000 Compatible Access

◆ Guests

◆ Users

The following sections describe the built-in Domain Local groups.

Account Operators

Members of the Account Operators group can create, delete, and modify user accounts and groups. Members cannot modify the Administrators group, Server Operators, Printer Operators, or Account Operators groups.

Server Operators

Members of the Server Operators group can manage disk resources, back up and restore file system resources, manage file system resources and manage system services and software.

Print Operators

Members of the Print Operators group can manage print resources. Members of this group also have the ability to add and remove printers.

Administrators

Membership in the Administrators groups enables a user to manage all aspects of the local operating system. Members of this group have the ability to manage user accounts, load and unload system drivers, and perform backups and restores of file systems.

Users with administrative authority have a great deal of privilege on a system. Membership does not, however, give the user automatic access to all resources on the system. If a user with administrative rights tries to access a resource that he or she does not have permission to use, he or she will get an access denied message. The user, however, does have the ability to take ownership of any resource, if the need arises. Once the user owns a resource he or she can change the permissions on the resource to allow access.

Membership in the Administrators groups should be managed very closely. Administrator access to the system should be limited to individuals who perform the following types of tasks:

NOTE

The Administrator User Account and the Administrators Group The Administrator user account is automatically made a member of the Administrators group. The Administrator user account cannot be removed from this group.

You also should note that the Domain Admins group is automatically added to the local Administrators group.

◆ Install the operating system and components (such as hardware drivers, system services, and so on)

◆ Install Service Packs and Windows Packs

◆ Upgrade the operating system

◆ Repair the operating system

◆ Configure critical operating system parameters (such as password policy, access control, audit policy, kernel mode driver configuration, and so on)

Guests

The Guests group is used to give someone limited access to resources on the system. The Guest account is automatically added to this group (but can be removed). You also will find that the Domain Guests and IIS Guest accounts are also made members of this group by default (and can be removed, if desired).

Replicator

The Replicator group is a group used by the Windows 2000 Directory Replication Service to replicate content between domain controllers.

Pre-Windows 2000 Compatible Access

Windows 2000 does not enable accounts logged on with anonymous access to view group membership, whereas Windows NT 4.0 did enable such operations. For compatibility reasons, you might want to add the Everyone group to the Pre-Windows 2000 Compatible

Access group to support legacy Windows NT resources in your environment. By adding the Everyone group to this group, you weaken the Windows 2000 security configuration, so legacy Windows NT resources can view group information before users are authenticated.

Backup Operators

Regular users have the ability to back up and restore files that they have permission to access without being part of the Backup Operators group. In most environments, however, backups are managed centrally so that they can be completed at set intervals with a high degree of reliability.

Membership in the Backup Operators group enables a user to back up and restore file systems regardless of permissions, ownership, encryption settings, or audit settings. Membership in this group enables you to assign users the authority to back up file systems without having to assign the users specific permissions to access the resources.

Users

The Users group includes domain user, interactive, and authenticated users as members. This group is used to give users rights to access the local operating system.

Ideally, all users will be able to run applications that have been installed on the local system by the Administrator or Server Operators groups. Users will not be able to run applications that have been installed on the local system by other users.

In addition, on volumes formatted with NTFS, members of the Users group are only able to access files that they have permission to use. For this reason, users are not able to see one another's files and folders. The default security configuration of Windows 2000 limits the ability of users to modify operating system files (i.e., a user cannot modify system critical files and configuration settings).

Built-in Global Groups

Built-in Global groups are used to provide users with rights and permissions to perform tasks on domain controllers in the domain environment. By default, Windows 2000 automatically adds members to some built-in Global groups. This enables Windows

NOTE   **Pre-Windows 2000 Compatible Access**   The Active Directory Installation Wizard offers you the opportunity to weaken dial-in permissions during install. Selecting this option will add the Everyone group to the Pre-Windows 2000 Compatible Access group.

N O T E

Built-in Global Groups There are a number of additional built-in Global groups in the Windows 2000 environment (for example, Cert Publishers, DnsAdmins, DnsUpdateProxy, Domain Computers, Domain Controllers, Schema Administrators, RAS, and IAS Servers). Each of these groups is used to manage access to a specific set of services and are beyond the scope of this book.

2000 to control the default administrative structure used to manage the Windows 2000 environment. Membership in these groups should be managed very carefully.

Four built-in Global groups added during installation are as follows:

◆ Domain Users

◆ Domain Admins

◆ Domain Guests

◆ Enterprise Admins

Domain Users

Windows 2000 automatically adds the Domain Users Global group to the Users Domain Local group. By default, the Administrator account is initially a member of the Domain Users Global group. Windows 2000 will automatically add each newly created Domain User account to the Domain Users Global group.

Domain Admin

Windows 2000 automatically adds the Domain Admins Global group to the Administrator Domain Local group so that the domain administrator can manage all local systems in the domain. This group is also added to the local Administrators group of all computers that are part of the domain. This gives the Domain Admins the capability to manage systems anywhere in the domain.

Domain Guests

Windows 2000 automatically adds the Domain Guests Global group to the Guests Domain Local group. By default, the Guest account is a member.

Enterprise Admin

You can add user accounts to the Enterprise Admin Global group who require administrator control over the entire network. Windows 2000 automatically adds the Enterprise Admin group to the Domain Admin Global group for all domains in the enterprise.

Special Groups

Windows 2000 supports a number of built-in groups that can be used for a variety of purposes. You cannot change the membership

of these groups; the assignment happens as an internal part of
Windows 2000.

Everyone

The Everyone group includes all current network users, including
guests and users from other domains. Whenever a user logs on to
the network, Windows 2000 automatically adds the user to the
Everyone group.

Authenticated Users

The Authenticated Users group includes all users with valid
user accounts on the computer or Active Directory. Use the
Authenticated User group instead of the Everyone group to
prevent anonymous access to a resource.

Creator Owner

The Creator Owner group includes the user account for the user
who created or took ownership of a resource. If a member of the
Administrators group creates a resource, the Administrators group
is the owner of the resource.

Interactive

The Interactive group includes all users currently logged on to a
particular computer. Whenever a user logs on to a system, they are
automatically added to the Interactive group.

Network

The Network group includes users currently accessing a
given resource over the network (as opposed to users who
access a resource by logging on locally to the computer on which
the resource resides). Whenever users access a given resource
over the network, Windows 2000 automatically adds them to
the Network group.

> **WARNING**
>
> **Use Authenticated Users when Granting Permissions** The default permissions used in Windows 2000 are that the Everyone group is given full control to resources. This assignment should be changed to the Authenticated Users group as soon as resources are created.

User Rights

In the previous section, you read about the rights that each of the
built-in groups has on a Windows 2000 Professional computer.
These groups receive their rights from a set of local user rights.
Local user rights can be modified, if need be.

You can view the current configuration of your system's local user rights from the Microsoft Management Console snap-in called Local Computer Policy.

Step by Step 7.5 provides details on how to view the Local Computer Policy settings.

STEP BY STEP

7.5 Viewing the Local Computer Policy Settings

1. From the Start menu, Select Run.

2. From the Open prompt of the Run dialog box, type MMC and click OK.

3. From the Console menu, select Add and Remove Snap-in.

4. In the Add/Remove Snap-in dialog box, click the Add button.

5. In the Add Standalone Snap-in dialog box, scroll down to the Group Policy snap-in. Highlight the Group Policy and click the Add button.

6. In the Select Group Policy Object window, click Finish.

7. In the Add Standalone Snap-in dialog box, click Close.

8. In the Add/Remove Snap-in dialog box, click the OK button. You will now have a Console window open with the Local Computer Policy snap-in enabled, as shown in Figure 7.23.

9. Click the plus sign on the Local Computer Policy object.

10. Click the plus sign on the Computer Configuration object.

11. Click the plus sign on the Windows Settings object.

12. Click the plus sign on the Security Setting object.

13. Click the plus sign on the Local Policies object.

14. Click the User Rights Assignments object.

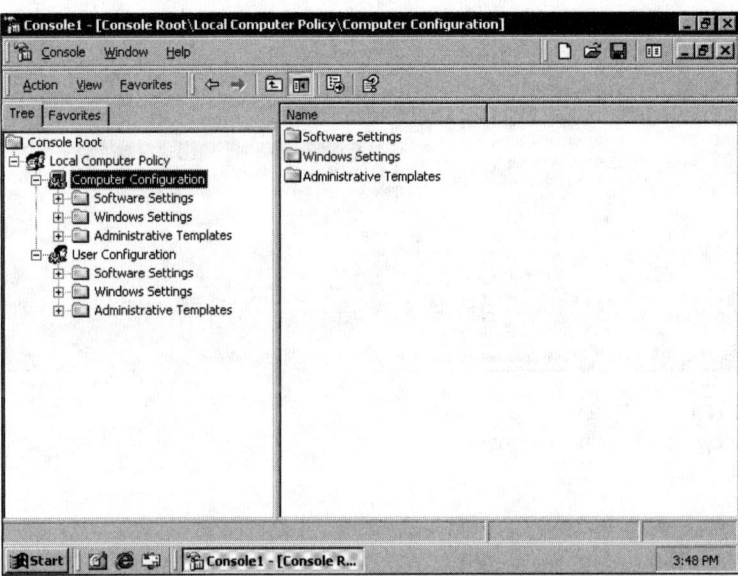

FIGURE 7.23
The Local Computer Policy snap-in.

You can now view the individual local user rights currently
configured on your system in the right-hand window of the console.
To see the rights' assignments for each policy, double-click the
policy. Figure 7.24 shows the users granted the right to log on
locally. Table 7.12 provides a description of the default user rights
assigned to the built-in Windows 2000 groups on Windows 2000
Professional (this is not a complete listing of all user rights, just the
most commonly used).

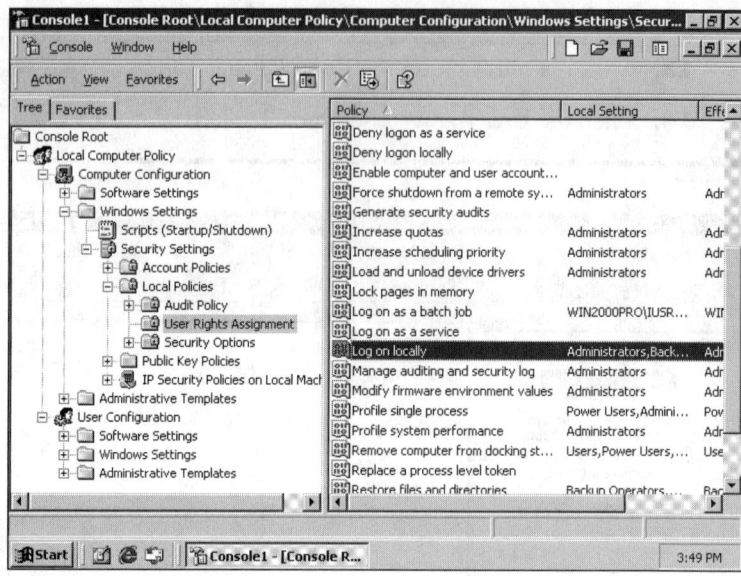

FIGURE 7.24
Viewing a specific user right.

TABLE 7.12

WINDOWS 2000 PROFESSIONAL USER RIGHTS

User Right	Description	Granted to
Access this computer from the network	Having this user right enables you to access resources from the network (for example, attach to a network share being hosted from a computer). Having this right does not give you the ability to access resources that your user account has not been given permission to use.	Everyone, User, Power Users, Backup Operators, Administrators

User Right	Description	Granted to
Back up files and directories	This user right enables users to back up file system resources regardless of permissions held by the user. Most users can only back up files that they have permission to use or own. This does not lend itself to the centralized management of backups.	Backup Operators, Administrators
Bypass traverse checking	This right enables a user to access a file resource deep in a directory structure even if the user does not have permission to the file's parent directory.	Everyone, Users, Power Users, Backup Operators, Administrators
Change the system time	This user right enables a user to change system time.	Power Users, Administrators
Create a pagefile	The user right enables a user to configure the virtual memory management of a system.	Administrators
Deny access to this computer from the network	This user right (or the lack of a right, as the case might be) restricts a user from accessing this computer over the network regardless of group membership. For example, the Joe user account has been granted the right to access this computer from the network through his membership in the Users group. If we wanted to override Joe's ability to access this computer from the network, we could explicitly restrict Joe from doing so by granting him this user right. This is a very powerful right for system and service accounts. Typically you do not want people using these accounts to access your systems over the network.	

continues

TABLE 7.12	*continued*

WINDOWS 2000 PROFESSIONAL USER RIGHTS

User Right	*Description*	*Granted to*
Deny logon locally	This user right explicitly restricts a user from logging onto a system from the local console.	
Force shutdown from a remote system	This user right enables a user to remotely shut down a system by using a remote shutdown utility (you can find the shutdown utility in the Windows 2000 Resource Kit).	Administrators
Increase quotas	This user right enables users to modify quota settings for NTFS-formatted partitions.	Administrators
Increase scheduling priority	This user right enables you to reschedule jobs that have been submitted to the scheduling service.	Administrators
Load and unload device drivers	This user right enables you to load and unload device drivers.	Administrators
Log on locally	This user right enables you to log on at the computer from the local computer console.	Guest, Users, Power Users, Backup Operators, Administrators
Manage auditing and security log	This user right enables a user to specify what type of resource access will by audited.	Administrators
Remove computer from docking station	This user right enables a user to undock a laptop from its docking station.	Users, Power Users, Administrators
Restore files and directories	This user right enables users to restore a backup of a file system of permissions held by the user.	Backup Operators, Administrators
Shut down the system	This user right enables a user to shut down the local system.	Users, Power Users, Backup Operators, Administrators

User Right	Description	Granted to
Take ownership of files or other objects	This user right enables a user to take ownership of files, directories, printers, and other objects on the computer. This right supersedes permissions protecting objects.	Administrators

When determining what group to add a particular user account to, remember the default assignments. If a group exists that has the rights required by a user, add them to that group. If a group does not exist with the appropriate privileges, create a new one. Be careful when assigning group membership: Do not use groups with too many rights; only give users the rights they need to get the job done (no more, no less).

It is helpful to remember the default rights assignments found in the built-in groups by default. Default rights assignments for Windows 2000 Professional are summarized in Table 7.13.

> **WARNING**
>
> **Windows 2000 Server versus Professional** By default, the Users and Guests groups have the capability to log on to Windows 2000 Professional and Windows 2000 Server (configured as stand-alone or member servers). This could be a potential security risk, as anyone with a valid user account can log on to your server(s).

TABLE 7.13

WINDOWS 2000 PROFESSIONAL DEFAULT RIGHTS ASSIGNMENTS

Right	Admin	Power Users	Users	Guests	Everyone	Backup Operators
Access this computer from the network	x	x	x		x	x
Back up files and directories	x					x
Bypass traverse checking	x	x	x		x	x
Change the system time	x	x				
Create a pagefile	x					
Deny access to this computer from the network						
Deny logon locally						

continues

TABLE 7.13	*continued*

WINDOWS 2000 PROFESSIONAL DEFAULT RIGHTS ASSIGNMENTS

Right	*Admin*	*Power Users*	*Users*	*Guests*	*Everyone*	*Backup Operators*
Force shutdown from a remote system	x					
Increase quotas	x					
Load and unload drivers	x					
Log on locally	x	x	x	x	x	x
Manage auditing and security	x					
Remove computer from docking station	x					
Restore files and directories	x					x
Shut down the system	x	x	x			x
Take ownership of files of other objects	x					

In addition to the default rights listed in Table 7.13, Windows 2000 also has built-in user capabilities. You cannot modify these built-in rights. The only way to give a user one of these rights is to put that user in a group that has the capability. If you want to give a user rights to create and manage user accounts, for example, you must put that user into either the Power Users or Administrators groups.

Table 7.14 lists the built-in capabilities on a Windows 2000 Professional computer.

TABLE 7.14

WINDOWS 2000 BUILT-IN USER CAPABILITIES

Right	Admin	Power Users	Users	Guests	Everyone	Backup Operators
Create and manage user accounts	x	x				
Create and manage Local groups	x	x				
Lock the workstation	x	x	x	x	x	x
Override the lock of a workstation	x					
Format a hard drive	x					
Share and stop sharing directories	x	x				
Share and Stop sharing printers	x	x				

LOCAL GROUP POLICY

Implement, configure, manage, and troubleshoot local Group Policy.

Securing a Windows 2000 environment involves many steps. In previous sections of this chapter, we looked at the management of users and groups and how they can be used to control access to the network. User and group management is a very important aspect of network management. If not managed correctly, network resources are impossible to secure.

After you develop an effective user and group management strategy, you need to consider the management of the computers in your environment. Specifically we are concerned with how a user (or group of users) can interact with the computer (i.e., reconfigure the computer).

Group Policy is a new set of technologies included with the Windows 2000 products. Group Policy is primarily used to manage the user and computer environment through the Active Directory database. A complete discussion of Group Policy is beyond the scope of this book, but we will look at local Group Policy and how it relates to Windows 2000 Professional.

N O T E **Local Policy versus Domain Level Group Policy** Because Group Policy objects associated with sites, domains, or organizational units can overwrite its settings, the local Group Policy object is the least influential one in an Active Directory environment. In a non-networked environment (or in a networked environment lacking a Windows 2000 domain controller), the local Group Policy object's settings are more important because they are not over-written by other Group Policy objects.

Each computer running Windows 2000 has a local Group Policy object associated with it. Using this object, Group Policy settings can be stored on individual computers whether or not they are part of an Active Directory environment or a networked environment.

Local Group Policy objects enable you to control the following components:

◆ **Administrative templates.** Registry-based settings that control access to various system settings.

◆ **Software settings.** Enables software to be assigned to users and computers so that it is available to users when they need it.

◆ **Security settings.** Security settings for computers and users.

◆ **Scripts.** User Logon/Logoff, Computer Startup/Shutdown scripts.

◆ **Folder redirection.** Enables data directories (usually part of a user's profile) to be placed on networked drives instead of the local computer.

LOCAL ACCOUNT POLICY

Implement, configure, manage, and troubleshoot local user accounts.

Account policies give administrators the ability to control how user passwords and lockouts are configured.

The following section provides details on password policy settings and account lockout policy settings.

Password Policies

Table 7.15 shows the Windows 2000 password policies. These policies enable you to manage the properties of a user's password (i.e., length or complexity).

TABLE 7.15	

PASSWORD POLICY SETTINGS

Policy Setting	*Description*
Enforce Password History	This setting tells the system to remember a user password so that it cannot be reused. This setting requires the administrator to input a value for the history length. Windows 2000 can track the history for your previous 24 passwords.
Maximum Password Age	This setting specifies the maximum age of a user password. Users are forced to change their passwords when the maximum age is met. The maximum value you can enter is 999 days.
Minimum Password Age	This setting specifies the minimum age of a user password. Users are not allowed to change their passwords unless the minimum password age has passed.
Minimum Password Length	This setting specifies the minimum length of the password (the value can be set between 0 and 14).
Password Must Meet Complexity Requirements	This setting implements the following password policy: Passwords must be at least six characters long. Passwords must contain characters from at least three of the following classes: Description (Examples) English uppercase letters (A, B, C, ... Z) English lowercase letters (a, b, c, ... z) Westernized Arabic numerals (0, 1, 2, ... 9) Non-alphanumeric ("special characters") such as punctuation symbols. Passwords may not contain your user name or any part of your full name. These requirements are hard-coded in the Passfilt.dll file and cannot be changed through the user interface or registry.

continues

TABLE 7.15	*continued*

PASSWORD POLICY SETTINGS

Policy Setting	Description
Store Password Using Reversible Encryption	This setting stores user passwords in encrypted, clear-text format.
User Must Log on to Change Password	This setting specifies that users must be logged on to the system to change their passwords. If users let their passwords expire, they will not be able to log on and will need the assistance of an administrator to reset their passwords.

Account Lockout Policy

Table 7.16 shows the Windows 2000 account lockout policies configuration settings.

TABLE 7.16

ACCOUNT LOCKOUT POLICY SETTINGS

Policy	Setting Description
Account Lockout Duration	If your account is locked out, this setting specifies the duration (can be set between 1 and 99,999 minutes).
Account Lockout Threshold	Specifies the number of times you can use an incorrect password before your account lockout is triggered. If this option were set to five, you could type your password incorrectly five times within the Reset Account Lockout Counter time period. This setting can be configured between 1 and 999 invalid logon attempts.
Reset Account Lockout Counter After	Specifies the number of minutes between resets of the account lockout counter (can be set between 1 and 99,999 minutes).

You should ensure that you use Account Lockout policy settings appropriately for your environment. You should ensure that you are using the auditing functions of Windows 2000 to detect invalid logon attempts. Account lockouts will go unnoticed in many environments in which the user account is enabled after the account lockout duration has passed.

MONITORING SECURITY EVENTS

As a network administrator, you might find that monitoring the activities of users, Windows 2000 system events, and application events is a powerful method of ensuring that your systems are secure and running properly. Windows 2000 enables you to monitor most events on a system. Events are user actions that are recorded, based on an audit policy, other significant occurrences in Windows 2000, or an application running on the system. Administrators need to monitor these events to track security, system performance, and application errors.

Events are recorded in event logs. You can view and analyze event logs to determine whether or not security breaches are occurring or system services are failing or to determine the nature of application errors. This section provides an overview of the Event Viewer, audit policies, the security log, categories of security events, object access events, and analyzing security events.

Event Logs and the Event Viewer

The Event Viewer is a tool that enables you to view three different logs that are stored by Windows 2000. The Event Viewer can be used to view the following logs:

◆ **System log.** The system log contains events logged by the Windows 2000 system components, such as drivers or other system components that failed to load during startup. Windows 2000 predetermines the event types logged by system components.

◆ **Application log.** The application log contains events logged by applications or programs. For example, a database program might record a file error in the application log. The program developer decides which events to record. Many Windows 2000 services (i.e., DHCP, DNS, File Replication Services, etc.) use the application log.

◆ **Security log.** The security log, if configured to do so, records security events, such as valid and invalid logon attempts. Events that are related to resource use such as creating, opening, or deleting files also can be logged. An administrator can specify what events are recorded in the security log policy.

The Event Viewer can be accessed through the Microsoft Management Console (MMC). The MMC enables management snap-ins to be added to a console. Step by Step 7.6 provides details on how to add the snap-in associated with the Event Viewer.

STEP BY STEP

7.6 Adding the ComputerManagement Snap-in to the Microsoft Management Console

1. Click Start and Run; in the Open dialog box, type MMC and click OK.

2. From the Console menu, select Add/Remove Snap-in.

3. In the Add/Remove Snap-in dialog box, click Add.

4. In the Add Standalone Snap-in dialog box, scroll down until you find the Computer Management snap-in and click Add.

5. You will be prompted to select the local computer or a remote machine. If you wanted to manage a remote system, you would provide the name here. In our case, however, select the local computer. The Computer Management is added to the list of snap-ins configured for this version of the MMC.

6. After all the required snap-ins have been added to your MMC, close the Add Standalone Snap-in dialog box and the Add/Remove Snap-in dialog box.

Your custom version of the MMC is now ready for use. You can save your version of the MMC from the Console menu if you wish.

By selecting the log type in the node pane (the left pane) of the MMC, the corresponding log data is displayed in the results pane (the right pane). Figure 7.25 shows the system log being displayed.

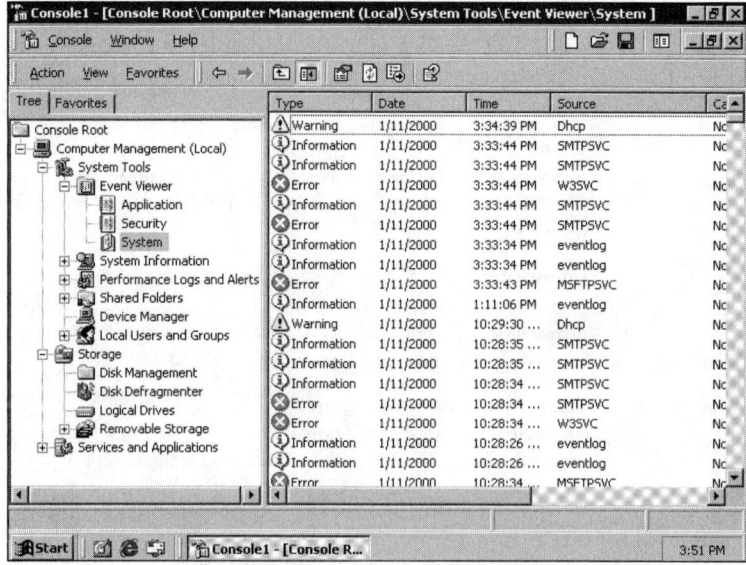

FIGURE 7.25
The Microsoft Windows 2000 Event Viewer.

The data being displayed can be sorted by selecting a column heading. You also have the ability to filter the results log entries being presented. To accomplish this, select Filter from the View menu. Figure 7.26 shows the options available when setting a filter.

You also can set the columns of data being presented by selecting Choose Columns from the View menu. Table 7.17 provides details regarding the column options.

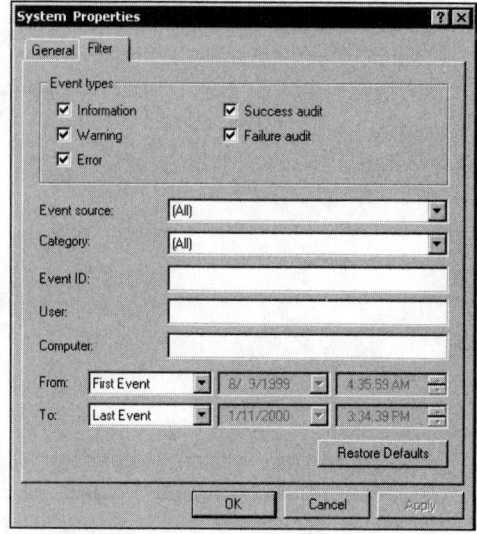

FIGURE 7.26
Microsoft Windows 2000 Event Viewer filter options.

TABLE 7.17

WINDOWS 2000 EVENT VIEWER

Name	*Definition*
Type	The Event Viewer tracks five basic types of events.
	Error A significant problem, such as loss of data or loss of functionality. For example, if a service fails to load during startup, an error will be logged.
	Warning An event that is not necessarily significant but might indicate a possible future problem. For example, when disk space is low, a warning will be logged.
	Information An event that describes the successful operation of an application, driver, or service. For example, when a network driver loads successfully, an Information event will be logged.
	Success Audit (security logs only) An audited security event in which a user's attempt to access a resource succeeds. For example, a user's successful attempt to log on to the system will be logged as a Success audit event.
	Failed Audit (security logs only) An audited security event in which a user's attempt to access a resource fails. For example, if a user tries to access a network drive and fails, the attempt will be logged as a Failed audit event.
Date	The date of the event.
Time	The time at which the event occurred.
Source	The source (typically a service or process) that reported the event to the Event Viewer.
Category	The category of the event. In many cases the category relates to the subsystem that reported the event. For example, when disk quotas are initialized, the Event Viewer application log has an entry stating that the operation has completed. The category of the event would be "Disk."
Event	The name of the event that was reported.
User	The user account associated with the event (this is not always applicable).
Computer	The computer on which the event occurred.

NOTE

Event ID The Event ID is a numeric code that can be used to obtain information from Microsoft regarding the event being logged. You can search Microsoft's Web site for the Event ID or Microsoft TechNet for details on each code.

Audit Policies

An audit policy defines the categories of user activities that Windows 2000 records in the security logs on each computer. Audit policies are set up to track authorized and unauthorized access to resources.

By default, auditing is not enabled. Before your organization enables auditing, you must define exactly what needs to be audited and why you want it to be audited. Auditing can slow down system performance.

Categories of Security Events

Security events are divided into categories. This enables the system administrator to configure audit policies to specific categories of events (based on your organization's auditing and security plan). When viewing the event logs, you can search for specific categories of events. Table 7.18 presents security event categories.

TABLE 7.18

CATEGORIES OF SECURITY EVENTS

Category	Description
Account logon	Logs an event each time a user attempts to log on. For example, specific events logged include: logon failures for unknown user accounts; time restriction violations; user account has expired; user does not have the right to log on locally; account password has expired; account is locked out. Successful logons also can be tracked through events.
Logon events	Logs an event for logon events that are occurring over the network or generated by service startup (for example, an interactive logon or service such as SQL starting).
Account management	Logs an event each time an account is managed. This is a useful function if you are concerned about changes being made to user accounts in your environment.
Directory service	Logs an event each time an event occurs within the Active Directory services—for example, successful or failed replication events.
Policy change	Logs an event each time a policy is successfully or unsuccessfully changed in your environment.

continues

| TABLE 7.18 | *continued* |

CATEGORIES OF SECURITY EVENTS

Category	*Description*
Process tracking	Logs an event for each program or process that a user launches while accessing a system. Administrators can use this information to track the details of a user's activities while accessing a system. Note that the event specifically tracks the creation of new processes and the exiting of processes.
Object access	Logs an event each time a user attempts to access a resource (i.e., printer, shared folder, etc.). These events provide a very effective way of monitoring access to sensitive data on your network.
Privilege use	Logs an event each time a user attempts, successfully or unsuccessfully, to use special privileges, such as changing system time. These events enable you to closely monitor the activities of the administrators in your environment.
System event	Logs a designated system event. Windows 2000 may log system events when a user restarts or shuts down a computer. These events provide a great deal of information regarding system services.

Auditing can be enabled for either success or failure of specific events. You need to decide what you want to use your log information for to determine whether logging successes or failures is most appropriate. For example, if you decide to audit account logons, you need to look at what the information will be used for. Your network Security group will most likely be interested in logging failed logon events (i.e., it can provide signs that someone is trying to log on with an account for which he or she does not have a correct password). This same Security group also might be interested in logging successful logons to determine whether users are accessing workstations in areas of the network that they should not be using.

Audit policies can be defined through Group Policy (either at the domain or computer level). Enabling auditing for Account Logon, Privilege Use, or System Events will automatically enable auditing of those events. Auditing of Object Access requires levels of configuration. The following section will review the configuration of Object Access audit policies.

Object Access Events

An audit policy can be configured to monitor access to objects such as files and folders, printers, and other objects. The audit policy defines what events will be entered in the event log. Table 7.19 presents a listing of the objects that can be audited and the type of events that can be audited for each.

TABLE 7.19

AUDITING OBJECT ACCESS

Object	Activities That Can Be Audited
File and Folders (files and folders can be audited only in a NTFS partition)	Displaying the contents of a file or folder. Changing the contents of a file or folder. Adding data to a file. Deleting a file or folder in a folder. Changing permissions for a file or folder.
Printers	Changing printer settings, pausing a printer, sharing a printer, or removing a printer. Changing job settings; pausing, restarting, or deleting documents. Changing printer properties.
Objects in the Active Directory	Viewing audited objects. Creating objects within an audited container. Deleting objects within an audited container (or an audited object). Changing the permissions for the audited object.

Setting Up Auditing

Setting up auditing is a two-step process. Step 1 involves enabling Auditing for the local policy of the computer (or domain). Step 2 requires you to configure auditing for each resource that you want to monitor.

To enable auditing for the local security policy, you need to access the computer's local policy. Step by Step 7.7 provides details on enabling object auditing. In this Step by Step, we will enable object auditing and account logon events in the local policy and then set up auditing on a folder. As you complete this Step by Step, notice that setting up auditing on an object is a two-step process.

STEP BY STEP

7.7 Enabling Auditing for a Computer

1. Click Start and Run; In the Open dialog box, type MMC and click OK.

2. From the Console menu, select Add/Remove Snap-in.

3. In the Add/Remove Snap-in dialog box, click Add.

4. In the Add Standalone Snap-in dialog box, scroll down until you find the Group Policy snap-in and click Add.

5. You will be prompted to select the local computer or a remote machine. If you wanted to manage a remote system, you would provide the name here. In this case, however, select the local computer.

6. After the required snap-in has been added to your MMC, close the Add Standalone Snap-in dialog box and the Add/Remove Snap-in dialog box.

7. We will now enable auditing. Auditing is configured through Group Policy. From the Group Policy snap-in, click Computer Configuration/Windows Settings/Security Settings/Local Policies/Audit Policies. This will expose the various types of auditing that are supported by Windows 2000. By double-clicking on one of the audit types, you can enable auditing for successful events or failure events.

8. Enable auditing for Account Logon events by double-clicking the Audit account logon events object. In the Local Security Policy Setting dialog box, check the Success and Failure checkboxes to enable account logon auditing.

9. Enable auditing for a file system share by double-clicking the Audit object access. In the Local Security Policy Setting dialog box, check the Success and Failure checkboxes to enable object access auditing.

10. Auditing is now enabled. To apply the policy, close the MMC.

11. We will now configure Auditing on a folder. Select a folder on a NTFS partition. Right-click the folder and select Properties from the secondary menu. Select the Security tab. Click the Advanced button on the bottom of the Securities tab to view the Access Control Settings dialog box for the folder. Select the Auditing tab. Figure 7.27 shows the Auditing tab of the Access Control Settings for a folder.

12. When you select the Auditing tab, you are presented with a list of all users who are currently being audited for this resource. Click the Add button and add the Everyone group to the list. Then select the specific events that you want to audit for this group of users (as shown in Figure 7.28). Notice that you can audit both successful and failed access. Select all of the checkboxes.

13. Close the dialog boxes.

14. Create a new file in the folder.

15. By accessing the folder, an audit event will be generated. To view the event logs, start the MMC and add the Computer Management snap-in (follow steps 1 through 6 if you can't remember how).

16. Access the security log. You should see a number of entries indicating a successful audit entry.

17. Log off of and on to your system. Check the security event to see the events that were generated.

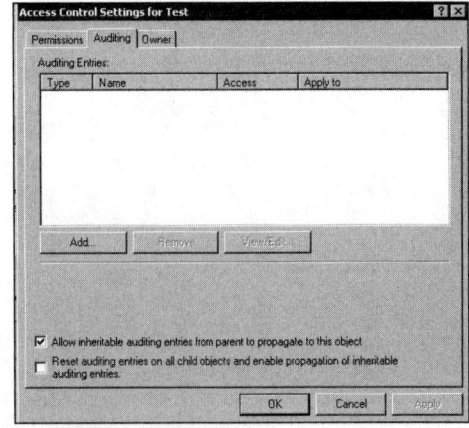

FIGURE 7.27
Auditing tab of the Access Control Settings for a folder.

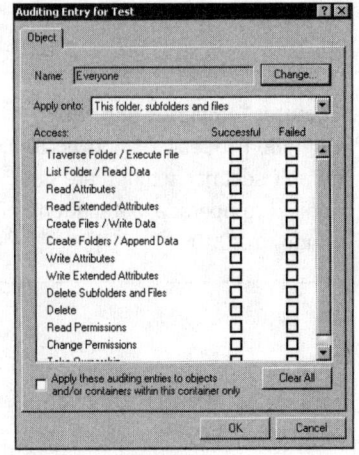

FIGURE 7.28
Select specific events in the Auditing Entry dialog box.

Windows 2000 Security Configurations

Implement, configure, manage, and troubleshoot a security configuration.

Windows 2000 supports the management of computers through security templates. Security templates are provided for common security scenarios. These can be assigned directly to a computer as is or modified to suit unique security requirements.

The predefined security templates are as follows:

- ◆ Default workstation (basicwk.inf)
- ◆ Default server (basicsv.inf)
- ◆ Default domain controller (basicdc.inf)
- ◆ Compatible workstation or server (compatws.inf)
- ◆ Secure workstation or server (securews.inf)
- ◆ Highly secure workstation or server (hisecws.inf)
- ◆ Highly secure domain controller (hisecdc.inf)
- ◆ Dedicated domain controller (dedicadc.inf)

By default, these templates are stored in the *systemroot*\security\ templates folder.

By default, Windows 2000 applies security templates to new installations of Windows 2000. The default templates are used to secure Windows.

If Windows 2000 is installed on a computer with FAT or FAT32 partitions, you should be aware that security configuration templates cannot be applied.

The following section looks at some of the security templates in more detail.

> **WARNING**
>
> **Security Templates and the Upgrade Process** Windows 2000 default security settings are not applied to upgrade installations of Windows 2000.

Basic and Advanced Security Templates

The basic configuration (basicwk.inf, basicsv.inf, basicdc.inf) templates are provided to assist you if you apply an inappropriate security configuration to your system. The basic configuration applies the Windows 2000 default security settings to all security areas except for sections covering user rights. User rights are not modified in the basic templates because application setup programs commonly modify user rights.

Compatible (compat*.inf)

Windows 2000 and Windows NT use different security settings to support applications running on them. Under Windows NT, applications were allowed a great deal of leeway regarding where they stored their configuration settings and registry entries. In many instances, users needed elevated privileges to install applications. Windows 2000 has changed this model and provided a more structured environment for the installation of applications. Windows 2000 applications (i.e., applications that use the Windows Installer service to install) are fully managed during installation, and users do not require elevated privileges as the application is installed in the security context of the installer service.

If you require compatibility with non-Windows 2000 applications in your environment, you might need to apply the compatible template. Under this template all users that are authenticated by Windows 2000 are automatically elevated to have the permissions associated with the Power Users group. This enables applications to access system files and registry keys that are required to operate properly.

Highly Secure (hisec*.inf)

The highly secure templates define a secure network communications environment for Windows 2000. The security areas are set to protect network traffic and protocols used between computers running Windows 2000. Computers configured with this template can communicate only with other Windows 2000 machines. This limits their capability to communicate with Windows NT and Windows 9x systems.

Dedicated Domain Controller (dedicadc.inf)

By default Windows 2000 domain controllers are configured to support legacy applications. Although Microsoft does not recommend this configuration, it might be required to support existing applications in your environment. Many applications running on Windows NT 4.0 need access to sections of the registry and system files to operate properly. If you are not going to be running legacy applications on your domain controllers, you can optimize their security configuration by implementing the dedicadc.inf security template. This template locks down the file system and registry permissions to secure your domain controller.

Configure System Security

The Security Templates snap-in enables you to manage security templates from the Microsoft Management Console (MMC). You can create or modify security templates by using this utility.

Step by Step 7.8 provides details on how a security template can be created.

STEP BY STEP

7.8 Creating Security Templates

1. Launch the Microsoft Management Console (MMC) by clicking the Start menu and selecting Run. In the Open dialog box, type MMC. Click OK. The MMC will launch.

2. Add the Security Templates snap-in to the MMC by clicking the Console/Add and Remove Snap-in menu. In the Add and Remove Snap-in dialog box, click Add. In the Add Standalone Snap-in dialog box, click Security Templates. Click Add and then click Close. Close the remaining windows to view the MMC with the snap-in added, as shown in Figure 7.29.

3. Open the Basicwk template in the left pane of the MMC. Opening the template exposes the settings that can be configured through the template.

4. If you were creating a new template, you would now edit the template and save the changes. You can save your changes from the Action menu.

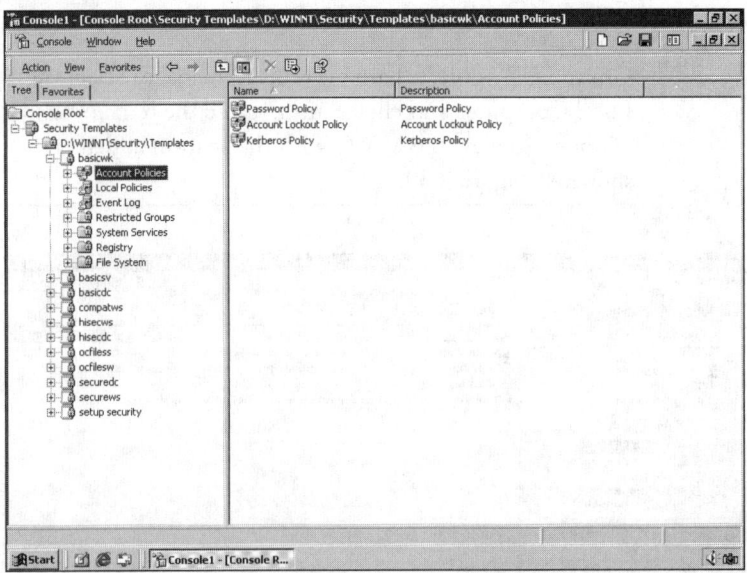

FIGURE 7.29
The Security Template MMC snap-in.

After you create a security template for your environment, you need to apply it to your computer. When you apply a template to existing security settings, the settings in the template are merged into the computer's security settings. Step by Step 7.9 demonstrates how to apply a security template to a Windows 2000 Professional system.

STEP BY STEP

7.9 Applying Security Templates

1. Launch the Microsoft Management Console (MMC) by clicking the Start menu and selecting Run. In the Open dialog box, type MMC. Click OK. The MMC will launch.

2. Add the Group Policy snap-in to the MMC by clicking the Console/Add and Remove Snap-in menu. In the Add and Remove Snap-in dialog box, click Add. In the Add Standalone Snap-in dialog box, click Group Policy. Click Add. You will be prompted to select the

continues

continued

Group Policy object that you want to manage. Select the Local Computer and click Finish. Close the remaining windows to view the MMC with the snap-in added, as shown in Figure 7.30.

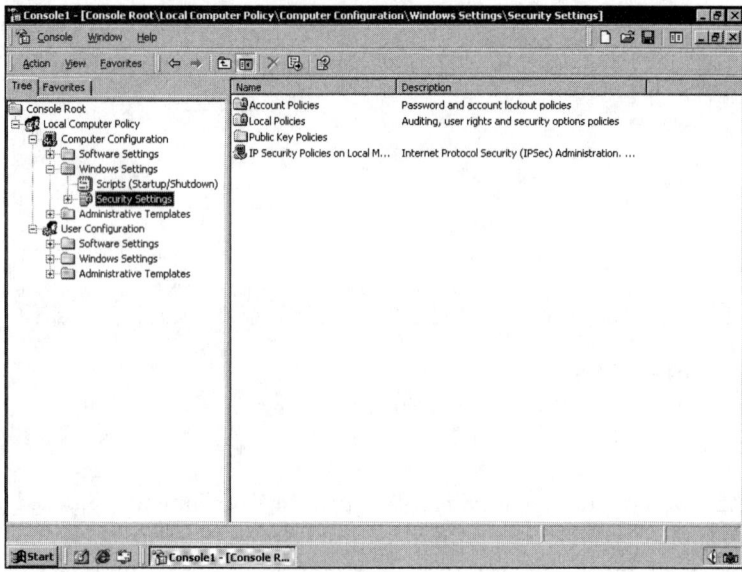

FIGURE 7.30
The Local Computer Policy MMC snap-in.

3. To import a new security template, open the Computer Configuration/Windows Settings options on the left side of the MMC. Right-click the Security Settings and select Import Policy from the secondary menu.

4. You will be prompted to select the template file that you want to import into your environment.

From the Group Policy snap-in, you are also able to export the security template for your system. Procedures to accomplish this are detailed in Step by Step 7.10.

STEP BY STEP

7.10 Exporting Security Templates

1. Launch the Microsoft Management Console (MMC) by clicking the Start menu and selecting Run. In the Open dialog box, type MMC. Click OK. The MMC will launch.

2. Add the Group Policy snap-in to the MMC by clicking the Console/Add and Remove Snap-in menu.

3. In the Add and Remove Snap-in dialog box, click Add. In the Add Standalone Snap-in dialog box, click Group Policy. Click Add.

4. You will be prompted to select the Group Policy object that you want to manage. Select the Local Computer and click Finish. Close the remaining windows to view the MMC with the snap-in added.

5. To export the existing security configuration for your system to a security template, open the Computer Configuration/Windows Settings options on the left of the MMC. Right-click the Security Settings and select Export Policy from the secondary menu.

6. The following are the two export options present:

- Export the local policy from your system. This will be the complete local policy regardless of whether or not it is currently effective for your system (policies need to be processed before they become effective).

- Export the effective policy from your local system. This will be the policy currently being applied by your system.

7. You will be prompted to select the name you want to store your template file under.

Validating a Security Configuration

The state of the operating system and applications on a computer is dynamic. For example, security levels might be required to change temporarily to enable immediate resolution of an administration or network issue; this change can often remain. This means that a computer might not meet the requirements for enterprise security any longer.

Regular analysis enables an administrator to track and ensure an adequate level of security on each computer. Analysis is provided at a micro level; information about all system aspects related to security is provided in the results. This enables an administrator to tune the security levels and, most important, to detect any security flaws that might open up in the system over time.

Security configuration and analysis enables quick review of security analysis results: Recommendations are presented alongside current system settings, and icons or remarks are used to highlight any areas where the current settings do not match the proposed level of security. Security configuration and analysis also offer the ability to resolve any discrepancies revealed by an analysis.

If frequent analyses of a large number of computers are required, as in a domain-based infrastructure, the secedit.exe command line tool may be used as a method of batch analysis. Analysis results still must be viewed, however, with security configuration and analysis.

Step by Step 7.11 provides details on how to use the Security Configuration and Analysis tool to compare the security configuration of a computer against a security template.

> **NOTE**
>
> **Secedit Help**   For more information on Secedit, type secedit.exe /help at the command prompt.

STEP BY STEP

7.11 Security Configuration and Analysis

1. Add the Security Configuration and Analysis snap-in to an MMC console (see Step by Step 7.1 for details on adding a snap-in).

2. Right-click Security Configuration and Analysis and then click Open database.

3. Select an existing database file or type a new name to create a new database, and then click Open.

4. If you open an existing database, it will already contain information regarding the template to which you are comparing your configuration. If you are creating a new database, you need to import the security template that you want to compare to your system configuration.

5. Right-click Security Configuration and Analysis and then click Analyze Computer Now.

6. In the Perform Analysis dialog box, choose a location for the analysis log and then click OK.

7. Windows 2000 will then compare the effective security configuration of your local computer against the security template. Any differences in your configuration will be shown with a red x, as shown in Figure 7.31.

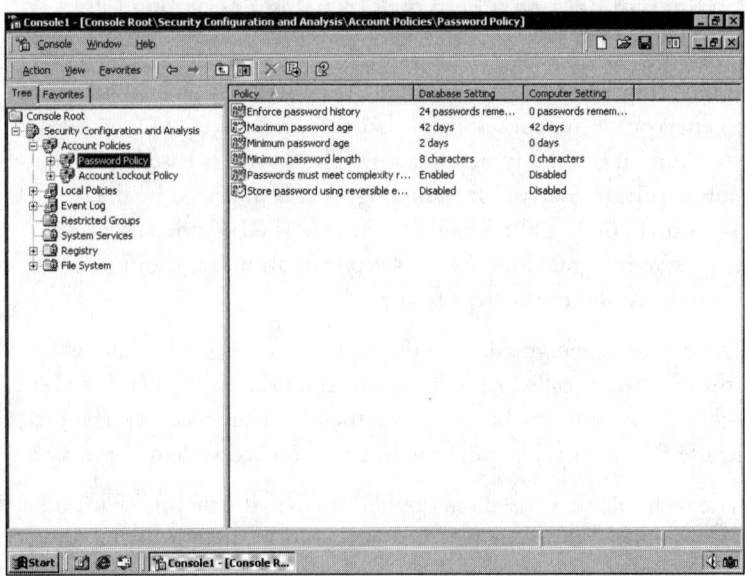

FIGURE 7.31
Completed security analysis.

After completing the analysis, you can perform a number of tasks, including the following:

- ◆ Eliminate discrepancies by configuring the settings in the database to match the current computer settings. To configure the database settings, double-click the setting in the detail pane of the MMC.

- ◆ Import another template file. This enables you to add additional security templates to the analysis.

- ◆ Export the current database setting to a template file. To export the template file, right-click Security Configuration and Analysis and then click Export Template.

ENCRYPTING FILE SYSTEM (EFS)

Encrypt data on a hard disk by using Encrypting File System (EFS).

Encrypting File System (EFS) is a system service that enables a user to encrypt file system resources that they have access to (you need a minimum of modify permissions). The service is based on public/private encryption technology and is managed by the Windows 2000 Public Key Infrastructure (PKI) services. Because EFS is an integrated service, it is very easy to manage, difficult to break into, and transparent to the user.

Once a file is encrypted, only the user who encrypted it (and a special account called recovery agent) can decrypt the file. If a user other then the user who encrypted the file or the recovery agent tries to use the resource, he or she will receive an access denied message.

The technology is based on a public key-based structure. Each user has a public and private key. The keys were created in such a way that anything encrypted with the private key can be decrypted only by using the public key and anything encrypted with the public key can be decrypted only by using the private key. As the names suggest, the public key is made available to any resource that requests it. The private key is kept secret and never exposed to non-authorized resources.

When the owner of a file encrypts a file system resource, a file encryption key is generated and used to encrypt the file. The file encryption keys are based on a fast symmetric key designed for bulk encryption. The file is encrypted in blocks with a different key for each block. All of the file encryption keys are then stored with the file (as part of the header of the file), the Data Decryption Field (DDF), and Data Recovery Field (DRF). Before the file encryption keys are stored, they are encrypted by using the public key of the owner, in the case of the DDF keys, and a recovery agent, in the case of the DRF keys. Because the keys are stored with the file, the file can be moved or renamed without impacting the recoverability of the file.

When a file is accessed, EFS detects the access attempt and locates the user's certificate from the Windows 2000 PKI and the user's associated private key. The private key is then used to decrypt the DDF to retrieve the file encryption keys used to encrypt each block of the file. The only key in existence with the capability to decrypt the information is the user who encrypted the file. Access to the file is denied to everyone else, as they do not hold the private key required for decrypting the file encryption keys.

If the owner's private key is not available for some reason (for example, the user account was deleted), the recovery agent can open the file. The recovery agent decrypts the DRF to unlock the list of file encryption keys. The recovery agent must be configured as part of the security policies of the local computer.

Step by Step 7.12 provides details for encrypting a file or folder within Windows 2000.

WARNING

Manage the Recovery Agent Properly The recovery agent can be configured through local policies (or Group Policy objects in the domain environment). If you change the recovery agent, you might not be able to recover encrypted files that were encrypted prior to the change (as the keys used to encrypt the sessions key in the recovery agent field were encrypted by using the old agent's key).

STEP BY STEP

7.12 Encrypting Files and Folders

1. Right-click on the file or folder that you want to encrypt.

2. Choose the Properties option from the secondary menu.

3. Click the Advanced button from the General tab.

4. Check the Encrypt contents to secure data checkbox from the Compress or Encrypt attributes section of the Advanced Attributes dialog box.

You also can manage the encryption attributes associated with files and folders on your system from the command prompt. The Cipher utility enables you to encrypt files and folders as well as check the compression statistics.

The syntax for the encryption utility is as follows:

```
CIPHER [/e¦ /d] [/s:dir] [/i] [/f] [/q] [filename [...]]
```
Where:

◆ /e encrypts the specified files or folders. Files added to the folder afterward will be encrypted.

◆ /d decrypts the specified files or folders. Files added to the folder afterward will not be encrypted.

◆ /s: *dir* performs the specified operation on files in the given directory and all subdirectories.

◆ /i continues performing the specified operation even after errors have occurred. By default, cipher stops when an error is encountered.

◆ /f forces the encryption or decryption of all specified files. By default, files that have already been encrypted or decrypted are skipped. This option forces files to be re-encrypted, even if they are currently encrypted. This would be important if a new recovery agent has been configured for your system, as the file(s) would be re-encrypted with a new key.

◆ /q reports only the most essential information.

◆ *Filename* specifies a pattern, file, or directory.

Step by Step 7.13 demonstrates how to use EFS.

STEP BY STEP

7.13 Using EFS

1. Create two new user accounts named EFSUser and Hacker on you computer.

2. Log on as user EFSUser.

3. Create a simple text file on a NTFS-formatted partition. Open the text file with Notepad. Enter a message in the file, save the file, and exit Notepad.

4. Right-click the file you just created and select Properties from the secondary menu. Click Advanced.

5. Check the Encrypt contents to secure data option box.

6. Log off of the system and log on as the Hacker account you created in Step 1.

7. Try to open the file that you created in Step 3. You will have been denied access to the file.

8. Log off and log on as the Administrator account.

9. We will now verify that the recovery agent can access the file. Access the Local Computer Policy and view the Encrypted Data Recovery Agents list (found under Computer Configuration/Windows Settings/Security Settings/Public Key Policies/Encrypted Data Recovery Agents). The default configuration has the local Administrator account in the list. This means that the administrator can access encrypted files.

10. Try to access the file you created in Step 3. You should be able to recover the file.

CASE STUDY: ABC COMPANY

ESSENCE OF THE CASE

Here are the essential elements in this case:

▶ Group strategy in a multi-domain environment

▶ Account policies

▶ Security template development

▶ Audit policies

▶ Company policies for EFS

SCENARIO

ABC Company is in the process of developing a network design for their Canadian operation. ABC Company has nine offices spread across Canada and employs 5,000 people. They are currently running a mix of Novell and Windows NT 3.51/4.0. The company is very concerned with the rising cost of managing their networked resources. The company has decided on a multiple domain design based on the legal organization of their company (i.e., one division in their company partners with a company in Europe and, therefore, requires lower levels of encrypting technology). Your job is to develop a complete security strategy plan for this company.

ANALYSIS

ABC Company is undertaking a major re-working of their network. This case focuses on security. To secure your environment, you need to manage your groups, account policies, security templates, and audit policies correctly.

Because we are dealing with a multi-domain environment, you need to develop a strategy for the management of groups. You should use Global groups to organize users in each domain. You then need to evaluate the resources to determine which staff need access. You will then create Domain Local groups and give these groups permission to the resources users need. Global groups are then placed in the Domain Local groups.

After you organize your users and groups, you should evaluate password policies. Does your company require complex passwords? What is the minimum length of passwords? How long

CASE STUDY: ABC COMPANY

can a user use a password before he or she must change it?

Now that the user accounts are protected, you will want to develop a strategy for securing individual systems. One of the most effective ways of doing this is through a security template

and by auditing access to resources.

Remember that each of the above features of Windows 2000 work together to secure your environment. Think of them as lines of defense. If one line fails another is there to protect your resources.

CHAPTER SUMMARY

In Chapter 7 we explored the tools built into Windows 2000 to secure the networked environment. The chapter started with an overview of the user account. User accounts are a very important aspect of network security, as they are your first line of defense against intruders. If your user accounts are not managed properly, it is impossible to secure the network. In the discussion of user accounts, we also reviewed the differences between a workgroup and a domain environment. Next, groups were covered in detail. Groups are a very powerful tool that can ease management and, if used properly, make implementing a secure environment easier. With a full understanding of users and groups, we then looked at local policies and account policies. Policies are tools that we can use to secure user accounts and computers.

Monitoring security events was also described, as was the process of defining an audit policy. Security templates and the Encrypting File System were discussed, as well.

KEY TERMS

- ▶ Workgroup
- ▶ Domain
- ▶ Active Directory
- ▶ User Account
- ▶ Group
- ▶ Security groups
- ▶ Distribution groups
- ▶ Local groups
- ▶ Domain Local groups
- ▶ Global group
- ▶ Universal group
- ▶ Built-in group
- ▶ Local Group policy
- ▶ Account policy
- ▶ Auditing
- ▶ Event logs
- ▶ Security template
- ▶ Encrypting File System

APPLY YOUR KNOWLEDGE

Exercises

7.1   Creating Local Users and Groups

In this exercise, you create a new local user account and group. You will then make the new user a member of the group.

Estimated Time: 10 Minutes

1. Click Start/Run. In the Open dialog box, type MMC and click OK.

2. From the Console menu, click the Add/Remove Snap-in menu.

3. In the Add/Remove Snap-in window, click Add.

4. In the Add Standalone Snap-in window, highlight the Computer Management snap-in and click Add.

5. In the Computer Management dialog box, select the local computer. Click Finish in the Computer Management window.

6. Close the Add Standalone Snap-in and Add/Remove Snap-in windows by clicking OK.

7. Open the Computer Management Snap-in by clicking the plus sign beside the snap-in.

8. Open the System Tools node of the Computer Management snap-in by clicking the plus sign beside the node.

9. Open the Local Users and Groups node of the Computer Management snap-in. From this location, you can create and manage users on the system.

10. To create a new local user, right-click the "Users" folder in the Local Users and Groups node. From the secondary menu, select New User. This action launches the New User dialog box.

11. Use the following information to create the account:

    - User name = Joe
    - Full name = Joe Smith
    - Description = Test User for Exercise 7.1
    - Password = password
    - Uncheck the User must change password on first logon box
    - Leave all other boxes unchecked

12. After you have entered the user configuration, click Create. Click Close to return to the MMC.

13. To create a new Local group, right-click the Groups folder in the Local Users and Groups node. From the secondary menu, select New Group. This action launches the New Group dialog box.

14. Enter the name of the group as Exercise 7.1 Test Group and enter Test group as the description.

15. After you have entered the group configuration, click Create. The New Group dialog box will reappear so you can create another group. Click Close to close the dialog box.

16. To add the user Joe to the membership of the group you just created, double-click the group. Click the Add button. In the Select Users or Groups dialog box, find Joe, click the Add button, and click OK.

17. Click OK to close the properties box for the group. Close the MMC. When prompted to save the changes say no.

APPLY YOUR KNOWLEDGE

7.2 Using Local Group Policy

In this exercise, you will configure the local Group Policy to remove the Run option from the Start menu of your computer.

Estimated Time: 15 Minutes

1. Click Start/Run. In the Open dialog box, type MMC and click OK.

2. From the Console menu, click the Add/Remove Snap-in menu.

3. In the Add/Remove Snap-in window, click Add.

4. In the Add Standalone Snap-in window, highlight the Group Policy snap-in and click Add.

5. In the Select Group Policy Object window, select the local computer. Click Finish in the Computer Management window.

6. Close the Add Standalone Snap-in and Add/Remove Snap-in windows by clicking OK.

7. Open the Local Computer Policy snap-in by clicking the plus sign beside the snap-in.

8. Open the User Configuration node of the Local Policy snap-in by clicking the plus sign beside the node.

9. Open the Administrative Templates node by clicking the plus sign beside the node.

10. Select the Start Menu & Taskbar folder in the scope pane. You should now see the individual policy settings in the results pane (the right-hand window).

11. Double-click on the Remove Run menu from Start menu and select Enable.

12. Exit the MMC (when you exit the MMC, you should save a copy on your desktop, as it is easier to launch it again later).

13. Log off of the system and log on again.

14. Check to see if the Run menu exists. It should be gone.

15. Launch the MMC and disable this policy setting.

7.3 Using Local Account Policies

In this exercise, you will configure the local account policy so the users can use incorrect passwords only three times within a ten-minute period. If users gets their passwords incorrect three times within this period, their accounts are locked out for 30 minutes.

Estimated Time: 15 Minutes

1. Click Start/Run. In the Open dialog box, type MMC and click OK.

2. From the Console menu, click the Add/Remove Snap-in menu.

3. In the Add/Remove Snap-in window, click Add.

4. In the Add Standalone Snap-in window, highlight the Group Policy snap-in and click Add.

5. In the Select Group Policy Object window, select the local computer. Click Finish in the Computer Management window.

6. Close the Add Standalone Snap-in and Add/Remove Snap-in Windows by clicking OK.

7. Open the Local Computer Policy snap-in by clicking the plus sign beside the snap-in.

8. Open the Computer Configuration node of the Local Policy snap-in by clicking the plus sign beside the node.

APPLY YOUR KNOWLEDGE

9. Open the Windows Settings node by clicking on the plus sign beside the node.

10. Open the Security Settings node by clicking on the plus sign beside the node.

11. In the scope pane, highlight Account Lockout Policies. You should now see the individual account lockout policies in the results pane.

12. Double-click the account lockout duration policy in the results pane. Enter 30 minutes as the account lockout duration. Click OK to close the policy.

13. The system will provide you with a list of suggested values for the other related account lockout policies. Click OK to accept them.

14. Change the values associated with the account lockout threshold (three bad logon attempts) and reset account lockout counter after values (ten minutes).

15. Log off of your system and try to log on as Joe. Type your password incorrectly and try to log on. Note the error message states that you provided an incorrect user name or password.

16. Continue to try to log on to the system with the incorrect password. After the third attempt, the system should issue a new error message stating that you are unable to log on because your account has been locked out.

7.4 Unlocking an Account

In this exercise, you will unlock the user account from Exercise 7.3.

Estimated Time: 5 Minutes

1. Log on as Administrator (or a user with administrative permissions).

2. Click Start/Run. In the Open dialog box, type **MMC** and click OK.

3. From the Console menu, click the Add/Remove Snap-in menu.

4. In the Add/Remove Snap-in window, click Add.

5. In the Add Standalone Snap-in window, highlight the Computer Management snap-in and click Add.

6. In the Computer Management window, select the local computer. Click Finish in the Computer Management window.

7. Close the Add Standalone Snap-in and Add/Remove Snap-in windows by clicking OK.

8. Open the Computer Management snap-in by clicking the plus sign beside the snap-in.

9. Open the System Tools node of the Computer Management snap-in by clicking the plus sign beside the node.

10. Open the Local Users and Groups node of the Computer Management snap-in.

11. Double-click the Joe user account. Uncheck the Account is locked out box to unlock Joe's account.

12. Click OK to close the Joe Property dialog box.

13. Log off as Administrator and log back on as Joe (this time with the correct password).

Review Questions

1. What utilities are used to create users and groups in a workgroup environment?

2. What utilities are used to create users and groups in a domain environment?

APPLY YOUR KNOWLEDGE

3. What is Microsoft's preferred strategy for groups in a domain environment?

4. What are the differences between a Global group and a Universal group?

5. When is it more appropriate to use a Global group over a Universal group?

6. What are the differences between a workgroup and a domain environment?

7. You want to stop hackers from trying to guess passwords in your environment; what feature of Windows 2000 should you use?

8. How does the Encrypting File System work and why would you want to use it?

9. What are local policies used for?

10. What is the secedit.exe utility used for?

11. What are user rights and how do they relate to built-in groups?

12. What types of events can be audited?

Exam Questions

1. You are working as a consultant for a small firm in Toronto, Canada. Your client wants to implement a Windows 2000 network but cannot decide if the workgroup or domain model is best suited for their environment. Which statements are true of the workgroup and domain models? (Select all that apply.)

   A. The workgroup model is best suited for large environments with centralized administration.

   B. The domain model is best suited for large environments with centralized administration.

   C. The workgroup model offers much tighter security and control over user accounts than the domain model does.

   D. The domain model offers much tighter security and control over user accounts than the workgroup model does.

   E. Generally, the workgroup model is limited to small environments with no centralized administration.

2. As the network administrator for your company, you find that you are spending a lot of time managing user accounts for temporary staff that work in your order-processing center. All temporary staff require the same level of access to network resources and only work at your organization for one or two weeks at a time. You also find that it is very difficult to keep up with the high turnover of temporary staff in this department. You need to develop a strategy to manage these users.

   Required Result:

   Security cannot be compromised on the network, as users access resources throughout the enterprise.

   Optional Desired Results:

   User accounts must be easily managed from a centralized location.

   You must be able to track each user based on a unique user name.

   Proposed Solution:

   You create a local user account on each local workstation in the order process center called "Temp". This account is then given access to all of the resources that order-processing staff require.

APPLY YOUR KNOWLEDGE

Given the proposed solution, which statement is true?

A. The proposed solution produces the required result and produces all of the optional desired results.

B. The proposed solution produces the required result and produces only one of the optional desired results.

C. The proposed solution produces the required result but does not produce any of the optional desired results.

D. The proposed solution does not produce the required result.

3. As the network administrator for your company, you find you are spending a lot of time managing user accounts for temporary staff that work in your order-processing center. All temporary staff require the same level of access to network resources and only work at your organization for one or two weeks at a time. You also find that it is very difficult to keep up with the high turnover of temporary staff in this department. You need to develop a strategy to manage these users.

Required Result:

Security cannot be compromised on the network, as users access resources throughout the enterprise.

Optional Desired Results:

User accounts must be easily managed from a centralized location.

You must be able to track each user based on a unique user name.

Proposed Solution:

You create a domain user account called "Temp". This account is then given access to all of the resources that order-processing staff require. The account is set up so that the user cannot change the password. All users from the order-processing center use this account to log on.

Given the proposed solution, which statement is true?

A. The proposed solution produces the required result and produces all of the optional desired results.

B. The proposed solution produces the required result and produces only one of the optional desired results.

C. The proposed solution produces the required result but does not produce any of the optional desired results.

D. The proposed solution does not produce the required result.

4. As the network administrator for your company you find you are spending a lot of time managing user accounts for temporary staff that work in your order-processing center. All temporary staff require the same level of access to network resources and only work at your organization for one or two weeks at a time. You also find that it is very difficult to keep up with the high turnover of temporary staff in this department. You need to develop a strategy to manage these users.

Required Result:

Security cannot be compromised on the network, as users access resources throughout the enterprise.

APPLY YOUR KNOWLEDGE

Optional Desired Results:

User accounts must be easily managed from a centralized location.

You must be able to track each user based on a unique user name.

Proposed Solution:

You assign one of your administrators the responsibility to manage user accounts for call center staff. You also develop a process whereby the Human Resources department forwards your administrative staff a copy of the contract for each call center person. A new domain user account is created for each call center person when the contract is received by network administration. The account is configured so that it will automatically expire when the user's contract expires.

Given the proposed solution, which statement is true?

A. The proposed solution produces the required result and produces all of the optional desired results.

B. The proposed solution produces the required result and produces only one of the optional desired results.

C. The proposed solution produces the required result but does not produce any of the optional desired results.

D. The proposed solution does not produce the required result.

5. You are the network administrator for a large corporate environment. You are developing a user and group management strategy for the executives at your company. Your environment consists of five domains, as shown in Figure 7.32. The executives' user accounts are spread across all of the domains. You need to give all executives access to a database in Domain A.

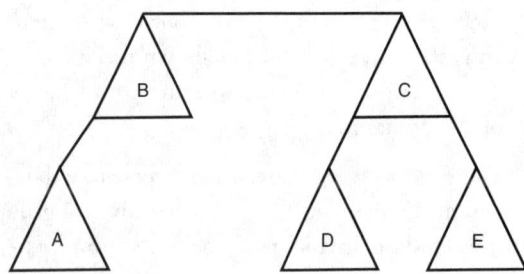

FIGURE 7.32
Sample domain structure.

You create a Domain Local group in each domain and place the users in their respective Domain Local groups. You then create a Global Group in Domain A and give it permission to use the database. You then place the Domain Local groups from Domain A, B, C, D, and E in the Global group. How effective is this strategy? Choose one of the following:

A. The proposed solution does not work.

B. It is not effective, although it does appear to work.

C. It is effective but could be improved upon through the use of Universal groups in each user domain.

APPLY YOUR KNOWLEDGE

D. It is effective but could be improved upon through the use of Domain Local groups in each user domain.

E. The proposed solution cannot be improved upon.

6. You are the network administrator for a large corporate environment. You are developing a user and group management strategy for the executives at your company. Your environment consists of five domains, as shown in Figure 7.32. The executives' user accounts are spread across all of the domains.

   You need to give all executives access to a database in Domain A. You create a Universal group in each domain and place the users from each domain in their respective Universal groups. You then create a Domain Local group in Domain A and give it permission to use the database. You then place the Universal groups from Domain A, B, C, D, and E in the Domain Local group. How effective is this strategy? Choose one of the following:

   A. The proposed solution does not work.

   B. It is not effective, although it does appear to work.

   C. It is effective but could be improved upon through the use of Global groups in each user domain.

   D. It is effective but could be improved upon through the use of Domain Local groups in each user domain.

   E. The proposed solution cannot be improved upon.

7. You are the network administrator for a large corporate environment. You are developing a user and group management strategy for the executives at your company. Your environment consists of five domains, as shown in Figure 7.32. The executives' user accounts are spread across all of the domains.

   You need to give all executives access to a database in Domain A. You create a Global group in each domain and place the users from each domain in their respective Global groups. You then create a Domain Local group in Domain A and give it permission to use the database. You then place the Global groups from Domain A, B, C, D, and E in the Domain Local group. How effective is this strategy? Choose one of the following:

   A. The proposed solution does not work.

   B. It is not effective, although it does appear to work.

   C. It is effective but could be improved upon through the use of Domain Local groups in each user domain.

   D. It is effective but could be improved upon through the use of Universal groups in each user domain.

   E. The proposed solution cannot be improved upon.

8. You are working as a help desk operator and receive a call from a user who cannot log on. The user explains that she just finished changing her password before lunch. The system accepted the password change. The user logged off of her workstation at lunchtime (like all good users do).

APPLY YOUR KNOWLEDGE

When she returned from lunch, the system indicated that the password she provided was incorrect. What is the most likely cause of the problem? (Choose the best answer.)

A. The password change has not replicated to the domain controllers yet.

B. The user has forgotten that passwords are case-sensitive and is not using the correct case.

C. The user account has been disabled, as the user is not a member of the Account Operators group, which is required to change the password.

D. The user is not allowed to log on from the workstation she attempted to log on from due to computer restrictions.

9. As the network administrator at a large insurance firm, you have installed a new Microsoft SQL Server to support a new billing system. The server is running on a Windows 2000 Advanced Server configured as a member server in your accounting domain. The users who need to access this server reside in another domain within the directory tree (i.e., the corporate domain). You create a Domain Local group called BILLING_USERS in the corporate domain and add all of the users who require access to the application to this group. You try to give the BILLING_USERS group permission to access the database, but you cannot. Why? (Choose two from the following.)

A. The group has not replicated to the domain controls and is, therefore, not available.

B. The group needs to be configured as a Universal group.

C. Domain Local groups can be used only to access resources in the domain in which they reside.

D. BILLING_USERS should have been configured as a Global group.

10. As the network administrator of your company's network, you are very concerned about security. Your predecessor was fired because users managed to hack their way into the Human Resources database. You don't want to have the same thing happen to you.

To help catch the hackers, you configure auditing. You set auditing so that the activities of the domain users group are monitored in the directories that contain the Human Resources database. Somehow hackers still manage to get in. Why didn't auditing help in this situation? (Choose three from the following.)

A. Configuration of auditing is a two-step process. You didn't set the local policy to include auditing.

B. You audited the wrong group. If you are auditing to determine unauthorized users who are accessing a resource, you should audit the Everyone group to ensure that all users (including those not authenticated to the network) are audited.

C. You cannot use auditing alone to secure resources.

D. Auditing cannot be set to track users who are accessing directories and files.

APPLY YOUR KNOWLEDGE

11. You are the administrator of a small network. The manager of the accounting department approaches you because one of her staff has encrypted all of their data in a shared folder. The user is sick and will not be back to work for an extended period. You are asked to decrypt the data. What is your best option?

    A. Take ownership of the files and change the permissions on them so that you own them. Then decrypt the files.

    B. Call the sick user and ask for her password. Log on as the user and decrypt the files.

    C. Log on as the administrator and decrypt the files.

    D. Log on as the recovery agent and decrypt the files.

12. As the network administrator of a large accounting firm, you configure all Windows 2000 servers in your environment to use the highly secure template. You receive a number of complaints from users that they are not able to connect to the servers from Windows 95/98 and Windows NT workstations. The workstations are able to connect to one another. How can the problem be corrected? (Choose two from the following.)

    A. Add the highly secure template to the Windows 95/98 and Windows NT workstations.

    B. Upgrade the Windows 95/98 and Windows NT workstations to Windows 2000 Professional.

    C. All users must have Power Users-(or Administrator) level access to attach to the servers configured with the highly secure template.

    D. Remove the highly secure template from the Windows 2000 Servers by re-applying the basic security template.

13. You are working as a support tech for a small manufacturing company in Toronto, Canada. You are servicing one server that starts without problems, but the IIS server will not start. The IIS server was running fine until the last day or so. As far as you know, no configuration changes have been made to the server. What should be your first course of action in solving this problem?

    A. Check to see if the server is running in the Services node of Computer Manager.

    B. Reboot the server.

    C. Check the Event Viewer to see of any error message has been logged.

    D. Check the audit logs to see if anyone has reconfigured the server.

14. As the system support specialist for the accounting department of your company, you have been asked to encrypt a large number of files and folders on a number of NTFS partitions on your servers. You spend an entire weekend encrypting the approximately 1,000 folders and 100,000 files. On Monday morning, users can no longer access the files that they need to do their jobs. You realize that because you used your account to encrypt the files, accounting staff will not be able to access the information unless they log on as your user account. For security reasons you don't want regular users logged on as an administrator.

    Your boss does not care about these technical problems and tells you to decrypt the files fast.

APPLY YOUR KNOWLEDGE

What is the fastest way to decrypt the files (remember that they are spread over multiple NTFS drives—it took you two days to encrypt the files by using Explorer)?

A. Have everyone log on to the system as the recovery agent (Administrator) and access the files.

B. Create a batch file with the following commands and execute it at the root of all NTFS volumes containing encrypted files: CIPHER /e /s

C. Create a batch file with the following commands and execute it at the root of all NTFS volumes containing encrypted files: CIPHER /d

D. Create a batch file with the following commands and execute it at the root of all NTFS volumes containing encrypted files: CIPHER /d /s /i

15. As the server administrator at your company, you install a new accounting package on your server. The software has a number of components that run as a service and require user accounts to operate. You company has a policy in place that requires users to change their passwords every 30 days. Every 30 days your accounting package fails to start because the logon account it uses must change its password. What should you do to correct the problem?

A. Set up the application so that it uses the Administrator account, as this account does not require password changes.

B. Write a script that will change the account password in both the account database and for the application every 30 days.

C. Configure the account so that its password does not expire.

D. Make sure that someone resets the password on the account each month.

Answers to Review Questions

1. The Computer Management snap-in is used to manage users and groups in a workgroup environment—in the Computer Management snap-in, there is a node called Local Users and Groups. For additional information see the section entitled "Creating Local User Accounts."

2. The Active Directory Users and Computer snap-in is used to manage users and groups in a domain environment. For additional information, see the section entitled "Creating Domain User Accounts."

3. Microsoft's preferred strategy is for accounts to be placed in Global groups. The Global groups are then placed in Domain Local groups. The Domain Local groups are then given permission to access resources. For additional information, see the section entitled "Groups."

4. Global groups can be used to assign permission to resources that are located in any domain. Membership in a Global group is limited to user accounts and Global groups from the domain in which the Global group resides. You can add Global groups to another Global group within the same domain or to Universal groups and Domain Local groups in other domains. For additional information, see the section entitled "Groups."

APPLY YOUR KNOWLEDGE

Universal groups can be used to assign permissions to resources that are located in any domain. You can add user accounts, Universal groups, and Global groups from any domain to its membership list. You can add a Universal group to Domain Local or Universal groups in any domain.

5. Global groups are used to organize user accounts within a domain. Global groups are then placed in the Domain Local groups to gain access to resources. Universal groups are used to grant access to resources that reside in multiple domains. You should not use Universal groups to organize user accounts (it can impact replication traffic). Instead, if you have resources that reside in multiple domains, place Global groups from each domain in a Universal group and then make the Universal group a member of a Domain Local group. For additional information, see the section entitled "Groups."

6. Under the workgroup model, each computer in your environment is responsible for the management of its own local account database. The workgroup model is meant for small environments. This model has a very high administrative cost, as user accounts must be managed on each computer in your environment. The workgroup model is very simple to implement and does not require that specialized computers manage a shared account database.

Under the domain model, a centralized database of user accounts is managed for a grouping (or domain) of computers. Domain user accounts contain information that defines users within the domain. In Windows 2000, all user account information for the domain is stored in the Active Directory database. Active Directory is

stored on a special computer called a domain controller. With a single domain user account, a user can log on to the domain and gain access to resources on any computer in the domain. The primary benefit of the domain model is that account management is simplified, as each user in your environment will have only a single user account defined. This model, however, is much more complex to set up, design, and configure. For additional information, see the sections entitled "The Domain Model" and "The Workgroup Model."

7. The local policy of a computer contains settings related to account policies. Under account policies you can configure an account lockout policy. These settings enable you to specify the total number of bad password attempts a user can have within a given period of time. If the number of bad password attempts is exceeded, the user account is locked. You also should consider auditing failed logins. For additional information, see the sections entitled "Local Group Policy" and "Audit Policies."

8. The Encrypting File System (EFS) enables a user to encrypt the contents of a file so that only that user (and a recovery agent) can access the file. This is helpful in environments in which users work with very sensitive data.

When a user encrypts a file, a session key is generated. This session key is used to encrypt the file. The session key is then encrypted by using the user's public key. The encrypted session key is then saved with the file. A version of the key encrypted by a recovery agent is also saved with the file so that it can be recovered if the user account (and corresponding private key required to retrieve the session key) is unavailable. For additional information, see the section entitled "Encrypting File System."

When a user attempts to open the file, the system will detect that it is encrypted and use the user's private key to decrypt the session key stored with the file. The session key is then used to decrypt the file.

9. Local Group Policy objects enable you to control the following components:

- **Administrative templates.** Registry-based setting that controls access to various system settings.

- **Software settings.** Enables software to be assigned to users and computers so that it is available to users when they need it.

- **Security settings.** Security settings for computers and users.

- **Scripts.** User Logon/Logoff, Computer Startup/Shutdown scripts.

- **Folder redirection.** Enables data directories (usually part of a user's profile) to be placed on networked drives instead of the local computer.

For additional information, see the section entitled "Local Group Policy."

10. The secedit.exe command line tool, when called from a batch file or automatic task scheduler, can be used to automatically create and apply templates and analyze system security. It can also be run dynamically from a command line.

This tool is useful when you have multiple computers on which security must be analyzed or configured and need to perform these tasks during off-hours. For additional information, see the section entitled "Windows 2000 Security Configurations."

11. User rights are specific permissions that can be assigned to users and groups. These permissions give users or groups the ability to manage various aspects of a system. Built-in groups relate to user rights because built-in groups get their rights from being assigned, by default, useful combinations of user rights. For additional information, see the section entitled "User Rights."

12. The following events can be audited:

- **Account logon.** Logs an event each time a user attempts to log on.

- **Logon events.** Logs an event for logon events that are occurring over the network or generated by service startup (for example, an interactive logon or a service such as SQL starting).

- **Account management.** Logs an event each time an account is managed. This is a useful function if you are concerned about changes being made to user accounts in your environment.

- **Directory service.** Logs an event each time an event occurs within the Active Directory services. For example successful or failed replication events.

- **Policy change.** Logs an event each time a policy is successfully or unsuccessfully changed in your environment.

APPLY YOUR KNOWLEDGE

- **Process tracking.** Logs an event for each program or process that a user launches while accessing a system. This information can be used by administrators to track the details of a user's activities while accessing a system.

- **Object access.** Logs an event each time a user attempts to access a resource (i.e., printer, shared folder, and so on.)

- **Privilege use.** Logs an event each time a user attempts, successfully or unsuccessfully, to use special privileges such as changing system time.

- **System event.** Logs designated system events. Windows 2000 may log system events when a user restarts or shuts down a computer.

Answers to Exam Questions

1. **B, D, E.** The key to this question is remembering where user accounts are stored under each model. Under the Workgroup model user accounts are stored and managed at the local machine. This model does not fit into environments with centralized Information System management. Under the domain model, user accounts stored in centralized locations are accessible throughout the domain. Generally, accounts stored and managed from a central location offer easier administration and better security. Answer A is not correct, as the workgroup model is not appropriate in large environments with centralized administration. Answer B is correct, as the domain model does work well in large environments with centralized administration. Answer C is not correct; the workgroup model does not offer better security. Answer D is correct; the domain model does offer better security. Answer E is also correct, as the workgroup model is limited to smaller environments. For additional information, see the sections entitled "The Workgroup Model" and "The Domain Model."

2. **D.** Scenario questions are popular on the Microsoft exams. The key to these questions is organizing the information presented and assessing each piece of it individually. Table 7.20 presents the answer to this question.

   For additional information, see the section entitled "User Accounts."

3. **B.** Scenario questions are popular on the Microsoft exams. The key to these questions is organizing the information presented and assessing each piece of it individually. Table 7.21 presents the answer to this question.

   For additional information, see the section entitled "User Accounts."

4. **A.** Scenario questions are popular on the Microsoft exams. The key to these questions is organizing the information presented and assessing each piece of it individually. Table 7.22 presents the answer to this question.

TABLE 7.20

QUESTION 2—RESULTS MATRIX

Result	Is this result met?	Rationale
Required Result: Security cannot be compromised on the network as users access resources throughout the enterprise.	No	The solution proposes that local user accounts be used on each workstation. Local accounts cannot be used to access resources across the enterprise.
Optional Result: User accounts must be easily managed from a centralized location.	No	The solution proposes that a location user account be used on each workstation. Local accounts do not allow for centralized administration.
Optional Result: You must be able to track each user based on a unique user name.	No	Each user is logging on as a user called "Temp".

TABLE 7.21

QUESTION 3—RESULTS MATRIX

Result	Is this result met?	Rationale
Required Result: Security cannot be compromised on the network, as users access resources throughout enterprise.	No	The solution proposes that a domain user account be used. Domain accounts can be given access to resources throughout the enterprise. The solution, however, requires that all users share the same user account. This type of environment would not be considered secure, as administrators cannot reliably determine which users are accessing the data.
Optional Result: User accounts must be easily managed from a centralized location.	Yes	The solution proposes that a domain user account be used. Domain accounts do allow for centralized administration.
Optional Result: You must be able to track each user based on a unique user name.	No	Each user is logging on as a user called "Temp".

APPLY YOUR KNOWLEDGE

TABLE 7.22

QUESTION 4—RESULTS MATRIX

Result	Is this result met?	Rationale
Required Result: Security cannot be compromised on the network, as users access resources throughout the enterprise.	Yes	The solution proposes that a domain user account be used. Domain accounts can be given access to resources throughout the enterprise. The solution also ensures that each user has their own account that is enabled only during the length of their contracts.
Optional Result: User accounts must be easily managed from a centralized location.	Yes	The solution proposes that a domain user account be used. Domain accounts do allow for centralized administration.
Optional Result: You must be able to track each user based on a unique user name.	Yes .	Each user is logging on with a unique user ID.

For additional information, see the section entitled "User Accounts."

5. **A.** The key to this question is understanding how groups work under Windows 2000. Answer A is correct, as you cannot take Domain Local groups from one domain and make them members of a group in another domain. Remember that Domain Local groups can be used only to access resources in the domain in which they reside. For additional information, see the section entitled "Groups."

6. **C.** The proposed solution does work but is not very effective. Universal groups from each user domain can be made a member of the Domain Local group in Domain A. This solution, however, is very inefficient, as Universal groups are not required at each user domain. Global groups should be used to organize the users, and the Global groups should be made a member of the Domain Local group in Domain A. Remember that Universal groups should not contain users in the membership list and is

appropriate only when the resource is located in a number of different domains. For additional information, see the section entitled "Groups."

7. **E.** This is the way Microsoft would like you to plan for access to resources. Accounts are placed into Global groups; Global groups are placed into Domain Local groups; and Domain Local groups are given permissions to the resource. Answers A and B are not correct, as the solution does work. Answers C and D are not correct, as using Domain Local groups or Universal groups in the user domains would not help with the solution. For additional information, see the section entitled "Groups."

8. **B.** Most likely the user reset her password with the CAPS lock on. Answer A is not correct, as passwords are considered priority changes and are replicated immediately. Answer C is not correct, as users do not need to be a member of the account operators group to change their passwords. Answer D is incorrect, as no mention was made that a workstation restriction was put

in place. For additional information, see the section entitled "User Accounts."

9. **C, D.** Domain Local groups can be used only to access resources in the domain that it is part of. You need to understand Microsoft's preferred method of using groups. Accounts are placed in Global groups, and Global groups are placed in Domain Local groups. Answer A is not correct, as replication usually occurs relatively quickly (approximately five minutes), and account information is not replicated between domains. Answer B is incorrect, as a Universal group would not be the preferred type of group (i.e., the resource is located in only one domain). For additional information, see the section entitled "Groups."

10. **A, B, C.** Remember that audit policies are configured in two places. You must enable auditing through a policy and then configure the resources that you want to be audited. When you configure the resource level, it is in your best interest to audit the Everyone group. The Everyone group includes all users (even users who are not authenticated to the network). You also should realize that auditing alone does not protect your resources. You generally use auditing to confirm that your security configuration is working properly. In this case, the network administrator should have reviewed the SQL database security, NFTS permissions, share permissions, and user password policies to ensure that the network is secure. Answer D is incorrect, as auditing can be used to track users accessing directories. For additional information, see the section entitled "Audit Policies."

11. **D.** The Encrypting File System supports a recovery agent account to assist if encrypted files need to be decrypted and the user is unavailable. Answer C is correct under the default installation of Windows 2000. The Administrator account is, by default, the recovery agent. Being the administrator, however, does not guarantee that you are also the recovery agent, if the default configuration has been changed. Answer A is incorrect because if you take ownership of the files, the encryption keys required to decrypt the file are not available to you. Answer B would work but is not an acceptable practice for network administrators. For additional information, see the section entitled "Encrypting File System."

12. **B, D.** You will need to remember the purpose of the security templates for the exam. The highly secure template configures secure network communications between Windows 2000-based systems and is supported only by Windows 2000-based systems. For this reason, answers B and D are correct. Answer B suggests upgrading the workstation so they have the ability to communicate with the servers. Answer D is less desirable but would work. In this case, we are going to apply the default security template to reset the servers to their default configuration, which does support communications with Windows 95/98 and Windows NT systems. Answer A is incorrect, as Windows 95/98 and Windows NT do not support security template configurations. Answer C is incorrect, as the user that is logged on does not impact on the secure communication channel required between client and server under the highly secure template. For additional information, see the section entitled "Windows 2000 Security Configurations."

APPLY YOUR KNOWLEDGE

13. **C.** In this question, you must be able to sort out the logical first place to look when troubleshooting a problem. Generally, the first place you will look for troubleshooting information is the Event Viewer. Remember that the Event Viewer shows information about services running on your servers. If the service is failing, you should see some information as to why in the event log. Answer A is another potentially correct answer. The Services node of Computer Manager, however, does not show any troubleshooting information (it only shows whether the service is running or not). Answer B is incorrect, as rebooting the server is generally considered a last resort when troubleshooting a problem (it also does not provide information as to the nature of the problem, if it does fix the problem). Answer D is incorrect, as the audit process will only show audit information about processes if you configured the server to audit for these events. For additional information, see the section entitled "Event Viewer."

14. **D.** This question requires that you understand how EFS works. Remember that the user who encrypts a file is the only user who can access the file (except for the recovery agent). In this scenario, we need a quick solution. The absolute fastest method we have available is to allow the users to log on as Administrator (i.e., the recovery agent). This solution would compromise network security and is totally inappropriate (therefore, answer A is incorrect). The next best solution is to write a batch file that runs the CIPHER command to decrypt the files. This involves mapping a drive to the root of each NTFS drive containing encrypted files and running the file. The only trick is getting the command syntax correct. Answer B is incorrect, as it uses the /e switch, which instructs CIPHER to encrypt files. Answer C is incorrect, as it does not include the /s switch, which tells CIPHER to decrypt files and sub-folders. Answer D is correct, as CIPHER is configured to decrypt files (/d), including subfolders (/s), and not stop on errors (/i). The /i option is important because when the command runs you might try to decrypt files you did not encrypt (i.e., files encrypted by other users). By default, CIPHER stops if it encounters an error. For additional information, see the section entitled "Encrypting File System."

15. **C.** This question requires that you put on your administrator's hat. Most administrators want things to be a simple as possible. In this scenario, you are having problems because the account policies in your environment require you to change your password every 30 days. This setting causes your service accounts to fail when their passwords expire. The simplest solution is C, set the service account so its password does not expire. Answer A is incorrect, as the Administrator also needs to reset passwords based on account policies. Answers B and D would work but would require more effort than necessary. For additional information, see the section entitled "Account Settings."

Suggested Readings and Resources

1. *Active Directory Overview*, White Paper. Microsoft Corporation, 2000. Available from www.microsoft.com.

2. *MS 2151—Supporting Windows 2000 Professional.* Microsoft Official Curriculum, Microsoft Corporation, 2000.

FINAL REVIEW

Fast Facts

Study and Exam Prep Tips

Practice Exam

The seven chapters of this book cover the objectives for the Windows 2000 Professional exam. After reading all of that, what are the important points that you really need to know? What should you review in that last hour prior to walking into the testing center to write your first (or next) Microsoft certification exam?

The following section covers the most significant points of the previous seven chapters and provides some insight into the information that makes particularly good exam material. There is no substitute for real-world, hands-on experience. However, knowing what to expect on the exam will go a long way toward a passing score. The information that follows provides the material that you must know to pass the exam. Don't memorize the concepts given; attempt to understand the reasons why they are so, and you will have no difficulty passing the exam.

INSTALLING WINDOWS 2000 PROFESSIONAL

Planning for and installing Windows 2000 Professional is naturally the first step to successfully using the product. The first consideration is the hardware requirements of the operating system and the application you plan on running.

Windows 2000 Professional requires a Pentium 133MHz or higher with 64MB of Memory, a system disk of at least 2GB with 650MB free space, a network adapter, VGA resolution graphics adapter or higher, a CD-ROM drive and finally, a keyboard and mouse.

System Configuration

The next task to installing Windows 2000 Professional is deciding on the disk layout. Windows 2000 Professional supports both basic disks and dynamic

Fast Facts

EXAM 70-210
INSTALLING, CONFIGURING, AND ADMINISTERING MICROSOFT WINDOWS 2000 PROFESSIONAL

disks. Basic disks use partitions (up to four per disk) and extended partitions with logical drives. Dynamic disks are broken up into logical volumes, with the disk configuration information being kept on the disk rather than in the Windows registry. Windows 9x and Windows NT 4.0 do not support dynamic disks, an important fact if you plan to implement a dual-boot system.

Once the layout is decided you need to choose the file system type. There are three types:

◆ FAT

◆ FAT32

◆ NTFS

File Allocation Table (FAT) supports the greatest number of operating systems and therefore is a good choice for dual-boot systems. It supports long filenames with spaces and additional periods, but it does not support encryption, disk quotas, or local security, and is inefficient for large partitions.

FAT32 was introduced to have a smaller cluster size to therefore support larger disk partitions. Otherwise, it suffers the same problems as FAT without the wide support. FAT32 does not support all versions of Windows 95, DOS, or Windows NT.

NTFS is the file system of choice for systems running Windows 2000. NTFS supports compression, encryption, quotas, file and folder level security, and uses transaction logging to support recoverability. NTFS supports sparse files (where only part of the file actually exists) and very large partitions (16 exabytes).

During the installation, you will be asked to select the network security group to install. The choices are workgroup and domain. The workgroup approach maintains a security database on each local machine in a grouping. This is naturally restricted to small groups of machines. The domain approach maintains a central database of security information. To join a domain, there must be a DNS name resolution system and a domain controller on your network.

Installation Methods

Manual (or automatic) installation of Windows 2000 Professional is completed in four steps. The first is to boot the computer from the CD or from a boot disk (made using the MAKEBOOT command). The installation enters the Text phase. In this phase you can select any third-party RAID/SCSI drivers, a boot partition, and file system type. The setup process copies files to the hard drive and reboots into graphical mode. In the graphical phase you are prompted for configuration information such as the local administrator's password and regional settings. The installation then configures the network adapters and selects a workgroup or domain to join. The final phase applies the configuration settings, cleans up any temporary files, and reboots the system.

If you wish to start the installation procedure from a running system, you would choose to run WINNT.EXE from DOS or WINNT32.EXE from Windows 95/98 or Windows NT.

Unattended Installation

Installation of Windows 2000 Professional can also be done without user intervention.

There are two different files used during unattended installation: the unattended text file (or answer file) and the uniqueness definition file (UDF). The first represents all the standard things in an installation and the second represents the unique settings found in each machine. The unattended text file is used to configure all of the standard options for each machine (one file for each type of hardware platform in your environment); the UDF file is used to configure the unique aspects of each individual computer (such as computer name, domain to join, and network configuration).

There is a tool in the Windows 2000 resource kit (SETUPMGR.EXE) that will create both the answer file and the UDF file as well as a batch file that will correctly apply the command switches to WINNT32.EXE to perform the unattended installation.

Remote Installation Services

Another way to install Windows 2000 Professional is by using Remote Installation Services (RIS). RIS runs on a server (domain controller or member server) and contains one or more operating system images that can be downloaded over the network. The Remote Image Preparation utility (RIPrep) is used to remove all SID, computer name, and registry information.

A RIS client uses the Pre-Boot Execution Environment (PXE) BIOS to obtain an address from DHCP and query DNS about the availability of RIS servers. You are prompted to log on and a list of RIS images to download is displayed.

A final way to install Windows 2000 Professional is by re-imaging a computer's hard drive with Sysprep and third-party disk imaging software.

IMPLEMENTING AND CONDUCTING ADMINISTRATION OF RESOURCES

This section deals with allowing and controlling access to network resources. The most often used and also the most complex network resource is that of file system access.

When a file is "shared" on the network, the owner is granting Read, Change, and Full Control permissions to users and groups. Read allows the user to read the contents of files and subfolders within the share and to execute programs held there. Change provides all the Read permissions as well as the ability to add files and subfolders to the share and append and delete from files already existing on the share. Full Control allows the user Read and Change privileges plus the ability to take ownership of the resource. It is also an option to deny access to the resource by a group.

Permissions are always cumulative with the exception of Deny, which overrides all others.

After a share has been created and access provided, the user can connect to it in one of four ways. The first is by using the command line net use x:*computer*\ *share* to link a drive letter to a shared resource. The same drive letter mapping can be done using the Windows Explorer under the Tools menu. Shares can also be accessed using My Network Places and by entering **computer****share** into the Windows Run menu.

Some default shares are automatically created when installing Windows 2000 Professional. These include *driveletter*$ (i.e., C$ or D$), which allows administrative personnel to attach to the root directory of a drive; ADMIN$ (used during remote administration), which is linked to the \WINNT subdirectory on the system drive; and IPC$, which is used as a communications link between programs.

Shared folder permissions provide very limited security; they protect resources only if they are accessed over the network. Shared folder permissions are also limited because they provide access to the entire directory structure from the share point down into the subdirectories. For these reasons, you will find that it is rare for shared folder permissions to be used in isolation, without NTFS permissions.

To secure folders and files on a NTFS partition, we assign NTFS permissions for each user or group that requires it. If a user does not have any permissions assigned to his user account, or does not belong to a group with permissions assigned, the user does not have access to the file or folder. The NTFS folder permissions available to set for users or groups are shown in the following list:

◆ **Read.** See the files and subfolders and view folder attributes, ownership, and permissions.

◆ **Write.** Create new files and subfolders, change folder attributes, and view folder ownership and permissions.

◆ **List Folder Contents.** See the names of files and subfolders in the folder.

◆ **Read and Execute.** The combination of the Read permission and the List Folder Contents permission and the ability to traverse folders. The right to traverse folders allows you to reach files and folders located in subdirectories even if the user does not have permission to access portions of the directory path.

◆ **Modify.** The combination of Read and Write permissions plus the ability to delete the folder.

◆ **Full Control.** Change permissions, take ownership, delete subfolders and files, and perform the actions granted by all other permissions.

The NTFS file permissions available to set for users or groups are shown in the following list:

◆ **Read.** Read a file and view file attributes, ownership, and permissions.

◆ **Write.** Overwrite a file, change file attributes, and view file ownership and permissions.

◆ **Read and Execute.** The combination of Read plus rights required to run applications.

◆ **Modify.** The combination of the Read and Execute permissions plus the ability to modify and delete a file.

◆ **Full Control.** Change permissions, take ownership, delete subfolders and files, and perform the actions granted by all other permissions.

File and folders permissions are cumulative exactly as described for file shares, and permissions can be inherited from the folder above. When you view the permissions of a file or folder, inherited permissions appear grayed out. Inheritance can also be blocked and inherited permissions removed from a file or folder. This would leave only the explicitly assigned permissions left. Permissions applied to the file level override permissions inherited from the folder level.

When you copy files or folders from one folder to another or from one partition to another, permissions may change. The following lists the results you can expect from various copy operations:

◆ When you copy a folder or file within a single NTFS partition, the folder or file inherits the permissions of the destination folder.

◆ When you move a folder or file within a single NTFS partition, the folder or file retains its original permissions.

◆ When you move or copy a folder or file between NTFS partitions, the folder or file inherits the permissions of the destination folder.

◆ When you move or copy a folder or file to a non-NTFS partition, all permissions are lost (this is because non-NTFS partitions do not support NTFS permissions).

Best Practices

Users will access network resources for a variety of purposes (home directories, shared files, or applications). Home directories, for example, are usually seen as the place where users keep their own documents. If this is on a server (as a shared resource), there are usually automatic backup and restore services provided. A user's files are also available even if the user is not at his normal workstation. Local home directories are available when the network is down or unavailable, but backups are left to the user (and that is usually not done regularly), so the information is at risk of disk failure.

Common files are usually shared at the top of the directory structure to provide a single starting point for all users. Access to individual files and folders is handled at the NTFS level to allow or deny access to individuals or groups.

Application shares allow common programs to be kept in one spot on the network. This allows for better control over versions and software upgrades and makes the application available even if the user is not at his normal workstation.

NTFS volumes also allow you to compress the data held on them to increase the amount of space available. This naturally increases the amount of time to access the file and uses some CPU power. However, in an emergency it can quickly provide some needed space. Compression can be enabled from the Windows Explorer from the Properties page of the volume. It can also be done using the COMPACT program from a command window.

One further step that you might want to take to secure information held locally on your computer is to encrypt the file or folder using the Encrypting File system provided by Windows 2000 Professional. Details on this feature are found in Chapter 7, "Implementing, Monitoring, and Troubleshooting Security."

Sharing Printer Resources

The four components that make up the Windows 2000 print environment are shown in the following list:

◆ **Printer.** A printer is a logical or software representation of a physical print device. You will find printers configured on computers so that print jobs can be sent to them.

◆ **Print driver.** A print driver is used to convert print requests into a format understood by the physical print device being used in the environment.

◆ **Print server.** A print server is a computer that receives and processes documents from client computers for processing.

◆ **Print device.** A print device is the physical device that produces the printed output.

Printers can be either local or network based. If you are installing a local printer, you are given the option of automatically creating a network share that would allow other users access to it. Access to shared printers is managed in the same fashion as shared files. In the case of printers, there are three types of permissions that you can assign to users or groups:

◆ Print

◆ Manage Documents

◆ Manage Printers

The various tasks that you may want to do with printers or print jobs will require different permissions. Table 1 outlines the permissions required to manage the printing environment.

TABLE 1
PERMISSIONS FOR THE PRINT ENVIRONMENT

Capabilities	Print Permission	Manage Documents Permission	Manage Printer Permission
Print documents	Yes	Yes	Yes
Pause, resume, restart, and cancel the user's own print jobs	Yes	Yes	Yes
Connect to the shared printer	Yes	Yes	Yes
Control job settings for all print jobs	No	Yes	Yes
Pause, resume, restart, and cancel all user's print jobs	No	Yes	Yes
Cancel all print jobs	No	Yes	Yes
Pause and resume a printer, and take a printer offline	No	No	Yes
Share a printer	No	No	Yes
Change printer properties	No	No	Yes
Delete a printer	No	No	Yes
Change printer permissions	No	No	Yes

Managing a printer environment can also include providing higher priority to some print jobs and providing greater capacity for some printers. Priority can be set by installing an additional printer pointing to the same physical printer as an existing printer, but with a higher priority.

Windows 2000 Professional allows you to create a printer pointing to a number of devices (print pooling), thereby providing a higher capacity than any one physical print device alone.

IMPLEMENTING, MANAGING, AND TROUBLESHOOTING HARDWARE DEVICES AND DRIVERS

Windows 2000 Professional supports Plug and Play (PnP), allowing you to add new hardware (or remove hardware) without making configuration changes. PnP will detect a new device both dynamically (adding a PCMCIA card) and at boot time (detecting a new video adapter).

Devices that are not Plug and Play compliant will have to be manually configured. Device drivers usually need configuration information on the following topics:

◆ **Interrupts.** An Interrupt Request (IRQ) is a way of determining which device is looking for service and what type of attention it needs. Windows 2000 provides interrupt numbers 0 through 15 to devices (IRQ 1 is always assigned to the keyboard).

◆ **Input/Output (I/O) ports.** I/O ports are areas of memory that the device uses to communicate with Windows 2000 Professional.

◆ **Direct Memory Access (DMA).** DMAs are channels that allow the hardware device to access memory directly. Windows 2000 Professional provides DMA channels 0 through 7.

◆ **Memory.** Many hardware devices have onboard memory or can reserve system memory for their use.

The Resource by Device display from the Device Manager shows the availability of resources in your computer system.

CD-ROM and DVD Devices

Current DVD and CD-ROM devices all support Plug and Play and should install automatically without intervention.

Hard Disk Devices

Conventional hard disks are either basic or dynamic. A basic disk is partitioned into up to four partitions (or three if an extended partition is configured). The partition information is kept on the disk in a partition table in the Master Boot Record (MBR). Each partition behaves as a separate device. Basic disks can also contain volume sets, mirrored volumes, striped volumes, and RAID-5 volumes created by NT 4.0 or earlier. You cannot create these structures on basic disks under Windows 2000. That capability is only supported under dynamic disks. Basic storage is supported by all versions of Microsoft Windows 3.x, Microsoft Windows 9x, and Windows 2000 Professional and Server.

A dynamic disk is divided into volumes rather than partitions. A volume consists of a part or parts of one or more physical disks laid out in five configurations (simple, spanned, mirrored, striped, and RAID-5). Dynamic disks keep the volume information on physical disks in a small, 1MB database at the end of the disk. Dynamic disks cannot contain partitions or logical drives and cannot be accessed by MS-DOS.

Simple volumes are made up of all or part of a single disk. Spanned volumes are made up of all or part of up to 32 disks. Stripped volumes are similar to spanned volumes with the data written across all disks at the same rate. A mirrored volume duplicates data onto two physical disks for fault tolerance. A RAID 5 structure is a fault-tolerant volume that spreads data and checksum information across three or more disk drives.

Removable Storage

Windows 2000 Professional supports Removable Storage Management (RSM) as the interface for accessing removable media, including automated devices such as changers, jukeboxes, and libraries. RSM is installed by default to control most types of removable media including CD-ROM, DVD-ROM, magneto-optical (MO) JAZ and ZIP drives in both standalone and library configurations. RSM can be used to manage anything except the A: and B: drives.

Multiple Displays

Windows 2000 Professional adds support for up to nine display adapters. This allows the desktop to extend to nine monitors supporting large graphical drawings (such as CAD displays) or topographical maps.

Power Management

Windows 2000 Professional supports the new Advanced Computer Power Interface (ACPI) and the older Advance Power Management (APM) system. ACPI provides the operating system control over power for every device installed on your computer. It also supports action on an event (like wake on LAN) or on a timer (like powering down a disk drive when it has been idle for a length of time).

Card Services

The CardBus interface allows PC cards to use a 32-bit connection and can operate up to speeds of 33MHz. This allows the cards to support things such as MPEG video, 100Mbit Ethernet, and Streaming Video. Windows 2000 Professional also supports power management and Plug and Play for these devices.

Input/Output devices

Windows 2000 Professional supports the Plug and Play standard and most new devices use this to standardize their installation steps.

Printers

The printing subsystem is modular and works hand in hand with other subsystems to provide printing services. When a printer is local and a print job is specified by an application, data is sent to the Graphics Device Interface (GDI) for rendering into a print job in the printer language of the print device. The GDI is the interface between the application and the printing subsystem. The print job is passed to the spooler and is written to disk as a temporary file so it can survive a power outage or system shutdown. Print jobs can be spooled in either the RAW or EMF printer language.

The spooling process is logically divided into two halves. The division between the client side and the server side allows the process to be on two different computers, allowing for the print process to use either local printer or remote.

Keyboards

Keyboards can be built in, connected with a specific device port, or operate as a USB device connected directly via a USB hub.

Keyboard Customizations

The Accessibility Options applet in the Control Panel also provides a number of ways to customize how your keyboard functions:

◆ **StickyKeys.** This option allows you to press a modifier key such as Ctrl, Alt, Shift, or the Windows Logo key and have it remain in effect until a non-modifier key is pressed.

◆ **FilterKeys.** This option allows you to ignore brief or repeated keystrokes.

◆ **ToggleKeys.** This option emits a sound when locking keys are pressed.

◆ **SerialKeys.** This option allows you to use an alternative input device instead of a keyboard and mouse.

Mouse

Like keyboards, mice can be directly connected to a mouse port, built into the keyboard as a piezoelectric control, connected to the serial port, or to a device on a USB port or USB hub. Once the mouse has been installed, you can adjust the characteristics of its action by using the Mouse applet in the Control Panel.

Multimedia

Categories of multimedia devices in Windows 2000 Professional include audio, video, and MIDI. In addition, the Microsoft Media Player can use the Web to access music files and radio stations that broadcast programming. The CD Player can be used to control the playback of music CD's from the system CD-ROM drive.

Smart Cards

Smart cards are credit card-sized programmable computing devices. Applications and data can be downloaded onto a card for a variety of uses including authentication, certificate storage, record keeping, and so on.

Although the processor included in the card can give it great capability, a smart card is not a stand-alone computer. It must be connected to other computers to be much use. Smart cards today contain an 8-bit micro-controller with 16KB or more of memory.

In the Windows 2000 operating system, smart cards and certificate-based logon are fully supported. In this architecture, the smart card contains the certificate and associated private key. A challenge is sent to the smart card when you are logging on to your Windows 2000 Professional computer. The private key signs the challenge and the result, along with the certificate, is submitted to the authentication service. The authentication service verifies the signature and permits or denies the logon request.

Modems

Modems are most commonly used to dial up remote systems or Internet service providers using speeds up to 56Kb over analog phone lines. Modems from different manufactures can achieve high speeds in different ways, causing compatibility problems for error correction and data compression. You may find that a high-speed modem will drop back to run at a lower speed because of compatibility differences with the modem at the other end of the phone line.

Infrared Devices

Windows 2000 Professional supports IrDA protocols that enable data transfer over infrared connections. The Windows 2000 Professional Plug and Play architecture will automatically detect and install the IrDA components for computers with built-in IrDA hardware.

Most laptops now ship with IrDA ports that provide either 115Kbps or 4Mbps transmission speeds.

Wireless Devices

The Wireless Link file transfer program, infrared printing functions, and image transfer capability are installed by default with your Windows 2000 Professional operating system. In addition, IrDA supports Winsock API calls to support programs created by other software and hardware manufacturers. The Winsock API calls can be used to provide infrared connections to printers, modems, pagers, PDA's, electronic cameras, cell phones, and hand-held computers.

Linking Infrared Devices

When communications are first established, the commanding station sends out a connection request at 9600Kbps. The responding station assumes the secondary role and returns information listing its capabilities. Both the primary and secondary stations then change the connection rate and link parameters to the common set established by this initial negotiation. With the connection established, data transfer is put under the control of the primary device.

A single IrDA device cannot link to more than one other IrDA device at a time. You can install multiple IrDA devices to provide simultaneous links to multiple remote devices. For example, you can have a desktop computer connect to a notebook and a digital camera simultaneously using two IrDA transceivers.

USB Devices

The Universal Serial Bus (USB) is a serial protocol that runs at up to 12Mb/sec, supporting Plug and Play and power management. USB is a token-based protocol that Windows 2000 Professional polls to detect changes to the devices connected.

Hubs can be self powered with an external power source or can be bus powered and get their power from the bus itself. The USB definition allows for a total of five tiers (such as hubs attached to hubs) in a USB network. With the Windows 2000 Professional computer acting as the USB host, that leaves a total of four tiers (or network segments) for actual devices.

Updating Drivers

When using WindowsUpdate, the hardware IDs for the devices installed are compared to what the Microsoft Web site has to offer. If an exact match is made, the new driver is downloaded and installed. If an update to an existing driver is found, the new software components will be listed on the Web site and a download button will load the updated drivers onto your Windows 2000 Professional computer into a temporary directory for installation.

Multiple Processing Units

Windows 2000 Professional is designed to run uniformly on a uniprocessor and symmetric multi-processor platforms.

Windows 2000 Professional supports the addition of a CPU under the following conditions:

◆ Both CPUs are identical and either have identical coprocessors or no coprocessors.

◆ Both CPUs can share memory and have uniform access to memory.

◆ In symmetric multiprocessor platforms, both CPUs can access memory, process interrupts, and access I/O control registers.

Network Adapters

If you install a new network adapter in your computer, the next time you start Windows 2000 Professional, a new local area connection icon appears in the Network and Dial-Up Connections folder. Plug and Play functionality finds the network adapter and creates a local area connection for it. You cannot manually add local area connections to the Network and Dial-up Connections folder. By default, the local area connection is always activated.

You must enable the network clients, services, and protocols that are required for each connection. When you do, the client, service, or protocol is enabled in all other network and dial-up connections.

Monitoring and Optimizing System Performance and Reliability

This section is concerned with the performance and reliability of your computer.

Driver Signing

Device drivers are a perennial source of problems in computer systems. Microsoft has instituted a certification program for device drivers and included a mechanism to enforce this on your computer. From the Systems applet in Control Panel, you can set driver signing to ignore an unsigned driver, warn you when one is installed, or block the installation altogether.

The Task Scheduler

The Task Scheduler is a graphical utility (run by a wizard) to allow you to schedule a task to be run on a scheduled basis. This replaces the older AT command that allowed you to run a command at a particular time. The problem with the AT command was its inflexibility (only based on date or time) and the fact that it ran everything under the SYSTEM account. This account does not have rights to your network files and therefore cannot be used to access shares. The Task Scheduler allows you to select the userid and pass-word under which to run the task. This provides your scheduled job with access to all the file shares the userid normally has available to it. Scheduled jobs are kept in the \\WINNT\Tasks folder with a .JOB extension.

Using and Synchronizing Offline Files

If you travel frequently and use your laptop for most of your work, offline files provide a way to ensure that the network files you are working with are the most current versions and that changes you make when offline will be synchronized when you reconnect to the network.

When you reconnect to the network (perhaps docking your portable computer), changes that you have made to the offline files are synchronized back to their original network files. If someone else has made changes to the same file, you have the option of saving your version of the file, keeping the other version, or saving them both.

Performance Monitoring

Windows 2000 Professional defines performance data in terms of objects, counters, and instances. An object is any resource, application, or service that you can measure. Each object has counters that are used to measure various aspects of performance such as transfer rates for disks, packet transmit rates for networks, or memory and processor time consumed by applications or services.

Each object will have at least one counter, although most have many different counters available. Each counter will have at least one instance (usually Total or Average) although some objects (such as Process) will have an instance for each process currently active on the computer.

Memory Performance

Memory usage in Windows 2000 Professional is divided into paged (can be written out to disk) or non-paged (must reside in memory). The paging file provides a place for memory in the paged pool to reside when not in use and extends the amount of virtual memory available. Memory not in use by processes is allocated to the file cache. This holds recently read or written data for quick access if required. The size of the file cache depends on the amount of physical memory available and the number of processes being run. You can find the current value for your computer by looking in the Performance tab in Task Manager.

The size of the paging file is set to the amount of physical memory plus 12MB, but its usage and size will be different on every system. If you configure your paging file too small, Windows 2000 Professional will spend more time looking for space and therefore run slower. You could also exhaust the amount of virtual memory available and generate errors when running applications. A best practice would be to move the paging file to a disk other than the one holding the system files and to set its minimum and maximum size to the same amount to prevent disk fragmentation.

Since Memory performance is tied to the paging file (and therefore disk performance), the most important counters to watch are Available Bytes (the amount of memory available) and Pages In and Pages Out (pages being written to and from the paging file).

The file system cache itself can't be a bottleneck. However, if there is not enough memory to make an effective cache area, the result is increased disk activity and perhaps, a disk bottleneck. An important counter to watch is Copy Read Hits %, which should be 80% or greater to be optimal. If your system is consistently below this value for long periods of time, you may have a memory shortage.

Processor Performance

The System, Processor, Process, and Thread objects contain counters that provide useful information about the work of your processor.

A processor bottleneck occurs when the processor is so busy that it cannot respond to an application that is requesting time. High activity may indicate that a processor is either handling the work adequately or it is a bottleneck and slowing down the system. The Processor Queue Length counter from the System object and the % Processor Time counter from the Processor object will indicate whether your processor is just busy, or overwhelmed by requests. The processor queue length should be less than 2 as an average. The % Processor Time should be less than 80% as an average.

If you determine that you do have a processor bottleneck, some of the following actions might shorten the processor queue and reduce the burden on your processor:

◆ Delete memory bottlenecks that might be consuming the processor.

◆ Upgrade your network or disk adapters to intelligent, 32-bit adapters.

◆ Try to obtain adapters that have optimization features.

◆ Upgrade to a faster processor.

◆ Add another processor.

Disk Performance

Disk performance counters can reflect both physical disk activity and logical disk and volume activity. To enable the logical disk counters you must run the command DISKPERF –yv and reboot your computer. When you next open the performance application, the logical disk object will be enabled.

Here are some important disk counters:

◆ **Avg. Disk Bytes/Transfer.** This counter measures the size of I/O operations.

◆ **Avg. Disk/Sec Transfer.** This counter measures the average time for each transfer regardless of the size.

◆ **Avg. Disk Queue Length.** This is the total number of requests waiting as well as the requests in service. If there are more that two requests continually waiting, then the disk might be a bottleneck.

◆ **Current Disk Queue Length.** This counter reports the number of I/O requests waiting as well as those being serviced.

◆ **Disk Bytes/Sec.** This is the rate at which data is being transferred to the disk. This is the primary measure of disk throughput.

◆ **Disk Transfers/Sec.** This is the number of reads and writes completed per second, regardless of the amount of data involved. This is the primary measure of disk utilization.

◆ **% Idle Time.** The percentage of time the disk subsystem was not processing requests and no I/O requests were queued.

It is important to monitor the amount of available storage space on your disks because a shortage of disk space can adversely affect the paging file and, as the disk space diminishes, disk fragmentation usually increases.

The % Free Space and Free Megabytes counters in the LogicalDisk object allow you to monitor the amount of available disk space. If the amount of available space is becoming low, then you may want to move some files to other disks if available and compress the disk and remove temporary files to free up some disk space.

If you think there is a disk bottleneck in your computer, then the following counters will be useful during analysis of the problem:

- **Paging counters (found in the Memory object).** Pages/Sec, Page Reads/Sec, Page Writes/Sec

- **Usage counters.** % Disk Time, % Disk Read Time, % Disk Write Time, % Idle Time, Disk Reads/Sec, Disk Writes/Sec, Disk Transfers/Sec

- **Queue-length counters.** Avg. Disk Queue Length, Avg. Disk Read Queue Length, Avg. Disk Write Queue Length, Current Disk Queue Length

- **Throughput counters.** Disk Bytes/Sec, Disk Read Bytes/Sec, Disk Write Bytes/Sec

Network Performance

As with other resources, when analyzing the performance of your Windows 2000 Professional computer network components, it is always best to establish a baseline for comparison. When performance data varies from your established baseline there may be a network resource bottleneck or a performance problem with some other resource that is having an impact on network performance. For that reason network counters should be viewed in conjunction with the % Processor Time (in the Processor object), the % Disk Time (in the PhysicalDisk object) and Pages/Sec (in the Memory object).

Network bottlenecks are typically caused by an overloaded processor, an overloaded network, or a problem on the network itself. Some of the approaches you can take to resolving network bottlenecks include the following:

- Use adapters with the highest bandwidth available for the best performance.

- Remove unused network adapters to reduce overhead.

- If your network uses multiple protocols, place each protocol on a different adapter.

- Use network adapters that support interrupt moderation to improve performance.

- Modify the protocol binding order on your Windows 2000 Professional computer to reflect the amount of use each protocols gets.

- Use offline folders to work on network applications without being connected to the network to help reduce network traffic.

Application Performance

Only a very few applications require the high performance of a real time data collection or a transaction system. It is therefore important to define what the required performance level is and to determine a way to measure it.

Application performance can be described from three points of view:

- **The real performance.** This is how fast the application actually performs its work.

- **The perceived performance.** This is how fast the application looks and feels to the user.

- **The consistency of the application's response.** This aspect of performance can be characterized in terms of the stability, scalability, and availability of the application.

The application that satisfies all three views will always be considered successful.

Here are some important counters for measuring Application performance. These are found in the Process object:

- **Memory.** Pool Paged Bytes, Pool Non-Paged, Non-Paged Bytes, Working Set, Working Set Peak

- **Processor.** % Privilege Time, % User Time, % Processor Time

- **I/O.** Read Bytes/Sec, Read Operations/Sec, Write Bytes/Sec, Write Operations/Sec

Hardware Profiles

Hardware profiles tell your Windows 2000 Professional computer which devices to start and what setting to use for each device.

You create hardware profiles from the System applet in the Control Panel. If there is more than one hardware profile, you can designate one as the default that will be loaded when you start your Windows 2000 Professional computer (assuming you don't make a choice manually). Once you create a hardware profile, you can use Device Manager to enable or disable devices in the profile. When you disable a device while a hardware profile is selected, that device will no longer be available and will not be loaded the next time you start your computer.

Recovering System and User Data Using Backup

A tested backup and recovery procedure is one of the most important administrative tasks to perform. When you are creating your backup policy, you must consider the following issues:

- How often should a backup be done?

- What type of backup is the most appropriate?

- How long should backup tapes be stored?

- How long will the recovery of lost data take?

There are five types of backups available through the Windows 2000 Backup utility:

- **Normal backup.** Copies all selected files and marks each as being backed up. With normal backups you can restore files quickly because the files on tape are the most current.

- **Copy backup.** Copies all the selected files but does not mark them as backed up.

- **Incremental backup.** Copies only those files created or changed since the last normal or incremental backup. A system restore would require a restore of the last normal backup and then all the incremental backups done since.

- **Differential backup.** Copies those files created or changed since the last normal backup. It does not mark the files as having been backed up.

- **Daily backup.** Copies those files that have been modified the day the daily backup is performed. The files are not marked as backed up.

Restoring Your Data

Windows 2000 Professional provides two ways to restore files using the Windows Backup utility: a wizard to walk you through the steps involved and a graphical interface to allow you to define the restore job manually.

When you wish to recover some or all of the files stored during a backup job, you must select the backup set to restore from and then the specific files (or all files) to restore. You can also restore the files to their original location or to an alternate location if you want to copy the recovered files by hand.

Booting your Computer Using Safe Mode

Press F8 during the operating system selection phase to display a screen with advanced options for booting Windows 2000. The following list describes the functions available from the advanced boot menu:

◆ **Safe Mode.** Loads only the basic devices and drivers required to start the system. This includes the mouse, keyboard, mass storage, base video, and the default set of system services.

◆ **Safe Mode with Networking.** Performs a Safe Load with the drivers and services necessary for networking.

◆ **Safe Mode with Command Prompt.** Performs a Safe Load but launches a command prompt rather than Windows Explorer.

◆ **Enable Boot Logging.** Logs the loading and initialization of drivers and services.

◆ **Enable VGA Mode.** Restricts the startup to use only the base video.

◆ **Last Known Good Configuration.** Uses the Last Known Good configuration to boot the system.

◆ **Directory Services Restore Mode.** Allows the restoration of the Active Directory (on Domain Controllers only).

◆ **Debugging Mode.** Turns on debugging.

When logging is enabled, the boot process writes the log information to \%systemroot%\NTBTLOG.TXT.

Last Known Good Configuration

Configuration information in Windows 2000 Professional is kept in a control set subkey. A typical Windows 2000 installation would have subkeys such as ControlSet001, ControlSet002, and

CurrentControlSet. The CurrentControlSet is a pointer to one of the ControlSetxxx subkeys. There is another control set named Clone that is used to initialize the computer (either the Default or LastKnownGood). It is re-created by the kernel initialization process each time the computer successfully starts.

The key HKEY_LOCAL_MACHINE\SYSTEM\Select contains subkeys named Current, Default, Failed, and LastKnownGood, which are described in the following list:

◆ **Current.** This value identifies which control set is the CurrentControlSet.

◆ **Default.** This value identifies the control set to use the next time Windows 2000 starts (unless you choose Last Known Good configuration during the boot process).

◆ **Failed.** This value identifies the control set that was the cause of a boot failure the last time the computer started.

◆ **LastKnownGood.** This value identifies the control set that was used the last time Windows 2000 was started successfully. After a successful logon, the Clone control set is copied to the LastKnownGood control set.

When you log on to a Windows 2000 Professional computer and modify its configuration by adding or removing drivers, the changes are saved in the Current control set. The next time the computer is booted, the kernel copies the information in the Current control set to the Clone control set. After the next successful logon to Windows 2000, the information in the Clone control set is copied to LastKnownGood.

If, when starting the computer, you experience problems that you think might be related to Windows 2000 configuration changes that you just made, restart the computer without logging on and press F8 during the initial boot phase. Selecting the Last Known Good configuration will restore the system configuration to the last one that Windows 2000 used to start successfully.

Configuring the Windows 2000 Recovery Console

To use the recovery console, you must first install it from the Windows 2000 CD. The Installation Wizard will create all the files necessary and modify boot.ini to provide an additional boot menu item that will allow you to select the recovery console while starting your system.

Installing the Recovery Console

The Recovery Console Wizard is started with the command

```
\I386\WINNT32 /cmdcons
```

where the \I386 is a subdirectory on the Windows 2000 CD.

CONFIGURING AND TROUBLESHOOTING THE DESKTOP ENVIRONMENT

This section reviews configuring and troubleshooting the desktop environment.

User Profiles

Windows 2000 is a multi-user operating system in that the expectation is that there will be more than one user who uses the system. Windows 2000 Professional supports this through user profiles. There are three different types of profiles:

◆ **Local profiles.** These profiles are stored on the local workstation and will not follow a user to another computer if they should log on to one.

◆ **Roaming profiles.** Roaming profiles are defined as a profile that is stored on a Windows 2000 server. This allows the profile to follow the user when logging on to a different computer.

◆ **Mandatory profiles.** This is a special variation of a roaming profile that will not save configuration changes made by the user.

Configuring Support for Multiple Languages

The starting point for multiple languages is the Regional Options applet of the Control Panel. This allows you to configure the appearance of numbers and date fields displayed by Windows 2000 Professional. In addition to being able to change the appearance of numbers, dates, and times, you can change the default input locale for a document. This allows you to enter letters and documents in a language other than the one your prompts and dialogs are in.

Windows Installer

Microsoft's Windows Installer technology is designed to address the limitations of software distribution:

◆ **On-demand installation of applications.** When an application is needed by the user, the operating system automatically installs the application from a network share, or by requesting the user insert the appropriate media.

◆ **On-the-fly installation of application components.** The Windows Installer technology allows applications to dynamically launch an installation to install additional components not initially installed on the computer.

◆ **Automatic application repair.** Windows applications are sometimes corrupted by users deleting some required files, or by errant installations of other software. The Windows installer can automatically repair damaged programs making your application more resilient.

Automatic installation is sometimes called Install on First Use. Some of the different options allowed when installing software by Windows Installer are as follows:

◆ **Run from My Computer.** This is the traditional installation method that loads the application onto the local hard drive.

◆ **Run from CD.** Run the component without installing any software on the local computer. This will cause the component to run slower, but will allow the component to be run when space is at a premium.

◆ **Install on First Use.** The component will be installed on its first use; in other words, if you never use a component, it won't be installed.

◆ **Not Available.** The component isn't installed. This option is useful when you don't want users to be able to install a feature on their own.

Configuring Desktop Settings

Windows 2000 Professional allows great latitude of choices and tastes when customizing the look of the desktop, including toolbars, shortcuts, wallpaper, desktop, and screen savers.

By effectively managing elements such as favorites, shortcuts, network connections, and desktop items, you can ensure that the most relevant and current information is easily accessible.

Setting a desktop standard within your company or workgroup can reduce support and training costs by eliminating the need to learn about the changes to each user's desktop. Windows 2000 allows you to create a unique standard operating environment including user interface (UI) standards, based on the needs of your organization.

Windows 2000 Professional in the Windows 2000 Server Network

When Windows 2000 Professional is part of a Windows 2000 Server network running Active Directory, powerful administrative functions such as Group Policy and Change and Configuration Management are available to customize and control the desktop.

Group Policy can be used to set and enforce policies on multiple workstations from a central location. There are more than 550 policies, including policies that help prevent users from making potentially counter-productive changes to their computers. You can optimize the desktop for the specific needs of each workgroup or department in your organization.

Comparing Stand-Alone and Active Directory-Based Management Features

All of the Group Policy snap-ins that can be used on a local computer can also be used when Group Policy is focused on an Active Directory container.

However, the following activities require Windows 2000 Server, an Active Directory infrastructure, and a client running Windows 2000:

◆ Centrally managed software installation and maintenance for groups of users and computers

- User data and settings management, including folder redirection, which allows special folders to be redirected to the network

- Remote operating system installation

Using Group Policy on Stand-Alone Computers

You will sometimes need to implement a Group Policy on a stand-alone computer. On a stand-alone computer running Windows 2000 Professional, local Group Policy objects are located at \\%*SystemRoot*%\System32\ GroupPolicy. The following settings are available on a local computer:

- **Security settings.** You can only define security settings for the local computer, not for a domain or network.

- **Administrative templates.** These allow you to set more than 400 operating system behaviors.

- **Scripts.** You can use scripts to automate computer startup and shutdown, as well as how the user logs on and off.

The following are examples of business rules that you might enforce through local Group Policy:

- The users cannot access the Run command.

- An anti-virus program runs every time the computer is restarted.

- Common program groups are hidden in the Start menu.

To manage Group Policy on local computers, you need administrative rights to those computers.

Desktop Control through Local Group Policies

There are a few simple rules to remember about the effects of Group Policies on user settings:

- The Group Policy always takes precedence. If it is set then the users covered by the policy will all have the setting specified.

- If the Group Policy doesn't have a value for a particular setting, or if there is no Group Policy, the user has the freedom to change the setting to whatever she would like.

- If a Group Policy is added to the system after the user has set up her environment, the Group Policy will take priority, and override any user settings.

Remember that when setting up Group Policies you may disable the user's ability to change something, but you may or may not disable the part of the user interface where changes to the setting are made. This sometimes causes confusion because the change just doesn't appear to have taken effect. See Chapter 5, "Configuring and Troubleshooting the Desktop Environment."

Configuring and Troubleshooting Fax Support

To send and receive faxes all you need is Windows 2000 and a fax device, such as a fax modem. Your fax device must support fax capabilities and not just data standards. While some modems offer both capabilities, the two are not interchangeable. Fax supports classes 1, 2, and 2.0. Fax for Windows 2000 does not support shared fax printers. This means you cannot share your fax printer with other users on a network.

Fax Service Management helps you to manage fax devices on your local computer or on other computers on your network. Using Fax Service Management, you can configure security permissions, determine how many rings occur before the fax is answered, set up a device to receive faxes, and set priorities for sending faxes.

Accessibility Services

Several built-in technologies and Windows Explorer options are available for administrators and users to configure their computers with the accessibility features they need. Many of these features have added function-ality beyond Microsoft Windows, including Magnifier, Narrator, On-Screen Keyboard, Utility Manager, high-visibility mouse pointers, and high-contrast color schemes. Again, see Chapter 5 for details on using the Accessibility Wizard to configure these services.

IMPLEMENTING, MONITORING, AND TROUBLESHOOTING NETWORK PROTOCOLS AND SERVICES

The bottom layers of the Windows 2000 network architecture include the network adapter card driver and the network interface card (NIC). NDIS supports both connection-oriented protocols such as ATM and ISDN, as well as the traditional connectionless protocols such as Ethernet, Token Ring, and Fiber Distributed Data Interface (FDDI). The mechanism that NDIS uses to bridge these two layers is the mini-port driver specification. The miniport drivers directly access the network adapters while providing common code where possible. Hardware vendors therefore do not have to write complete Media Access Control (MAC) drivers, and protocols can be substituted without changing network adapter card drivers.

NDIS 5.0 is the current level supported by Windows 2000 Professional and adds new functionality to networking. The following list describes some of the new features of NDIS 5.0:

◆ **Power management and network wake-up.** NDIS power management can power down network adapters at the request of the user or the system. The system can also be awakened from a lower power state based on network events like a cable reconnect or the receipt of a network wakeup frame or a Magic Packet packet (16 contiguous copies of the receiving system's Ethernet address).

◆ **NDIS Plug-and-play.** Installs, loads, and binds miniports when a new adapter card is introduced.

◆ **Task Offload.** Available if the network adapter card has the capability to support check-summing and forwarding for performance enhancements.

◆ **Support for Quality of Service (QoS) and connection-oriented media such as ATM and ISDN.** QoS allows for bandwidth to be reserved for uses like video conferencing. Protocols like ATM do not support features like broadcasts used by TCP/IP (broadcasts for a DHCP server). This must be emulated in connection-oriented media.

TCP/IP

Transmission Control Protocol/Internet Protocol (TCP/IP) is the default protocol for Windows 2000 Professional and is an industry standard suite of protocols available for wide area networks (WAN) and the Internet.

NWLink IPX/SPX Compatible Transport

NWLink is an NDIS-compliant, native 32-bit implementation of Novell's IPX/SPX protocol.

NetBIOS Extended User Interface (NetBEUI)

NetBEUI is a simple non-routable protocol designed for peer-to-peer Networks that requires little memory overhead.

Adding and Configuring Network Components

You can configure all your network components when you first install Windows 2000 Professional. If you want to examine how your network components are configured or make changes to your network identification, double-click the System applet in the Control Panel and select the Network Identification tab.

Identification Options

Use the Network Identification option in the System applet to view your computer name and your workgroup or domain information.

To configure network options, open the Network and Dial-Up connection folder in Control Panel, right-click a connection, and select Properties.

Protocol Options

To configure Protocols, click the Install button. This brings up the Select Network Component Type button.

Service Options

Click on the Install button and select a service to add to display all the available services not currently installed.

Client Options

Select the Client entry and click the Add button to show the clients available to install on your computer.

IP Addressing

Each TCP/IP connection must be identified by an address. The address is a 32-bit number that is used to uniquely identify a host on a network. The TCP/IP address has no dependence on the Data-Link layer address such as the MAC address of a Network adapter. Although the IP address is 32 bits, it is customary to break it into four 8-bit numbers expressed in decimal and separated by dots. This can be referred to in dotted decimal format and is expressed as $w.x.y.z$.

This addressing scheme is again broken down into two halves: a network ID (also known as the network address) and the host ID (also known as the host address). The network ID must be unique in the Internet or intranet, and the host ID must be unique to the network ID. The network portion of the $w.x.y.z$ notation is separated from the host through the use of the subnet mask.

The Internet community was originally divided into five address classes. Microsoft TCP/IP supports class A, B, and C addresses assigned to hosts.

The class of address defines which bits are used for the network ID and which bits are used for the host ID. It also defines the possible number of networks and the number of hosts per network. Here is a rundown of the five classes:

◆ **Class A addresses.** The high order bit is always binary 0 and the next seven bits complete the network ID. The next three octets define the host ID. This represents 126 networks with 16,777,214 hosts per network.

◆ **Class B addresses.** The top two bits in a class B address are always set to binary 1 0. The next 14 bits complete the network ID. The remaining two octets define the host ID. This represents 16,384 networks with 65,534 hosts per network.

◆ **Class C addresses.** The top three bits in a class C address are always set to binary 1 1 0. The next 21 bits define the network ID. The remaining octet defines the host ID. This represents 2,097,152 networks with 254 hosts per network.

◆ **Class D addresses.** Class D addresses are used for multicasting to a number of hosts. Packets are passed to a selected subset of hosts on a network. Only those hosts registered for the multicast address accept the packet. The four high-order bits in a class D address are always set to binary 1 1 1 0. The remaining bits are for the address that interested hosts will recognize.

◆ **Class E addresses.** Class E is an experimental address that is reserved for future use. The high-order bits in a class E address are set to 1 1 1 1.

Table 2 shows the most common address classes and the number of networks and hosts supported by them.

Subnet Mask

Once an IP address from a particular class has been decided upon, it is possible to divide it into smaller segments to better utilize the addresses available. Each segment is bounded by an IP router and assigned a new subnetted network ID that is a subset of the original class-based network ID.

A subnet mask (also known as an address mask) is defined as a 32-bit value that is used to distinguish the network ID from the host ID in an IP address. The bits of the subnet mask are defined as follows:

◆ All bits that correspond to the network ID are set to 1.

◆ All bits that correspond to the host ID are set to 0.

The subnet mask is broken down to four 8-bit octets in the same fashion as the class addresses.

Table 3 shows the default subnet mask and the dotted notation used to describe them to Windows 2000 Professional.

TABLE 2
ADDRESS CLASSES, NETWORKS, AND HOSTS

Class	Network ID	Network Portion	Host Portion	Number of Networks	Number of Hosts
A	1.126	w.	x.y.z	126	16,777,214
B	128.191	w.x	y.z	16,384	65,534
C	192.168.23	w.x.y	z	2,097,152	254

TABLE 3
DEFAULT SUBNET MASK AND DOTTED NOTATION EQUIVALENT

Address Class	Bits for Subnet Mask	Subnet Mask
Class A	11111111 00000000 00000000 00000000	255.0.0.0
Class B	11111111 11111111 00000000 00000000	255.255.0.0
Class C	11111111 11111111 11111111 00000000	255.255.255.0

Default Gateway (Router)

This optional setting is the IP address of the router for this subnet segment. Each subnet segment is bounded by a router that will direct packets destined for segments outside the local one to the correct segment or to another router that can complete the connection. If this address is left blank, this computer will be able to communicate only with other computers on the same network segment.

Windows Internet Name Service (WINS)

Computers may use IP addresses to identify one another, but users generally prefer to use computer names. Windows 2000 Professional allows Windows 9x and Windows NT 4 clients to use NetBIOS names to communicate and therefore requires a means to resolve NetBIOS names to IP addresses. WINS provides a dynamic database that replaces the static LMHOST file and maintains mappings of computer names to IP addresses.

Domain Name Systems (DNS) Server Address

DNS is an industry-standard distributed database that provides name resolution and a hierarchical naming system (Fully Qualified Domain Name) for identifying TCP/IP hosts on Internets and private networks that replaces the static HOST file.

Understanding DHCP

One way to avoid the possible problems of administrative overhead and incorrect settings for the TCP/IP protocol (which are usually caused by manual configurations) is to use DCHP. DHCP centralizes and manages the allocation of the TCP/IP settings required for proper network functionality for computers that have been configured as DHCP clients.

Virtual Private Networks (VPN)

A Virtual Private Network (VPN) allows the computers in one network to connect to the computers in another network by the use of a tunnel through the Internet or other public network. The VPN provides the same security and features formerly available only in private networks.

A VPN connection allows you to connect to a server on your corporate network from home or when traveling using the routing facilities of the Internet. The connection appears to be a private point-to-point network connection between your computer and the corporate server.

Additionally, VPNs can be used to connect remote office LANs to the corporate LAN or to other remote LANs to share resources and information using direct connect or dial-up access.

The basic functions managed by VPNs are the following:

◆ **User authentication.** Verify the user's identity and restrict VPN access to authorized users only.

◆ **Address management.** Assign the client's address on the private net and ensure that private addresses are kept private.

◆ **Data encryption.** Data carried on the public network must be unreadable to unauthorized clients on the network.

◆ **Key management.** Encryption keys must be refreshed for both the client and the server.

◆ **Multiprotocol support.** The most common protocols used in the public network are supported.

A VPN is not a protocol in itself, but rather the encapsulation of existing protocols and the encryption of the data being transmitted.

Windows 2000 Professional provides two encapsulation methods for VPN connections, Point-to-Point Tunneling Protocol and Layer 2 Tunneling Protocol.

Point-to-Point Tunneling Protocol (PPTP)

This protocol enables the secure transfer of data from your computer to a remote computer on TCP/IP networks. PPTP tunnels, or encapsulates, IP, IPX, or NetBEUI protocols inside of PPP datagrams.

PPTP Encryption

The PPP frame is encrypted with Microsoft Point-to-Point Encryption (MPPE) by using encryption keys generated from the MS-CHAP or EAP-TLS authentication process.

Layer 2 Tunneling Protocol (L2TP)

L2TP is an Internet tunneling protocol with roughly the same functionality as PPTP. The Windows 2000 implementation of L2TP is designed to run natively over IP networks.

L2TP Encryption

The L2TP message is encrypted with IPSec encryption mechanisms by using encryption keys generated from the IPSec authentication process. The portion of the packet from the UDP header to the IPSec ESP Trailer inclusive is encrypted by IPSec.

Connecting to Computers by Using Dial-Up Networking

Dial-Up Networking enables you to extend your network to unlimited locations. The Microsoft RAS protocol is a proprietary protocol that supports the NetBIOS standard.

Dial-Up to the Internet

This option is used to connect to an Internet Service Provider (ISP).

The Internet Connection Wizard also allows you to enter email configuration information to allow Outlook Express to connect to an Internet mail service. Outlook Express is configured when Windows 2000 Professional is installed, and can be used to connect to POP3, IMAP4, or HTTP mail servers.

Internet Connection Sharing

With the Internet connection-sharing feature of Network and Dial-Up Connections, you can use Windows 2000 to connect your home network or small office network to the Internet.

A computer with Internet connection sharing needs two connections: one to the internal LAN and one to the Internet. Internet connection sharing is enabled on the Internet connection. This shared connection will allow your internal network to receive its addresses using DHCP, provide a DNS service to resolve names, and provide a gateway service to access computer systems outside your home network. The network address translation (NAT) service allows your home network to use any addressing scheme you want because the internal addresses are not broadcast onto the Internet.

The NAT is transparent to both the client and server. The client appears to be talking directly with the external server and the external server behaves as though the NAT is the end client. To the client, the NAT may be its default gateway (as is the case with Internet connection sharing) or, in a larger network, the router that connects to the Internet.

When the NAT is performing address and port translation, all internal addresses will be mapped to the single IP address of the NAT's external network card or dial-up interface. Ports will be mapped so that they remain unique.

Connecting to Shared Resources

Windows 2000 provides different methods to work with network resources and to determine what network resources are available.

Browsing

Users on a Windows 2000 network often need to know what domains and computers are accessible from their local computers.

Universal Naming Convention

The Universal Naming Convention (UNC) is a standardized way to specify a share name on a specific computer. The share name can refer to folders or printers. The UNC path takes the form of \\computer_name\share_name.

NET USE Command

You can assign network resources to drive letters from the command prompt as well as from the Tools menu from Windows Explorer. To connect drive letter X: to a share called GoodStuff on a server named SERVER1, for example, you would type the following command at the command prompt:

```
C:\Net Use X: \\SERVER1\GoodStuff
```

You can also use the NET USE command to connect clients to network printers. If you want to connect port LPT1: to a network printer named HP5 on a server named SERVER1, use the following command:

```
Net Use LPT1: \\SERVER1\HP5
```

To disconnect the network resources for these two, use the following two commands:

```
Net Use X: /d
Net Use LPT1: /d
```

Troubleshooting TCP/IP Connections

The first thing to do when troubleshooting TCP/IP networking connections is to use IPCONFIG /all to obtain the local TCP/IP configuration.

Typical problems found in the configuration are duplicate IP addresses with other computers on the network, or a subnet mask of 0.0.0.0.

PING is a tool that will help to verify connectivity at the IP level. The best process to follow when using PING to detect network problems is to use IP addresses only (so as not to confuse name resolution errors with network errors) and to ping progressively more remote computers.

Using Tracert

The Tracert diagnostic utility determines the route taken to a destination by sending Internet Control Message Protocol (ICMP) echo packets with varying IP Time-to-Live (TTL) values to the destination. Each router along the path is required to decrement the TTL on a packet by at least 1 before forwarding it. When the TTL on a packet reaches 0, the router should send an ICMP Time Exceeded message back to the source computer.

Resolve a NetBIOS Name to an IP Address

Resolving a NetBIOS name means successfully mapping a 16-byte NetBIOS name to an IP address. The File and Printer Sharing for Microsoft Networks service in Windows 2000 Professional uses NetBIOS name resolution. When your computer starts up, this service registers a unique NetBIOS name based on the name of your computer (padded out to 15 characters if it is shorter than that) with 0x20 as the 16th character.

Resolve a Host or Domain Name to an IP Address

Host names are resolved by using the HOSTS file or by querying a DNS server. Problems in the HOSTS file usually involve spelling errors and duplicate entries. The Nslookup utility or the Netdiag resource kit utility can be used to diagnose host name resolution problems.

Determine Whether the Address Is Local

The subnet mask along with the IP address are used to determine whether the IP address is local or on a remote subnet.

A misconfigured subnet mask can result in the system's inability to access any other system on the local subnet while still being able to communicate with remote systems.

If the IP address is local, ARP is used to identify the destination MAC address.

Determine the Correct Gateway

If the IP address is remote from the local subnet, the gateway to use to reach the remote address must be determined. If the network has a single router, this problem is straightforward. In a network with more than one router connected, additional steps must be taken.

To solve this problem, the system uses the routing table. The entries in the routing table enable IP to determine which gateway to send outgoing traffic through. The routing table has many entries for individual routes, each one consisting of a destination, network mask, gateway interface, and hop count (metric).

IMPLEMENTING, MONITORING, AND TROUBLESHOOTING SECURITY

A user account contains information about a person who can gain access to your network. Information stored in a user account includes the user's name and password as well as other information that describes the configuration of the user. User accounts are used to represent people in your networked environment. Accounts allow users to identify themselves when they log on to the local computer or domain. Users accounts are also used to grant (or deny) access to resources. Through user accounts you can control how a user gains access to a resource.

The Workgroup Model

Under the Workgroup model each computer in your environment is responsible for the management of its own local account database. Local user accounts contain information that define users for the local computer. With a local user account, a user can log on to the local computer and gain access to local resources. To gain access to resources on another computer, a user must use an account on the other computer.

The Domain Model

Under the Domain model, a centralized database of user accounts is managed for a grouping (or domain) of computers. Domain user accounts contain information that defines users within the domain.

User Accounts

Windows 2000 automatically creates two user accounts called built-in accounts when it is installed. The Administrator account is the account that is used to manage the configuration of the computer and users stored on the computer. The Administrator account has the capability to manage all aspects of the computer so access to this account must be protected. You can rename the Administrator account but it cannot be deleted. Guest is also a built-in account. The Guest account can be used to grant occasional users access to resources. The Guest account is disabled by default.

Local User Accounts

Local user accounts are typically associated with the Workgroup model. Local user accounts can be used to access the computer on which the account physically resides and resources on the local machine. Local user accounts are limited to local resources.

Creating Domain User Accounts

Domain user accounts are very similar to local user accounts. The primary difference between a local user account and a domain user account is that a domain account can be used to gain access to resources throughout a domain or through an Active Directory environment.

Account Settings

A set of default properties is associated with each domain user account you create. You can use these properties to define how users can access the network. After you create a domain user account you will need to configure the account.

Personal Properties

The most common tabs in the Properties dialog box that contain personal information about each user account are the General, Address, Telephones, and Organization tabs.

Account Properties

You can also manage a user's logon name, password settings, the hours during which the user can logon, and the computers from which the user can logon.

Setting logon hours give administrators the ability to control when a user account is allowed to logon to the network. For example, if you know a user is only going to be accessing the network during business hours the account can be set to only allow logon during those hours.

Dial-Up Properties

Configuring dial-up properties for a user account allows you to control how a user can connect to a network through a remote access server (a dial-up). Configuration of settings can be managed from the Dial-Up tab of the properties of a user account.

Group Membership

Groups are used to simplify resource access. The Member Of tab allows you to manage the group membership of a user account. From this tab you can click the Add or Remove button to modify group membership.

Groups

Groups are used to simplify the overall management of accounts in your environment. In most environments users can be grouped into categories of user account (such as Accountants, Sales People, and so on). These categories of user accounts generally define common access needs for groups of users in your environment.

Being a member of a group automatically grants you the same rights as the group object. Depending on the type of group, you can also make groups members of other groups.

There are different groups within Windows 2000 Professional that reflect the scope of the group within the domain.

Global Groups

The most common use of global groups is to organize users who share similar network access requirements.

Domain Local Groups

The most common use of a domain local group is to assign permissions to resources.

Universal Groups

The most common use of a universal group is to assign permissions to resources in multiple domains.

Group Strategies

If you are in a single domain environment, for example, you can use Global Groups to organize your users into logical groupings. You would then create local groups to provide access to resources (such as assign permissions to the domain local groups). You would then make the appropriate Global Groups members in the Domain Local Group with access to required resources. The short form for this is A → GG → LG → Permissions or "put accounts into global groups, global groups into local groups, and assign permissions to local groups."

Built-In Groups

Windows 2000 systems have a number of built-in groups associated with them. These groups provide a powerful tool for the management of resources on the local system/domain. Membership in one (or more) of these groups gives users rights to access (and manage) the local operating system depending on the group. Each group is, by default, assigned a useful collection of rights and privileges.

The five built-in local groups added during installation are as follows:

◆ **Administrators.** Membership in the Administrators group allows a user to manage all aspects of the local operating system. Members of this group have the ability to manage user accounts, load and unload system drivers, and perform backups and restores of file systems.

◆ **Backup Operators.** Regular users have the ability to back up and restore files that they have permission to access without being part of this group. In most environments, however, backups are managed centrally so that they can be completed by set intervals with a high degree of reliability.

◆ **Guests.** The guests group is used to give someone limited access to resources on the system. The guest account is automatically added to this group.

◆ **Power Users.** Members of the Power Users group have more permission than members of the Users group and less permission than members of the Administrators group. Power Users can perform most operating system tasks (share resources, install or remove applications, and customize system resources).

◆ **Users.** By default all users (with the exception of the built-in Administrator and Guest accounts) created on the local system are made members of the Users group. The users group provides the user with all of the necessary rights to run the computer as an end user.

Built-In Domain Local Groups

The seven built-in local groups added during installation are as follows:

◆ **Account Operators.** Members of the Account Operators group can create, delete, and modify users' accounts and groups. Members cannot modify the Administrators, Server Operators, Printer Operators, or Account Operators groups.

◆ **Server Operators.** Members of the Server Operators group can manage disk resources, back up and restore file system resources, and manage files system resources.

◆ **Print Operators.** Members of the Print Operators group can manage print resources.

◆ **Administrators.** Membership in the Administrators group allows a user to manage all aspects of the local operating system. Members of this group can manage user accounts, load and unload system drivers, and perform backups and restores of file systems.

◆ **Backup Operators.** Regular users can back up and restore files that they have permission to access without being part of this group. In most environments, however, backups are managed centrally so that they can be completed at set intervals with a high degree of reliability.

◆ **Guests.** The Guests group is used to give someone limited access to resources on the system. The Guest account is automatically added to this group.

◆ **Users.** By default all users (with the exception of the built in Administrators and Guest accounts) created on the local system are made members of the Users group. The Users group provides the user with all of the necessary rights to run the computer as an end user.

Built-In Global Groups

The four built-in Global Groups added during installation are as follows:

- **Domain Users.** Windows 2000 automatically adds the Domain Users global group to the User domain local group. By default, the Administrator account is initially a member of the Domain Users global group. Windows 2000 also adds each domain user to the Domain Users group when each domain user is created.

- **Domain Admins.** Windows 2000 automatically adds the Domain Admins global group to the Administrator domain local group so that the Domain Administrator can manage all local systems in the domain.

- **Domain Guests.** Windows 2000 automatically adds the Domain Guests global group to the Guests domain local group. By default, the Guest account is a member.

- **Enterprise Admins.** You can add user accounts to the Enterprise Admin global group for those users who require administrator control over the entire network. Windows 2000 automatically adds the Enterprise Admin group to the Domain Admin global group for all domains in the enterprise. The Enterprise Admins group will only appear in your root domain.

User Rights

Table 4 lists the rights assigned to the various built-in groups.

TABLE 4
RIGHTS FOR THE VARIOUS BUILT-IN GROUPS

User Right	Description	Granted To
Access This Computer from the Network	Allows you to access resources from the computer over the network but does not give you the capability to access resources that your user account has not been given permission to use.	Everyone, Users, Power Users, Backup Operators, Administrators
Back Up Files and Directories	Allows you to back up file system resources regardless of permissions held by the user.	Backup Operators, Administrators
Bypass Traverse Checking	Gives you the ability to access a file resource deep in a directory structure even if the user does not have permission to the file's parent directory.	Everyone, Users, Power Users, Backup Operators, Administrators
Change the System Time	Allows you to change system time.	Power Users, Administrators
Create a Page file	Allows you to configure the virtual memory management of a system.	Administrators
Deny Access to This Computer from the Network	Restricts a user from accessing this computer over the network regardless of group membership.	None
Deny Logon Locally	Explicitly restricts a user from logging on to a system from the local console.	None
Force Shutdown from a Remote System	Allows a user to remotely shut down a system using a remote shutdown utility.	Administrators
Increase Quotas	Allows users to modify quota settings for NTFS-formatted partitions.	Administrators
Increase Scheduling Priority	Allows you to reschedule jobs that have been submitted to the scheduling service.	Administrators

continues

TABLE 4 *continued*
RIGHTS FOR THE VARIOUS BUILT-IN GROUPS

User Right	Description	Granted To
Load and Unload Drivers	Allows you to load and unload device drivers.	Administrators
Log On Locally	Allows you to log on at the computer from the local computer console.	Guests, Users, Power Users, Backup Operators, Administrators
Manage Auditing and Security log	Allows a user to specify what type of resource access will be audited.	Administrators
Remove Computer from Docking Station	Allows a user to undock a laptop from its docking station.	Users, Power Users, Administrators
Restore File and Directories	Allow users to restore a backup of a file system of permissions held by the user.	Backup Operators, Administrators
Shut Down the System	Allows a user to shut down the local system.	Users, Power Users, Backup Operators, Administrators. (On Windows 2000 Server, members of the Users group do not have this ability.)
Take Ownership of Files of Other Objects	Allows a user to take ownership of files, directories, printers and other objects on the computer. This right supersedes permissions protecting objects.	Administrators

Audit Policies

An audit policy defines the categories of user activities that Windows 2000 records in the security logs on each computer. Audit policies are set up to track authorized and unauthorized access to resources.

Categories of Security Events

Security events are divided into categories. This allows the system administrator to configure audit policies to specific categories of events (based on your organization's auditing and security plan). When viewing the event logs you can search for specific categories of events.

Object Access Events

An audit policy can be configured to monitor access to objects such as files and folders, printers, and other objects. The audit policy defines what events will be entered in the event log.

Windows 2000 Security Configurations

Windows 2000 Professional manages security configurations through the use of templates. There are eight predefined templates, with four that relate to Windows 2000 Professional. They define default, compatible, secure, and highly secure configurations. The default configuration can be used to return your computer to the default Windows 2000 security configuration. The compatible template provides NT 4.0 backward compatibility for the Power Users group (for development of applications destined to run on Windows NT 4.0). The secure template implements all recommended security settings for Windows 2000 Professional. The highly secure configuration provides the greatest protection for Network traffic. This is reserved for

Windows 2000 to Windows 2000 communication and will not allow your computer to communicate with NT 4.0 or Windows 9x machines.

Encrypting File System

Encrypting File System (EFS) allows the owner of a file system resource to encrypt it. The service is based on public/private encryption technology and is managed by the Windows 2000 Public Key Infrastructure (PKI) services.

The technology is based on a public key-based structure. Each user has a public and private key. The keys were created in such a way that anything encrypted using the private key can be decrypted only using the public key and anything encrypted using the public key can be decrypted only using the private key.

When the owner of a file encrypts a file system resource, a file encryption key is generated and used to encrypt the file. The file encryption keys are based on a fast symmetric key designed for bulk encryption. The file is encrypted in blocks with a different key for each block. All of the file encryption keys are then stored with the file (as part of the header of the file).

When a file is accessed, EFS detects the access attempt and locates the user's certificate from the Windows 2000 PKI and the users associated private key. The private key is then used to decrypt the Data Decryption Field (DDF) to retrieve the file encryption keys used to encrypt each block of the file. The only key in existence with the ability to decrypt the DDF information is the private key of the owner of the file. Access to the file is denied to anyone else, as they do not hold the private key required for decrypting the file encryption keys.

File encryption can be managed using Windows Explorer or the CIPHER program.

This element of the book provides you with some general guidelines for preparing for a certification exam. It is organized into four sections. The first section addresses your learning style and how it affects your preparation for the exam. The second section covers your exam preparation activities and general study tips. This is followed by an extended look at the Microsoft Certification exams, including a number of specific tips that apply to the various Microsoft exam formats and question types. Finally, changes in Microsoft's testing policies, and how these might affect you, are discussed.

LEARNING STYLES

To better understand the nature of preparation for the test, it is important to understand learning as a process. You probably are aware of how you best learn new material. You may find that outlining works best for you, or, as a visual learner, you may need to "see" things. Whatever your learning style, test preparation takes place over time. Obviously, you shouldn't start studying for these exams the night before you take them; it is very important to understand that learning is a developmental process. Understanding it as a process helps you focus on what you know and what you have yet to learn.

Thinking about how you learn should help you recognize that learning takes place when you are able to match new information to old. You have some previous experience with computers and networking. Now you are preparing for this certification exam. Using this book, software, and supplementary materials will not just add incrementally to what you know; as you study, the organization of your knowledge actually restructures as you integrate new information into your existing knowledge base. This will lead you to a more comprehensive understanding of the tasks and concepts

Study and Exam Prep Tips

outlined in the objectives and of computing in general. Again, this happens as a result of a repetitive process rather than a singular event. Keep this model of learning in mind as you prepare for the exam, and you will make better decisions concerning what to study and how much more studying you need to do.

STUDY TIPS

There are many ways to approach studying just as there are many different types of material to study. However, the tips that follow should work well for the type of material covered on the certification exams.

Study Strategies

Although individuals vary in the ways they learn information, some basic principles of learning apply to everyone. You should adopt some study strategies that take advantage of these principles. One of these principles is that learning can be broken into various depths. Recognition (of terms, for example) exemplifies a more surface level of learning in which you rely on a prompt of some sort to elicit recall. Comprehension or understanding (of the concepts behind the terms, for example) represents a deeper level of learning. The ability to analyze a concept and apply your understanding of it in a new way represents a further depth of learning.

Your learning strategy should enable you to know the material at a level or two deeper than mere recognition. This will help you perform well on the exams. You will know the material so thoroughly that you can easily handle the recognition-level types of questions used in multiple-choice testing. You will also be able to apply your knowledge to solve new problems.

Macro and Micro Study Strategies

One strategy that can lead to this deeper learning includes preparing an outline that covers all the objectives and subobjectives for the particular exam you are working on. You should delve a bit further into the material and include a level or two of detail beyond the stated objectives and subobjectives for the exam. Then expand the outline by coming up with a statement of definition or a summary for each point in the outline.

An outline provides two approaches to studying. First, you can study the outline by focusing on the organization of the material. Work your way through the points and sub-points of your outline with the goal of learning how they relate to one another. For example, be sure you understand how each of the main objective areas is similar to and different from another. Then, do the same thing with the subobjectives; be sure you know which subobjectives pertain to each objective area and how they relate to one another.

Next, you can work through the outline, focusing on learning the details. Memorize and understand terms and their definitions, facts, rules and strategies, advantages and disadvantages, and so on. In this pass through the outline, attempt to learn detail rather than the big picture (the organizational information that you worked on in the first pass through the outline).

Research has shown that attempting to assimilate both types of information at the same time seems to interfere with the overall learning process. Separate your studying into these two approaches, and you will perform better on the exam.

Active Study Strategies

The process of writing down and defining objectives, subobjectives, terms, facts, and definitions promotes a more active learning strategy than merely reading the material. In human information-processing terms, writing forces you to engage in more active encoding of the information. Simply reading over it exemplifies more passive processing.

Next, determine whether you can apply the information you have learned by attempting to create examples and scenarios on your own. Think about how or where you could apply the concepts you are learning. Again, write down this information to process the facts and concepts in a more active fashion.

The hands-on nature of the step-by-step tutorials and exercises at the ends of the chapters provide further active learning opportunities that will reinforce concepts as well.

Common-Sense Strategies

Finally, you should also follow common-sense practices when studying. Study when you are alert, reduce or eliminate distractions, and take breaks when you become fatigued.

Pre-Testing Yourself

Pre-testing allows you to assess how well you are learning. One of the most important aspects of learning is what has been called "meta-learning." Meta-learning has to do with realizing when you know something well or when you need to study some more. In other words, you recognize how well or how poorly you have learned the material you are studying.

For most people, this can be difficult to assess objectively on their own. Practice tests are useful in that they reveal more objectively what you have learned and what you have not learned. You should use this information to guide review and further studying. Developmental learning takes place as you cycle through studying, assessing how well you have learned, then reviewing, and then assessing again until you feel you are ready to take the exam.

You may have noticed the practice exam included in this book. Use it as part of the learning process. The *ExamGear, Training Guide Edition* test simulation software included on the CD also provides you with an excellent opportunity to assess your knowledge.

You should set a goal for your pre-testing. A reasonable goal would be to score consistently in the 90-percent range.

See Appendix C, "Using the *ExamGear, Training Guide Edition* Software," for more explanation of the test simulation software.

Exam Prep Tips

Having mastered the subject matter, the final preparatory step is to understand how the exam will be presented. Make no mistake: A Microsoft Certified Professional (MCP) exam will challenge both your knowledge and your test-taking skills. This section starts with the basics of exam design, reviews a new type of exam format, and concludes with hints targeted to each of the exam formats.

The MCP Exam

Every MCP exam is released in one of three basic formats. What's being called exam format here is really little more than a combination of the overall exam structure and the presentation method for exam questions.

Understanding the exam formats is key to good preparation because the format determines the number of questions presented, the difficulty of those questions, and the amount of time allowed to complete the exam.

Each exam format uses many of the same types of questions. These types or styles of questions include several types of traditional multiple-choice questions, multiple-rating (or scenario-based) questions, and simulation-based questions. Some exams include other types of questions that ask you to drag and drop objects on the screen, reorder a list, or categorize things. Still other exams ask you to answer these types of questions in response to a case study you have read. It's important that you understand the types of questions you will be asked and the actions required to properly answer them.

The rest of this section addresses the exam formats and then tackles the question types. Understanding the formats and question types will help you feel much more comfortable when you take the exam.

Exam Format

As mentioned above, there are three basic formats for the MCP exams: the traditional fixed-form exam, the adaptive form, and the case study form. As its name implies, the fixed-form exam presents a fixed set of questions during the exam session. The adaptive form, however, uses only a subset of questions drawn from a larger pool during any given exam session. The case study form includes case studies that serve as the basis for answering the various types of questions.

Fixed-Form

A fixed-form computerized exam is based on a fixed set of exam questions. The individual questions are presented in random order during a test session. If you take the same exam more than once, you won't necessarily see the exact same questions. This is because two or three final forms are typically assembled for every fixed-form exam Microsoft releases. These are usually labeled Forms A, B, and C.

The final forms of a fixed-form exam are identical in terms of content coverage, number of questions, and allotted time, but the questions are different. You may notice, however, that some of the same questions appear on, or rather are shared among, different final forms. When questions are shared among multiple final forms of an exam, the percentage of sharing is generally small. Many final forms share no questions, but some older exams may have a 10–15 percent duplication of exam questions on the final exam forms.

Fixed-form exams also have a fixed time limit in which you must complete the exam. The *ExamGear, Training Guide Edition* software on the CD-ROM that accompanies this book provides fixed-form exams.

Finally, the score you achieve on a fixed-form exam, which is always reported for MCP exams on a scale of 0 to 1,000, is based on the number of questions you answer correctly. The passing score is the same for all final forms of a given fixed-form exam.

The typical format for the fixed-form exam is as follows:

- ◆ 50–60 questions.
- ◆ 75–90 minute testing time.
- ◆ Question review is allowed, including the opportunity to change your answers.

Adaptive Form

An adaptive-form exam has the same appearance as a fixed-form exam, but its questions differ in quantity and process of selection. Although the statistics of adaptive testing are fairly complex, the process is concerned with determining your level of skill or ability with the exam subject matter. This ability assessment begins with the presentation of questions of varying levels of difficulty and ascertaining at what difficulty level you can reliably answer them. Finally, the ability assessment determines whether that ability level is above or below the level required to pass that exam.

Examinees at different levels of ability will see quite different sets of questions. Examinees who demonstrate little expertise with the subject matter will continue to be presented with relatively easy questions. Examinees who demonstrate a high level of expertise will be presented progressively more difficult questions. Individuals of both levels of expertise may answer the same number of questions correctly, but because the higher-expertise examinee can correctly answer more difficult questions, he or she will receive a higher score and is more likely to pass the exam.

The typical design for the adaptive form exam is as follows:

◆ 20–25 questions.

◆ 90 minute testing time (although this is likely to be reduced to 45–60 minutes in the near future).

◆ Question review is not allowed, providing no opportunity for you to change your answers.

The Adaptive-Exam Process

Your first adaptive exam will be unlike any other testing experience you have had. In fact, many examinees have difficulty accepting the adaptive testing process because they feel that they were not provided the opportunity to adequately demonstrate their full expertise.

You can take consolation in the fact that adaptive exams are painstakingly put together after months of data gathering and analysis and that adaptive exams are just as valid as fixed-form exams. The rigor introduced through the adaptive testing methodology means that there is nothing arbitrary about the exam items you'll see. It is also a more efficient means of testing, requiring less time to conduct and complete than traditional fixed-form exams.

As you can see in Figure 1, a number of statistical measures drive the adaptive examination process. The measure most immediately relevant to you is the ability estimate. Accompanying this test statistic are the standard error of measurement, the item characteristic curve, and the test information curve.

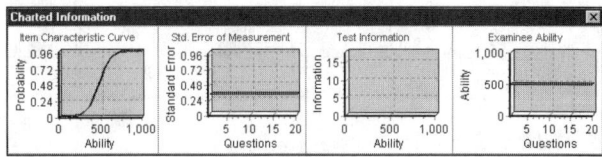

FIGURE 1
Microsoft's adaptive testing demonstration program.

The standard error, which is the key factor in determining when an adaptive exam will terminate, reflects the degree of error in the exam ability estimate. The item characteristic curve reflects the probability of a correct response relative to examinee ability. Finally, the test information statistic provides a measure of the information contained in the set of questions the examinee has answered, again relative to the ability level of the individual examinee.

When you begin an adaptive exam, the standard error has already been assigned a target value below which it must drop for the exam to conclude. This target value reflects a particular level of statistical confidence in the process. The examinee ability is initially set to the mean possible exam score (500 for MCP exams).

As the adaptive exam progresses, questions of varying difficulty are presented. Based on your pattern of responses to these questions, the ability estimate is recalculated. At the same time, the standard error estimate is refined from its first estimated value of one toward the target value. When the standard error reaches its target value, the exam is terminated. Thus, the more consistently you answer questions of the same degree of difficulty, the more quickly the standard error estimate drops, and the fewer questions you will end up seeing during the exam session. This situation is depicted in Figure 2.

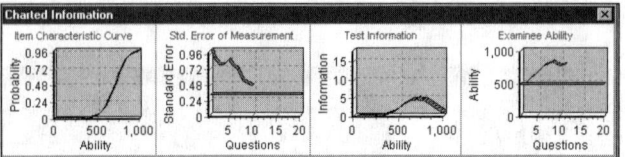

FIGURE 2
The changing statistics in an adaptive exam.

As you might suspect, one good piece of advice for taking an adaptive exam is to treat every exam question as if it were the most important. The adaptive scoring algorithm attempts to discover a pattern of responses that reflects some level of proficiency with the subject matter. Incorrect responses almost guarantee that additional questions must be answered (unless, of course, you get every question wrong). This is because the scoring algorithm must adjust to information that is not consistent with the emerging pattern.

Case Study Form

The case study-based format first appeared with the advent of the 70-100 exam (Solution Architectures). The questions in the case study format are not the independent entities that they are in the fixed and adaptive formats. Instead, questions are tied to a case study, a long scenario-like description of an information technology situation. As the test taker, your job is to extract from the case study the information that needs to be integrated with your understanding of Microsoft technology. The idea is that a case study will provide you with a situation that is more like a "real life" problem situation than the other formats provide.

The case studies are presented as "testlets." These are sections within the exam in which you read the case study, then answer 10 to 15 questions that apply to the case study. When you finish that section, you move onto another testlet with another case study and its associated questions. There may be as many as five of these testlets that compose the overall exam. You will be given more time to complete such an exam because it takes time to read through the cases and analyze them. You may have as much as three hours to complete the exam—and you may need all of it. The case studies are always available through a linking button while you are in a testlet. However, once you leave a testlet, you cannot come back to it.

Figure 3 provides an illustration of part of a case study.

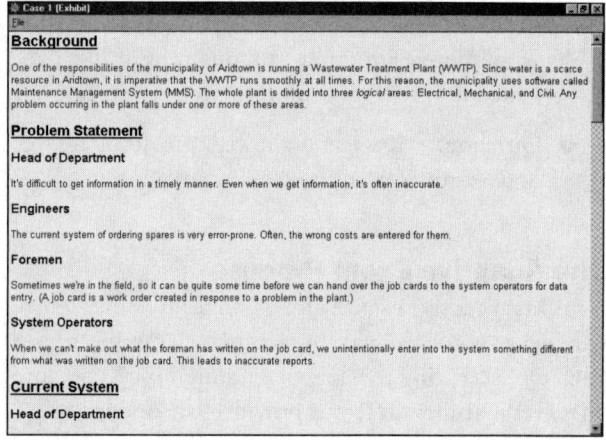

FIGURE 3
An example of a case study

Question Types

A variety of question types can appear on MCP exams. Examples of many of the various types appear in this book and the *ExamGear, Training Guide Edition* software. We have attempted to cover all the types that were available at the time of this writing. Most of the question types discussed in the following sections can appear in each of the three exam formats.

The typical MCP exam question is based on the idea of measuring skills or the ability to complete tasks. Therefore, most of the questions are written so as to present you with a situation that includes a role (such as a system administrator or technician), a technology environment (100 computers running Windows 98 on a Windows 2000 Server network), and a problem to be solved (the user can connect to services on the LAN, but not the intranet). The answers indicate actions that you might take to solve the problem or create setups or environments that would function correctly from the start. Keep this in mind as you read the questions on the exam. You may encounter some questions that just call for you to regurgitate facts, but these will be relatively few and far between.

In the following sections we will look at the different question types.

Multiple-Choice Questions

Despite the variety of question types that now appear in various MCP exams, the multiple-choice question is still the basic building block of the exams. The multiple-choice question comes in three varieties:

- ◆ **Regular multiple-choice.** Also referred to as an alphabetic question, it asks you to choose one answer as correct.

- ◆ **Multiple-answer multiple-choice.** Also referred to as a multi-alphabetic question, this version of a multiple-choice question requires you to choose two or more answers as correct. Typically, you are told precisely the number of correct answers to choose.

- ◆ **Enhanced multiple-choice.** This is simply a regular or multiple-answer question that includes a graphic or table to which you must refer to answer the question correctly.

Examples of such questions appear at the end of each chapter.

Multiple-Rating Questions

These questions are often referred to as scenario questions. Similar to multiple-choice questions, they offer more extended descriptions of the computing environment and a problem that needs to be solved. Required and desired optional results of the problem-solving are specified, as well as a solution. You are then asked to judge whether the actions taken in the solution are likely to bring about all or part of the required and desired optional results. There is, typically, only one correct answer.

You may be asking yourself, "What is multiple about multiple-rating questions?" The answer is that rather than having multiple answers, the question itself may be repeated in the exam with only minor variations in the required results, optional results, or solution introduced to create "new" questions. Read these different versions very carefully; the differences can be subtle.

Examples of these types of questions appear at the end of the chapters.

Simulation Questions

Simulation-based questions reproduce the look and feel of key Microsoft product features for the purpose of testing. The simulation software used in MCP exams has been designed to look and act, as much as possible, just like the actual product. Consequently, answering simulation questions in an MCP exam entails completing one or more tasks just as if you were using the product itself.

The format of a typical Microsoft simulation question consists of a brief scenario or problem statement, along with one or more tasks that you must complete to solve the problem. An example of a simulation question for MCP exams is shown in the following section.

A Typical Simulation Question

It sounds obvious, but your first step when you encounter a simulation question is to carefully read the question (see Figure 4). Do not go straight to the simulation application! You must assess the problem that's presented and identify the conditions that make up the problem scenario. Note the tasks that must be performed or outcomes that must be achieved to answer the question, and then review any instructions you're given on how to proceed.

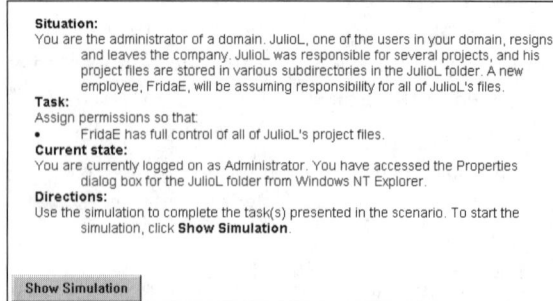

FIGURE 4
A typical MCP exam simulation question with directions.

The next step is to launch the simulator by using the button provided. After clicking the Show Simulation button, you will see a feature of the product, as shown in the dialog box in Figure 5. The simulation application will partially obscure the question text on many test center machines. Feel free to reposition the simulator and to move between the question text screen and

the simulator by using hotkeys or point-and-click navigation, or even by clicking the simulator's launch button again.

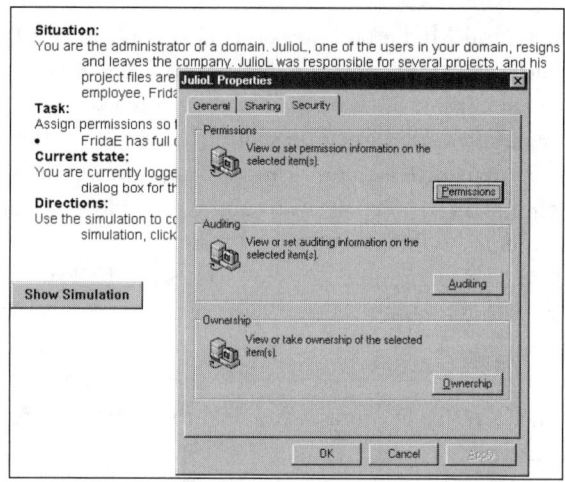

FIGURE 5
Launching the simulation application.

It is important for you to understand that your answer to the simulation question will not be recorded until you move on to the next exam question. This gives you the added capability of closing and reopening the simulation application (using the launch button) on the same question without losing any partial answer you may have made.

The third step is to use the simulator as you would the actual product to solve the problem or perform the defined tasks. Again, the simulation software is designed to function—within reason—just as the product does. But don't expect the simulator to reproduce product behavior perfectly. Most importantly, do not allow yourself to become flustered if the simulator does not look or act exactly like the product.

Figure 6 shows the solution to the example simulation problem.

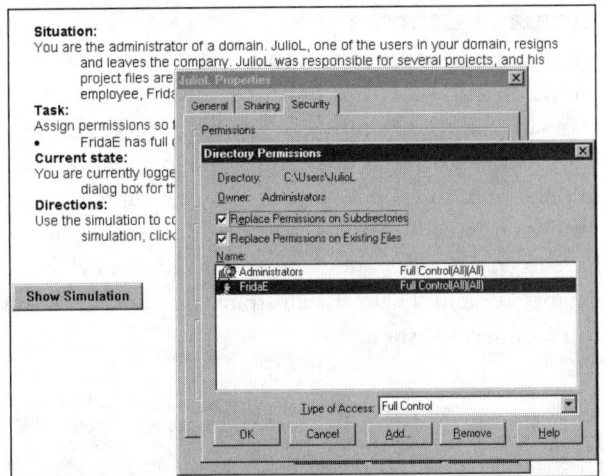

FIGURE 6
The solution to the simulation example.

Two final points will help you tackle simulation questions. First, respond only to what is being asked in the question; do not solve problems that you are not asked to solve. Second, accept what is being asked of you. You may not entirely agree with conditions in the problem statement, the quality of the desired solution, or the sufficiency of defined tasks to adequately solve the problem. Always remember that you are being tested on your ability to solve the problem as it is presented.

The solution to the simulation problem shown in Figure 6 perfectly illustrates both of those points. As you'll recall from the question scenario (refer to Figure 4), you were asked to assign appropriate permissions to a new user, Frida E. You were not instructed to make any other changes in permissions. Thus, if you were to modify or remove the administrator's permissions, this item would be scored wrong on an MCP exam.

Hot Area Question

Hot area questions call for you to click on a graphic or diagram in order to complete some task. You are asked a question that is similar to any other, but rather than clicking an option button or check box next to an answer, you click the relevant item in a screen shot or on a part of a diagram. An example of such an item is shown in Figure 7.

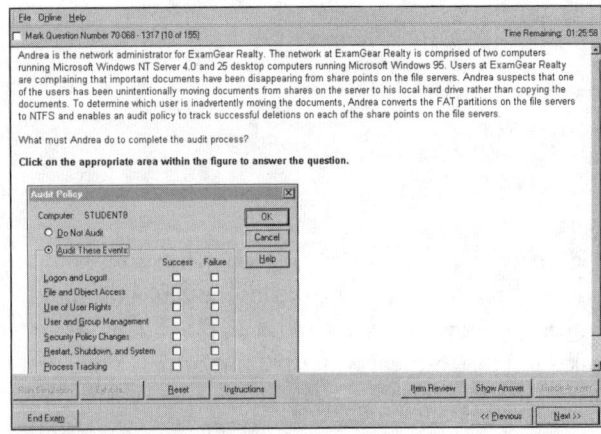

FIGURE 7
A typical hot area question.

Drag and Drop Style Questions

Microsoft has utilized two different types of drag and drop questions in exams. The first is a Select and Place question. The other is a Drop and Connect question. Both are covered in the following sections.

Select and Place

Select and Place questions typically require you to drag and drop labels on images in a diagram so as to correctly label or identify some portion of a network. Figure 8 shows you the actual question portion of a Select and Place item.

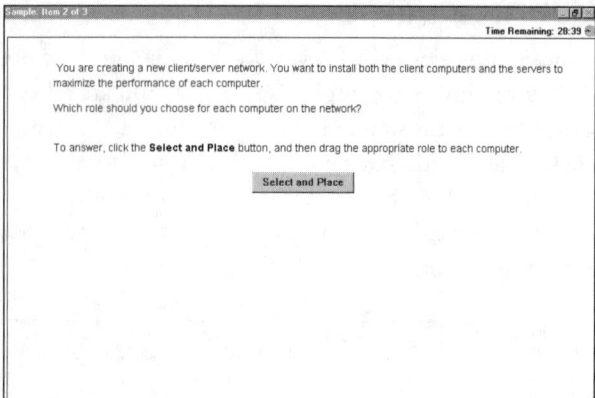

FIGURE 8
A Select and Place question.

Figure 9 shows the window you would see after you chose Select and Place. It contains the actual diagram in which you would select and drag the various server roles and match them with the appropriate computers.

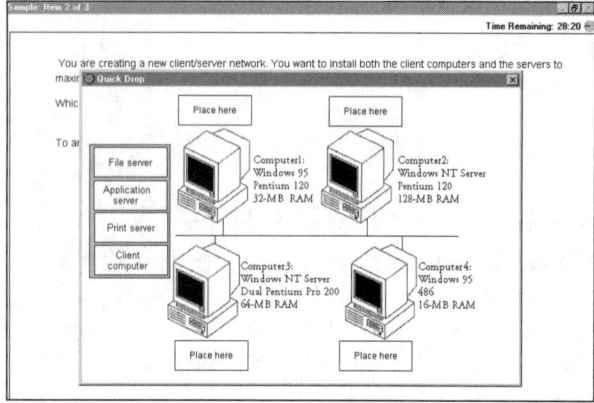

FIGURE 9
The window containing the diagram.

Drop and Connect

Drop and Connect questions provide a different spin on the drag and drop question. The question provides you with the opportunity to create boxes that you can label, as well as connectors of various types with which to link them. In essence, you are creating a model or diagram in order to answer the question. You might have to create a network diagram or a data model for a database system. Figure 10 illustrates the idea of a Drop and Connect question.

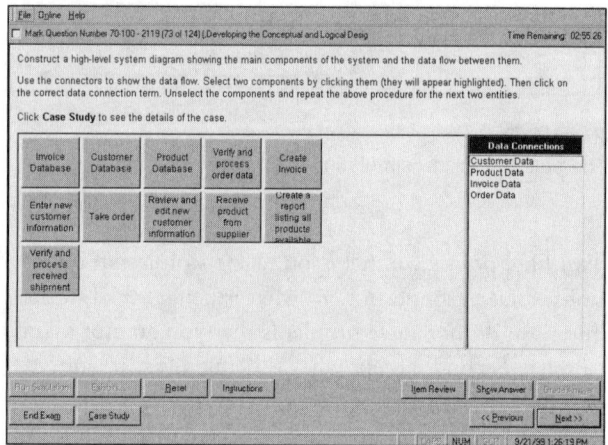

FIGURE 10
A Drop and Connect question.

Ordered List Questions

Ordered list questions simply require you to consider a list of items and place them in the proper order. You select items and then use a button to add them to a new list in the correct order. You have another button that you can use to remove the items in the new list in case you change your mind and want to reorder things. Figure 11 shows an ordered list item.

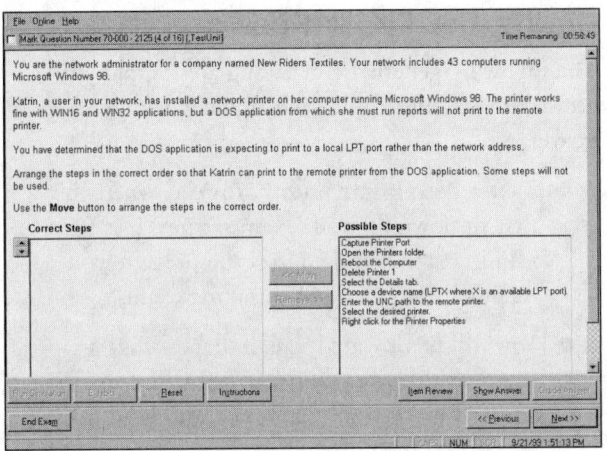

FIGURE 11
An ordered list question.

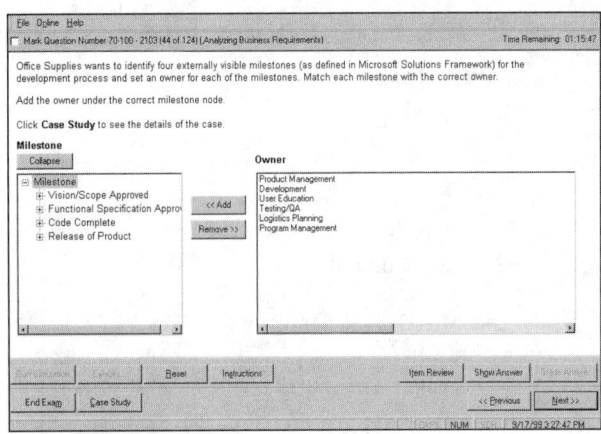

FIGURE 12
A tree question.

Tree Questions

Tree questions require you to think hierarchically and categorically. You are asked to place items from a list into categories that are displayed as nodes in a tree structure. Such questions might ask you to identify parent-child relationships in processes or the structure of keys in a database. You might also be required to show order within the categories, much as you would in an ordered list question. Figure 12 shows a typical tree question.

As you can see, Microsoft is making an effort to utilize question types that go beyond asking you to simply memorize facts. These question types force you to know how to accomplish tasks and understand concepts and relationships. Study so that you can answer these types of questions rather than those that simply ask you to recall facts.

Putting It All Together

Given all these different pieces of information, the task now is to assemble a set of tips that will help you successfully tackle the different types of MCP exams.

More Exam Preparation Tips

Generic exam-preparation advice is always useful. Tips include the following:

◆ Become familiar with the product. Hands-on experience is one of the keys to success on any MCP exam. Review the exercises and the Step by Steps in the book.

◆ Review the current exam-preparation guide on the Microsoft MCP Web site (www.microsoft.com/mcp/examinfo/exams.htm). The documentation Microsoft makes available over the Web identifies the skills every exam is intended to test.

◆ Memorize foundational technical detail, but remember that MCP exams are generally heavier on problem solving and application of knowledge than on questions that require only rote memorization.

◆ Take any of the available practice tests. We recommend the one included in this book and the ones you can create using the *ExamGear* software on the CD-ROM. As a supplement to the material bound with this book, try the free practice tests available on the Microsoft MCP Web site.

◆ Look on the Microsoft MCP Web site for samples and demonstration items. These tend to be particularly valuable for one significant reason: They help you become familiar with new testing technologies before you encounter them on MCP exams.

During the Exam Session

The following generic exam-taking advice that you've heard for years also applies when you're taking an MCP exam:

◆ Take a deep breath and try to relax when you first sit down for your exam session. It is very important that you control the pressure you may (naturally) feel when taking exams.

◆ You will be provided scratch paper. Take a moment to write down any factual information and technical detail that you committed to short-term memory.

◆ Carefully read all information and instruction screens. These displays have been put together to give you information relevant to the exam you are taking.

◆ Accept the non-disclosure agreement and preliminary survey as part of the examination process. Complete them accurately and quickly move on.

◆ Read the exam questions carefully. Reread each question to identify all relevant detail.

◆ Tackle the questions in the order in which they are presented. Skipping around won't build your confidence; the clock is always counting down (at least in the fixed form exams).

◆ Don't rush, but also don't linger on difficult questions. The questions vary in degree of difficulty. Don't let yourself be flustered by a particularly difficult or wordy question.

Fixed-Form Exams

Building from this basic preparation and test-taking advice, you also need to consider the challenges presented by the different exam designs. Because a fixed-form exam is composed of a fixed, finite set of questions, add these tips to your strategy for taking a fixed-form exam:

◆ Note the time allotted and the number of questions on the exam you are taking. Make a rough calculation of how many minutes you can spend on each question, and use this figure to pace yourself through the exam.

◆ Take advantage of the fact that you can return to and review skipped or previously answered questions. Record the questions you can't answer confidently on the scratch paper provided, noting the relative difficulty of each question. When you reach the end of the exam, return to the more difficult questions.

◆ If you have session time remaining after you complete all the questions (and if you aren't too fatigued!), review your answers. Pay particular attention to questions that seem to have a lot of detail or that require graphics.

◆ As for changing your answers, the general rule of thumb here is *don't*! If you read the question carefully and completely and you felt like you knew the right answer, you probably did. Don't second-guess yourself. If, as you check your answers, one clearly stands out as incorrect, however, of course you should change it. But if you are at all unsure, go with your first impression.

Adaptive Exams

If you are planning to take an adaptive exam, keep these additional tips in mind:

◆ Read and answer every question with great care. When you're reading a question, identify every relevant detail, requirement, or task you must perform and double-check your answer to be sure you have addressed every one of them.

◆ If you cannot answer a question, use the process of elimination to reduce the set of potential answers, and then take your best guess. Stupid mistakes invariably mean that additional questions will be presented.

◆ You cannot review questions and change answers. When you leave a question, whether you've answered it or not, you cannot return to it. Do not skip any question, either; if you do, it's counted as incorrect.

Case Study Exams

This new exam format calls for unique study and exam-taking strategies. When you take this type of exam, remember that you have more time than in a typical exam. Take your time and read the case study thoroughly. Use the scrap paper or whatever medium is provided to you to take notes, diagram processes, and actively seek out the important information. Work through each testlet as if each were an independent exam. Remember, you cannot go back after you have left a testlet. Refer to the case study as often as you need to, but do not use that as a substitute for reading it carefully initially and for taking notes.

FINAL CONSIDERATIONS

Finally, a number of changes in the MCP program will impact how frequently you can repeat an exam and what you will see when you do.

◆ Microsoft has instituted a new exam retake policy. The new rule is "two and two, then one and two." That is, you can attempt any exam twice with no restrictions on the time between attempts. But after the second attempt, you must wait two weeks before you can attempt that exam again. After that, you will be required to wait two weeks between subsequent attempts. Plan to pass the exam in two attempts or plan to increase your time horizon for receiving the MCP credential.

◆ New questions are being seeded into the MCP exams. After performance data is gathered on new questions, the examiners will replace older questions on all exam forms. This means that the questions appearing on exams will regularly change.

◆ Many of the current MCP exams will be republished in adaptive form. Prepare yourself for this significant change in testing; it is entirely likely that this will become the preferred MCP exam format for most exams. The exception to this may be the case study exams because the adaptive approach may not work with that format.

These changes mean that the brute-force strategies for passing MCP exams may soon completely lose their viability. So if you don't pass an exam on the first or second attempt, it is likely that the exam's form will change significantly by the next time you take it. It could be updated from fixed-form to adaptive, or it could have a different set of questions or question types.

Microsoft's intention is not to make the exams more difficult by introducing unwanted change, but to create and maintain valid measures of the technical skills and knowledge associated with the different MCP credentials. Preparing for an MCP exam has always involved not only studying the subject matter, but also planning for the testing experience itself. With the recent changes, this is now more true than ever.

This exam consists of 58 questions reflecting the material you have covered in the chapters and which are representative of the types of questions that you should expect to see on the actual exam.

The answers to all questions appear in their own section following the exam. It is strongly suggested that when you take this exam, you treat it just as you would the actual exam at the test center. Time yourself, read carefully, and answer all the questions to the best of your ability.

Most of the questions do not simply require you to recall facts but require deduction on your part to come up with the best answer. Most questions require you to identify the best course of action to take in a given situation. Many of the questions are verbose, requiring you to read them carefully and thoroughly before you attempt to answer them. Run through the exam, and for questions you miss, review any material associated with them.

Practice Exam

EXAM QUESTIONS

1. A brand new top-of-the-line workstation has just arrived in your office and you are about to install Windows 2000 Professional for the first time. The system contains a new SCSI controller interface that is not on the HCL, but a driver has been provided by the manufacturer of the system. You tried to install Windows 2000 following the basic steps, but each time the system restarts, it stops. It seems the system cannot access any of the SCSI drives since the driver is not installed. What should you do to load the new SCSI driver during the installation of Windows 2000?

   A. Boot from the driver disk that the manufacture provided. Windows 2000 will recognize the SCSI devices and continue with the setup properly.

   B. During the final phase of setup, press F8 to install additional drivers for mass storage.

   C. During the first phase of setup, press F6 to load additional drivers for mass storage.

   D. Install the manufacturer's drivers on the boot disk using the makeboot.exe utility.

   E. Windows 2000 cannot be installed on a system with hardware that is not on the HCL.

2. Your new summer intern has been asked to prepare unattended answer files to help in the installation of Windows 2000 on several new computers. However, he cannot find the Setup Manager utility on the Windows 2000 Professional computer you provided for him. Where can you tell him to look to find this utility? Select the best answer.

   A. The utility is found in the winnt\system32 directory. It does not have an icon in the Start menu. Simply change to this directory and run Setupmgr.exe.

   B. Setup Manager is only available on a Windows 2000 server. You must install the Windows 2000 Server Tools on the Windows 2000 Professional system to have access to Setupmgr.exe.

   C. Setup Manager must be downloaded from Microsoft Web site.

   D. Setup Manager is part of the resource kit. Simply install the resource kit and the utility will show up under Start, Programs.

   E. Setup Manager is part of the add-ons that are available in the add-on folder of the Windows 2000 Professional CD.

3. A new technician in the company has read all about RIS automated installs and would like to implement the procedure in your network. What basic components must be present in the network to allow a RIS-based implementation? Select three answers.

   A. A DHCP server

   B. A DNS server

   C. A WINS server

   D. A server running Active Directory

   E. A Browser server

   F. An IPsec server

4. A small computer training company has decided to install the software and operating system needed every day for the next day's class. This process involves 125 identical computers that need Windows 2000 Professional and Office 2000. The setup process manually takes over eight hours to perform.

You are hired as a setup consultant to provide a solution for this small training company.

Required Results:

- Provide an easy installation that will guarantee that each system is set up with the same operating system and application configuration.

- Maintain a secured copy of a base system that can be downloaded at a moment's notice even during the day, in case of a system crash.

Optional Desired Results:

- Network storage requirements for the image should be minimal.

- The setup person will require only one visit to each computer to setup the software.

- The systems must have a unique computer name and ID on the network.

Proposed Solution:

Install a basic system manually with all the settings and applications required for a course.

Using a third party disk imaging product, create a single image that will be placed in a read-only shared folder on a server.

Create a batch file that the setup person can invoke at each system to download the image to each computer each night.

Which result(s) does the proposed solution produce?

A. The proposed solution produces all the required results and all of the optional desired results.

B. The proposed solution produces one of the required results and all of the optional desired results.

C. The proposed solution produces all the required results and one of the optional desired results.

D. The proposed solution produces all the required results and none of the optional desired results.

E. The proposed solution produces none of the required results and none of the optional desired results.

5. You want to safely upgrade your 50 Windows 95 computers to Windows 2000 Professional. What steps could you take to ensure that the computers are compatible with Windows 2000 prior to performing the upgrade? Select all possible answers.

A. Run the HCL.exe program to create a compatibility report.

B. Run Winnt.exe or Winnt32.exe with the /upgradetest switch.

C. Run the Winnt.exe or Winnt32.exe with the /checkupgradeonly switch.

D. Use the Checkupgrade.exe utility from the resource kit.

E. Use the Chkupgrd.exe utility from the resource kit.

F. Running a trial upgrade using Winnt.exe or Winnt32.exe with the /trial switch.

6. A client tries to upgrade his Windows 98 computer to Windows 2000 Professional and fails. The client calls you at the help desk and asks you why he was unable to join the domain. He is using the same domain, computer, and user name as he had in Windows 98. What would you tell him?

A. Windows 2000 Professional system must be upgraded by administrators only.

B. A computer account must be created in the domain to allow Windows 2000 Professional system to join.

C. You cannot use the same computer name for Windows 2000 as you had for Windows 98. Computer names are registered in the domain and cannot be shared.

D. Microsoft is marketing Windows 98 and Windows 2000 Professional to two very separate segments of the market. They are not compatible and therefore you cannot upgrade a Windows 98 computer to Windows 2000 Professional.

E. To upgrade to Windows 2000 Professional, an upgrade file must be copied to the client system. You will send him one today and he should copy it to the %systemroot% folder.

7. There are several computers in the network running Windows 95 and Windows NT Workstation 4.0 that do not meet the requirements for Windows 2000 Professional. Therefore, they will not be upgraded just yet. Alexander, your boss, has asked you to come up with a plan that will allow the use of these legacy systems until their hardware can be updated.

Required Results:

All systems must be able to access shared folders on Windows 2000 servers.

All systems must be able to log on to the Windows 2000 network and be validated.

Optional Desired Results:

All systems must be able to make use of Active Directory to log on and locate resources.

All systems must be able to access the Windows 2000 Server computers fault tolerant DFS roots.

Proposed Solution:

All Windows 2000 Server shares are created with the Windows NT 4.0 and 95 compatibility turned on.

The client account in Active Directory that will be used on legacy systems is set to Windows NT 4.0 Domain compatibility.

Which result(s) does the proposed solution produce?

A. The proposed solution produces all the required results and all of the optional desired results.

B. The proposed solution produces one of the required results and all of the optional desired results.

C. The proposed solution produces all the required results and one of the optional desired results.

D. The proposed solution produces all the required results and none of the optional desired results.

E. The proposed solution produces none of the required results and none of the optional desired results.

8. Sara needs to update all the Windows 2000 Professional computers in her network to the latest service pack of the operating system. What method of deployment can she use? Select all that apply.

A. Windows Installer can be used to upgrade applications.

B. Microsoft's SMS software.

C. Windows 2000 Professional Update Manager.

D. Windows 2000 group policies.

E. Microsoft's Site Server software.

9. During a planning session you are asked what would be the best way to allow clients to have access to their files from any system in the network while still maintaining a secured environment. What would you propose? Select two answers.

   A. Set up roaming profiles.

   B. Have all users save their files in the Mydocuments folder.

   C. Set up a home share on an NTFS partition on the server. Allow everyone full control over the share.

   D. Configure each user with a Home directory that points to \\server\home\%username%, where \\server is a network server and \home is a shared folder.

   E. Set up a home share on a FAT partition. Allow everyone full control over the share.

   F. Configure each user account to use redirected folders as their home directories.

10. Alexander is a member of the Sales and the Accounting groups. You have given the Sales group Read permission and the Accounting group Change permission. Alexander is unable to access the folder. What is the most likely cause of the problem?

   A. The folder is marked as Read Only at the NTFS level.

   B. The files in the folder are marked as Read Only at the NTFS level.

   C. Alexander has not been added to the list of users with at least Read access.

   D. Alexander must have No Access assigned to his user account.

   E. The group Everyone has been removed from the list of users with access.

11. You are the network administrator for Balzac Petroleum. You are concerned that certain files are being accessed on your network without proper permissions. What can you do to prevent unauthorized users access?

   A. Change the default permission to Everyone Denied Access and only add groups as needed with the appropriate permissions.

   B. Remove the default group Everyone and delete the Guest account.

   C. Remove the default group Everyone and only add groups as needed with the appropriate permissions.

   D. Remove the default Guest Accounts permissions on all files and only add groups as needed with the appropriate permissions.

   E. Remove the default group Authenticated Users and only add groups as needed with the appropriate permissions.

12. You are the administrator of a very large multi-national organization with users all over the world. In the Sales department, most users work from home. All users need to be able to access files from any server in the world. You hired a consulting firm to suggest possible solutions.

   Required Results:

   ◆ A secure connection must be made for all folder access.

   ◆ All users must be able to access any folder on any server in the organization. Un-authenticated users will not be able to connect using the guest account.

   Optional Desired Results:

   ◆ At-home clients should be able to access files through their Web browsers

◆ Network clients should be able to access files from their network neighborhood.

Proposed Solution:

Set up a RAS server with dial-in as well as VPN capability and enforce security with IPSEC.

All resources that need to be made available over the network will be shared. The default permission Everyone Full Control is removed and replaced with appropriate groups and the guest account is disabled.

At-home clients are configured to connect to the closest office using a dial-up or VPN connection.

Which results does the proposed solution produce?

A. The proposed solution produces all the required results and all of the optional desired results.

B. The proposed solution produces one of the required results and all of the optional desired results.

C. The proposed solution produces all the required results and one of the optional desired results.

D. The proposed solution produces all the required results and none of the optional desired results.

E. The proposed solution produces none of the required results and none of the optional desired results.

13. You are the administrator of a very large multi-national organization with user all over the world. In the Sales department, most users work from home. All users need to be able to access files from any server in the world. You hired a consulting firm to suggest possible solutions.

Required Results:

A secure connection must be made for all folder access.

All users must be able to access any folder on any server in the organization. Un-authenticated users will not be able to connect using the guest account.

Optional Desired Results:

At-home clients should be able to access files through their Web browsers

Network clients should be able to access files from their network neighborhood.

Proposed Solution:

Set up a RAS server with dial-in as well as VPN capability and enforce security with IPSEC.

All resources that need to be made available over the network will be shared. The default permission Everyone Full Control is removed and replaced with appropriate groups and the Guest account is disabled.

Set up Web sharing as well as network sharing for all resources that are to be accessed remotely.

At-home clients are configured to connect to the closest office using a dial-up or VPN connection.

Select the answer that best describes the proposed solution.

A. The proposed solution produces all the required results and all of the optional desired results.

B. The proposed solution produces one of the required results and all of the optional desired results.

C. The proposed solution produces all the required results and one of the optional desired results.

D. The proposed solution produces all the required results and none of the optional desired results.

E. The proposed solution produces none of the required results and none of the optional desired results.

14. A client would like to send you a report but tells you her email is unavailable, although she still has access to the Internet for Web browsing. You do not want her to dial in to your office. How can she send you a copy of the report without the risk of sending a virus to your servers?

A. She can connect to your Web server and upload the file.

B. She can connect to your FTP site and upload the file.

C. She can connect to your intranet site server and upload the file.

D. She can print to one of your office printers that has been shared over the Internet.

E. She cannot send the report until her email has been fixed.

15. There are several users and several identical printers in an office. You need to make sure that if your printer is unavailable, the other printers will take over. You also need to make sure that the executives in the company never have to wait for a print job. What can you do to accommodate everyone? Select two answers.

A. Create a print job with high priority for executives.

B. Create a printer redirection on all printers to each other.

C. Set up a printer pool with several print devices of the same type.

D. Create a second printer with a higher job priority and share it only to executives.

E. Set up one printer exclusively for executives and one printer for all users.

16. Your office is setting up several new laptop computers with Windows 2000 Professional for the VPs in the company. The CIO is concerned someone might steal a laptop and copy files to a FAT partition and read its content. How can you make sure the files are secure? Select all that apply.

A. Install Windows 2000 Professional using RIS.

B. Make sure all local drives on the laptop computers are NTFS.

C. Enable DFS on the files you want protected.

D. Make sure all local drives are configured so only owners have full access.

E. Enable EFS on all folders you want protected.

17. In what situations should the APM support be disabled? Select three.

    A. The computer is a desktop.

    B. The laptop computer is set up to dual boot with Windows 98 and Windows 2000 Professional.

    C. The computer has multiple CPUs.

    D. The computer has multiple video devices.

    E. The laptop is running a lot of software as background applications.

    F. The laptop is always used as a standalone unit.

18. A new Windows 2000 Professional system has arrived in your office with a DVD drive. What are the names of the new formats used for hardware decoders providing full motion video and surround-sound capability used by DVDs? Select all that apply.

    A. DVD

    B. NTFS

    C. UDF

    D. MPEG-2

    E. AC-3

19. While working with disk partitions, you notice your disk administrator showing that you have a Basic disk. What features are not supported by a Basic disk? Select three.

    A. Create and delete primary and extended partitions and logical drives.

    B. Mark a partition as active.

    C. Create simple, spanned, striped, mirrored, and RAID-5 volumes.

    D. Delete spanned volumes, striped volumes, mirrored volumes, and RAID-5 volumes.

    E. Break a mirror from a mirrored volume.

    F. Extend volumes and volume sets.

    G. Add a mirror to a simple volume.

20. You have installed a PCI video adapter in your new Windows 2000 Professional computer that already had an on-board video adapter. Which of the following statements is true?

    A. The on-board video adapter will be the primary adapter.

    B. The on-board video adapter will be the secondary adapter.

    C. Windows 2000 Professional can configure each adapter to be primary or secondary using the Display applet in the Control Panel.

    D. The system's BIOS must be used to set the on-board adapter as secondary; otherwise, it will be primary.

    E. PCI cards cannot be used in a multi-adapter implementation.

21. Your small network has been upgraded and added to over the years by many different consultants and administrators. There are several segments connected by routers. You believe there are a lot of inefficiencies and would like to clean it up. Some servers require IPX, and others require TCP/IP, but none use only NetBEUI. All clients are set up with all three protocols.

    Required Results:

    Simplify network protocols.

    Maintain connectivity for all desktops to all servers.

Optional Desired Results:

Reduce network broadcast on segments.

Improve desktops connection time to servers they use most often.

Proposed Solution:

Simply remove the NetBEUI protocol from all systems in the network. Configure the routers not to forward broadcasts of any type.

Which results does the proposed solution produce?

A. The proposed solution produces all the required results and all of the optional desired results.

B. The proposed solution produces one of the required results and one of the optional desired results.

C. The proposed solution produces all the required results and one of the optional desired results.

D. The proposed solution produces all the required results and none of the optional desired results.

E. The proposed solution produces none of the required results and none of the optional desired results.

22. You have been monitoring your Windows 2000 Professional system and want to verify whether the processor is overburdened. What counters would you be looking at, and what values would help you decide if another processor is required?

A. If processor time is more than 90 percent and the interrupt time is greater than 15 percent.

B. If the system time is more than 90 percent.

C. If the processor time is more than 90 percent and the hard page faults are greater than 2.

D. If the percentage of user time is more than 90 percent.

E. If processor time is more than 90 percent and the average queue length is more than 1.

23. A user calls the help desk for help in setting up a digital camera on Windows 2000 Professional computer. He tells you the device is PnP, and has plugged it into the system, but he is getting errors such as You do not have sufficient rights to perform such a task. What could be the problem be and how would you solve it?

A. The user is unable to access the Windows 2000 Professional source files on the server with his/her logon name. Change the shared permission to allow this user access to the files.

B. Plug and Play assumes the user's logon rights. You must be logged on as an administrator to install hardware.

C. Disconnect the device and install the drivers first. Once the drivers are on the computer, plug in the device and Plug and Play will connect properly.

D. Windows 2000 Professional does not support Plug and Play. Disable the PnP on the camera and reinstall.

E. All digital cameras use the Infrared protocol. Make sure it is installed first and then install the camera.

24. As a junior network administrator you have been asked to install Windows 2000 Professional on several types of laptop computers. You notice that the APM features are enabled on some laptops and disabled on others. What could be the reason for this inconsistency? Select two answers.

    A. The laptop computer is ACPI compliant only.

    B. The laptop computer's BIOS need to be upgraded to a Windows 2000 Professional-compatible version.

    C. Microsoft has determined that some laptop computers will not support APM properly and therefore does not install APM support.

    D. During the installation, some laptop computers must have been set up with the Mobile option, whereas others have been set up using the Typical setting.

    E. The Windows 2000 Professional software was not installed for mobile users. Rerun the setup and choose Mobile Users.

25. A client has installed several new drivers from Microsoft and a few third-party drivers without his realizing it. One of the new third-party drivers has caused damage to his Windows 2000 Professional computer. He calls you at the help desk and asks "Why did the system not warn me when I installed this third-party driver?" How should you respond?

    A. Driver verification is done automatically and the system did not find any errors with the third-party drivers.

    B. A policy governing whether the verification of signatures is to be applied is not enabled.

    C. Each driver must be tested manually before being installed. The Windows 2000 Professional operating system cannot verify each file as it is installed.

    D. All drivers in Windows 2000 are pre-tested by Microsoft and will not install otherwise. He must be mistaken; there were no third-party drivers installed.

    E. Windows 2000 Professional will repair any damaged files if he uses the repair process off the emergency repair disk.

26. You are responsible for all new drivers that are introduced into your network comprised of 100 Windows 2000 Professional computers. How can you ensure that only drivers that have been tested by Microsoft are installed?

    A. From the System icon in the Control Panel set the digital signature to Block—Prevent the installation of all unsigned files.

    B. From the Security icon in the Control Panel set the digital signature to Block—Prevent the installation of all unsigned files.

    C. From the System icon in the Control Panel set the digital signature to Warn—Display a message before installing unsigned files.

    D. From the Security icon in the Control Panel set the digital signature to Warn—Display a message before installing unsigned files.

    E. This cannot be done. You cannot prevent non-Microsoft driver files from being installed. The only control you have is on the signature of a file, not the origin.

27. Your predecessor had created a series of automated tasks that are running on your Windows 2000 Professional system each day. You are using the Find command to locate these task files on the workstation. What file extension are you looking for?

    A. .Tas

    B. .Job

C. .At

D. .Inf

E. .Bat

28. To maintain systems, your IT department chooses to use automated tasks. Using the Task Scheduler in Windows 2000 Professional and the AT command, entries are added to various systems. On occasion you try to modify an existing task using the AT command, but are unable to. This problem does not seem to appear for all tasks. What could be the problem and how would you solve it?

A. The AT command is a Windows NT 4.0 command and will not work in Windows 2000 Professional.

B. The AT command cannot edit a task that was scheduled with the Tasks Scheduler. Once a task has been created or modified using Windows 2000 Professional Tasks Scheduler, you must continue to use it.

C. The Windows 2000 Professional Task Scheduler can be configured to maintain backward compatibility with the AT command. Once this option is set, you will be able to edit and view all tasks using either tool.

D. Use the WINAT command from the resource kit. It can read or edit any type of task that was created or edited by any tool.

29. The administrator from your remote office sends you the following capture as seen in Figure PE.1. What type of bottleneck is present, if any?

A. There is no bottleneck.

B. A Process bottleneck.

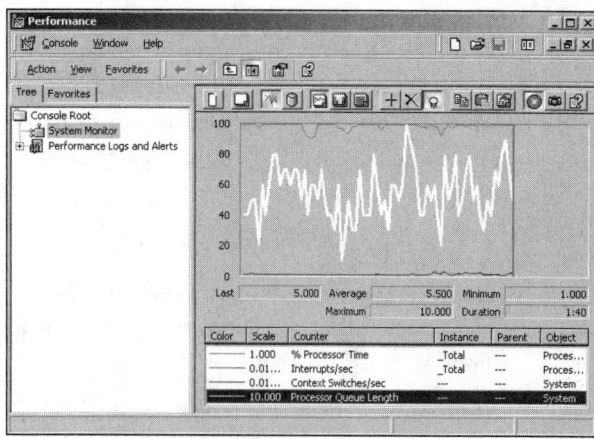

FIGURE PE.1
Figure for question 29.

C. A Disk bottleneck.

D. A Processor bottleneck.

E. A memory bottleneck.

30. Your colleagues in the remote office are trying to capture disk activity and find that all the counters are set to zero. What do you tell them?

A. There is no additional disk activity. The counters automatically filter out basic operating system activity.

B. The SNMP agent must be installed to add the disk counters to the system.

C. There is no bottleneck on the system; therefore, the disk activity is low.

D. The disk counters have not been enabled. Use the DISKPERF command to enable them.

E. They are using logical disk counters when they should be using physical disk counters, as they are more accurate.

31. A client sends you their system and tells you there are several errors coming up when she starts up. You believe it is a faulty driver for a new piece of hardware she installed. How can you best troubleshoot the problem? Select two answers.

    A. Create a hardware profile called test.

    B. Boot the system in the test profile and disable the device and/or services you believe to be at fault.

    C. Boot the system in safe mode and disable the device and/or service you believe to be at fault.

    D. Create a drivers disk to update all drivers to the latest for each device.

    E. Create a hardware service called test.

32. You need to decide the type of media to use to perform your daily backups. What media type does Windows 2000 Professional support? Select all that apply.

    A. CD-ROMs

    B. Hard drives

    C. Floppy disk drives

    D. Network drives

    E. Tape drives

    F. Modems

    G. DVD-ROM drives

33. As the administrator of a small legal firm, you want to maintain certain desktop configuration standards in the organization. What tool can you use to maintain control?

    A. Group policy

    B. Remote access control

    C. System management

    D. Intellimirror

    E. Roaming profiles

34. You have decided to implement policies that will allow users to maintain a certain desktop configuration standard. You want to allow users the ability to change some personal settings, however. What do you need to do to make sure each user maintains his own settings if he shares a computer?

    A. Change each user to roaming profiles.

    B. Do nothing; roaming profiles are on by default.

    C. Do nothing; local profiles will take care of each user's settings.

    D. Each user must save his settings to his home folder.

    E. This cannot be done. All users on a system will share settings.

35. Two users are sharing a Windows NT account. You want to prevent the two from changing the settings that might confuse the other. What can be done?

    A. Change NTUser.dat to Ntuser.one.

    B. Restrict roaming profiles.

    C. Disable profiles.

    D. Copy NTUser.dat to Ntuser.man.

    E. Rename Ntuser.dat to Ntuser.man.

36. A user calls and complains that she does not have the multiple languages indicator in the Taskbar like her colleagues. Where can you direct her to make this indicator appear?

A. Right-click on the task bar and select it.

B. From the Tools, Options menu of the Office 2000 application she is using.

C. From the languages icon in the Control Panel.

D. From the properties of the My Computer icon.

E. From the Regional Settings icon in the Control Panel.

37. A traveling salesman in your company tells you he is tired of configuring his system's dial-out properties each time he changes hotels. What feature in Windows 2000 Professional would you suggest he use?

A. Win Fax software.

B. Multi-location tools.

C. Choose dialing rules from the Fax Wizard.

D. Dialing locations.

E. Dialing Wizard.

38. Several hearing-impaired individuals in your department have approached you about the benefits of Windows 2000. What new features can you tell them about that would improve their working conditions? Select all that apply.

A. Sound surround setups

B. Dictation software

C. ShowSounds

D. SoundSentry

E. Auto volume control

39. You need to make sure that all users have the same applications ready for them to use regardless of which computer they use in the office. Which Windows 2000 Professional feature would you implement?

A. Group policy

B. Remote software installation

C. System management server installations

D. RIS (Remote Installation Server)

E. Roaming profiles

40. Windows 2000 Professional systems can be controlled with custom desktops through Active Directory. Which other operating systems can be controlled in the same way? Select all that apply.

A. UNIX

B. Novell NetWare

C. Windows NT 4.0

D. Apple Macintosh

E. Windows 95

41. You are in charge of configuring TCP/IP for all the clients and servers on your network. All clients are DHCP enabled. When you first installed the DCHP Server, a Class B subnet mask was chosen. You have reconfigured the DHCP server to use a Class C subnet mask. A user calls and says she cannot connect to any servers on the network. What command would you tell the user to type to find out her IP Address?

A. Nbtstat –c.

B. Ipconfig /all

C. Ipconfig /release

D. Ping Servera

42. You are troubleshooting a connectivity problem and a Windows 2000 Professional computer. Using the PING command, place the following steps in the recommended order.

    Ping the remote host.

    Ping the address of 127.0.0.1.

    Ping the local host.

    Ping the gateway.

    1st _____

    2nd _____

    3rd _____

    4th _____

43. You are a senior IT consultant working on a network of 200 Windows 2000 Professional computers, 50 Windows 2000 servers, and 10 UNIX servers. You are tasked with configuring the TCP/IP setting on the Windows 2000 Professional computer with the following guidelines:

    Required Results:

    Automatic IP addressing of Windows 2000 Professional clients

    Dynamic name resolution of Windows 2000 servers

    Optional Desired Results:

    Name resolution of all the UNIX servers on your network

    Proposed Solution:

    At each Windows 2000 Professional computer, you configure the computer to use DHCP and a WINS server. You also place all of the UNIX server's names and IP addresses in the HOST file on each Windows 2000 Professional computer.

Which result(s) does the proposed solution produce?

A. The proposed solution produces the required results and all of the optional desired results.

B. The proposed solution produces one of the required results and all of the optional desired results.

C. The proposed solution produces the required results but none of the optional desired results

D. The proposed solution does not produce the required results or the optional desired results.

44. You are an administrator of a small office. There are 10 Windows 2000 Professional computers. To connect to the Internet, you have shared an Internet connection. One of the users in the office cannot connect to your computer to access the Internet. When you run ipconfig on his computer, you see that the address assigned to his computer is 10.1.54.232. Which of the following address ranges should his IP address fall between?

A. 1.0.0.1 and 1.255.255.254

B. 192.168.0.1 and 192.168.255.254

C. 191.191.0.1 and 191.194.0.1

D. 224.224.244.1 and 224.224.244.254

45. You are the network administrator for a network that has 50 users who dial in from home. A help desk analyst has asked you to explain the differences between SLIP and PPP. Which of the following would you tell the analyst apply only to PPP? Select two.

A. Supports TCP/IP, IPX, and NetBEUI.

B. Passwords are sent as clear text.

C. Usually needs scripting to complete log on.

D. Supports encryption for authentication.

E. No error detection.

F. Can only be used for dial out.

46. As the help manager, you need to explain to all the new help desk support staff the different ways to resolve computer names. Which of the following would you tell them can be used for NetBIOS name resolution? Choose all that apply.

A. lmhosts

B. wins

C. lmhosts.sam

D. hosts cache

E. names

F. DHCP

G. hosts

47. You are the network administrator of an office that consists of three Window 2000 Servers computers, one Novell 3.12 file server computer, and 50 Windows 2000 Professional computers. Of the Windows 2000 Professional computers, 25 are running NetBEUI and IPX/SPX. The rest of the Windows 2000 Professional computers are running TCP/IP. Users are complaining that they cannot communicate with one another across your network.

You need to fix the problem.

Required Results:

All clients must be able to communicate with one another.

All clients must be able to access the Internet.

Optional Desired Results:

All clients must be able to communicate with the Novell server.

Proposed Solution:

On each client computer, install TCP/IP only.

Which results does the proposed solution produce?

A. The proposed solution produces the required results and all of the optional desired results.

B. The proposed solution produces one of the required results and all of the optional desired results.

C. The proposed solution produces the required results but none of the optional desired results.

D. The proposed solution does not produce the required results or the optional desired results.

48. You are the network administrator of a network that spans two cities. There are 10 Windows 2000 servers and 200 Windows 2000 Professional computers. To implement name resolution, you decided on LMHOSTS files. Users are complaining that when they try to connect to a server called \\vcrmail in a remote location, it takes a long time to connect. Which of the following could you add to the LMHOSTS file to make the connections faster? Select the best answer.

A. 121.45.6.201   vcrmail   #load

B. 121.45.6.201   #PRE   vcrmail

C. #Dom121.45.6.201   vcrmail

D. 121.45.6.201   vcrmail   #PRE

49. You are a network consultant who has been asked to install a new network for an office of 10 users.

Required Results:

Centralized administration.

Users can log on to any Windows 2000 Professional machine with the same user name.

Optional Desired Results:

Reduce administration work as much as possible.

Proposed Solution:

You install and configure 10 Windows 2000 Professional computers and one Windows 2000 Server computer. You have configured the server as a Domain controller. You then show the office administrator how to create and administrate domain user accounts.

Which results does the proposed solution produce?

A. The proposed solution produces the required results and all of the optional desired results.

B. The proposed solution produces one of the required results and all of the optional desired results.

C. The proposed solution produces the required results but none of the optional desired results

D. The proposed solution does not produce the required results or the optional desired results.

50. You are a network administrator. Jane Smith in accounting has moved on to new opportunities. Fred Jones, a new employee, has replaced Jane in accounting. Which one of the following actions would you take to allow Fred access to all of Jane's resources?

A. Delete Jane's account and create Fred's account.

B. Rename Jane's account to Fred's name.

C. Tell Fred to use Jane's account and password.

D. Create an account for Fred and tell him to re-create everything.

51. You are a local network administrator. Your network is made up of three Windows 2000 domains with 2000 Windows 2000 Professional computers and 250 Windows 2000 Server computers. The local HR manager has asked you to configure his Windows 2000 Professional computer so that people across the enterprise can access a specific folder called statsdata.

Required Results:

All HR managers from all domains should be able to access the data.

When a new HR manager is hired, all administration will be done through groups.

Optional Desired Results:

Reduce Active Directory traffic as much as possible.

Proposed Solution:

On the Windows 2000 Professional computer, create a local group called statdata. In Active Directory, create a universal group called All Managers. Assign each HR manager into the universal group. Make the universal group a member of the local group statdata. You then assign statdata to the folder statsdata.

Which results does the proposed solution produce?

A. The proposed solution produces the required results and all of the optional desired results.

B. The proposed solution produces one of the required results and all of the optional desired results.

C. The proposed solution produces the required results but none of the optional desired results

D. The proposed solution does not produce the required results or the optional desired results.

52. You are a local network administrator. Your network is made up of three Windows 2000 domains with 2000 Windows 2000 Professional computers and 250 Windows 2000 Server computers. The local HR manager has asked you to configure his Windows 2000 Professional computers so that people across the enterprise can access a specific folder called statsdata.

Required Results:

All HR managers from all domains should be able to access the data.

When a new HR manager is hired, all administration will be done through groups.

Optional Desired Results:

Reduce Active Director traffic as much as possible.

Proposed Solution:

On the Windows 2000 Professional computer, create a local group called statdata. In Active Directory, create a global group called HR Managers for each domain. Assign HR managers into their respective global groups. Also, create a universal group called allHRmanagers. Make the local group statdata a member of the universal group allHRmanagers. Then assign statdata to the folder statsdata.

Which results does the proposed solution produce?

A. The proposed solution produces the required results and all of the optional desired results.

B. The proposed solution produces one of the required results and all of the optional desired results.

C. The proposed solution produces the required results but none of the optional desired results

D. The proposed solution does not produce the required results or the optional desired results.

53. You are an administrator of a network that consists of 50 Windows 2000 Professional computers and six Windows 2000 Server computers. The network was just upgraded to Windows 2000 from Windows NT 4.0. The users are complaining that they cannot run all the applications that used to run on their Windows NT 4.0 workstations. What group would you add them to so they can run all the applications that they used to run?

A. Users

B. Guests

C. Backup Operators

D. Power Users

54. You are the help desk manager. You are creating a chart that will allow the help desk analysts to understand the differences between built-in global groups and built in local groups. Which of the following are built-in local groups? Select all that apply.

A. Guests

B. Administrators

C. Domain Admins

D. Power Users

E. Everyone

F. Domain Users

G. Managers

55. As the network administrator, you are auditing specific folders on users' Windows 2000 Professional computers. A user asks you to explain where she can find out who has been accessing the audited folder on her computer. You tell her about Event view and the security log. When she tries to read the security log, it denies the user access. To what group would she have to be added so she can access the security log?

    A. Guest

    B. Administrators

    C. Auditors

    D. Power Users

56. You are the network administrator who has been tasked with setting up security on the Windows 2000 Professional computers on your network. The network consists of the 600 Windows 2000 Professional computers, 100 Windows NT Workstation 4.0 computers, 250 Windows 98 computers, and 80 Windows 2000 Server computers in a single domain environment.

    Required Results:

    All users must be able to run applications designed for Windows NT 4.0.

    All Windows 2000 Professional computers must be able to communicate with Windows NT 4.0 and Windows 98 computers.

    Optional Desired Results:

    Users should not be able to load and unload applications.

    Proposed Solution:

    Place the global group Domain Users into each one of the Windows 2000 Professional computer's local group Power Users.

Which results does the proposed solution produce?

    A. The proposed solution produces the required results and all of the optional desired results.

    B. The proposed solution produces one of the required results and all of the optional desired results.

    C. The proposed solution produces the required results but none of the optional desired results

    D. The proposed solution does not produce the required results or the optional desired results.

57. You are the network administrator who has been tasked with setting up security on the Windows 2000 Professional computers on your network. The network consists of the 600 Windows 2000 Professional computers, 100 Windows NT Workstation 4.0 computers, 250 Windows 98 computers, and 80 Windows 2000 Server computers in a single domain environment.

    Required Results:

    All users must be able to run applications designed for Windows NT 4.0.

    All Windows 2000 Professional computers must be able to communicate with Windows NT 4.0 and Windows 98 computers.

    Optional Desired Results:

    Users should not be able to install and uninstall applications.

    Proposed Solution:

    Assign the security template called Compatible Workstation to each Windows 2000 Professional computer.

Which results does the proposed solution produce?

A. The proposed solution produces the required results and all of the optional desired results.

B. The proposed solution produces one of the required results and all of the optional desired results.

C. The proposed solution produces the required results but none of the optional desired results

D. The proposed solution does not produce the required results or the optional desired results.

58. You are a desktop support analyst. A user has asked for EFS to be configured on his Windows 2000 Professional computer. What would you enable on the computer to be able to unencrypt files if the user's private key has been deleted?

A. unecrypt.exe

B. recovery agent

C. unlock files agent

D. decrypt agent

ANSWERS TO EXAM QUESTIONS

1. **C.** There will always be new devices introduced and Windows 2000 will be compatible with them if the manufacturer provides the appropriate drivers. In the first phase, the installation program will try to detect the SCSI interface and will fail. At this point you can press the F6 key to install additional drivers. The boot disk created with Makeboot.exe cannot be altered with any new drivers. For more information see "Installing Windows 2000 Professional Manually " in Chapter 1, "Installing Windows 2000 Professional."

2. **D.** Once the resource kit is installed, the Setup Manager will be listed in the Resource Kit menu within the Start program's menu. The correct file name is setupmgr.exe. For more information see "Using the Setup Manager" in Chapter 1, "Installing Windows 2000 Professional."

3. **A, B, D.** The RIS server will require a DHCP server to hand out TCP/IP addresses and allow clients to boot up. It will also require a DNS server to locate the RIS server and a server running Active Directory to determine what operating system image to install. For more information see "Remote Installation Services (RIS)" in Chapter 1, "Installing Windows 2000 Professional."

4. **C.** The solution will create desktop systems with duplicate computer names and SIDs. The setup person will have to visit each desktop to initiate the install, and make a second visit to perform final configuration changes after the install is complete. For more information see "Imaging Windows 2000 Professional Installs" in Chapter 1, "Installing Windows 2000 Professional."

5. **C, E.** The winnt.exe and winnt32.exe using the /checkupgradeonly switch as well as the Chkupgrd.exe utility will generate a report showing any incompatibilities. No software will be installed onto the existing Windows 95 computer. For more information see "Upgrading to Windows 2000 Professional" in Chapter 1, "Installing Windows 2000 Professional."

6. **B.** Windows 95 and 98 systems are not really part of the domain and, therefore, do not require a computer account. Windows NT 4.0 and 2000 must have a valid computer name and user name before a client can join the domain. For more information see "Upgrading to Windows 2000 Professional" in Chapter 1, "Installing Windows 2000 Professional."

7. **D.** Windows 95 and Windows NT Workstation 4.0 are compatible with Windows 2000 for folder sharing and logon, but they cannot make use of Active Directory options such as locating resources. Fault-tolerant DFS roots can only be accessed through Active Directory. For more information see "Incompatible Systems" in Chapter 1, "Installing Windows 2000 Professional."

8. **B, D.** The Windows Installer can be used only for applications, not operating systems. SMS can deploy any type of package, including service packs. Windows 2000 group policies have a section on deploying software to systems based on user names or computer names. Site Server is to configure and manage Web sites. For more information see "Service Pack Deployment" in Chapter 1, "Installing Windows 2000 Professional."

9. **C, D.** Using an NTFS share and %username% will create a folder for each user with full control assigned only to them. The shared folder on the server does not need to be protected much since the local NTFS permissions are more restrictive. Roaming profiles and Mydocuments would allow users to access files, but this is an unsecured method and copies all files to and from the server each time the clients log on or off of the system. This can be very slow. For more information see "Developing an Efficient Directory Structure" in Chapter 2, "Implementing and Conducting Administration of Resources."

10. **D.** A No Access setting will override any other permissions. The Sales and Accounting groups would give Alexander an effective permission of Change; however, No Access will override that. For more information see "File Resources" in Chapter 2, "Implementing and Conducting Administration of Resources."

11. **C.** The default permission on all shares is Everyone has Full Control; this includes the guest account as well. Remove this permission and add only groups with the appropriate permissions. For more information see "File Resources" in Chapter 2, "Implementing and Conducting Administration Resources."

12. **C.** All clients can connect with a secured connection internally, automatically, and externally through the VPNs using IPSEC. For more information see "File Resources" in Chapter 2, "Implementing and Conducting Administration of Resources."

13. **A.** All clients can connect with a secured connection internally, automatically, and externally through the VPNs using IPSEC. Clients at home will be able to use their Web browsers to connect to or use regular network shares. For more information see "File Resources" in Chapter 2, "Implementing and Conducting Administration of Resources."

14. **D.** Sending the file through the Web or FTP servers will carry the risk of sending a virus. Using Internet-based printing, the report can be sent safely. For more information see "The Print Environment" in Chapter 2, "Implementing and Conducting Administration of Resources."

15. **C, D.** All print devices can be set up and shared in a printer pool, which would prevent any one print device failure from causing downtime. The same print device can be set up with two printers,

each with different permissions and properties. The Executives will print with a higher priority and therefore will jump the queue. For more information see "The Print Environment" in Chapter 2, "Implementing and Conducting Administration of Resources."

16. **B, E.** NTFS can be used to implement local permissions on files. With the help of EFS, additional encryption can be added to files so that, even if they are copied to a FAT partition, they cannot be viewed by anyone but the owner. For more information see "Managing File Resources" in Chapter 2, "Implementing and Conducting Administration of Resources."

17. **A, C, D.** A desktop will not need to conserve energy since it is not running on batteries. Multiple CPUs and multiple video cards are not stable under the APM environment. Windows 98 and Windows 2000 Professional both support APM. For more information see "Power Management" in Chapter 3, "Implementing, Managing, and Troubleshooting Hardware Devices and Drivers."

18. **D, E.** MPEG-2 and AC-3 are decoder formats that allow DVDs to bypass the standard PCI controllers and access the display adapters. For more information see "Installing Hardware" in Chapter 3, " Implementing, Managing, and Troubleshooting Hardware Devices and Drivers."

19. **C, F, G.** Basic disks are supported for backward compatibility. They cannot be used to create mirrors or volumes. For more information see "Installing Hardware" in Chapter 3, "Implementing, Managing, and Troubleshooting Hardware Devices and Drivers."

20. **B.** There are no configuration tools to change the primary adapter. It will be the first PCI card detected. Some system's BIOSs can be set to deactivate the on-board card but not to set it as

primary. It will always be a secondary adapter. For more information see "Display Devices" in Chapter 3, "Implementing, Managing, and Troubleshooting Hardware Devices and Drivers."

21. **C.** Removing the NetBEUI protocol simplifies protocols on the network and reduced local broadcasts. Each system will broadcast its server services on each protocol that is installed every 15 minutes, and the services will not be forwarded by router by default. Reducing the number of protocols will help in this situation. For more information see "Network Adapters" in Chapter 3, " Implementing, Managing, and Troubleshooting Hardware Devices and Drivers."

22. **A.** If the processor is busy with any type of activity at a level of 90% or more over an extended period of time, it is common to have the processor spike to 100%. The interrupts per second show how many requests are coming in. The queue length should not be more than 2 for any long period of time. For more information see "Monitoring Multiple CPUs" in Chapter 3, "Implementing, Managing, and Troubleshooting Hardware Devices and Drivers."

23. **B.** You must be logged on with a user ID that has administrator privileges to complete this procedure. If your camera supports Plug and Play, Windows 2000 Professional will detect it and install the correct drivers automatically. For more information see "Cameras" in Chapter 3, "Implementing, Managing, and Troubleshooting Hardware Devices and Drivers."

24. **A, C.** On the Windows 2000 Professional CD, a file called Biosinfo.inf has a list of laptops that will be set up with AutoEnable and AutoDisable for APM. ACPI-only systems do not support APM either. For more information see "Power Management" in Chapter 3, "Implementing, Managing, and Troubleshooting Hardware Devices and Drivers."

25. **B.** The system must be configured to prevent installation or provide a warning when an unsigned file is being installed. For more information see "Managing and Troubleshooting Driver Signing" in Chapter 4, "Monitoring and Optimizing System Performance and Reliability."

26. **E.** All drivers and files that are signed will be installed automatically. Non-signed files may be blocked or the installer will get a warning if the signature policy is in place. For more information see "Managing and Troubleshooting Driver Signing" in Chapter 4, "Monitoring and Optimizing System Performance and Reliability."

27. **B.** Search for files with a .Job extension in the Winnt\tasks folder. For more information see "Configuring, Managing, and Troubleshooting the Task Scheduler" in Chapter 4, "Monitoring and Optimizing System Performance and Reliability."

28. **B.** Windows 2000 Professional will continue to accept and allow you to edit tasks using the AT command. However, once the tasks are modified in the Task Scheduler, their format is changed and can no longer be read by the older AT command. For more information see "Configuring, Managing, and Troubleshooting the Task Scheduler" in Chapter 4, "Monitoring and Optimizing System Performance and Reliability."

29. **D.** A processor bottleneck occurs if the percentage of processor time is above 90% and the disk queue length is above 2. For more information see "Optimizing and Troubleshooting Performance of the Windows 2000 Professional Desktop" in Chapter 4, "Monitoring and Optimizing System Performance and Reliability."

30. **D.** Disk counters are disabled by default and must be enabled before monitoring. Counters are enabled using the Devices applet in the Control Panel, or the Diskperf command.

For more information see "Optimizing and Troubleshooting Performance of the Windows 2000 Professional Desktop" in Chapter 4, "Monitoring and Optimizing System Performance and Reliability."

31. **A, B.** By creating a test hardware profile, you do not risk losing the original configuration. Once the system has been restarted in the test configuration, you can disable devices or services. If the desired results occur, you make these changes permanent in the original configuration. For more information see "Managing Hardware Profiles" in Chapter 4, "Monitoring and Optimizing System Performance and Reliability."

32. **B, C, D, E.** CD-ROMs and DVD-ROMs are read only and therefore cannot be written to from the backup utility. Modem cannot be used in backup at this point. Windows 2000 Professional can be configured to use any writable device connected to the system. For more information see "Recovering System and User Data by Using Windows Backup" in Chapter 4, "Monitoring and Optimizing System Performance and Reliability."

33. **A.** Group policies from Active Directory can help maintain a standard desktop and reduce administration cost. For more information see "The Desktop Environment" in Chapter 5, "Configuring and Troubleshooting the Desktop Environment."

34. **C.** Local profiles are always enabled on a Windows 2000 Professional system. As long as the users do not change computers, roaming profiles are not needed. For more information see "Configuring and Managing User Profiles" in Chapter 5, "Configuring and Troubleshooting the Desktop Environment."

35. **E.** Ntuser.dat can be renamed to NTUser.man and it will make the profile mandatory. Users can change settings but will not be able to save them

upon exiting. Unlike Windows 9x, you cannot disable profiles in Windows 2000 Professional. For more information see "Mandatory User Profiles" in Chapter 5, "Configuring and Troubleshooting the Desktop Environment."

36. **E.** If the input locale indicator is not on your taskbar, click Start, point to Settings, click Control Panel, and then double-click Regional Options. On the Input Locales tab, select Enable Indicator on Taskbar. For more information see "Configuring Support for Multiple Languages or Multiple Locations in Windows 2000" in Chapter 5, "Configuring and Troubleshooting the Desktop Environment."

37. **D.** Dialing locations allow a user to save settings of commonly used configurations. If the user is dialing from home or the same hotel, the settings are saved. For more information see "Fax Overview" in Chapter 5, "Configuring and Troubleshooting the Desktop Environment."

38. **C, D.** ShowSounds and SoundSentry give people with hearing impairments control of their audio environments. For more information see "Accessibility Benefits with Windows 2000" in Chapter 5, "Configuring and Troubleshooting the Desktop Environment."

39. **A.** Group policies from Active Directory can help publish and assign applications to users. For more information see "The Desktop Environment" in Chapter 5, "Configuring and Troubleshooting the Desktop Environment."

40. **A, B, C.** Several other operating systems other than Windows 2000 including UNIX, Novell NetWare, and Windows NT 4.0 can be controlled. For more information see "The Desktop Environment" in Chapter 5, "Configuring and Troubleshooting the Desktop Environment."

41. **B.** To find out IP information on a computer that is DHCP enabled, you use the ipconfig command. The /all switch will show you all the IP information. For more information see "Understanding DHCP" in Chapter 6, "Implementing, Managing, and Troubleshooting Network Protocols and Services."

42. The correct order is as follows:

Ping the address of 127.0.0.1

Ping the local host

Ping the gateway

Ping the remote host.

The order reflects the path information must travel through when communicating over TCP/IP: first the stack (127.0.0.1), then the card, the gateway, and the remote host. For more information see "Configuring the TCP/IP Protocol" in Chapter 6, "Implementing, Managing, and Troubleshooting Network Protocols and Services."

43. **A.** By configuring Windows 2000 Professional to use DHCP and WINS, you are allowing for automatic IP addressing and dynamic name resolution of the Windows 2000 servers. By using the host file, you are allowing the UNIX server's name to be resolved. For more information see "Configuring the TCP/IP Protocol" in Chapter 6, "Implementing, Managing, and Troubleshooting Network Protocols and Services."

44. **B.** When you share an Internet connection on a Windows 2000 computer, it will automatically assign DHCP addresses to clients. The addresses that it assigns are between 192.168.0.1 and 192.168.255.254. For more information see "Internet Connection Sharing" in Chapter 6, "Implementing, Managing, and Troubleshooting Network Protocols and Services."

45. **A, D.** Only PPP supports IPX and NetBEUI as well as TCP/IP. PPP also supports encryption of logon information if configured. For more information see "Serial Line Internet Protocol (SLIP)" and "Point-to-Point Protocol (PPP)" in Chapter 6, "Implementing, Managing, and Troubleshooting Network Protocols and Services."

46. **A, B, G.** The LMHOSTS file is used to statically map IP addresses to NetBIOS names. WINS is a service that is installed on a server to create a database, a NetBIOS name, and associated IP addresses. Clients can query the database to find names to IP address mappings. If the first two methods fail, then Windows will read the HOST file to see if there is a host name that is the same as the NetBIOS name. For more information see "Resolve a NetBIOS Name to an IP Address" in Chapter 6, "Implementing, Managing, and Troubleshooting Network Protocols and Services."

47. **C.** By installing only TCP/IP, the Windows 2000 clients cannot connect to the Novell server. To connect to the Novell server, you would require IPX/SPX. For more information see "NWLink IPX/SPX Compatible Transport" in Chapter 6, "Implementing, Managing, and Troubleshooting Network Protocols and Services."

48. **D.** By adding the #PRE switch to the end of the line, you are telling Windows to load the name mapping into the NetBIOS name cache. This cache can be checked running the nbtstat –c command. For more information see "LMHOSTS File Errors" and "Understanding DHCP" in Chapter 6, "Implementing, Managing, and Troubleshooting Network Protocols and Services."

49. **A.** By installing and configuring a Windows 2000 Domain, you have allowed for centralized administration and single-user ID logon. Because each user account must be created only once, you have also reduced administration of user accounts as well. For more info see "User Accounts" in Chapter 7, "Implementing, Monitoring, and Troubleshooting Security."

50. **B.** The correct method is to rename Jane's account to Fred's login name. Because user access is really controlled by SID, the name is just to make it easier to see and control. Answer A is incorrect because Fred will not have access to Jane's resources. B is incorrect because it is a security risk. Answer D is too much work. For more information see " Groups" in Chapter 7, "Implementing, Monitoring, and Troubleshooting Security."

51. **C.** The solution does not satisfy the optional desired results because placing the managers in the Universal group will cause more Active Directory traffic. This is the case because not only will the user and group account be updated, but there will be a synchronization with the Global Catalog server. For more information see "Groups" in Chapter 7, "Implementing, Monitoring, and Troubleshooting Security."

52. **D.** The proposed solution does not satisfy any of the required or optional desired results. Proper group management can be summed up by the following acronym: AGDLP (**a**ccounts in **g**lobal groups placed in **d**omain **l**ocal groups and given **p**ermissions). For more information see "Groups" in Chapter 7, "Implementing, Monitoring, and Troubleshooting Security."

53. **D.** Applications that were written for Windows NT 4.0 do not know about the Windows 2000 security model. By adding the users into the Power Users group, they should be able to run all applications. For more information see "Groups" in Chapter 7, "Implementing, Monitoring, and Troubleshooting Security."

54. **A, B, D.** Answers C and F are built-in Global groups. Everyone is a System group. Managers is not a built-in group; it is a group that was created by an administrator. For more information see "Create and Manage Local Users and Groups" in Chapter 6, "Implementing, Managing, and Troubleshooting Network Protocols, and Services."

55. **B.** Only administrators can access the security log on Windows 2000 Professional computers. For more information see "Setting up Auditing" in Chapter 7, "Implementing, Monitoring, and Troubleshooting Security."

56. **C.** Power users have the ability to load and unload applications. Users cannot perform such tasks. For more information see in "Windows 2000 Security Configurations" in Chapter 7, "Implementing, Monitoring, and Troubleshooting Security."

57. **A.** When the compatible workstation template is assigned to Windows 2000 Professional computers, it reduces the level of security required for the components of applications designed for Windows NT 4.0. It does not allow the users to have the same level of rights that a power user has, so they cannot install or uninstall applications. For more information see "Windows 2000 Security Configurations " in Chapter 7, "Implementing, Monitoring, and Troubleshooting Security."

58. **B.** The recovery agent must be configured in the security policies of the local computer for it to work. For more information see "Encrypting File System" in Chapter 7, "Implementing, Monitoring, and Troubleshooting Security."

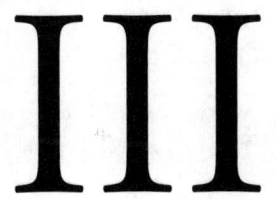

APPENDICES

Overview of the Certification Process

You must pass rigorous certification exams to become a Microsoft Certified Professional. These closed-book exams provide a valid and reliable measure of your technical proficiency and expertise. Developed in consultation with computer industry professionals who have experience with Microsoft products in the workplace, the exams are conducted by two independent organizations. Virtual University Enterprises (VUE) testing centers offer exams at more than 2,700 locations in 128 countries. Prometric offers the exams at more than 2,000 authorized Prometric Testing Centers around the world, as well.

To schedule an exam, call Sylvan Prometric Testing Centers at 800-755-EXAM (3926) (or register online at http://www.2test.com/register) or VUE at 888-837-8734 (or register online at http://www.vue.com/ms/msexam.html). At the time of this writing, Microsoft offered eight types of certification, each based on a specific area of expertise. Please check the Microsoft Certified Professional Web site for the most up-to-date information (www.microsoft.com/mcp/).

TYPES OF CERTIFICATION

◆ **Microsoft Certified Professional (MCP).** Persons with this credential are qualified to support at least one Microsoft product. Candidates can take elective exams to develop areas of specialization. MCP is the base level of expertise.

◆ **Microsoft Certified Professional+Internet (MCP+Internet).** Persons with this credential are qualified to plan security, install and configure server products, manage server resources, extend service to run CGI scripts or ISAPI scripts, monitor and analyze performance, and troubleshoot problems. Expertise is similar to that of an MCP but with a focus on the Internet.

◆ **Microsoft Certified Professional+Site Building (MCP+Site Building).** Persons with this credential are qualified to plan, build, maintain, and manage Web sites using Microsoft technologies and products. The credential is appropriate for people who manage sophisticated, interactive Web sites that include database connectivity, multimedia, and searchable content.

◆ **Microsoft Certified Database Administrator (MCDBA).** Qualified individuals can derive physical database designs, develop logical data models, create physical databases, create data services by using Transact-SQL, manage and maintain databases, configure and manage security, monitor and optimize databases, and install and configure Microsoft SQL Server.

◆ **Microsoft Certified Systems Engineer (MCSE).** These individuals are qualified to analyze the business requirements for a system architecture; design solutions; deploy, install, and configure architecture components; and troubleshoot system problems.

◆ **Microsoft Certified Systems Engineer+Internet (MCSE+Internet).** Persons with this credential are qualified in the core MCSE areas and also are qualified to enhance, deploy, and manage sophisticated intranet and Internet solutions that include a browser, proxy server, host servers, database, and messaging and commerce components. An MCSE+Internet-certified professional is able to manage and analyze Web sites.

◆ **Microsoft Certified Solution Developer (MCSD).** These individuals are qualified to design and develop custom business solutions by using Microsoft development tools, technologies, and platforms. The new track includes certification exams that test the user's ability to build Web-based, distributed, and commerce applications by using Microsoft products such as Microsoft SQL Server, Microsoft Visual Studio, and Microsoft Component Services.

◆ **Microsoft Certified Trainer (MCT).** Persons with this credential are instructionally and technically qualified by Microsoft to deliver Microsoft Education Courses at Microsoft-authorized sites. An MCT must be employed by a Microsoft Solution Provider Authorized Technical Education Center or a Microsoft Authorized Academic Training site.

NOTE
For up-to-date information about each type of certification, visit the Microsoft Training and Certification Web site at `http://www.microsoft.com/mcp`. You can also contact Microsoft through the following sources:

- Microsoft Certified Professional Program: 800-636-7544

- `mcp@msource.com`

- Microsoft Online Institute (MOLI): 800-449-9333

CERTIFICATION REQUIREMENTS

The following sections describe the requirements for the various types of Microsoft certifications.

NOTE
An asterisk following an exam in any of the following lists means that it is slated for retirement.

How to Become a Microsoft Certified Professional

To become certified as an MCP, you need only pass any Microsoft exam (with the exceptions of Networking Essentials, #70-058* and Microsoft Windows 2000 Accelerated Exam for MCPs Certified on Microsoft Windows NT 4.0, #70-240).

How to Become a Microsoft Certified Professional+Internet

To become an MCP specializing in Internet technology, you must pass the following exams:

◆ Internetworking with Microsoft TCP/IP on Microsoft Windows NT 4.0, #70-059*

◆ Implementing and Supporting Microsoft Windows NT Server 4.0, #70-067*

◆ Implementing and Supporting Microsoft Internet Information Server 3.0 and Microsoft Index Server 1.1, #70-077*

   OR Implementing and Supporting Microsoft Internet Information Server 4.0, #70-087*

How to Become a Microsoft Certified Professional+Site Building

To be certified as an MCP+Site Building, you need to pass two of the following exams:

◆ Designing and Implementing Web Sites with Microsoft FrontPage 98, #70-055

◆ Designing and Implementing Commerce Solutions with Microsoft Site Server 3.0, Commerce Edition, #70-057

◆ Designing and Implementing Web Solutions with Microsoft Visual InterDev 6.0, #70-152

How to Become a Microsoft Certified Database Administrator

There are two MCDBA tracks, one tied to Windows 2000, the other based on Windows NT 4.0.

Windows 2000 Track

To become an MCDBA in the Windows 2000 track, you must pass three core exams and one elective exam.

Core Exams

The core exams required to become an MCDBA in the Windows 2000 track are as follows:

◆ Installing, Configuring, and Administering Microsoft Windows 2000 Server, #70-215

   OR Microsoft Windows 2000 Accelerated Exam for MCPs Certified on Microsoft Windows NT 4.0, #70-240 (only for those who have passed exams #70-067*, #70-068*, and #70-073*)

◆ Administering Microsoft SQL Server 7.0, #70-028

◆ Designing and Implementing Databases with Microsoft SQL Server 7.0, #70-029

Elective Exams

You must also pass one elective exam from the following list:

◆ Implementing and Administering a Microsoft Windows 2000 Network Infrastructure, #70-216 (only for those who have *not* already passed #70-067*, #70-068*, and #70-073*)

OR Microsoft Windows 2000 Accelerated Exam for MCPs Certified on Microsoft Windows NT 4.0, #70-240 (only for those who have passed exams #70-067*, #70-068*, and #70-073*)

◆ Designing and Implementing Distributed Applications with Microsoft Visual C++ 6.0, #70-015

◆ Designing and Implementing Data Warehouses with Microsoft SQL Server 7.0 and Microsoft Decision Support Services 1.0, #70-019

◆ Implementing and Supporting Microsoft Internet Information Server 4.0, #70-087*

◆ Designing and Implementing Distributed Applications with Microsoft Visual FoxPro 6.0, #70-155

◆ Designing and Implementing Distributed Applications with Microsoft Visual Basic 6.0, #70-175

Windows NT 4.0 Track

To become an MCDBA in the Windows NT 4.0 track, you must pass four core exams and one elective exam.

Core Exams

The core exams required to become an MCDBA in the Windows NT 4.0 track are as follows:

◆ Administering Microsoft SQL Server 7.0, #70-028

◆ Designing and Implementing Databases with Microsoft SQL Server 7.0, #70-029

◆ Implementing and Supporting Microsoft Windows NT Server 4.0, #70-067*

◆ Implementing and Supporting Microsoft Windows NT Server 4.0 in the Enterprise, #70-068*

Elective Exams

You must also pass one elective exam from the following list:

◆ Designing and Implementing Distributed Applications with Microsoft Visual C++ 6.0, #70-015

◆ Designing and Implementing Data Warehouses with Microsoft SQL Server 7.0 and Microsoft Decision Support Services 1.0, #70-019

◆ Internetworking with Microsoft TCP/IP on Microsoft Windows NT 4.0, #70-059*

◆ Implementing and Supporting Microsoft Internet Information Server 4.0, #70-087*

◆ Designing and Implementing Distributed Applications with Microsoft Visual FoxPro 6.0, #70-155

◆ Designing and Implementing Distributed Applications with Microsoft Visual Basic 6.0, #70-175

How to Become a Microsoft Certified Systems Engineer

You must pass operating system exams and two elective exams to become an MCSE. The MCSE certification path is divided into two tracks: Windows 2000 and Windows NT 4.0.

The following lists show the core requirements for the Windows 2000 and Windows NT 4.0 tracks and the electives.

Windows 2000 Track

The Windows 2000 track requires you to pass five core exams (or an accelerated exam and another core exam). You must also pass two elective exams.

Core Exams

The Windows 2000 track core requirements for MCSE certification include the following for those who have *not* passed #70-067, #70-068, and #70-073:

◆ Installing, Configuring, and Administering Microsoft Windows 2000 Professional, #70-210

◆ Installing, Configuring, and Administering Microsoft Windows 2000 Server, #70-215

◆ Implementing and Administering a Microsoft Windows 2000 Network Infrastructure, #70-216

◆ Implementing and Administering a Microsoft Windows 2000 Directory Services Infrastructure, #70-217

The Windows 2000 Track core requirements for MCSE certification include the following for those who have passed #70-067*, #70-068*, and #70-073*:

◆ Microsoft Windows 2000 Accelerated Exam for MCPs Certified on Microsoft Windows NT 4.0, #70-240

All candidates must pass one of these three additional core exams:

◆ Designing a Microsoft Windows 2000 Directory Services Infrastructure, #70-219

   OR Designing Security for a Microsoft Windows 2000 Network, #70-220

   OR Designing a Microsoft Windows 2000 Infrastructure, #70-221

Elective Exams

Any MCSE elective exams that are current (not slated for retirement) when the Windows 2000 core exams are released can be used to fulfill the requirement of two elective exams. In addition, core exams #70-219,

#70-220, and #70-221 can be used as elective exams, as long as they are not already being used to fulfill the "additional core exams" requirement outlined previously. Exam #70-222 (Upgrading from Microsoft Windows NT 4.0 to Microsoft Windows 2000), can also be used to fulfill this requirement. Finally, selected third-party certifications that focus on interoperability may count for this requirement. Watch the Microsoft MCP Web site (www.microsoft.com/mcp) for more information on these third-party certifications.

Windows NT 4.0 Track

The Windows NT 4.0 track is also organized around core and elective exams.

Core Exams

The four Windows NT 4.0 track core requirements for MCSE certification are as follows:

◆ Implementing and Supporting Microsoft Windows NT Server 4.0, #70-067*

◆ Implementing and Supporting Microsoft Windows NT Server 4.0 in the Enterprise, #70-068*

◆ Microsoft Windows 3.1, #70-030*

   OR Microsoft Windows for Workgroups 3.11, #70-048*

   OR Implementing and Supporting Microsoft Windows 95, #70-064*

   OR Implementing and Supporting Microsoft Windows NT Workstation 4.0, #70-073*

   OR Implementing and Supporting Microsoft Windows 98, #70-098

◆ Networking Essentials, #70-058*

Elective Exams

For the Windows NT 4.0 track, you must pass two of the following elective exams for MCSE certification:

◆ Implementing and Supporting Microsoft SNA Server 3.0, #70-013

   OR Implementing and Supporting Microsoft SNA Server 4.0, #70-085

◆ Implementing and Supporting Microsoft Systems Management Server 1.2, #70-018

   OR Implementing and Supporting Microsoft Systems Management Server 2.0, #70-086

◆ Designing and Implementing Data Warehouse with Microsoft SQL Server 7.0, #70-019

◆ Microsoft SQL Server 4.2 Database Implementation, #70-021*

   OR Implementing a Database Design on Microsoft SQL Server 6.5, #70-027

   OR Implementing a Database Design on Microsoft SQL Server 7.0, #70-029

◆ Microsoft SQL Server 4.2 Database Administration for Microsoft Windows NT, #70-022*

   OR System Administration for Microsoft SQL Server 6.5 (or 6.0), #70-026

   OR System Administration for Microsoft SQL Server 7.0, #70-028

◆ Microsoft Mail for PC Networks 3.2-Enterprise, #70-037*

◆ Internetworking with Microsoft TCP/IP on Microsoft Windows NT (3.5–3.51), #70-053*

   OR Internetworking with Microsoft TCP/IP on Microsoft Windows NT 4.0, #70-059*

◆ Implementing and Supporting Web Sites Using Microsoft Site Server 3.0, #70-056

◆ Implementing and Supporting Microsoft Exchange Server 4.0, #70-075*

   OR Implementing and Supporting Microsoft Exchange Server 5.0, #70-076

   OR Implementing and Supporting Microsoft Exchange Server 5.5, #70-081

◆ Implementing and Supporting Microsoft Internet Information Server 3.0 and Microsoft Index Server 1.1, #70-077*

   OR Implementing and Supporting Microsoft Internet Information Server 4.0, #70-087*

◆ Implementing and Supporting Microsoft Proxy Server 1.0, #70-078

   OR Implementing and Supporting Microsoft Proxy Server 2.0, #70-088

◆ Implementing and Supporting Microsoft Internet Explorer 4.0 by Using the Internet Explorer Resource Kit, #70-079

   OR Implementing and Supporting Microsoft Internet Explorer 5.0 by Using the Internet Explorer Resource Kit, #70-080

◆ Designing a Microsoft Windows 2000 Directory Services Infrastructure, #70-219

◆ Designing Security for a Microsoft Windows 2000 Network, #70-220

◆ Designing a Microsoft Windows 2000 Infrastructure, #70-221

◆ Upgrading from Microsoft Windows NT 4.0 to Microsoft Windows 2000, #70-222

How to Become a Microsoft Certified Systems Engineer+Internet

You must pass seven operating system exams and two elective exams to become an MCSE specializing in Internet technology.

Core Exams

The following seven core exams are required for MCSE+Internet certification:

◆ Networking Essentials, #70-058*

◆ Internetworking with Microsoft TCP/IP on Microsoft Windows NT 4.0, #70-059*

◆ Implementing and Supporting Microsoft Windows 95, #70-064*

 OR Implementing and Supporting Microsoft Windows NT Workstation 4.0, #70-073*

 OR Implementing and Supporting Microsoft Windows 98, #70-098

◆ Implementing and Supporting Microsoft Windows NT Server 4.0, #70-067*

◆ Implementing and Supporting Microsoft Windows NT Server 4.0 in the Enterprise, #70-068*

◆ Implementing and Supporting Microsoft Internet Information Server 3.0 and Microsoft Index Server 1.1, #70-077*

 OR Implementing and Supporting Microsoft Internet Information Server 4.0, #70-087*

◆ Implementing and Supporting Microsoft Internet Explorer 4.0 by Using the Internet Explorer Resource Kit, #70-079

 OR Implementing and Supporting Microsoft Internet Explorer 5.0 by Using the Internet Explorer Resource Kit, #70-080

Elective Exams

You must also pass two of the following elective exams for MCSE+Internet certification:

◆ System Administration for Microsoft SQL Server 6.5, #70-026

 OR Administering Microsoft SQL Server 7.0, #70-028

◆ Implementing a Database Design on Microsoft SQL Server 6.5, #70-027

 OR Designing and Implementing Databases with Microsoft SQL Server 7.0, #70-029

◆ Implementing and Supporting Web Sites Using Microsoft Site Server 3.0, # 70-056

◆ Implementing and Supporting Microsoft Exchange Server 5.0, #70-076

 OR Implementing and Supporting Microsoft Exchange Server 5.5, #70-081

◆ Implementing and Supporting Microsoft Proxy Server 1.0, #70-078

 OR Implementing and Supporting Microsoft Proxy Server 2.0, #70-088

◆ Implementing and Supporting Microsoft SNA Server 4.0, #70-085

How to Become a Microsoft Certified Solution Developer

The MCSD certification has undergone substantial revision. Listed below are the requirements for the new track (available fourth quarter 1998) as well as the old.

New Track

For the new track, you must pass three core exams and one elective exam.

Core Exams

The core exams are as follows. You must pass one exam in each of the following groups:

Desktop Applications Development (one required)

- ◆ Designing and Implementing Desktop Applications with Microsoft Visual C++ 6.0, #70-016

  OR Designing and Implementing Desktop Applications with Microsoft Visual FoxPro 6.0, #70-156

  OR Designing and Implementing Desktop Applications with Microsoft Visual Basic 6.0, #70-176

Distributed Applications Development (one required)

- ◆ Designing and Implementing Distributed Applications with Microsoft Visual C++ 6.0, #70-015

  OR Designing and Implementing Distributed Applications with Microsoft Visual FoxPro 6.0, #70-155

  OR Designing and Implementing Distributed Applications with Microsoft Visual Basic 6.0, #70-175

Solution Architecture (required)

- ◆ Analyzing Requirements and Defining Solution Architectures, #70-100

Elective Exam

You must pass one of the following elective exams:

- ◆ Designing and Implementing Distributed Applications with Microsoft Visual C++ 6.0, #70-015

- ◆ Designing and Implementing Desktop Applications with Microsoft Visual C++ 6.0, #70-016

- ◆ Designing and Implementing Data Warehouses with Microsoft SQL Server 7.0, #70-019

- ◆ Developing Applications with C++ Using the Microsoft Foundation Class Library, #70-024

- ◆ Implementing OLE in Microsoft Foundation Class Applications, #70-025

- ◆ Implementing a Database Design on Microsoft SQL Server 6.5, #70-027

- ◆ Implementing a Database Design on Microsoft SQL Server 7.0, #70-029

- ◆ Designing and Implementing Web Sites with Microsoft FrontPage 98, #70-055

- ◆ Designing and Implementing Commerce Solutions with Microsoft Site Server 3.0, Commerce Edition, #70-057

- ◆ Programming with Microsoft Visual Basic 4.0, #70-065*

- ◆ Application Development with Microsoft Access for Windows 95 and the Microsoft Access Developer's Toolkit, #70-069

- ◆ Designing and Implementing Solutions with Microsoft Office 2000 and Microsoft Visual Basic for Applications, #70-091

- ◆ Designing and Implementing Database Applications with Microsoft Access 2000, #70-097

◆ Designing and Implementing Collaborative Solutions with Microsoft Outlook 2000 and Microsoft Exchange Server 5.5, #70-105

◆ Designing and Implementing Web Solutions with Microsoft Visual InterDev 6.0, #70-152

◆ Designing and Implementing Distributed Applications with Microsoft Visual FoxPro 6.0, #70-155

◆ Designing and Implementing Desktop Applications with Microsoft Visual FoxPro 6.0, #70-156

◆ Developing Applications with Microsoft Visual Basic 5.0, #70-165

◆ Designing and Implementing Distributed Applications with Microsoft Visual Basic 6.0, #70-175

◆ Designing and Implementing Desktop Applications with Microsoft Visual Basic 6.0, #70-176

Old Track

For the old track, you must pass two core technology exams and two elective exams for MCSD certification. The following lists show the required technology exams and elective exams needed for MCSD certification.

Core Exams

You must pass the following two core technology exams to qualify for MCSD certification:

◆ Microsoft Windows Architecture I, #70-160*

◆ Microsoft Windows Architecture II, #70-161*

Elective Exams

You must also pass two of the following elective exams to become an MSCD:

◆ Designing and Implementing Distributed Applications with Microsoft Visual C++ 6.0, #70-015

◆ Designing and Implementing Desktop Applications with Microsoft Visual C++ 6.0, #70-016

◆ Designing and Implementing Data Warehouses with Microsoft SQL Server 7.0, #70-019

◆ Microsoft SQL Server 4.2 Database Implementation, #70-021*

   OR Implementing a Database Design on Microsoft SQL Server 6.5, #70-027

   OR Implementing a Database Design on Microsoft SQL Server 7.0, #70-029

◆ Developing Applications with C++ Using the Microsoft Foundation Class Library, #70-024

◆ Implementing OLE in Microsoft Foundation Class Applications, #70-025

◆ Programming with Microsoft Visual Basic 4.0, #70-065

   OR Developing Applications with Microsoft Visual Basic 5.0, #70-165

   OR Designing and Implementing Distributed Applications with Microsoft Visual Basic 6.0, #70-175

◆ Designing and Implementing Desktop Applications with Microsoft Visual Basic 6.0, #70-176

◆ Microsoft Access 2.0 for Windows-Application Development, #70-051*

  OR Microsoft Access for Windows 95 and the Microsoft Access Development Toolkit, #70-069

  OR Designing and Implementing Database Applications with Microsoft Access 2000, #70-097

◆ Developing Applications with Microsoft Excel 5.0 Using Visual Basic for Applications, #70-052*

◆ Programming in Microsoft Visual FoxPro 3.0 for Windows, #70-054*

  OR Designing and Implementing Distributed Applications with Microsoft Visual FoxPro 6.0, #70-155

  OR Designing and Implementing Desktop Applications with Microsoft Visual FoxPro 6.0, #70-156

◆ Designing and Implementing Web Sites with Microsoft FrontPage 98, #70-055

◆ Designing and Implementing Commerce Solutions with Microsoft Site Server 3.0, Commerce Edition, #70-057

◆ Designing and Implementing Solutions with Microsoft Office (code-named Office 9) and Microsoft Visual Basic for Applications, #70-091

◆ Designing and Implementing Collaborative Solutions with Microsoft Outlook 2000 and Microsoft Exchange Server 5.5, #70-105

◆ Designing and Implementing Web Solutions with Microsoft Visual InterDev 6.0, #70-152

Becoming a Microsoft Certified Trainer

To fully understand the requirements and process for becoming an MCT, you need to obtain the Microsoft Certified Trainer Guide document from the following WWW site:

    http://www.microsoft.com/mcp/certstep/mct.htm

At this site, you can read the document as a Web page or display and download it as a Word file. The MCT Guide explains the process for becoming an MCT. The general steps for the MCT certification are as follows:

1. Complete and mail a Microsoft Certified Trainer application to Microsoft. You must include proof of your skills for presenting instructional material. The options for doing so are described in the MCT Guide.

2. Obtain and study the Microsoft Trainer Kit for the Microsoft Official Curricula (MOC) courses for which you want to be certified. Microsoft Trainer Kits can be ordered by calling 800-688-0496 in North America. Those of you in other regions should review the MCT Guide for information on how to order a Trainer Kit.

3. Take and pass any required prerequisite MCP exam(s) to measure your current technical knowledge.

4. Prepare to teach a MOC course. Begin by attending the MOC course for which you want to be certified. This is required so that you understand how the course is structured, how labs are completed, and how the course flows.

5. Pass any additional exam requirement(s) to measure any additional product knowledge that pertains to the course.

6. Submit your course preparation checklist to Microsoft so that your additional accreditation may be processed and reflect on your transcript.

> **WARNING** You should consider the preceding steps a general overview of the MCT certification process. The precise steps that you need to take are described in detail on the Web site mentioned earlier. Do not misinterpret the preceding steps as the exact process you must undergo.

If you are interested in becoming an MCT, you can obtain more information by visiting the Microsoft Certified Training WWW site at `http://www.microsoft.com/train_cert/mct/` or by calling 800-688-0496.

What's on the CD-ROM

This appendix is a brief rundown of what you'll find on the CD-ROM that comes with this book. For a more detailed description of the newly developed *ExamGear, Training Guide Edition* exam simulation software, see Appendix C, "Using the *ExamGear, Training Guide Edition* Software." All items on the CD-ROM are easily accessible from the simple interface. In addition to *ExamGear, Training Guide Edition*, the CD-ROM includes the electronic version of the book in Portable Document Format (PDF) as well as several utility and application programs.

EXAMGEAR, TRAINING GUIDE EDITION

ExamGear is an exam environment developed exclusively for New Riders Publishing. It is, we believe, the best exam software available. In addition to providing a means of evaluating your knowledge of the *Training Guide* material, *ExamGear, Training Guide Edition* features several innovations that help you to improve your mastery of the subject matter.

For example, the practice tests allow you to check your score by exam area or category to determine which topics you need to study more. In another mode, *ExamGear, Training Guide Edition* allows you to obtain immediate feedback on your responses in the form of explanations for the correct and incorrect answers.

Although *ExamGear, Training Guide Edition* exhibits most of the full functionality of the retail version of *ExamGear*, including the exam format and question types, this special version is written to the Training Guide content. It is designed to aid you in assessing how well you understand the Training Guide material and enable you to experience most of the question formats you will see on the actual exam. It is not as complete a simulation of the exam as the full *ExamGear* retail product. It also does not include some of the features of the full retail product, such as access to the mentored discussion groups. However, it serves as an excellent method for assessing your knowledge of the Training Guide content and gives you the experience of taking an electronic exam.

Again, for a more complete description of *ExamGear, Training Guide Edition* features, see Appendix C, "Using the *ExamGear, Training Guide Edition* Software."

EXCLUSIVE ELECTRONIC VERSION OF TEXT

The CD-ROM also contains the electronic version of this book in Portable Document Format (PDF). The electronic version comes complete with all figures as they appear in the book. You will find that the search capabilities of the reader come in handy for study and review purposes.

Copyright Information and Disclaimer

New Riders Publishing's *ExamGear* **test simulator:**
Copyright ©2000 by New Riders Publishing. All rights
reserved. Made in U.S.A.

Using the ExamGear, Training Guide Edition Software

This training guide includes a special version of *ExamGear*—a revolutionary new test engine that is designed to give you the best in certification exam preparation. *ExamGear* offers sample and practice exams for many of today's most in-demand technical certifications. This special Training Guide edition is included with this book as a tool to utilize in assessing your knowledge of the Training Guide material while also providing you with the experience of taking an electronic exam.

In the rest of this appendix, we describe in detail what *ExamGear, Training Guide Edition* is, how it works, and what it can do to help you prepare for the exam. Note that although the Training Guide edition includes nearly all the test simulation functions of the complete, retail version, the questions focus on the Training Guide content rather than on simulating the actual Microsoft exam. Also, this version does not offer the same degree of online support that the full product does.

EXAM SIMULATION

One of the main functions of *ExamGear, Training Guide Edition* is exam simulation. To prepare you to take the actual vendor certification exam, the Training Guide edition of this test engine is designed to offer the most effective exam simulation available.

Question Quality

The questions provided in the *ExamGear, Training Guide Edition* simulations are written to high standards of technical accuracy. The questions tap the content of the Training Guide chapters and help you review and assess your knowledge before you take the actual exam.

Interface Design

The *ExamGear, Training Guide Edition* exam simulation interface provides you with the experience of taking an electronic exam. This enables you to effectively prepare for taking the actual exam by making the test experience a familiar one. Using the this test simulation can help eliminate the sense of surprise or anxiety that you might experience in the testing center, because you will already be acquainted with computerized testing.

STUDY TOOLS

ExamGear provides you with several learning tools to help prepare you for the actual certification exam.

Effective Learning Environment

The *ExamGear, Training Guide Edition* interface provides a learning environment that not only tests you through the computer, but also teaches the material you need to know to pass the certification exam. Each question comes with a detailed explanation of the correct answer and provides reasons why the other options were incorrect. This information helps to reinforce the knowledge you have already and also provides practical information you can use on the job.

Automatic Progress Tracking

ExamGear, Training Guide Edition automatically tracks your progress as you work through the test questions. From the Item Review tab (discussed in detail later in this appendix), you can see at a glance how well you are scoring by objective, by unit, or on a question-by-question basis (see Figure C.1). You can also configure *ExamGear* to drill you on the skills you need to work on most.

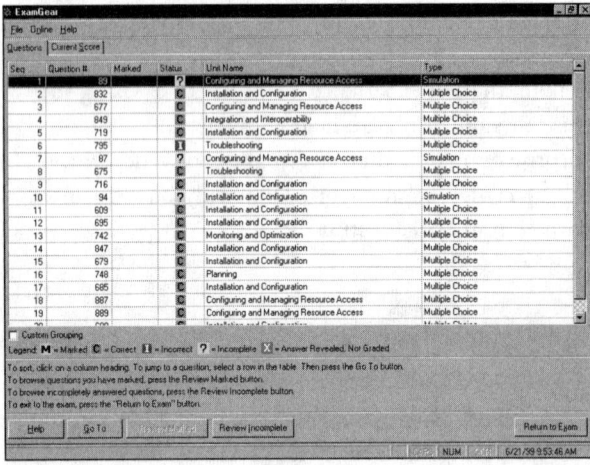

FIGURE C.1
Item review.

HOW EXAMGEAR, TRAINING GUIDE EDITION WORKS

ExamGear comprises two main elements: the interface and the database. The *interface* is the part of the program that you use to study and to run practice tests. The *database* stores all the question-and-answer data.

Interface

The *ExamGear, Training Guide Edition* interface is designed to be easy to use and provides the most effective study method available. The interface enables you to select from the following modes:

◆ **Study Mode.** In this mode, you can select the number of questions you want to see and the time you want to allow for the test. You can select questions from all the chapters or from specific chapters. This enables you to reinforce your knowledge in a specific area or strengthen your knowledge in areas pertaining to a specific objective. During the exam, you can display the correct answer to each question along with an explanation of why it is correct.

◆ **Practice Exam.** In this mode, you take an exam that is designed to simulate the actual certification exam. Questions are selected from all test-objective groups. The number of questions selected and the time allowed are set to match those parameters of the actual certification exam.

◆ **Adaptive Exam.** In this mode, you take an exam simulation using the adaptive testing technique. Questions are taken from all test-objective groups. The questions are presented in a way that ensures your mastery of all the test objectives. After you have a passing score or if you reach a point where it is statistically impossible for you to pass, the exam is ended. This method provides a rapid assessment of your readiness for the actual exam.

Database

The *ExamGear, Training Guide Edition* database stores a group of test questions along with answers and explanations. At least three databases are included for each Training Guide edition product. One includes the questions from the ends of the chapters. Another includes the questions from the Assessment Exam. The third is a database of new questions that have not appeared in the book. Additional exam databases may also be available for purchase online and are simple to download. Look ahead to the section "Obtaining Updates" in this appendix to find out how to download and activate additional databases.

INSTALLING AND REGISTERING EXAMGEAR, TRAINING GUIDE EDITION

This section provides instructions for *ExamGear, Training Guide Edition* installation and describes the process and benefits of registering your Training Guide edition product.

Requirements

ExamGear requires a computer with the following:

◆ Microsoft Windows 95, Windows 98, Windows NT 4.0, or Windows 2000.

A Pentium or later processor is recommended.

◆ Microsoft's Internet Explorer 4.01 or later version.

Internet Explorer 4.01 (or a later version) must be installed. (Even if you use a different browser, you still need to have Internet Explorer 4.01 or later installed.)

◆ A minimum of 16MB of RAM.

As with any Windows application, the more memory, the better your performance.

◆ A connection to the Internet.

An Internet connection is not required for the software to work, but it is required for online registration, product updates, downloading bonus question sets, and for unlocking other exams. These processes are described in more detail later.

Installing ExamGear, Training Guide Edition

Install *ExamGear, Training Guide Edition* by running the setup program that you found on the *ExamGear, Training Guide Edition* CD. Follow these instructions to install the Training Guide edition on your computer:

1. Insert the CD in your CD-ROM drive. The Autorun feature of Windows should launch the software. If you have Autorun disabled, click Start, and choose Run. Go to the root directory of the CD and choose START.EXE. Click Open and OK.

2. Click the button in the circle, and you see the welcome screen. From here you can install *ExamGear*. Click the ExamGear button to begin installation.

3. The Installation Wizard appears onscreen and prompts you with instructions to complete the installation. Select a directory on which to install *ExamGear, Training Guide Edition* (the Installation Wizard defaults to `C:\Program Files\ExamGear`).

4. The Installation Wizard copies the *ExamGear, Training Guide Edition* files to your hard drive, adds ExamGear, Training Guide Edition to your Program menu, adds values to your Registry, and installs test engine's DLLs to the appropriate system folders. To ensure that the process was successful, the Setup program finishes by running *ExamGear, Training Guide Edition*.

5. The Installation Wizard logs the installation process and stores this information in a file named `INSTALL.LOG`. This log file is used by the uninstall process in the event that you choose to remove *ExamGear, Training Guide Edition* from your computer. Because the *ExamGear* installation adds Registry keys and DLL files to your computer, it is important to uninstall the program appropriately (see the section "Removing *ExamGear, Training Guide Edition* from your Computer").

Registering ExamGear, Training Guide Edition

The Product Registration Wizard appears when *ExamGear, Training Guide Edition* is started for the first time, and *ExamGear* checks at startup to see whether you are registered. If you are not registered, the main menu is hidden, and a Product Registration Wizard appears. Remember that your computer must have an Internet connection to complete the Product Registration Wizard.

The first page of the Product Registration Wizard details the benefits of registration; however, you can always elect not to register. The Show This Message at Startup Until I Register option enables you to decide whether the registration screen should appear every time *ExamGear, Training Guide Edition* is started. If you click the Cancel button, you return to the main menu. You can register at any time by selecting Online, Registration from the main menu.

The registration process is composed of a simple form for entering your personal information, including your name and address. You are asked for your level of experience with the product you are testing on and whether you purchased *ExamGear, Training Guide Edition* from a retail store or over the Internet. The information will be used by our software designers and marketing department to provide us with feedback about the usability and usefulness of this product. It takes only a few seconds to fill out and transmit the registration data. A confirmation dialog box appears when registration is complete.

After you have registered and transmitted this information to New Riders, the registration option is removed from the pull-down menus.

Registration Benefits

Remember that registration allows you access to download updates from our FTP site using *ExamGear, Training Guide Edition* (see the later section "Obtaining Updates").

Removing ExamGear, Training Guide Edition from Your Computer

In the event that you elect to remove the *ExamGear, Training Guide Edition* product from your computer, an uninstall process has been included to ensure that it is removed from your system safely and completely. Follow these instructions to remove *ExamGear* from your computer:

1. Click Start, Settings, Control Panel.

2. Double-click the Add/Remove Programs icon.

3. You are presented with a list of software that is installed on your computer. Select ExamGear, Training Guide Edition from the list and click the Add/Remove button. The *ExamGear, Training Guide Edition* software is then removed from your computer.

It is important that the INSTALL.LOG file be present in the directory where you have installed *ExamGear, Training Guide Edition* should you ever choose to uninstall the product. Do not delete this file. The INSTALL.LOG file is used by the uninstall process to safely remove the files and Registry settings that were added to your computer by the installation process.

USING EXAMGEAR, TRAINING GUIDE EDITION

ExamGear is designed to be user friendly and very intuitive, eliminating the need for you to learn some confusing piece of software just to practice answering questions. Because the software has a smooth learning curve, your time is maximized because you start practicing almost immediately.

General Description of How the Software Works

ExamGear has three modes of operation: Study Mode, Practice Exam, and Adaptive Exam (see Figure C.2).

All three sections have the same easy-to-use interface. Using Study Mode, you can hone your knowledge as well as your test-taking abilities through the use of the Show Answers option. While you are taking the test, you can expose the answers along with a brief description of why the given answers are right or wrong. This gives you the ability to better understand the material presented.

The Practice Exam section has many of the same options as Study Mode, but you cannot reveal the answers. This way, you have a more traditional testing environment with which to practice.

The Adaptive Exam questions continuously monitor your expertise in each tested topic area. If you reach a point at which you either pass or fail, the software ends the examination. As in the Practice Exam, you cannot reveal the answers.

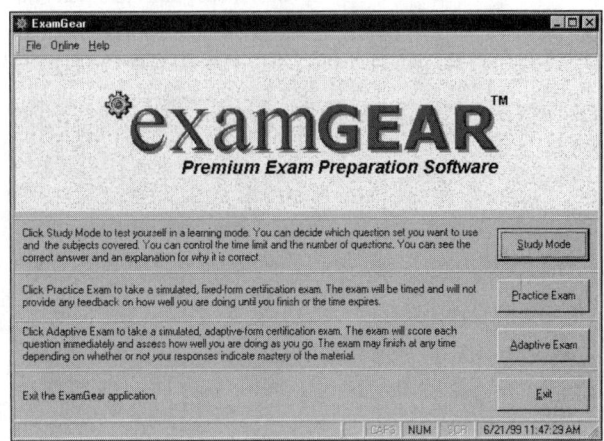

FIGURE C.2
The opening screen offers three testing modes.

Menu Options

The *ExamGear, Training Guide Edition* interface has an easy-to-use menu that provides the following options:

Menu	Command	Description
File	Print	Prints the current screen.
	Print Setup	Allows you to select the printer.
	Exit ExamGear	Exits the program.
Online	Registration	Starts the Registration Wizard and allows you to register online. This menu option is removed after you have successfully registered the product.
	Check for Product Updates	Downloads product catalog for Web-based updates.
	Web Browser	Opens the Web browser. It appears like this on the main menu, but more options appear after the browser is opened.
Help	Contents	Opens *ExamGear, Training Guide Edition*'s help file.
	About	Displays information about *ExamGear, Training Guide Edition*, including serial number, registered owner, and so on.

File

The File menu allows you to exit the program and configure print options.

Online

In the Online menu, you can register *ExamGear, Training Guide Edition*, check for product updates (update the *ExamGear* executable as well as check for free, updated question sets), and surf Web pages. The Online menu is always available, except when you are taking a test.

Registration

Registration is free and allows you access updates. Registration is the first task that *ExamGear, Training Guide Edition* asks you to perform. You will not have access to the free product updates if you do not register.

Check for Product Updates

This option takes you to *ExamGear, Training Guide Edition*'s Web site, where you can update the software. Registration is required for this option to be available. You must also be connected to the Internet to use this option. The *ExamGear* Web site lists the options that have been made available since your version of *ExamGear* was installed on your computer.

Web Browser

This option provides a convenient way to start your Web browser and connect to the New Riders Web site while you are working in *ExamGear, Training Guide Edition*. Click the Exit button to leave the Web browser and return to the *ExamGear* interface.

Help

As it suggests, this menu option gives you access to *ExamGear's* help system. It also provides important information like your serial number, software version, and so on.

Starting a Study Mode Session

Study Mode enables you to control the test in ways that actual certification exams do not allow:

◆ You can set your own time limits.

◆ You can concentrate on selected skill areas (units).

◆ You can reveal answers or have each response graded immediately with feedback.

◆ You can restrict the questions you see again to those missed or those answered correctly a given number of times.

◆ You can control the order in which questions are presented—random order or in order by skill area (unit).

To begin testing in Study Mode, click the Study Mode button from the main Interface screen. You are presented with the Study Mode configuration page (see Figure C.3).

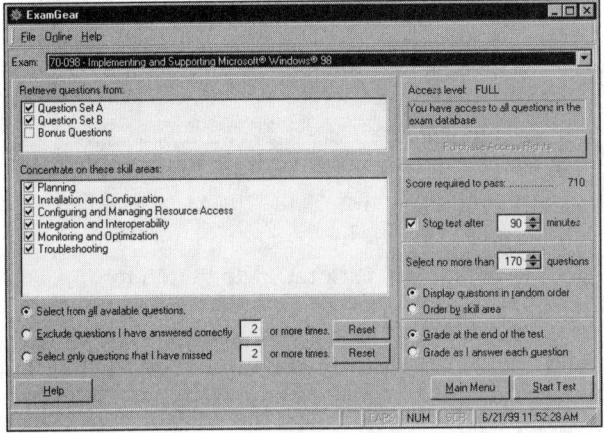

FIGURE C.3
The Study Mode configuration page.

At the top of the Study Mode configuration screen, you see the Exam drop-down list. This list shows the activated exam that you have purchased with your *ExamGear, Training Guide Edition* product, as well as any other exams you may have downloaded or any Preview exams that were shipped with your version of *ExamGear*. Select the exam with which you want to practice from the drop-down list.

Below the Exam drop-down list, you see the questions that are available for the selected exam. Each exam has at least one question set. You can select the individual question set or any combination of the question sets if there is more than one available for the selected exam.

Below the Question Set list is a list of skill areas or chapter on which you can concentrate. These skill areas or chapters reflect the units of exam objectives defined by Microsoft for the exam. Within each skill area you will find several exam objectives. You can select a single skill area or chapter to focus on, or you can select any combination of the available skill areas/chapters to customize the exam to your individual needs.

In addition to specifying which question sets and skill areas you want to test yourself on, you can also define which questions are included in the test based on your previous progress working with the test. *ExamGear, Training Guide Edition* automatically tracks your progress with the available questions. When configuring the Study Mode options, you can opt to view all the questions available within the question sets and skill areas you have selected, or you can limit the questions presented. Choose from the following options:

◆ **Select from All Available Questions.** This option causes *ExamGear, Training Guide Edition* to present all available questions from the selected question sets and skill areas.

◆ **Exclude Questions I Have Answered Correctly *X* or More Times.** *ExamGear* offers you the option to exclude questions that you have previously answered correctly. You can specify how many times you want to answer a question correctly before *ExamGear* considers you to have mastered it (the default is two times).

◆ **Select Only Questions That I Have Missed *X* or More Times.** This option configures *ExamGear, Training Guide Edition* to drill you only on questions that you have missed repeatedly. You may specify how many times you must miss a question before *ExamGear* determines that you have not mastered it (the default is two times).

At any time, you can reset *ExamGear, Training Guide Edition*'s tracking information by clicking the Reset button for the feature you want to clear.

At the top-right side of the Study Mode configuration sheet, you can see your access level to the question sets for the selected exam. Access levels are either Full or Preview. For a detailed explanation of each of these access levels, see the section "Obtaining Updates" in this appendix.

Under your access level, you see the score required to pass the selected exam. Below the required score, you can select whether the test will be timed and how much time will be allowed to complete the exam. Select the Stop Test After 90 Minutes check box to set a time limit for the exam. Enter the number of minutes you want to allow for the test (the default is 90 minutes). Deselecting this check box allows you to take an exam with no time limit.

You can also configure the number of questions included in the exam. The default number of questions changes with the specific exam you have selected. Enter the number of questions you want to include in the exam in the Select No More than *X* Questions option.

You can configure the order in which *ExamGear, Training Guide Edition* presents the exam questions. Select from the following options:

◆ **Display Questions in Random Order.** This option is the default option. When selected, it causes *ExamGear, Training Guide Edition* to present the questions in random order throughout the exam.

◆ **Order by Skill Area.** This option causes *ExamGear* to group the questions presented in the exam by skill area. All questions for each selected skill area are presented in succession. The test progresses from one selected skill area to the next, until all the questions from each selected skill area have been presented.

ExamGear offers two options for scoring your exams. Select one of the following options:

◆ **Grade at the End of the Test.** This option configures *ExamGear, Training Guide Edition* to score your test after you have been presented with all the selected exam questions. You can reveal correct answers to a question, but if you do, that question is not scored.

◆ **Grade as I Answer Each Question.** This option configures *ExamGear* to grade each question as you answer it, providing you with instant feedback as you take the test. All questions are scored unless you click the Show Answer button before completing the question.

You can return to the *ExamGear, Training Guide Edition* main startup screen from the Study Mode configuration screen by clicking the Main Menu button. If you need assistance configuring the Study Mode exam options, click the Help button for configuration instructions.

When you have finished configuring all the exam options, click the Start Test button to begin the exam.

Starting Practice Exams and Adaptive Exams

This section describes practice exams and adaptive exams, defines the differences between these exam options and the Study Mode option, and provides instructions for starting them.

Differences Between the Practice and Adaptive Exams and Study Modes

Question screens in the practice and adaptive exams are identical to those found in Study Mode, except that the

Show Answer, Grade Answer, and Item Review buttons are not available while you are in the process of taking a practice or adaptive exam. The Practice Exam provides you with a report screen at the end of the exam. The Adaptive Exam gives you a brief message indicating whether you've passed or failed the exam.

When taking a practice exam, the Item Review screen is not available until you have answered all the questions. This is consistent with the behavior of most vendors' current certification exams. In Study Mode, Item Review is available at any time.

When the exam timer expires, or if you click the End Exam button, the Examination Score Report screen comes up.

Starting an Exam

From the *ExamGear, Training Guide Edition* main menu screen, select the type of exam you want to run. Click the Practice Exam or Adaptive Exam button to begin the corresponding exam type.

What Is an Adaptive Exam?

To make the certification testing process more efficient and valid and therefore make the certification itself more valuable, some vendors in the industry are using a testing technique called *adaptive testing*. In an adaptive exam, the exam "adapts" to your abilities by varying the difficulty level of the questions presented to you.

The first question in an adaptive exam is typically an easy one. If you answer it correctly, you are presented with a slightly more difficult question. If you answer that question correctly, the next question you see is even more difficult. If you answer the question incorrectly, however, the exam "adapts" to your skill level by presenting you with another question of equal or lesser difficulty on the same subject. If you answer that question correctly, the test begins to increase the difficulty level again. You must correctly answer several questions at a predetermined difficulty level to pass the exam. After you have done this successfully, the exam is ended and scored. If you do not reach the required level of difficulty within a predetermined time (typically 30 minutes) the exam is ended and scored.

Why Do Vendors Use Adaptive Exams?

Many vendors who offer technical certifications have adopted the adaptive testing technique. They have found that it is an effective way to measure a candidate's mastery of the test material in as little time as necessary. This reduces the scheduling demands on the test taker and allows the testing center to offer more tests per test station than they could with longer, more traditional exams. In addition, test security is greater, and this increases the validity of the exam process.

Studying for Adaptive Exams

Studying for adaptive exams is no different from studying for traditional exams. You should make sure that you have thoroughly covered all the material for each of the test objectives specified by the certification exam vendor. As with any other exam, when you take an adaptive exam, either you know the material or you don't. If you are well prepared, you will be able to pass the exam. *ExamGear, Training Guide Edition* allows you to familiarize yourself with the adaptive exam testing technique. This will help eliminate any anxiety you might experience from this testing technique and allow you to focus on learning the actual exam material.

ExamGear's Adaptive Exam

The method used to score the adaptive exam requires a large pool of questions. For this reason, you cannot use this exam in Preview mode. The adaptive exam is presented in much the same way as the practice exam. When you click the Start Test button, you begin answering questions. The adaptive exam does not allow item review, and it does not allow you to mark questions to skip and answer later. You must answer each question when it is presented.

Assumptions

This section describes the assumptions made when designing the behavior of the *ExamGear, Training Guide Edition* adaptive exam.

- ◆ You fail the test if you fail any chapter or unit, earn a failing overall score, or reach a threshold at which it is statistically impossible for you to pass the exam.

- ◆ You can fail or pass a test without cycling through all the questions.

- ◆ The overall score for the adaptive exam is Pass or Fail. However, to evaluate user responses dynamically, percentage scores are recorded for units and the overall score.

Algorithm Assumptions

This section describes the assumptions used in designing the *ExamGear, Training Guide Edition* Adaptive Exam scoring algorithm.

Unit Scores

You fail a unit (and the exam) if any unit score falls below 66%.

Overall Scores

To pass the exam, you must pass all units and achieve an overall score of 86% or higher.

You fail if the overall score percentage is less than or equal to 85% or if any unit score is less than 66%.

Inconclusive Scores

If your overall score is between 67 and 85%, it is considered to be *inconclusive*. Additional questions will be asked until you pass or fail or until it becomes statistically impossible to pass without asking more than the maximum number of questions allowed.

Question Types and How to Answer Them

Because certification exams from different vendors vary, you will face many types of questions on any given exam. *ExamGear, Training Guide Edition* presents you with different question types to allow you to become familiar with the various ways an actual exam may test your knowledge. The Solution Architectures exam, in particular, offers a unique exam format and utilizes question types other than multiple choice. This version of *ExamGear* includes cases—extensive problem descriptions running several pages in length, followed by a number of questions specific to that case. Microsoft refers to these case/question collections as *testlets*. This version of *ExamGear, Training Guide Edition* also includes regular questions that are not attached to a case study. We include these question types to make taking the actual exam easier because you will already be familiar with the steps required to answer each question type. This section describes each of the question types presented by *ExamGear* and provides instructions for answering each type.

Multiple Choice

Most of the questions you see on a certification exam are multiple choice (see Figure C.4). This question type asks you to select an answer from the list provided. Sometimes you must select only one answer, often indicated by answers preceded by option buttons (round selection buttons). At other times, multiple correct answers are possible, indicated by check boxes preceding the possible answer combinations.

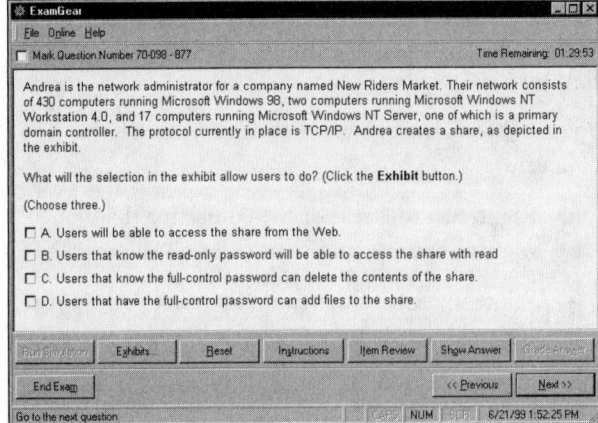

FIGURE C.4
A typical multiple-choice question.

You can use three methods to select an answer:

◆ Click the option button or check box next to the answer. If more than one correct answer to a question is possible, the answers will have check boxes next to them. If only one correct answer to a question is possible, each answer will have an option button next to it. *ExamGear, Training Guide Edition* prompts you with the number of answers you must select.

◆ Click the text of the answer.

◆ Press the alphabetic key that corresponds to the answer.

You can use any one of three methods to clear an option button:

◆ Click another option button.

◆ Click the text of another answer.

◆ Press the alphabetic key that corresponds to another answer.

You can use any one of three methods to clear a check box:

◆ Click the check box next to the selected answer.

◆ Click the text of the selected answer.

◆ Press the alphabetic key that corresponds to the selected answer.

To clear all answers, click the Reset button.

Remember that some of the questions have multiple answers that are correct. Do not let this throw you off. The *multiple correct* questions do not have one answer that is more correct than another. In the *single correct* format, only one answer is correct. *ExamGear, Training Guide Edition* prompts you with the number of answers you must select.

Drag and Drop

One form of drag and drop question is called a *Drop and Connect* question. These questions present you with a number of objects and connectors. The question prompts you to create relationships between the objects by using the connectors. The gray squares on the left side of the question window are the objects you can select. The connectors are listed on the right side of the question window in the Connectors box. An example is shown in Figure C.5.

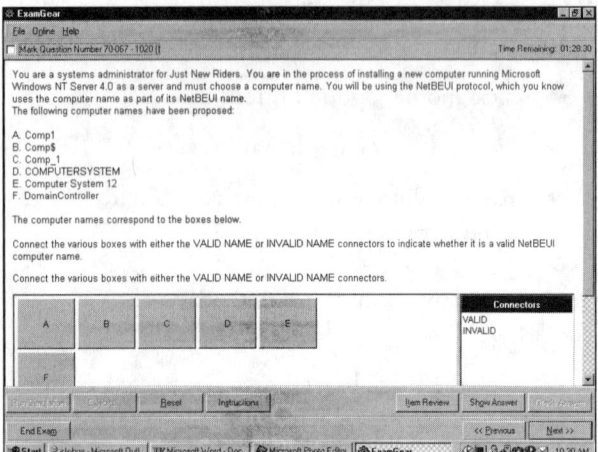

FIGURE C.5
A typical Drop and Connect question.

To select an object, click it with the mouse. When an object is selected, it changes color from a gray box to a white box. To drag an object, select it by clicking it with the left mouse button and holding the left mouse button down. You can move (or drag) the object to another area on the screen by moving the mouse while holding the left mouse button down.

To create a relationship between two objects, take the following actions:

1. Select an object and drag it to an available area on the screen.

2. Select another object and drag it to a location near where you dragged the first object.

3. Select the connector that you want to place between the two objects. The relationship should now appear complete. Note that to create a relationship, you must have two objects selected. If you try to select a connector without first selecting two objects, you are presented with an error message like that illustrated in Figure C.6.

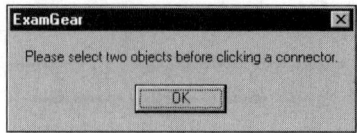

FIGURE C.6
The error message.

Initially, the direction of the relationship established by the connector is from the first object selected to the second object selected. To change the direction of the connector, right-click the connector and choose Reverse Connection.

You can use either of two methods to remove the connector:

◆ Right-click the text of the connector that you want to remove, and then choose Delete.

◆ Select the text of the connector that you want to remove, and then press the Delete key.

To remove from the screen all the relationships you have created, click the Reset button.

Keep in mind that connectors can be used multiple times. If you move connected objects, it will not change the relationship between the objects; to remove the relationship between objects, you must remove the connector that joins them. When *ExamGear, Training Guide Edition* scores a drag-and-drop question, only objects with connectors to other objects are scored.

Another form of drag and drop question is called the *Select and Place* question. Instead of creating a diagram as you do with the Drop and Connect question, you are asked a question about a diagram. You then drag and drop labels onto the diagram in order to correctly answer the question.

Ordered-List Questions

In the *ordered-list* question type (see Figure C.7), you are presented with a number of items and are asked to perform two tasks:

1. Build an answer list from items on the list of choices.

2. Put the items in a particular order.

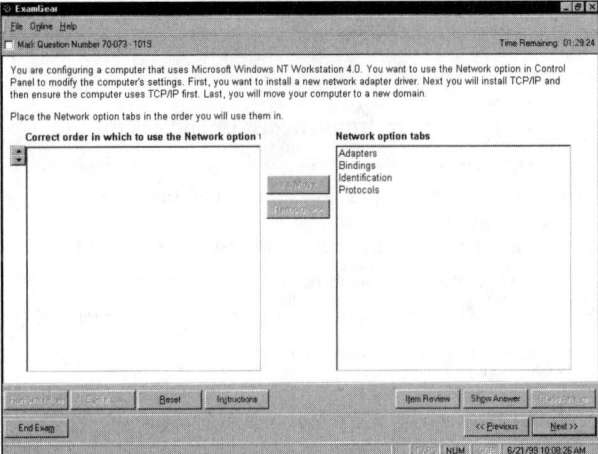

FIGURE C.7
A typical ordered-list question.

You can use any one of the following three methods to add an item to the answer list:

◆ Drag the item from the list of choices on the right side of the screen to the answer list on the left side of the screen.

◆ From the available items on the right side of the screen, double-click the item you want to add.

◆ From the available items on the right side of the screen, select the item you want to add; then click the Move button.

To remove an item from the answer list, you can use any one of the following four methods:

◆ Drag the item you want to remove from the answer list on the left side of the screen back to the list of choices on the right side of the screen.

◆ On the left side of the screen, double-click the item you want to remove from the answer list.

◆ On the left side of the screen, select the item you want to remove from the answer list, and then click the Remove button.

◆ On the left side of the screen, select the item you want to remove from the answer list, and then press the Delete key.

To remove all items from the answer list, click the Reset button.

If you need to change the order of the items in the answer list, you can do so using either of the following two methods:

◆ Drag each item to the appropriate location in the answer list.

◆ In the answer list, select the item that you want to move, and then click the up or down arrow button to move the item.

Keep in mind that items in the list can be selected twice. You may find that an ordered-list question will ask you to list in the correct order the steps required to perform a certain task. Certain steps may need to be performed more than once during the process. Don't think that after you have selected a list item, it is no longer available. If you need to select a list item more than once, you can simply select that item at each appropriate place as you construct your list.

Ordered-Tree Questions

The *ordered-tree* question type (see Figure C.8) presents you with a number of items and prompts you to create a tree structure from those items. The tree structure includes two or three levels of nodes.

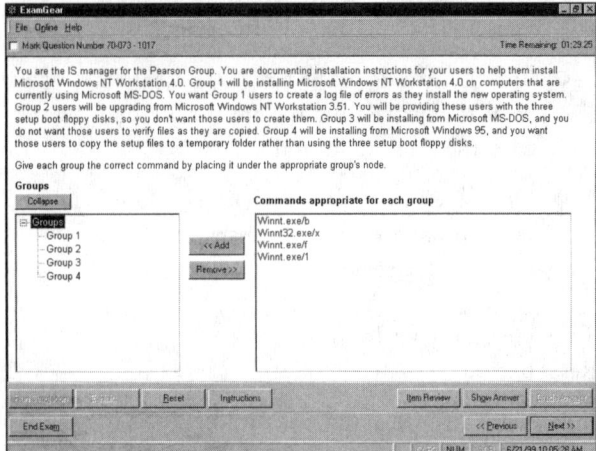

FIGURE C.8
A typical ordered-tree question.

An item in the list of choices can be added only to the appropriate node level. If you attempt to add one of the list choices to an inappropriate node level, you are presented with the error message shown in Figure C.9

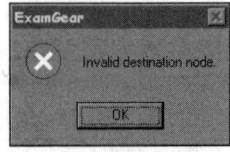

FIGURE C.9
The Invalid Destination Node error message.

Like the ordered-list question, realize that any item in the list can be selected twice. If you need to select a list item more than once, you can simply select that item for the appropriate node as you construct your tree.

Also realize that not every tree question actually requires order to the lists under each node. Think of them as simply tree questions rather than ordered-tree questions. Such questions are just asking you to categorize hierarchically. Order is not an issue.

You can use either of the following two methods to add an item to the tree:

◆ Drag the item from the list of choices on the right side of the screen to the appropriate node of the tree on the left side of the screen.

◆ Select the appropriate node of the tree on the left side of the screen. Select the appropriate item from the list of choices on the right side of the screen. Click the Add button.

You can use either of the following two methods to remove an item from the tree:

◆ Drag an item from the tree to the list of choices.

◆ Select the item and click the Remove button.

To remove from the tree structure all the items you have added, click the Reset button.

Simulations

Simulation questions (see Figure C.10) require you to actually perform a task.

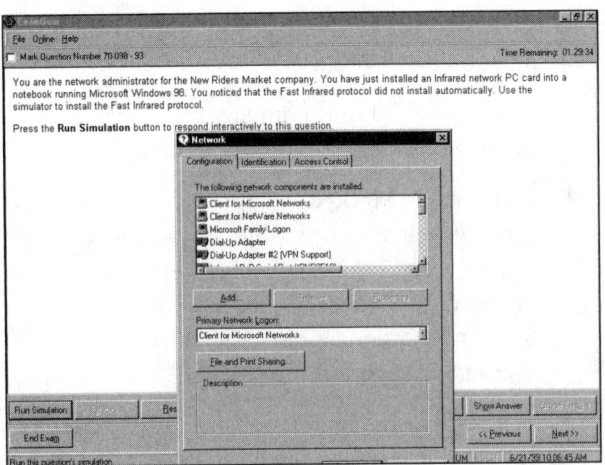

FIGURE C.10
A typical simulation question.

The main screen describes a situation and prompts you to provide a solution. When you are ready to proceed, you click the Run Simulation button in the lower-left corner. A screen or window appears on which you perform the solution. This window simulates the actual software that you would use to perform the required task in the real world. When a task requires several steps to complete, the simulator displays all the necessary screens to allow you to complete the task. When you have provided your answer by completing all the steps necessary to perform the required task, you can click the OK button to proceed to the next question.

You can return to any simulation to modify your answer. Your actions in the simulation are recorded, and the simulation appears exactly as you left it.

Simulation questions can be reset to their original state by clicking the Reset button.

Hot Spot Questions

Hot spot questions (see Figure C.11) ask you to correctly identify an item by clicking an area of the graphic or diagram displayed. To respond to the question, position the mouse cursor over a graphic. Then press the right mouse button to indicate your selection. To select another area on the graphic, you do not need to deselect the first one. Just click another region in the image.

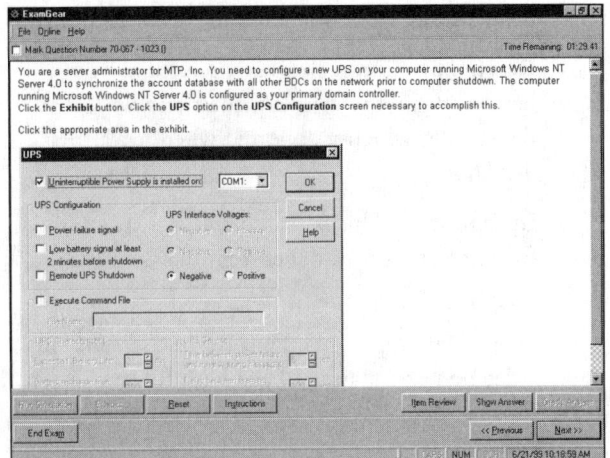

FIGURE C.11
A typical hot spot question.

Standard ExamGear, Training Guide Edition Options

Regardless of question type, a consistent set of clickable buttons enables you to navigate and interact with questions. The following list describes the function of each of the buttons you may see. Depending on the question type, some of the buttons will be grayed out and will be inaccessible. Buttons that are appropriate to the question type are active.

◆ **Run Simulation.** This button is enabled if the question supports a simulation. Clicking this button begins the simulation process.

◆ **Exhibits.** This button is enabled if exhibits are provided to support the question. An *exhibit* is an image, video, sound, or text file that provides supplemental information needed to answer the question. If a question has more than one exhibit, a dialog box appears, listing exhibits by name. If only one exhibit exists, the file is opened immediately when you click the Exhibits button.

◆ **Reset.** This button clears any selections you have made and returns the question window to the state in which it appeared when it was first displayed.

◆ **Instructions.** This button displays instructions for interacting with the current question type.

◆ **Item Review.** This button leaves the question window and opens the Item Review screen. For a detailed explanation of the Item Review screen, see the "Item Review" section later in this appendix.

◆ **Show Answer.** This option displays the correct answer with an explanation of why it is correct. If you choose this option, the current question will not be scored.

◆ **Grade Answer.** If Grade at the End of the Test is selected as a configuration option, this button is disabled. It is enabled when Grade as I Answer Each Question is selected as a configuration option. Clicking this button grades the current question immediately. An explanation of the correct answer is provided, just as if the Show Answer button were pressed. The question is graded, however.

◆ **End Exam.** This button ends the exam and displays the Examination Score Report screen.

◆ **<< Previous.** This button displays the previous question on the exam.

◆ **Next >>.** This button displays the next question on the exam.

◆ **<< Previous Marked.** This button is displayed if you have opted to review questions that you have marked using using the Item Review screen. This button displays the previous marked question. Marking questions is discussed in more detail later in this appendix.

◆ **<< Previous Incomplete.** This button is displayed if you have opted to review questions that you have not answered using the Item Review screen. This button displays the previous unanswered question.

◆ **Next Marked >>.** This button is displayed if you have opted to review questions that you have marked using the Item Review screen. This button displays the next marked question. Marking questions is discussed in more detail later in this appendix.

◆ **Next Incomplete>>.** This button is displayed if you have opted to review questions, using the Item Review screen, that you have not answered. This button displays the next unanswered question.

Mark Question and Time Remaining

ExamGear provides you with two methods to aid in dealing with the time limit of the testing process. If you find that you need to skip a question or if you want to check the time remaining to complete the test, use one of the options discussed in the following sections.

Mark Question

Check this box to mark a question so that you can return to it later using the Item Review feature. The adaptive exam does not allow questions to be marked because it does not support item review.

Time Remaining

If the test is timed, the Time Remaining indicator is enabled. It counts down minutes remaining to complete the test. The adaptive exam does not offer this feature because it is not timed.

Item Review

The Item Review screen allows you to jump to any question. *ExamGear, Training Guide Edition* considers an *incomplete* question to be any unanswered question or any multiple-choice question for which the total number of required responses has not been selected. For example, if the question prompts for three answers and you selected only A and C, *ExamGear* considers the question to be incomplete.

The Item Review screen enables you to review the exam questions in different ways. You can enter one of two *browse sequences* (series of similar records): Browse Marked Questions or Browse Incomplete Questions. You can also create a custom grouping of the exam questions for review based on a number of criteria.

When using Item Review, if Show Answer was selected for a question while you were taking the exam, the question is grayed out in item review. The question can be answered again if you use the Reset button to reset the question status.

The Item Review screen contains two tabs. The Questions tab lists questions and question information in columns. The Current Score tab provides your exam score information, presented as a percentage for each unit and as a bar graph for your overall score.

The Item Review Questions Tab

The Questions tab on the Item Review screen (see Figure C.12) presents the exam questions and question information in a table. You can select any row you want by clicking in the grid. The Go To button is enabled whenever a row is selected. Clicking the Go To button displays the question on the selected row. You can also display a question by double-clicking that row.

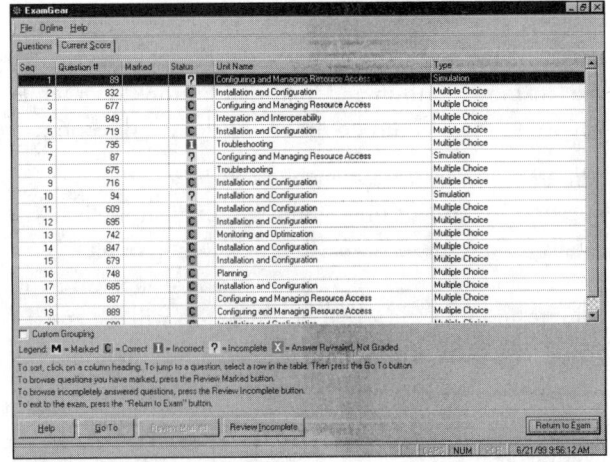

FIGURE C.12
The Questions tab on the Item Review screen.

Columns

The Questions tab contains the following six columns of information:

- ◆ **Seq.** Indicates the sequence number of the question as it was displayed in the exam.

- ◆ **Question Number.** Displays the question's identification number for easy reference.

- ◆ **Marked.** Indicates a question that you have marked using the Mark Question check box.

- ◆ **Status.** The status can be M for Marked, ? for Incomplete, C for Correct, I for Incorrect, or X for Answer Shown.

◆ **Unit Name.** The unit associated with each question.

◆ **Type.** The question type, which can be Multiple Choice, Drag and Drop, Simulation, Hot Spot, Ordered List, or Ordered Tree.

To resize a column, place the mouse pointer over the vertical line between column headings. When the mouse pointer changes to a set of right and left arrows, you can drag the column border to the left or right to make the column more or less wide. Simply click with the left mouse button and hold that button down while you move the column border in the desired direction.

The Item Review screen enables you to sort the questions on any of the column headings. Initially, the list of questions is sorted in descending order on the sequence number column. To sort on a different column heading, click that heading. You will see an arrow appear on the column heading indicating the direction of the sort (ascending or descending). To change the direction of the sort, click the column heading again.

The Item Review screen also allows you to create a *custom grouping*. This feature enables you to sort the questions based on any combination of criteria you prefer. For instance, you might want to review the question items sorted first by whether they were marked, then by the unit name, then by sequence number. The Custom Grouping feature allows you to do this. Start by checking the Custom Grouping check box (see Figure C.13). When you do so, the entire questions table shifts down a bit onscreen, and a message appear at the top of the table that reads Drag a column header here to group by that column.

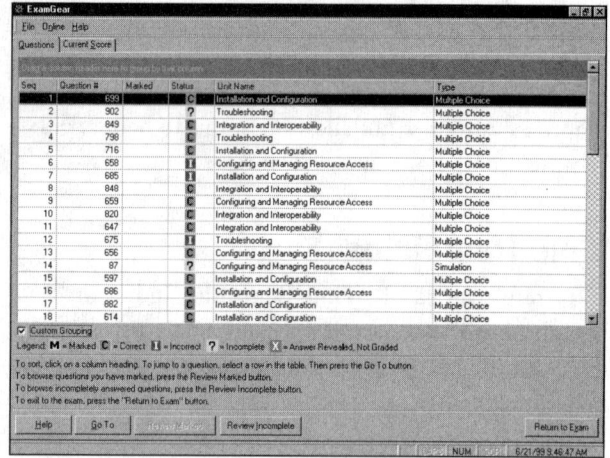

FIGURE C.13
The Custom Grouping check box allows you to create your own question sort order.

Simply click the column heading you want with the left mouse button, hold that button down, and move the mouse into the area directly above the questions table (the custom grouping area). Release the left mouse button to drop the column heading into the custom grouping area. To accomplish the custom grouping previously described, first check the Custom Grouping check box. Then drag the Marked column heading into the custom grouping area above the question table. Next, drag the Unit Name column heading into the custom grouping area. You will see the two column headings joined together by a line that indicates the order of the custom grouping. Finally, drag the Seq column heading into the custom grouping area. This heading will be joined to the Unit Name heading by another line indicating the direction of the custom grouping.

Notice that each column heading in the custom grouping area has an arrow indicating the direction in which items are sorted under that column heading. You can reverse the direction of the sort on an individual column-heading basis using these arrows. Click the column heading in the custom grouping area to change the direction of the sort for that column heading only. For example, using the custom grouping created previously, you can display the question list sorted first in descending order by whether the question was marked, in descending order by unit name, and then in ascending order by sequence number.

The custom grouping feature of the Item Review screen gives you enormous flexibility in how you choose to review the exam questions. To remove a custom grouping and return the Item Review display to its default setting (sorted in descending order by sequence number), simply uncheck the Custom Grouping check box.

The Current Score Tab

The Current Score tab of the Item Review screen (see Figure C.14) provides a real-time snapshot of your score. The top half of the screen is an expandable grid. When the grid is collapsed, scores are displayed for each unit. Units can be expanded to show percentage scores for objectives and subobjectives. Information about your exam progress is presented in the following columns:

◆ **Unit Name.** This column shows the unit name for each objective group.

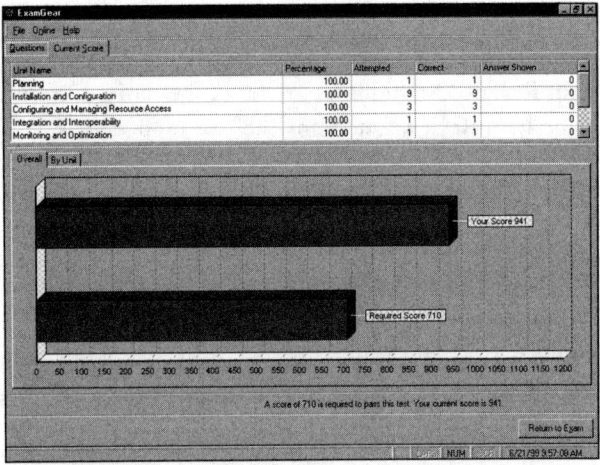

FIGURE C.14
The Current Score tab on the item review screen.

◆ **Percentage.** This column shows the percentage of questions for each objective group that you answered correctly.

◆ **Attempted.** This column lists the number of questions you answered either completely or partially for each objective group.

◆ **Correct.** This column lists the actual number of questions you answered correctly for each objective group.

◆ **Answer Shown.** This column lists the number of questions for each objective group that you chose to display the answer to using the Show Answer button.

The columns in the scoring table are resized and sorted in the same way as those in the questions table on the Item Review Questions tab. Refer to the earlier section "The Item Review Questions Tab" for more details.

A graphical overview of the score is presented below the grid. The graph depicts two red bars: The top bar represents your current exam score, and the bottom bar represents the required passing score. To the right of the bars in the graph is a legend that lists the required score and your score. Below the bar graph is a statement that describes the required passing score and your current score.

In addition, the information can be presented on an overall basis or by exam unit. The Overall tab shows the overall score. The By Unit tab shows the score by unit.

Clicking the End Exam button terminates the exam and passes control to the Examination Score Report screen.

The Return to Exam button returns to the exam at the question from which the Item Review button was clicked.

Review Marked Items

The Item Review screen allows you to enter a browse sequence for marked questions. When you click the Review Marked button, questions that you have previously marked using the Mark Question check box are presented for your review. While browsing the marked questions, you will see the following changes to the buttons available:

◆ The caption of the Next button becomes Next Marked.

◆ The caption of the Previous button becomes Previous Marked.

Review Incomplete

The Item Review screen allows you to enter a browse sequence for incomplete questions. When you click the Review Incomplete button, the questions you did not answer or did not completely answer are displayed for your review. While browsing the incomplete questions, you will see the following changes to the buttons:

◆ The caption of the Next button becomes Next Incomplete.

◆ The caption of the Previous button becomes Previous Incomplete.

Examination Score Report Screen

The Examination Score Report screen (see Figure C.15) appears when the Study Mode, Practice Exam, or Adaptive Exam ends—as the result of timer expiration, completion of all questions, or your decision to terminate early.

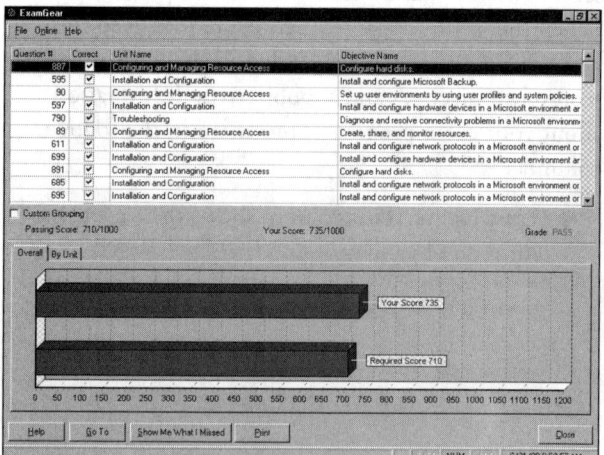

FIGURE C.15
The Examination Score Report screen.

This screen provides you with a graphical display of your test score, along with a tabular breakdown of scores by unit. The graphical display at the top of the screen compares your overall score with the score required to pass the exam. Buttons below the graphical display allow you to open the Show Me What I Missed browse sequence, print the screen, or return to the main menu.

Show Me What I Missed Browse Sequence

The Show Me What I Missed browse sequence is invoked by clicking the Show Me What I Missed button from the Examination Score Report or from the configuration screen of an adaptive exam.

Note that the window caption is modified to indicate that you are in the Show Me What I Missed browse sequence mode. Question IDs and position within the browse sequence appear at the top of the screen, in place of the Mark Question and Time Remaining indicators. Main window contents vary, depending on the question type. The following list describes the buttons available within the Show Me What I Missed browse sequence and the functions they perform:

◆ **Return to Score Report.** Returns control to the Examination Score Report screen. In the case of an adaptive exam, this button's caption is Exit, and control returns to the adaptive exam configuration screen.

◆ **Run Simulation.** Opens a simulation in Grade mode, causing the simulation to open displaying your response and the correct answer. If the current question does not offer a simulation, this button is disabled.

◆ **Exhibits.** Opens the Exhibits window. This button is enabled if one or more exhibits are available for the question.

◆ **Instructions.** Shows how to answer the current question type.

◆ **Print.** Prints the current screen.

◆ **Previous or Next.** Displays missed questions.

Checking the Web Site

To check the New Riders Home Page or the *ExamGear, Training Guide Edition* Home Page for updates or other product information, choose the desired Web site from the Web Sites option of the Online menu. You must be connected to the Internet to reach these Web sites. When you select a Web site, the Internet Explorer browser opens inside the *ExamGear, Training Guide Edition* window and displays the Web site.

OBTAINING UPDATES

The procedures for obtaining updates are outlined in this section.

The Catalog Web Site for Updates

Selecting the Check for Product Updates option from the Online menu shows you the full range of products you can either download for free or purchase. You can download additional items only if you have registered the software.

Product Updates Dialog Box

This dialog box appears when you select Check for Product Updates from the Online menu. *ExamGear, Training Guide Edition* checks for product updates from the New Riders Internet site and displays a list of products available for download. Some items, such as *ExamGear* program updates or bonus question sets for exam databases you have activated, are available for download free of charge.

Types of Updates

Several types of updates may be available for download, including various free updates and additional items available for purchase.

Free Program Updates

Free program updates include changes to the *ExamGear, Training Guide Edition* executables and runtime libraries (DLLs). When any of these items are downloaded, *ExamGear* automatically installs the upgrades. *ExamGear, Training Guide Edition* will be reopened after the installation is complete.

Free Database Updates

Free database updates include updates to the exam or exams that you have registered. Exam updates are contained in compressed, encrypted files and include exam databases, simulations, and exhibits. *ExamGear, Training Guide Edition* automatically decompresses these files to their proper location and updates the *ExamGear* software to record version changes and import new question sets.

CONTACTING NEW RIDERS PUBLISHING

At New Riders, we strive to meet and exceed the needs of our customers. We have developed *ExamGear, Training Guide Edition* to surpass the demands and expectations of network professionals seeking technical certifications, and we think it shows. What do you think?

If you need to contact New Riders regarding any aspect of the *ExamGear, Training Guide Edition* product line, feel free to do so. We look forward to hearing from you. Contact us at the following address or phone number:

New Riders Publishing
201 West 103 Street
Indianapolis, IN 46290
800-545-5914

You can also reach us on the World Wide Web:

http://www.newriders.com

Technical Support

Technical support is available at the following phone number during the hours specified:

317-581-3833

Monday through Friday, 10:00 a.m.–3:00 p.m. Central Standard Time.

Customer Service

If you have a damaged product and need a replacement or refund, please call the following phone number:

800-858-7674

Product Updates

Product updates can be obtained by choosing *ExamGear, Training Guide Edition*'s Online pull-down menu and selecting Products Updates. You'll be taken to a private Web site with full details.

Product Suggestions and Comments

We value your input! Please email your suggestions and comments to the following address:

  `certification@mcp.com`

LICENSE AGREEMENT

YOU SHOULD CAREFULLY READ THE FOLLOWING TERMS AND CONDITIONS BEFORE BREAKING THE SEAL ON THE PACKAGE. AMONG OTHER THINGS, THIS AGREEMENT LICENSES THE ENCLOSED SOFTWARE TO YOU AND CONTAINS WARRANTY AND LIABILITY DISCLAIMERS. BY BREAKING THE SEAL ON THE PACKAGE, YOU ARE ACCEPTING AND AGREEING TO THE TERMS AND CONDITIONS OF THIS AGREEMENT. IF YOU DO NOT AGREE TO THE TERMS OF THIS AGREEMENT, DO NOT BREAK THE SEAL. YOU SHOULD PROMPTLY RETURN THE PACKAGE UNOPENED.

LICENSE

Subject to the provisions contained herein, New Riders Publishing (NRP) hereby grants to you a nonexclusive, nontransferable license to use the object-code version of the computer software product (Software) contained in the package on a single computer of the type identified on the package.

SOFTWARE AND DOCUMENTATION

NRP shall furnish the Software to you on media in machine-readable object-code form and may also provide the standard documentation (Documentation) containing instructions for operation and use of the Software.

LICENSE TERM AND CHARGES

The term of this license commences upon delivery of the Software to you and is perpetual unless earlier terminated upon default or as otherwise set forth herein.

TITLE

Title, ownership right, and intellectual property rights in and to the Software and Documentation shall remain in NRP and/or in suppliers to NRP of programs contained in the Software. The Software is provided for your own internal use under this license. This license does not include the right to sublicense and is personal to you and therefore may not be assigned (by operation of law or otherwise) or transferred without the prior written consent of NRP. You acknowledge that the Software in source code form remains a confidential trade secret of NRP and/or its suppliers and therefore you agree not to attempt to decipher or decompile, modify, disassemble, reverse engineer, or prepare derivative works of the Software or develop source code for the Software or knowingly allow others to do so. Further, you may not copy the Documentation or other written materials accompanying the Software.

UPDATES

This license does not grant you any right, license, or interest in and to any improvements, modifications, enhancements, or updates to the Software and Documentation. Updates, if available, may be obtained by you at NRP's then-current standard pricing, terms, and conditions.

LIMITED WARRANTY AND DISCLAIMER

NRP warrants that the media containing the Software, if provided by NRP, is free from defects in material and workmanship under normal use for a period of sixty (60) days from the date you purchased a license to it.

THIS IS A LIMITED WARRANTY AND IT IS THE ONLY WARRANTY MADE BY NRP. THE SOFTWARE IS PROVIDED "AS IS" AND NRP SPECIFICALLY DISCLAIMS ALL WARRANTIES OF ANY KIND, EITHER EXPRESS OR IMPLIED, INCLUDING, BUT NOT LIMITED TO, THE IMPLIED WARRANTY OF MERCHANTABILITY AND FITNESS FOR A PARTICULAR PURPOSE. FURTHER, COMPANY DOES NOT WARRANT, GUARANTEE, OR MAKE ANY REPRESENTA-TIONS REGARDING THE USE, OR THE RESULTS OF THE USE, OF THE SOFTWARE IN TERMS OR CORRECTNESS, ACCURACY, RELIABILITY, CURRENTNESS, OR OTHERWISE AND DOES NOT WARRANT THAT THE OPERATION OF ANY SOFTWARE WILL BE UNINTERRUPTED OR ERROR FREE. NRP EXPRESSLY DISCLAIMS ANY WARRANTIES NOT STATED HEREIN. NO ORAL OR WRITTEN INFORMATION OR ADVICE GIVEN BY NRP, OR ANY NRP DEALER, AGENT, EMPLOYEE, OR OTHERS SHALL CREATE, MODIFY, OR EXTEND A WARRANTY OR IN ANY WAY INCREASE THE SCOPE OF THE FOREGOING WARRANTY, AND NEITHER SUBLICENSEE OR PURCHASER MAY RELY ON ANY SUCH INFORMATION OR ADVICE. If the media is subjected to accident, abuse, or improper use, or if you violate the terms of this Agreement, then this warranty shall immediately be terminated. This warranty shall not apply if the Software is used on or in conjunction with hardware or programs other than the unmodified version of hardware and programs with which the Software was designed to be used as described in the Documentation.

LIMITATION OF LIABILITY

Your sole and exclusive remedies for any damage or loss in any way connected with the Software are set forth below.

UNDER NO CIRCUMSTANCES AND UNDER NO LEGAL THEORY, TORT, CONTRACT, OR OTHERWISE, SHALL NRP BE LIABLE TO YOU OR ANY OTHER PERSON FOR ANY INDIRECT, SPECIAL, INCIDENTAL, OR CONSEQUENTIAL DAMAGES OF ANY CHARACTER INCLUDING, WITHOUT LIMITATION, DAMAGES FOR LOSS OF GOODWILL, LOSS OF PROFIT, WORK STOPPAGE, COMPUTER FAILURE OR MALFUNCTION, OR ANY AND ALL OTHER COMMERCIAL DAMAGES OR LOSSES, OR FOR ANY OTHER DAMAGES EVEN IF NRP SHALL HAVE BEEN INFORMED OF THE POSSIBILITY OF SUCH DAMAGES, OR FOR ANY CLAIM BY ANOTHER PARTY. NRP'S THIRD-PARTY PROGRAM SUPPLIERS MAKE NO WARRANTY, AND HAVE NO LIABILITY WHATSOEVER, TO YOU. NRP's sole and exclusive obligation and liability and your exclusive remedy shall be: upon NRP's election, (i) the replacement of our defective media; or (ii) the repair or correction of your defective media if NRP is able, so that it will conform to the above warranty; or (iii) if NRP is unable to replace or repair, you may terminate this license by returning the Software. Only if you inform NRP of your problem during the applicable warranty period will NRP be obligated to honor this warranty. SOME STATES OR JURISDICTIONS DO NOT ALLOW THE EXCLUSION OF IMPLIED WARRANTIES OR LIMITATION OR EXCLUSION OF CONSE-QUENTIAL DAMAGES, SO THE ABOVE LIMITATIONS OR EXCLUSIONS MAY NOT APPLY TO YOU. THIS WARRANTY GIVES YOU SPECIFIC LEGAL RIGHTS AND YOU MAY ALSO HAVE OTHER RIGHTS WHICH VARY BY STATE OR JURISDICTION.

MISCELLANEOUS

If any provision of the Agreement is held to be ineffective, unenforceable, or illegal under certain circumstances for any reason, such decision shall not affect the validity or enforceability (i) of such provision under other circumstances or (ii) of the remaining provisions hereof under all circumstances, and such provision shall be reformed to and only to the extent necessary to make it effective, enforceable, and legal under such circumstances. All headings are solely for convenience and shall not be considered in interpreting this Agreement. This Agreement shall be governed by and construed under New York law as such law applies to agreements between New York residents entered into and to be performed entirely within New York, except as required by U.S. Government rules and regulations to be governed by Federal law.

YOU ACKNOWLEDGE THAT YOU HAVE READ THIS AGREEMENT, UNDERSTAND IT, AND AGREE TO BE BOUND BY ITS TERMS AND CONDITIONS. YOU FURTHER AGREE THAT IT IS THE COMPLETE AND EXCLUSIVE STATE-MENT OF THE AGREEMENT BETWEEN US THAT SUPERSEDES ANY PROPOSAL OR PRIOR AGREEMENT, ORAL OR WRITTEN, AND ANY OTHER COMMUNICATIONS BETWEEN US RELATING TO THE SUBJECT MATTER OF THIS AGREEMENT.

U.S. GOVERNMENT RESTRICTED RIGHTS

Use, duplication, or disclosure by the Government is subject to restrictions set forth in subparagraphs (a) through (d) of the Commercial Computer-Restricted Rights clause at FAR 52.227-19 when applicable, or in subparagraph (c) (1) (ii) of the Rights in Technical Data and Computer Software clause at DFARS 252.227-7013, and in similar clauses in the NASA FAR Supplement.

Index

M

Solutions from experts you know and trust.

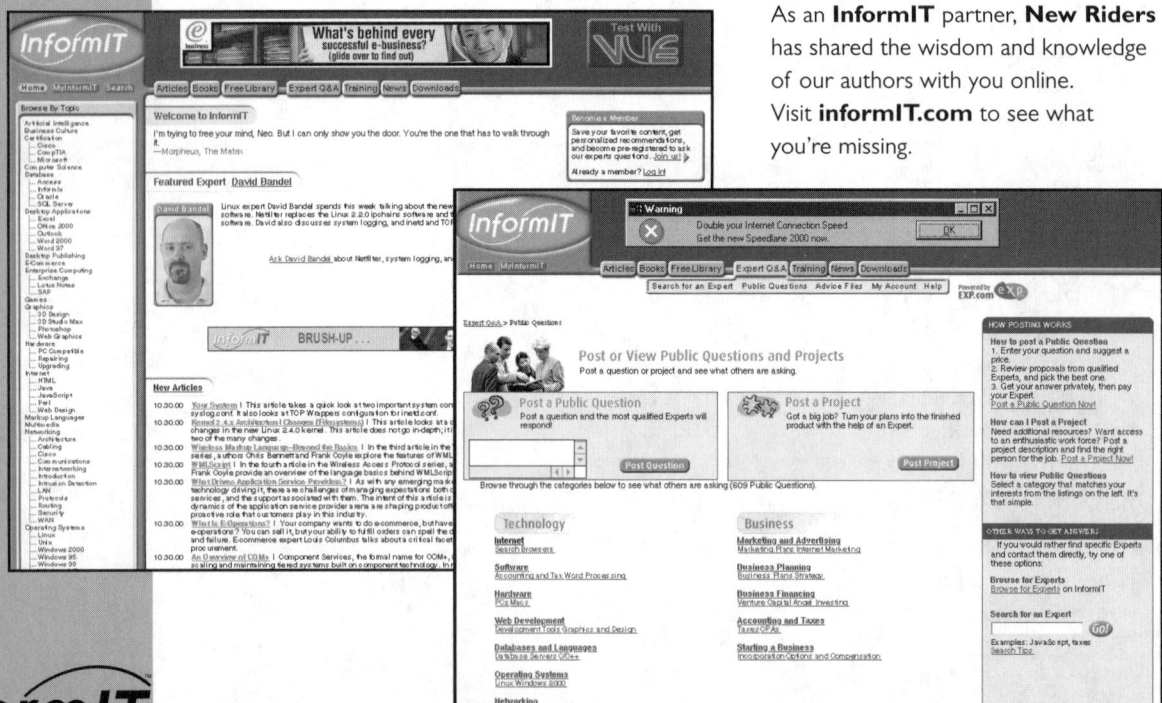

When IT really matters, test with VUE

You've studied the *Training Guide*. Tested your skills with *ExamGear*.™ Now what? Are you ready to sit the exam?
If the answer is yes, be sure to test with VUE.

Why VUE? Because with VUE, you get the best technology and even better service. Some of the benefits are:

- **VUE allows you to register and reschedule your exam in real-time, online, by phone, or at you local testing center**

- **Your test is on time and ready for you, 99% of the time**

- **Your results are promptly and accurately provided to the certifying agency, then merged with your test history**

VUE has over 2,400 quality-focused testing centers worldwide, so no matter where you are, you're never far from a VUE testing center.

VUE is a testing vendor for all the major certification vendors, including Cisco®, Microsoft®, CompTIA® and Novell®. Coming soon, you'll find New Riders
questions and content on the VUE web site, and you'll be able to get your next *Training Guide* at www.vue.com.

HURRY! SIGN UP FOR YOUR EXAM NOW!
TEST WITH VUE. WHEN *IT* REALLY MATTERS.

www.newriders.com

W W W . V U E . C O M

Additional Tools for Certification Preparation

Taking the author-driven, no-nonsense approach that we pioneered with our *Landmark* books, New Riders proudly offers something unique for Windows 2000 administrators—an interesting and discriminating book on Windows 2000 Server, written by someone in the trenches who can anticipate your situation and provide answers you can trust.

INSIDE

Windows 2000 Server

New Riders

William Boswell

ISBN: 1-56205-929-7

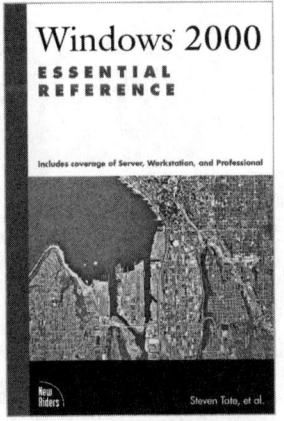

Windows 2000
ESSENTIAL REFERENCE

Includes coverage of Server, Workstation, and Professional

New Riders

Steven Tate, et al.

Architected to be the most navigable, useful, and value-packed reference for Windows 2000, this book uses a creative "telescoping" design that you can adapt to your style of learning. It's a concise, focused, and quick reference for Windows 2000, providing the kind of practical advice, tips, procedures, and additional resources that every administrator will need.

ISBN: 0-7357-0869-X

Understanding the Network is just one of several new titles from New Riders' acclaimed *Landmark Series*. This book addresses the audience in practical terminology, and describes the most essential information and tools required to build high-availability networks in a step-by-step implementation format. Each chapter could be read as a stand-alone, but the book builds progressively toward a summary of the essential concepts needed to put together a wide area network.

Understanding the Network
A Practical Guide to Internetworking

New Riders

Michael J. Martin

ISBN: 0-7357-0977-7

New Riders
Windows 2000 Resources

Advice and Experience for the Windows 2000 Networker

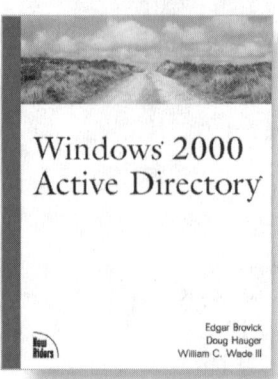

LANDMARK SERIES

We know how important it is to have access to detailed, solution-oriented information on core technologies. *Landmark* books contain the essential information you need to solve technical problems. Written by experts and subjected to rigorous peer and technical reviews, our *Landmark* books are hard-core resources for practitioners like you.

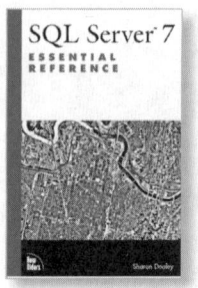

ESSENTIAL REFERENCE SERIES

The *Essential Reference* series from New Riders provides answers when you know what you want to do but need to know how to do it. Each title skips extraneous material and assumes a strong base of knowledge. These are indispensable books for the practitioner who wants to find specific features of a technology quickly and efficiently. Avoiding fluff and basic material, these books present solutions in an innovative, clean format—and at a great value.

CIRCLE SERIES

The *Circle Series* is a set of reference guides that meet the needs of the growing community of advanced, technical-level networkers who must architect, develop, and administer Windows NT/2000 systems. These books provide network designers and programmers with detailed, proven solutions to their problems.

The Road to MCSE Windows 2000

The new Microsoft Windows 2000 track is designed for information technology professionals working in a typically complex computing environment of medium to large organizations. A Windows 2000 MCSE candidate should have at least one year of experience implementing and administering a network operating system.

MCSEs in the Windows 2000 track are required to pass **five core exams and two elective exams** that provide a valid and reliable measure of technical proficiency and expertise.

See below for the exam information and the relevant New Riders title that covers that exam.

Core Exams

New MCSE Candidates (Who Have Not Already Passed Windows NT 4.0 Exams) Must Take All 4 of the Following Core Exams:

Exam 70-210: Installing, Configuring and Administering Microsoft® Windows® 2000 Professional

Exam 70-215: Installing, Configuring and Administering Microsoft Windows 2000 Server

Exam 70-216: Implementing and Administering a Microsoft Windows 2000 Network Infrastructure

Exam 70-217: Implementing and Administering a Microsoft Windows 2000 Directory Services Infrastructure

ISBN 0-7357-0965-3   ISBN 0-7357-0968-8

ISBN 0-7357-0966-1   ISBN 0-7357-0976-9

or

MCPs Who Have Passed 3 Windows NT 4.0 Exams (Exams 70-067, 70-068, and 70-073) Instead of the 4 Core Exams at Left, May Take:

Exam 70-240: Microsoft Windows 2000 Accelerated Exam for MCPs Certified on Microsoft Windows NT 4.0.

(This accelerated, intensive exam, which will be available until December 31, 2001, covers the core competencies of exams 70-210, 70-215, 70-216, and 70-217.)

ISBN 0-7357-0979-3

MCSE Training Guide: Core Exams (Bundle)

ISBN 0-7357-0988-2

PLUS - All Candidates - 1 of the Following Core Elective Exams Required:

***Exam 70-219:** Designing a Microsoft Windows 2000 Directory Services Infrastructure

***Exam 70-220:** Designing Security for a Microsoft Windows 2000 Network

***Exam 70-221:** Designing a Microsoft Windows 2000 Network Infrastructure

ISBN 0-7357-0983-1   ISBN 0-7357-0984-X   ISBN 0-7357-0982-3

PLUS - All Candidates - 2 of the Following Elective Exams Required:

Any current MCSE electives (visit www.microsoft.com for a list of current electives)

Selected third-party certifications that focus on interoperability will be accepted as an alternative to one elective exam. Please watch for more information on the third-party certifications that will be acceptable.)

Exam 70-219: Designing a Microsoft Windows 2000 Directory Services Infrastructure

Exam 70-220: Designing Security for a Microsoft Windows 2000 Network

Exam 70-221: Designing a Microsoft Windows 2000 Network Infrastructure

Exam 70-222: Upgrading from Microsoft Windows NT 4.0 to Microsoft Windows 2000

ISBN 0-7357-0983-1   ISBN 0-7357-0984-X   ISBN 0-7357-0982-3

Core exams that can also be used as elective exams may only be counted once toward a certification; that is, if a candidate receives credit for an exam as a core in one track, that candidate will not receive credit for that same exam as an elective in that same track.

New Riders

WWW.NEWRIDERS.COM

 **Books for Networking Professionals**

Windows NT/2000 Titles

Windows 2000 TCP/IP
By Karanjit Siyan, Ph.D.
2nd Edition
900 pages, $39.99
ISBN: 0-7357-0992-0

Windows 2000 TCP/IP cuts through the complexities and provides the most informative and complex reference book on Windows 2000-based TCP/IP topics. The book is a tutorial-reference hybrid, focusing on how Microsoft TCP/IP works, using hands-on tutorials and practical examples. Concepts essential to TCP/IP administration are explained thoroughly, and are then related to the practical use of Microsoft TCP/IP in a serious networking environment.

Windows 2000 DNS
By Roger Abell, Herman Knief, Andrew Daniels, and Jeffrey Graham
2nd Edition
450 pages, $39.99
ISBN: 0-7357-0973-4

The Domain Name System is a directory of registered computer names and IP addresses that can be instantly located. Without proper design and administration of DNS, computers wouldn't be able to locate each other on the network, and applications like email and Web browsing wouldn't be feasible. Administrators need this information to make their networks work. *Windows 2000 DNS* provides a technical overview of DNS and WINS, and how to design and administer them for optimal performance in a Windows 2000 environment.

Windows 2000 Server Professional Reference
By Karanjit Siyan, Ph.D.
3rd Edition
1800 pages, $75.00
ISBN: 0-7357-0952-1

Windows 2000 Server Professional Reference is the benchmark of references available for Windows 2000. Although other titles take you through the setup and implementation phase of the product, no other book provides the user with detailed answers to day-to-day administration problems and tasks. Real-world implementations are key to help administrators discover the most viable solutions for their particular environments. Solid content shows administrators how to manage, troubleshoot, and fix problems that are specific to heterogeneous Windows networks, as well as Internet features and functionality.

Windows 2000 Professional
By Jerry Honeycutt
350 pages, $34.99 US
ISBN: 0-7357-0950-5

Windows 2000 Professional explores the power available to the Windows workstation user on the corporate network and Internet. The book is aimed directly at the power user who values the security, stability, and networking capabilities of NT alongside the ease and familiarity of the Windows 95/98 user interface. This book covers both user and administration topics, with a dose of networking content added for connectivity.

Windows NT Power Toolkit
By Stu Sjouwerman and Ed Tittel
1st Edition
800 pages, $49.99
ISBN: 0-7357-0922-X

This book covers the analysis, tuning, optimization, automation, enhancement, maintenance, and troubleshooting of Windows NT Server 4.0 and Windows NT Workstation 4.0. In most cases, the two operating systems overlap completely. Where the two systems diverge, each platform is covered separately. This advanced title comprises a task-oriented treatment of the Windows NT 4.0 environment. By concentrating on the use of operating system tools and utilities, resource kit elements, and selected third-party tuning, analysis, optimization, and productivity tools, this book will show you how to carry out everyday and advanced tasks.

Windows 2000 User Management
By Lori Sanders
300 pages, $34.99
ISBN: 1-56205-886-X

With the dawn of Windows 2000, it has become even more difficult to draw a clear line between managing the user and managing the user's environment and desktop. This book, written by a noted trainer and consultant, provides comprehensive, practical advice to managing users and their desktop environments with Windows 2000.

Windows 2000 Deployment & Desktop Management
By Jeffrey A. Ferris, MCSE
1st Edition
400 pages, $34.99
ISBN: 0-7357-0975-0

More than a simple overview of new features and tools, *Windows 2000 Deployment & Desktop Management* is a thorough reference to deploying Windows 2000 Professional to corporate workstations. Incorporating real-world advice and detailed excercises, this book is a one-stop resource for any system administrator, integrator, engineer, or other IT professional.

Planning for Windows 2000

By Eric K. Cone, Jon Boggs, and Sergio Perez
1st Edition
400 pages, $29.99
ISBN: 0-7357-0048-6

Windows 2000 is poised to be one of the largest and most important software releases of the next decade, and you are charged with planning, testing, and deploying it in your enterprise. Are you ready? With this book, you will be. *Planning for Windows 2000* lets you know what the upgrade hurdles will be, informs you of how to clear them, guides you through effective Active Directory design, and presents you with detailed rollout procedures. Eric K. Cone, Jon Boggs, and Sergio Perez give you the benefit of their extensive experiences as Windows 2000 Rapid Deployment Program members by sharing problems and solutions they've encountered on the job.

Inside Windows 2000 Server

By William Boswell
2nd Edition
1533 pages, $49.99
ISBN: 1-56205-929-7

Finally, a totally new edition of New Riders' best-selling *Inside Windows NT Server 4*. Taking the author-driven, no-nonsense approach pioneered with the *Landmark* books, New Riders proudly offers something unique for Windows 2000 administrators—an interesting, discriminating book on Windows 2000 Server written by someone who can anticipate your situation and give you workarounds that won't leave a system unstable or sluggish.

SQL Server System Administration

By Sean Baird,
Chris Miller, et al.
1st Edition
352 pages, $29.99
ISBN: 1-56205-955-6

How often does your SQL Server go down during the day when everyone wants to access the data? Do you spend most of your time being a "report monkey" for your coworkers and bosses? *SQL Server System Administration* helps you keep data consistently available to your users. This book omits introductory information. The authors don't spend time explaining queries and how they work. Instead, they focus on the information you can't get anywhere else, like how to choose the correct replication topology and achieve high availability of information.

Internet Information Services Administration
By Kelli Adam
1st Edition,
200 pages, $29.99
ISBN: 0-7357-0022-2

Are the new Internet technologies in Internet Information Services giving you headaches? Does protecting security on the Web take up all of your time? Then this is the book for you. With hands-on configuration training, advanced study of the new protocols, the most recent version of IIS, and detailed instructions on authenticating users with the new Certificate Server and implementing and managing the new e-commerce features, *Internet Information Services Administration* gives you the real-life solutions you need. This definitive resource prepares you for upgrading to Windows 2000 by giving you detailed advice on working with Microsoft Management Console, which was first used by IIS.

SMS 2 Administration
By Michael Lubanski and Darshan Doshi
1st Edition
350 pages, $39.99
ISBN: 0-7357-0082-6

Microsoft's new version of its Systems Management Server (SMS) is starting to turn heads. Although complex, it allows administrators to lower their total cost of ownership and more efficiently manage clients, applications, and support operations. If your organization is using or implementing SMS, you'll need some expert advice. Michael Lubanski and Darshan Doshi can help you get the most bang for your buck with insight, expert tips, and real-world examples. Michael and Darshan are consultants specializing in SMS and have worked with Microsoft on one of the most complex SMS rollouts in the world, involving 32 countries, 15 languages, and thousands of clients.

SQL Server 7 Essential Reference
By Sharon Dooley
1st Edition
500 pages, $35.00 US
ISBN: 0-7357-0864-9

SQL Server 7 Essential Reference is a comprehensive reference of advanced howtos and techniques for SQL Server 7 administrators. This book provides solid grounding in fundamental SQL Server 7 administrative tasks to help you tame your SQL Server environment. With coverage ranging from installation, monitoring, troubleshooting security, and backup and recovery plans, this book breaks down SQL Server into its key conceptual areas and functions. This easy-to-use reference is a must-have for any SQL Server administrator.

UNIX/Linux Titles

Solaris Essential Reference
By John P. Mulligan
1st Edition
300 pages, $24.95
ISBN: 0-7357-0023-0

Looking for the fastest and easiest way to find the Solaris command you need? Need a few pointers on shell scripting? How about advanced administration tips and sound, practical expertise on security issues? Are you looking for trustworthy information about available third-party software packages that will enhance your operating system? Author John Mulligan—creator of the popular "Unofficial Guide to The Solaris™ Operating Environment" Web site (sun.icsnet.com)—delivers all that and more in one attractive, easy-to-use reference book. With clear and concise instructions on how to perform important administration and management tasks, and key information on powerful commands and advanced topics, *Solaris Essential Reference* is the book you need when you know what you want to do and only need to know how.

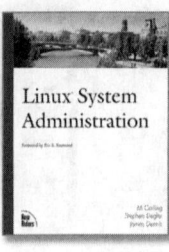

Linux System Administration
By M. Carling, Stephen Degler, and James Dennis
1st Edition
450 pages, $29.99
ISBN: 1-56205-934-3

As an administrator, you probably feel that most of your time and energy is spent in endless firefighting. If your network has become a fragile quilt of temporary patches and work-arounds, this book is for you. Have you had trouble sending or receiving email lately? Are you looking for a way to keep your network running smoothly with enhanced performance? Are your users always hankering for more storage, services, and speed? *Linux System Administration* advises you on the many intricacies of maintaining a secure, stable system. In this definitive work, the authors address all the issues related to system administration, from adding users and managing file permissions, to Internet services and Web hosting, to recovery planning and security. This book fulfills the need for expert advice that will ensure a trouble-free Linux environment.

GTK+/Gnome Application Development
By Havoc Pennington
1st Edition
492 pages, $39.99
ISBN: 0-7357-0078-8

This title is for the reader who is conversant with the C programming language and UNIX/Linux development. It provides detailed and solution-oriented information designed to meet the needs of programmers and application developers using the GTK+/Gnome libraries. Coverage complements existing GTK+/Gnome documentation, going into more depth on pivotal issues such as uncovering the GTK+ object system, working with the event loop, managing the Gdk substrate, writing custom widgets, and mastering GnomeCanvas.

Developing Linux Applications with GTK+ and GDK
By Eric Harlow
1st Edition
490 pages, $34.99
ISBN: 0-7357-0021-4

We all know that Linux is one of the most powerful and solid operating systems in existence. And as the success of Linux grows, there is an increasing interest in developing applications with graphical user interfaces that take advantage of the power of Linux. In this book, software developer Eric Harlow gives you an indispensable development handbook focusing on the GTK+ toolkit. More than an overview of the elements of applica-tion or GUI design, this is a hands-on book that delves into the technology. With in-depth material on the various GUI programming tools and loads of examples, this book's unique focus will give you the information you need to design and launch professional-quality applications.

Linux Essential Reference
By Ed Petron
1st Edition
350 pages, $24.95
ISBN: 0-7357-0852-5

This book is all about getting things done as quickly and efficiently as possible by providing a structured organization for the plethora of available Linux information. We can sum it up in one word—value. This book has it all: concise instructions

on how to perform key administration tasks, advanced information on configuration, shell scripting, hardware management, systems management, data tasks, automation, and tons of other useful information. This book truly provides groundbreaking information for the growing community of advanced Linux professionals.

Lotus Notes and Domino Titles

Domino System Administration
By Rob Kirkland, CLP, CLI
1st Edition
850 pages, $49.99
ISBN: 1-56205-948-3

Your boss has just announced that you will be upgrading to the newest version of Notes and Domino when it ships. How are you supposed to get this new system installed, configured, and rolled out to all of your end users? You understand how Lotus Notes works—you've been administering it for years. What you need is a concise, practical explanation of the new features and how to make some of the advanced stuff work smoothly by someone like you, who has worked with the product for years and understands what you need to know. *Domino System Administration* is the answer—the first book on Domino that attacks the technology at the professional level with practical, hands-on assistance to get Domino running in your organization.

Lotus Notes & Domino Essential Reference
By Tim Bankes, CLP
and Dave Hatter, CLP, MCP
1st Edition
650 pages, $45.00
ISBN: 0-7357-0007-9

You're in a bind because you've been asked to design and program a new database in Notes for an important client who will keep track of and itemize myriad inventory and shipping data. The client wants a user-friendly interface that won't sacrifice speed or functionality. You are experienced (and could develop this application in your sleep), but feel you need something to facilitate your creative and technical abilities—something to perfect your programming skills. The answer is waiting for you: *Lotus Notes & Domino Essential Reference*. It's compact and simply designed. It's loaded with information. All of the objects, classes, functions, and methods are listed. It shows you the object hierarchy and the relationship between each one. It's perfect for you. Problem solved.

Networking Titles

Network Intrusion Detection: An Analyst's Handbook
By Stephen Northcutt
1st Edition
267 pages, $39.99
ISBN: 0-7357-0868-1

Get answers and solutions from someone who has been in the trenches. The author, Stephen Northcutt, original developer of the Shadow intrusion detection system and former director of the United States Navy's Information System Security Office at the Naval Security Warfare Center, gives his expertise to intrusion detection specialists, security analysts, and consultants responsible for setting up and maintaining an effective defense against network security attacks.

Understanding Data Communications, Sixth Edition
By Gilbert Held
Sixth Edition
600 pages, $39.99
ISBN: 0-7357-0036-2

Updated from the highly successful fifth edition, this book explains how data communications systems and their various hardware and software components work. More than an entry-level book, it approaches the material in textbook format, addressing the complex issues involved in internetworking today. A great reference book for the experienced networking professional that is written by the noted networking authority, Gilbert Held.

Other Books By New Riders

Switched, Fast and Gigabit Ethernet, Third Edition
1-57870-073-6 • $50.00 US / $74.95 CAN
Wireless LANs: Implementing Interoperable Networks
1-57870-081-7 • $40.00 US / $59.95 CAN
Local Area High Speed Networks
1-57870-113-9 • $50.00 US / $74.95 CAN
Wide Area High Speed Networks
1-57870-114-7 • $50.00 US / $74.95 CAN
The DHCP Handbook
1-57870-137-6 • $55.00 US / $81.95 CAN
Designing Routing and Switching Architectures for Enterprise Networks
1-57870-060-4 • $55.00 US / $81.95 CAN
Network Performance Baselining
1-57870-240-2 • $50.00 US / $74.95 CAN
Economics of Electronic Commerce
1-57870-014-0 • $49.99 US / $74.95 CAN

SECURITY

Intrusion Detection
1-57870-185-6 • $50.00 US / $74.95 CAN
Understanding Public-Key Infrastructure
1-57870-166-X • $50.00 US / $74.95 CAN
Network Intrusion Detection: An Analyst's Handbook, 2E
0-7357-1008-2 • $45.00 US / $67.95 CAN
Linux Firewalls
0-7357-0900-9 • $39.99 US / $59.95 CAN
Intrusion Signatures and Analysis
0-7357-1063-5 • $39.99 US / $59.95 CAN
Hackers Beware
0-7357-1009-0 • $45.00 US / $67.95 CAN
• Available July 2001

LOTUS NOTES/DOMINO

Domino System Administration
1-56205-948-3 • $49.99 US / $74.95 CAN
Lotus Notes & Domino Essential Reference
0-7357-0007-9 • $45.00 US / $67.95 CAN

PROFESSIONAL CERTIFICATION

TRAINING GUIDES

MCSE Training Guide: Networking Essentials, 2nd Ed.
1-56205-919-X • $49.99 US / $74.95 CAN
MCSE Training Guide: Windows NT Server 4, 2nd Ed.
1-56205-916-5 • $49.99 US / $74.95 CAN
MCSE Training Guide: Windows NT Workstation 4, 2nd Ed.
1-56205-918-1 • $49.99 US / $74.95 CAN
MCSE Training Guide: Windows NT Server 4 Enterprise, 2nd Ed.
1-56205-917-3 • $49.99 US / $74.95 CAN
MCSE Training Guide: Core Exams Bundle, 2nd Ed.
1-56205-926-2 • $149.99 US / $223.95 CAN
MCSE Training Guide: TCP/IP, 2nd Ed.
1-56205-920-3 • $49.99 US / $74.95 CAN
MCSE Training Guide: IIS 4, 2nd Ed.
0-7357-0865-7 • $49.99 US / $74.95 CAN
MCSE Training Guide: SQL Server 7 Administration
0-7357-0003-6 • $49.99 US / $74.95 CAN
MCSE Training Guide: SQL Server 7 Database Design
0-7357-0004-4 • $49.99 US / $74.95 CAN
MCSD Training Guide: Visual Basic 6 Exams
0-7357-0002-8 • $69.99 US / $104.95 CAN
MCSD Training Guide: Solution Architectures
0-7357-0026-5 • $49.99 US / $74.95 CAN
MCSD Training Guide: 4-in-1 Bundle
0-7357-0912-2 • $149.99 US / $223.95 CAN
A+ Certification Training Guide, Second Edition
0-7357-0907-6 • $49.99 US / $74.95 CAN
Network+ Certification Guide
0-7357-0077-X • $49.99 US / $74.95 CAN
Solaris 2.6 Administrator Certification Training Guide, Part I
1-57870-085-X • $40.00 US / $59.95 CAN

Solaris 2.6 Administrator Certification Training Guide, Part II
1-57870-086-8 • $40.00 US / $59.95 CAN
Solaris 7 Administrator Certification Training Guide, Part I and II
1-57870-249-6 • $49.99 US / $74.95 CAN
MCSE Training Guide: Windows 2000 Professional
0-7357-0965-3 • $49.99 US / $74.95 CAN
MCSE Training Guide: Windows 2000 Server
0-7357-0968-8 • $49.99 US / $74.95 CAN
MCSE Training Guide: Windows 2000 Network Infrastructure
0-7357-0966-1 • $49.99 US / $74.95 CAN
MCSE Training Guide: Windows 2000 Network Security Design
0-73570-984X • $49.99 US / $74.95 CAN
MCSE Training Guide: Windows 2000 Network Infrastructure Design
0-73570-982-3 • $49.99 US / $74.95 CAN

MCSE Training Guide: Windows 2000 Directory Svcs. Infrastructure
0-7357-0976-9 • $49.99 US / $74.95 CAN

MCSE Training Guide: Windows 2000 Directory Services Design
0-7357-0983-1 • $49.99 US / $74.95 CAN
MCSE Training Guide: Windows 2000 Accelerated Exam
0-7357-0979-3 • $69.99 US / $104.95 CAN
MCSE Training Guide: Windows 2000 Core Exams Bundle
0-7357-0988-2 • $149.99 US / $223.95 CAN

FAST TRACKS

CLP Fast Track: Lotus Notes/Domino 5 Application Development
0-73570-877-0 • $39.99 US / $59.95 CAN
CLP Fast Track: Lotus Notes/Domino 5 System Administration
0-7357-0878-9 • $39.99 US / $59.95 CAN
Network+ Fast Track
0-7357-0904-1 • $29.99 US / $44.95 CAN
A+ Fast Track
0-7357-0028-1 • $34.99 US / $52.95 CAN
MCSD Fast Track: Visual Basic 6, Exam #70-175
0-7357-0019-2 • $19.99 US / $29.95 CAN
MCSD FastTrack: Visual Basic 6, Exam #70-175
0-7357-0018-4 • $19.99 US / $29.95 CAN

SOFTWARE ARCHITECTURE & ENGINEERING

Designing for the User with OVID
1-57870-101-5 • $40.00 US / $59.95 CAN
Designing Flexible Object-Oriented Systems with UML
1-57870-098-1 • $40.00 US / $59.95 CAN
Constructing Superior Software
1-57870-147-3 • $40.00 US / $59.95 CAN
A UML Pattern Language
1-57870-118-X • $45.00 US / $67.95 CAN

HOW TO CONTACT US

IF YOU NEED THE LATEST UPDATES ON A TITLE THAT YOU'VE PURCHASED:

1) Visit our Web site at www.newriders.com.

2) Enter the book ISBN number, which is located on the back cover in the bottom right-hand corner, in the site search box on the left navigation bar.

3) Select your book title from the list of search results. On the book page, you'll find available updates and downloads for your title.

IF YOU ARE HAVING TECHNICAL PROBLEMS WITH THE BOOK OR THE CD THAT IS INCLUDED:

1) Check the book's information page on our Web site according to the instructions listed above, or

2) Email us at userservices@macmillanusa.com, or

3) Fax us at 317-581-4663 ATTN: Tech Support.

IF YOU HAVE COMMENTS ABOUT ANY OF OUR CERTIFICATION PRODUCTS THAT ARE NON-SUPPORT RELATED:

1) Email us at nrfeedback@newriders.com, or

2) Write to us at New Riders, 201 W. 103rd St., Indianapolis, IN 46290-1097, or

3) Fax us at 317-581-4663.

IF YOU ARE OUTSIDE THE UNITED STATES AND NEED TO FIND A DISTRIBUTOR IN YOUR AREA:

Please contact our international department at international@mcp.com.

IF YOU ARE INTERESTED IN BEING AN AUTHOR OR TECHNICAL REVIEWER:

Email us at opportunities@newriders.com. Include your name, email address, phone number, and area of technical expertise.

IF YOU WISH TO PREVIEW ANY OF OUR CERTIFICATION BOOKS FOR CLASSROOM USE:

Email us at nrmedia@newriders.com. Your message should include your name, title, training company or school, department, address, phone number, office days/hours, text in use, and enrollment. Send these details along with your request for desk/examination copies and/or additional information.

IF YOU ARE A MEMBER OF THE PRESS AND WOULD LIKE TO REVIEW ONE OF OUR BOOKS:

Email us at nrmedia@newriders.com. Your message should include your name, title, publication or website you work for, mailing address, and email address.

To better serve you, we would like your opinion on the content and quality of this book. Please complete this card and mail it to us or fax it to 317-581-4663.

Name _____

Address _____

City _____ State _____ Zip _____

Phone _____ Email Address _____

Occupation _____

Which certification exams have you already passed? _____
_____
_____
_____

Which certification exams do you plan to take? _____
_____
_____
_____

What influenced your purchase of this book?
❏ Recommendation   ❏ Cover Design
❏ Table of Contents   ❏ Index
❏ Magazine Review   ❏ Advertisement
❏ Reputation of New Riders ❏ Author Name

How would you rate the contents of this book?
❏ Excellent   ❏ Very Good
❏ Good   ❏ Fair
❏ Below Average   ❏ Poor

What other types of certification products will you buy/have you bought to help you prepare for the exam?
❏ Quick reference books   ❏ Testing software
❏ Study guides   ❏ Other

What do you like most about this book? Check all that apply.
❏ Content   ❏ Writing Style
❏ Accuracy   ❏ Examples
❏ Listings   ❏ Design
❏ Index   ❏ Page Count
❏ Price   ❏ Illustrations

What do you like least about this book? Check all that apply.
❏ Content   ❏ Writing Style
❏ Accuracy   ❏ Examples
❏ Listings   ❏ Design
❏ Index   ❏ Page Count
❏ Price   ❏ Illustrations

What would be a useful follow-up book to this one for you?_____

Where did you purchase this book? _____

Can you name a similar book that you like better than this one, or one that is as good? Why?_____
_____
_____

How many New Riders books do you own? _____

What are your favorite certification or general computer book titles? _____

What other titles would you like to see us develop?_____
_____

Any comments for us? _____
_____
_____

Fold here and tape to mail

- -